PCWEEK
Guide to Lotus Notes
Release 4

PCWEEK
Guide to Lotus Notes Release 4

WorkGroup Systems, Inc.

Eric Mann and Gerry Litton

Ziff-Davis Press
An imprint of Macmillan Computer Publishing USA
Emeryville, California

Acquisitions Editor	Lysa Lewallen
Development Editor	Paula Hardin
Copy Editor	J. Smith
Technical Reviewers	Sue Reber and Stephanie Preston
Proofreader	Morton Flask
Cover Design	Megan Gandt
Book Design	Paper Crane Graphics, Berkeley
Technical Illustration	Ryan Oldfather
Word Processing	Howard Blechman
Page Layout	ZD Press Staff
Indexer	Ted Laux

Ziff-Davis Press, ZD Press, the Ziff-Davis Press logo, PC Magazine, and the PC Magazine logo, PC Week and the PC Week logo are trademarks or registered trademarks of, and are licensed to Macmillan Computer Publishing USA by Ziff-Davis Publishing Company, New York, New York.

Ziff-Davis Press imprint books are produced on a Macintosh computer system with the following applications: FrameMaker®, Microsoft® Word, QuarkXPress®, Adobe Illustrator®, Adobe Photoshop®, Adobe Streamline™, MacLink®Plus, Aldus® FreeHand™, Collage Plus™.

Ziff-Davis Press, an imprint of
Macmillan Computer Publishing USA
5903 Christie Avenue
Emeryville, CA 94608

ISBN 1-56276-378-4

Manufactured in the United States of America
10 9 8 7 6 5 4 3 2 1

■ Dedication

This book is dedicated to my grandfather,
Nathan Fleischer, who taught me about
kindness, humor, and enjoying life.
Thank you for all of the lessons and the
love you have given me.

—Eric Mann

To CS.

—Gerry Litton

■ Contents at a Glance

■ Table of Contents

**PART 2   Advanced Application
                   Development Features**   295

Chapter 9:   Designing Navigators   297

Chapter 21: Deploying InterNotes and Web Publisher — 657

Chapter 22: Migration — 699

■ Acknowledgments

To my family and friends, who have bolstered my spirits through many crazy ideas, this book included. In particular—Gram, Mom, Dad, Kevin, Jane, Dave, and Ralph—your support means a great deal to me. Finally, I can't forget the folks at Ziff-Davis who put up with this rookie author and helped me get the book out the door!

—Eric Mann

A book is the creation of a great many people: editors, managers, proofreaders, computer experts, and others. Oh yes, and the authors, who according to tradition get to have their names on or near the cover. But don't be impressed by that, because without all the rest of the cast, the author is like a sailboat without wind.

Thanks are certainly due to Paula Hardin for her role as development editor, and also to Jeannie Smith for her editing skills. Thanks are also due to Howard Blechman for word processing and to the ZD Press staff for page layout.

—Gerry Litton

■ Introduction

It's always exciting to see a good product become even better, and that's what has happened to Lotus Notes. Lotus Notes 4.0 is a major improvement on a software product that was already unique, with something new for everybody.

If you're a seasoned Notes user, much of the functionality of Lotus Notes 4.0 will be familiar, except that just about every feature has been recast. For example, Notes views have been given a major face-lift; and although fundamentally the same, they are much more user-friendly. Similarly, you'll find that all the menu items from Notes 3.0 have either been repositioned on other menus or they have been replaced by other options.

Lotus Notes 4.0 contains a cornucopia of new features, which add immensely to Notes' functionality and versatility. The result is a rich and complex system that encompasses document and information management, e-mail, and workflow. For system administrators, Notes 4.0 offers great new management tools, vastly improved security, and performance and capacity breakthroughs.

■ What This Book Covers

This book is intended primarily for designers of Notes applications and Notes system administrators. It provides in-depth coverage of both areas. Rather than try to introduce the features that are new to Notes 4.0, we have included extensive coverage of these important topics. Our aim is to include the old information in a single integrated package that will get you up and running quickly, regardless of your current knowledge level.

The first part of the book is devoted to describing the various design features available to Notes application developers. If you have had experience with designing Notes applications, you'll probably recognize a good deal of this material, although you may be surprised at the degree to which many features have been extended. On the other hand, if you're new to Notes design, you'll probably benefit from spending a good deal of time at the computer, using the examples in the book as the basis for your own practice.

The second part of the book is for system administrators. These two sections will teach you how to deploy a Notes 4.0 network and how to manage a Notes 4.0 network. The chapters are broken down logically so you can easily understand what chapters relate to what job functions. If you are already a seasoned Notes administrator, each chapter will guide you to the relevant new information. If you have little or no Notes experience, you will get step-by-step instructions for setting up and managing the Notes system. In addition, you will get helpful background information so that you understand what is happening, not just how to do it.

■ What This Book Doesn't Tell You

This book is not intended to be used by end-users who are seeking an introduction to working with Notes. Many excellent references dealing with the day-to-day use of Notes already exist on the shelves, and they speak to a group that's different from the intended audience of this book.

Neither is the book intended to delve into the mysteries of how to use any particular operating system. Operating systems require special expertise, which is not germane to the subject matter of this book. This book assumes that the computers that will be used are running with a Notes supported operating system, network protocol, and whatever physical connections will be used to communicate (LAN, WAN, or telephone).

Finally, this book does not attempt to cover the topic of LotusScript—a rich and powerful programming language that can be used for creating highly sophisticated Notes applications. Fortunately, the vast majority of Notes applications—probably 90 to 95 percent—can be developed without recourse to using LotusScript. Those are the applications to which this book is addressed. Regrettably, the other 5 to 10 percent are beyond our present scope.

P A R T

1

Application Development

- *The Elements of a Notes Database*
- *The Components of a Notes Document*
- *The Database User Interface*
- *Working with Notes Databases*
- *Introducing the InfoBox*

CHAPTER

1

Exploring Notes Databases

Whether you're a novice or an experienced user needing to get up to speed with Lotus Notes 4.0, this chapter can be helpful to you, because it provides a nicely paced overview of the main elements of Notes applications. In particular, the chapter focuses on two areas: the new user interface with which you'll be confronted when you start to work with Notes 4.0, and the various design features available for building applications.

Although Notes 4.0 contains all of the old Notes 3.0 functionality, and although the new Notes workspace is similar (but not identical) to the old one, the main database interface is entirely different. In fact, it's so different that if you've worked with earlier Notes releases, the first time you open a Notes 4.0 database you'll probably wonder if you accidentally opened the wrong software. This chapter devotes a lot of space to discussing this interface.

Notes 4.0 contains a wealth of new design features, including not only significant additions to content of databases, but also the tools for working with these databases. This chapter provides a comfortable overview of these design features; later, other parts of the book describe them in detail.

■ The Elements of a Notes Database

Each Notes 4.0 database consists of several types of components. If you have experience with earlier Notes versions, you'll recognize many of these database components—such as documents, forms, and views. However, Notes 4.0 databases contain a whole new array of useful elements, which we present briefly here and then discuss in depth later, throughout the book.

Every Notes 4.0 database contains some or all of the following components:

- *Documents.* Just as with earlier Notes versions, the document is the heart of the database, and Notes 4.0 is particularly flexible in the type of information that you can store within its documents. In fact, a document can contain just about any type of machine-readable information.

  A single database can contain any number of different *types* of documents. For instance, one database may contain one set of documents containing name and address information; another set might contain confidential financial information; and still another set of documents might be devoted to personal, historical information—all in the same database!

  As a simple example, Figure 1.1 shows a relatively straightforward Notes document containing simple name-and-address information. This document contains various fields, each of which contains one or more pieces of information.

- *Forms.* Within a database, you create different forms for generating documents. You use a particular form to create a particular type of document. You can create any number of forms within each database, and then select the one you want whenever you create a new document.

  Figure 1.2 shows a simple form, which was used to create the document shown in Figure 1.1. Although you can't tell by looking at Figure 1.2, Notes 4.0 provides many new design features for creating forms, offering you greatly improved flexibility in generating documents.

Figure 1.1

This Notes document
contains name and
address information.

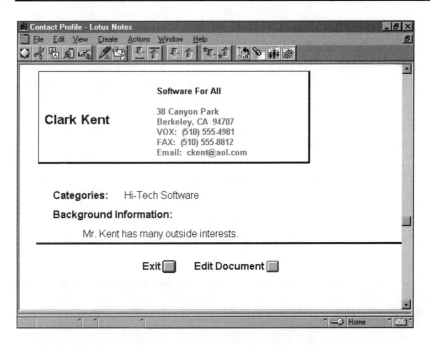

Figure 1.2

This Notes form was
used to generate the
document shown in
Figure 1.1.

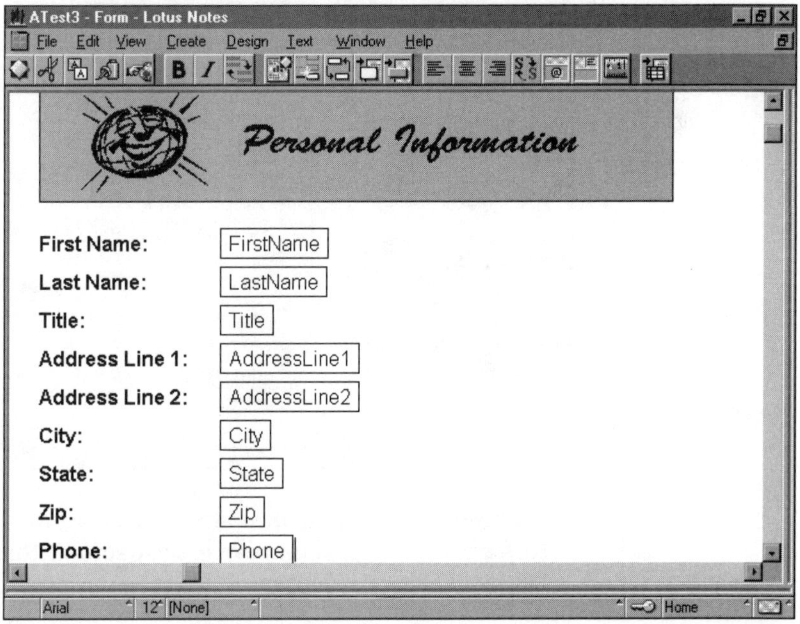

Within Notes 4.0, you can also create one or more *subforms* as part of a database design. A subform is like a miniform that's used globally. That is, you can incorporate a subform into one or more of your standard forms. This can be a great convenience if you plan to use the same group of elements (fields and so forth) in several forms within a database.

- *Views.* A database view is a window into the documents stored in a database. Views are somewhat analogous to the indexes used with the older, traditional types of databases, such as dBASE, Paradox, and so on. However, Notes views (a brilliant development by the authors of Notes) are infinitely more user-friendly than traditional indexes. Each view shows a particular subset of all the documents in a database, and it also shows selected data from those documents.

  Figure 1.3 shows how a typical view appears. Like all views, this one contains several columns, each of which displays one or more data items for each document. You can customize a view to contain as many columns as you wish.

Figure 1.3

A typical user interface, displaying both a custom view and a custom navigator.

Navigator ——

View ——

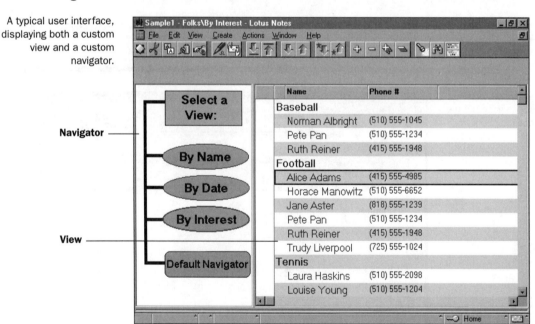

- *Navigators.* One of the new innovations appearing in Notes 4.0, navigators are custom tools that can greatly simplify the work of end users. With the help of one or more navigators—which the database designer creates—users can simply point and click to perform routine (and not-so-routine) tasks, such as switching views, deleting old documents, printing selected database information, and so on. The left part of Figure 1.3 shows a custom navigator. Navigators are briefly described later in this chapter in the section "Custom Navigators," and also in great detail in Chapter 9.

- *Agents.* An agent is the new term for what was previously known as a *macro.* The new term was probably chosen to send a strong message to the Notes community that macros are not what they used to be—they are much, much more. Simply stated, an agent is a set of instructions—written by the database developer—that tells Notes to perform a set of operations. However, a Notes agent can now consist of anything from a simple, one-line instruction to a complex program written in the new LotusScript language. You can write agents for many different purposes within a database, just as you could with Notes 3.0. However, Notes 4.0 offers many new opportunities for using agents to customize and automate your databases.

- *Folders.* The folder is also a Notes 4.0 innovation. Within a given database, you can create as many folders as you wish, storing different groups of documents in each one. By selecting a particular folder, you can view the documents it contains.

- *Indexes.* A database may contain one or more indexes. For instance, Notes automatically maintains an index for each view within a database. In addition, you can create a full-text index for a database, which you can then use for sophisticated text searches.

■ The Components of a Notes Document

As we mentioned earlier, Notes offers an amazing degree of flexibility regarding the type of information that you can store in your documents. Also, Notes offers a wide array of tools for creating complex and interesting forms—the structures within which you create your documents.

Invariably, a Notes document contains an assortment of fields, in which various bits and pieces of information are stored, including text, graphics, numbers, OLE objects, and so on. In addition, a Notes document may contain other design elements that enhance its appearance and utility.

NOTE. *Be sure that you understand the difference between a* document *and a* document form. *As the designer of a database, you create one or more forms, each of which can then be used to create a particular type of new document. When we refer to the design of a document, we're really referring to the design of the underlying form.*

Fields

If your experience has been with other types of databases, you'll be amazed at the flexibility offered by Notes' array of field types. On the other hand, if you've been using an earlier version of Notes, you'll recognize all of the Notes 4.0 field types. However, you now have a great deal of control over formatting the fields at your disposal. You also have much more control over where you can position fields on your forms.

Using the various field types, you can store the following types of information in Notes documents:

Note. Chapter 6 discusses each of these field types in more detail.

- Text

- Numbers

- Graphics

- Keywords

- Time and date values

- Personal names

- OLE-embedded objects

Notes fields have some very unusual characteristics that distinguish them from those used by other database systems. First of all, fields are variable-length. The significant advantages of this feature are twofold: First, each document takes up only as much hard-disk space as it needs; the wasted disk space normally incurred when using fixed-length fields is gone.

Secondly, the sizes of the same field in different documents don't have to be the same, so you can enter as much information as you wish into a field—which automatically expands as needed—and there's no wasted space in the corresponding fields in other documents.

At the option of the database designer, some fields can be set to take multiple values. If you choose to enter several values into one of these fields, each value can be a different length. Except for one type of field, all the values within a single field must be the same type (the exception is discussed next).

One field type—called *rich text*— is amazingly flexible, having the following characteristics:

- It can contain one or several graphics, intermixed with text.

- Users can format selected text blocks within the field, assigning custom fonts and paragraph characteristics (such as line spacing and so on).

- A rich text field can store either an embedded or linked OLE object. This could be, for example, part or all of a Word Pro document, an Excel spreadsheet, or a complete Freelance presentation. To access the object, the user simply double-clicks on the representation of the object in the document.

As an example, Figure 1.4 shows a Notes document that includes a rich text field. This field contains an embedded 1-2-3 worksheet, which you can edit by double-clicking on it.

Figure 1.4

This document includes a rich text field containing an embedded 1-2-3 spreadsheet.

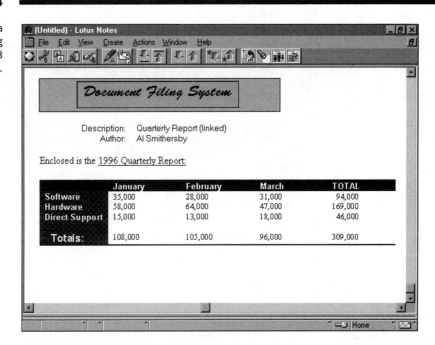

Buttons and Hotspots

Notes offers a number of features that provide users with point-and-click operations when reading or editing documents. *Buttons,* which are inherited from earlier Notes versions, are simple and self-explanatory tools for performing a wide variety of operations. *Text hotspots,* which are new to Notes 4.0, also provide several different types of tools: When a user clicks on a text hotspot, something happens, depending on how the designer set up the hotspot.

By clicking on a text hotspot, you can

- Pop up a special information message while viewing a document

- Perform a special action, programmed by the database designer

- Jump to another document—either in the same database or a different one

The bottom of Figure 1.1 shows two buttons on a form. Note that the designer has thoughtfully labeled each button, so that the user knows its purpose. For example, to make changes to the document, the user would click the button labeled Edit Document.

As an alternative to using buttons, Figure 1.5 shows a document containing two different text hotspots—labeled Exit and Edit Document. To perform one of these actions, the user simply clicks on the corresponding hotspot.

Figure 1.5

You can use the text hotspots shown in this document to perform different operations.

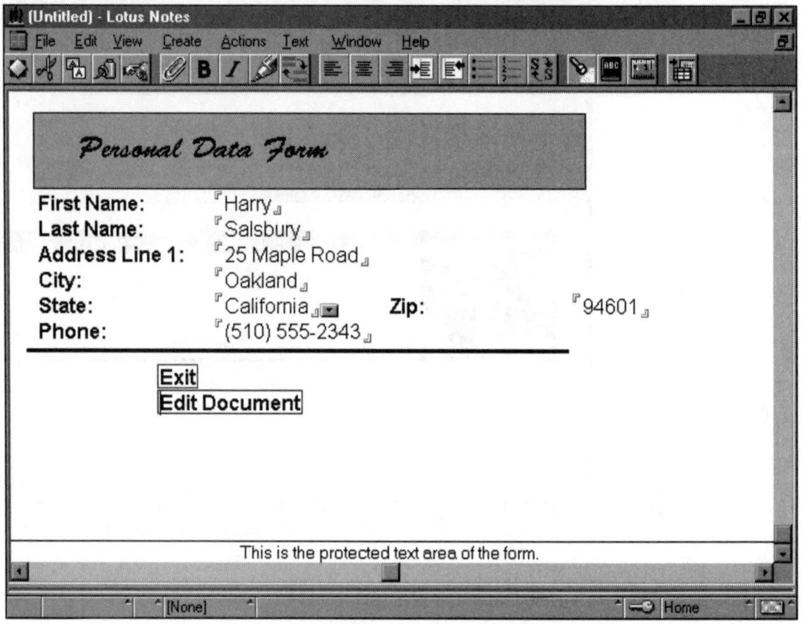

Text hotspot pop-ups are a convenient way of displaying information to the person reading or editing a document. For example, when a user clicks on the text pop-up shown in Figure 1.6(a), the text shown in Figure 1.6(b) appears.

Link hotspots are a handy way of creating hypertext-type links to other Notes documents and to particular views and folders. The amazing thing is that you can use this tool to link documents to different Notes databases; you're offered a tool for creating your own hypertext systems.

Figure 1.7 shows a document containing a link hotspot. When the user double-clicks on the text "Double-click here…" Notes loads and displays the document linked to this hotspot. The user can display both the original and linked documents simultaneously.

Figure 1.6

(a) A user can click on the text pop-up shown here; (b) this information is displayed when the user clicks on the text pop-up.

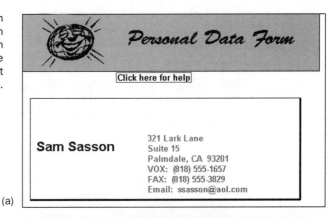

(a)

(b)

Hotspots have one particularly interesting and important characteristic: They can be created either by the database designer as part of an underlying form, or by the person editing a particular document. In other words, a hotspot can be either part of a form or part of a document.

For example, the link hotspot in Figure 1.7 is probably part of the basic form underlying the document; that is, it was created by the database designer. On the other hand, users could create their own link hotspots (or other types of hotspots) within documents that they are creating or editing.

Sections, Layout Regions, and Subforms

Although older versions of Notes supported *sections* within documents, Notes 4.0 has added three major extensions to the original concept. First, sections are now *collapsible*, so that a user can either hide or display the information contained within a section. This innovation offers users a handy tool

Figure 1.7

This document contains a link hotspot to another Notes document.

Hotspot

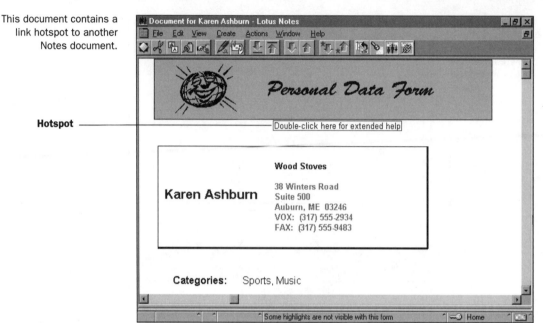

for hiding information that's not of immediate interest. For example, the two parts of Figure 1.8 illustrate how the information within a section can be either displayed or hidden. To hide or display the section, you click on the little arrow at the top of the section.

This type of section can contain all of the components available within other parts of a document: fields, graphic elements, and so on. Moreover, the designer can set each section so that it is automatically either displayed or hidden whenever a document is opened. The designer can also write a formula that specifies that a section is hidden whenever a particular set of conditions is true.

The type of section just described is designed and implemented by the database designer. For instance, the section shown in Figure 1.8 has been set up by the database designer. However, Notes 4.0 also offers another new type of collapsible section that's originated by the person creating or editing a document. Here, the user can select one or more paragraphs within a rich text field and instruct Notes to treat them as a collapsible field. Again, this serves as a handy device whereby a user can simplify the reading or editing of a document by selectively hiding text blocks that aren't immediately needed.

Figure 1.8

(a) A section with all of
its information displayed;
(b) the user has chosen
to hide the section's
information.

Section

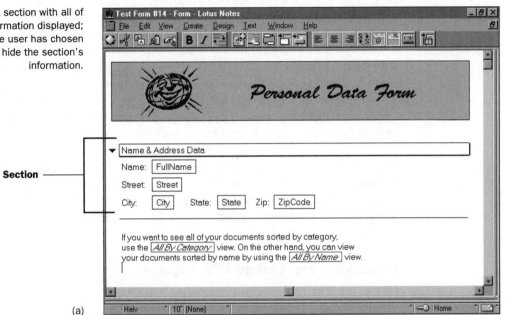

(a)

Section title

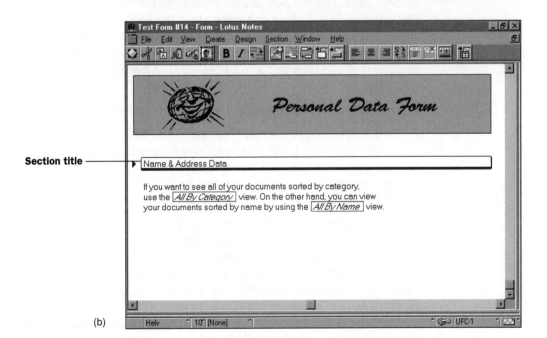

(b)

Layout regions offer another new design tool. The database designer can create one or more layout regions within each form, and each region can contain fields, graphic objects, and buttons. Here's the big advantage: When designing a new form, you can click and drag each object within a layout region to exactly where you want it. This is a terrific improvement over working with forms in earlier Notes versions, where you were extremely limited in how you could position the various objects on a form.

As an example, the top, shaded part of the form shown in Figure 1.2 was created as a separate layout region; the graphic and text were entered as two objects, each of which was separately positioned within the region.

Subforms offer the database designer still another new tool. If a designer expects to use the same group of design elements in several forms, he or she can save considerable effort by creating that group of elements once, saving it as a subform. Then, whenever the designer wants to use that particular group of design elements as part of a new form, he or she can simply copy the subform onto the form.

Embedded and Linked OLE Objects

One of the features that gives Notes databases so much flexibility is that a document can contain one or more linked or embedded OLE objects. Each of these objects can be part of a document created by any software package that supports OLE linking and embedding. The result is that you can create a Notes database that consists of a set of just about any type of document, such as spreadsheets, Freelance presentations, documents created by word processors, sound clips, and so on. Each OLE object can be either of the following:

- An embedded object, which is part of the Notes document.

- A linked object; in this case, the Notes document contains links to the original document, which is stored in a separate file. You would choose this type of object if you expected the information it represented to change over the course of time, and you wanted the Notes document always to display the most current information.

There are two main advantages of using OLE objects within Notes databases. First, you can combine diverse types of information into a single integrated Notes document. This feature is not unique to Notes, but when combined with the second advantage, it is tremendous: You can use Notes views—and all their associated features—to organize, display, and retrieve large numbers of different types of documents.

As an example, suppose that you want to create a Notes database of training documents, consisting of Word Pro documents and Freelance presentations.

You could create a set of Notes documents similar to the one shown in Figure 1.9. The first data line in this document identifies the type of information it contains: In this example it's a Word Pro document. The icon below this line represents the actual Word Pro document. To view it, the user simply double-clicks the icon. Notes then loads Word Pro and displays the document.

Figure 1.9

This document contains an embedded Word Pro training document.

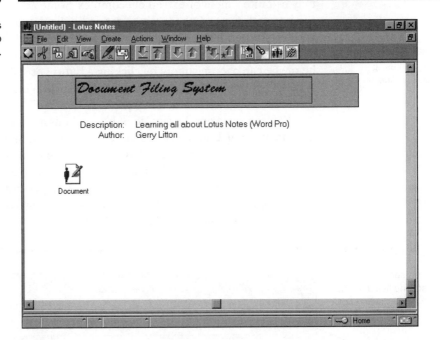

In some cases, the designer may choose to display the actual data within the Notes document—rather than displaying an icon that represents the data (like the one shown in Figure 1.9). This could be useful, for example, if the object to be displayed were a relatively small part of a 1-2-3 worksheet and fit in nicely with the rest of the document.

There are a couple of reasons why the database designer might choose to display the entire contents of a word-processed document within a Notes document. First, the user can scan the document in place, without needing to load the software that originally created the document.

The second reason is a little less obvious: If the actual word-processed document is displayed, a full-text search will include the contents of that document! This offers you a terrific search tool that can scan multiple documents of different types, such as text documents, spreadsheets, and so on.

Actions

Notes contains an incredibly powerful set of features for working with its databases, but many of these operations require a good deal of specialized knowledge that's often beyond the scope of the daily end-users. To give these users more direct access to some of this power, Notes 4.0 has introduced a new feature called *actions*. Each action represents a set of operations, which may be quite simple or extremely complex. Some actions are supplied out-of-the-box with Notes. Others can be set up by the database designer—often with very little work, although sometimes with a great deal of design effort.

Note. For details about creating and using actions, see Chapter 5.

Each database can present to the end user a set of actions, from which he or she can choose simply by clicking a button or selecting a menu option. A set of actions can be set up by the database designer for one or more forms and views within the database.

You can see a good example of how actions are used by starting to create a mail menu: Use the command Create, Mail, Memo, which displays a new memo as shown in Figure 1.10. The action bar, near the top of the form, displays a set of buttons (which are supplied by the Notes designers for this form). The user can select a particular button to perform a specific action. For example, clicking the button labeled Address displays the list of names stored in the current Notes Address Book.

Figure 1.10

The user can use the actions listed on the action bar.

Action bar

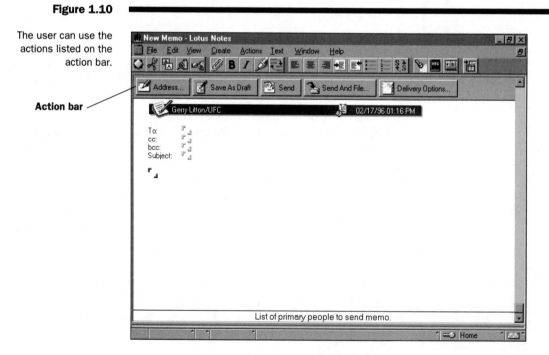

The set of actions assigned to a form or view is also available from the Actions menu. For example, Figure 1.11 shows the contents of the Actions menu for the form shown in Figure 1.10.

Figure 1.11

The Actions menu displays the actions currently available to the user.

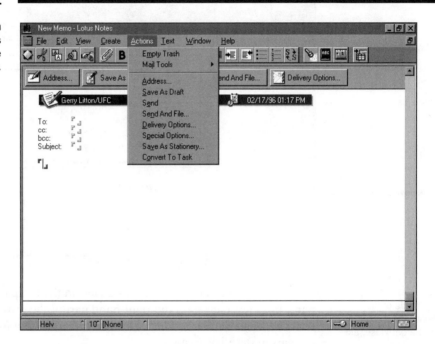

■ The Database User Interface

Notes 4.0 takes full advantage of modern computer software technology and ideas, and this is clearly demonstrated by the main database display presented to the user. Figure 1.12 shows an example of this display, which contains three basic parts:

• Navigator pane

• View pane

• Preview pane

The Navigator pane, on the upper-left part of the display, is an innovation new to Notes 4.0. The top part of this pane displays the names of all the views and folders available in the current database. For example, the database in Figure 1.12 has views named People by Category, People by Name, and People by Company. The database also contains a couple of folders named Important People and Out-of-Date.

Figure 1.12

The main database
display shows a great
deal of useful information.

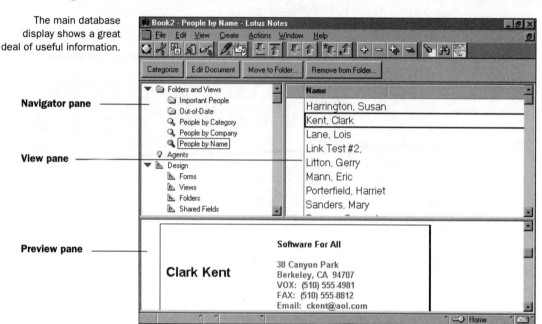

Navigator pane ————

View pane ————

Preview pane ————

Note. You can also use
the right side of the
display to show other
parts of a database, as
discussed next.

When you click on the name of a view in the top part of the Navigator
pane, the View pane—on the right-hand part of the display—displays that
database view. Similarly, when you click the name of a folder, its contents
appears in the View pane.

By default, the Navigator pane displays Notes' built-in navigator called
Folders, as shown in Figure 1.12. However, you can also create your own custom navigators to be displayed in this pane.

Note. Chapter 5
describes how to design
and work with views.

If you examine the View pane in Figure 1.12, you'll see that Notes 4.0
views have strong similarities to those of earlier Notes releases. However,
several extremely important changes have been incorporated into views,
offering users a great deal of increased flexibility. For instance, users can
change the width of selected columns; and each row can occupy more than a
single line.

As with earlier Notes releases, each view must be custom designed, by
either the database designer or an experienced user. If you're familiar with
creating views, you can cook up a new one in about two or three minutes.

The bottom of the Navigator pane lists the various types of design elements that can be incorporated into each database: forms, views, and so on.
By clicking on a particular element type, you can display the corresponding
parts of the current database in the View pane. For instance, if you click on

Views, the View pane then displays the names of all the views available for the database, as shown in Figure 1.13.

Figure 1.13

The right side of this display lists the views contained in the current database.

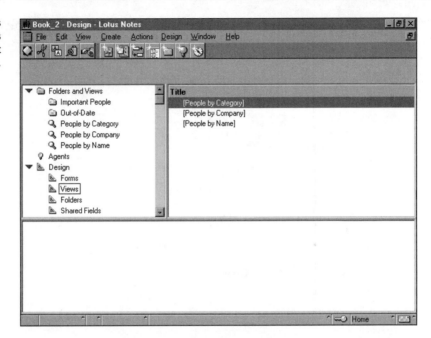

The bottom part of the main database display is the Preview pane—which may or may not be displayed on your screen. When you've selected a view in the Navigator pane, and you then select a particular document in the View pane, the Preview pane displays part of that document. This is a very handy innovation because it allows you to quickly browse through a group of documents.

Customizing the Main Display

Notes offers a variety of ways in which you—as a user—can customize the main database display. For instance, you can adjust the relative sizes and locations of the three panes in just about any way you wish. You can even remove any of the panes from the display, and to some extent, you can control the relative positions of the panes.

To change the size of a pane, use the mouse to grab the edge between that pane and one of its neighbors and then drag the edge one way or the other to expand or contract the pane. Figure 1.14 shows the mouse dragging the edge between the View and Navigator panes. To remove a pane altogether, simply drag an edge until that pane disappears. The pane's edge is still visible, so you can later redisplay the pane by clicking and dragging the edge.

Figure 1.14

You can adjust the size of each of the panes.

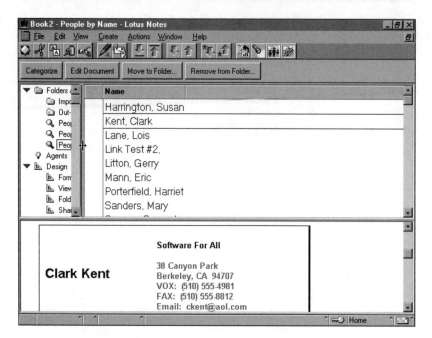

You can also remove the Preview pane by clicking View, Document Preview. This is a handy way to completely remove that pane when you want to maximize the available screen real estate for working with just the Navigator and View panes.

To accommodate your view preferences, Notes allows you to choose where to display the Preview pane:

1. Make sure that the Preview pane is displayed (the Document Preview option should be checked on the View menu).

2. Select View, Arrange Preview, displaying the dialog box shown in Figure 1.15.

3. Click on your choice for the Preview pane position and then click OK.

TIP. *Here's a handy way to preview a group of documents: Place the Preview pane on the right side of the display, minimize the size of the Navigator pane, and reduce the width of the View pane, as shown in Figure 1.16. You can then use most of the screen for previewing documents.*

Figure 1.15

Use this dialog box to select a position for the Preview pane.

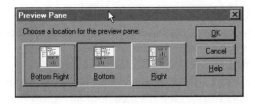

Figure 1.16

This arrangement of panes offers a convenient method for previewing documents.

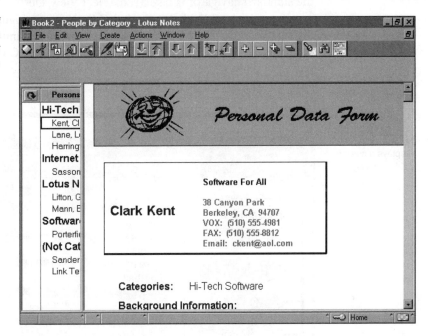

Custom Navigators

The Navigator pane shown in Figure 1.12 displays the *standard Notes navigator*, which we described earlier. You use this navigator to display different views, as well as other parts of a database. However, you can also use the Navigator pane to display custom navigators, which you can create as part of a database. The main purpose of this type of navigator is to provide users with a set of simple-to-use tools for working with a database.

Typically, a navigator contains a set of *hotspots*, which are areas sensitive to mouse clicks. When you click on a hotspot, Notes performs whatever actions are associated with that hotspot, such as the following:

- Switch to a particular view or folder in the current database

- Switch to another navigator in the database

- Perform the operations programmed into a custom formula or script

Since you can program just about any set of Notes operations into a formula or script, navigator hotspots can be extremely powerful, while at the same time being a piece of cake for the end users.

As an example, the Navigator pane shown in Figure 1.17 displays a custom navigator. You can tell it's a custom navigator because it's not the standard Notes navigator shown in Figure 1.12. (If you want to make sure that the standard navigator is displayed, select View, Design.)

If you click on the hotspot labeled By Name in Figure 1.17, Notes will display the view called By Name, in the View pane. Similarly, if you click on the hotspot labeled By Company, the view called By Company will be displayed. Finally, if you click on Default Navigator, Notes will display the standard navigator, as shown in Figure 1.12.

Figure 1.17

The Navigator pane here displays a custom navigator.

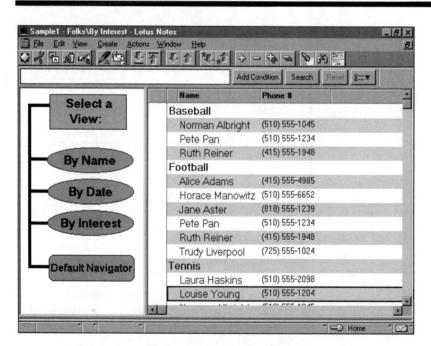

You can see another example of custom navigators in action by displaying the Help index (click Help, Help Topics), as shown in Figure 1.18. If you click on the topics labeled How Do I, Tell Me About, and so on, you'll see that the display in the Navigator pane changes with each click. Here's why: Each time you click on a particular item, a new custom navigator is displayed.

For instance, if you click on How Do I, the pane changes to show the custom navigator shown in Figure 1.19. Notice that the only difference between the two custom navigators in Figure 1.18 and 1.19 seems to be that different book icons are open. However, on closer inspection, you'll notice that different views (in the View pane) have also been selected.

Figure 1.18

The Navigator pane here displays a custom navigator used by Notes Help.

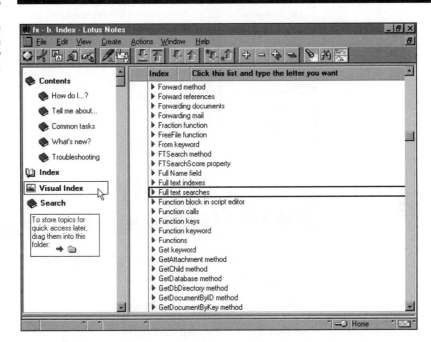

By cleverly designing a set of custom navigators for a database, you can simplify things for end users so that they need to learn very little about Notes before being able to work with its databases. For example, a designer can set up a set of custom navigators as a group of menus. By making a series of menu choices, a user can carry out whatever activity is needed.

■ Working with Notes Databases

This section describes the steps you need to follow in order to open and work with Notes databases. If you're a seasoned Notes user, much of this material will be somewhat familiar because many of the basic operations are similar—although for the most part the details are all new in Notes 4.0.

Figure 1.19

When you click on How
Do I, in Figure 1.18, this
display appears.

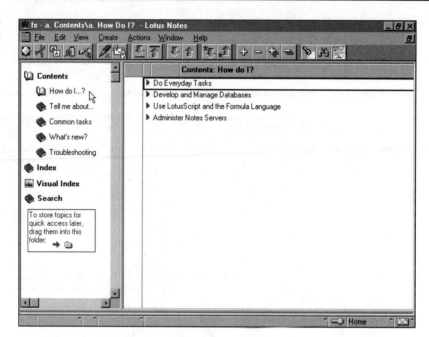

In this section we'll cover the following topics:

- Opening a database

- Browsing through a database

- Viewing and editing documents

Opening a Database

In keeping with prior versions of Notes, to *open* a database means to set up
an icon for it on your Notes workspace. Unlike previous versions of Notes,
however, Notes 4.0 helps you search for databases by browsing any directory
to which you have read/write access. These directories can be on your local
workstation, your home server, or on any other server to which you have access—even remote servers accessible by telephone. When you find the database you want, you can then set up its icon on your workspace. From then
on, you can access the database by double-clicking on its icon.

NOTE. *Notes uses the phrase "opening a database" in two different contexts:
to place the icon for a database on the Notes workspace, and to access the
contents of a database by double-clicking on its icon on the workspace. We use
this terminology throughout this book; the context always clearly indicates the
meaning.*

Here's how to open a database; that is, add its icon to your workspace:

1. Make sure that your screen displays your Notes workspace, as shown in Figure 1.20.

2. Select File, Database, Open, displaying the dialog box shown in Figure 1.21.

3. To select the server containing the database that you want to open, pull down the top list box, labeled Server, and then make your choice. If the database is on your local workstation, choose Local.

Figure 1.20

A typical Notes workspace

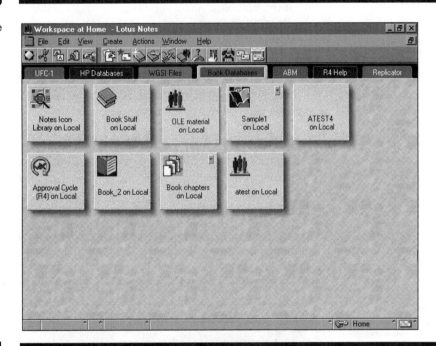

Figure 1.21

Use this dialog box to begin choosing a database that you wish to place on your workspace.

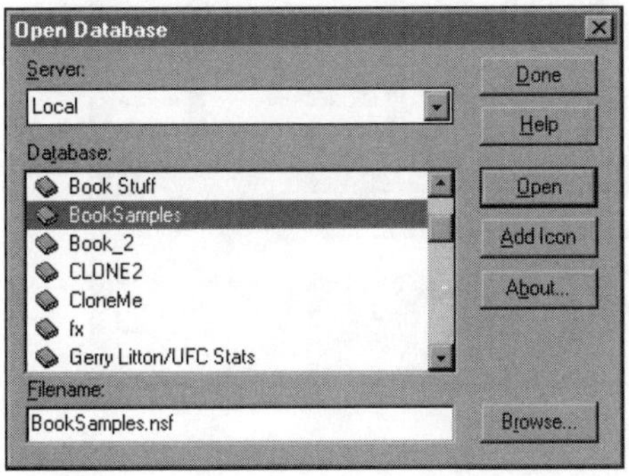

4. If the database is not in the \Data subdirectory under the main Notes directory or in a subdirectory under \Data, skip to the following section, "Searching Other Drives and Directories." Otherwise, go on to step 5.

5. Use the middle list box and the bottom edit box to locate the name of the database that you want. Notice that when you click on a file description in the middle list box, the bottom edit box displays the name of that file. For instance, in Figure 1.21 the file description BookSamples is selected, and the corresponding file name BOOKSAMPLES.NSF is shown in the bottom edit box.

6. If the database is in a subdirectory under \Data, scroll down in the middle window until the name of that subdirectory is displayed and then double-click that name. Then select the database that you want, as described in step 5.

7. After you've selected the database that you want, click the Open button. Notes will then install the icon for that database on your workspace, under the tab that's currently selected.

Searching Other Drives and Directories

If the database that you want to open is neither in the Notes\Data directory nor in one of its subdirectories, you can search other disk drives and directories to which you have read/write or read access. To accomplish this, begin by displaying the Open Database dialog box shown in Figure 1.21. Then:

1. To browse the current server, click the Browse button, displaying the dialog box shown in Figure 1.22.

Figure 1.22

Use this dialog box to browse the current server or workstation.

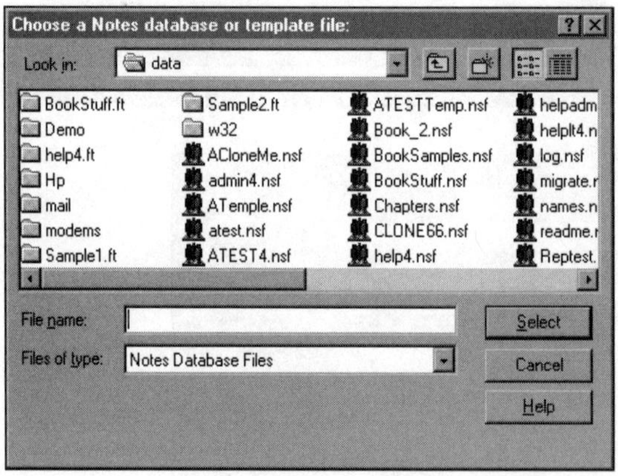

Choose a Notes database or template file:			? X

Look in: data

BookStuff.ft	Sample2.ft	ATESTTemp.nsf	helpadm
Demo	w32	Book_2.nsf	helplt4.n
help4.ft	ACloneMe.nsf	BookSamples.nsf	log.nsf
Hp	admin4.nsf	BookStuff.nsf	migrate.r
mail	ATemple.nsf	Chapters.nsf	names.n
modems	atest.nsf	CLONE66.nsf	readme.r
Sample1.ft	ATEST4.nsf	help4.nsf	Reptest.

File name: Select

Files of type: Notes Database Files   Cancel

Help

2. Use the top (LookIn) pull-down list box to select a disk drive.

3. Use the middle list box to select the directory and database that you want. Note that this dialog box does not display file descriptions, in contrast to the Open Database dialog shown in Figure 1.21.

4. After you've selected the database, and its file name appears in the edit box labeled File Name, click the Select button.

5. When the Open Database dialog reappears, click the Open button.

Viewing and Editing Documents

After you have installed the icon for a database on your Notes workspace, you can then open the database by double-clicking its icon. The main Notes display for that database then appears, and typically it looks something like that shown in Figure 1.12.

NOTE. *When you open a database, the display that you see may look very different from that shown in Figure 1.12. The main reasons for this are*

- *The database design may include a custom navigator that has been set up to appear automatically each time you open the database.*

- *A database option was selected by the database designer, telling Notes to open the database with the same main display that appeared when the database was last closed.*

Selecting a View

To open a particular document, you must first select the database view that you want to use. You can then use that view to choose the document that you want to view and/or edit.

You can select the view you want from either a custom navigator or the Notes standard navigator for the current database.

Using the Standard Navigator   If the custom navigator that's displayed does not point to the view that you want, you must switch to another navigator that does. If you don't know which navigator to use, you can switch to the standard Notes navigator by clicking View, Show, Folders. The standard navigator will then appear, similar to that shown in Figure 1.12.

When the standard navigator for a database is displayed, the top part will display the names of the database views and folders—unless that part is collapsed, so that only the title Folders And Views appears, as shown below:

To expand this part of the navigator, click anywhere on the title Folders And Views, so that the names of the database views and folders appear, as shown below:

To select the view that you want, simply click on its name under Folders And Views.

NOTE. *The Folders And Views part of the standard navigator displays the names of both folders and views for the current database. You can distinguish them because the name of each view is preceded by the following icon:*

Tip. If you can't get the names of any views or folders to appear under Folders And Views, you probably do not have adequate access to the database. If this happens, consult your database administrator.

Using a Custom Navigator   You can use a custom navigator to select a view, provided all of the following apply:

- A custom navigator has been designed for the database that you're using

- That navigator is currently displayed in the Navigator pane

- The navigator contains a hotspot that points to the view you want to use

If all of the preceding are true, you can simply click on the hotspot pointing to the view. The View pane will then change to display the view that you selected. For instance, the navigator shown in Figure 1.17 contains hotspots pointing to three different views called By Name, By Date, and By Interest.

Finding the Documents You Want

The View pane of the main database display shows the view that you most recently selected. If you plan to use this view for a while, you may want to maximize its size. To accomplish this, grab the vertical bar at the left end of the View pane and then drag the bar all the way to the left edge of the display, as shown in Figure 1.23. (Later, if you want to use part of the Navigator pane, you can redisplay it by repositioning that edge.)

Figure 1.23

You can maximize the size of the View pane.

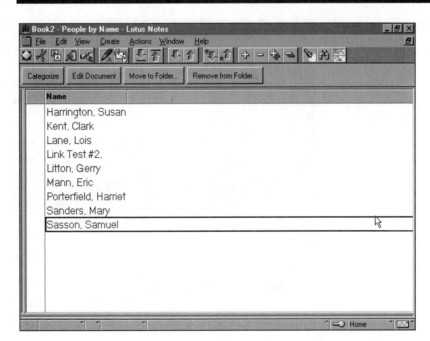

NOTE. *If you decide that the views available to you are inadequate, you can design your own. For details, see Chapter 7.*

To help you find the document you want, several options are available. You can

- Scroll through the view, using the displayed information to help you find the document you want.

- Use Quick Search, which searches a particular column to help you locate the appropriate document.

- Use the Find facility, which searches the view for selected words or phrases.

- Use full-text searching to look through the contents of each document for the word or phrase that you want.

If the view does not contain enough information to help you find the document you're looking for, you may want to display the Preview pane, as shown in Figure 1.24. When you highlight a document in the View pane, Notes automatically displays the top of that document in the Preview pane.

Figure 1.24

The Preview pane can help you find the documents you want.

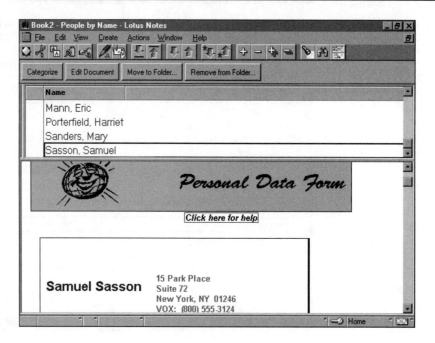

To display the Preview pane, you can click View, Document Preview, or you can use the mouse to drag up the horizontal bar at the bottom of the display. (If you have previously rearranged the positions of the three panes, the Preview pane may be somewhere other than at the bottom of the display—in which case, the bar that you drag will also be somewhere else.)

Using Quick Search   If the documents in the current view are sorted or categorized, you can simply type in the first few letters of the sorted value that you want. As you begin to type, the Quick Search edit box appears:

After typing in as many characters as you think you need to uniquely identify the document you want, click OK. If the view contains one or more sorted columns, Notes searches the first of them, highlighting the first document whose column value matches the characters that you entered. On the other hand, if the view contains one or more categorized columns, Notes searches the first of them, highlighting the first value containing the characters that you entered.

Using Find   You can use the Find mechanism to search for words displayed in the current view. This type of search is more comprehensive than Quick Search, because it looks in all the columns displayed in the view.
To use Find:

1. Click on the top document displayed in the current view.

2. Select Edit, Find/Replace, or click the Edit Find icon (below), displaying the Find dialog box.

3. Enter the text, word, or phrase that you want to search for.

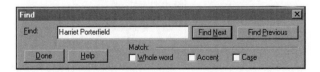

4. Click Find Next. Notes will search the view and highlight the first entry containing the text that you typed.

5. To search backward from the view entry that's currently highlighted, you can use the Find Previous button.

Displaying, Editing, and Deleting Documents

When you've found the document that you want, you can open it for browsing and editing by double-clicking on its entry in the current view. The document will appear on the screen, where you can then

- Read it

- Edit it and save your changes, provided you have proper access rights

- Delete it—again, provided you have adequate access

To read through a document, you can use the vertical scroll bar or the PgDn and PgUp keys. If you have editing rights, you can switch to edit mode and modify the document: Either double-click anywhere in the document; choose Actions, Edit Document; or click the Actions Edit SmartIcon. You can then modify the contents of the fields within the document. To save your changes, either choose File, Save or press the Esc key (in which case, Notes asks you if you want save your changes).

Deleting Documents   You can delete documents in several different ways. First, if you're currently reading or editing a document, you can delete it as follows:

1. Make sure that the document is not in edit mode: Open the Actions menu and make sure that the Edit option is available and *deselected*.

2. Either press the Del key or select Edit, Clear. Notes will then mark the document for deletion, close it, and open the next document in the view. The document will be marked for deletion in the view, as shown below. The actual deletion will occur when you next close the database.

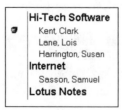

You can also delete one or more documents from a view. To do so, click in the leftmost column next to each document that you want to delete, so that a check mark appears, as shown in Figure 1.25. Then:

- To delete those documents immediately, select Edit, Cut.

- To mark the documents for later deletion (when you close the database), either select Edit, Clear or press Del.

Figure 1.25

A group of documents are
selected.

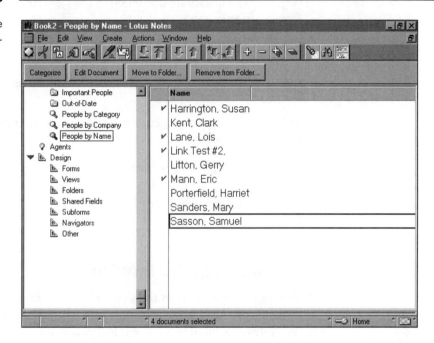

If a document is marked for deletion, you can undo its curse: Click on the document so that it becomes highlighted in the view and then select Edit, Undo Delete. You can also press the Del key—provided there are no check marks appearing next to any documents in the view.

Warning! This is an irreversible process.

Instead of merely marking documents in a view for deletion (so that they are subsequently deleted when you close the database), you can immediately remove them: Click the ones that you want to delete and then select Edit, Cut. Notes immediately removes the selected documents from the database.

Browsing by the Buttons

When you finish viewing and/or editing a particular document, you can use a couple of different techniques to browse and edit other documents. First, you can return to the current view, either by clicking the Esc key or by selecting

File, Close. You can then use a view to resume browsing through the documents, as described earlier in the section "Finding the Documents You Want."

Alternatively, while you still have an open document displayed, you can use the buttons on the SmartIcon bar to browse directly to other documents that are shown in the current view. The following table shows the icons you can use for browsing:

Icon	Displays This Document
	The next main document in the view (that is, skipping response documents)
	The previous main document in the view
	The next document (main document or response document)
	The previous document (main document or response document)
	The next unread document
	The previous unread document

■ Introducing the InfoBox

As part of its ongoing effort to increase the user-interface consistency for all of its major products, Lotus Development has added the Database InfoBox to the Notes arsenal of tools. The InfoBox is a one-stop shopping tool that you can use for assigning properties to the various bits and pieces that make up the overall design of a database.

Remember this distinction: You can use the InfoBox to set *design properties* of your databases; on the other hand, you do not use the InfoBox to assign *values* to the fields within your documents. For instance, to assign or change the features of a database, such as its name, its replication settings, and so on, you can use the InfoBox. Similarly, if you want to assign various properties to a particular view, such as its name or the colors used when it is displayed, you can also use the InfoBox.

The InfoBox is modeless. That is, while it's displayed on the screen, you can switch back and forth between it and whatever else is displayed within the Notes window. This is handy, because it means that you can leave the InfoBox displayed on the screen while you perform other Notes tasks. Then, whenever you need to use the InfoBox, it's right there.

To illustrate how the InfoBox works, let's suppose that your Notes work-space is currently displayed on the screen. Here's how to display the InfoBox for any of your databases:

1. Right-button-click on the database, displaying the pop-up menu shown in Figure 1.26.

2. Choose the option Database Properties, and the InfoBox for that data-base will appear, as shown in Figure 1.27.

Figure 1.26

You can use this pop-up menu to display the InfoBox.

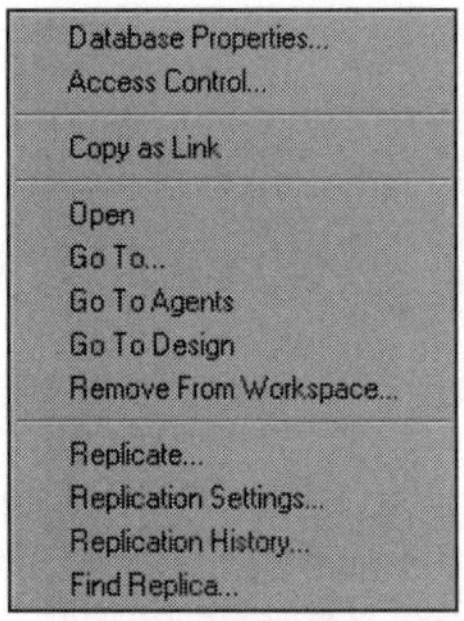

Figure 1.27

You can use this InfoBox to assign properties to the selected database.

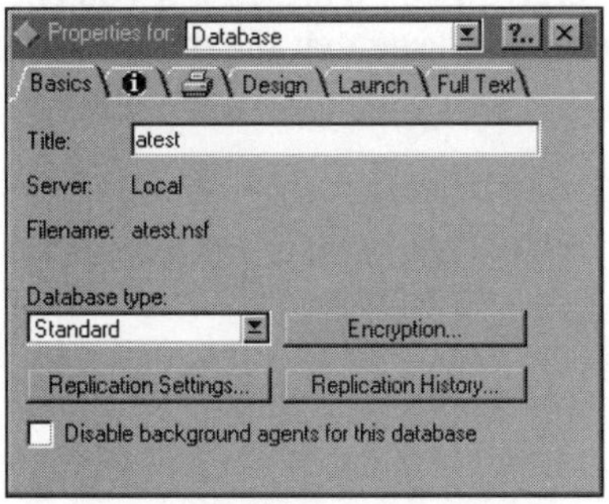

Notice that the InfoBox displays several different tabs. When you click a tab, a different page of the InfoBox appears, displaying different groups of database properties. To change a property, you simply delete the current value and enter a new one. For example, to change the descriptive name of the data-base, click the tab labeled Basics, type in the new name in the edit box labeled Title, and then click the check mark at the right end of the edit box.

As another example, here's how you can assign a template from which the current database will inherit its design:

1. Click the tab labeled Design, displaying the InfoBox shown in Figure 1.28.

Figure 1.28

Use this page of the
InfoBox to assign a
design template to the
current database.

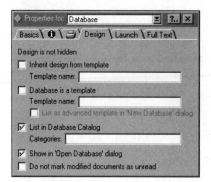

2. In the edit box labeled Template name (under the Inherit design from Template option), type in the name of the template database that you want to use and then click the corresponding check box.

The InfoBox always applies to the object that you're currently working with. For example, referring to Figure 1.27, if you click on another database icon in the workspace, you'll see that the database name on the Basics page of the InfoBox changes to the name of that database.

- *Creating a Database with a New Design*
- *Creating a Copy of Another Database*
- *Creating a Descriptive Database Icon*
- *Assigning Database Properties*
- *Setting Up Inheritance*

C H A P T E R

2

Creating a Database

CREATING A NEW DATABASE CAN BE A SIMPLE PROCESS, OR IT MAY involve months of design and testing. It all depends on how much database design material you can borrow from existing databases.

There are a number of different ways in which you can create new databases; the way you choose will depend on your intentions for the database:

- Will you be creating the design for the new database from scratch?

- Is the new database to be a replica copy of an existing one?

- Will the design for the new database be copied from an existing database or template?

- If you copy the design from another database, will you then want to make design modifications, or will you want the design of the new database to continue to inherit changes made to the design of the original one?

If your answer to the first question was "yes," then the design process may be quite lengthy, depending on its complexity. You'll need to design new forms, views, and possibly navigators and agents for the database. You'll also need to go through debugging and testing phases to ensure the completeness and accuracy of the design.

On the other hand, if you plan to copy the design of an existing database or template, your design process may be extremely short, inasmuch as some or all of the design work will essentially be done for you. This is particularly true when you either create a replica copy of a database or set up the new database so that it inherits all of its design features from a design template.

The first part of this chapter describes the various ways in which you can create new databases—whether from scratch or by copying existing designs. The latter part covers setup procedures common to all new databases.

Whenever you create a new database, Notes inserts an icon for it on your workspace. If the new database is a copy of an existing one, Notes also copies the little descriptive icon onto the new database icon, as shown below. You can leave this descriptive icon as is, or you can replace it with another one.

Descriptive icon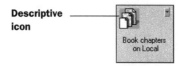

NOTE. *Notes unfortunately uses the term* database icon *in two different contexts. The first meaning refers to the little squares on the Notes workspace, each of which represents a database and is called the icon for that database. Notes also uses the term* database icon *to refer to the little identifying picture that you can attach to each database icon on the workspace. To help eliminate this confusion, we'll call the little pictures* descriptive database icons, *or simply* descriptive icons.

■ Creating a Database with a New Design

When you create a database completely from scratch, you begin by creating a new database file and assigning various options to the database. These options include the following:

- Selecting where you want to install the database: either on a server to which you have access or on your local workstation.

- Assigning a file name and descriptive title for the new database.

- Selecting whether or not to have Notes automatically encrypt the database. This can be particularly important if others can gain access to the workstation or server where the database is located.

- Assigning a maximum size to the database—either 1, 2, 3, or 4 gigabytes. Notes will impose this size limit on the database size for the entire lifetime of the database.

To create a new database and select any or all of the preceding options, follow these steps:

1. From the workspace, either click the New Database SmartIcon or select File, Database, New, displaying the dialog box shown in Figure 2.1.

Figure 2.1

Use this dialog box to begin creating a new database.

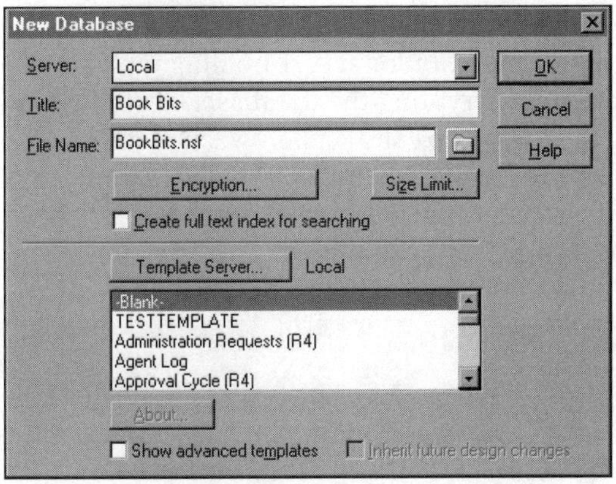

2. In the pull-down list box at the top, choose where you want to install the new database—either on a server or your workstation. If you intend to develop the database design at your workstation, install the database

there. Later, when the design is ready to be rolled out, you can transfer it to a server.

3. Click the button next to the File Name edit box and then select the disk drive and directory in which you want to save the new database file. When you're done, click OK to return to the New Database dialog box.

4. Enter a name for the new database file. Be sure to conform to the file-naming conventions for your particular system.

Note. If you enter a title before entering a file name, Notes copies the title as the file name, but you can override this default and enter whatever file name you wish.

5. Enter a title for the new database, which can include spaces and special characters—up to a maximum length of 32.

6. By default, Notes assigns a maximum, lifetime database size of 1 gigabyte. To select another size, click the Size Limit button, displaying the dialog box shown below, and then make your choice from the pull-down list box.

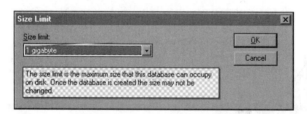

7. By default, the new database will be available to any user having access to the workstation or server holding the database. You can limit this access by encrypting the database: Click the Encryption button, displaying the dialog box shown below; click the lower radio button; and then select the level of encryption that you want. (You can also allow selected users access to the encrypted database. For details, see "Local Database Encryption," later in this chapter.)

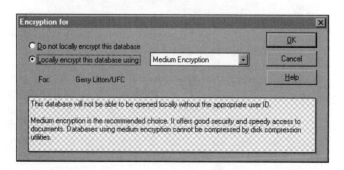

8. When you're finished selecting options, click OK. Notes will create the new database file; it will also insert a new database icon for it on your workspace.

NOTE. *Most of the options you select while creating the database can be changed at any time during the life of the database—with one exception. The maximum size that you set for the database (the preceding step 6) is fixed for the lifetime of the database. Later, if you need to increase the database size beyond the limit you select here, you will have to create a replica copy of the current database (see "Creating a Replica Copy of a Database," later in the chapter), specifying a larger limit for the copy, and then you can delete the original database.*

Because you're creating a brand new database from scratch, you'll need to design all of its forms, views, navigators, and so on. Database design covers a variety of topics, which are covered in the following chapters.

■ Creating a Copy of Another Database

There are three situations in which you may want to use the design of an existing database as the basis for the one you're creating:

- You want to make a replica copy of an existing database. Subsequently, you'll use Notes' replication procedures to keep the new database synchronized with the original one.

- You are lucky enough to stumble across an existing database whose design contains one or more elements that you can use.

- You want the design of the new database to duplicate that of a database template. The latter can be either a standard template supplied by Notes or one that you previously created.

Creating a Replica Copy of a Database

You create a replica copy of a database when you want both the design and contents of the new database to be kept synchronized with the original. (By contrast, you create a copy of a design template when you want only the design of the original to be kept in sync with the new one.) For instance, if you routinely work remotely on a laptop, you might want to create a replica copy of a database stored on your home server. Then you could periodically replicate between the two copies.

When you create a replica copy of an existing database, Notes copies both the original design and the contents of the original database (that is, all of its data). As part of the creation process, you have the following options:

- Whether or not to copy the original access control list.

- Whether to copy the database immediately or wait until the next regularly scheduled replication. If you choose the latter, only an icon for the new database will be created now on your workspace. During replication, the rest of the database will be copied.

- Whether to encrypt the new replica copy.

  To create a new replica copy of an existing database, follow these steps:

1. To begin, display your Notes workspace.

2. If the original database (that is, the one you want to create a copy of) is displayed on your workspace, click on it and then select File, Replication, New Replica. Notes then displays the dialog box shown in Figure 2.2. *Now skip to step 8.*

Figure 2.2

Use this dialog box to select a new file name and a new descriptive name for the replica database that you're creating.

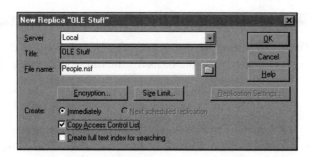

3. If the original database is *not* on your workspace, click anywhere on your workspace *except on a database icon* and then select File, Replication, New Replica, and you'll see the Choose Database dialog box shown in Figure 2.3.

Figure 2.3

Use this dialog box to select an existing database.

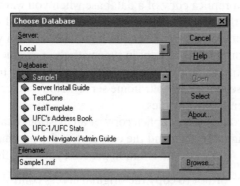

4. Using the Choose Database dialog box, select the server that contains the database from which you want to create a replica copy.

5. If you know the full name (including complete path) of the database file that you want to copy, type it into the Filename edit box and then skip to step 7. Otherwise, go to step 6.

6. To locate the database file that you want to replicate, click the Browse button, displaying the dialog box shown in Figure 2.4. Select the disk drive and directory containing the database, make sure that the database's file name appears in the File Name edit box, and then click the Select button.

Figure 2.4

Use this dialog box to select the disk drive, directory, and file name for the database that you want to copy.

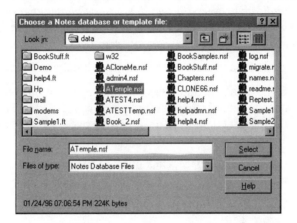

7. When the complete file name (including path) appears in the Filename edit box in the Choose Database dialog box, click the Select button, and you'll see the New Replica dialog box shown in Figure 2.2.

8. In the New Replica dialog box, if you want to, enter a file name and title for the new database that you're creating.

9. Select size limit and encryption options, as described in the previous section, "Creating a Database with a New Design." Note that the size limit you select is fixed for the lifetime of the database, although you can circumvent this limitation (see the last Note in the previous section).

10. Select the access control and indexing options that you want, at the bottom of the dialog box. (If you're not sure about these, just leave them as they are.)

11. Click OK. Notes will create the new database replica and an icon for it on your workspace.

The new database will be an exact duplicate of the original one. Any changes that you subsequently make to the new copy may or may not be replicated to the original, depending on the replication settings in both copies.

Creating a Normal Copy of Another Database

In contrast to creating a *replica copy* of a database, you may want to create just a normal copy of another database. You can then modify the design of the new copy in any way you wish, and your changes will have no effect on the original database.

NOTE. *Here's the difference between a replica copy of a database and a normal copy: When you create a replica copy, the replica ID numbers of the original and new databases are identical. Because of this identification, Notes can replicate between the two databases. On the other hand, when you create a normal copy of a database, Notes assigns it a new, unique replica ID number. Consequently, replication cannot occur between the two.*

To make a normal copy of another database, follow these steps:

1. If the database that you want to copy is not on your workspace, you'll have to place it there before going on. (For details on adding the icon for the original database to your workspace, see the later section "Opening a Database on Your Workspace.")

2. On your workspace, click once on the icon for the database that you want to copy.

3. Select File, Database, New Copy, and you'll see the dialog box shown in Figure 2.5.

4. In the top pull-down list box, select where you want to create the new database. This can be either on a server to which you have access or on your local workstation.

Figure 2.5

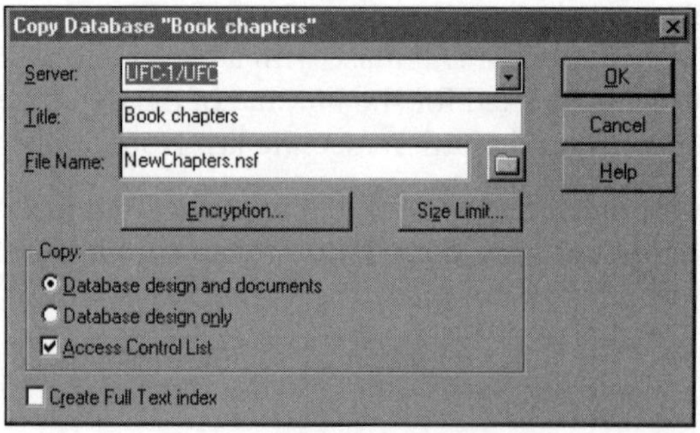

Use this dialog box to assign a new file name and description to a database copy that you're creating.

5. In the File Name edit box, enter the complete path and file name for the new database. If necessary, you can click the Browse button to help you choose the appropriate disk drive and directory.

6. Enter a title for the new database, which can include spaces and special characters—up to a maximum length of 32.

7. Select size limit and encryption options. For details see the previous section "Creating a Database with a New Design."

8. Select the access control and indexing options that you want at the bottom of the dialog box. (If you're not sure about these, just leave them as they are.)

9. Select size limit and encryption options as described in the previous section.

10. Click OK. Notes will create the new database copy on the disk drive and directory that you selected; it will also create an icon for the new database on your workspace.

You can now make whatever design changes you want to the new database. The following chapters deal with the various aspects of database design.

Opening a Database on Your Workspace

If you want to gain access to an existing database, such as for making a copy of it as described in the previous section, you need to create a database icon for it on your workspace.

Here's how to accomplish this:

1. Click the workspace tab where you want to place the database icon.

2. Select File, Database, Open, and you'll see the Open Database dialog box shown in Figure 2.6.

Note. If you enter a title before entering a file name, Notes copies the title as the file name, but you can override this default and enter whatever file name you wish.

Figure 2.6

Use this dialog box to place an icon for an existing database on your Notes workspace.

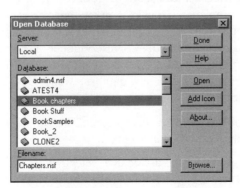

3. Using the pull-down list box at the top, select the location of the database. This could be either your local workstation or a server to which you have access.

4. Using the Browse button, locate and select the disk drive, directory, and file name containing the database that you want to open. Then click your way back to the Open Database dialog box. If you're more familiar with the title of the database than its filename, you can use the Database list box in the Open Database dialog box to locate the database by title.

5. From the Open Database dialog box, click the Open button, and Notes will create an icon on the workspace for the database that you selected.

This procedure allows you to create icons on your workspace for Notes databases only—not for databases defined as templates, because the names of template databases do not appear on the Open Database dialog box. The following section describes how to create a new database that's a copy of a template.

Creating a New Database from a Template

You can create a new database whose design is an exact copy of an existing database template. Because a Notes template is really a Notes database with a special file-name extension, you might wonder what the difference is between making a copy of a database and making a copy of a template.

For ordinary templates, there will be no difference. For example, Notes supplies several standard database designs which it assigns the status of templates by giving them each the .NTF file name extension. One of these is the Discussion database, which you can use as the starting point to create your own discussion database, whose design you can then customize in any way you wish.

However, some templates are raised to the status of *design templates*. When you create a new database by copying a design template, you have one important option: You can set up your database so that any changes made to the original template—either by you or someone else—are automatically copied to your own database. (The Notes server program called Design is responsible for maintaining this correspondence, although you can perform the process manually as well.)

Here's how to create a new database whose design is based on that of an existing template:

1. From your Notes workspace, select File, Database, New, and you'll see the dialog box shown in Figure 2.1.

2. In the top part of the dialog box, select where you want the new database to reside. This can be either a server to which you have access or your local workstation.

Note. If you enter a title before entering a file name, Notes copies the title as the file name, but you can override this default and enter whatever file name you wish.

3. In the File Name edit box, enter the complete path and file name for the new database. If necessary, you can click the Browse button to help you choose the appropriate disk drive and directory. When selecting a file name, be sure to conform to the file-naming conventions of your system.

4. Enter a descriptive title for the database. This can contain just about any combination of letters, digits, and so on.

5. Select size limit and encryption options. For details see the previous section "Creating a Database with a New Design."

6. Select the location that contains the template file you want to copy: Click the Template Server button and then select either Local (your workstation) or the name of the server.

7. Click the button labeled Advanced Templates, to show all of the available templates on the server or workstation that you selected.

8. In the bottom list box, select the template (when you highlight the descriptive name of each template, its file name appears underneath the list box).

9. If you're not sure which template you want to select, you can highlight a likely candidate and then press the About button. Notes will display a window of information about the template.

10. If you want the new database to inherit any changes made to the design of the template that you selected, select the option Inherit Future De- sign Changes. If this option is not available, the template that you chose is not a design template.

11. Click OK. Notes will create the new database copy on the disk drive and directory that you selected; it will also create an icon for the new data- base on your workspace.

■ Creating a Descriptive Database Icon

Your Notes workspace probably contains an assortment of database icons similar to those shown in Figure 2.7, and most of them contain little descrip- tive pictures that help you identify the different databases. When you create a database icon on your workspace for a database supplied by Notes, the descriptive icon is included. However, when you create a new database that's not a copy of an existing one, you'll need to supply your own descriptive icon.

There are several techniques available to you for creating descriptive icons for your databases. First, you can scan the Notes database called ICONS.NSF; if you see an icon that you like, you can use it for one of your databases. You can also use a variety of techniques for creating your own icons, such as Notes' own icon editor.

Figure 2.7

You can attach a
descriptive icon to each
of your databases.

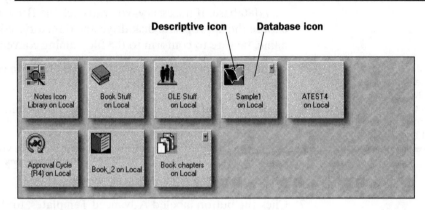

NOTE. *You can use the techniques described in the following sections either for new databases or for a database whose descriptive icon you want to replace.*

Using the Notes Icon Database

The Notes icon database, which is supplied along with the Notes software in the file ICONS.NSF, contains a large number of icons covering a wide variety of topics. To use this database, you'll need to begin by opening it on your workspace. You can then browse through it to see if it contains any icons you like. If you find one, you can copy it to your system clipboard; and from there you can paste it as a descriptive icon for your own database.

Finding the Icon You Want

Note. If you can't find the ICONS.NSF database, consult your Notes administrator. The database may have been stuffed into some out-of-the-way corner.

Here's how to use Notes' handy treasure trove of icons:

1. To begin, you'll need to find the icon database, whose name is ICONS.NSF, and whose descriptive title is Notes Icons Library. This database normally lives in either the Notes \Data subdirectory or one of its subdirectories although it may also be stored on a Notes server.

2. Open ICONS.NSF on your workspace.

3. After you've installed the new database icon, double-click on it to open the main database view, similar to the one shown in Figure 2.8.

4. In the upper part of the Navigator pane, click on Main View, so that the View pane looks like that shown in Figure 2.8.

5. Scroll through the View pane. If you see a likely looking topic, double-click on it. Notes will then display that document, which contains a set of icons related to the topic that you just selected. Figure 2.9 shows a typical document.

Figure 2.8

Using the View pane, double-click on a category that might contain icons of interest.

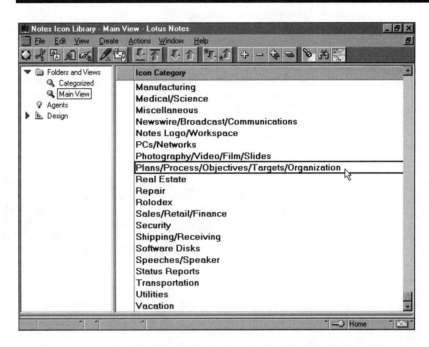

Figure 2.9

Each document in the ICONS.NSF database displays a sample of similar icons, such as this one.

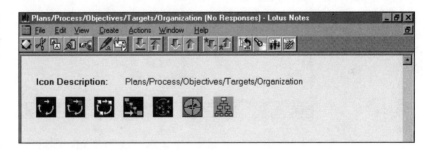

6. Enter edit mode: Either double-click anywhere in the document or choose Actions, Edit Document.

7. If you see an icon that you want to use as the descriptive icon for your new database, click on it; then copy it to the clipboard by selecting Edit, Copy.

Installing the Icon

If you found an icon of interest in Notes' database of icons, and if you copied the icon to the Clipboard by following the preceding steps, you can now set up that icon so that it appears as the descriptive icon for your new database. Here's how to proceed:

1. Display your Notes workspace and then double-click on the database where you want to install the icon.

2. When the main display for your database appears, make sure that the Design option (in the lower part of the Navigator pane) is expanded; if it isn't, click once on Design.

3. Click on Other in the Navigator pane, so that the View pane resembles that shown below:

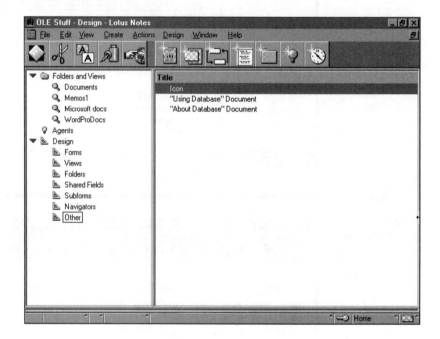

4. In the View pane, double-click on Icon, and you'll see a display similar to that shown in Figure 2.10. This is the Notes icon editor, which you can use to create new descriptive icons.

5. The main part of the display should be blank, since presumably you're creating an icon for a database that doesn't yet have one. However, if a picture does appear, then it's the descriptive icon for the current database. To replace that picture with the one you selected earlier, click the Clear button and then go on to step 6.

6. Click the Paste button; the icon that you selected earlier and saved on your system's Clipboard will be pasted into the icon editor.

Figure 2.10

You can use the Notes
icon editor either to
insert icons that you
obtained elsewhere or to
create your own
descriptive database
icons.

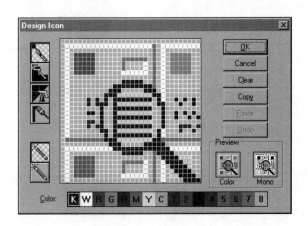

Note. For details about
using Notes' icon editor,
see "Creating Your Own
Icons," later in this
chapter.

7. If you're artistically inclined, you may want to use the icon editor to enhance the icon. Note that the little icons labeled Preview in the lower-
right-hand corner show how the icon will appear in the database icon on
your workspace.

8. When you're done, click OK.

The descriptive icon is now stored as part of the current database, and it
will appear within the database icon on your workspace.

Copying an Icon from Another Database

There's no law against using the same descriptive icon for two different databases. If you find an existing database that contains a descriptive icon you
would like to use for your own database, you can easily copy that icon, using
your system's Clipboard and the Notes' icon editor.

Here's how to copy the descriptive icon from another database (which
we'll call the *source database*) onto your own (the *target database*):

1. To begin, you'll need to open the source database onto your Notes
workspace, so that its icon appears there.

2. Then, double-click on the icon for the source database, so that its main
display appears (View pane, Navigator pane, and so on).

3. Make sure that the Design option (in the lower part of the Navigator
pane) is expanded; if it isn't, click once on Design.

4. Click on Other in the Navigator pane.

5. Double-click on Icon in the View pane, displaying the Notes icon editor (Figure 2.10). The picture that appears is the descriptive icon for the current database.

6. Save a copy of the descriptive icon to your system Clipboard: Click the Copy button.

7. Exit from the icon editor (click OK) and then click your way back to your Notes workspace.

8. Find the database icon for the target database.

9. Using the procedure outlined in steps 2 through 5, display the icon editor.

10. If the target database already contains a descriptive icon, it will appear here; click the Clear button to delete this icon.

11. Click the Paste button to retrieve the icon you copied from the source database. Then finish up by clicking OK.

The descriptive icon that you copied will now appear on the target database's icon on your workspace.

Using Icons from Other Sources

If you have access to other sources of bitmapped icons—perhaps your own clip art collection—you may be able to use them as descriptive icons for your databases. Naturally, there are restrictions on what you can use, but within these limitations you may be able to choose from zillions of computerized art images.

There are two main restrictions on the type of images that you can use as descriptive icons for Notes databases: The first is that an image must be in .BMP format. This means that if an image is stored in a file with a .BMP file-name extension, Notes can probably use it. Alternatively, if an image is stored as part of a group of pictures within a single graphics file, when you select the image and copy it to your system's Clipboard, the image must be recognized as a .BMP bitmapped image.

The second restriction is that the image can't be any larger than 32 by 32 pixels, because that's how much space Notes allocates for each descriptive database icon.

Here's an outline of the steps that you need to follow in order to use a .BMP image from another source:

1. Using whatever software is appropriate, display the image that you want to use. For example, if the image is stored as a .BMP file, and if you're using Windows 95, you can use the Paint applet to load the file.

2. Make sure that the image fits within the 32 by 32 size limit. If necessary, crop the image.

3. Copy the image to the system Clipboard.

4. Paste the image into the database. For details, see "Installing the Icon," earlier in this chapter.

Creating Your Own Icons

If you have artistic abilities, you may want to create your own custom icons for your databases. You can use any available software, or you can use the Notes icon editor.

If you use an external software package to create an icon, the result must be bitmapped (.BMP-type format), and its size must be equal to or less than 32 by 32 pixels. The end result of your efforts must be copied to the system Clipboard. After that, you can follow the steps in the earlier section "Installing the Icon."

You can also use the Notes icon editor to create your own masterpieces. This editor offers a standard assortment of icon-editing tools, and you're automatically confined to a 32 by 32 palette.

Here's how to use the icon editor to create your own descriptive database icon:

1. To begin, display your workspace; then double-click on the icon of the database to which you want to add a descriptive icon.

2. Make sure that the Design option (in the lower part of the Navigator pane) is expanded; if it isn't, click once on Design.

3. Click on Other in the Navigator pane.

4. Double-click on Icon in the View pane, displaying the Notes icon editor (Figure 2.10).

5. Using the various drawing tools, draw the icon. (For details about using these tools, see the following section, "Using the Drawing Tools.")

6. When your drawing is finished, click OK. The new icon will be displayed within the database icon on your workspace.

Using the Drawing Tools

The upper-left part of the icon editor window (see Figure 2.10) contains buttons for the available drawing tools, which are summarized in the following table. To use a tool, simply click on it then use the mouse to draw or erase pixels. For each operation, you begin by selecting either the Draw Mode or

Erase Mode tool. Next, select the tool that you want to use for drawing or erasing. Finally, use the mouse to color or erase pixels.

Icon	Purpose
	Paint tool: Use to draw one pixel at a time
	Fill Straight tool: Use to fill in straight lines
	Fill tool: Use to fill an enclosed area
	Draw Straight tool: Use to draw a straight line
	Draw Mode tool: Use for drawing and filling
	Erase Mode tool: Use for erasing lines and fill areas

Here's a synopsis of the operations you can perform:

- To draw pixels or fill enclosed regions with color, click the Draw Mode tool.
- To erase pixels, click the Erase Mode tool.
- To select the current color, click on it at the bottom of the window.
- To color a pixel with the current color, click on that pixel.
- To draw lines of pixels using the current color, place the mouse cursor where you want to draw, hold down the mouse button, and then drag the mouse.
- To erase pixels one at a time, select the Erase Mode tool and then click on each pixel to be erased. You can also hold down the mouse button and drag the mouse across the pixels that you want to erase.
- To fill an enclosed area with the current color, use the Fill tool or the Fill Straight tool (be sure that the Draw Mode tool is also selected).
- To erase the color from an enclosed area, click the Erase Mode tool and then use the Fill tool.

■ Assigning Database Properties

As part of creating a new database, you must assign it various properties. Some of these, like the database title, are informational and have little effect on the performance of the database. However, some database properties—like the access control list—are quite important and can have a significant impact on the database.

Your choices for the different database properties aren't written in stone; during the lifetime of a database, you can change the properties at any time. Some changes, such as the choice of the database's design template, can have immediate and significant effect on the database. Other changes are more or less cosmetic.

With the exception of the access control settings, you use the Database InfoBox—shown in Figure 2.11—to set the various database properties. You can display this InfoBox from any part of a database using any of the following:

- If your Notes workspace is displayed, right-button-click on the icon of the database whose properties you want to choose and then select Database Properties from the popup menu that appears.

- From anywhere within the database, choose File, Database, Properties.

- If the InfoBox for any part of the database (Form, View, or whatever) is currently displayed, pull down the list box at the top of the InfoBox and then click on Database.

Figure 2.11

You use the database InfoBox to assign various properties to a database.

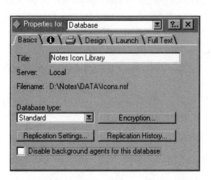

NOTE. *In all of the following sections, we'll assume that the InfoBox for the current database is displayed.*

Basic Properties

Some database properties are pretty mundane: Once you assign values for them, you'll probably never need to change them—although you wouldn't want to swear to this. For example, the database title helps you to identify the database when you're trying to find it among thousands of others. Although you probably will never need to change the title, there's no rule that says you can't.

Database Title and Type

The title of a database appears on the database's icon on your workspace; the title also appears in the Open Database dialog box (click on File, Database, Open). In both circumstances, the title can help you to identify the database that you're seeking.

To assign a title to a database, follow these easy steps:

1. Click the database InfoBox tab labeled Basics.

2. Type in a descriptive title for the database. You can use just about any characters you can find on the keyboard—up to a maximum length of 32.

The Basics tab on the InfoBox also offers three selections for the database *type*. Almost invariably, you should select Standard, which happens to be the default. The Library option is only for special types of databases that contain lists of other databases. The Personal Journal option is only for databases created with the Journal 4 template.

Selecting Database-Wide Printing Properties

If you intend to print any part of the database, to a limited extent you can format the pages by designing a header and footer, specifying page numbering, and setting the page size and margins.

For printing various parts of the database, you can use the database InfoBox for formatting the headers and footers. These options provide you with a handy way to preformat *anything* you ever print from the database—forms, documents, or lists of documents from a view. However, you can always override these default database print options by assigning special formatting options for particular documents or forms.

Here's how to assign header and footer formatting that applies to anything you print from a database:

1. Click the third tab from the left on the Database InfoBox, displaying the options shown in Figure 2.12.

2. To format the header or footer, click the appropriate radio button.

3. Type in the text that you want to appear within the header or footer.

4. You can also insert tabs, page numbering, and other assorted special text. See the following section, "Special Formatting Tips," for details.

5. Use the options at the bottom of the InfoBox to assign a special font to the text in the header or footer.

Figure 2.12

Use these options to
format headers and
footers of printouts.

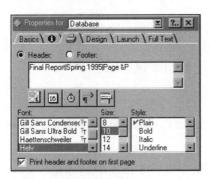

Special Formatting Tips   To insert special text, you can use the icons shown
in the following table.

To Insert	Use This Button
Page numbers	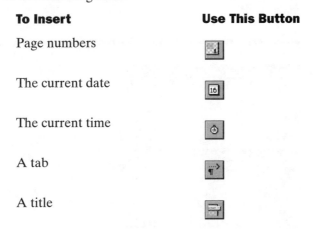
The current date	
The current time	
A tab	
A title	

When you click on one of the buttons listed in the preceding table, Notes
inserts a special code into the header or footer space. For example, the code
for page numbers is &P, whereas &D is the code for the current date. Except
for these special codes, whatever text you type into the header or footer
space will appear as is when printed. Thus, for example, you could insert
page numbers by typing in "Page " (including the space) and then clicking
the Page Number button.

You can also insert multiple lines in headers and footers: press the Enter
key to begin a new line.

Here are a few other handy tips to help you do your formatting:

•   Notes provides for two fixed tab positions: a center tab and a right-align
     tab. When you click the Tab icon, Notes displays the I symbol in the
     header or footer space.

- To center a text block, insert one tab, type the text, and then insert a second tab.

- To right-align a text block, insert two tabs and then type in the text.

- To left-align one text block and then right-align the rest of the text on the line, type in the first block, insert one tab, and then type in the remaining text.

- You can left-align one text block, center a second one, and right-align a third block: Type in the first block, click the Tab button, type in the second block, again click the Tab button, and then type in the last block.

Other Formatting Options   You can also choose several other database-wide print-formatting options, such as the starting page number, the header and footer sizes, and the margin settings. To adjust any of these options, select File, Page Setup, displaying the options shown in Figure 2.13; then make your choices.

Figure 2.13

Use these options to set various page-layout features.

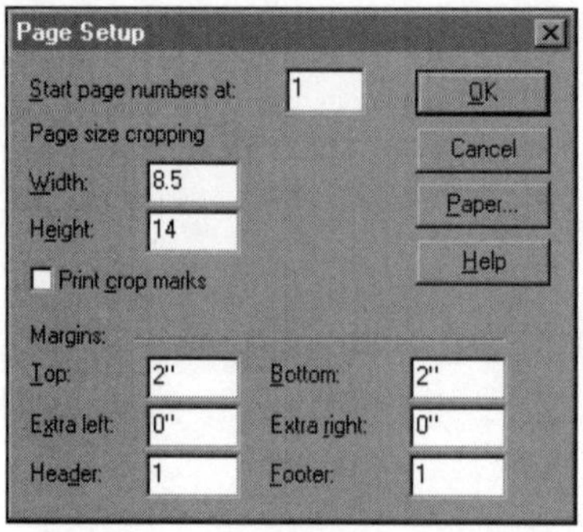

You can also change the page orientation for printing:

1. Make sure that something other than your workspace is displayed.

2. Select File, Print.

3. Click the Printer button.

4. Click the Setup button.

5. Select the page orientation that you want.

Local Database Encryption

When you're designing a new database, you'll probably be working on your local workstation. To protect against fidgety fingers (someone else's, of course) accidentally trashing your design work, you might wish to encrypt your local copy during the design phase. Then, only you—or someone who knows your password—can access the database on your workstation. In addition to yourself, you can allow a select few to access an encrypted database.

Here's how to provide for encryption of a database that's stored at your workstation:

1. Make sure that you're logged on with your own user ID (or whichever ID you plan to use while working on the database).

2. Click the Basics tab on the Database InfoBox, displaying the options shown in Figure 2.11.

3. Click the button labeled Encryption, displaying the following dialog box:

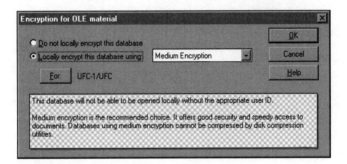

4. Click the lower of the two radio buttons and then choose a level of encryption.

5. If you want to allow another person to access the database: Click the button labeled For, displaying the list of names in your Notes Names & Address book (Figure 2.14); select a name from this list; and then click OK.

Template Issues

Occasionally, when you create a new database you'll want its design to be an exact copy of another *template* database. In the earlier section "Creating a New Database from a Template," we described how to copy the design of an existing template to a new database. You may want to use this design simply as a starting point, from which you plan to customize the new database design.

Alternatively, you may want the database design to continue to follow the design of the original template, so that whenever the template is redesigned by you or someone else, its changes will propagate to the new database. In "Creating a New Database from a Template," we also described how to accomplish this when you first create the new database. However, you may not have chosen to do this at that time, but second thoughts have led

Figure 2.14

Select the name of whomever you want to grant access to a locally encrypted database.

you to change your mind. If this is the case, you can set a database option so that the database inherits whatever changes are made to the original design template.

There may also be circumstances in which you may be designing a new database that you plan to use as a template—either a normal template or a design template. In either case, you need to set appropriate database options.

■ Setting Up Inheritance

To set up a database so that it continues to inherit its design from a design template, follow these steps:

1. Make sure the Database InfoBox is displayed and then click on the Design tab, displaying the dialog box shown in Figure 2.15.

Figure 2.15

Use these options to establish inheritance between the current database and another one.

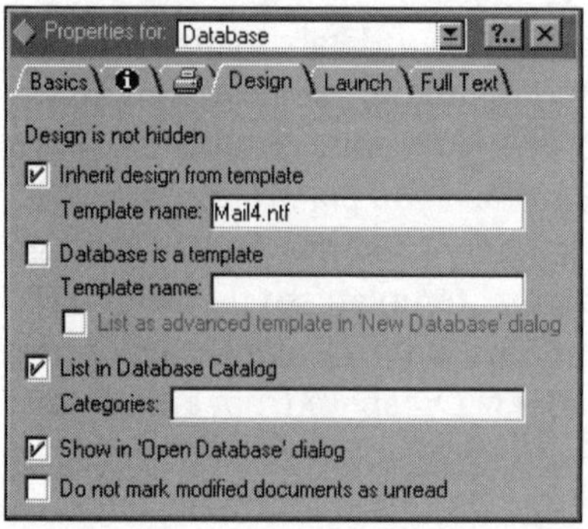

2. Select the option Inherit Design From Template. Then, in the edit box immediately below, type in the name of the template whose design is to be inherited. Note that this is the special template name assigned to that template; *you do not type in either the name or the title of the template* (see the discussion in the following section on assigning template names).

If you're not sure about the template name, you can find out as follows: Install the database icon for the template on your workspace; display the Database InfoBox for that database; and then click the Design InfoBox tab, displaying the options shown in Figure 2.15. The template name will appear in the edit box labeled (strangely enough) Template Name.

NOTE. *Instead of having a database inherit its entire design from a template, you can arrange for it to inherit only selected design elements, such as specific views, forms, and so on. Techniques for accomplishing this will be discussed in appropriate chapters later in the book.*

Establishing a Database as a Template

You can set up the current database to be a template—either a regular template or a design template—so that you or others can easily copy its design for new databases. When a database is set up as a template, it appears in the New Database dialog box (select File, Database, New), in the list of templates at the bottom of the window, as shown in Figure 2.1. In addition, if a database is a design template, changes made to its design can be inherited by other databases.

In order for Notes to recognize a database as a template, two things must be true:

- The file-name extension for the database must be .NTF (as opposed to .NSF for ordinary databases).

- The database must be in the \Data subdirectory under the main Notes directory.

If either of the preceding conditions is not present, here's how to correct the situation:

1. Deselect the database; that is, be sure that you click somewhere on your workspace other than the icon for that database.

2. Temporarily exit back to your operating system.

3. Using the appropriate system tools, rename the database file, changing its file-name extension to .NTF. Furthermore, if necessary, move or copy the database file to the \Data subdirectory under the main Notes directory.

4. Return to Notes.

If you have used the preceding steps to change either the name or location of the database, and if your workspace currently displays an icon for the database, you'll need to delete that icon because Notes still associates it with the original database name and location—which no longer exist. You can then create a new icon on the workspace, selecting the new database file name and location.

Instead of establishing a database as an ordinary template, as just described, you may want to set it up as a design template. In order to accomplish this, you must give the database an .NTF file-name extension and place it in the \Data subdirectory, as previously described. In addition, you must assign it a template name, as follows:

1. On the Database InfoBox, click the Design tab, displaying the options shown in Figure 2.15.

2. Select the option Database Is A Template. Then, in the edit box directly below, type in a unique template name. This can be any combination of characters, including blanks. For various practical reasons, it's a good idea to limit this name to 25 or 30 characters.

- *Creating a New Form*
- *Copying Forms*
- *Setting the Form Properties*

3

Creating Forms

*F*ORMS ARE ONE OF THE MAJOR BUILDING BLOCKS OF A DATABASE. When you want to create a group of documents of a particular type, you must first create a corresponding form. The form determines not only the type of information you can insert into the documents, but also the layout of this information.

You can create as many different forms as you wish for each database, and each form can be just about as long as you like.

In addition to creating your own forms, you can borrow from previous work. If another database contains a form whose design is close to the one you have in mind, you can copy and paste it into your database. You can then either use the form as is, or you can make whatever modifications you wish.

You can also selectively copy one or more forms from either a template or a design template. In the latter case, you can establish a link from the database to the design template so that future changes to the form in the template are automatically inherited by your database.

When creating a new form, you must assign it various properties, such as its name, background color, and a myriad of other options. Notes sets default values for nearly all of these options, so you can ignore most of them when you first begin to design a new form. However, you'll need to understand the purpose of these options, so that if and when a problem arises you'll be able to fix things up by setting the appropriate options.

■ Creating a New Form

When creating a new form, the steps you take will depend on whether you intend to build the form from scratch, or whether you'll be copying an existing form from another database or template. This section concentrates on creating a new form from the ground up. Later sections discuss how to copy existing forms.

To begin creating a new form in a database, follow these steps:

1. If your workspace is currently displayed, click on the database and then select View, Design, so that the Navigator and View panes for that database are displayed.

2. Select Create, Design, Form. Notes will create a new form and display it in the Form Design window, as shown in Figure 3.1.

The top half of this window, which we'll refer to as the *Layout pane*, is where you'll be inserting the various bits and pieces that constitute the new form. The bottom half, which is called the *Design pane*, is where you'll be supplying details for new fields, actions, and other parts of the form.

Maximizing the Design Space

When you first begin laying out a new form, you may find it helpful to maximize the amount of screen real estate available for the Layout pane, because this is where you'll be arranging the various form elements. To accomplish this, you can hide the Design pane by pulling down the View menu and deselecting

Figure 3.1

Start here to begin creating a new form.

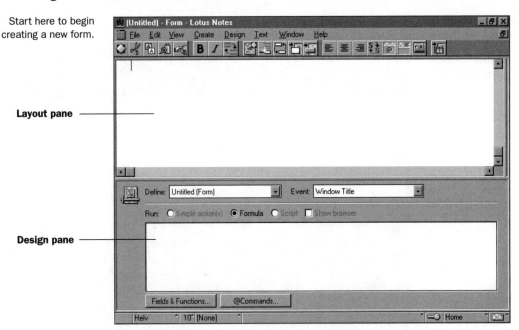

Layout pane

Design pane

the Design Pane option. Or you can reduce the size of the Design pane but still leave it visible: Click and drag down the top border of the Design pane until just a little bit of the pane remains visible.

TIP. *For various reasons (such as that you accidentally hit the wrong set of keystrokes), the form display may also include the Action pane on the right, as shown in Figure 3.2. If this occurs, you can free up that screen space by hiding the pane, which you won't need for a while: Pull down the View menu and then deselect the Action Pane option.*

After creating the new, empty form, you are ready to assign it various properties. The latter part of this chapter is devoted to a discussion of form properties; the next chapter describes how to add design elements to the form.

■ Copying Forms

If you're lucky enough, you may be able to find a form in another database or template whose design is close to a new form you intend to create. Or you may even be able to use a form exactly as is from another database. If that database is a design template, you can optionally set up the new form so that it inherits changes made in the future to the original one.

Figure 3.2

The Action pane takes up valuable screen space that you can better use for designing the layout of a new form.

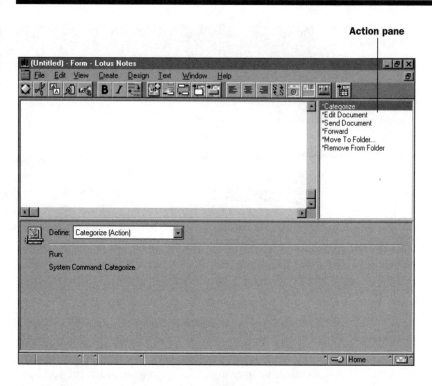

Copying a Form from a Database or Template

Note. When you copy a form, you're copying only the design—not any of the documents created with the original form.

You can easily copy a form from a database or template to the database that you're designing. After you copy a form, you can then modify it any way you wish—both its structure and its properties. You can also make a copy of a form already in your database. For instance, you might want a database to have two versions of the same form, one slightly different from the other.

Copying from Another Database

To copy a form, follow these steps:

1. From your Notes workspace, select the database containing the form that you want to copy and then select View, Design, displaying the main display for that database.

2. In the middle of the Navigator pane, click on Forms, so that the View pane (the one on the right) displays a list of the forms in this database.

3. Click once on the form that you want to copy.

4. Copy the form to the Clipboard: Select Edit, Copy. Now you're ready to copy the new form into the database you're designing.

5. Return to your workspace and then click on the icon for that database.

6. Again select View, Design and then click on Forms in the Navigator pane.

7. Copy the new form into the database: Select Edit, Paste.

The name of the new form will appear in the list of forms for the database. You can now open that form and change it in any way you wish. (For details about designing forms, see Chapter 4.)

Copying from the Same Database

Making a duplicate copy of a form that's already in your database is a straightforward copy-and-paste operation:

1. If the database isn't currently open, select it on your workspace.

2. Select View, Design, displaying the main database display.

3. In the lower part of the Navigator pane, click on Forms.

4. In the View pane, single-click the name of the form that you want to copy.

5. Copy the form to the Clipboard: select Edit, Copy.

6. Now paste the duplicate back into the database: Select Edit, Paste.

The name of the new, duplicate form will appear in the list of forms, and its name will be "Copy of *Original Form Name*."

Copying from a Template

You can copy a particular form to a new database either from an ordinary template or from a design template. In the latter case, you can optionally link the form to the design template. Then the form in the new database will inherit any design changes made in the future to the form in the template. For instance, suppose that your company wants to use a standard form for inputting client name-and-address information. After finalizing the design for the form, you can place it in a design template and then copy and link the form to the various appropriate databases within the company. Later, if design changes are made to the original form, they will be automatically propagated to the other databases, maintaining consistency for that form across all databases.

Accessing the Template   In order to copy a form from a template or design template, you must have that template open on your Notes workspace. If it isn't, follow these steps:

1. Make sure that your workspace is displayed.

2. Select File, Database, Open.

3. When the Open Database dialog box appears, select either your workstation or the server containing the template or design template that you want to access.

4. Click the Browse button, displaying the following dialog box:

5. In the bottom pull-down list box, labeled Files Of Type, select Notes Template Files.

6. Using the upper part of the dialog box, select the appropriate disk drive and directory and then choose the template.

7. Click the Select button and then, when the Open Database dialog reappears, click the Add icon button and then click the Done button.

Copying the Form The icon for the template that you selected will now appear on your workspace. You can proceed to select the form(s) you want to copy—or copy and link—from the template to the database that you're designing. Here are the steps:

1. In the Notes workspace, click the icon for the template.

2. Select View, Design, displaying main database window for the template.

3. Click on Forms in the middle of the Navigator pane, so that the View pane displays the current list of forms.

4. Click once on the form that you want to either copy or copy and link.

5. Copy the form to the Clipboard: Select Edit, Copy. Now you're ready to copy the new form into the database that you're designing.

6. Exit back to your workspace by pressing Esc.

7. Click on the icon for the database.

8. Select View, Design.

9. Click on Forms in the middle of the Navigator pane.

10. Copy the new form: Select Edit, Paste.

11. If the original template was a design template, you'll see the following dialog box:

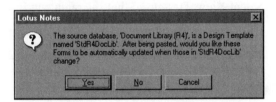

12. Select Yes to copy the form and establish the link between the form in the template and the copy in the database.

When you're done copying the form, remember to remove the template icon from your workspace—unless, of course, you plan to use it in the fore-seeable future.

■ Setting the Form Properties

As part of creating a new form, you'll need to assign various properties. Some of these determine how users will be able to interact with the form. For instance, you can limit who can read or create documents created with the form. Other properties determine how the form interacts with other parts of the database. For example, you can specify whether a form will be used for creating documents, response documents, or response-to-response documents.

As with most other design elements within Notes, you can change any of the properties of a form at any time during its life. For instance, if you decide that you just can't stand the current name of a particular form, you can change it to something else. On the other hand, changing some properties could have a noticeable effect on your database. For instance, if you change the form type from Document to Response Document, you may cause a great deal of confusion among the current database users.

In this section, we describe the properties that you can assign to a form. If you're familiar with Notes, many of these properties will be familiar to you, al-though they have been recast in a new and improved format. For convenience, we've categorized the different options according to use and context.

TIP. *Take some time to familiarize yourself with the various form options. As your design experience increases, you'll find yourself using a great many of them.*

Displaying the Form's Design Window

Before going on, be sure that the design window for the form is displayed, as shown in Figure 3.1. If it isn't, here's how to display it:

1. Make sure that the database you want is selected.

2. Select View, Design, so that the main window for the database is shown.

3. Click on Forms in the middle of the Navigator pane.

4. Double-click on the name of the form in the View pane.

Displaying the Form InfoBox

To assign the various properties to a form, you use the Form InfoBox, which is new to Notes 4.0. The InfoBox simplifies the form design process, because it provides a central location where you can assign nearly all of a form's properties.

In order to display the InfoBox for a particular form, you'll first need to display the design window for that form (steps 1 through 3 above).

To display the Form InfoBox (shown in Figure 3.3), you can do either of the following:

- Select Design, Form Properties.

- Right-click anywhere in the Layout pane, displaying the pull-down menu shown below, and then select Form Properties.

Figure 3.3

Use the Form InfoBox to
assign various properties
to the current form.

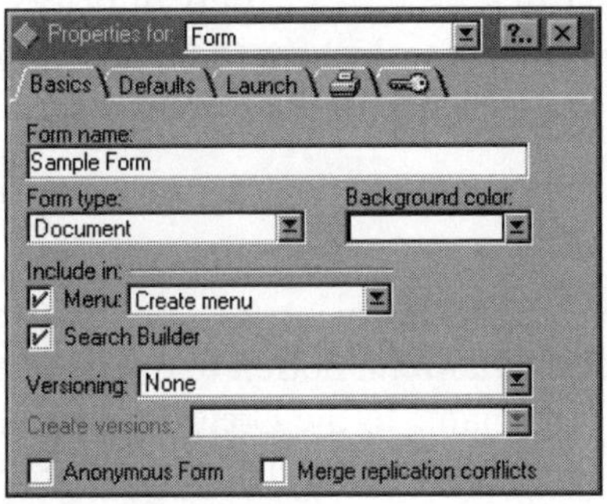

Basic Options

The Basic options, which appear on the Basics page of the InfoBox (Figure 3.3) are fundamental to each form. If you don't want to bother with any of the other options before jumping into designing your form, take a few minutes to select values for these options.

Form Name

You must assign a name to each new form. You can use just about any characters on the keyboard, and the maximum length is more than you'll ever conceive of needing. However, remember that if you choose the option that places the form name on the Create menu, the *entire* name will appear, so keep it short enough so that the Create menu doesn't overwhelm the entire screen!

Form Type

There are three different types of forms: Document, Response, and Responses To Response. If the form is going to be used for creating main documents within the database, select Document. For responses to main documents, choose Response; and if the documents will be responses to either main documents or other response documents, choose Response To Response. Note that the default option is Document, because most forms are in fact main documents.

Background Color

The color that you select for Background Color will be the background of every document you create with this form. Be warned that jazzy colors such as bright red or blue will get very tiresome, very quickly.

Menu Options

The name of a form can appear in a variety of places within your database. To some extent, you can control where the name appears: Two options on the InfoBox affect the inclusion of the form name on menus, dialog boxes, and pull-down lists.

Include In Menu

By default, the name of each form appears on the Create menu. However, you can use the Include In Menu option to override the default, choosing either to move the form name to the Create, Other dialog box or to remove it completely from the Create menu structure. This is a handy option for those forms that you want either to remain partially hidden from users (by putting the form names in the Create, Other dialog box instead of on the Create menu) or totally hidden (by deselecting the Include In Menu option). For example, some forms in a complex application may be used only indirectly by other forms, or they may be used only by an agent or script.

Include In Search Builder

Search Builder is a highly flexible query system, which you can use to perform various types of searches for words, phrases, and so on, within a database. One type of search is *query by example,* in which your query is based on values that you enter into a blank form.

By default, each new form is made available to Search Builder for query-by-example searches. However, if you do not want the current form to be available for this type of search, you can deselect the option Include In Search Builder. You might do this, for example, if the form is completely inappropriate for this type of database searching.

Versioning Options

When you make a set of changes to a document created with this form, you can optionally have those changes written to a new copy of the document, called a *version*. In that case, the original document is unchanged. There are two main reasons for using versioning. First, it provides for a history of changes to each document. Second, some types of versioning can eliminate replication and thereby save conflicts.

Notes provides three different options on the Form InfoBox for controlling how versioning occurs.

Versioning

By using the Versioning option, you can avoid the replication and save conflicts that would normally occur when two users make changes to the same document either on two different replica copies of the same database or on the same copy at the same time. This option offers four choices:

- *None*. This option prevents versioning from occurring; replication conflicts may occur.

- *New Versions Become Responses*. This option prevents replication and save conflicts from occuring. Whenever you make a set of changes to a document created with this form, the original document remains unchanged; the changes are saved as a separate document, which Notes treats as a response document to the original one.

    If two users make changes to the same document on two different replica copies, then after replication, each set of changes is treated as a response document to the original one and is listed in chronological order on your views; that way, no replication or save conflicts occur.

- *Prior Versions Become Responses*. This option also preserves the original document when you make a set of changes to it, but in this case, replication or save conflicts may occur. Here's what happens: When you edit a document and then save your changes, the original remains untouched, and the changes are saved as a separate document. However, the newest document—the altered one, in this case—is treated as the main document, and the original document appears as a response to the altered one.

    If two users make changes to the same document on different replica copies, then after replication the two new versions will appear as a main document with a replication or save conflict; the original document will show up as a response document.

- *New Versions Become Siblings*. If you select this option, each set of revisions to a document results in a new document, but no hierarchy is established: Both the original and the new document are treated as main documents and displayed chronologically in the views. This is advantageous when you don't want to display a hierarchy of documents in your views. Also, in this scenario there are no replication or save conflicts.

Create Versions

The Create Versions option offers users a choice of whether or not to save a set of changes as a new version. This option becomes available only when you select something other than None for the Versioning option described previously, and it gives users a chance to manually override that option. Here are the choices for this option:

- *Automatic - File, Save*. Each time the user makes changes and then selects File, Save, the changes are incorporated into a new document, which is saved according to your choice for the Versioning option.

- *Manual - File, New Version.* To save a set of changes, a user can select either File, Save or File, Save As New Version. The File, Save option saves the changes to the original file; whereas File, Save As New Version incorporates the changes into a new copy of the document.

Merge Replication Conflicts

Unless you select the appropriate version option, as previously described, then whenever two users make changes to the same document on two different replica copies of the database, a replication conflict will occur during replication. The database views will then show one version of the document as a main document and the other as a replication conflict—marked by a diamond.

However, if you select the option Merge Replication Conflicts, Notes automatically merges all the changes in the conflicting documents into a single main document. This is a double-edged sword: It saves you the trouble of looking through the individual sets of changes, but on the other hand, you won't have a record of who made which changes.

Inheritance Options

When you highlight a document in a view and then create a new document (via the Create menu), the new document may inherit some field values from the selected document, or it may inherit the entire contents of the selected document—depending on how you set up the two options dealing with inheritance.

To access these options, click the Defaults tab on the Form InfoBox, as shown in Figure 3.4.

Figure 3.4

More options for selecting form properties.

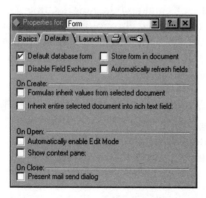

Formulas Inherit Values From Selected Document

Selecting the option Formulas Inherit Values From Selected Document allows fields in the new document to inherit values from the selected document. However, this inheritance is not then automatic; you must write appropriate formulas in the form for the new document for the fields that you want to inherit values.

As an example, suppose that a user creates a new document containing a field called FullName, and suppose that this field contains the simple formula "Name." If, when the user creates this document, he or she has selected a document (in a view) whose field called Name contains the value "Thomas Q. Bergonovich," then the FullName field in the new document will inherit that value. Note that inheritance does not depend on the commonality of field names, but rather on the name of one field appearing in the formula of another field.

Inherit Entire Selected Document Into Rich Text Field

The option Inherit Entire Selected Document Into Rich Text Field allows you to import the entire contents of the currently selected document into a rich text field within the new document. For instance, when you're creating a response to a short memo you might want the entire contents of that memo to appear at the top of the response document.

When you select this option, you must also choose the name of the rich text field to use in the new document, and you must choose the connection as one of the following types:

- A link to the original document

- A display of the original document within the rich text field

- A display of the original document within a collapsible section containing the rich text field

NOTE. *A collapsing section is one in which part of a document can be hidden, with only its title remaining visible. For details, see the next chapter.*

Options for Opening and Closing

You can select various options to control specific actions that Notes may or may not take each time you open or close a document. These options are displayed on the Defaults page of the Form InfoBox (Figure 3.4).

Automatically Enable Edit Mode

The option Automatically Enable Edit Mode overrides the Notes default, which is to open documents in view mode. If this option is selected, Notes will instead open the document in edit mode.

Show Context Pane

Setting the Show Context Pane option allows you a preview of a document related to the current one: When you open a document, a separate pane will be displayed at the bottom of the window (see Figure 3.5) for viewing either the parent of the document or the document to which the current one is linked. If the document has both a parent and a link to another document, you can use the View menu to select which of them should be displayed in the lower pane: Select either Parent Preview or DocLink.

Figure 3.5

The lower pane previews either the parent document or the document to which the current one is linked.

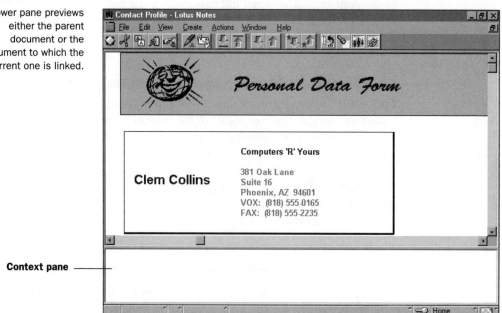

Context pane ———

Present Mail Send Dialog

If you select the Present Mail Send Dialog option, then whenever you close a document that you've created or edited, the Close Window dialog box (see below) will be displayed. Note that in order to select either of the Send options in this dialog box, the document must have a SendTo field. Otherwise, Notes will not allow you to select either of those options.

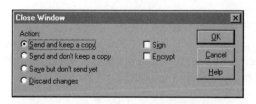

Launch Options

If a document contains attachments or links to other documents, you can choose whether or not Notes automatically launches any of them when opening the document. (By default, nothing is launched.) Furthermore, if a document contains an OLE object, you can choose when to launch it automatically.

To display these options, click the Launch tab on the Form InfoBox, showing the options in Figure 3.6.

Figure 3.6

Options for launching objects within documents.

Auto Launch

The Auto Launch option allows you to choose which—if any—attachment or object within a document is automatically launched. Here are the choices for this option:

- *First Attachment.* When a document containing attachments is opened, Notes will automatically launch the server program for the first attachment in the document and then load that attachment. For instance, if a document contains an attached file containing a 1-2-3 worksheet, Notes will launch 1-2-3 and open the worksheet.

- *First Document Link.* When a user opens a document containing one or more links, Notes will automatically display the first document linked to the current document.

- *First OLE Object.* The first OLE object stored within the document will be launched under the conditions that you specify in the Launch When option (see the following section, "Launch When"). When you select this option, other options appear in the Form InfoBox (Figure 3.7).

Launch When

The Launch When option allows you to choose under which circumstances to launch the first OLE object in a document. Pull down the Launch When list and then select one or more of the following:

- Creating
- Editing
- Reading

Figure 3.7

Select when and how to
auto-launch the first OLE
object in a document.

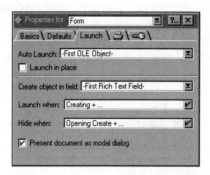

For example, if you select the last option, then each time you open a document for reading, Notes will launch the OLE object.

Hide When

Use the Hide When option to specify when to hide the Notes document window when an OLE object is auto-launched. You can select one or more of the following conditions:

- Opening Create

- Opening Edit

- Opening Read

- Closing Create

- Closing Edit

- Closing Read

For example, if you select the Launch When Editing option and also the Hide When Opening Edit option, then whenever a user opens a document in edit mode, Notes will launch the OLE object and also hide the Notes document window. Furthermore, if you have also selected the Closing Edit condition, then when a user closes the OLE object, the Notes document will automatically be closed.

By selecting a pair of Opening and Closing options together, you can make a set of Notes documents appear entirely as a set of documents generated by the OLE server. For instance, you could create a database of documents, each of which contains a single 1-2-3 worksheet. Then, whenever a user opens one of these documents, she or he sees only the corresponding worksheet—not the underlying Notes document.

Security Options

You can choose which users have read access to documents created with the current form. You can also control who can create documents with the form. To view these options, click the rightmost tab of the Form InfoBox, shown in Figure 3.8. Here's a general description of these options:

- *Read access.* By default, anyone with at least Reader access can read documents in the database. To override this default, use the top list box to select the names of those persons whom you want to have read access. To extend your search, you can click the icon to the right of the list box to access the available Address Books.

- *Author access.* By default, anyone with at least Author access to the database can create new documents. However, you can override this default and restrict access to only specific persons and groups. In the list box labeled Who Can Create Documents With This Form, click those persons or groups to whom you want to grant Author access. You can also search the available Address Books by clicking the icon to the right of the list box and then selecting the people or groups that you want.

Figure 3.8

Use these options to
control access to
documents created with
the current form.

Miscellaneous Options

The options described in this section do not fall conveniently into any of the categories described up to now. They cover a range of features, and you might want to take a few minutes to glance through them—just in case you ever need to use them.

Anonymous Form

The Anonymous Form option instructs Notes not to record the names of authors and editors of documents created with this form. These documents will contain an $Anonymous field containing the value 1, but they will not contain an $UpdatedBy field (which normally contains the names of authors and editors of each form).

Default Database Form

The Default Database Form option makes the current form the default for the current database. The default form will be used by Notes to display any database document whose form no longer exists. For instance, you might have decided to delete a form that's no longer needed, but the database may still contain documents created with that form. In that case, Notes will use the default form to display those documents. Only one default form is allowed per database.

Note. Field Exchange is discussed in Chapter 12.

Disable Field Exchange

Notes normally enables the exchange of information between forms and various fields contained in embedded OLE objects. The Disable Field Exchange option prevents that exchange.

Store Form In Document

When the Store Form In Document option is selected, then each time a person uses this form to create a document, the form will be stored as part of the document. This is very handy when you plan to mail or otherwise send documents to a location that doesn't contain a copy of this form. Those documents will then be self-formatting, because they contain a copy of the form. However, be aware that this option can use up a great deal of disk space because of the extra size of each document, so use it only when absolutely necessary.

A stored form takes precedence over any form formulas stored in views; that is, the stored form is always used for displaying the document.

Automatically Refresh Fields

Normally, a document is recalculated either when you save the document or when you force a recalculation (by pressing F9, for example). For some types of forms, however, you may wish to use the Automatically Refresh Fields option so that users can immediately see the results of changing one or more field values within a document.

This option could be helpful with documents containing a field whose value is used as the basis for calculating several other field values. As an example, you could design a form having fields for a person's identification number, name, address, and other basic information. You could automate this form so that as soon as a user enters a person's identification number, Notes provides the other field values automatically by performing a table lookup.

Before implementing a new form with this option selected, you might want to do a little experimenting, to make sure that the automation does not force users to wait for an unreasonably long time. This would occur, for example, if a document contained a very large number of calculated fields. Or, if an automatic table lookup required a large amount of data transmission from a remote database, the time delays could be prohibitive.

Printing Options

You can choose various options for printing documents created with the current form. These options are available by clicking the Print tab on the Form InfoBox (the fourth one from the left, as shown in Figure 3.9). They override any print options that you may have selected for the entire database. As an example, the options selected in Figure 3.9 will print a header containing a title and page number. (For a discussion of print options, see "Selecting Database-Wide Printing Properties," in Chapter 2.)

Figure 3.9

Use these options to control the appearance of documents printed with the current form.

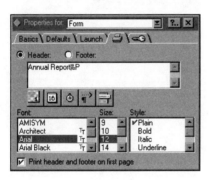

- *Getting Started*
- *Working with Static Text*
- *Adding New Fields*
- *Adding Graphics*
- *Hotspots and Buttons*
- *Tables*

C H A P T E R

Tools for Building Forms

Notes offers a wide array of design tools, providing you
the means to create attractive and easy-to-use forms. Many of
these tools are new to Notes 4.0, and if you're coming from earlier
Notes versions, you'll be pleased at the increased flexibility in
form design.

This chapter describes the more basic design elements at your disposal for designing forms; Chapter 5 will then focus on the more sophisticated design tools you can use for creating professional-looking forms.

The design tools we describe in this chapter include the following:

- Static text and fields, the most basic of all the design elements

- Customized and imported graphics for enhancing forms

- Hotspots and buttons for automating common actions

- Automated text pop-ups for supplying special information

- Automated links to other documents and databases

- Tables for creating special effects

Of course, static text and fields are the fundamental building blocks of every form. This chapter describes how to handle them in Notes 4.0. (Chapter 6 describes the features of the different types of fields.) We also describe the different ways you can add graphics to your forms.

Hotspots and buttons offer several types of point-and-click regions for performing different operations. By clicking on a link hotspot, a user can immediately access information in other parts of the database, or even in different databases; in fact, these links can be used to create customized hypertext documents. Other types of hotspots include pop-ups for providing context-sensitive information, and action hotspots and buttons for performing just about any type of simple or complex task.

Notes 4.0 has retained the table as a design element, and it still can be extremely useful for certain design situations. By making use of the InfoBox, Notes has improved—and at the same time simplified—how you can create and customize tables.

■ Getting Started

Before going any further, be sure that the form you want to work with is displayed in the Form Design window. Here's how to accomplish this:

1. If your workspace is displayed, click on the database that you want to work with and then select View, Design to display the main database display.

2. If you're in some other part of the database, use the Esc key to click your way back to the main database display and then—if necessary—select View, Show, Folders, so that the standard navigator is displayed.

3. Make sure the lower part of the standard navigator is expanded and then click on Forms.

4. In the View pane (on the right side of the display), double-click on the name of the form that you want to work with.

5. Maximize the area available for designing the form layout: When the Form Design window appears, pull down the View menu and then deselect the option Design Pane. The window should then appear as shown in Figure 4.1.

Figure 4.1

Use this design window to edit a form.

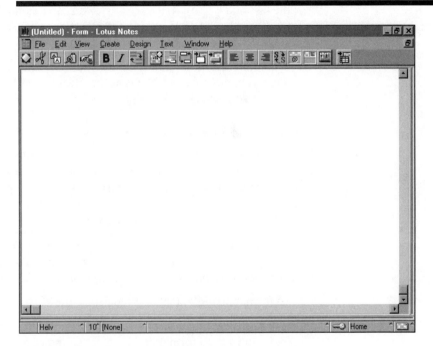

■ Working with Static Text

You can insert text anywhere you wish on a form. The main purposes of text are to act as field labels and to supply informative captions and titles to various parts of a form. For example, you'll probably want to insert a heading at the top of each major section on a form.

Using the Text InfoBox, you can format individual characters, words, or other contiguous groups of characters, assigning the font, size, color and attributes. You can also set the alignment of a title line—either left-justified, right-justified, or centered.

NOTE. *The techniques described here apply to text anywhere on a form except in a layout region. For a description of working with layout regions, see Chapter 5.*

Adding New Text

You can add a new block of text just about anywhere on a form. As with other form-design elements, the text that you insert will appear on every document you create with the form.

To add text somewhere on the form, follow these steps:

1. Move the insertion point to where you want to insert the text. Note that you can't move the insertion point past the bottom of the form (that is, the last blank line); so if necessary, you can extend the bottom by using the Enter key. And to extend the insertion point to the right on the line you select, use either the spacebar or the Tab key.

2. When the insertion point is where you want it, type in the text. For long lines, you either can let Notes automatically word-wrap for you, or you can set your own breaks by pressing Enter.

Editing and Formatting Text

You can easily edit text you've added on a form, using standard word processing operations. For instance, you can cut and paste or copy and paste text from one location to another on a form. (You can't, however, click and drag text blocks from one place to another.) You can also format individual text blocks, assigning custom fonts, sizes, styles, and colors.

NOTE. *All of the text-formatting techniques described next apply to text that you're creating as part of a form. However, these methods also can be used by document authors and editors on text contained within rich text fields.*

To format an individual text block, use the Text InfoBox as follows:

1. If the InfoBox is not displayed, right-button-click anywhere on the text that you want to format and then, when the pop-up menu appears, select Text Properties, displaying the options shown in Figure 4.2.

Figure 4.2

Use the Text InfoBox to assign properties to text.

2. If the InfoBox is already displayed, make sure that Text appears in the top edit box labeled Properties For. If it doesn't, pull down that list box and click on Text.

3. Using the mouse, highlight the text that you want to format.

4. Using the options on the InfoBox, select the font, size, style, and color for the text that you selected.

■ Adding New Fields

As with earlier Notes releases, you can insert any number of fields on a form. Each field can be either local to the form, or it can be a shared field that's available to any form in the database. Adding a local field (which we'll refer to simply as a field) is quite straightforward: You place the insertion point where you want to place the field, and then you make a few mouse selections. Adding a shared field is also quite easy, being a matter of selecting the one that you want from a list of those available in the database.

The more interesting part of creating a new field is assigning its properties. However, this is such an involved subject that we'll defer it completely to Chapter 6, which is entirely devoted to describing the various types of Notes fields.

Adding Fields

To add a new field onto the form, follow these steps:

1. Move the insertion point to where you want to insert the new field. If necessary, you can extend the bottom of the form by moving the insertion point there and then pressing the Enter key once for each new line.

2. To create the field, you can either click the Create Field SmartIcon or select Create, Field. The new field will appear at the insertion-point position, labeled "Untitled," and the Field InfoBox will appear, as shown in Figure 4.3.

3. Make sure that the Basics tab of the InfoBox is selected and then insert a name for the field.

4. Use the InfoBox to assign other properties to the field (see Chapter 6 for details about designing fields).

Figure 4.3

Use the Field InfoBox
to assign the name
and other properties
to a new field.

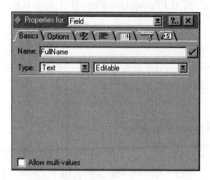

Adding Shared Fields to a Form

Note For a description
of creating shared fields,
see Chapter 6.

A *shared field* is one whose complete definition is available to any form within a database. If you're going to use the same field for several forms, define it once as a shared field for the current database. Then you can simply copy the field into each form that uses it.

Here's how to insert a shared field onto a form:

1. Position the insertion point where you want to add the field.

2. Select Create, Insert Shared Field, or click on the Shared Field SmartIcon, displaying the following dialog box:

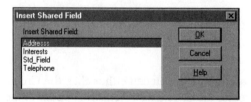

3. Select the field that you want to insert and then click OK.

■ Adding Graphics

Graphics can make all the difference between an ordinary-looking form and one that catches your eye, and you can easily insert graphic images as part of the forms you design. If you can copy an image to the Clipboard from another application, you can probably paste it onto a form.

NOTE. *The techniques described here apply to adding graphics anywhere on a form except in a layout region. For a description of working with layout regions, see Chapter 5.*

You can also import pictures stored in various flavors of graphic files, including the following:

• Lotus PIC files (.PIC)

• ANSI metafiles (.CGM, .GMF)

• JPEG files (.JPG)

• TIFF 5.0 files (.TIF)

• Miscellaneous bitmap formats, including .BMP, .GIF, and .PCX

After you copy an image onto a form, you can then resize it to match the rest of the contents of the form.

TIP. *When you paste a graphic image directly onto a form, you have very limited options for repositioning it. To get around this limitation, you can insert your images onto layout regions. For details, see Chapter 5.*

To insert a picture onto a form, place the insertion point where you want the image to appear. You can insert an image either on a line by itself or on a line containing text, fields, or other graphics. Typically (but not always), the lower-left corner of the image will appear at the insertion-point position. If necessary, the current contents of the line will be pushed down to make room for the image.

The steps that you take to place the image on the form depend on whether you're using the Clipboard to copy and paste, or whether you're importing the contents of a graphics file.

Copying an Image from Another Program

If you have access to clip art software, you may have a deluge of pictures from which to choose. Or, if you're artistically inclined, you can use a drawing program to generate your own masterpieces.

In either case, here's how to get the image you want onto a Notes form:

1. Temporarily exit from Notes and then launch the drawing or clip art software.

2. Retrieve or draw the image that you want on the screen and then copy it to the Clipboard.

3. Return to Notes.

4. Place the insertion point where you want the image to appear; usually, the lower-left-hand corner of the image will appear where the insertion point is located.

5. Select Edit, Paste.

If the image does not appear on the form, you'll need to take alternative steps, as follows:

1. Select Edit, Paste Special, displaying the following dialog box:

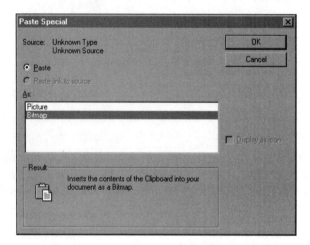

2. Select one of the image types displayed in the middle list box and then click OK. Keep trying different image types until you find the one that works—or that works best. (If you can't stand the sight of an image you've pasted, you can delete it by clicking on it and then pressing Del).

Importing a File

Importing any of the file types listed earlier is straightforward:

1. Place the insertion point where you want the image to appear.

2. Select File, Import, displaying the dialog box shown in Figure 4.4.

3. Select the graphics file and then click the Import button.

The entire image in the file will be imported and displayed at the position of the insertion point.

Figure 4.4

Select the graphics file
that you want to import.

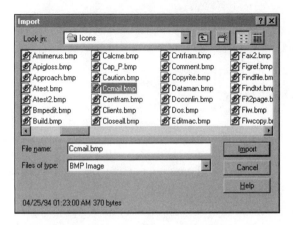

WARNING! *The size of the image that appears in the form is unpredictable. It may be quite small, or it may overwhelm your screen. In any case, see the next section for information on resizing the image.*

Repositioning and Resizing an Image

After you paste or import an image onto the form, you can resize it and—to a limited extent—reposition it. Before going on, display the InfoBox for the image (Figure 4.5): Right-button-click anywhere on the picture and then choose Picture Properties from the menu that appears. (Alternatively, you can left-button-click on the image and then select Picture, Picture Properties.)

Figure 4.5

Use the InfoBox to help
you resize an image.

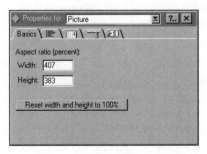

To resize an image, you can either do it freehand or use the InfoBox:

1. To resize the image using freehand: Click anywhere on the image, and a handle will appear in the lower-right corner of the image (Figure 4.6); then click on the handle and drag it in or out to resize the image.

Figure 4.6

You can use an image's
handle to resize it.

2. To resize the image more precisely, you can change the numbers shown in the InfoBox for the width and height. For example, to reduce the picture's size by 50 percent, change the two numbers from 100 to 50.

You can also reposition an image; however, your options are somewhat limited. Basically, you can think of an image as a giant character whose baseline is where you positioned the insertion point just before placing the image. (In fact, you can insert characters or fields to either the left or right of an image.)

If there's nothing to either the left or right of the image, you can use the InfoBox to reposition it:

Tip. Because of the line-based nature of forms, you're quite limited in how you can reposition images. However, Notes 4.0 contains a new feature—the layout region—that solves this problem, because within a layout region, you can freely position graphic images, fields, and other objects. Chapter 5 describes layout regions in detail.

1. Make sure that the top of the InfoBox displays "Picture." If it doesn't, pull down the InfoBox list box labeled Properties For and choose Picture.

2. Click the Alignment InfoBox tab (the second from the left).

3. To left-align, right-align, or center the image, click the appropriate button labeled Alignment.

4. To indent the image by a certain distance from the left edge of the window:
   - Click the left-align button;
   - In the edit box labeled Left Margin, type in the amount that you want indented.

If the line containing the image also contains other text, graphics, or fields, you can reposition the image on the line by inserting blank spaces between it and whatever is to its immediate left: Click to the left of the image so that the insertion point appears there,then press the spacebar or Tab key as many times as you wish.

You can also reposition an image up or down, just as you would any other character. For example, to move the image down, click to its immediate left so that the insertion point appears, then press Enter to insert a blank line above the image.

Deleting an Image

You can delete an image in any of the following ways:

- Click on the image and then press either the Backspace key or Del.

- Reposition the insertion point just to the left of the image and then press Del.

- Reposition the insertion point just to the right of the image and then press the Backspace key.

- Select (highlight) the image—either alone or as part of a text block—and then select Edit, Cut, or press either Del or the Backspace key.

    Note that Edit, Undo works for some—but not all—of the preceding methods.

■ Hotspots and Buttons

A *hotspot* is a region within a form that is associated with a particular action or set of Notes operations. When a reader clicks on a particular hotspot within a document created with the form, Notes performs the set of associated operations. As a form designer, you create each hotspot and decide which operations are associated with it.

Notes 4.0 provides a number of different types of hotspots:

- *Hotspot pop-ups* are a convenient way of displaying information to the person reading or editing a document. When a user clicks on a hotspot pop-up within a document, an informative message (preprogrammed by the form designer) appears.

- *Formula hotspots* also provide a point-and-click area that the user can utilize to perform a set of operations programmed into a Notes formula.

- *Action hotspots* are a more general form of formula hotspots; each action hotspot can be associated with either a formula, a script, or a built-in Notes action (actions are described in Chapter 5).

- *Buttons,* which are inherited from earlier Notes versions, are an alternative form of an action hotspot: You can associate a button with a formula, a script, or a Notes action.

- *Link hotspots* offer point-and-click access to other views and documents—either in the same database or a different one.

NOTE. *In addition to the various flavors of hotspots and buttons—all of which can be placed anywhere in a document—you can create action buttons, which appear on the button bar at the top of a document. Just as with hotspots,* *you associate each action button with a formula, script, or Notes action. Action buttons are described in Chapter 5.*

Except for buttons, each of the types of hotspots in the preceding list appears as ordinary text in a document. You can optionally enclose a text hotspot in a box, so that the reader can more easily recognize it as a hotspot. However, you can't tell what type a hotspot is from its appearance, because one block of text looks pretty much like another. However, the text of a hotspot should clarify its purpose. For instance, if the text of an enclosed hotspot is "Press here to exit from Notes," there shouldn't be much doubt in a user's mind as to the hotspot's purpose.

The various types of hotspots—including buttons—all have one very interesting and important characteristic in common: They can be created either by the database designer as part of an underlying form (so that they appear on every document created with the form) or by a user as part of a particular document. In other words, a hotspot can be either part of a form or part of a document.

As an example of the latter, a user—while creating or editing a document—could insert a link hotspot to another document. Or, he or she could insert a hotspot pop-up, which when clicked by a reader would display a special message. There's one limitation to this powerful feature: A user can create a hotspot only within a rich text field in a document. Consequently, the form designer must make advance provision for this possibility by including rich text fields at appropriate places in forms.

The following sections describe how to include the various types of hotspots as part of a form design. The techniques presented here apply as well to creating hotspots within a rich text field of a document.

Hotspot Pop-ups

A hotspot pop-up is a handy way of displaying information to the person reading or editing a document. For example, when a user clicks on the hotspot pop-up shown in Figure 4.7(a), the text shown in Figure 4.7(b) appears.

Here's how to insert a hotspot pop-up onto a form:

1. Position the insertion point on the form exactly where you want the hotspot pop-up to appear and then type in the text that you want to become the hotspot. For example, in Figure 4.7, the text pop-up is "Click here for help."

2. Highlight the text.

3. Select Create, Hotspot, Text Pop-up.

Figure 4.7

(a) A user can click on the hotspot pop-up shown here; (b) information displayed when the user clicks on the hotspot pop-up.

(b) Information displayed when the user clicks on the hotspot pop-up.

4. If the Hotspot Pop-up InfoBox does not appear as shown in Figure 4.8, right-button-click anywhere on the hotspot pop-up and then select Hotspot Properties.

5. In the InfoBox edit box labeled Popup Text, type in the text that you want to pop up whenever a user clicks on the hotspot.

6. If you want a box drawn around the text hotspot on each document created with this form, select the InfoBox option Show Border Around Hotspot.

Figure 4.8

Insert the text for the
hotspot pop-up.

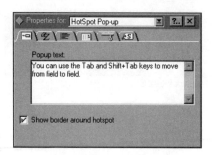

You can format the hotspot text by using the various options on the InfoBox. However, you can't change the font, attributes, or color of the text
that actually pops up when you click on the hotspot.

Formula Hotspots

A *formula hotspot* is a block of text that's part of a form. When a user clicks
on that hotspot in a document created with the form, Notes carries out the
formula associated with the hotspot.

NOTE. *Unfortunately, Notes refers to formula hotspots both as* hotspot pop-
ups *and* formula pop-ups. *We'll stick to the term* formula hotspot.

As an example, Figure 4.9 shows two formula hotspots, "Exit" and "Edit
Document," appearing in a document. When a user clicks on Exit, Notes
runs the associated formula, which closes the document. Similarly, when a
user clicks the hotspot Edit Document, its associated formula switches Notes
to edit mode.

To create a formula hotspot, you begin by typing the text to be used as
the hotspot in the form. Then you create the formula that you want to associate with that hotspot. Here are the steps:

1. Move the insertion point to exactly where you want the formula hotspot
    to be and then type in the text that's to become the hotspot.

2. Highlight the text.

3. Select Create, Hotspot, Formula Popup.

4. Make sure that the Design pane is displayed at the bottom of the win-
    dow, as shown in Figure 4.10.

5. In the Design pane, type in the formula that you want to associate with
    the hotspot. This is the formula that Notes will execute whenever a
    reader clicks on the hotspot in a document. For instance, the formula

Figure 4.9

You can use the hotspots
shown in this document
to perform different
operations.

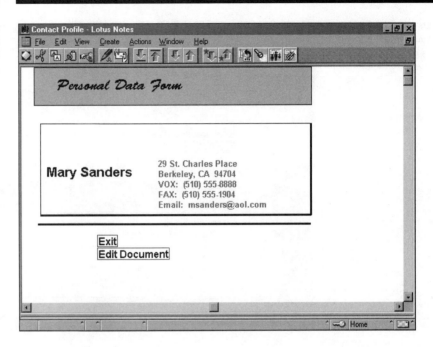

shown in Figure 4.10 will close the current document whenever a user
clicks on the hotspot.

Note. For information
about using formulas,
see Chapter 10.

6. If you want a box to appear around the text hotspot on each document
created with this form, select the InfoBox option Show Border Around
Hotspot (click the leftmost tab to display the option).

Notice that designing this type of hotspot is somewhat more complicated
than a text hotspot pop-up, because in this case you must use both the InfoBox and the Design pane. Furthermore, designing formulas can be quite
complex, depending on your level of ambition.

Action Hotspots and Buttons

An *action hotspot* is similar to a formula hotspot, but the action hotspot is
more general. Whereas a formula hotspot can be associated only with a formula, an action hotspot can be associated with either a formula, a script, or a
Notes action.

TIP. *If you plan to associate a formula with a hotspot, you can use either an
action hotspot or a formula hotspot. An action hotspot is actually a misnomer
because you can associate an action hotspot with either an action, a formula,
or a script.*

Figure 4.10

Enter the formula that
you want to associate
with the current formula
hotspot.

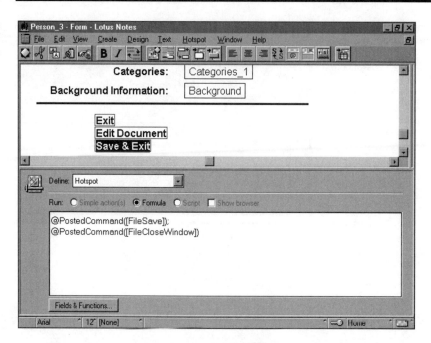

A *button hotspot* (or simply *button,* for short) is similar to an action hotspot, in that it can be associated with either a formula, action, or script. However, a button looks like a button on the form, whereas an action hotspot appears as a text block.

You can take your pick when designing forms, because buttons and action hotspots can be used interchangeably.

Creating an Action Hotspot

Here's how to begin creating an action hotspot:

1. Position the insertion point exactly where you want to place the hotspot.

2. Type in the text that you want displayed as the hotspot. Highlight the text, and then select Create, Hotspot, Action Hotspot. If the InfoBox isn't visible, select Hotspot, Hotspot Properties. The top of the InfoBox should display "Properties For Hotspot Button."

3. If you want a box to appear around the hotspot on each document created with this form, select the option Show Border Around Hotspot on the InfoBox.

4. Make sure that the Design pane is displayed at the bottom of the window, as shown in Figure 4.10.

After creating the basic hotspot, you must now either assign it an action or create a formula or script for it. For details, see the section "Putting Power into Buttons and Action Hotspots."

Creating a Button

You can also use a button as a hotspot on a form. However, setting up a button is a bit different from setting up other types of hotspots. Here are the details:

1. Position the insertion point exactly where you want to place the button.

2. Select Create, Hotspot, Button. The button will appear at the insertion-point position, and the Button InfoBox should also appear. If it doesn't, right-button-click on the button and then select Button Properties. Alternatively, you can click on the button and then select Button, Button Properties (did you notice that the Button menu appeared when you clicked on the button?).

3. To add text to the face of the button, click the leftmost InfoBox tab, displaying the options shown in Figure 4.11.

Figure 4.11

Use these options to assign text to a button.

4. To limit the width of the button, select the option Wrap Text and then type the maximum allowable width into the lower edit window. If you don't select the Wrap Text option, Notes ignores the number that you enter.

5. Type in the text that you want to appear on the button face. If necessary, Notes will insert soft returns so that the button width is no greater than the value you assigned in step 4.

After creating the button, you must either assign it an action or create a formula or script for it. For details, see the following sections.

Note. For details about creating your own actions, see "Actions and Action Buttons" in Chapter 5.

Putting Power into Buttons and Action Hotspots

After creating a new action hotspot or button, you can associate it with a formula, a script, or an action as described in the following two sections.

Note. For details about using formulas, see Chapter 10.

Creating a Formula   After creating a new button or action hotspot, you can associate it with a formula. Here's how to proceed:

1. Make sure that the Design pane is displayed at the bottom of the window.

2. At the top of the Design pane, click the Formula radio button.

3. In the Design pane, type the formula that you want to associate with the hotspot. This is the formula that Notes will execute whenever a user clicks on the hotspot.

Note. Scripts allow highly complex sets of operations that can be performd automatically; although they are touched upon here and there, an in-depth treatment is beyond the scope of this book.

Creating a Script   Using the LotusScript language, you can create a script to be associated with a button or an action hotspot that you've created. Lotus-Script is a complex language, far beyond the scope of this book. However, rather than skipping this topic entirely, we'll compromise by indicating the general steps you need to follow after creating a button or action hotspot, and we'll also show a simple script.

Here's how to attach a script to a button or action hotspot that you've created:

1. Click on the button or hotspot and then make sure that the Design pane is displayed (if it isn't, you can select View, Design Pane).

2. At the top of the Design pane, click the Script radio button.

3. Using the lower part of the design pane, enter the script.

The button in Figure 4.12 is attached to the simple script shown in the Design pane. When a user creates a document with this form and then clicks the button, the simple message box shown below will appear.

Link Hotspots

A link hotspot offers a quick path from a document to any of the following:

- Another document, in either the current database or another one

- A view in either the current database or another one

- Another database (opens to the most recently used view)

Like every other type of hotspot—except, of course, buttons—a link hotspot is a special block of text that you enter onto a form. To emphasize

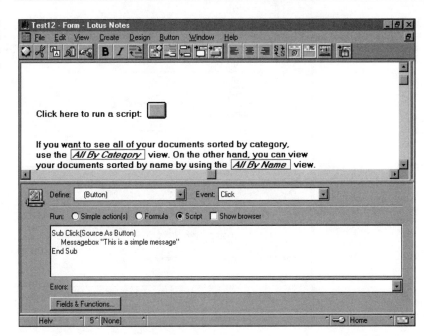

the link, you can draw a box around the text block. When a user clicks on a
link hotspot in a document created with the form, a special message pops up,
displaying the details of the link. For example, Figure 4.13 shows that single-
clicking on the hotspot All By Category indicates that it is connected to the
view People By Category in the database Sample1.

When a user double-clicks on a link hotspot, Notes transfers control to the
linked object—either another document, a view, or another database (in
the latter case, Notes opens the database to the last-used view). Then, after the
transfer has been completed, the user can return to the original document by
pressing Esc.

To create a link hotspot, follow these steps:

1. To begin, you must set up the document, view, or database to which you
   want to attach the link, as follows:

   - *To establish a link to another document:* Open the database contain-
     ing the document, display a view containing the document, and then
     click on the document in the view.

   - *To establish a link to a view:* Open the database containing the view,
     make sure that the main database window is displayed (select View,
     Design), pull down the lower half of the Navigator pane labeled

Figure 4.13

Clicking on a link hotspot displays where the link is connected.

Pop-up text

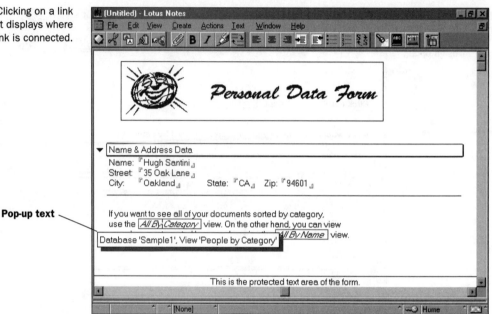

Design, click on Views, and finally click on the name of the view that you want to set up as the link.

- *To establish a link to another database:* Return to your workspace and then click once on the icon for that database.

2. Now select Edit, Copy As Link and then choose the appropriate option: Document Link, View Link, or Database Link.

3. Return to the form in which you want to create the link hotspot.

4. Move the insertion point to where you want to insert the link hotspot and then type in the hotspot text.

5. Highlight the hotspot text.

6. Select Create, Hotspot, Link Hotspot.

Deleting and Modifying Hotspots

After creating a hotspot, you can easily change its text (both for buttons and text hotspots), reposition it, or delete it. If you've gone to a lot of work to create a formula or script for a hotspot, make a backup of your database before deleting a hotspot, just in case you later change your mind. However, if you accidentally delete a hotspot and immediately realize the error of your ways, you can usually recover by using the Edit, Undo option.

Deleting Hotspots

To delete a button hotspot, click on it and then either press Del or select Edit, Cut.

You can delete a text hotspot in either of two ways:

• Delete both the hotspot and its associated text

• Delete the hotspot, but leave the text behind as ordinary text

To remove the text hotspot but leave the text in place, click anywhere on the hotspot and then select Hotspot, Remove Hotspot. If you also want to remove the text, you can then use standard word processing operations.

Editing, Copying, and Moving Hotspots

You can edit the text within a text hotspot just as you would ordinary text: First place the insertion point anywhere within the text and then use standard word processing operations to add or delete characters.

Editing the label appearing on the face of a button is a wee bit more complicated:

1. Click anywhere on the button.

2. Display the InfoBox for the button and then click on the leftmost InfoBox tab.

3. Edit the button text appearing on the InfoBox.

You can also move or copy any type of hotspot from one position to another within a document. Here's how:

1. Click at one end of the hotspot, hold down the mouse button, and then drag the cursor across the hotspot until it's entirely highlighted. Or, in the case of a button, you can simply click on it.

2. Select Edit, Cut or Edit, Copy.

3. Click where you want to paste the hotspot and then select Edit, Paste.

A Hotspot Summary

Hotspots offer a wealth of tools for performing different types of operations. To help you choose the right hotspot for the right job, Table 4.1 presents a handy hotspot summary.

Table 4.1

A Summary of
Hotspot Uses.

FOR	USE
Displaying helpful pop-up information	Text pop-up
Running a formula or script	Formula hotspot, action hotspot, or button
Running a simple Notes action	Action hotspot
Link to a document, a view, or another database	Link hotspot

■ Tables

Tables are a carryover from earlier Notes versions, and functionally they are more or less the same in Notes 4.0. However, as with other Notes tools, the current incarnation of tables is much easier to use than earlier ones.

You might recall that if two or more fields exist on the same line, then whenever a user enters data into the first field, the others are pushed over to the right—and perhaps down to the next line. In earlier Notes versions, the standard solution to this problem was to use a table, in which two or more columns of fields would continue to line up when a user entered data into them.

As an example, Figure 4.14 shows a simple table design for holding name and address information. When a user enters a value for the State field, the text and field to the right will not be repositioned.

Tables may not be as useful for data input as one might first imagine—for two reasons. First, having the data fields arranged in multiple columns during data entry may not be particularly convenient for the data-entry person.

Note. For a discussion of layout regions, see Chapter 5.

The second reason is the introduction in Notes 4.0 of layout regions. Here's why: Within a layout region, you can arrange fields any way you wish; perhaps, for example, in multiple columns. Manipulating text and fields within a layout region is much simpler for the form designer than in tables.

Nevertheless, you may still find occasion to put tables to good use. For example, you could use tables to display columnar information in read mode—hiding the table in edit mode. Chapter 5 discusses hiding and displaying objects in a form.

Having now presented the possible reasons for not using tables, let's consider the positive side by looking at an example of a database whose forms are built almost exclusively with tables—one of Notes' own internal databases—the Address Book, which is usually stored in a file called NAMES.NSF. If you have sufficient access privileges, you can open the forms for this database and get a direct look at how tables can be used.

Figure 4.14

You can use a table to create columnar information.

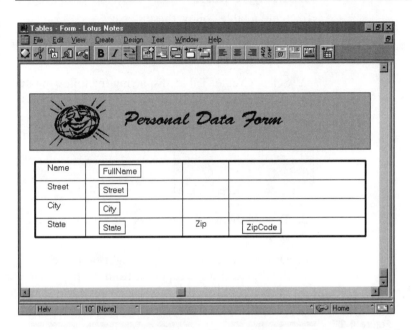

As an example, the following illustration shows the top part of the form named Person. The portion of the form starting with the line labeled "Name…Mail" and ending with the line labeled "Work…Home" consists of a single table. The heavy lines are created as part of the table.

Creating a Table

To create a table, follow these steps:

1. Place the insertion point where you want to insert a new table—preferably at the beginning of a blank line.

2. Select Create, Table, displaying the following dialog box:

3. Type in the number of rows and columns of the new table and then click OK.

4. Display the Table InfoBox: Right-button-click anywhere on the table and then select Table Properties from the pop-up menu that appears. Click the leftmost InfoBox tab, displaying the options shown in Figure 4.15.

Figure 4.15

Use these options to assign borders to a set of table cells.

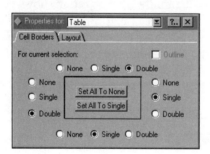

Customizing a Table

You can format the appearance of a table by assigning single lines, double lines, or no lines to selected cells. You can also add extra space between rows and columns by adjusting the row and column spacing. And you can set the left margin of the table and change the individual column widths:

- To format the borders of a group of cells, highlight the cells that you want to format and then use the InfoBox options shown in Figure 4.15.

- To set the table margin, the row and column spacing, and the column widths, click the tab labeled Layout and then make your selections.

You can also add or delete rows or columns, using options on the Table menu, which appears only when you click on a table, as follows:

- To add a new row, click on the row above which you want to add a new one and then select Table, Insert Row.

- To add a new column, click on the column to the left of which you want to add a new one and then select Table, Insert Column.

- To insert two or more rows or columns at once, click as described in the preceding instruction and then select Table, Insert Special to select the number of rows or columns to insert.

- To delete one or more rows or columns, highlight them and then make the appropriate selection from the Table menu.

- To insert rows or columns at the bottom or right of the table, use the Append options on the Table menu.

- *Preliminaries*
- *Sections*
- *Layout Regions*
- *Subforms*
- *Actions and Action Buttons*
- *Techniques for Formatting Forms*

5

Advanced Form-Design Tools

CHAPTER 4 INTRODUCED THE BASIC BUILDING BLOCKS FOR DESIGN-ing forms, and using only those tools, you can create reasonably effective forms. However, in order to take full advantage of Notes 4.0, you'll need to add several important form-design tools to your arsenal.

These tools are

- Sections that collapse, for hiding unwanted information
- Layout regions for creating highly customized design elements
- Subforms for storing groups of frequently used design elements
- Action bars and menus for performing common operations

Collapsible sections offer end users the means to hide information of no immediate interest, thereby simplifying the appearance of the form while users read or edit it. Notes provides two different types of sections—*standard* and *controlled access*. The latter is similar to the section field in earlier releases, in which the designer or end users can specify those users who can edit the information within the section.

A *layout region* is a new innovation to Notes 4.0, and it provides a solution to a serious design restriction that exists in previous releases—the inability to freely reposition and manipulate fields, text, and graphics within a form. Within a layout region, you can insert text, graphics, fields, and buttons; in addition, you can freely reposition these objects within the layout region, thereby providing a new level of design flexibility.

Subforms offer a way to reuse groups of common design elements. For example, if you want name and address fields to appear exactly the same on all your standard forms, you can create a subform containing those fields—including descriptive text and graphics. The subform becomes part of the database. Then you can copy the contents of the subform onto any form in any of your databases.

An *action,* which is a new design feature in Notes 4.0, is a set of preset operations that you define either with a formula or script, or from a list of common operations provided by Notes. You make each action available to users by means of an Action button bar and also via the Actions menu. Whenever a user selects an action from the button bar or Actions menu, Notes performs the set of operations assigned to that action.

■ Preliminaries

When creating or modifying a form, you must first display it in design mode:

1. From the main database display, select View, Design.
2. Pull down the lower half of the Navigator pane (by clicking on Design).
3. Select Forms (under Design) and then in the View pane double-click on the name of the form that you want to modify.

4. Until you need them, hide the Design pane and Action pane by deselecting the Design Pane and Action Pane options on the View menu.

5. Display the Form InfoBox: Right-click anywhere on the form and then select Form Properties from the pop-up menu that appears.

■ Sections

A *section* is a special area that you can insert onto a form. The main purpose of a section is to allow a reader to optionally hide or display that part of a document; if the contents of a particular section within a document are not of importance to a user, he or she can collapse the section to simplify the document's appearance.

When you collapse a section within a document, all of its contents become hidden—except the section title, which identifies the nature of the information that's hidden. If you decide to view the contents of a collapsed section, you simply click on its title.

After creating a new section within a form, you can then insert within it any of the standard design elements: fields, text, graphics, hotspots, buttons, and layout regions. You can even insert one or more collapsible sections within another, providing a great tool for users to selectively hide parts within parts of documents.

Figure 5.1 shows a form design that contains two collapsible sections, with the top one expanded. The top of the section displays the section title, which you create as part of the section. Also, a single line indicates the lower boundary of the section—although you can optionally remove this line.

Note. You can insert either type of section into either a form or a subform. However, you can't insert a section into a layout region.

Notes provides two different types of sections—*standard* and *controlled access.* Here's the major difference between the two: Anyone with sufficient access privileges can read or edit the information contained in a standard section. However, the situation is different with a controlled access section: Either the form designer or document users can override the ACL (access control list) by specifying who can edit the contents of this type of section. (In this sense, a controlled access section is similar to the section type of field in earlier Notes releases.)

When designing a section, you can specify whether it will automatically expand or collapse when a document is opened for reading, editing, or previewing.

TIP. *Create a standard section when you want to make part of a form optionally available to readers. In the extreme, you could create a form that consisted entirely of collapsible sections, so that whenever a reader opened a document, all he or she would see at first would be the section titles.*

You can see a good example of how sections are used in the Server/Servers section of your Name & Address Book. Each Server document contains several collapsible sections, near the bottom of the document.

Figure 5.1

A collapsible section within a form provides users with a tool for selectively hiding information on a document.

Section title ──────

Lower limit of section ──────

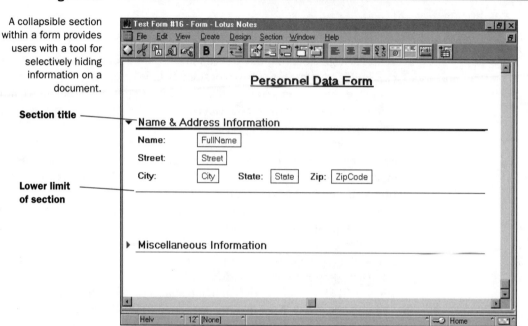

Standard Sections

After creating a standard section, you can fill it with text, fields, and other form elements. You can also customize it as follows:

- Create a descriptive section title

- Select the font, size, and color of the title text

- Select conditions (reading, previewing, or editing) where the section should be automatically expanded or collapsed

- Specify when the section title should be hidden

Creating a Standard Section

To create a standard section within a form, follow these steps:

1. Place the insertion point exactly where you want it on the form. This should be at the beginning of a blank line.

2. Select Create, Section, Standard. Notes will insert a new, empty section labeled Untitled Section, as shown here:

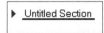

3. To display the Section InfoBox, right-button-click anywhere on the section label and then select Section Properties.

4. Click the InfoBox tab labeled Title, displaying the options shown in Figure 5.2.

Figure 5.2

Use these options to customize a section.

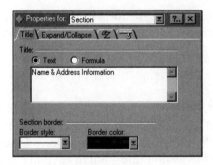

Note. Later, you can delete the border if you don't want it to appear on documents.

5. To help you work with the section, add a border, which will create a box around the title and a line at the bottom of the section: Pull down the list labeled Border Style (see below) and then choose the top border on the list.

6. Enter a title for the new section: Click the radio button labeled Text and then type in the title. (This title will appear when the section is collapsed.) Alternatively, you can enter a formula for the title. For an example, see the following section, "Creating a Title with a Formula."

7. Try clicking a few times on the section title on the form; notice that when you expand the section:

Note. This behavior is the same whether you click on a section title on a form or on a document created with the form.

- A solid line appears at the bottom, defining the lower limit of the section.
- The little triangle to the left of the section points downward instead of sideways.

Creating a Title with a Formula   Instead of typing in a section title (step 6 in the preceding list), you can type in a formula to determine the contents of the title. For instance, the title could be based on the contents of each document created with the form. To use a formula, click the radio button labeled Formula (Figure 5.2) and then type in the formula in the space below the radio button.

As an example, suppose the form contains a field called FullName. If you create a section containing salary information, you can use the following formula:

```
"Salary Information for " + FullName.
```

Customizing the Section

To assign a special font to the section title, click the third tab from the left on the InfoBox and then select the font, size, color, and so on. Your selections will apply only to the section title—not to anything else within the section, such as text, fields, and other elements.

To specify when the section will automatically be expanded or collapsed, follow these steps:

1. Click the InfoBox tab labeled Expand/Collapse, displaying the following options:

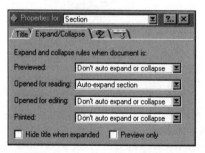

2. Pull down each of the four list boxes in turn and then make your selection. For instance, to expand the section automatically whenever a document is opened for reading, pull down the second list box from the top and select Auto-Expand Section.

You can choose when the section title is hidden, independent of whether the section is expanded or collapsed; just follow these steps:

1. Click the rightmost InfoBox tab.

2. Select the conditions under which you want the section title to be hidden. For instance, if you don't want to display the title while editing, select the option Opened For Editing.

3. You can also write a formula that specifies other conditions when the title should be hidden; to do so, select the option Hide Paragraph If Formula Is True and then type in the formula. For instance, the following formula would hide the section title if the current user's name were Joan Jones:

```
@UserName = "Joan Jones"
```

TIP. *You can set up a section so that it's completely hidden—including the title—whenever a document is in edit mode, making it impossible for users to modify the section's contents. Here's how: First, with the Expand/Collapse tab selected, choose Auto-Collapse Section for the option Opened For Editing. Then choose the option that hides the section title whenever a document is opened for editing (see preceding steps 1 and 2).*

Adding Elements to the Section

Within a section, you can add all the design elements that make up a form—text, fields, graphics, hotspots, buttons, and other sections—working with each element in exactly the same way that you normally would.

TIP. *If you can't see where a section ends, it can be difficult to figure out where to add elements. To eliminate this problem, create a border around the section, as described earlier in the section "Creating a Standard Section." The bottom line that's part of the border will then help you lay out elements within the section.*

Here's how to add elements to a section:

1. To begin, make sure that the section is expanded, as shown next:

Click here to insert a new design element

Bottom of section

▼ Personal Information

2. Click between the section's title and its bottom line.

3. Press Enter once or twice to enlarge the section a bit, so you can more easily place new elements (later, you can delete any extra vertical space in the section).

4. Click on where you want to insert the new element. If necessary, you can press Tab or the spacebar to move the insertion point to the right.

5. Insert the new element (field, text, or whatever) using the same steps that you would for inserting the element anywhere else on a form.

Controlled Access Sections

A controlled access section is different from a standard section: Each controlled access section in a document has an access list of people who have edit access to the section's contents. There are two ways to create this list: First, you can define the section type to be Computed and then write a formula that calculates the list of authorized editors for all documents created with the form. Alternatively, you can define the section type to be Editable, so that when someone creates a document with the form, that person can define his or her own edit access list for the section.

In either case, the list of authorized editors cannot override the ACL for the database; it can only create a subset of users who are already assigned at least Editor access.

To create a new controlled access section, select Create, Section, Controlled Access. The new section will then appear at the insertion-point position. You can then customize the section and add text, fields, and other elements to it; the techniques are basically the same as those for standard sections.

Controlling Edit Access to the Section

Note. By default, all users having Editor or higher access can edit a controlled access section.

You can either create a formula that specifies a list of valid editors, or you can let the author of each new document create the list for that document. The list can contain any combination of individuals, groups, and roles. For example, if you want only those persons working within a particular division to have access to a section, you can set up a group within the database's ACL, containing only the names of those people.

Using a Formula   To create a formula to define a list of authorized section editors, do the following:

1. Display the InfoBox for the section and then click the Formula tab, displaying the options shown in Figure 5.3.

2. Pull down the list box labeled Type and then select Computed.

3. In the bottom edit box labeled Access Formula, type in the formula whose results are the list of valid editors. For instance, the formula in Figure 5.3 calculates that three users can edit this section in any documents created with the form.

Figure 5.3

You can write a formula
to create a list of valid
editors for a section
within documents created
with the current form.

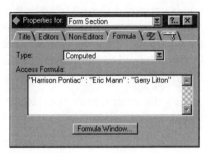

Setting Up for an Author-defined Editor List   You can allow the author of
each document created with the form to create a list of authorized editors
for the section:

1. Display the InfoBox for the section and then click the Formula tab,
   displaying the options shown in Figure 5.3.

2. Pull down the list box labeled Type and select Editable.

3. You can optionally create a formula to assign a default list, using the bottom edit box. This is the default list that will appear for each document.
   The author of each document can override this list.

Defining the List during Document Creation   If you set up a controlled
access section to be editable, then whenever an author creates a new
document, that author defines the list of authorized users as follows:

1. Double-click anywhere on the section title, and the following dialog box
   appears:

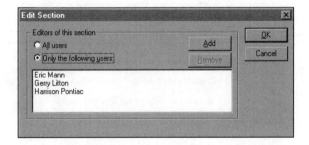

2. Enter the names of those users who will have edit access to the section:
   Click the Add button and then select names in the Address Book to add
   to the list.

Setting Up for User-defined Sections

Note. For details about rich text fields, see Chapter 6.

A *user-defined section* is entirely different from both types of sections described previously, because here the author or user of a document defines the section. A user-defined section can be one or more adjacent paragraphs, and it can optionally be collapsed for easier document reading.

Note these relevant points:

- While creating a new document, an author can create a collapsible section and assign it an access list.

- A person who subsequently opens the document can also create a collapsible section, provided that person has at least edit access to the document.

- A user-defined section can be defined only within a rich text field. The bottom line here is that it's up to the form designer to judiciously insert rich text fields wherever appropriate.

Figure 5.4 illustrates an expanded user-defined section, which is headed by a title. Notice that the bottom of the section is defined by a horizontal line (which is optional, as is the box surrounding the title).

Figure 5.4

A user-defined section can be expanded or collapsed.

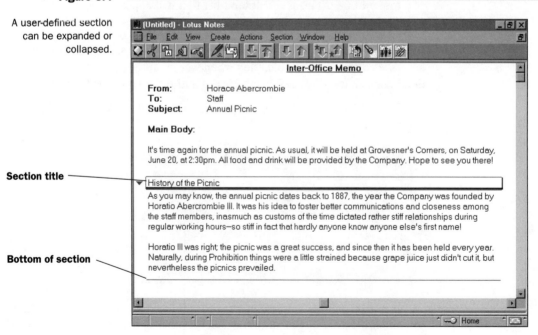

Section title

Bottom of section

Here's how either the author of a document or a subsequent user can create a collapsible section:

1. Make sure that the document is in edit mode and then find the rich text field that you want to edit.

2. Highlight the text you want to make into a collapsible section.

3. Select Create, Section. Notes will hide all but the top line of the selected text, which becomes the default title. Don't panic! You can create your own custom title.

4. Display the Section InfoBox: Right-button-click on the section title and then select Section Properties.

5. Click the leftmost tab, displaying the options shown below:

6. Delete the default title and type in one that's short but descriptive.

7. To create a border around the section title, as well as a line at the bottom of the section, pull down the list box labeled Border Style and select the style that you want. You can also assign a color to the border, using the right-hand pull-down color palette.

8. Click the tab labeled Expand/Collapse, displaying the following options:

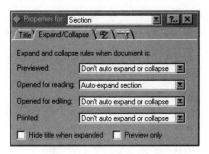

9. Using the four pull-down list boxes, select when you want the section to be automatically expanded, hidden, or neither. For instance, to have the section automatically expanded whenever the document is opened in read mode, pull down the second-from-the-top list box and select Auto-Expand Section.

10. To hide the title when the section is expanded, click the appropriate option at the bottom of the InfoBox.

WARNING! *If you select the option Preview Only, the title of the section is hidden when you open the document in either read or edit mode. If you select this option, but you also want the section to be visible in either read or edit mode, you'll need to set the options (in step 10 of the preceding list) to auto-expand the section in either mode. Also, once you select the Preview Only option, you can't deselect it!*

■ Layout Regions

Layout regions provide form designers a new level of flexibility. Within each region, you can insert text, graphics, fields, and buttons, each of which is treated as a separate design object. The huge advantage of using layout regions is that you can freely reposition each design object within the layout region, thereby eliminating the line-by-line design restriction of earlier Notes releases.

When creating a new form, you can insert as many layout regions as you wish. Wherever you want to do especially nice layout work on a form, insert a layout region there and then do your design work within it. For example, you can use a layout region at the top of a form to create an especially attractive logo.

One traditional approach to form design has been to create two separate parts to each form—one for data input and the other for reading documents—hiding one section during data input and the other during reading. This method has been somewhat clumsy, partially because the smallest unit that you can hide on a form is the paragraph.

For example, consider the following line (really a paragraph) on a form:

Name: Name

During data input, you want both the label and the field to be displayed, but in read mode you want to display only the field. In Notes 3 and earlier releases, you can't accomplish this directly; instead, you must create two lines:

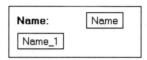

The top line is displayed in edit mode, and the bottom line in read mode. Although this approach can be used with great success, it does tend to lead to long forms.

Layout regions offer some relief from this problem, because within a layout region you specify whether each individual object is either displayed or hidden in read mode and edit mode.

As an example, you could display various buttons whenever a document is being edited, but hide the buttons when the document is displayed in read mode. The result is that you don't need to create duplicate objects in a layout region—one for read mode and the other for edit mode.

Although layout regions offer several huge design advantages, they have a few restrictions. The following table lists what you can and cannot insert into a layout region.

Objects You Can Insert into a Layout Region	Objects You Cannot Insert into a Layout Region
Fields	Shared fields
Graphic objects	Sections
Hotspot buttons	Hotspots: link, text, formula, and action
Graphic buttons	Tables
	Subforms
	OLE objects

Creating a Layout Region

When you create a new layout region, it initially extends across the entire width of the window. Although you can reduce the width of the layout region, you can't insert anything to the left or right of it. The maximum size you can make a layout region is 22.75 by 22.75 inches.

Here's how to create and size a new layout region:

1. Place the insertion point where you want to insert the new region. Be sure that the insertion point is at the beginning of a line—not anywhere in the middle.

2. Select Create, Layout Region, New Layout Region. The new region will appear as a rectangular box on the form, extending downward from the original position of the insertion point:

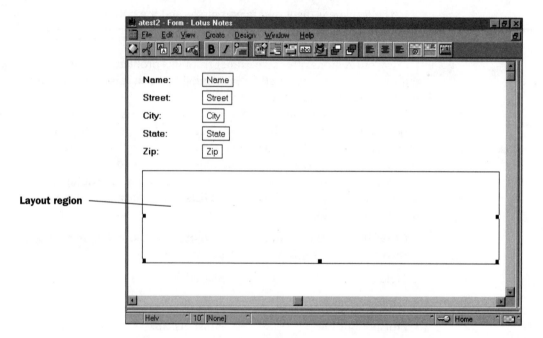

Layout region

3. To resize the layout region, grab a handle on the side or the bottom and then drag it in or out to extend or reduce the width or height.

4. For more precise sizing of the layout region, you can use the InfoBox:

   - Right-button-click anywhere in the layout region and then select Layout Properties from the pop-up menu that appears.
   - When the Layout InfoBox appears (Figure 5.5), enter values for the options labeled Left, Width, and Height.

TIP. *If you have trouble extending the right edge, use the Infobox to set the width.*

Other Layout Region Options

You can use the options shown in Figure 5.5 to customize the appearance of a layout region, as follows:

- To create a box around the layout region, select the option Show Border.

- To make the layout region stand out even more against other parts of the form, select the option 3D Style. Figure 5.6 illustrates an example of using this option.

After creating a layout region, you can insert text blocks, fields, graphics, and buttons, which you can then freely reposition within the confines of the region.

Figure 5.5

Use these options to customize a layout region.

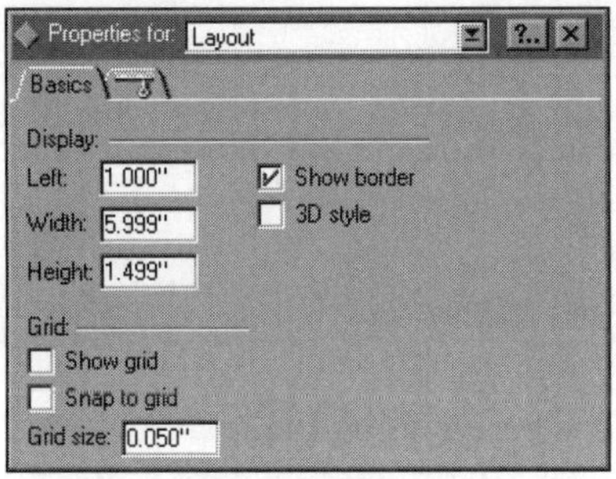

Inserting Fields

Note. For details about working with fields, refer to Chapter 6.

Fields in a layout region are pretty much like those on other parts of a form: After creating a new field, you can assign it properties just as you would for a field inserted on other parts of a form. However, there's one important difference: Within a layout region, you can click and drag a field freely from one position to another.

Here's how to create a new field in a layout region:

1. Select the layout region by clicking anywhere on it.

2. Either click the New Field icon (below) or select Create, Field.

NOTE. *Each new field begins life in the middle of the layout region, so if you create two fields without repositioning either one, they'll completely overlap, and you will not be able to see the one underneath.*

Figure 5.6

A customized layout
region can enhance the
appearance of
documents.

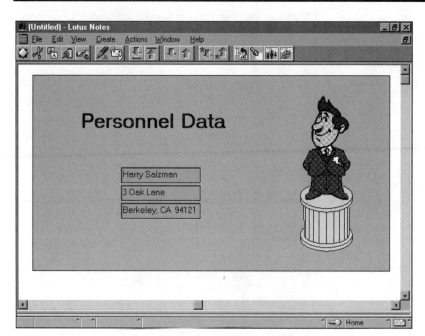

3. When the field box containing the text "Untitled (edit control)" appears, as shown in Figure 5.7, drag it to where it doesn't overlap any other objects on the layout region.

Figure 5.7

Use the InfoBox to assign
properties to the new
field.

Layout region ——

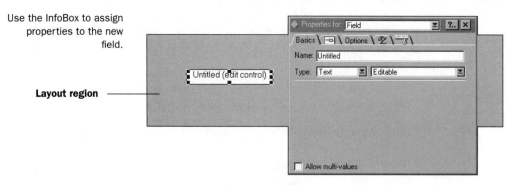

4. If necessary, double-click on the new field object so that its InfoBox appears, as shown in Figure 5.7.

Note. See Chapter 6 for
details about assigning
field properties.

5. Using the InfoBox, assign the various field properties.

You can resize the field by grabbing one of its handles and dragging it away from the field center. You would need to do this, for example, if you assigned a larger font to the field.

For more precise field repositioning and sizing, you can use the InfoBox: Click the second tab from the left on the InfoBox (Figure 5.8) and then enter new values for field size and position.

Figure 5.8

Use the Layout options for sizing and positioning a field.

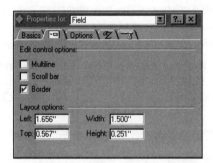

You can also use the grid for lining up groups of fields. For details, see the later section "Repositioning Objects."

Creating Text Blocks

You can create a text block consisting of one or more lines within a layout region. Using the various options on the Text InfoBox, you can format the text just as you would ordinary text, changing its font, size, attributes, and color. You can also reposition the text with standard click-and-drag operations.

Here's how to insert and format a text block in a layout region:

1. Click anywhere on the layout region.

2. Select Create, Layout Region, Text. Notes will display a new text box, containing the text "Untitled."

3. If the InfoBox is not displayed, double-click on the text block.

4. Be sure that the top of the InfoBox displays Properties For Control (if not, pull down the top list box and select Control), as shown in Figure 5.9.

5. In the edit window within the InfoBox labeled Text (and which initially contains "Untitled"), type in the text that you want. To create a hard return, press the Enter key.

6. To left-align, right-align, or center the text block within the text box, select the appropriate alignment option on the InfoBox.

7. To vertically center the text block within the text box, select the option Center Vertically.

8. To set the font, attributes, and color of the text block, click the middle tab on the InfoBox, as shown in Figure 5.10.

9. To assign a background color to the text block, deselect the Transparent option and then select the background color.

Note. You can force a text block to break at a word boundary by reducing the width of the text box.

10. If you resized the text in step 8, it may now be too large to fit in the text box. If so, grab a corner of the box and then enlarge it. Alternatively, you can use InfoBox options to resize the text box: Click the leftmost InfoBox tab and then change the Width and Height values.

11. To reposition the text block, click and drag it to any position within the layout region. (For more information about repositioning objects in layout regions, see the later section "Repositioning Objects.")

Figure 5.9

You can use the InfoBox to assign properties to a new text block.

Layout region

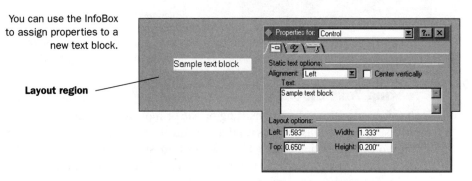

Figure 5.10

Use these options to change the characteristics of a text block.

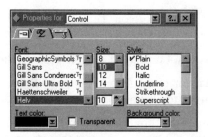

Inserting Graphic Images and Buttons

You can import into a layout region graphic images from other software packages. These can be either clip art images or images you create, and you can insert any number of them onto a layout region. However, unlike other parts of a form, you can insert only images that you have previously copied to the Clipboard. After inserting an image, you can reposition it anywhere within the layout region by clicking and dragging.

Unfortunately, you cannot resize an image within a layout region. Instead, you must set the size in the software in which you create or obtain the image and then copy and paste it into the layout region. In many cases, you may have to go through a couple of trial-and-error cycles in order to get the size just right.

You can also create *graphic buttons* and *plain buttons* in a layout region. A graphic button behaves exactly like an action button: You can attach just about any type of Notes operation to the button, so that when a user clicks on it, Notes performs the attached operation. A plain button (referred to by Notes simply as a *button*) is like a graphic button, but its face displays text instead of a graphic.

Using Graphic Images

You can use graphics to create static images or graphic buttons within a layout region. To insert a graphic image, follow these steps:

1. Temporarily exit from Notes and then launch whatever drawing or clip art software you have at your fingertips.

2. Display or create the image that you want and then copy it to the Clipboard.

3. Exit from the software, back to Notes.

4. Click anywhere on the layout region where you want to insert the image.

5. To insert the graphic image, select Create, Layout Region, Graphic.

After inserting an image, you can reposition it anywhere within the layout region by clicking and dragging.

You can also use a graphic image from another source to create a graphic button—one that's mouse-sensitive, as described previously. To accomplish this, begin by following steps 1 through 4 above. Next, select Create, Layout Region, Graphic Button. Then display the the Design pane, select the appropriate radio button (Action, Formula, or Script), and finish up either by selecting an action or writing a formula or script.

Inserting Buttons

A button within a layout region behaves just like an ordinary button on any other part of a form: With each button, you can associate either a simple Notes action, a formula, or a script, so that when a user clicks on the button, Notes will perform the associated operation.

Like other objects within a layout region, you can place a button anywhere you wish by clicking and dragging. For easy identification, you can attach a text label either to the top of the button or as a separate text block.

Here's how to create a button:

1. Click anywhere in the layout region.

2. Select Create, Hotspot, Button.

3. To display the InfoBox for the button (Figure 5.11), double-click on it.

Figure 5.11

You can use the InfoBox to assign text properties to a button.

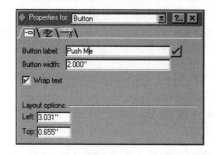

Tip. To set the width of a button having no label, type in as many spaces as needed.

4. Type the button label into the InfoBox. If you want the text to automatically wrap on the button, select the appropriate option.

5. If you selected the Wrap Text option in step 4, you can then select a maximum width for the button. (If you did not select Wrap Text, Notes ignores the width you specify here.)

6. To customize the text, click on the middle InfoBox tab and then choose options for the text font, size, and so on.

7. Make sure that the Design pane appears at the bottom of the window, as shown in Figure 5.12.

Note. For details about assigning button operations, see "Action Hotspots and Buttons," in Chapter 4.

8. Select the type of operation that you want to associate with the button— either a simple Notes action, a formula, or a script. Notes will perform this operation whenever a user clicks the button.

9. Depending on your choice in step 8, fill in the necessary details (write a formula, or whatever).

Repositioning Objects

One of the chief advantages offered by a layout region is that you can easily rearrange the objects within it. By using the mouse, you can drag the objects from one position to another—even overlapping them for special effects.

Figure 5.12

Use the bottom Design
pane to associate an
operation with the current
button.

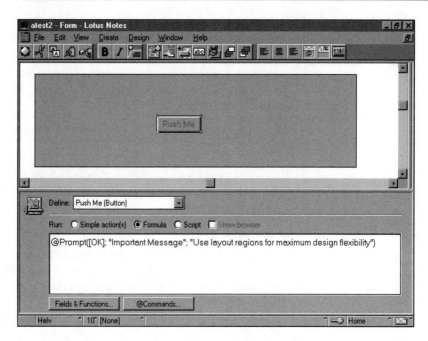

Figure 5.12

Use the bottom Design
pane to associate an
operation with the current
button.

To reposition an object, simply click on it, hold down the mouse button,
and then drag the object to where you want it. Overlapping offers a very
clever way to create two different designs—one for viewing and another for
editing—within the same physical space on the form.

Overlapping Text

You can overlap text onto a picture to create a special effect, such as the one
shown in Figure 5.13. Here, the text object labeled "Fast Results!" is placed
on top of the picture.

Figure 5.13

You can overlap text onto
a picture to create a
special effect.

Here are a few tips for when you're creating this type of effect:

1. Before dragging the text on top of the image, click the text block and then select Design, Bring To Front. This will ensure that the text will lie on top of the image and will therefore be visible.

2. Using the InfoBox for the text block, select the middle tab, deselect the option Transparent, and then select colors for the text and background.

3. Assign a font and a large enough text size to stand out against the picture.

4. If the text disappears as soon as you drag it on top of the picture, you can easily fix things up: Click anywhere on the picture and then select Design, Sent To Back.

Using the Grid

To create designs in which the various objects are precisely lined up, you can use the grid that lies dormant in each layout region. When you activate the grid, each object you reposition will snap to the nearest grid line. Similarly, when you resize an object, the edge you're repositioning will snap to the nearest grid line. The figure below shows how the grid appears when displayed in a form.

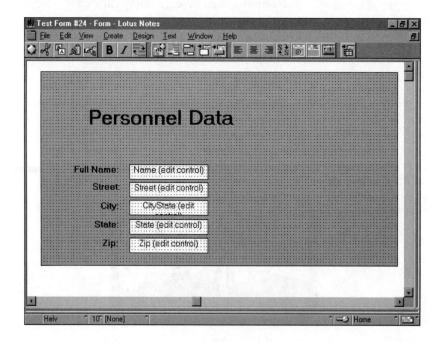

Here's how to use the grid within a layout region:

1. Display the InfoBox for the layout region (as shown in Figure 5.6) by right-button-clicking anywhere in the region and then selecting Layout Properties from the pop-up menu that appears.

2. At the bottom of the InfoBox, select the options Show Grid and Snap To Grid.

3. If you wish, you can customize the size of the grid spacing by entering a value in the edit box labeled Grid Size.

Displaying and Hiding Objects

By default, each object that you create in a layout region is visible under all conditions. However, you can optionally select whether an object should be visible only when reading the document or only when editing it. This is a terrific tool you can use to great advantage when designing forms, because you can make a single layout region within a document appear one way in edit mode and another way in read mode. This technique is very similar to that available in earlier Notes releases, but with one important difference: In earlier releases, you could display or hide only entire paragraphs in a document; within a layout region, you can display or hide individual objects.

You can selectively hide or display objects in design, edit, and preview modes. You can also write a formula for an object that determines when the object is hidden.

To selectively hide and display a particular object in a layout region, follow these steps:

1. Click on the object that you want to customize.

2. If the InfoBox for the object is not visible, double-click on the object.

3. Click on the rightmost InfoBox tab, displaying the options shown in Figure 5.14.

4. Select when you want the object to be hidden. For example, to make the object visible only when viewing documents in read mode, select all the options except Opened For Reading.

To illustrate how you can use selective hiding of objects within a layout region, we'll use a simple form consisting of a single layout region. Figure 5.15 shows a document created with this form. Part (a) of the figure shows how the document appears in edit mode; part (b) shows it in read mode.

To understand the design of the layout region shown in Figure 5.15, note that the layout region consists of the two sets of objects shown in Figure 5.16 parts (a) and (b): One set is visible only in read mode, and the other only in

Figure 5.14

Use these options to
selectively hide and
display layout region
objects.

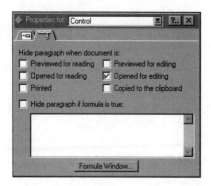

edit mode. Note that although these figures show the two different sets of
objects individually, in actuality they are superimposed on top of one another
in the layout region.

You can also create a formula that specifies special conditions under
which an object is hidden. To do so, click the option Hide Paragraph If Formula Is True and then type in the formula. For instance, you can hide an
object whenever one or more fields in a document have specific values. As an
example, here's a formula that will hide an object whenever the value of the
FirstName and LastName fields have specific values:

```
FirstName = "Henry" & LastName = "Aldrich"
```

Setting the Tab Order in a Layout Region

You can assign the order in which the focus moves from object to object
within a layout region when a user presses the Tab key. Here, *object* refers to
fields, buttons, and graphic buttons, which are the only types of objects available to users when creating and editing documents.

This feature can be very useful for simplifying the work of data-entry
personnel. For instance, if you know the order in which data values will be
listed on hard copy, you can set the tab order to match that order.

Here's how to set the tab order:

1. Click on the first object that you want to have the focus. This will be the
   first object reached when the focus is on a field above the layout region
   and a user then presses Tab.

2. Select Design, Bring To Front.

3. Click on the next object that you want to have the focus and then select
   Design, Bring To Front.

4. Repeat step 3 for each object in the layout region.

Figure 5.15

(a) The contents of a
document displayed in
edit mode; (b) the same
layout region displayed in
read mode.

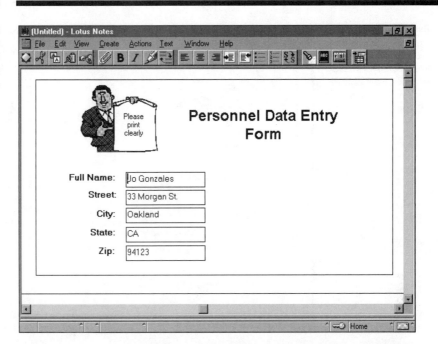

(a)

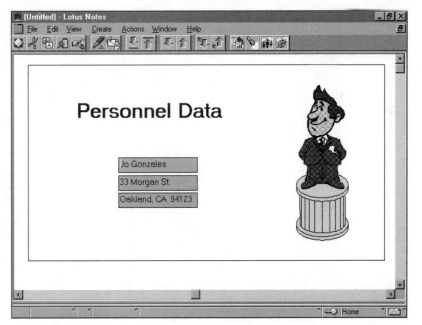

(b)

Figure 5.16

Part of the underlying layout region for the document shown in Figure 5.15: (a) These objects appear only in edit mode; (b) these objects appear only in read mode.

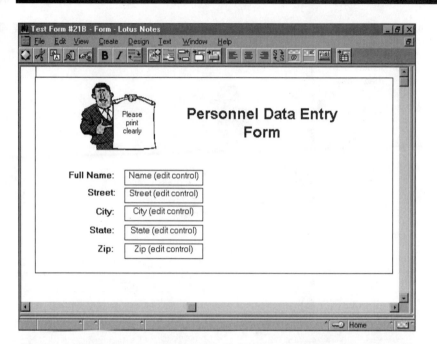

(a)

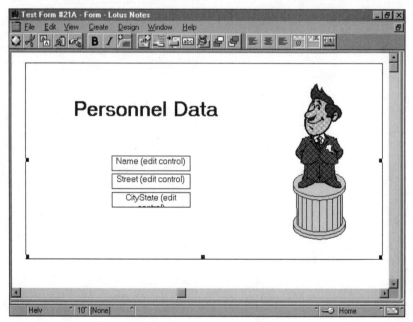

(b)

Manipulating Layout Regions

You can delete, move, or copy a layout region from one position to another within a document. You can even copy a layout region from one form to another, using the operating system's Clipboard.

WARNING! *When you delete a layout region, you delete all of its contents as well. Unfortunately, you cannot use Edit, Undo to reverse the deletion, so be careful about pressing Del or the Backspace key after selecting a layout region.*

Deleting a layout region is extremely easy, and with a couple of mouse clicks, you can destroy a great deal of work.

To delete the layout region (and all of its contents), click anywhere on it and then press either Del or the Backspace key. You can also select Edit, Cut to delete a layout region. This is somewhat safer, in case you change your mind, because you can recover by using Edit, Paste—until you put something else on the Clipboard.

You can copy and paste or cut and paste the layout region, again using the Clipboard. This is a handy way to save work by copying a set of design elements from one part of a form to another, or from one form to another—even in different databases. (You can also accomplish this by using subforms, which are discussed in the next section.)

If a layout region contains a field, and you copy the entire region from one part of a form to another, Notes automatically renames the field in the new copy (remember, you can't have two fields with the same name in a form). For instance, if the original layout region contains a field named City, the corresponding field in the copy of the layout region will be named City_1.

TIP. *If you create a layout region that you think you might want to use in other forms—perhaps even in other databases—copy and paste the layout region into a template database that you use for saving useful odds and ends. Then, whenever you want to use the layout region, you can easily copy and paste it from the template database.*

■ Subforms

One of the many new features of Notes 4.0, subforms may prove to be a handy tool if you find yourself designing forms for many different databases. If you plan to use the same group of design elements in several forms, you can save yourself considerable effort by creating that group of elements once, saving it as a subform with a unique name. Then, whenever you want to use that particular group of design elements as part of a new form, you can simply insert the subform onto the form.

A subform can contain just about all of the design elements available for ordinary forms—fields, text, graphics, layout regions, and so on. However, there's one exception: You can't insert one subform into another.

Each subform is saved as part of a particular database. However, if you create a subform that you really like, you can easily copy and paste it into other databases.

You can edit a subform whenever you wish. However, this can be a double-edged sword, because your changes will automatically be reflected in every form in the database containing the subform. This particular characteristic can be used as a method for helping to maintain uniformity among the various forms used by a company. For instance, you could create a subform consisting of basic name-and-address information—perhaps including custom graphic elements. You could then copy the subform into other databases used within the company, so that name and address information would always appear in the same way—in every form that uses the subform. Later, if you decided to alter the format of the name and address information, you would make the changes on one copy of the subform and then paste the new version of the subform to all the other relevant databases. The changes would then be reflected in every form using the subform.

> **Note.** If you copy a subform from one database to another, changes to the subform in one database will not automatically be carried over to those in other databases.

WARNING! *Modifying a subform is an excellent way to lose track of a great deal of data. For instance, if you delete a field from a subform, the corresponding field values will no longer appear on the forms containing that subform, although the data values will still be stored within the documents.*

Creating a Subform

A subform exists as a separate entity within a database. Here's how to create one:

1. Make sure that the main database display is shown: From your workspace, you can select the database in which you want to create the subform and then select View, Design.

2. Select Create, Design, Subform, displaying the design window shown in Figure 5.17.

3. Display the InfoBox for the subform (see Figure 5.17): Right-button-click anywhere on the subform and then choose Subform Properties.

4. Type in a unique name for the subform; that is, one not assigned to any other subform in the current database.

5. Be sure to select the option Include In Insert Subform Dialog.

6. Insert the design elements that you want to be part of the subform.

Figure 5.17

Use this design window
to create a new subform.

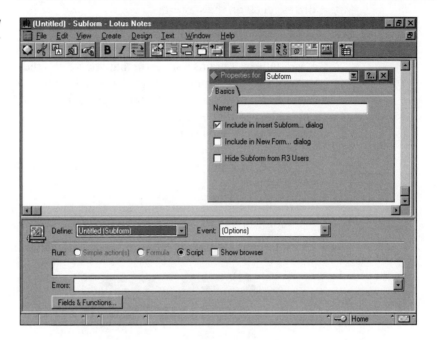

7. Save the subform by selecting File, Save.

The subform becomes a permanent part of the current database.

Editing a Subform

You can easily make changes to a subform, such as adding or deleting text, fields, and other design elements.

To edit a subform:

1. From your workspace, select the database containing the subform and then select View, Design.

2. Make sure that the lower part of the Navigator pane is expanded; if it isn't, click once on Design (in the middle of the pane).

3. Click on Subforms; the list of subforms in the current database is then displayed in the View pane.

4. Double-click on the name of the subform that you want to edit, displaying the subform design.

5. Make whatever changes you want to the subform and then save them (select File, Save).

You can also edit a subform from a form that contains the subform: double-click on the subform.

Using a Subform

If a database contains a subform that you've created, you can include the contents of that subform as part of any form you create within the database. You can also write a formula that specifies the conditions under which different subforms will be inserted into each document created with this form. For instance, you could insert one subform for certain classes of users, and another subform for others.

Here's how to add the contents of a subform to the current form that you're editing:

1. Position the insertion point on a blank line, where you want to insert the subform.

2. Select Create, Insert Subform, displaying the list of available subforms:

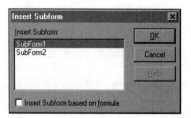

3. If you want to add a specific subform, choose it from the list; the contents of the subform will then appear on the current form. Otherwise, to write a formula to choose which subform to add to the form, go on to step 4.

4. To write a formula, select the option Insert Subform Based On Formula and then click OK. The form will then display the following object:

   `<Computed Subform>`

5. In the Design pane, write a formula to specify the conditions under which different subforms will be inserted into new documents.

As an example, suppose that you're building a form to contain information about your acquaintances, who fall into two categories: "business" and "personal friends." As part of the form, you would like to include one set of fields for friends, and another set for business associates, but you would like each of these two sets of fields to appear only under the appropriate circumstances. That is, the fields for friends would appear only when you're creating a document about one of your friends, and similarly for the other set of fields.

Here's how to accomplish this: First, include a special keyword field named Type, which will contain one of two values—Friends or Business. Then create two subforms named FriendsFields and BusinessFields, each containing the fields for the appropriate type of acquaintance. Finally, insert a computed subform at the appropriate position on the form that you're building, and assign it the following formula:

```
@If(Type = "Friends"; "FriendsFields"; "BusinessFields")
```

Editing a Subform from within a Form

If you click anywhere on the copy of a subform within a form, a box appears completely around the subform, but you can't access the individual elements. However, you can easily access the subform itself by double-clicking anywhere on the subform contents on the form. The subform will then appear, and you can make whatever changes you want to it, then select File, Close and save the changes to return to the original form.

■ Actions and Action Buttons

An *action* is something that you as a form designer create as a shortcut tool for users. When you create an action, you attach it either to a formula or script you write, or to one of Notes' built-in simple actions. Because of the power of formulas and scripts, you can incorporate just about any set of Notes operations into an action button or menu option.

After creating a new action, you can make it available to users for point-and-click operation in any of the following ways:

- As an action button on the action bar, which appears at the top of each document created with the form in which you define the action button. To perform an action, the user clicks the appropriate action button. Figure 5.18 shows a document displaying the action bar.

- As an option on the Actions menu, which also appears when a document is opened.

- As an action hotspot or button, which can be located anywhere on a form, and which appear in the corresponding locations on documents created with the form. (Chapter 4 describes how to set up action hotspots and buttons.)

NOTE. *Notes uses an unfortunate choice of terminology that can be extremely confusing: A* simple Notes action *is a predefined operation provided by Notes, such as switching to edit mode, saving the current document, and so on. On the other hand, an* action *is something that you create as part of a form. You*

Figure 5.18

The Action bar offers point-and-click operation for common database functions.

Action button bar

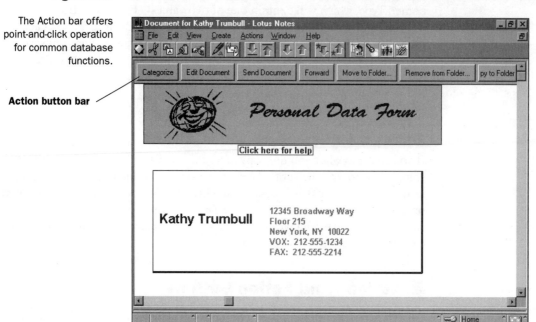

attach each action to either a formula, a script, or a simple Notes action. For example, you can create an action and attach it to the simple Notes action to switch to edit mode.

After you create a new action as part of a form, you can choose whether it will appear as an action button on the action bar, and whether it will also appear on the Actions menu. Here's an important point to bear in mind: The action bar and Actions menu appear only on documents created with the form—they do not appear on the form itself.

Each action that you create is specific to the form in which you create it. However, you can easily copy and paste an action from one form to another.

Creating a New Action

Building a new action involves two steps. First, you create the action and customize its various options, such as assigning it a name and deciding whether it will appear on the action bar or Actions menu. The second part of the process is to define what the action does; to accomplish this, you assign the action either to a simple Notes action or to a formula or script that you write.

The following steps outline the first part of this process—setting the new action's options:

1. Make the sure that the form you want to edit is selected and displayed in design mode (in the main database display, click on Forms in the Navigator pane and then double-click on the name of the form).

2. When the form is displayed, select View, Action Pane. The Action pane appears on the right side of the window, displaying a list of the actions currently associated with the form (see Figure 5.19).

NOTE. *In the Action pane, the actions whose names are preceded by an asterisk are automatically attached to each form.*

Figure 5.19

The Action pane displays the names of actions attached to the current form.

Action pane

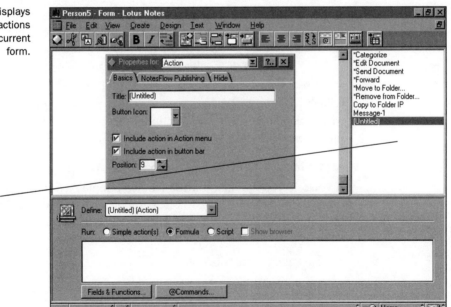

3. To begin attaching a new action to the form, select Create, Action. You'll see the following:

   - The Action InfoBox appears, as shown in Figure 5.19.

   - A new action called "(Untitled)" appears in the Action pane.

   - The title "(Untitled)" appears in the InfoBox.

   - The edit box at the top of the Design pane displays "(Untitled) (Action)."

Note. The Define edit box in the Design pane always shows the design element that you're currently working with.

4. Make sure that the Design pane is displayed at the bottom; if it isn't, select View, Design Pane.

5. In the InfoBox, type in a short but descriptive name for the new action. When you finish typing the title and clicking the check box to the right, you'll see the new title appear in the Action pane.

6. At the top of the Design pane, select whether you're going to attach the new action to a simple Notes action (select Simple Action), a formula (which you'll write), or a script (ditto).

Now you can choose where the action should appear on documents created with the form:

1. Make sure that the name of the new action is highlighted in the Action pane and that the Basics tab on the InfoBox is selected.

2. To include the action on the action bar and/or the Actions menu, select the corresponding option(s) on the InfoBox. Remember: You don't see the action bar or Actions menu while working on the form; they appear only when a user creates, edits, or views a document.

After defining a new action, you must attach it either to a simple action (which you select from a list), to a formula you write, or to a script you write—depending on your selection in the preceding step 6. Each of these three operations is described in the following sections.

Attaching a Simple Notes Action to an Action

If you selected the radio button labeled Simple Action in step 6, you must now attach the new action to one (or more) of the simple actions provided by Notes. Each simple actions represents a standard operation on a document, such as the following:

- Save the current document

- Delete the current document

- Copy the current document to a particular folder

- Mail the current document

Here's how to select a simple action to attach to the new action:

1. Click the Add Action button, displaying the dialog box shown in Figure 5.20.

2. Pull down the top list box, scroll through the various items, and then select the operation you want. (For an explanation of these operations, see the later section "Selecting an Action.")

3. For many operations, you'll need to supply additional information in the dialog box. For example, if you select Copy To Folder, you'll then need to select the name of the folder, as shown in Figure 5.21.

4. When you exit from the Edit Action dialog box, you'll see the operation you selected shown in the Design pane.

In some circumstances, you may want to attach more than one simple Notes action to an action you've created. For instance, you can attach a new action to the following two simple Notes actions:

• Copy the current document to a special folder

• Enter edit mode for the document

Figure 5.20

Use this dialog box to define an action.

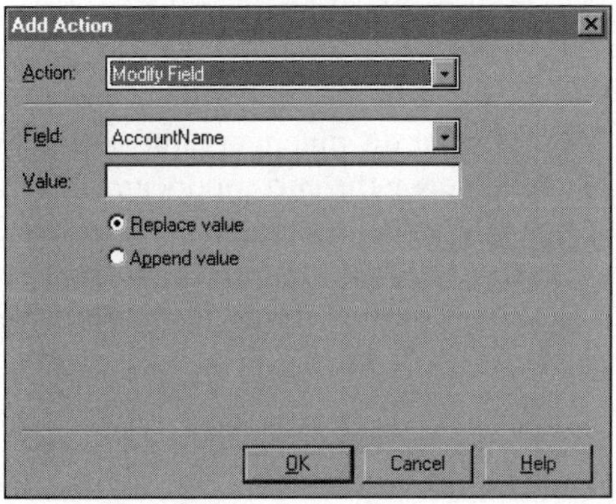

Figure 5.21

Select the name of the folder that you want as the recipient.

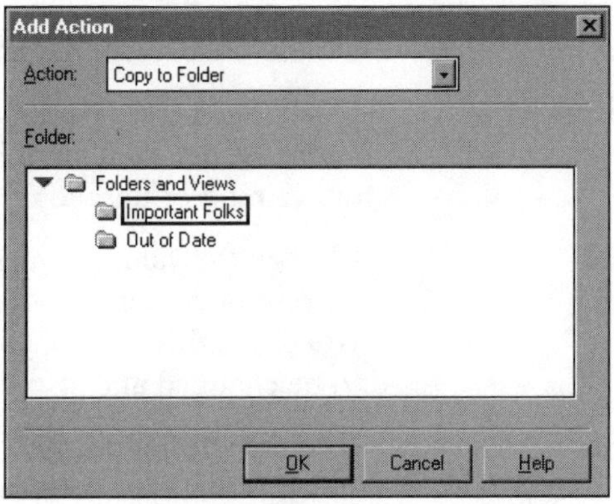

To assign another operation to the current action, click in the Design pane to the left or right of the operation listed there—but don't highlight that operation—click the button labeled Add Action, and then proceed as described in the preceding steps 1 through 4. You can assign as many operations as you want to an action.

NOTE. *Although you're free to combine as many simple actions as you wish, in practice this will probably not be very useful, because the simple actions are more or less independent. In general, if you need to create an action that performs complex operations, more than likely you'll need to write either a formula or a script.*

Selecting an Action   The top list box in the Add Action dialog box (Figure 5.20) displays the list of the simple Notes actions from which you can choose. To understand how these actions work, you need to remember that most actions specifically apply to the document that's currently open. For example, suppose you select the action Copy To Folder from this list and then also choose the folder named Important People. Now suppose that later a user is working with a particular document created with this form. If the user runs this action, Notes will copy the current document to the folder named Important People. (Actually, a new document is not created; only the name of this document is added to the folder, from which users can access that document.)

Here's a partial list of the actions available in the Add Action dialog box, with a brief explanation of each:

Action	Operation
Copy To Database	Copy the current document to the selected database (when you select this option, you must also select the database to which you want to copy documents)
Delete From Database	Delete the current document from the database
Mark Document Read	Mark the current document as read (remember that each document in a view is marked as either read or unread)
Modify Field	Change the value of the selected field in the current document to the specified value (when you select this option, you must select the field to be changed and also the new value)
Run Agent	Run the specified agent (which you must also specify when you select this option)
Send Document	Mail the current document to the person listed in the SendTo field in the current document

Attaching a Formula or Script to an Action

By writing a formula or script, you can attach just about any set of Notes operations to an action. Then you place this entire set of operations at users' fingertips by displaying the action on the action bar and the Actions menu.

Here's how to attach a formula or script to a new action:

1. Make sure that the Design pane is displayed at the bottom of the window.

Note. For details about using formulas, see Chapter 10.

2. At the top of the Design pane, click the Formula or Script radio button.

3. In the Design pane, type in the formula or script.

LotusScript is a complex language, far beyond the scope of this book. However, just to whet your appetite, Figure 5.22 shows a simple script attached to the action Message-1. When a user clicks the corresponding action button, the following message box appears:

Figure 5.22

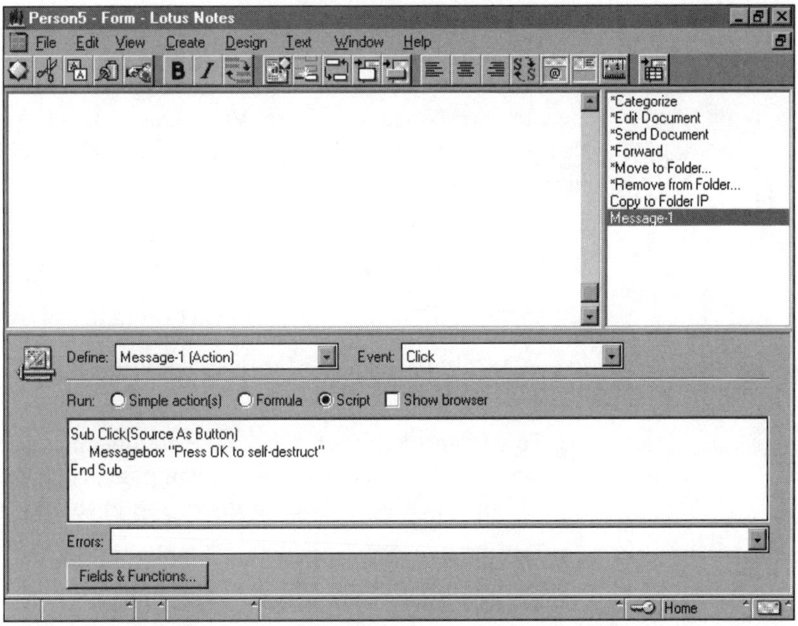

Running the Message-1 action executes the script shown in the Design pane.

![Screenshot of the Person5 - Form - Lotus Notes window showing the Design pane with a LotusScript action. The right panel lists: *Categorize, *Edit Document, *Send Document, *Forward, *Move to Folder..., *Remove from Folder..., Copy to Folder IP, Message-1. The Define field shows "Message-1 (Action)", Event "Click", Run options show Simple action(s), Formula, Script (selected), Show browser. The script reads: Sub Click(Source As Button) / Messagebox "Press OK to self-destruct" / End Sub]

Note. For a review of action hotspots and buttons, see Chapter 4.

The preceding sections have described how to attach a simple Notes action to an action that you create as part of a form. You can also attach a simple Notes action to either an action hotspot or a regular button. (Remember that unlike actions, which appear on the action bar at the top of a document as well as on the Actions menu, action hotspots and buttons can appear anywhere in a document.) Then, whenever you click the hotspot or button, Notes will perform the simple action that's attached.

Here's how to attach an action hotspot or button to a simple Notes action:

1. To create an action hotspot, select the text that you want as the hotspot and then select Create, Hotspot, Action Hotspot. Or, to create a button, position the insertion point and then select Create, Hotspot, Button.

2. Display the Design pane.

3. At the top of the Design pane, click the Simple Action radio button.

4. Select the simple action that you want to assign to the hotspot or button. For details about selecting actions, see "Attaching a Simple Notes Action to an Action," earlier in this chapter.

Editing, Deleting, and Copying Actions

If an action outlives its usefulness, you can either modify it or delete it entirely from the form. You can also copy an action from one form to another— even a form in a different database.

To perform any type of operation on an action, you must first display the form containing the action: With the main database display visible, display the standard Navigator (select View, Design); pull down the lower half of the Navigator pane labeled Design if necessary; click on Forms; and then double-click on the form name in the View pane.

To modify an action:

1. Display both the Action pane and the Design pane.

2. In the Action pane, select the action that you want to modify.

3. To delete part of an action, highlight those parts in the Design pane and then press Del.

4. To add another operation to the action, click at one end or the other of the operations listed in the Design pane, click the Add Action button, and then select the operations you want to add.

5. To edit an existing operation, highlight it in the Design pane, click the Edit Action button, and then make the changes you want.

Here's how to perform other handy operations on an action:

- To delete an action, highlight it in the Action pane and then press Del or select Edit, Cut.

- To copy the action to another form, highlight the action; select Edit, Copy; switch to the other form (in design mode), which can even be in another database; and then select Edit, Paste.

■ Techniques for Formatting Forms

Several useful techniques are available for customizing the appearance of forms, many of which are borrowed straight out of the repertoire of modern word processors. For instance, you can format paragraphs by setting the line spacing, aligning text, inserting tabs, and assigning other features. You can also create bulleted and numbered lists on a form, using groups of adjacent paragraphs.

Notes 4.0 even allows you to create paragraph styles, which can greatly simplify your work when formatting long and complicated forms.

One of Notes' most powerful formatting features allows you to selectively display and hide paragraphs. This technique—a carryover from earlier Notes releases—allows you to create two or more forms in one. For instance, you can display one part of a form when in edit mode and another part in view mode. You can also hide or display a paragraph, depending on the outcome of a formula that you write. This powerful new feature allows you to customize the appearance of a form based on current circumstances, such as the values of particular fields or the name of the current author or editor.

Formatting Paragraphs

Notes provides a great many paragraph-formatting options. You can

- Format the alignment and spacing of individual paragraphs

- Control page breaks before and after paragraphs

- Assign custom tabs to individual paragraphs

- Create groups of numbered and bulleted lists

- Create custom styles and apply them to individual paragraphs

In this context, a *paragraph* is any collection of design elements—text, fields, graphics, buttons, and hotspots—between two hard returns. Unfortunately, you can't see hard returns on a form, so you'll sometimes need to use your judgment or trial-and-error to figure out where they are. Here's one sure-fire way to guarantee there's a hard return where you want it:

1. Place the insertion point where you think the end of the paragraph is.

2. Press Del a few times—until the beginning of the following line jumps up to the end of the one where the insertion point is located.

3. Now press Enter once.

You can use the InfoBox to format entire paragraphs. For instance, you can left-align, center, or right-align a title (which usually consists of a one-line paragraph). Here are some of your options (in these examples, we'll assume that you have highlighted one or more paragraphs that you want to format):

• To set the paragraph alignment, click the InfoBox tab that's second from the left, displaying the options shown in Figure 5.23, and then make your selections.

• To set the paragraph spacing—including extra space above and below—use the bottom options on the InfoBox, as shown in Figure 5.23.

• To control page breaks before and after a paragraph, click the third-from-left InfoBox tab, displaying the options shown in Figure 5.24.

Figure 5.23

Use these options to customize the appearance of a paragraph.

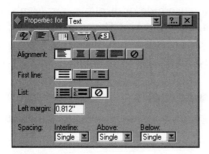

Figure 5.24

Use these options to control page breaks and set tabs for individual paragraphs.

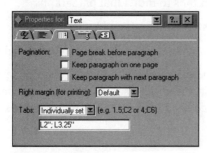

You can also set the alignment of a paragraph with Notes' ruler. To begin, display the ruler at the top of the window by selecting View, Ruler (see Figure 5.25). Next, select the paragraph that you want to format. Then:

- To change the left margin of the entire paragraph, drag the left-margin marker (see Figure 5.25) to where you want it.

- To set the left margin of the first line only, click and drag the first-line marker.

- To create a hanging indent, click and drag the left-margin marker to where you want to place the indent and then drag the first-line marker back to its original position.

Figure 5.25

You can use the ruler to assign alignment and tabs to a paragraph.

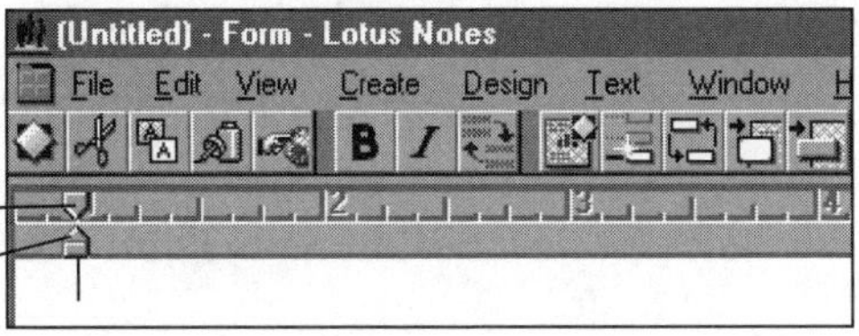

First-line alignment mark

Left-margin marker

Setting Tabs

By default, each paragraph is assigned a set of tabs, evenly spaced at 0.5-inch intervals. You can override this default for individual paragraphs, assigning custom tabs instead. You can assign left tabs (the default), center, right, and decimal tabs, and you can use either the Text InfoBox or the ruler to assign tabs.

TIP. *As soon as you create a new tab for a paragraph, Notes removes all the default tabs to the left of the new one. For instance, if you insert a new tab at 1.25 inches, the default tabs at 0.5 inch and 1 inch are removed. If you still want a tab at 0.5 inch, insert a new custom one.*

To use the Text InfoBox to assign a set of custom tabs to a set of paragraphs you've highlighted, follow these steps:

1. Click the third InfoBox tab from the left, displaying the options shown in Figure 5.24.

2. In the edit box labeled Tabs, select Individually Set.

3. In the bottom edit box, type in the tab positions that you want, following these rules:

   - Each tab position is relative to the left edge of the window—not to the left margin.

- You must separate each tab position from the next with a semicolon.
- To create a left tab (the default), use either the format 2.5 or L2.5 (a left tab at 2.5 inches).
- To create a center tab, use the format C3 (a center tab at 3 inches).
- To create a right tab, use the format R3.
- To create a decimal tab (one in which the decimal point is positioned at the tab setting), use the format D4.
- To create a set of evenly spaced tabs, select the option Evenly Spaced in the Tabs edit window and then type in the spacing that you want.

You can also use the ruler to insert left, center, or right tabs, as follows:

1. Highlight the paragraph(s) to which you want to add tabs.
2. Select View, Ruler (see Figure 5.25) to display the ruler at the top of the window.
3. To insert a left tab, click the left mouse button at the appropriate position on the ruler.
4. To insert a right tab, right-button-click at the desired position on the ruler.
5. Do delete a tab you've inserted, left-button-click on it.
6. To change a tab that you've inserted to a different type of tab (center, right, or decimal), right-click on it and then select the new tab type from the pop-up menu that appears (see below).

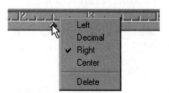

If you later want to change the tabs in a paragraph to which you've already added tabs, highlight part or all of the paragraph and then make your changes, following the preceding rules. If you want to be able to easily reformat a group of paragraphs at a later time—changing their tabs or other formatting features—use *paragraph styles,* which are described later in this chapter.

Creating Numbered and Bulleted Lists

Notes 4.0 is rapidly catching up with the paragraph-formatting capabilities found in modern word processors. For example, you can transform a group of paragraphs into a bulleted or numbered list, as follows:

1. Highlight the paragraphs that you want to change.

2. Display the Text InfoBox and then click on the Alignment tab (second from the left), displaying the options shown in Figure 5.23.

3. To create either a bulleted or numbered list, click the appropriate button on the line labeled List.

If you change your mind about the numbered or bulleted list that you've set up, you can easily unformed the paragraphs. To do that, highlight the paragraphs and then click the rightmost button on the line labeled List.

Creating and Using Styles

A *paragraph style* (or *style,* for short) is a set of special paragraph-formatting characteristics to which you assign a unique style name. These characteristics can be any combination of the formatting features described in the earlier sections: text font and size, left margin, indents, and so on. For example, you could define a style to consist of the following formatting features: boldface, with a custom tab at 2 inches.

NOTE. *All of the techniques described in this section for creating and using styles apply to text that you're creating as part of a form. However, these methods can also be used by document authors and editors on text and graphics contained within rich text fields.*

To explain the use of styles, let's take the following example: Suppose that you plan to use several titles in a particular form, and for the sake of uniformity and consistency you plan to format all of them in the same way: Arial 12-point, boldface, and centered on the line.

Instead of formatting each new title individually, you can create a special style named something appropriate, like Main Title, with the previously mentioned features (Arial 12-point and so on). Then, each time you type in a new title, you simply assign the style Main Title to it.

Here are a few things to keep in mind about using styles:

- To create a new style, you set up a model paragraph, which incorporates all the formatting features that you want to include in the new style, and then you create the style based on the model paragraph.

- When creating a new style, you can optionally exclude all of the font characteristics in the model paragraph from the style definition.

- You can apply a paragraph style only to complete paragraphs—not to parts of one.

- After applying a style to a paragraph, you can then apply additional formatting to individual parts of the paragraph.

- By default, each style that you create is restricted to the current form. However, you can also set an option making the style available to any form in the database.

Creating a New Style

To illustrate the steps for creating a style, we'll describe how to create the Main Title style described in the previous section. First, you create a paragraph and format it just the way you want it. Then you use that paragraph as a model for creating the new style.

Here are the details:

1. Create a model title. Format it exactly the way you want; for example, boldfaced, 12-point Arial font, and centered on the line. Remember, to center a line, you click the Alignment tab on the Text InfoBox and then click the Center Alignment button.

2. Make sure that the insertion point is still on the title line and then click the Styles tab on the InfoBox (the rightmost tab), displaying the options shown in Figure 5.26. The displayed list shows the current styles available to the form; the ones with asterisks are supplied automatically by Notes.

Figure 5.26

Start here to create or modify a paragraph style.

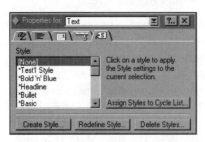

3. Click the button labeled Create Style, displaying the following dialog box:

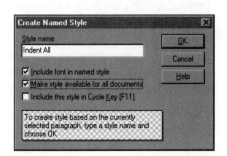

4. In the top edit box, type in a unique name for the new style (Main Title, in this example). The name can be up to 35 characters in length, and it can include spaces and special characters.

5. To make this style available to all the forms in the current database, select the middle check-box option.

6. To include the text font characteristics in the definition of the new style, select the top check-box option.

7. Click OK to close the dialog box.

Modifying and Deleting Styles

You can modify the characteristics of an existing style, or you can delete it entirely from the form. Here's how to modify a style:

1. To begin, find a paragraph that's been assigned the style. Or you can simply create a new paragraph.

2. Reformat the paragraph, adding all the changes that you want to incorporate into the modified style.

3. Display the InfoBox and select the Styles tab (the one farthest to the right).

4. Click the button labeled Redefine Style.

5. When the Redefine dialog box shown below appears, select the style and then click OK.

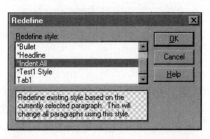

To delete a style, display the Text InfoBox and then click the Styles tab. Click the button labeled Delete Styles and then select the style you want to trash.

Using Styles

After creating a style, you can use it (as well as any of the others available to the current form) to format any paragraph you wish. To accomplish this, you can use either the Text InfoBox or the pop-up list on the Status Bar.

To use a style to format a paragraph:

1. Click anywhere on the paragraph. Or, to format several adjacent paragraphs at the same time, highlight them.

2. To select the style from the status bar, click on the Styles button, popping up the list of available styles (see below), and then click the one you want to apply to the paragraph(s).

3. Alternatively, you can use the Text InfoBox to select a style: Click the Styles tab and then select the style from the list that appears, as shown in Figure 5.26.

Copying a Style

You can make a style available to any form in the current database, as described in the previous section, "Creating a New Style" (step 5). You can't directly copy a style to another database; however, you can get around this restriction with a tiny bit of work:

1. Highlight any paragraph that's assigned the style that you want to copy to another database.

2. Copy the paragraph to the Clipboard.

3. Switch to the other database and then open up any of its forms.

4. Paste the paragraph onto that form; anywhere at all will do, because it's only there temporarily.

5. Now create a new style, using that paragraph as the template. Set the option to make that style available to any form in the database.

6. To finish up, delete the paragraph.

The new style is identical to the original one, and it's available to any form in this database.

Hiding Paragraphs

Often, you'll want to present one form to users for creating and editing documents, and an entirely different form for reading the same documents. In earlier versions of Notes, your chief tool was the ability to selectively hide paragraphs. That is, you could specify which paragraphs were displayed or hidden during editing and reading. This tool has been carried over to Notes 4.0, and you may still find it to be useful in many situations.

As in earlier releases, the smallest unit that you can hide or display in a Notes 4.0 form is the paragraph, which could be as small as a single line. A paragraph can contain text, fields, and graphic objects, all of which can be hidden or displayed.

NOTE. *There's one important exception to the preceding rule regarding hiding objects on a form: Within a layout region, you hide or display individual objects, which can be text blocks, fields, graphic images, or buttons.*

As an example of how effective this tool can be, Figure 5.27 shows how the same document appears in edit mode (a) and view mode (b).

By default, every paragraph within a document is always displayed— both when in view mode and when in edit mode. You can, however, override this default for various paragraphs. To specify when a paragraph should be hidden or displayed, follow these steps:

1. Click anywhere on the paragraph. Or, for multiple, adjacent paragraphs, highlight all of them.

2. Display the Text InfoBox: Right-click anywhere on the highlighted paragraphs and then select Text Properties from the pop-up menu that appears.

3. When the InfoBox appears, click the fourth tab from the left (displaying the icon shaped like a window shade), so that the options shown in Figure 5.28 appear.

4. Using the various options, choose when the paragraph(s) should be hidden. For example, to hide the paragraph when a document is displayed in view mode, select the option Opened For Reading.

Figure 5.27

(a) A document displayed in edit mode; (b) the same document in view mode.

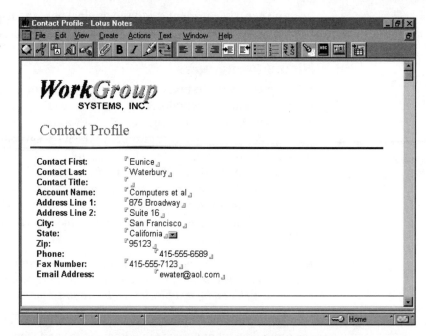

(a)

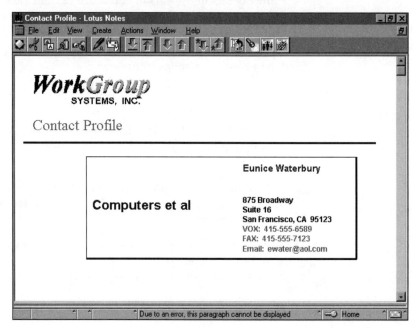

(b)

Figure 5.28

Use these options to
select when a paragraph
should be hidden.

5. You can also write a formula that can specify a set of conditions under which a document is hidden. To do so, select the option Hide Paragraph If Formula Is True and then type in the formula in the bottom edit window. For instance, to hide a particular paragraph for only those people who live in California, you could write the following formula:

```
ContactState="California"
```

- *Creating and Using Fields*

- *Assigning Basic Field Options*

- *The Field Types*

- *Selecting How Field Values Are Supplied*

- *Multi-Valued Fields*

- *Reserved Fields*

- *Shared Fields*

- *Inheritance*

Designing Fields

FIELDS ARE THE BASIC BUILDING BLOCKS OF NOTES FORMS, AND learning to work with fields is a vital part of database design. Notes provides several different field types to accommodate the various types of information that you may want to store. If you've had experience with other database systems, you may be amazed at the flexibility offered by these field types. One type in particular—rich text fields—can hold just about any kind of information that you can possibly imagine, including embedded or linked OLE objects. Rich text fields also have other features that make them a jack-of-all-trades that you'll find invaluable.

Most fields that you design can be either single-valued or multi-valued. And all fields are variable-length, which means that each field value takes up only as much disk space as it needs.

For most types of fields, values can either be input by users or calculated according to formulas created by the form designer. Formulas can be based on other field values—either in the same form or on another one. In the latter case, the form can be in either the same database or a different one. Formulas can incorporate a wide variety of built-in Notes functions, and for still more flexibility, the designer can write entire LotusScript programs as the basis of field calculations.

A *keyword field* is a special type of field that presents users with a list of preset values from which to choose. This list, which can optionally be sorted, can be either a fixed group of values supplied by the form designer or a set of values existing in another database. The latter type of list is dynamic, in that it always displays the current contents of that database. For either type of keyword list, the form designer can optionally allow users to enter values not on the list.

As you design each field, you'll need to assign it various features or characteristics, such as the field name, type, whether its values are to be input or calculated, and so on. You select all of these features from the Field InfoBox—the convenient, one-stop design tool that's prevalent throughout Notes 4.0.

When designing a field, you can make it *single-use*, which means that its definition is restricted to the form in which you design it; or you can make the field a *shared field*, in which case its design is available to any form in the database. Shared fields provide a convenient mechanism for maintaining design uniformity in fields that are used in several different forms.

Notes provides several reserved fields for special purposes. You can insert these fields onto your forms and take advantages of their unique features. For instance, some fields are used for routing documents, while others are involved with security features.

As you design each field, you'll need to consider a variety of issues, such as the following:

- What type of data values will be stored in the field?

- Does the field need to accept single or multiple values?

- Will field values be entered by users or computed within Notes? If the latter, then what type of computation is involved?

- Should input values be formatted in any way?

- Are only certain input values to be considered valid?

- Are there security issues associated with the field?

- Is the field going to be a shared field or limited to the current form?

- Is the form mail-enabled, and if so, are the correct mail-associated fields defined on the form?

- Do any other special fields need to be defined?

Clearly, there's a lot to learn about Notes fields, and this chapter provides the important groundwork.

■ Creating and Using Fields

Note. This section deals only with single-use fields; that is, those limited to the form in which they are created. A special section later in this chapter deals with shared fields.

You can create a new field on just about any part of a form: within the main part of the form, or in a layout region or collapsible section.

After creating a field, you can copy and paste it or cut and paste it from one part of a form to another. You can also copy a field from one form to another—either in the same database or in another one.

Creating a Field

Regardless of where you're placing a field, the steps for creating it are similar: To insert a field anywhere on a form—except within a layout region—place the insertion point where you want to insert the field. For a layout region, simply click anywhere on the region. Then either click the Create Field SmartIcon or select Create, Field.

The new field, which is initially labeled Untitled, will appear at the insertion-point position (or in the center of the layout region, in which case it appears as a *field object*), and you can then proceed to define the field.

Copying and Deleting Fields

You can copy a field from one form to any other form in your Notes universe. When you make a copy of a field within the same form, Notes automatically changes the name of the copy—because field names within a form must be unique.

To begin copying a field, position the insertion point just to the left (or right) of the field on the form, use the mouse to highlight the entire field, and then select Edit, Copy, placing a copy of the field on the Clipboard. If you're a little casual, you might pick up a blank space or two to the right or left of

Note. To copy a field in a layout region to the Clipboard, simply click in the field and then select Edit, Copy.

the field during this procedure, but this is of little consequence, because you can easily delete the extra space later.

After copying the field to the Clipboard, switch to wherever you want to place the copy and then select Edit, Paste. If you're copying to another form, the new copy will retain the original field name.

Besides copying a single field, you can perform other similar operations, including the following:

- Cut and paste a field from one position to another on a form.

- Highlight and then cut and paste or copy and paste two or more fields at the same time. You can even include blocks of text as part of this type of operation.

Note that you can't copy fields from a layout region to other parts of a form and vice-versa.

Deleting Fields

You can easily delete a field from a form. This is not as serious as it may seem: When you use a form to create a new document, the field values become part of the document—not the form. Remember that a form is simply a window into a group of documents. If you delete a field from the form, you're not deleting any corresponding field values; you're simply reducing the visibility offered by that particular form.

The field values are still in their respective documents, and you can view them either by adding the field back to the form or by creating a new form that contains a field with the same name and type.

To delete a field on a form, simply click on that field and then either press Del or select Edit, Cut. The latter is slightly safer, in case you immediately realize that you have made a mistake, because you can use Edit, Paste to recover the deleted field—as long as you haven't in the meantime copied something else to the Clipboard.

■ Assigning Basic Field Options

After creating a new field on a form, you must then assign its various characteristics, which you select from the Field InfoBox.

To begin, make sure that the Field InfoBox is displayed, and then select the Basics tab, as shown in Figure 6.1.

Figure 6.1

Select field names that
are short, unique, and
descriptive.

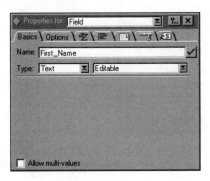

Field Name

For each new field, assign a name that you can easily recognize and that conveys
the type of information to be stored in the field. The name can be up to 32 characters long, and it can contain only letters, digits (0–9), underscores, dollar signs,
and periods—no spaces or hyphens are allowed. Don't worry about forgetting
these rules; Notes will tell you when you try to create a name that's too fancy.

You can't create two fields with the same name within the same form;
this applies both to local fields (those defined only for the current form) and
shared fields (those available to any form in the database). Moreover, Notes
ignores capitalization in field names; for example, you can't name one field
FirstName and another one Firstname, on the same form.

Text Characteristics

You can use the Field InfoBox to assign the font, size, attributes, and color of
the text in a field. Your selections will apply both to the field as it appears on
the form, and to the field contents on documents created with the form. The
default is 10-point Helv black.

To customize the field text, click the Fonts tab (third from the left) on
the InfoBox, displaying the options shown in Figure 6.2.

Field Help

You can use two different techniques to supply users with online information
about the purpose of each field. First, you can enter a short description about
the field into the InfoBox; this text will appear at the bottom of each document
whenever the field is selected while a document is being created or edited.

To insert a help description: Click the Options tab on the InfoBox, displaying the choices shown in Figure 6.3. Then type in a short but informative
description about the field. Notes will display only a single line at the bottom
of a document, no matter how much help text you enter.

Figure 6.2

Use these options to customize the text in a field.

Figure 6.3

Type in a helpful message for users.

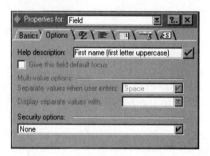

There's another way in which you can display helpful information about a field: Add a hotspot pop-up immediately adjacent to the field. When a user clicks on the pop-up, your message will appear. Chapter 4 describes how to create hotspot pop-ups.

Special Options for Layout Regions

Fields created within a layout region have one basic difference from those created elsewhere: Each field in a layout region exists within the confines of a fixed-dimension field object, and you specify those dimensions as part of the field design. This is the field size that a user will see when creating documents; in other words, within a field in a layout region, you can't see very much text at the same time. However, the field contents is still variable-length, and you can enter as much information as needed; you just can't see much of it at once.

Note. All the text within the fields in a layout region is searchable.

Notes provides options to ensure that readers can view the entire contents of the field, regardless of its length. These options include

- Handles on the field object, which the designer can use to adjust the object's default size so that more than one line of text can be seen

- Provision for automatic text-wrap within the field object

- A scroll bar to facilitate reading long, multiline values

If you expect that data values within a field in a layout region will require several lines of text, here's how to utilize these special options:

1. Click on the field.

2. To increase the length of the field object, drag one of its handles outward.

3. Using a handle, expand the field object's height so that two or more lines of text will be visible.

4. In the Field InfoBox, click on the second tab from the left, as shown below:

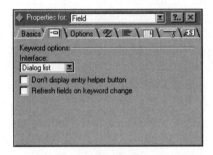

Note. You can also use the InfoBox to set the size and position of the field.

5. To provide for multiple lines, choose the Multiline option.

6. To allow users to read long field values, select the Scroll Bar option.

■ The Field Types

When creating a new field, you must assign it an option that determines the kind of information that can be stored in the field. Notes provides eight different field types, but they offer enough variety to accommodate just about any type of information you could possibly want to place in a document.

Selecting a field type can have many subtle implications for the documents that you create. For example, one type of field is used for determining who can edit documents, while another type helps to specify who can read documents.

The field types are

* Text

* Number

* Time

* Rich text

* Keyword

* Authors

- Readers

- Names

NOTE. *If you have used earlier versions of Notes, you may have noticed that the Section field type is missing from the preceding list. In Notes 4.0, sections still exist, but not as fields. Instead, they are treated as a special type of building block—controlled access sections—for creating forms containing parts with restricted access. For details about creating and using sections, see Chapter 5.*

To assign a type to a new field, display the Field InfoBox options shown in Figure 6.1, pull down the list box labeled Type, and then make your selection.

The following sections describe each of the field types in detail, indicating when you would use each one. As you'll see, some field types require only a few words of explanation; others require pages.

Text Fields

A *text field* can contain just about any combination of letters, digits, and special characters. In a typical application, the majority of fields are text. If you expect a field to contain numeric values, but they will not be used mathematically, you should probably define the field as text.

TIP. *Use a text field for zip code information, because leading zeros will be retained (unlike with number fields, where leading zeros are discarded). Also, some international zip codes contain letters.*

Like other types of Notes fields, each text field is variable-length, so you can enter as much information as you wish.

Number Fields

Use a *number field* for storing numeric information—especially information that you plan to either treat or sort numerically. You can select from several schemes for formatting numbers:

- *Fixed*. Each number is rounded to contain a fixed number of decimal digits that's set by the form designer.

- *Currency*. Each number is preceded by a dollar sign.

- *Scientific*. Notes formats each number to appear as x.xxE+xx. For instance, if a user enters 25.2, Notes will reformat it to 2.5E+01.

- *General*. No formatting is applied to input values.

- *Percentage*. Notes multiplies each input value by 100 and appends the percentage sign.

In addition to the preceding choices, you can set an option so that Notes inserts commas in large numbers and displays negative numbers in parentheses.

To select the formatting options for a number field, select Number as the field type on the Field InfoBox and then make your choices from the numeric options that appear (see below).

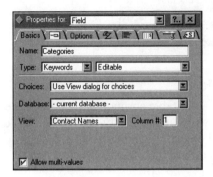

Time Fields

If you plan to store either time or date information, use the *Time field type,* which encompasses both. Within a time field, you can store either time values, date values, or combinations of both. The options that you select on the Field InfoBox determine how the input values are displayed.

As an example, you could input complete time-date values for a field. For output, you could display only the date portion on one form, but the full time-date values on another.

Here are a few samples of valid time and date values you can input:

3:00	1/2/96	1/2/96 3:00
3:00am	01/02/96	3:00 1/2/96
3:00AM	01-02-96	3:00 Today

On the other hand, here are a few formats that Notes will not recognize:

3am (minutes must be included)

3:am

3:00a.m. (no periods allowed)

01.02.03 (separator must be either a forward slash or a hyphen)

To select the formatting options for a time field, select Time as the field type in the InfoBox and then make your selections from the options that appear (see below).

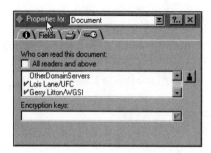

Rich Text Fields

A *rich text field* is a veritable cornucopia of possibilities for document authors and editors, who can use this type of field to hold just about any type of machine-readable objects. Each rich text field is like an open drawer whose capacity stretches almost to infinity, and which can hold any combination of the following:

- *Text.* Users can format text within a rich text field in a document, selecting different fonts, sizes, attributes (bold, and so on), and colors.

- *Graphics.* Users can either import the contents of a graphics file (select File, Import) or paste a graphic image from the Clipboard.

- *Attachments.* Using the File, Attach command, a user can attach a file to the current document, using a rich text field as the receptacle.

- *Embedded OLE objects.* Users can embed or link OLE objects.

- *Collapsible sections.* A user can define any part of a rich text field to be a collapsible section—even portions that include graphics or other objects.

- *Hotspots and buttons.* A user can insert any type of hotspot, even attaching a formula or action to one.

Note. Chapter 11 describes using OLE objects within Notes documents.

Note. Collapsible sections, hotspots, and buttons are described in Chapter 4.

As usual, there's no free lunch, and rich text fields have a major restriction: Notes can't evaluate the contents of this type of field (if this weren't true, you might be tempted to dump the entire contents of every document into a single rich text field, because of its versatility). There are several implications to this restriction: You can't use the contents of a rich text field in a database view, nor can you use a formula to evaluate the contents of a rich text field.

Keyword Fields

You use a *keyword field* to present users with a list of items from which to choose. This is very convenient for a number of reasons. First, it relieves the user from having to make arbitrary decisions when none is needed; secondly, it imposes data consistency within a set of related documents; and finally, it increases the speed of data input.

For example, you might want to use a keyword field named Region to display the values East, West, North, and South, from which the user makes the appropriate selection for each new document. Notice that a keyword field not only restricts the input values, it also enforces correct spelling and capitalization.

As a form designer, you can set up each keyword field so that its values are created in any of the following ways:

- Predefined by you, so that the same list is always displayed to users. You can optionally sort the list.

- Taken from the personal names in the user's Address Book.

- Taken from the contents of the access control list for the current database.

- Taken from a specified column of a particular view, in either the current database or another one.

- Created by a formula.

When a keyword field is set up as a sorted list that's predefined by the designer, data entry is particularly easy: A user can select a particular value simply by typing in the first few letters.

You can optionally allow a user to enter a value that's not in the list; this value is *not* added to the keyword list. You can also set up the field to accept multiple values, mixing user-input values with others selected from the standard list (see "Multi-Valued Fields," later in this chapter).

Normally, a keyword list appears in a pop-up dialog box, which the user displays either by pressing Enter or by clicking the little button adjacent to the field (which you can optionally hide). However, if the list consists of a fixed group of items, the form designer can optionally display them as either a group of check box or radio button options. However, these two options are not available under any of the following conditions:

- The field contains multiple values (that is, the user can select more than one item from the list).

- The users can enter values that are not on the list.

- The keyword list is taken from either the Address Book or the database's access control list.

To customize the various options unique to keyword fields, you use the first two tabbed pages on the Field InfoBox, shown on the following page.

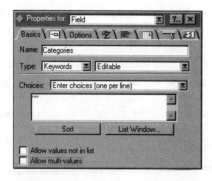

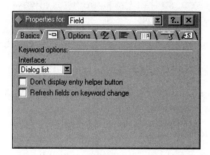

When making your selection for the Choices option, you can use the following table as a guide:

To	Choices Option
Type in a group of values for the keyword list	Enter choices (one per line)
Define a formula to supply the values for a keyword	Use formula for choices
Use the values in the Address Book	Use address dialog for choices
Use the values in the ACL	Use access control list for choices
Use the values defined in the column of a database view	Use View dialog box for choices (see the example in the next section)

As you make your selections, here are a few other helpful hints:

- Assign the keyword field to be Editable. Otherwise, users won't be able to make any selections!

- Unless the keyword list is very short, don't use check boxes or radio buttons, because they'll take up too much room on a document.

- When entering a list of items for a keyword field, you can enlarge the edit box in which you're working by clicking the List Window button. Similarly, if you're creating a formula to display the list, you can get more working room by clicking the Formula Window button.

- If other field values depend on the value of the keyword field, you can choose the option Refresh Fields On Keyword Change. This will cause the entire document to be recalculated whenever a new value is selected for the field.

Example: Using a View Column to Supply Values

Suppose that you're designing a new database form, and you want to include a keyword field where a document author can select the name of a particular business contact from a list. Let's also suppose that you maintain a separate database of business contacts, and you would like to use the names in this database as the basis for the list in the keyword field.

To begin setting up the keyword field, you must first switch to the business contacts database and create a new view—call it Contact Names—containing a single column that displays the personal names in the database.

After creating the special view, you're ready to define the keyword field in the form that you're designing:

1. Insert the keyword field where you want it, and make sure that the Field InfoBox is displayed with the Basics tab displayed.

2. Select the options Keywords and Editable.

3. For the Choices option, choose Use View Dialog For Choices; the InfoBox options will change to display the following:

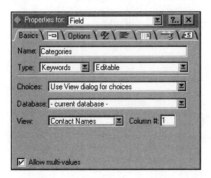

4. Select the name of the database containing the view that you want to use.

5. Select the name of the view (in this example, it's Contact Names).

6. Select the number of the column containing the values that you want to display (in this example, its the first column).

NOTE. *If you're a seasoned Notes developer, you may have realized by now that the technique just described is a replacement for the old method of using the DbColumn function to access a column of values in a database view. This is only a modest shortcut, and it's not likely to put you out of work.*

Supplying User-Friendly Values

Suppose you create a keyword field whose list contains the names of the 50 U.S. states. To make things easy for users, you would like to display the full state names, but you would like the final field values to be the two-letter abbreviations. In other words, the user would see a list something like the following:

Alabama

Arizona

Arkansas

.

.

But, you want Notes to store values as AL, AZ, and so on. Here's how you can accomplish this:

1. Create the new field and select the type to be Keywords, Editable.

2. For Choices, select Enter Choices (One Per Line).

3. Make sure to *deselect* the option Allow Values Not In List.

4. Enter the state values as follows:

Alabama | AB

Arizona | AZ

Arkansas | AK

.

.

.

When a new document is created, the user will see a list consisting of the first item in each pair of values, but when the user selects a state, the corresponding two-letter code will be stored internally. However, the full state name will be displayed in the documents, making them more easily understood.

Authors Field

The purpose of a field whose type is *authors* is to restrict edit access of documents to a select few users having only Author access. In other words, this field is used to override the ACL by allowing selected authors to edit documents created by someone else. An authors field contains a list of names—which can be any combination of individuals, group names, and roles. In a document containing an authors field, users having Author database access can edit the document provided their names appear in that field.

If a form does not contain an authors field, then edit access to documents is restricted either by the database's ACL or by controlled-access sections within the documents.

If users have Reader access to a database, they can never edit documents there, even if their names appear in an authors field. On the other hand, users listed in the ACL with Editor or higher access can always edit a document.

A forms designer can set up an authors field so that its values are specified in one of three ways:

- Define the field to be Computed and create a field formula that generates a list of author names. These will be the only people allowed to edit documents created with this form.

- Define the field to be Editable. Then when an author creates a new document, he or she can supply the names of authorized editors for the document.

- A combination of the above two: Make the field Editable, but supply a formula that creates a default list of people who have edit access to all documents. Each document author can then edit the list as needed.

If you use a formula to create a list of names, they should be separated by colons, such as the following:

```
"Jack Payle" : "Jill Hill"
```

You can set up a form to have more than one authors field. For instance, one field could be defined as editable, so that authors could create their own access list; another authors field could be set up as Computed When Composed, having the formula @UserName. The purpose of this field is twofold: It displays the name of the document author, and it also adds that name to the list of authorized editors.

To customize the options unique to authors fields, you use the first tabbed page on the Field InfoBox. As you begin to select options for an authors field, you can use Table 6.1 as a guide.

Table 6.1

Setting options for an authors field.

TO	CHOICES OPTION	FIELD TYPE
Allow authors to type in an access list for each document	None	Editable
Allow authors to build the access list from entries in the Address Book	Use Address Dialog Box For Choices	Editable
Allow authors to build the access list from entries In the database ACL	Use Access Control List For Choices	Editable
Allow authors to select access list from a column in a database view	Use View Dialog Box For Choices	Editable
Provide a fixed access list as part of the form design	None	Computed (user also supplies a formula)

The $UpdatedBy Field

Notes provides a convenient tool for tracking document editors: If a document contains an authors field, Notes automatically inserts the field $UpdatedBy into the document and stores there the name of each person who has edited the document. To view the contents of this field, open the document (or select it in a view), display the Document InfoBox, click the Fields tab, and then scroll down and select the $UpdatedBy field. Its contents will be displayed in the right-hand part of the InfoBox.

Instead of going through the preceding steps, you can also take a convenient shortcut—if the document is open in read mode. To do this, click on the authors field and hold down the mouse button for a second or two; Notes will display the names of those who have edited the document (see below). A user's name will be added to this list only if he or she actually makes changes to a document (reading a document does not count).

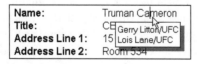

Readers Fields

The purpose of a *readers field* is to restrict read access of documents. A readers field contains a list of names—which can be any combination of individuals, group names, and roles. When a document contains a readers field, users whose names appear in that field will have read access to the document.

When you create a new form, Notes automatically establishes a default list of authorized readers, which will apply to every document created with the form. If you add a readers field to the form, the names that it contains in a document are added to the original default list.

NOTE. *You can modify the original default list for a form by displaying its InfoBox and then clicking the Security tab, showing the following options:*

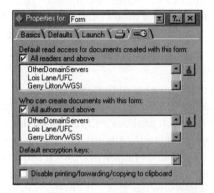

If a user's name does not appear on the combined list of authorized readers for a document, then he or she cannot read that document; in fact, that document won't even be visible on any of the database views—even if the user has Manager access to the database!

A readers field can never override the ACL of the database. That is, if a user has either No Access or Depositor access to a database, that person can never read documents there, even if his or her name appears in a readers field.

NOTE. *If a user tries unsuccessfully to open a document, he or she probably doesn't have read access. Unfortunately, Notes doesn't display a descriptive message—it just locks the reader out.*

Similarly, users with read access to a document may or may not also have edit access—depending on their database ACL rights. Users with read-only access to a document also have copy access; they can copy selected parts of the document to the Clipboard, for pasting elsewhere.

As part of designing a form, you can set up a readers field so that its values are specified in one of three ways:

- Define the field to be Computed and then create a field formula that generates a list of authorized names. Authors then have no way to modify the access list for individual documents.

- Let the author create the read-access list for individual documents: Define the field to be Editable. Then when an author creates a new document, he or she supplies the names of people who have read access to that particular document.

- Same as preceding, but supply a formula that creates a default list of authorized readers for the form—which becomes the default list for every new document. However, each document author can then edit this list as needed.

If you select either of the latter two options, you must then choose the way in which authors build or modify the access list. The options are exactly the same as those described in Table 6.1 (earlier in this chapter).

Names Fields

A *names field* is a convenient tool that you can use to store personal names in full canonical form but to display the names in abbreviated form. This is similar to the way in which authors and readers fields manipulate names, but names fields are not associated with any kind of access controls.

Note. Authors and readers fields both handle names exactly as described here.

To illustrate how a names field works, we'll use a specific example. Suppose that you create a field called Company People, assigning the Names type for the field. When you use this field in documents, you can enter names in canonical form, like some of those shown in the first column of Table 6.2. However, regardless of how you enter a name in the field, it appears in abbreviated form when the document is opened, as shown in the second column of Table 6.2.

Table 6.2

How a Names Field Displays Values.

INPUT VALUE	VALUE DISPLAYED IN READ MODE
Alice Jones	Alice Jones
CN=Alice Jones	Alice Jones
CN=Alice Jones/O=The ABC Company	Alice Jones/The ABC Company
CN=Alice Jones/OU=Accounting/O=The ABC Company	Alice Jones/Accounting/The ABC Company
CN=Alice Jones/O=The ABC Company/ OU=Accounting	Alice Jones/Accounting/The ABC Company

■ Selecting How Field Values Are Supplied

When creating a new field, you must select the manner in which its data values will be supplied. For instance, in most documents the majority of field values are input by authors and editors. On the other hand, you'll sometimes need to set up a field so that its values are automatically calculated, the results depending on a variety of circumstances such as values of other fields, the current date, or the phase of the moon.

As with other field options, you use the Field InfoBox (see Figure 6.4) to specify how a field's values are supplied. The choices are Editable, Computed, Computed When Composed, and Computed For Display. The following sections describe these four field options.

Figure 6.4

Select how a field's values are to be supplied—either by user input or automatically by Notes.

Fields with User-Supplied Input

If you want authors and editors to be able to input and modify the values of a field, select the Editable option for it. You can assign this option to any of the eight field types.

If a field is editable, then a user can modify its contents, provided that he or she has Editor or higher access in the database's ACL, or—if the user has Author access—provided that he or she is listed in an authors field in specific documents.

Note. For information about using formulas, see Chapter 10.

You can optionally write a formula that assigns a default value to an editable field in each new document. You can also write formulas to modify field values input by users, and to verify that those values conform to a set of predetermined rules.

Fields Assigned the Computed Option

When you assign the Computed option to a field, its values cannot be changed by users. Instead, values are calculated by a formula attached to the field. You can assign the Computed option to any field, although you probably won't ever find a reason for doing so with either keyword fields or rich text fields.

Computed fields in a document are recalculated under each of the following conditions:

- When the document is opened for reading or editing
- When the document is saved
- In edit mode, when a user either presses F9 or selects View, Refresh
- Whenever a field value is changed—if the option Automatically Refresh Fields has been selected for the underlying form

During a recalculation, every field in a document is recomputed. You can't selectively recalculate specific fields.

Following are a couple of examples in which computed fields are used.

Duplicating a Field Value

A standard form-design technique is to create two different sections—one for data input and another for data display. For example, in the data input section, you might use the field FullName to input a person's name. In the data display part of the same form, you could create a field Name2 to display the same name. The formula for Name2 would be simply FullName (a formula can consist entirely of a field name).

Displaying Full Names

You could create two fields for inputting personal names: FirstName and LastName. Then, you could create another field, CompleteName, with the following formula:

```
FirstName + " " + LastName
```

A formula can consist of a combination of field values, with other things thrown in as well. Here, the quantity {" "} inserts a blank space between the first and last names.

Fields Computed When Documents Are Composed

Using the Computed When Composed option, you can create a field that calculates a value only once—when a document is first composed. This type of field is never recalculated, no matter how many times you press F9 while a document is open. You can assign the Computed When Composed option to any type of field except a rich text field, although you'll probably never use this option for keyword fields either.

Note. Because they don't exist until displayed, these types of values are not included in full-text searches.

As an example of using this option, you could create a field to display the date on which a document was created. To accomplish this, assign the field the following formula: @Today.

Another common use of this type of field is to display the name of the document author. When creating this field, you can assign it the following formula: @UserName. This is a built-in function that returns the name of the current user.

Fields Computed Only for Display

Another convenient computed field is the type Computed For Display, which you can use to save disk space. When a document contains this type of field, no field value is stored as part of the document (hence, the saved disk space). Instead, Notes calculates a field value whenever the document is recalculated: when the document is opened or saved, when you press F9, and so on. You can assign the Computed For Display option to any type of field except rich text fields.

As an example, suppose that you routinely create personnel documents and that for each new document, you enter values for the fields FirstName and LastName. Now suppose that you want to display the following title at the top of each document: "Information for *Jane Doe*." To accomplish this, you can create a field at the top of the document, having the following formula:

```
"Information for " + FirstName + " " + LastName
```

Instead of wasting disk space for this field, you can assign it the type Computed For Display; each time a document is opened, Notes will calculate and display the field value, using the current values in the fields FirstName and LastName.

■ Multi-Valued Fields

A *multi-valued field* is one that can hold more than one value, and Notes is particularly adept at handling this field option. You can define any type of field to be multi-valued—except rich text fields. (By definition, a rich text field can hold any number of objects—text, graphics, and so on—so it hardly makes sense to think of it in any terms other than multi-valued.)

As an example, suppose that you want to define a text field called Children to hold one or more names. Here's how to go about it:

1. Insert the new field where you want it and then display its InfoBox and click the Basics tab.

2. Select the check box option Allow Multi-Values.

3. Click the Options tab on the InfoBox.

4. Now specify how you would like to separate two or more input values: Pull down the list labeled Separate Values When User Enters and then click as many of the options as you wish (see below). As an example, you could choose to separate input values either with commas or semicolons.

> **WARNING!** *If you deselect every option on this list, the list will immediately become unavailable, because Notes will automatically deselect the Allow Multi-Values option.*

5. Select how you would like multiple values to be separated on display: Pull down the lower list box and then select an option (you can select only one in this case).

Note. Reserved fields are described in detail in the next section.

TIP. *Suppose that a group of documents contain the multi-valued field called Vals, and suppose that the field is used as the basis for a Notes view column. If that column is categorized, then each document will be listed in the view once for each value in its Vals field. For example, the categorized view shown below displays documents containing the multi-valued field Interests. As you can see, some documents are referenced more than once.*

■ Reserved Fields

Notes uses a wide array of *reserved fields* for various purposes. Some fields provide information to users; for others, users must provide values.

Note. Reserved fields are not included in a full-text search.

In some circumstances, Notes will automatically add certain reserved fields to a document and provide values for those fields. These are called *internal fields,* because they don't appear on the underlying form. For instance, Notes often attaches an internal field named Form to a document, containing the name of the form with which the document was created. The field does not appear directly on the document; instead, it's lurking in the background.

Even if a reserved field is not displayed on a document—that is, it's an internal field—you can display that field's value:

1. Either click on the document in a view or open the document in read mode.

2. Display the InfoBox for the document and click on the Fields tab, as shown in Figure 6.5.

Figure 6.5

You can use the InfoBox to display field values.

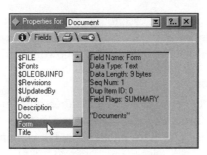

3. The left-hand list displays the names of all fields in the document—both the ones that you created and those supplied automatically by Notes.

4. Click on the name of a field, and its value will appear near the bottom of the right-hand pane.

In some situations, you may want to create a reserved field directly on the form that you're building. This is perfectly acceptable, provided that you spell the field name correctly and assign it the proper type (text, number, or whatever). Notes will recognize that field in documents and supply appropriate values.

Reserved fields can be divided into the following categories:

- Mail

- Security

- Historical

- Others

The following sections describes each of these groups of important and useful fields.

Mail Fields

Note. For a discussion of using Notes mail, see Chapter 20.

Notes recognizes the following special fields, which help you to create and manage mail-enabled documents:

- SendTo
- CopyTo
- BlindCopyTo
- MailOptions
- SaveOptions
- Encrypt
- Sign

Some of these fields are essential, while others are optional, providing information that may or may not be useful in a particular application. We describe each of these special fields in the following sections.

Addressing Fields

Notes provides three reserved fields for addressing, which you can incorporate into mail-enabled forms. These fields are SendTo, CopyTo, and BlindCopyTo.

When designing a form for mail-enabled documents, you should include a field named SendTo. Each time a user creates a new document, this field is used for recipient names, which can be individuals, groups, or mail-in databases. Later, when the user mails a document, Notes uses those recipient names for routing.

You can optionally include CopyTo and BlindCopyTo fields, which have the traditional meanings.

Values in each of these three fields must be text; and you can assign field types of either text, keyword, authors, readers, or names. Fields can be either editable or computed.

When creating any of these fields, keep in mind the following:

- Define the field to be either editable or computed, depending on whether you want users or a field formula to supply the recipient names.

- If you want users to select names from a predefined list, select the keywords field type. As the form designer, you can either type in the list yourself or use another source of values, such as the ACL, the user's Address Book, or a column of values within a database view.

- If a document can have multiple recipients, select the Allow Multi-Values option.

Fields That Control Mailing

You can design a set of documents so that they can be easily mailed. That is, they are *mail-enabled*. One way to mail-enable a set of documents is to select the option On Close, Present Mail Send Dialog, which is on the Defaults page of the Form InfoBox. Then, each time a document is closed after editing, Notes will display the following dialog box, in which you make various choices regarding the disposition of the document:

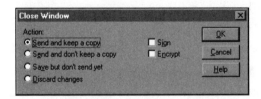

For example, to mail the document, a user would select either of the options Send And Keep A Copy or Send And Don't Keep A Copy.

As a designer, you can have users bypass this dialog box and automate the mailing process by incorporating one or more of three reserved fields. If you include them on a form, you can then deselect the On Close, Present Mail Send Dialog option, bypassing the Close Window dialog box just shown.

Table 6.3 shows these three field names and their options.

Table 6.3

Fields That Control Mailing.

FIELD	VALUE	RESULT
MailOptions	"1"	The document is automatically mailed when it's closed.
	"0"	The document is not mailed.
SaveOptions	"1"	The document is automatically saved when it's mailed.
	"0"	The document is not automatically saved.
Encrypt	"1"	The document is encrypted during mailing.
	"0"	No mail encryption is performed.
Sign	"1"	The document is signed when mailed.
	"0"	The document is not signed.

If you use any of the preceding three fields, follow these guidelines:

- Assign the field type to be either editable or computed text, or editable keywords. The final value of each field must be either "0" or "1" (text values, not numbers).

- If you assign the field to be computed text, enter a formula whose final value is always either "0" or "1." (You need the quotes, because the field types are textual, not numeric.)

- If you want the user to be able to choose whether or not to mail each new document, assign the MailOptions field to be editable keywords and then create the following list:

  Mail|1

  Do not mail|0

Be sure to *deselect* both of the options Allow Values Not In List and Allow Multi-Values.

Other Mail Fields

You can incorporate various other mail-oriented fields into your forms; Table 6.4 summarizes their properties.

MailFormat

If you use cc:Mail to send documents to both Notes mail users and cc:Mail users, you can use the MailFormat field to help format the documents for both classes of recipients. If a recipient is using Notes mail, your documents will be legible, although reformatted to some extent.

Note. For more information, see "Hiding Paragraphs," in Chapter 5.

To set up a field named MailFormat on a form that you're creating, place the field somewhere out of the way—at the end of the form, for example. Put it on a line by itself and select the options to hide it both in read and edit modes. Assign it the options Text and Computed and then create a formula whose value depends on how you want the documents to be formatted; these options are described in Table 6.5.

All of the conversions described in Table 6.5 take place regardless of whether the intended recipients use cc:Mail or Notes mail. Consequently, the transmitted documents may appear differently to Notes users than they would if only Notes mail were involved from one end to the other.

Other Special Fields

Notes also provides an array of special fields for purposes other than document routing. Most of these fields are automatically added to documents

Table 6.4

Options for Various
Mail Fields.

FIELD NAME	VALUE	PURPOSE
DeliveryPriority	H	High: Forces immediate delivery of the document via the Router.
	N	Normal: Notes waits until next scheduled service by the Router.
	L	Low: Notes holds mail for "low-cost" routing (usually, late at night).
DeliveryReport	N	No report: Notes never returns a report about the outcome of the routing process.
	C	Confirmed: Notes will always deliver a report about the routing outcome.
	B	Basic: Notes delivers a report only if the document couldn't be mailed.
ReturnReceipt	1	Notes will send a return receipt to the document sender, indicating that the intended recipient received and opened the document.
	0	Notes does not deliver a return receipt to the document sender.
PostedDate	-	When a document has been successfully mailed, Notes attaches this field to the document; the value indicates the date and time of delivery.
RouteServers	-	If the document has been routed through a group of servers, Notes attaches this field, which contains a list of the servers used.
FromCategories	-	If the original document contains a field named Categories, then its value is stored in a new field named FromCategories, which Notes inserts into the copy of the document that's mailed.
DeliveredDate	-	When a document has been delivered, Notes adds this field to the original form, containing the date of delivery.
Subject	-	If a mailed document contains this field, its contents will be displayed in the Subject column of the recipient's mail database views. This is especially convenient when you mail a document whose fields are entirely different from those in a standard mail database: The recipient will be able to see at least the subject of the transmitted document.

Table 6.5

Options for the
MailFormat Field.

MAILFORMAT VALUE	OPERATION
"E"	Each document is encapsulated in a Notes database, and the document appears as an icon in the cc:Mail memo that's created and sent to the recipient. However, in order for this method to work properly, the cc:Mail recipient must have Notes installed on his or her workstation. When the recipient opens the memo and double-clicks the Notes database icon, Notes is launched, and the database containing the original document is displayed.
T	This type of formatting takes up a good deal of disk space, because each document is wrapped up in a complete Notes database—with all of its attendant disk-space overhead. Consequently, you should use this format only if information in documents would be lost if they were to be converted to Text or Memo format (see the following table entries).
	If you select this formatting option, you must also select the option Store Form In Document (in the Form InfoBox), so that the form is included with the encapsulated document. If you do not select this option, recipients may not be able to read the document.
"T"	The entire contents of each document is converted to text, which is then pasted into the body of the cc:Mail memo that's sent. In this case, the cc:Mail recipient can read the document directly in cc:Mail—that is, without needing Notes.
"B"	This option combines both the "E" and "T" options: The document is converted to text, and it's also encapsulated in a Notes database. This is a cover-all-your-bets option, because the cc:Mail recipients can either read the document directly in the cc:Mail memo, or they can double-click on the database icon in the memo, to launch Notes and read the document in its original format.
"M"	This option behaves in a manner similar to the "T" option; however, in this case, only the Body field of the document is converted to text and then pasted into the cc:Mail memo. This option makes sense only if the original document contains a Body field.

whenever appropriate, although there a couple that you must add to the forms yourself.

Categories

Notes includes an extremely useful facility for categorizing documents. To make use of this feature with a particular set of documents, you include a field named Categories on the underlying form. Then, by using a view containing a column whose values are based on the Categories field, users can assign categories to various documents *from within the view*.

If you do not include a Categories field on a form, you can still use the categorizing feature. In this case, Notes will automatically add an internal Categories field to a document when you categorize it in a view.

For example, assume that a form named Contacts holds information about users' sales contacts. As part of the form, you want to create a field that categorizes the information about your contacts' professional interests. However, most of these people work in rapidly changing industries, and their interests change weekly. To keep up with this volatile information, you would like users to be able to display their contacts' documents in a view and from there change the values in the categorizing field.

Here's how you can accomplish this:

Note. For details about designing views, see Chapter 7.

1. As part of the underlying form, create a field named Categories. Define it to be Keyword and Editable, select the option allowing multiple values, and then enter a list of keywords that define your contacts' interests.

2. Define the rest of the form—fields, graphics, and so on.

3. Next, create a view named Contacts By Interest for displaying the documents created with the Contacts form. As part of the view, define a column having the following properties:

    *   Formula: Categories

    *   Sorting: Sorted and Categorized

    *   Width: 1

4. Define a column to display the person's name in each record.

5. Define whatever other columns that appeal to you.

When you display the Contacts view (after creating a few documents), it will look something like the first illustration on the next page.

To change the value for the Categories field in a document—directly from the view:

1. Click on a document that you want to edit.

2. Select Action, Categorize, and you'll see the dialog box shown on the next page.

3. Select the current categories that apply to the person whose document you selected. In addition, you can type in one or more other categories, separated by commas, in the New Categories edit box.

The categories that you select become the current values in the Categories field of the document you selected.

Form

The *form* field is one of the most important fields available. You can create this field as part of a form, or you can let Notes insert an internal field named Form on each new document.

Whenever you create a new document, and if the underlying form does not contain a field named Form, Notes inserts an internal field named Form in the document, assigning the field value to be the name of the form used to create the document. The main purpose of this field is to tell Notes which form to use when displaying the document.

Example: Creating a Form Field   In some situations, you may want to insert a field named Form as part of a form design. You would do this for a variety of reasons. For example, you might want to use that form to create documents, but use another form to display those documents. Here's how to accomplish this:

1. Insert a field named Form somewhere out of the way on the form— perhaps at the very bottom.

2. Select the options to hide this field both when viewing and when editing documents.

3. Assign the field options to be Text and Computed.

4. Place the field on a line by itself and make it hidden—both for reading and editing.

5. Create a formula for the field, which generates the name of the form that you want to be used for displaying documents created with this form—not the name of the current form.

Whenever you open a document created with the original form, Notes will use the form specified in the field named Form.

Example: A More Complex Form Field   You can create a complicated formula for a Form field that you include as part of a form, specifying different form names under different conditions. For example, suppose the documents you'll be creating contain information about your acquaintances—some of whom are business associates with whom you have close business relationships, and some of whom are more casual acquaintances. Different fields in the form are filled in for the two types of associates.

You would like to use one form named BusinessDocs and another one named CasualDocs, for displaying documents of each type. Here's how you can accomplish this:

1. Create the two forms, BusinessDocs and CasualDocs, for displaying the two groups of documents.

2. Insert a field named Status on the form, having the attributes Keyword and Editable.

3. Type in the following two values for the keyword list: Business and Casual. Whenever you create a new document, you'll choose one value or the other from the keyword list.

4. Create a Form field, assigning it the following attributes:
   - Type: Text, Computed When Composed
   - Formula: @If(Status="Business"; "BusinessDocs"; "CasualDocs")

Here's how this formula works: Each time a user creates a new document, he or she selects either Business or Casual for the Status field. Then the formula in the Form field examines the Status field: If its value is Business, then the value BusinessDocs is assigned as the value of the Form field; otherwise the value CasualDocs is assigned. Because you assigned the option

Computed When Composed to the Form field, this calculation occurs only once—when you save the document for the first time.

FolderOptions

FolderOptions is a reserved field, which you can include as part of a form design. This field can then be used by document authors to save new documents to selected folders. If this field is included in a document, it must have a value of "1" or "2." You can either assign a default value as part of the field definition in a form, or you can make the field a keywords type and let each user decide how to handle new documents.

Table 6.6 describes the effect of using a FolderOptions field.

When creating a FolderOptions field, you can set it up in either of the following ways:

- Assign the field to be the text type, and then assign it a default value of "1" or "2."

- Assign the field to be the keyword type, and then create a list something like the following:

Select a folder for saving document | 1

Save document in current folder | 2

Then, when a user creates a new document, he or she can select the appropriate option for the field. If "1" is selected, the dialog shown in Figure 6.6 will appear when the document is saved.

Figure 6.6

Use this dialog box to select the disposition of the current document.

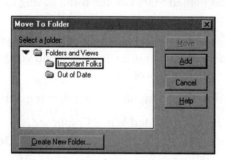

Fields for Storing Forms in Documents

When creating a form, you can select an option that stores the form itself as part of each document created with the form. This option, which is available on the Form InfoBox, is called Store Form In Document. You would select

Table 6.6

Effect of including
a FolderOptions
Field in Form.

VALUE OF THE FOLDEROPTIONS FIELD	CONSEQUENCES
"1"	When a new document is saved, Notes displays the dialog box shown in Figure 6.6. You can then either select a folder where Notes will store a copy of the document or press Cancel to skip the process.
"2"	Notes will automatically copy the current document to the folder that's currently open.

this option, for example, when you knew that authors would be sending documents to other Notes users who might not have access to the original form.

If you choose to use the Store Form In Document option as part of a form, then Notes does not include an internal Form field as part of each new document. Instead, Notes adds one or more of the following fields, which together contain the necessary information to rebuild the original form design:

- Body
- $TITLE
- $Info
- $WindowTitle

NOTE. *When you select the option Store Form In Document as part of a form design, be sure* not *to include a field named Form as part of the design. Here's why: When Notes displays a document, it first looks for a field named Form in the document; if the field exists, and if it contains the name of a form, then Notes uses that form to display the document. Otherwise, Notes uses the form that's stored as part of the document.*

It is important to be familiar with the four fields named Body, $TITLE, $Info, and $WindowTitle. Here's why: If you need to remove the form that's stored as part of a document, you can do so by deleting whichever of these four fields are stored in the document. You must also insert a new Form field into the document, supplying it with the name of the form that you want to be used for displaying the document. To accomplish these operations, you'll need to create an agent that you can then run manually.

Historical Fields

Notes provides two internal fields that track revisions to a document. These are extremely useful if you need to keep track of document revisions by author and date.

The two fields are the following:

- *$Revisions*. Maintains a list of dates and times on which a document was revised.

- *$UpdatedBy*. Maintains a list of authors who have made revisions.

Each field is multi-valued; whenever a user modifies a document, Notes adds a new value to each of these fields, so users can easily see when each editor made changes to a particular document. However, one entry at most is made in a particular document for a given user on a particular day—even if that user modifies a document several times.

■ Shared Fields

Typically, most fields in a form are *single-use*, which means that they are unique to the form in which they are created. However, there may be times when you want to use the same field definition for several different forms within a database. This would be convenient, for instance, to maintain consistency in field design across a group of forms. For example, if several forms included a field containing a list of U.S. states, a user would appreciate seeing the same drop-down list—typeface, color, formatting, and so on—no matter which type of document was being created.

You can impose this type of uniformity by using *shared fields*. When you define a shared field, it's stored as part of the database—not as part of a particular form. Then, after creating a shared field, you can use it in any form you create within that database.

When you insert a copy of a shared field onto a form, the field definition is still retained by the database—not by the individual form. This means that if you modify the definition of a shared field, your changes automatically propagate to all the forms using that field within the database.

You can even distribute shared fields to other databases, using standard copy-and-paste operations. However, when you make changes to a copy of a shared field in one database, those changes are not automatically circulated to the other copies.

When you create a shared field, most of the single-use options are available: You can select from among the same field types, and you can make the field either Editable, Computed, Computed When Composed, or Computed For Display.

You can insert a shared field onto a form, a subform, or a section—but not on a layout region. You can distinguish a shared field from single-use fields on a form because the outline of the shared field is boldface (see the illustration below). However, when a user creates a new document, the two types of fields are indistinguishable.

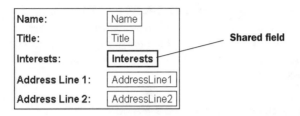

Shared field

Creating a Shared Field

You can create a shared field from just about anywhere within a database, as follows:

1. Select Create, Design, Shared Field, displaying the dialog box shown in Figure 6.7.

Figure 6.7

Use this display to create and edit shared fields.

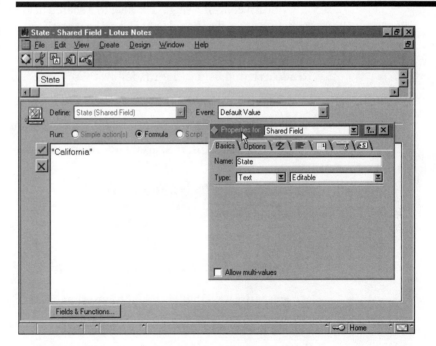

2. Define the field characteristics, using the first three tabbed InfoBox pages (counting from the left).

3. If appropriate, write a field formula in the Design pane.

4. When you're done, save the field: Click File, Save and then either press Esc or click File, Close.

NOTE. *Although the Field InfoBox for a shared field displays several tabbed pages, only the first three are used. Don't bother assigning other options—such as font, text color, alignment, and so on—because Notes ignores your selections. To assign a font or color to a shared field, do it on the form containing the field.*

Working with Shared Fields

While designing a form, you can insert any shared field that is part of the current database. You can also copy a shared field only from one database to another.

You can delete a shared field from a database when it's outlived its usefulness. If you delete a shared field only from a particular form, the original shared field remains part of the database. Also, the information for that field is still retained in the documents. To access that information, you'll need to use a form having a field with the same name and characteristics as the one that was deleted. However, this new field can be either single-use or shared.

You can convert a single-use field to a shared field for the database, and you can take a copy of a shared field and make it single-use on a particular form.

Adding a Shared Field to a Form

To add a shared field to a form, follow these steps:

1. Make sure that the Form Design window is open.

2. Position the insertion point exactly where you want to insert the field.

3. Select Create, Insert Shared Field, displaying the following dialog box:

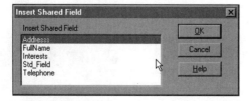

4. Select the field that you want to insert and then click OK.

Editing a Shared Field

Because a shared field is global to a database, you can edit it without needing to open a particular form. You can also edit a shared field from within a form on which the field is being used. Any changes you make will automatically appear in each form using the field.

To edit a shared field, follow these steps:

1. Display the default database navigator and make sure the lower half of the pane is opened (see below).

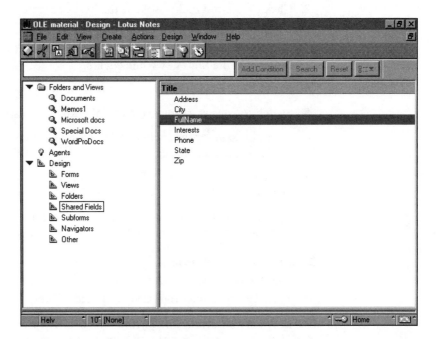

2. Click on Shared Fields, and Notes will display a list of the shared fields in the current database.

3. Double-click on the name of the shared field that you want to edit. When the display shown in Figure 6.7 appears, make whatever changes you want.

4. To finish up, select File, Close.

To edit a shared field directly from a form containing the field: Open the form for editing and then double-click on the field. Notes will switch to the display shown in Figure 6.7, where you can make the changes.

Copying Shared Fields

It does not make sense to copy a shared field from one part of a database to another, because the field is already global to that database. However, you can copy shared fields from one database to another—a convenient way to control uniformity across the databases in an organization. Remember, though, that after copying a shared field from one database to another, the two copies are independent. That is, changes that you make to the field in one database will not be transmitted to other copies of the field.

Here's how to copy one or more shared fields from one database to another:

1. Display the default database navigator and make sure the lower half—labeled Design—is opened.

2. Click on Shared Fields, so that the list of shared fields in the current database appears in the View pane.

3. Click on the field that you want to copy. To select more than one field, hold down the Shift key while clicking.

4. Select Edit, Copy, which copies the field to the system Clipboard.

5. Switch to your workspace (select Window, Workspace At...).

6. Click the icon for the recipient database and then select View, Design, displaying the default navigator.

7. Make sure that the lower part of the navigation pane—labeled Design—is pulled down and then click on Shared Fields.

8. Paste the shared field into this database: Select Edit, Paste. The new field name will then appear in the list of shared fields shown in the View pane.

Deleting a Shared Field

You can delete a shared field from a form, just as you would delete a single-use field. However, the original shared field remains as part of the database.

NOTE. *When you delete a field from a form—whether it's a single-use field or a shared one—you're not touching the corresponding field values in the documents. Instead, you're simply making those values inaccessible through that particular form.*

You can also completely delete a shared field from the database. Naturally, you want to exercise a certain amount of discretion here, because the corresponding field values created and stored in documents become inaccessible. However, you can make this information accessible again by creating a form containing a field that has the same name as the deleted field.

Deleting a Field from a Form   You can use a couple of different methods to delete a shared field from a form:

- Click once on the field and then press Del. Note that you can't use Edit, Undo to reverse this process; however, this is not a problem, because it's so easy to add the field back onto the form.

- Highlight the field—either by itself or as part of a selected block that includes other elements—and select Edit, Cut.

Deleting a Field from the Database   If you're absolutely positive that you want to delete a particular field, follow these steps:

1. Display the default database navigator and make sure the lower half—labeled Design—is opened.

2. Click on Shared Fields, so that the list of shared fields in the current database appears in the View pane.

3. Click on the field that you want to delete.

4. Select Edit, Cut.

Switching Field Types

When working with fields, you will occasionally find yourself in the position of finding the grass greener on the other side. Notes nicely accommodates you by allowing you to convert a single-use field to shared status, and almost vice-versa.

Single-Use to Shared   If you decide that a field in one of your forms is so useful that you'd like to distribute it to other forms in the database, you can change its status from single-use to shared. Here's how to accomplish this:

1. Click once on the field.

2. Select Design, Share This Field.

The box around the field on the form will become boldface, indicating that the field has now reached shared status. Moreover, the field name will appear in the list of shared fields (in the database's View pane).

Shared to Single-Use   Suppose you copy a shared field onto a form, only to discover later that you want to modify the field. However, you want to change only the local copy of the field on the form—not the original shared field. You can accomplish this by making a single-use copy of the shared field, as follows:

1. Highlight the entire shared field on the form.

2. Select Edit, Cut, which deletes the field from the form and copies it to the system Clipboard.

3. Move the insertion point to a blank spot on the form and then select Edit, Paste.

4. Remember to save the form before doing anything else.

The new copy of the field will be single-use.

Special Considerations

Because shared fields are part of a database, and not part of any particular form, you need to consider what happens when you copy a form containing a shared field. For example, let's say that a form in one of your databases contains the shared field PersonalName, and you copy the form to another database—which does not contain a shared field with the same name. When you create a new document from that form, Notes displays a message saying that it can't find a definition for that particular field, which Notes will consequently ignore.

There's a simple solution to this problem: You must also copy the shared field to the new database. If the copied form contains two or more shared fields, you'll have to copy them all. This isn't as bad as it seems, because you can copy and paste them all in a single operation. For details, see "Copying Shared Fields," earlier in this chapter.

■ Inheritance

You can set up a form so that when you create a new document, one or more fields will inherit values from another document. The ability of Notes to automatically copy field values from an existing document into a new one is called *inheritance*.

When a new document inherits values from another document, the original is called the *parent* document; and the new document is called the *child*. Furthermore, a document can become a parent only if you select it in a Notes view or open it just before creating the new document.

Notes provides two other types of inheritance, as well:

- A rich text field in a new document can inherit the entire contents of a parent document.

- One or more fields in a new document can inherit values of other fields in the same document.

In all of these situations, the inheritance must be built into the underlying form of the documents being created.

Inheriting Field Values from an Existing Document

When you create a new document, Notes can automatically copy field values from an existing document—the parent. This convenient feature can save you composition time; it can also provide for data consistency between two or more documents.

Here's an example of how this feature can be useful: Suppose you're browsing through a Notes view that displays your incoming memos. Finding one that needs an answer, you create a response document for it. To speed up your creation effort, Notes can automatically fill in the name of the recipient for your response by copying the name of the sender on the original memo. For instance, if your response document contains a field named SendTo, and if the original memo contains a field called From, you can set up Notes to copy the From field value into SendTo.

To illustrate how to accomplish this, we'll use the preceding example: You're creating a form named Replies, which you plan to use for creating responses to memos that you receive. You want to set up the field SendTo in the Replies form so that when you create a reply, Notes will copy the value in the From field from the original memo into the SendTo field of the reply.

Here's how to set up the Replies form to accomplish this:

1. Open the Replies form for editing.

2. Display the Form InfoBox and select the tab labeled Defaults.

3. Select the option Formulas Inherit Values From Selected Document.

4. Create the field SendTo (unless, of course, it already exists). Assign it the following two options: Text, and Computed When Composed.

5. Using the Design pane, write the following formula: From (which is the name of the field in the memos from which the SendTo field will inherit values).

6. If you want replies to appear as response documents in Notes views, select the Basic InfoBox tab and then choose the form type to be Response.

Here are some important points to remember about this type of inheritance:

- You can set up field inheritance in any type of form: Document, Response, or Response To Response (you select the form type on the Basics page of the Form InfoBox).

- Each Field that is set up for inheritance must have a formula that names the field in the parent document from which the value is to be copied.

- To be safe, assign the option Computed When Composed to the inheriting field.

Inheritance occurs only once for a document: when it is first composed. Consequently, if the name of the inheriting field is not the same as the field name in the original document, you must assign the option Computed When Composed. Here's why: Using the previous example, if you assign the new field SendTo to be Computed (instead of Computed When Composed), then whenever the response document is recalculated, the value of that field will be set to null, because there's no field named FROM in the document (because the field formula is FROM).

Inheriting an Entire Document

The previous section described how to set up inheritance for individual fields. You can also set up a form so that each new document inherits the entire contents of a parent document. For example, when creating a reply to a memo, you can include the entire contents of the original memo as a prelude to your reply.

To set up this type of inheritance, you include a rich text field as part of the form, and you choose one of the following options:

- Insert the entire contents of the parent document into the rich text field of the new document. Optionally, you can set up the rich text field to be in a collapsible section.

- Create a link between the rich text field and the parent document. When linked, the parent will appear as an icon in the rich text field (to display the parent, you double-click on the icon).

Here's how to set up this type of inheritance in a form:

1. Insert the rich text field where you want it on the form; it can be at the top of the form or anywhere else you wish.

2. Display the Form InfoBox and then select the tab labeled Defaults.

3. Select the option Inherit Entire Selected Document Into Rich Text Field.

4. Pull down the list of rich text fields, as shown below, and then select the one that you want to use.

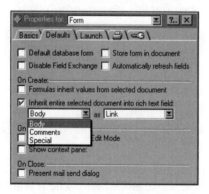

5. Pull down the list box labeled As and then select how you want a parent document to be attached to each new document created with this form.

Tip.

Linking a parent document into a rich text field of a new document is convenient, because only an icon appears until you double-click on it to display the parent. However, in some circumstances, document linking will not work—such as if you forward a document to someone who doesn't have access to the database containing the original parent document.

To get around this problem you can use one of the other options to copy the entire parent document into each new document. This solution, however, introduces a new problem: Whenever a child document is opened, the parent document will automatically be displayed; this can easily confuse the reader, who may not be able to figure out what he or she is viewing.

You can solve this potential dilemma as follows: Create a collapsible section into which you insert the rich text field; select the option that displays the parent document directly in the rich text field (the Rich Text option in the preceding step 5); finally, display the Section InfoBox and select the option that automatically forces the section to be collapsed whenever documents are opened. With a clearly labeled section, the user can then optionally expand it to display the parent document, thereby avoiding confusion.

Inheriting Values from Fields in the Same Document

Part of the power of a Notes form is that you can design it as a collection of several pieces, each of which is displayed to users under special circumstances. For instance, you can design one part to be visible only for data entry, and another part visible only for viewing. As part of this type of design, you can create a set of fields within the viewing portion that inherit their values from the fields in the data-entry portion.

Suppose you want Field_B in a form to inherit its value from Field_A. You can accomplish this as follows:

1. Assign the attribute Computed For Display to Field_B.

2. Create a formula for Field_B that contains a reference to Field_A. The simplest formula would be just "Field_A" by itself.

3. As a general rule, try to work out the design so that Field_B is either to the right of Field_A on the same line or physically below it on the form.

If you don't adhere to the rule in step 3, and if Field_A is itself a computed field, there are situations in which Field_B will not be properly calculated. Here's why: When recalculating the fields in a document, Notes works its way down the form, line by line and left to right on each line. If Field_B is above Field_A on the form (or to the left of Field_A, on the same line), then

Field_B will be recalculated before Field_A. So if Field_A changes as the result of the recalculation, the new value won't be displayed in Field_B.

If you need to have Field_B above Field_A on the form, you can get around this problem by introducing a third field that's below Field_A on the form. Then you can write a formula for this third field that assigns the recalculated value of Field_A to Field_B.

- *Introduction*
- *Creating Views and Folders*
- *Customizing Views and Folders*
- *Creating and Working with Columns*

7

Designing Views and Folders

THE PREVIOUS CHAPTERS DESCRIBED HOW TO DESIGN FORMS AND fields—two necessary building blocks for Notes databases. However, you can design the best-looking documents in the world, but without Notes *views* and *folders,* you can't see the documents.

■ Introduction

Each database view and folder presents users with a window into that database, displaying selected groups of documents.

You can easily design a view displaying every document in a database. However, this is usually impractical because databases can contain hundreds or even thousands of documents. Instead, a database designer typically sets up each view to display only a particular subset of documents within a database. On the other hand, each folder is a receptacle for a special group of documents—usually hand-selected by users.

Views and folders have some of the features of conventional database indexes—but they are much more versatile and easy to use.

New Features

Although views in earlier Notes releases were powerful and effective, they had several limitations. Notes 4.0 views have gone a long way toward eliminating those limitations; if you have had design experience with Notes, you'll appreciate the new features in Release 4. For instance, users can now change column widths and sort documents on the fly (neither of these features was available with earlier releases). Another new innovation is that documents are no longer limited to one line per view.

The view-design user interface has been completely redone; this interface, together with Notes' ever-present InfoBox, greatly simplifies the task of designing views and folders.

Design Features

You can design a view or folder to display just about any subset of documents that you can think of. For example, suppose one of your databases contained thousands of personnel documents. You could design views to display information for each of the following groups of people:

- Managers within the organization

- Terminated employees

- Employees within two years of retirement

- Employees earning less than $25,000 per year

- Employees who are managers and who also earn more than $50,000 per year

- Employees who have not received a bonus within the past two years

You can create views and folders that select documents for display based on complex conditions. For example, suppose that a group of personnel documents contained a field named CompanyPosition, and that the values of the field included titles such as Finance Officer, Personnel Officer, and so on. You could create a view that displayed only those documents whose CompanyPosition field contained the word *Officer.*

Each row in a view or folder displays information from a single document (see Figure 7.1 for an example). By default, a row consists of a single line; however, you can change this so that a view can accommodate long field values by allowing multiple lines per document. Each column displays similar information from each document. For example, the second column of the view shown in Figure 7.1 displays a telephone number for each displayed document. In the simplest situation, a column value displays a field value for a document. However, you can design columns to hold a wide variety of other types of information as well.

Figure 7.1

A view displays a subset of the documents in a database.

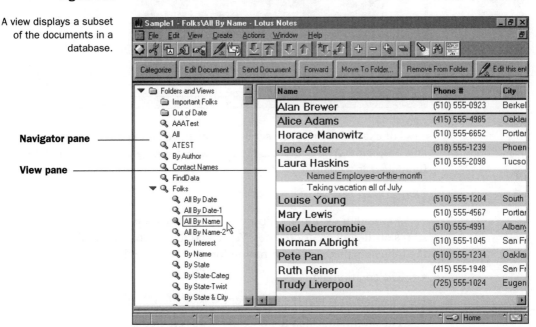

Navigator pane

View pane

Columns

Columns are the heart of each Notes view and folder, and most of the work in designing views and folders involves building columns to display exactly the right information for users. Most columns display simple field values, such as those shown in Figure 7.1 and Figure 7.2. You can also create formulas to display information in columns.

Figure 7.2

This view categorizes documents.

Categories

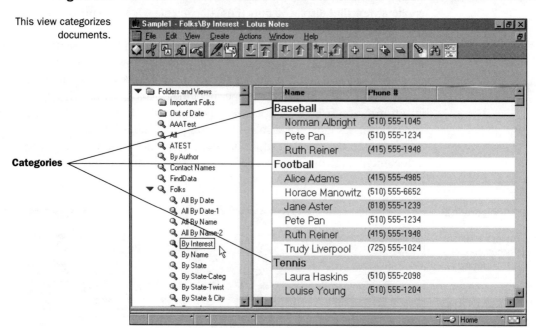

For example, suppose a set of documents contained the fields FirstName and LastName. You could use the following formula to calculate and display full names in a column:

```
FirstName + " " + LastName
```

As another example, suppose a set of documents contains a field that stores document creation dates. You could design columns to display each of the following pieces of information for each document:

- The creation date
- The year in which the document was created
- The month in which the document was created
- How long ago the document was created

You can use columns to display information other than field values. For instance, for some types of information you may prefer to display a set of icons in place of specific values. As an example, suppose that a field named

Status can take on the values Inactive, Pending, or Closed. You could improve the communicative value of a view by displaying illustrative icons instead of those values.

Notes provides an extensive array of built-in icons from which to choose. To display a particular one, you simply supply its corresponding internal number.

Sorting and Categorizing

You can set up a view or folder to sort the information that's displayed. For instance, the documents in Figure 7.1 are sorted by city. In fact, you can sort on as many columns in a view as you wish.

Notes automatically maintains an index for each view and folder, and this index includes the list of documents displayed in the view—in sorted order. By default, the index is automatically updated whenever you add, modify, or delete documents. However, you can override this default by setting special options to control when the index is updated, to best meet the users' needs.

Notes views and folders also provide an extremely valuable feature called *categorizing*, which is a kind of sorting—but is often more useful. To see how this tool operates, notice that the view in Figure 7.1 contains a column listing people's interests. Instead of using this view, you can create one that lists people according to their interests, as shown in Figure 7.2. Here, each different interest (baseball, and so on) is set up as a separate category, and the appropriate documents are listed under each one.

Categories are sorted in a view—either ascending or descending (your choice); and you can set up a view to be categorized on the values of several different fields. For instance, you could design a view to categorize a group of documents first by state and secondarily by city.

The index for a view or folder automatically maintains categories in sorted order when a user adds, deletes, or modifies documents. For example, if you change the category of a document from Dogs to Cats, Notes will automatically reposition the document in the view under Cats instead of Dogs.

Views and folders can also display document hierarchies, as shown by the example in Figure 7.3. Notice that two indented documents are listed below the main document for Laura Haskins. The indenting indicates that these two documents are response documents to the main one for Laura Haskins. A view can display up to 32 levels of responses—each level indented below the one above it.

Figure 7.3

A view displaying
document hierarchies.

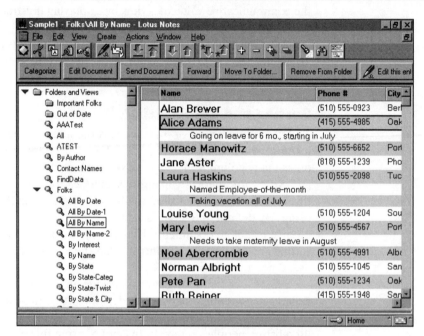

Folders

A folder is similar to a view, in that it displays a group of documents stored in a database. However, unlike a view, a folder does not include a formula that selects which documents are to be displayed. Instead, users must populate each folder by copying database documents into it—either manually or with the help of agents. Except for this difference, you design views and folders exactly the same way.

NOTE. *When a document is "copied" into a folder, a new, individual copy of the document is not made. Instead, the folder's index is updated to include a reference to the document.*

Users can copy documents into folders in a number of different ways:

- By clicking and dragging individual documents from the view in the View pane to the name of the folder in the Navigator pane.

- By executing an appropriate action—either from the button bar or the Action menu—that copies the current document to the folder named by the user.

- By executing an agent to copy a preselected set of documents to a particular folder.

Displaying Views and Folders

Notes displays the names of the current database's views and folders in the Navigation pane, as shown in Figure 7.3. You can differentiate folders and views by the icons preceding them:

 View

 Folder

If a database contains many views or folders, you can arrange them in hierarchies, using one of Notes' built-in graphical tools. You can either hide or display each hierarchy in the Navigation pane simply by clicking on the parent. (If a view or folder name is accompanied by a little "twistie" icon, then it's the parent to one or more views or folders.)

To display a particular view or folder, you simply click on its name in the upper half of the Navigation pane. To change from one view or folder to another, click on the appropriate name.

Shared and Private Views and Folders

When you create a new view or folder, you can set it up to be either *shared* or *private*. Here's the difference: A shared view or folder is accessible to anyone who has adequate access to the database. On the other hand, a private view or folder is for your own personal use, and it's not accessible to anyone else on the system.

You can also create a shared view or folder that's *personal on first use*. Here's how this works: This type of view or folder is accessible to anyone who has adequate database access. However, the first time a person uses that view or folder, Notes creates a private copy just for that person. Any changes subsequently made to that copy are not reflected anywhere else. Similarly, any changes made to the original copy of the view or folder are not reflected in the private copies.

If a user wants to keep his or her copy of the view up to date, she or he will need to delete the current private copy and then access the original one again—making a new private copy.

Access Rights

The use of views and folders is regulated primarily by a database's ACL (access control list). For instance, if a user has read-only access to a database, he or she may be able to display views and folders but not edit any of the displayed documents. The database designer can further restrict access to a view or folder by assigning it a special read-access list. Of course, each document can also have its own private read-access list, which takes precedence: If a user does not have read access to a particular document, she or he won't find the document on any view or folder.

View and Folder Limitations

Information from any type of field can be the basis of the values in a column, with a couple of exceptions: Values in rich text fields are not available in views. The reason is that a rich text field is really more than a simple field; it's a general-purpose container that can hold any combination of text, graphics, OLE objects, and so on.

Also, if the information in a field is encrypted, then it can't be displayed in a view or folder, because the purpose of encryption is to protect information from prying eyes.

Setting Up Basic Designs

Creating a new view or folder involves several steps. First, you assign various basic properties to the view or folder, such as a name, width, colors, and so on. Fortunately, most of these options have default values that you can provisionally accept, changing them later as needed. If you need to create a new view in a hurry to get a quick-and-dirty look at some important information, you can usually ignore most of the options.

As part of a view (but not folder) design, you must specify which documents in the database are to be displayed. By default, each new view will display every document in the database, but you'll often want to change this to limit the view to a particular subset of documents. Notes provides a number of ways for doing this—most of them reasonably straightforward.

Form Formulas

You can create a special view whose only purpose is to use a specific form to display documents. To accomplish this, you write a *form formula* for the view. Whenever a document is opened from the view, the specified form will be used—regardless of which form was used to create the document.

■ Creating Views and Folders

When creating a new view or folder, you can either start from scratch or you can make a copy of an existing view or folder either from the same database or a different one—and then modify the copy as needed.

Copying a View or Folder in the Same Database

If the database where you plan to create a new view or folder contains a view or folder with design elements that you can use, you can make a copy of the original and then use the copy as the basis for the new design.

NOTE. *You can use a folder design as the basis for a new view, and vice versa.*

Here's how to proceed:

1. Either display your Notes workspace and select the icon of the database you want to work with, or display the main display for that database.

2. Select Create, View or Create, Folder, displaying a dialog box similar to that shown in Figure 7.4.

3. Click the Options button, displaying the dialog box shown in Figure 7.5.

4. Select the view or folder that you want to copy: The large pane in the middle of the dialog box displays all the views and folders in the database; click on the one you want and then click OK.

Figure 7.4

Use this dialog box to select the location in the Navigator pane for a new view.

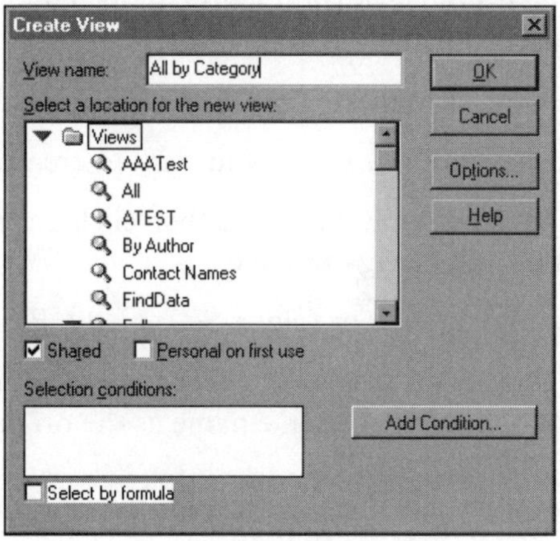

Figure 7.5

Use this dialog box to
select the view or folder
to copy.

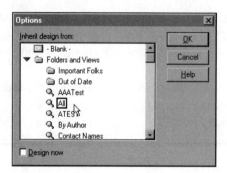

5. In the Create view dialog box (see Figure 7.4), click on which branch of the navigator tree you want the new view to be displayed; then click OK. To customize the view or folder, see the section "Customizing Views and Folders" later in this chapter.

Copying a View or Folder from a Different Database

You can use a view or folder in a different database as the basis for creating a new view or folder. Here's an outline of the steps to follow:

1. Switch to the database containing the view or folder that you want to copy.

2. Display the default navigator in the main database window (select View, Design).

3. Display the list of views (or folders) in the database and then click in the View pane on the one you want to copy.

4. Copy the view or folder to the Clipboard: Select Edit, Copy.

5. Return to the database where you want to create a new view or folder.

6. Display the default navigator and then click on Views (or Folders) in the lower part of the Navigator pane.

7. Copy the original view or folder: Select Edit, Paste.

The new copy of the original view or folder will now appear in the list of views (or folders), having the same name as the original one, and—if necessary—prefixed by "Copy of."

You can now modify the new view in any way you wish, as described throughout the remainder of this chapter.

Creating a New View or Folder from Scratch

If you can't find a view or folder with any design elements you could use conveniently as a starting point, you'll need to create a new one from the ground up. The first step is to assign the view (or folder) a name and position it in the existing hierarchy of views—that is, the hierarchy that appears in the Navigator pane.

Here are the steps to the follow:

1. Either display your Notes workspace and select the icon of the database you want to work with, or display the main display for that database.

2. Select Create, View or Create, Folder, displaying the dialog box shown in Figure 7.4.

3. Click the Options button, displaying the dialog box shown in Figure 7.5.

4. Select Blank and then click OK.

5. Enter a name for the new view or folder. (See the discussion on names in the following section.)

6. If the new view or folder is to be shared, click the appropriate option.

7. If you selected the Shared option, and if you want to make the view or folder Personal On First Use, select that option as well.

8. In the middle pane, select on which branch of the navigator tree you want the new view name to appear. To insert the view or folder as a child under an existing view or folder, simply click on the latter. Or, to insert the view or folder directly in the main tree, click on the very top of the hierarchy in the display.

NOTE. *By default, the entire tree structure of view (or folder) names is displayed in the Create View (or Create Folder) dialog box. If you accidentally hide any of the names by collapsing that part of the tree structure, you can redisplay that part of the structure by clicking on the "twistie" icon next to the parent name.*

View and Folder Names

Like other Notes names, a view (or folder) name can optionally include synonyms. In the absence of a synonym, any formula that refers to the view must use the main view name. The problem with this is that if you or someone else changes the name of the view, that new name must be inserted into every formula that refers to the view.

You can eliminate this major handicap by using a synonym for each view (and folder) name. Then, you use the synonym instead of the main name in all

Note. You can also use the View InfoBox to modify a view name.

formulas that refer to the view. You never change the name of the synonym, so even if you change the main name of the view, you'll never to need to re-write formulas that refer to the view.

To include a synonym as part of a view or folder name, separate the synonym from the view or folder, with a vertical bar. Here's an example, where PI is the synonym for the view named Personal Information:

```
Personal Information|PI
```

You can use any combination of characters in a view or folder name—including blanks and special characters. However, the total length of a view name can't exceed 130 characters; this includes the name of the parent view (if you chose to insert the view as a child underneath a parent view), the main view name, and the synonym.

As an example, suppose that when you create a view you name it Personal Information|PI, and you insert it as a child under the existing view named Folks. As far as Notes is concerned, the full name of the new view is the following:

```
Folks\Personal Information|PI
```

The total length of this name is 29 characters.

■ Customizing Views and Folders

When you first create a new view or folder, it's nothing but an empty shell, and you'll need to assign it various options. Some affect the appearance of the view or folder, while others determine how the view or folder behaves within Notes.

You can set the row spacing in a view (or folder), and you can also select the maximum number of lines per row—a very handy feature to accommodate long field values. You can set the amount of indentation for response documents, and you can also select options to control the flagging of unread documents. You can set an option that determines whether a view is fully collapsed or expanded each time it is opened, and you can also set options to control when view reindexing occurs—a very convenient time-saver when working with very large databases.

As part of designing a view, you must specify which documents are to be displayed. To accomplish this, you write a *view selection formula*. The situation is different for folders, where you do not write any such formula. Instead, documents are placed in a folder by users or agents—usually on a document-by-document basis.

Opening a View or Folder in Edit Mode

When you want to customize a view or folder, you must begin by opening it in edit mode, as follows:

1. Display the default navigator for the database. One way to accomplish this is to click on the database icon in your workspace and then select View, Design.

Note. If you're viewing the contents of a view (or folder) in the View pane, you can easily open that view in edit mode by selecting Actions, View Options, Design.

2. Make sure that the lower half of the navigator is pulled down and then click on Views or Folders.

3. In the list of views or folders appearing in the View pane, double-click on the name of the view or folder. Notes will switch to edit mode for the view or folder, displaying a window something like that shown in Figure 7.6.

Figure 7.6

A view opened in edit mode.

Refresh icon

Title bar for first column

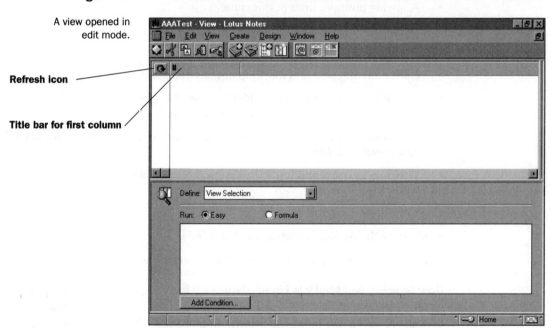

NOTE. *When a view is open in edit mode, you can refresh the upper part of the window to display the view, just as it will normally appear in the View pane in the main database window. This is an extremely handy feature to have, because as you're designing a new column you can see the immediate results of your efforts—without needing to switch back to the View pane.*

To display the view contents here, simply press F9 or click on the Refresh icon in the upper-left corner of the window.

There is one difference between the standard display of the view in the View pane and the one that you see in edit mode: From the view pane, you can open a document by double-clicking on its row. In edit mode, you can't do this.

Setting the Basic Options

Even before designing the columns for a view or folder, you can make some preliminary design decisions that affect its behavior and appearance. Later, you can change any of these options as the need arises.

Appearance

Notes provides a wide assortment of options for customizing the overall appearance of a view (or folder), including the following:

- Row spacing
- Allowing multiple lines per document
- Optionally displaying or hiding the selection margin
- Optionally indenting response documents
- Optionally flagging and marking unread documents
- Assigning a default view or folder to a database—the view or folder a user sees the first time the user opens the database
- Assigning the design of a view or folder to be the default design for each new view and folder
- Placing each view and folder in the hierarchy displayed in the Navigator pane
- Restricting read access
- Setting the options affecting the View index

These various options are discussed in the following sections.

Row Spacing and Multiple Lines   Notes 4.0 has added a long-needed design feature: the ability to define multiple lines, both for column titles and individual rows—a *row* being the information displayed for a single document.

Using the Lines Per Heading option—on the InfoBox page labeled S—you can assign up to five lines for column headings. Note, however, that the value that you select applies to all the columns.

Using the option Lines Per Row, you can expand the amount of space available for displaying document information. This feature becomes even more useful if you also select the option Shrink Rows To Content, so that each document takes up only as much space as it needs. Here's how these two options work together: By default, one line will be assigned to each row.

However, if any value in that row requires more space than is available on a single line, the row will automatically expand to accommodate that value—up to the maximum you specify.

You can also adjust the spacing between rows, using the Row Spacing option. This option applies only to the space between different rows—not the spacing between multiple lines in the same row—which are always single-spaced.

Displaying the Selection Margin   When it's displayed, the selection margin is the leftmost column in a view. It is mainly used for two purposes:

- To show which documents are currently selected (to select a document, you click on its row in the selection margin).

- To indicate (by asterisks) which documents have not been read.

If you don't plan to use either of these features for a particular view, you can liberate a tiny bit of horizontal space by deselecting the option Show Selection Margin, on the InfoBox page labeled S.

Indenting Response Documents   By default, Notes indents by three spaces a response document under its parent document. This type of formatting allows users to easily distinguish between parents and their siblings. It's particularly useful when a view displays several levels in a document hierarchy.

However, for some types of applications you may not want to display the hierarchical nature of documents. For instance, you may want to display all of the memos—and their responses—in a view without regard to which memo was a response to another memo.

To set up this type of view, deselect the option Show Response Documents In A Hierarchy, on the Options page of the InfoBox.

Tracking Unread Documents   You can set up a view so that it will highlight *unread documents,* which by definition are those that you have not yet read in their current form. This includes, for example, new documents created or sent to you by someone else. It could also include documents that you haven't viewed since they were last changed—again, by someone else.

Notes provides two different types of markings for flagging unread documents, which you can set up as part of the view design. First, you can assign a special color—red is a typical choice—that makes unread documents stand out. Second, Notes can also display an *unread mark* (an asterisk) in the selection margin (the leftmost edge of the view) for unread documents. You can exercise some control over which unread view entries are flagged.

Here's how to assign a special color to unread documents:

1. Display the InfoBox for the view.

2. Click the middle tab (labeled S).

3. Select the color that you want for the unread rows.

The color you select will apply only to unread documents; if the view is categorized, a category is never colored, even if it contains one or more unread documents.

To a limited extent, you can specify which rows in a view Notes marks as unread:

1. Display the infoBox for the view and then click on the tab shaped like a hat.

2. Make your selection for the option Unread Marks.

Your selections for this option are the following:

- *None.* No unread marks are displayed.

- *Standard* (compute in hierarchy). All unread documents are marked—at all levels in a document hierarchy. In addition, if a collapsed category contains any unread documents, that category is marked as unread.

- *Unread Documents Only.* The same as the previous option, but with one difference: Collapsed categories containing unread documents are not marked as unread.

Other Options

Beyond those options that affect the appearance of a view, there are others whose influences are more subtle.

Assigning a Default View   You can assign a default view or folder to a database. This is the view a new user will see the first time he or she opens the database. To select a database default view (or folder), choose the option "Default when database is first opened"—on the Options page of the View InfoBox.

Assigning a Default Design   You can select a view or folder as the default design for each new view or folder. This means that each time you start to create a new view or folder, Notes will assign the design of the default view to it. You can override this default, selecting the design of another view or folder—or selecting None—as the basis for the new view or folder.

To select a view or folder as the default, choose the option Default Design For New Folders And Views (on the Options page of the View InfoBox).

NOTE. *If there is already a default view and design assigned, these options are not available.*

Selecting the Initial State of a View or Folder By default, each time you open a view (or folder), all of its documents are displayed—both main documents and all of their descendants. However, you can change this default by selecting the option Collapse All When Database Is First Opened (on the Options page of the View InfoBox). Then, each time you open a view, only the main documents will be displayed. Or, if the view is categorized, only the top-level group of categories is displayed. (To expand part or all of a view that's collapsed, you can either double-click on individual categories or select View, Expand All.)

You can also select which row is displayed each time a view or folder is opened. Your choices are either the first row, the last row, or the row that was selected when the view or folder was last closed. To make your selection, use the option On Open (on the Options page of the View InfoBox).

Placing a View or Folder in a Hierarchy Typically, as your database grows you'll want to create separate hierarchies for the views and folders—just to maintain order and simplify your work when you want to locate a particular one. The top part of the default navigator for each database displays these hierarchies, as shown in the following illustration.

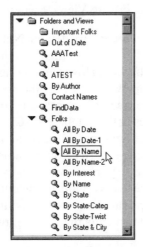

Notes maintains four different sets of hierarchies: one each for public views and public folders; and two more sets for each user—for private views and private folders.

When you create a new view or folder, you can optionally position it within the appropriate hierarchy. However, the choice you make then is not written in stone, and you can later reposition the view or folder elsewhere within the hierarchy. If you're not satisfied with the depth of the current hierarchy, you can create a new branch.

Here's how to reposition an existing view or folder within the appropriate hierarchy:

1. Open the view or folder by clicking on it in the upper half of the default navigator.

2. Select Actions, View Options, Move, displaying the following dialog box.

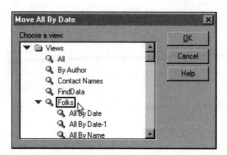

3. To reposition the view or folder as a child under an existing view or folder, simply click on that view or folder. Or, to place the view or folder on the main stem of the hierarchy, click on the topmost member of the tree (labeled either Views, Private Views, Folders, or Private Folders).

Limiting Access to a View or Folder   By default, Notes sets up each new view so that users having Reader access or higher in the database's access control list (ACL) can open the view. However, you can override this default and set up a user access list for a view, selecting the people and groups that you want to have access to the view. When setting up this list, you can select from any of the current entries in the database's ACL.

It's important to note that limiting the access to a particular view is not a way of implementing database security. For example, suppose that a particular user is excluded from every shared view that you create for a database. If that user has adequate access rights to the database by virtue of the ACL, he or she can create a private view to display the contents of the database—except for those documents that contain read-access lists that exclude the user.

Here's how to set up an access list for a view:

1. Make sure that the view is open in edit mode.

2. Display the View InfoBox and then click on the Security tab (see below).

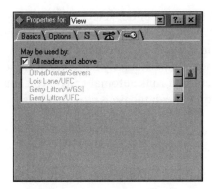

3. Deselect the option All Readers And Above.

4. Scroll through the list, clicking on those entries that you want to add to the read-access list.

5. If you want to add an entry that's not on the list, click the Address Book icon to the right of the list, displaying your current Address Book. Then, using the entries that are displayed, select those you want to add to the view's access list.

You can use the preceding steps to add or delete entries from a view's access list any time you wish.

Index Options   Notes maintains a separate index for each view and folder. Each index keeps track of all the information needed to ensure that the view or folder displays what it's supposed to. This information includes a record of which documents are displayed, the sorting and categorizing orders of these documents, which field values are displayed, and so on.

Whenever you add or delete documents that are displayed in a particular view or folder, the corresponding index must be refreshed so that the view or folder continues to display the correct information. Similarly, if you change the value of a field displayed in a view or folder, the corresponding index must again be refreshed.

By default, Notes maintains these indexes automatically, refreshing them every time a view or folder is opened. However, in some circumstances you may want to take control over when a particular view or folder index is refreshed. For example, if you're maintaining several views that display large numbers of documents, refreshing all the indexes can take as long as several minutes, and this may significantly impact database users. Obviously, if other users are also on line, the impact of delays will be proportionately worse.

Also by default, Notes never deletes an index. However, if an index is particularly large, and if disk space is at a premium, you can optionally have

Notes discard the index under selected conditions. Rebuilding an index for a large database can take several minutes, so you should be careful when deciding to set up an index to be automatically deleted.

For instance, if a particularly large index is used infrequently—and then only by an agent that runs automatically—you could set up the index to be deleted each time the database is closed, releasing the disk space used by the index.

Here's how you can change the way in which Notes refreshes the index for a particular view or folder:

1. Open the view or folder in edit mode.

2. Display the InfoBox and then select the tab displaying a hat (second from the right).

3. Select the appropriate options for refreshing and discarding the index (see the two following sections for details).

Options for Index Refreshing   By making the appropriate choice for the option Refresh Index, you can set the index to refresh either automatically, semiautomatically, or under user control, as follows:

- *Automatic*. Notes will automatically refresh the index each time you open the view or folder. Note that this is true for any other user who opens the view while you're using it. This could cause unexplainable delays if the database is very large, because the refresh could take a noticeable amount of time.

- *Automatic, after first use*. This is the same as the preceding option, except that the index is not refreshed the first time you open the view or folder.

- *Manual*. Select this option if you're working with a large database, when refreshing a view could severely limit your ability to work interactively with the database. In particular, this option can be successful if you don't need to have the view completely up to date when you use it.

  When this option is selected, the user can manually refresh the view, either by selecting View, Refresh or by clicking on the Refresh button whenever it appears in the upper-left corner of the view.

- *Auto, at most every xx hours*. Notes will automatically refresh the index at this interval. As an example, you could use this option if you knew that a particular agent updated the database periodically and if this were the primary means by which the contents of a particular view were changed; you could select this option to refresh the index, using the same time interval as that for the agent.

Options for Discarding an Index   By selecting the appropriate choice for the option Discard Index, you can control if and when Notes discards an index, as follows:

- *Never*. The index is perpetually maintained by Notes. This is the default, and you should probably have a good reason for changing it.

- *After each use*. Notes will discard the index each time you close the database containing the view or folder. The next time the view or folder is opened, Notes will rebuild the index—even if you have selected Manual for the Refresh Index option. Save this option for those situations satisfying all of the following conditions:

  - The index takes up a great deal of disk space.

  - Disk space is at a premium on your system.

  - The database is used infrequently and predictably, and rebuilding the index on demand (such as by a periodic agent) will not affect human usage.

- *If inactive for xx days*. This is a compromise between the other two options. Use it primarily for large views or folders that aren't used a great deal, and whose index gobbles up an incredible amount of disk space.

Selecting the Documents to Display in a View

Only occasionally will you want to use a view to display all of the documents in a database. Instead, you'll usually select a particular subset of documents to suit users' needs. In fact, one of the most important purposes of a view is to select which documents in a database to display. Notes refers to this as the *view selection*.

NOTE. *This section applies only to views—not to folders. You must individually select the documents to be placed in each folder.*

The possibilities are just about endless for the types of document groupings you may want to select for display in a view. For example, some databases contain many different types of documents, created from a variety of forms; and a typical view might display only those documents created with a particular form.

As an example, suppose that a personnel department maintains various types of documents within a database. Some documents contain basic name-and-address information, others contain salary information, and still others contain historical data. You could create a different view to display only the information for each type of document. You could also create a single view to display bits and pieces of information from all of the documents.

Here are a few more examples of the different types of documents for which you might create views:

- Documents you receive via electronic mail
- Documents you receive from Joan Jones
- Documents you've mailed to Harriet Smith
- Documents marked "Pending"

To specify which documents to display in a view, you either build a set of search conditions based on field values, or you write a formula.

To begin setting up the view selection, follow these steps:

1. Display the view in edit mode.

2. Click anywhere in the top half of the display. The edit box labeled Define (in the bottom part of the display) will then show "View Selection," indicating that you're ready to set up the selection criteria.

NOTE. *You use the bottom half of the edit-mode display to build the view selection. This part of the window is called the* Design *pane.*

Notes provides two mechanisms for setting up view selection: (1) the Easy method and (2) writing formulas. The following section describes how to use the Easy method; formulas are discussed later, in the section "Creating Formulas to Select Documents."

Selecting Documents the Easy Way

Using the Easy method, you can select the documents to be displayed in a view using any of the following criteria:

- *By form.* You select only those documents created with specific forms. For example, if your database contains a wide variety of different types of documents, you might want to use a view to display only those created with one, two, or just a small number of those forms.

- *By author.* You can display only documents created by specific authors— perhaps only yourself.

- *By date.* You can display only those documents created before or after a particular date, or within a specific date range.

- *By field value.*

Selecting documents by field values is a particularly powerful tool, and in many circumstances, you'll want to display only those documents that contain specific field values. For instance, suppose that you maintain a database of client information. Here are a few subsets of documents you might like to display in some of the views you create:

- Clients living in Nebraska

- Clients who owe you money

- Clients who don't owe you money

- Clients over the age of 16

- Clients over the age of 16 who live in Nebraska

Using the Easy method, you can specify a condition for any type of field except rich text. For fields containing text, you can use either an "includes the string" or "does not include the string" condition to select documents. For instance, you can select documents whose City field does not include the string "field."

NOTE. *When doing string comparisons, Notes includes case sensitivity, so you'll need to include not only the correct spelling but also the correct case.*

For numeric fields, you can use any of the standard comparison operators: "is equal to," "is less than," and so on.

Note. To use conditions in the logical OR sense, you'll need to write a formula.

For fields containing time-date information, you can use various types of date comparisons. For instance, here are a few examples you could use for a field named DateOfCreation:

- Is on 01/01/96

- Is before 5/6/96

- Is after 5/6/96

- Is after the next 3 (days)

You can combine conditions on two or more fields, but only in the logical AND sense. For example, you can select documents satisfying both of these conditions:

- The value of the Age field is greater than 21

- The value of the City field contains "San Francisco"

NOTE. *The Easy method is easy partly because you don't have a lot of options to fiddle with. This means that searches involving sophisticated search criteria are excluded. For instance, you can't search for documents containing two strings that are "close to each other." In order to use more search conditions* *that are more complex than those allowed by the Easy method, you'll need to write a formula. This topic is described later, in the section "Creating Formulas to Select Documents."*

The Easy method involves using Notes' Search Builder to create a view selection. To begin using this method, follow these steps:

1. Click on the radio button labeled Easy in the bottom half of the view design window.

2. Click the button labeled Add Condition, displaying the dialog box shown in Figure 7.7. This is the Search Builder dialog box, where you create the view selection for a view.

Figure 7.7

Use this dialog box to select the documents to display in a view.

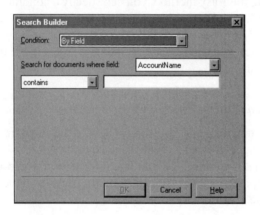

NOTE. *To illustrate the various ways in which you can set up view selection, we'll use several examples, to follow. Each of these examples uses the Search Builder dialog box.*

Example: Displaying All Documents Created with Particular Forms   You can set up a view selection that will display only documents created with one of the forms you choose:

1. Pull down the list box labeled Condition and then select By Form Used.

2. In the drop-down list that appears (see Figure 7.8), click on the names of the forms that you want to select.

3. Click OK to exit from the Search Builder.

Figure 7.8

Select the form(s) used to create the documents to be displayed.

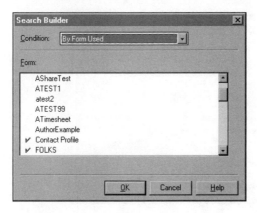

The Design pane will now display the result of your selection—something like that shown below:

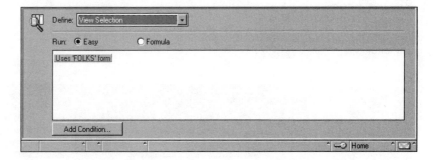

TIP. *If you decide that you want to delete a selection shown in the Design pane, click on it and then select Edit, Cut. If you want to edit an existing selection in the Design pane, double-click it.*

Example: Selecting All Documents Created by a Specific Author   Each time a new document is created, Notes attaches a field named $UpdatedBy and inserts the name of the author. Using the Search Builder, you can have Notes select documents based on a particular author name, as follows:

1. Pull down the top list box in the Search Builder and then select By Author, so that the dialog box shown in Figure 7.9 appears.

2. In the option labeled Search For Documents, select Contains.

3. To select an author name from the current Address Book, go on to step 4. Otherwise, skip to step 7.

Figure 7.9

Select the document
author that you want to
appear in the view.

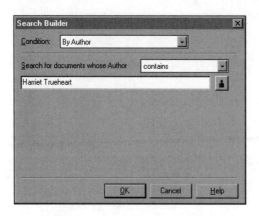

Warning! You can select
more than one name;
however, if you do, the
view probably will not
select the correct
documents, because the
Easy method doesn't
work properly for OR-type
operations.

4. To display the Address Book, click the Person icon at the right side of
   the dialog box, so that the list of names in the Address Book appears, as
   shown below.

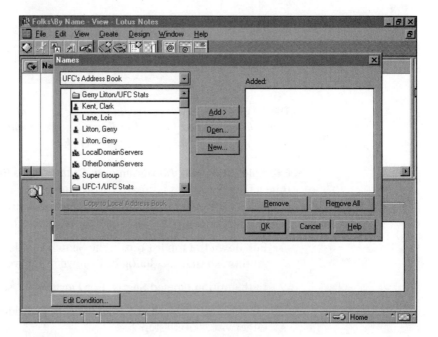

5. To select a name, click on it and then click the Add button.

6. Click OK to return to the Search Builder dialog box.

7. To enter a name directly, type it into the bottom edit window.

8. Click OK to return to the view design window.

TIP. *Be very careful about capitalization when entering values, because text comparisons made when searching documents are case-sensitive.*

Example: Displaying Documents According to Creation Date   You can use the Search Builder to select a group of documents based on their creation date (Notes automatically inserts the date of creation into each document). For instance, you could select all documents created either before or after a specified date, or within a particular range of dates. Here's how:

1. Pull down the top list box in the Search Builder dialog box and then select By Date.

2. In the drop-down list box Search For Documents Whose, select Date Created.

3. Pull down the leftmost drop-down list (see below) and then select the conditions that you want to apply.

4. In the lower-right edit box, type in the appropriate date. If you selected either Is Between or Is Not Between in step 3, you'll need to enter two dates.

Tip. You can sort documents in a view by date. For details, see Chapter 8.

5. Click OK to return to the view design window.

Example: Displaying Documents for Clients Living in California   To have Notes display all the documents for clients who live in California, follow these steps:

1. Pull down the top list box in the Search Builder dialog and then select By Field.

2. Pull down the drop-down list Search For Documents and then select the field State (see the note, to follow).

3. In the lower-left list box, select Contains.

4. In the lower-right edit box, type California. This will select documents whose State field contains the string California.

5. Click OK to return to the view design window.

NOTE. *In the preceding step 2, the list of fields contains every field in the entire database—including those that were once used but no longer exist. Be sure that you select the correct field name.*

Example: Multiple Conditions   You can set up a view selection that's based on two or more different criteria. To accomplish this, you simply use the Search Builder once for each criterion that you want to establish. This technique works well for AND-type conditions; that is, those in which all of the conditions must be true for each document that's displayed. However, the Easy method does not work properly for most OR-type conditions.

For example, you could set up a view selection to include only documents created by Joe Smith after January 1, 1996. Here's an outline of the steps to follow:

1. Click the Add Condition button to display the Search Builder.

2. Pull down the top list box in the Search Builder and then select By Author.

3. Select the name of the author (Joe Smith in this example) whose documents you want to display.

4. Click OK to return to the view design window.

5. Now click the Add Condition button again to return to the Search Builder dialog box.

6. Pull down the top list box and, this time, select By Date.

7. Set up the following condition: "Search for documents whose date created is after 1/1/96."

8. Click OK to exit from the Search Builder.

TIP. *To use OR-type conditions, or more complex multiple conditions, you'll need to write a formula. For examples, see the section "Creating Formulas to Select Documents."*

Example: Using Query By Example   You can select the documents you want to display by filling in a blank form. First you select the name of the form that you want to fill in, and then you fill in whatever fields you want. The field values that you enter will become the basis of the view selection.

As an example, suppose that one of the forms in your database is called Folks, and you use it to create personnel documents. Here's how you can create the view selection to display documents only for people living in California:

1. Display the Search Builder dialog box.

2. Pull down the top list box and then select By Form.

3. Pull down the list box labeled Form and then choose the name of the form that you want to use; in this example, the form is called Folks. A blank Folks document will then appear.

4. Scroll down so that the field State is shown and then type in **California**.

5. Exit from the Search Builder.

When using the Query By Example method, you can fill in as many fields as you wish. Notes will use them all in the AND sense. For instance, if you fill in "California" for the State field and also "San Francisco" for the City field, the view will display only those documents for which the State field value is California *and* the City field value is San Francisco.

You can't use the Query By Example method to specify OR-type conditions. For instance, suppose you want to display documents for people living in either Berkeley or San Francisco. You'll need to write a formula for the view selection to accomplish this.

Although you must use a particular form to enter the search values, the documents displayed in the view are not confined to that form. For instance, suppose you use the Folks form to specify the value of California for the State field, as in the previous example. The view will then display all documents whose State field value is California—regardless of which form was used to create the documents.

Creating Formulas to Select Documents

The methods described in the preceding examples for setting up view selections are reasonably straightforward to use, but they do have limitations. For instance, if you want to specify multiple conditions using different field values in the OR sense, Notes does not work reliably. Also, you can't use the Easy method to specify really complicated and sophisticated search conditions.

When the Easy method fails, you'll need to write a formula to specify the view-selection criteria.

For example, you'll need to write formulas for the following types of view-selection criteria:

- Case-insensitive conditions on text

- Complex multivalue conditions, perhaps involving the use of temporary variables and multiple conditional tests

NOTE. *The following discussion assumes that you understand the basics of writing Notes formulas. Even if this is not the case, you might want to read through the following examples. Some of them are quite simple, and you may get a good idea of the syntax that's used.*

Here's an outline of the steps to follow when writing a formula to specify the view selection:

1. Make sure that the correct view is open in edit mode and that the Design pane is displayed.

2. Click anywhere in the upper part of the window, so that View Selection appears in the list box labeled Define (in the Design pane).

3. Click the radio button labeled Formula.

4. Write the formula in the Design pane.

Note. For information about formulas, see Chapter 10.

Example: Selecting All Documents   The simplest formula that you can create selects all the documents in a database—regardless of content or origin. The following illustration shows how this formula appears in the Design pane.

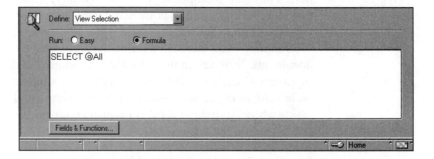

Typically, each selection formula contains the keyword SELECT. If a formula is complex, you can create temporary variables to hold values needed later on in the formula. However, the last line of the formula must begin with SELECT and specify the conditions that documents must satisfy in order to be displayed.

For example, the following formula returns one of two form names—PendingForm or RegularForm—depending on the value of the field Status:

```
SELECT Form = @If(Status = "Pending"; "PendingForm"; "RegularForm")
```

Note that this is not an assignment statement. Instead, it returns a simple condition: either Form = "PendingForm" or Form = "RegularForm." The view will display all documents created with either of these forms.

Example: Displaying Documents According to a Field Value   Suppose that
your documents contain the keywords field named Status, whose values can
be either Open, Pending, or Closed. Here's a view-selection formula to display only those documents that are pending:

```
SELECT Status = "Pending"
```

Example: Displaying Documents and Responses to Them   To create a view
that displays both documents and the responses to them, you can write a fairly
simple formula. As an example, suppose that you maintain a database of information about your office staff. One set of documents, created with the form
named Folks, contains basic personnel information. From time to time, you insert comment documents about various staff members; each of these comments is inserted as a response to the corresponding Folks document.

Figure 7.10 shows a view that displays both the original documents and
responses to them. The selection formula for this view must specify that the
view is to include only (1) documents created with the Folks form and (2) responses to these documents.

Figure 7.10

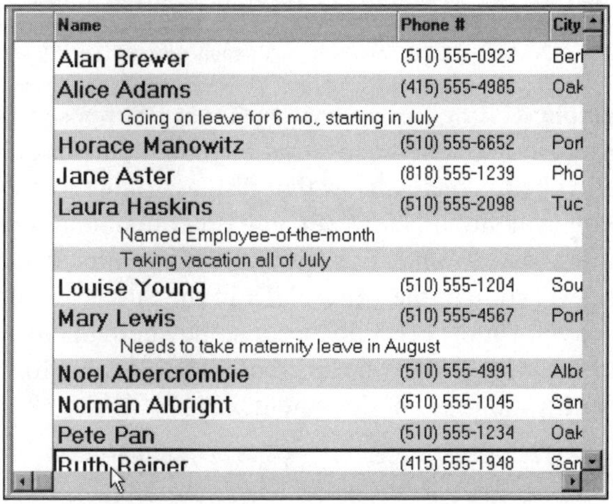

This view displays
documents and
responses to them.

Here's the formula to accomplish this:

```
SELECT Form = "Folks" | @AllChildren
```

The first part of this formula, Select Form = "Folks", will choose only
those documents created with the Folks form. The second part, @AllChil-
dren, has the following meaning: Display all response documents attached to

every "Folks" document displayed in the form—regardless of the form used to create those responses.

TIP. *The function @AllChildren is a replacement for the older function @IsResponseDoc. For a discussion of these functions, and also of the new function @AllDescendants, see Chapter 10.*

Example: Using Multiple Conditions   Suppose that you maintain a database of your customers, and that the database contains balance-due information. You would like to create a view that displays customers living either in California or Oregon, and who have outstanding balances of more than $1,000.

You can't use the Easy method to set this up, because the conditions are too complicated. However, you can write the following formula for the view selection:

```
SELECT (State = "California" | State = "Oregon") & (BalanceDue > 1000)
```

The | and & symbols stand for the logical OR and AND operations. The parentheses helps to define the groupings of the different operations.

By the way, you can use Notes's convenient shorthand for writing lists to abbreviate the preceding formula to the following:

```
SELECT (State = "California" : "Oregon") & BalanceDue > 1000
```

Example: Listing Documents by Topic   Suppose that your database contains a group of documents that include the fields Subject and Body. You would like to create a view that displays only those documents dealing with the topic of violins. However, you don't maintain strict control over the content of these documents, so you can't guarantee that every relevant document will contain the word *violin* in the Subject field. However, the word *violin* will almost certainly occur somewhere in either the Subject or Body field. Consequently, you can create the following formula to select and display only the relevant documents:

```
SELECT @Contains(Subject; "violin") | @Contains(Body; "violin")
```

The expression @Contains(Subject; "violin") will return the value True only if the contents of the Subject field contains the string "violin."

There's a potential problem with the preceding formula. Whenever Notes compares two strings, it always includes case-sensitivity; so if a document happens to include the word *violin*, it will not be included in the view.

You can correct this problem by using the following formula instead of the previous one:

```
Hold1 := @UpperCase(Subject);
Hold2 := @UpperCase(Body)
SELECT @Contains(Hold1; "VIOLIN") | @Contains(Hold2; "VIOLIN")
```

Here, two temporary variables—Hold1 and Hold2—are used to hold the uppercase equivalent of the values in the Subject and Body fields.

Example: Selecting Documents Relevant to Individuals   Suppose that your company maintains a centralized database of sales information—consisting of many different types of documents. Furthermore, suppose that one group of documents, created with a form named Sales, deals with information about individual sales; and one field in these documents is called Salesperson.

You would like to create a view that displays only those sales documents for which you are the salesperson. Assuming that your name is Tammy Jones, here's how the selection formula would appear:

```
SELECT (Form = "Sales") & (Salesperson = "Tammy Jones")
```

Selecting Forms for Viewing and Creating Documents

Note. You'll find that most views do not contain a form formula, in which case the default form (specified by the hierarchy shown in this list) is used for displaying documents.

Normally, when you double-click a document that's shown in a view, Notes opens the document, selecting a form according to the following hierarchy:

* The form stored with the document

* The form with which the document was created

* The default database form

For example, if a form is stored with a document, then that form is always used to display the document.

In some circumstances, you may want to specify that a particular form is used when displaying documents. To accomplish this, you can create a new view and write a *form formula* for it. This formula specifies that a particular form is to be used when opening any document from within that view.

This technique has limitations: If a document contains a stored form, then Notes uses that form to display the document, ignoring the form formula (if any) in the view.

You can also use a form formula in a view to specify that whenever that view is open and a new document is created, a particular form is used—regardless of the user's selection from the Create menu. This option is particularly useful when you're using a macro or script to programmatically create new documents.

A form formula can be as complicated as you wish, but its result must always be the name of a form that exists in the current database. If the formula produces the name of a nonexistent form, Notes will display a message something like "Cannot locate form." It will then use the default database form to display documents.

Form names are case-sensitive. For instance, if a form formula is MY-FIRSTFORM, but the actual form name is spelled MyFirstForm, then Notes will not find the form!

TIP. *If you're not sure of the name or capitalization of a particular form, you can easily display the list of forms in the database: Display the default navigator (select View, Design), pull down the bottom part of the Navigator pane, and then click on Forms. The view pane will display the complete list of forms.*

Here's how to create a form formula for a view:

1. Display the View InfoBox and select the tab displaying a little hat.

2. Click the button labeled Formula Window, displaying the window shown below:

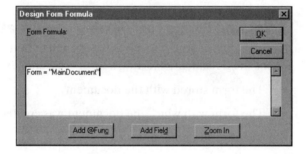

3. Type in the form formula.

4. Click on OK.

Example: Choosing a Single Form for Displaying Documents   As an example, suppose you want to use the form named Special5 to display documents that are opened from within a particular view. To accomplish this, you could write the following simple form formula:

```
Special5
```

Example: A More Complicated Formula   Let's suppose that you maintain a group of personnel documents that fall into two broad categories: those for temporary employees and others for permanent employees. Each document contains a field called Type, containing either the value Temporary or Permanent.

You are creating a view to display all of these documents; however, when you open a document by selecting it in the view, you would like to use one of two forms—either TempFolks or PermFolks, depending on whether the document contains information about a temporary or permanent employee.

To accomplish this, write the following form formula:

```
@If(Type="Temporary"; "TempFolks"; "PermFolks")
```

Example: A Formula for Creating New Documents Here's a form formula that will force Notes to use a particular form named UseMe when creating a new document—regardless of which form is selected on the Create menu:

```
@If(@IsNewDoc; "UseMe"; "RegularForm")
```

The @IsNewDoc function returns the value True only when a new document is being created.

■ Creating and Working with Columns

Note. The details of designing columns for views and forms are identical.

Each view and folder consists of one or more columns, which you design either for displaying document information or for other purposes.

When designing a new column, you begin by assigning its basic features, such as the column title, column width, and other basic characteristics. Most important, you must select the method by which the column values will be calculated.

You can create as many columns as you wish for a view or folder—but only the leftmost 22.75 inches will print. Although you assign each new column a width, you can optionally set up the column so that users can adjust the width.

A column can display text, numeric, and time-date values; and you can select the formatting for these values. You can also sort the displayed documents according to the values in one or more columns. If a field contains multiple values, you can set up the column to display any or all of them. A column can display values from any field type except rich text.

Not all columns display field information; you can set up a column to display any of the following:

- *Totals*. Statistics on numbers of displayed documents.

- *Icons*. Special symbols, each of which represents either a particular field value or a special condition. For example, you can display an icon that shows whether or not a particular document has any associated response documents that are currently hidden in the view.

In some circumstances, you may want to create a column but hide its values. You would do this, for example, with a column whose values are used as the basis for sorting the documents, but where you don't want those values to be displayed in the view.

Creating a New Column

In order to create a new column for a view, you'll need to open the view in design mode. If you're working with a brand new view, its design window looks similar to that shown in Figure 7.6. Notes automatically inserts one column into each new view, indicated by the # symbol at the top of the column. This column contains the formula @DocNumber, which displays the position of each document in the view: The top main document is number 1, the next one down is 2, and so on. Unless you happen to want this column in your view, delete it: Select the column by clicking on its title bar and then press Del.

To create a new column, follow these steps:

1. Either click the New Column SmartIcon or select Create, Insert New Column. A new, blank column will appear, as indicated in Figure 7.11.

Figure 7.11

Use the InfoBox to assign properties to a new column.

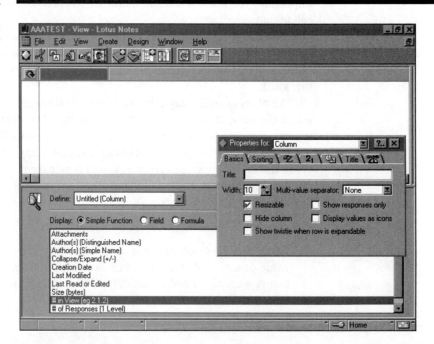

2. Display the InfoBox for the new column: You can either double-click on the title bar for the new column, or you can select Design, Column Properties.

If you're adding a column to a view that contains other columns, you can add a new column either to the left of a column that you select, or to the right of the last one. In the former case, use the preceding list of steps. Otherwise, select Create, Append New Column.

TIP. *To simplify your work when adding new columns, add a new, blank one to the right-hand end of whatever view or folder you're creating or editing. To accomplish this, select Create, Append New Column. You can add a descriptive label to it; something like Blank or Dummy. Whenever you want to add a new column to the right-hand end of the view, you can simply click on that column and then click on the Create New Column SmartIcon.*

When you're finished designing the view or folder, you can then delete the Dummy column.

Customizing a Column

After creating a new column, you can set its basic features, such as typing in a title, customizing its appearance, and so on. You can assign one set of text characteristics to the column title and another set to the column values. You must select the way in which Notes calculates the values to appear in the column; you can also set up a column so that its values are used as the basis for sorting the documents in the view.

Basic Column Characteristics

You can use the Column InfoBox to assign the column title, width, and other basic features.

Note. You can assign up to five lines for the column titles.

Column Title   Use the Basics page of the Column InfoBox to assign a title to a new column. The title can be as long as you wish; make it meaningful, but keep it short enough to fit within the column width and height that you select.

You can assign the text characteristics to a column title. For instance, you could choose a large font and perhaps a striking color. To set these features, click the Title tab of the InfoBox and then make your selections. You can also use an option on this InfoBox page to align (justify) the column title.

TIP. *You can format the titles for all of the existing columns in the same way, saving yourself some steps: Select one column, select the formatting options that you want, and then click the button labeled Apply To All.*

Column Width   Using the Basics page of the Column InfoBox, you can set the width for a column, but don't worry about getting it exactly right. Not only can you change the width at any time, but also by selecting the appropriate option (resizable) on this page of the InfoBox, you can give users the option to adjust the column width.

Displaying Multiple Values   If this column will be displaying the contents of a multivalue field (or if for some other reason you expect the column to be displaying multiple values in a single entry—perhaps as the result of the column formula), you can select the separator to use between values. This option is on the Basics page of the Column InfoBox. If you leave the default value of None for this option, blanks will be used when necessary.

Note that one of the options for the multivalue separator is New Line. If you select this option, you must also set the view's option to allow for multiple lines, as follows:

1. In the InfoBox, pull down the top list box labeled Properties For and then select View.

2. Click the InfoBox tab labeled S.

3. For the option labeled Lines Per Row, select a number between 1 and 9.

Assigning Column Values

You must specify how the values of each column are to be calculated. Notes provides three basic options, from which you can select the one to use:

- *Field*. You can display the values of a selected field.

- *Simple function*. Notes provides a list of commonly used operations, from which you can select the one to be used for displaying values for this column.

- *Formula*. You can write a formula to calculate the column values.

To select your choice, click the appropriate radio button at the top of the Design pane:

Using Field Values   Probably the most common selection for column values is to display the values for a particular field. This is particularly useful for on-the-fly columns that you want to quickly throw together in order to display a particular set of information.

Here's how to set up a column to display field values: In the Design pane, select the radio button labeled Field; when the list of fields appears, click on the name of the field whose values you want to display.

TIP. *The list of field names displayed by Notes includes every field that ever existed in the database—even those no longer used. Be careful to select exactly the right field name. If you're not sure of which field to select, open the corresponding form or forms to investigate.*

Selecting a Simple Function Notes includes a list of built-in calculations from which you can choose one for a column. If you click the radio button labeled Simple Function, this list will appear. Scroll through it to familiarize yourself with the various choices. If you're not sure about the meaning of one, select it and then either press F9 or click the Recalculate icon (in the upper-left corner of the window). Notes will make the appropriate calculation for each document selected for the view you're working with. For instance, if you select the function "Authors(s) (Simple Name)" and then press F9 to recalculate the view, the upper pane will display the author name for every document displayed in the view. Table 7.1 lists a few of these functions.

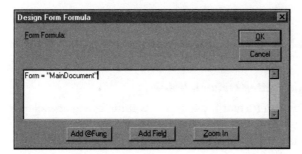

Using Formulas If you don't want to use a set of field values for a column, and if you can't find a simple function to supply the column values that you want, you'll need to write a formula to calculate the column values. Notes contains a wide array of programmable functions, providing you the tools for designing just about any type of calculations you can think of.

NOTE. *The simple functions described in the previous section are not the same as the programmable functions mentioned in the preceding paragraph. The latter are much more general, and there are literally hundreds of them.*

The basic steps for creating a formula are quite simple: Click the radio button labeled Formula and then type in the formula for calculating the column values.

Table 7.1

Some Simple Functions
You Can Use for Column
Calculations.

SIMPLE FUNCTION	COLUMN VALUE
Attachments	The number of attachments a document contains
Author(s) (Simple Name)	The name of a document's author(s)
Collapse/Expand (+/-)	Displays + if a document has responses that are not displayed (that is, the document is collapsed). Otherwise, displays -
Creation Date	Date on which a document was created
# Responses (All Levels)	The total number of descendants of a document, including responses, responses to responses, and so on

As a simple example, suppose that your documents contained two fields named FirstName and LastName. You would like to create a column that displays the full name of each person. Here's a simple formula to accomplish this:

```
FirstName + " " + LastName
```

The middle item inserts a blank space between the first and last names.

NOTE. *Chapter 8 provides several examples of the types of column formulas you can create.*

Formatting Column Values

You can format the text in a column of values, selecting the font, size, and so on. If your column contains numeric or time-date information, you can also select the format in which you want these values to appear.

Text Characteristics   To customize the text in a column, display the Column InfoBox; click on the Fonts tab (third from the left), and then make your selections. Note that your choices apply only to the column values, not to the column title (which you can format separately, as described earlier).

TIP. *If you want to format the values for all of the existing columns in the same way, you can save yourself some steps: Select one column, select the text-formatting options that you want, and then click the button labeled Apply To All.*

Numeric Formatting   If a column displays numeric information, you can format those values in various ways: Click the Numeric Formats tab (labeled 2_1) and then make your formatting selections.

If you're not sure about the meaning of one of the options, select it and then click the Recalculate icon in the upper-left corner of the window (or press F9). The column values will be reformatted according to your selections.

Time-Date Formatting If a column displays time-date information, you have a wide array of formatting choices. For example, typically a time-date value contains both the time and date. You can choose whether to display just the time or date—or both. You can also select from a limited number of time and date display formats. To choose the format you want, click the Time/Date tab (third from the right-hand end) and then make your selections. Your choices affect only the display—the original values stored in the documents remain unchanged.

Sorting the Values in a Column

You can use the values in a column as the basis for sorting the documents appearing in the view. In fact, you can use several columns for sorting. When more than one column is used, Notes works from left to right, sorting first on the leftmost column designated for sorting, then the next one to the right, and so on. For instance, if you set up two columns for sorting, Notes sorts the documents first by the values in the leftmost of the two columns and then by the values in the other one.

You can sort columns whose values are numeric, time-date, or text; the latter includes fields of types Text, Keywords, Authors, Names, or Readers.

To use a column for sorting, display the InfoBox page labeled Sorting. Then, to set up a column to sort either in ascending or descending order, select the appropriate option on the top line. We'll refer to your selection here as the *default sort order*.

Setting Up for User-Selected Sorting You can set up a column so that a user can either turn sorting on or off, or switch from ascending to descending sorting. To accomplish this, you select the option Click On Column Header To Sort. The user can then switch between the selection that you make here and the default sort order—the choice you make for the Sort option at the top of the InfoBox.

Here are your choices:

- *Descending.* A user can switch between the default sort order and a descending sort. For example, if you select None as the default, then the users' choices are no sorting or descending order.

- *Ascending.* A user can switch between the default sort order and an ascending sort.

- *Both.* A user can switch between ascending, descending, or the default (which you should set to None, in this case).

How does a user switch the sorting order? By clicking on the column title in the view, as shown below. A little triangle indicates that a choice of sorting options is available by clicking the column title.

Selecting a Secondary Sort Column   If you set up a column for user-selectable sorting, you can also use the Secondary Sort Column option to specify another column on which the view will be secondarily sorted. When you select this option, you can then select the name of the secondary column and whether the sorting is to be ascending or descending (see below).

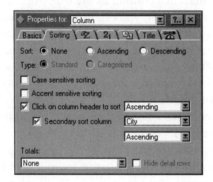

Here are a couple of points to keep in mind about secondary sorting:

- When you set up a column for secondary sorting, your sort choice for this column overrides whatever choice you make for the column directly.

- Secondary sorting takes place only when a user clicks the column title bar in the View pane and turns on the optional sort—that is, when the little triangle in the title bar changes from dark to light.

Copying, Moving, and Deleting Columns

You can easily copy or move columns from one view to another—even in different databases. When you copy a column, the new one has exactly the same characteristics as the original, including the same title. This is true even if you make a copy of a column in the same view, because there's nothing to prevent a view from having two or more identical columns.

After you make a copy of a column, the original and the new one are not connected in any way; changes that you make to either one are not reflected in the other.

TIP. *If you're building a view that's wider than a full screen width, you can help users keep track of important column information by repeating the column periodically. This could be useful, for example, with personal names or identification numbers.*

To copy or move a column of the view that's currently open, follow these steps:

1. Click on the title bar of the column that you want to copy or move.

2. Select either Edit, Copy or Edit, Move.

3. Now switch to the database and view in which you want to copy the column; select the view for editing.

4. Click on the title bar of the column *to the left of which* you want to insert the new column.

5. Select Edit, Paste to insert the column.

TIP. *The preceding technique works unless you happen to want to paste the new column at the right-hand end of the view, in which case things become a bit complicated, because you can't very easily paste a column there. However, if you took our earlier advice to keep a dummy column at the right-hand end of the view, you can use the preceding steps to paste a column just to the left of the dummy column. If you do not have a dummy column placed at the right-hand end of the view, then place one there before carrying out the preceding steps.*

As you can see from the preceding discussion, deleting a column is almost too easy: Click on its title bar and then either press Del or select Edit, Cut. Worse yet, you can't use Edit, Undo to recover from an accidental deletion. Develop the habit of using Edit, Cut to delete columns—instead of using the Del key. Then, if you realize that you've made a mistake, you may be able to recover the column by selecting Edit, Paste—provided you haven't in the meantime copied something else to the Clipboard.

- *Using Columns Effectively*
- *Categorizing Documents*
- *Displaying Response Documents*
- *Automating Views and Folders*
- *Copying and Deleting Actions*
- *Customizing the Action Bar*
- *Views for Special Purposes*

C H A P T E R

8

Using Views and Folders

CHAPTER 7 DESCRIBED THE BASIC TOOLS AVAILABLE FOR CREATING database views and folders within Notes. Although you can use those tools to build a variety of views and folders, you'll find that there's still a lot to learn.

In fact, creating views and folders is as much an art as a science, and there's probably no substitute for experience, which brings us to this chapter, where we describe a wide variety of different types of views and folders that you can create.

Along the way, we illustrate how to use views and folders to categorize documents—a very nice method for simplifying the manner in which information is displayed. We also show how to use views and folders to display both main documents and responses to them. In fact, these topics are so vital to the success of Notes databases that this chapter devotes quite a bit of space to them.

Besides displaying document information directly, a view or folder can also display other, related objects and material. For instance, a column can display different icons, each representing a particular circumstance. Views and folders can also take on a bit of a "reporting" flavor by including statistical information such as totals and percentages.

Notes provides a set of tools—called *actions*—for automating your views and folders. These actions offer users single-click operation for accomplishing a wide variety of common—but not necessarily simple—tasks. We describe how to use Notes' built-in actions, and how to create your own customized ones.

By the time you finish reading this chapter, you should have a much better understanding of the wide variety of options available to you when designing views and folders.

Before making any type of change to the design of a view, you must first open that view in edit mode. To review how to accomplish this, see "Opening a View or Folder in Edit Mode" in Chapter 7.

Also, remember that the top part of the edit mode window shows how the view will appear in the regular View pane, although when you first enter edit mode, you'll have to either press F9 or click the Refresh icon (in the upper-left corner of the window) to see the full view display. You'll also need to refresh after you make any kind of design change to the view.

■ Using Columns Effectively

The easiest type of columns to design are those displaying simple field values. For example, one column might display the values from a City field, another from a State field, and so on. But that's just the beginning, because columns are much more flexible.

For example, each column value could consist of any of the following:

- Field values plus text

- Multiple field values

- Conditional formulas

- Icons

Field Values and Text

You can attach one or more text strings to each column value by including the strings in the column formula. As an example, suppose that you're building a column to display the values in a TotalSales field. Instead of using the simple column formula TotalSales, you could be a little more creative and try the following:

```
"Total sales: " + TotalSales
```

Because of this formula, each column will display values like the following:

```
Total sales: 45,320
```

Multiple Field Values in Columns

You can combine two or more field values to produce each value in a column. For instance, if a set of documents contained the fields FirstName and LastName, you could display the full names in a column by using the following formula:

```
FirstName + " " + LastName
```

Or, if you wanted to display names more formally, you could use this formula:

```
LastName + ",  " + FirstName
```

Notice that each of the above two sample formulas contains three separate items separated by commas: two field values and a string value enclosed in quotes.

Here's another example of how to incorporate two field values into each column value: Suppose that your database contained Sales documents, each of which contained the name of a salesperson (the FullName field) and the total units that the salesperson has sold (TotalUnits field). You could create a column that displayed both the person's name and the number of units sold, using the following formula:

```
FullName + " has sold " + TotalUnits + "."
```

If a single field contains multiple values, you can display them in a column. To accomplish this, display the Column InfoBox page labeled Basics. Pull down the list labeled Multi-Value Separator and then select how you want the values displayed in the column to be separated. Your choices are the following:

- Space
- Comma

- Semicolon
- New Line

If you select the option New Line, then you must also select the option that allows multiple lines for each document displayed in a view. To accomplish this, display the View InfoBox, click the tab labeled S, and then select a number other than 1 for the option Lines Per Row.

Using Conditional Column Formulas

You can create a column whose values depend on circumstances. For example, suppose your Sales database contains documents that include a field named TotalSales, which contains the total dollar of sales to date. Here's a formula that will display the field value if it's non-zero; otherwise, it displays "No sales":

```
@If(TotalSales>0; TotalSales; "No sales")
```

Here's a more complicated example. Your sales force receives bonuses commensurate with their total sales, according to the following scale:

Total Sales	Bonus
0–2,500	0
2,501–5,000	100
5,001–10,000	250
>10,000	3% of sales

The following column formula will compute and display bonuses according to the preceding table:

```
@If(TotalSales>10000; 0.03*TotalSales; TotalSales>5000; 250;
TotalSales>2500; 100; 0)
```

This formula works because Notes evaluates an @If function starting at the left end and working to the right.

Using a Column to Display Icons

Notes provides a wide variety of built-in icons that you can display as column values. For instance, if a particular field contains only a couple of possible values—Yes or No, for example—you might prefer to display either of two icons instead of the values.

A common use of icons is to indicate whether or not a document contains an attachment. The standard icon used for this purpose is shown below.

Figure 8.1 shows the icons that you can use. Each icon corresponds to a particular numeric value between 1 and 169. Referring to Figure 8.1, the icons whose numbers are 1–20 are listed in the second column from the left: The top icon corresponds to number 1, the next one down to number 2, and so on. Then, in the third column, the top icon corresponds to number 21, and then number 22, and so on.

Figure 8.1

You can display any of these icons in a view.

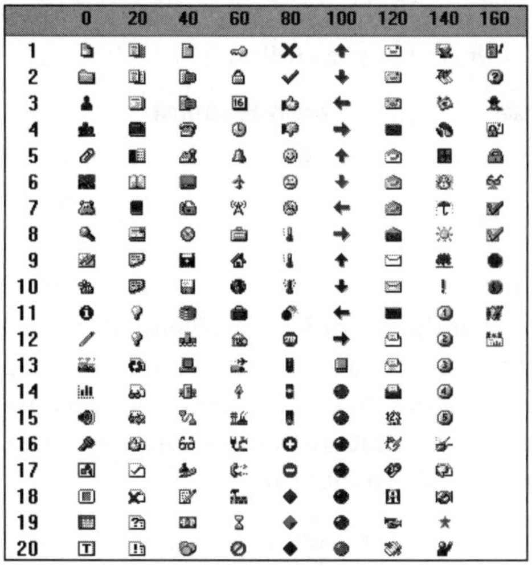

	0	20	40	60	80	100	120	140	160
1									
2									
3									
4									
5									
6									
7									
8									
9									
10									
11									
12									
13									
14									
15									
16									
17									
18									
19									
20									

In order to display icons in a column, you first set up the appropriate column option that tells Notes to display icons in this column. Then you arrange for the column to display the values that correspond to the icons you want to display.

Here's how to set the column option that specifies that icons are to be displayed:

1. Open the view in edit mode.

Note. To select a column, click on its title bar.

2. Select the column in which you want to display icons.

3. Display the InfoBox for that column, click the Basics tab, and then select the option Display Values As Icons.

The more interesting part of the work is arranging for the column to display the values corresponding to the icons that you want displayed. As a simple (but very instructive!) example, let's suppose that you want to display the same icon for every document that appears in a view. Let's also suppose that this icon corresponds to number 5 (this happens to be the Contains An Attachment icon, which you can see in Figure 8.1).

To arrange this, insert the column formula that consists of the single number 5.

This formula tells Notes to calculate the number 5 for every document shown in the view; however, because you also select the option Display Values As Icons for the column, Notes displays the corresponding icon instead of the value 5.

Now let's use a more realistic example. Suppose your personnel documents contain a keywords field named EmployeeLevel, which indicates whether employees are top-level management, middle-level, or neither. You could set up a column for these field values, but display icons instead of the field values in the column, as follows:

Field Value	Icon Number
Top-Level	85
Middle-Level	87
Standard	86

If you consult the list of icons in Figure 8.1, you'll see that these numbers correspond to icons that are either smiling, frowning, or neutral.

To set up a column to display one of these icons for each document that's displayed, first select the option Display Values As Icons. Then assign the following formula to the column:

```
@If(EmployeeLevel ="Top-Level"; 85;
EmployeeLevel="MiddleLevel"; 87; EmployeeLevel="Standard";
86; 0)
```

The final value in the formula, 0, corresponds to no icon being displayed, which is what will happen if the EmployeeLevel field contains any value other than Top-Level, Middle-Level, or Standard.

Using a Hidden Column for Sorting

Sometimes you may want to set up a special column just for sorting the documents in a view, but you don't want that column of values to be visible to users.

As an example, suppose that your documents contain a keywords field named Status, which can contain only one of the following values: Open-Inactive, Pending, or Closed. You would like to create a view displaying these documents—but in a specific order: first, the pending documents; then, those that are open and inactive; and finally, the closed documents.

To begin, you can set up the leftmost column to display the Status field values. However, if you select the Sort Ascending option for this column, all the closed documents will be displayed at the top of the view, because Closed comes before either Open-Inactive or Pending in the standard sort order.

The way around this is not to display the field values in this column, but instead to assign the following formula to the column:

```
@If(Status="Pending"; "1"; Status=" Open-inactive "; "2";
Status="Closed"; "3";"")
```

The result of this formula is that the column values will be either 1, 2, or 3, depending on the field values.

Now select the following options for the column:

- Sort Ascending

- Hide Column

The column will be sorted—not on the original field values, but on the values generated by the preceding formula: 1, 2, and 3. Consequently, the pending documents will appear at the top of the view, and so on.

By making the column values hidden, the numbers 1, 2, and 3 don't appear in the view, because they wouldn't have a great deal of meaning to users. However, you would still like to see the status of each document, so you can create a *second column* just to the right of the first, hidden one, displaying the actual document status—Pending, Open-Inactive, or Closed.

The only problem with this view is that the word Pending will appear a great many times—once for each pending document. The view would look a lot cleaner if Pending, Open-Inactive, and Closed each appeared only once. You can accomplish this by categorizing the documents, a process which is described further on in this chapter, in "Categorizing Documents."

Displaying Totals

If a column displays numeric values, you can set an option so that the column also shows either the total value or the average value. If a view displays categories, you can display incremental values for each category, as well as final totals, averages, and other statistical quantities.

As an example, the following illustration shows a simple view displaying the total value of the sales figures.

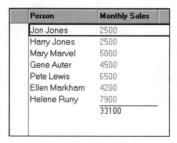

Here's how to display the totals for a column:

1. Select the column, display the Column InfoBox, and click the Sorting tab on the InfoBox (see Figure 8.2).

Figure 8.2

Use these column options to set up categorizing.

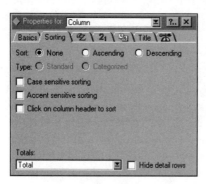

2. Pull down the list box labeled Totals (see below) and select the option Total.

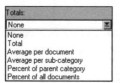

Now let's look at a view that displays categories (see the illustration at the top of the next page). Here, the subtotal for each category is displayed, as well as the grand total for all documents. Again, you select the Total option for the categorized column. (Categorizing is described later in this chapter.)

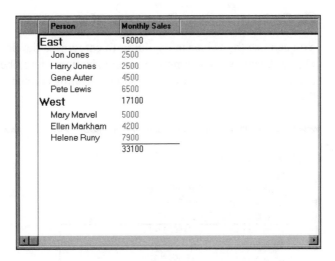

You can create a view that displays totals for a column, but suppresses its details, as shown below.

To accomplish this type of column display, select the option Hide Detail Rows on the Sorting page of the Column InfoBox.

Besides totals, you can also display several other statistical quantities—most of which are best used with categorized information. To select the type of calculation that you want for a column, pull down the Totals list on the Sorting page of the Column InfoBox and then make your choice.

■ Categorizing Documents

You can use the values in a column to categorize the documents in a view; Figure 8.3 shows an example of categorization. Here, the values in the first column are sorted but are also used as headings under which documents are listed.

Figure 8.3

Figure 8.3

Categorizing can help to clarify the contents of a view.

Name	Phone #	
Baseball		
Clark Kent	(415) 555-2346	
Norman Albright	(510) 555-1045	
Pete Pan	(510) 555-1234	
Ruth Reiner	(415) 555-1948	
Football		
Alice Adams	(415) 555-4985	
Clark Kent	(415) 555-2346	
Horace Manowitz	(510) 555-6652	
Jane Aster	(818) 555-1239	
Pete Pan	(510) 555-1234	
Ruth Reiner	(415) 555-1948	
Trudy Liverpool	(725) 555-1024	
Tennis		

If a document contains multiple values in a column that's categorized, the document will appear once under each category. For example, in Figure 8.3, Pete Pan is listed under both Baseball and Football.

Here's how to use the values in a column for categorizing a view:

1. Open the view in edit mode.

2. Display the View InfoBox and click on the Sorting InfoBox tab.

3. Select a sorting option: either Ascending or Descending.

4. Select the option Categorized. Note that this option is available only if you select either Sort Ascending or Sort Descending.

5. Be sure to *deselect* the option Click On Column Header To Sort. If you select this option, column categorizing will not work properly.

TIP. *If you select a column for categorizing a view, position that column near the leftmost end of the view. Otherwise, the appearance of the view will probably be confusing to users.*

You can categorize the documents in a view on the basis of one, two, or several columns. For example, suppose that your documents contained the fields City and State. You could categorize the documents first on the values in the State column and then, secondarily, by city within each state.

Be sure to position the columns in the order in which you want the categorization to take place. Here's why: When categorizing a view, Notes searches from left to right, using the first categorized column it finds, and then the next one, and so on.

Example: Categorizing by State and City

One common way in which documents are sorted is by city, state, or both. Using categorization can help the appearance of views displaying this type of information.

By State Only

Suppose that you have a group of documents containing the fields State and City, and you want to display the documents sorted in order by state.

To begin, create a new view and set up columns for displaying whatever document information you wish. Set up the leftmost column to display the values of the State field, using the following formula:

```
State
```

Also, select the Sort Ascending option for this column.
The new view will appear something like the following:

State	Name	Phone	City
AZ	Jane Aster	(818) 555-1239	Phoenix
AZ	Laura Haskins	(510) 555-2098	Tucson
CA	Alan Brewer	(510) 555-0923	Berkeley
CA	Alice Adams	(415) 555-4985	Oakland
CA	Clark Kent	(415) 555-2346	San Ramon
CA	Louise Young	(510) 555-1204	South San Franci
CA	Noel Abercrombie	(510) 555-4991	Albany
CA	Norman Albright	(510) 555-1045	San Francisco
CA	Pete Pan	(510) 555-1234	Oakland
CA	Ruth Reiner	(415) 555-1948	San Francisco
OR	Horace Manowitz	(510) 555-6652	Portland
OR	Mary Lewis	(510) 555-4567	Portland
OR	Trudy Liverpool	(725) 555-1024	Eugene

Although the documents are sorted in ascending order, the format of the view leaves something to be desired, because each state value is listed more than once. Categorizing the column will take care of this deficiency: Select the Categorized option on the InfoBox. The view will then take on the appearance shown in Figure 8.4.

Figure 8.4

The values in the first column are categorized.

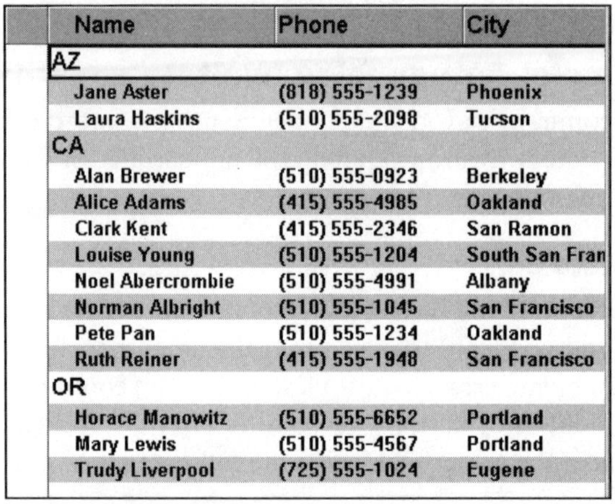

Name	Phone	City
AZ		
Jane Aster	(818) 555-1239	Phoenix
Laura Haskins	(510) 555-2098	Tucson
CA		
Alan Brewer	(510) 555-0923	Berkeley
Alice Adams	(415) 555-4985	Oakland
Clark Kent	(415) 555-2346	San Ramon
Louise Young	(510) 555-1204	South San Fran
Noel Abercrombie	(510) 555-4991	Albany
Norman Albright	(510) 555-1045	San Francisco
Pete Pan	(510) 555-1234	Oakland
Ruth Reiner	(415) 555-1948	San Francisco
OR		
Horace Manowitz	(510) 555-6652	Portland
Mary Lewis	(510) 555-4567	Portland
Trudy Liverpool	(725) 555-1024	Eugene

As you can see, this display is much superior to the previous one: Each state is set off by itself, with the appropriate documents listed underneath it. Note the following enhancements that we have made to this view:

- A somewhat larger font is used for the state values.

- The title of the first column has been deleted. You don't really need it now, because the values are self-evident. (Also, the name of the view appears in the title bar, and this name is usually pretty descriptive.) As a side benefit, you can reduce this column width to 1, leaving more room for other columns. In addition, this small width positions the values in the second column to be partially beneath the state values—an aesthetically pleasing effect.

TIP. *When you categorize the first column and assign it a width of 1, Notes automatically indents the values of the second column, as shown in Figure 8.4. If you want to indent these values even more, choose a larger width for the categorized column.*

By State and City

Let's expand on the previous example and change the view so that the documents are categorized first by state and then, within each state, by city. Here's how to accomplish this, starting with the view shown in Figure 8.4:

Note. For details about moving columns, see Chapter 7.

- Move the City column so that it's just to the right of the State column.

- Assign the Categorized option to the City column.

- Remove the title from the column.

- Reduce the column width to 1.

- Increase the font size of the values, and underline them to stand out a bit.

  The result is shown below.

	Name	Phone	
AZ			
Phoenix			
	Jane Aster	(818) 555-1239	
Tucson			
	Laura Haskins	(510) 555-2098	
CA			
Albany			
	Noel Abercrombie	(510) 555-4991	
Berkeley			
	Alan Brewer	(510) 555-0923	
Oakland			
	Alice Adams	(415) 555-4985	
	Pete Pan	(510) 555-1234	
San Francisco			
	Norman Albright	(510) 555-1045	
	Ruth Reiner	(415) 555-1948	
San Ramon			

Indicators for Collapsed and Expanded Categories

Notes provides several methods by which users can collapse categories displayed in a view. (When a category is fully collapsed, the category itself is displayed, but all of its child categories and documents are hidden from view.)

You can set up a view so that it displays a special marker—called a _twistie_—next to each category. This marker has two purposes. First, you can click the marker next to a category either to collapse or expand that category. Second, each marker indicates whether a category is either collapsed or expanded. For instance, in the illustration that follows, a twistie marker is displayed next to each category; and the one next to the category CA indicates that it's collapsed; that is, there are rows belonging to this category that are hidden from view (compare the twistie with the others in this illustration).

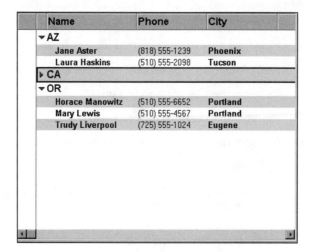

Here's how to attach a group of twisties to a column that displays categories:

1. Make sure the view is open in edit mode.

2. Select the column to which you want to attach twisties. This column must be set up as categorized; otherwise, no twisties will appear.

3. Display the Column InfoBox and then click the tab labeled Basics.

4. Select the option Show Twistie When Row Is Expandable.

TIP. *You can also use twisties to indicate that a main document has one or more response documents. See "Displaying Response Documents," later in this chapter.*

Example: Categorizing by Date

Another common type of view categorizing is by date. This could be either creation date, date of last update, or some other set of dates contained in a field that you include in your documents. The creation date and the date of last update are particularly useful—so much so that Notes provides internal fields for those values in every document.

You can easily sort a set of documents based on the date values in a field: Design the first column in the view so that it displays those field values and then assign either ascending or descending sorting to that column. (Use the Sort tab on the Column InfoBox to display the sorting options.)

Although you can categorize on a set of date values in a field, the resulting view is not particularly appealing, because every different date value will generate a separate category, and you'll wind up with almost as many categories as documents.

However, with a little ingenuity you can categorize a group of documents by year and month. Figure 8.5 shows an example of this type of categorizing. To create this type of view, you need to design formulas that pull out the year and month for each date value and then categorize on those individual values. This is a bit complicated, because it requires three separate columns whose values are based on the original values in a date field.

Figure 8.5

A set of documents categorized by year and by month.

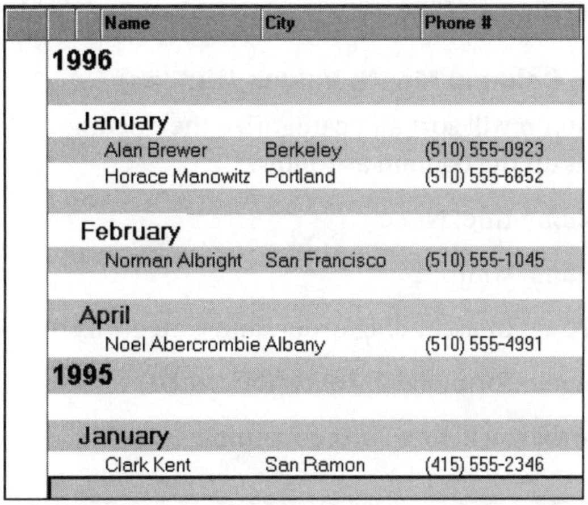

Name	City	Phone #
1996		
January		
Alan Brewer	Berkeley	(510) 555-0923
Horace Manowitz	Portland	(510) 555-6652
February		
Norman Albright	San Francisco	(510) 555-1045
April		
Noel Abercrombie	Albany	(510) 555-4991
1995		
January		
Clark Kent	San Ramon	(415) 555-2346

As an example, let's suppose that your database contains a group of documents, and you want to set up a view to display and categorize the documents according to the dates on which they were created.

To begin, here is a list of built-in Notes functions that we can use to help build the view:

- @Created. Returns the date and time on which a document was created.

- @Year(*Date-value*). Extracts the year from the value *Date-value* and returns it as a four-digit number.

- @Month(*Date-value*). Extracts the month value from *Date-value* and returns it as a number between 1 and 12.

- @Select(*Position, Val1, Val2, Val3…*). If the value of *Position* is 1, then the function returns *Val1*; If *Position* is 2, then the function returns *Val2*; and so on.

Using the preceding formulas, you can set up a view to categorize documents both by year and month. The next sections describe the steps for carrying this out.

First Column: Year Values

Create the leftmost column to categorize the year values, as follows:

- Column title: None

- Column width: 1

- Sorting: In descending order, and Categorized

- Column formula: @Year(@Created)

The year values (1994, 1995, and so on) will be displayed as the categories.

Second Column: Month Values (Hidden)

This column will sort and categorize the documents by month—within each year. Set up the column as follows:

- Column title: None

- Column width: 1

- Sorting: In ascending order, and Categorized

- Column formula: @Month(@Created)

  The view will now look something like this:

You may have noticed that the preceding view is a bit hard to read, because the months—although listed in ascending order—are listed by their numbers instead of their names. This is necessary in order to have the months arranged chronologically. However, what we really want to see is month *names*, not numbers.

We can arrange this as follows: First, make the values of this column *hidden*, by selecting the Hide Column option on the Basics page of the Column InfoBox. Then use the instructions in the following section to create still another column to display the month values.

Third Column: Month Names

Set up the third column to have the following attributes:

- Column title: None.

- Column width: 1.

- Sorting: In either ascending or descending order, and Categorized. The sorting option doesn't matter here—as long as you select one. (If you don't, then you won't be able to select the Categorized option.)

- Column formula: @Select(@Month(@Created);"January"; "February"); "March"; "April"; "May"; "June"; "July"; "August"; "September"; "October"; "November"; "December").

This column is actually a little tricky to understand. Because of the way in which Notes sorts and categorizes, there's a one-to-one correspondence between the values in this column and those in the second column. For instance, consider the entries under 1996: For the month January, the second column displays (hidden) the sorted value 1. Then, the third column displays (visibly) the value January. Because there's only one entry in the third column for each entry in the second one, your choice of either ascending or descending sort is immaterial.

Categorizing Documents from within Views

You can set up Notes to categorize a set of documents based on the values in *any* field. However, Notes provides a bonus if you add a field named Categories to your forms. Then, when a user displays the documents in a view, he or she can change the values in this field *directly from the view*, by making a simple menu selection. This procedure is significantly faster than opening individual documents.

To see how this works, suppose that you maintain a group of personnel documents. The underlying form includes the field Categories, which contains the interests of each person. You can create a view that sorts and categorizes these documents, based on the values in the Categories field, similar to the one shown in Figure 8.3.

Suppose that you want to make changes to the Categories field for several people. Instead of opening each document to make the changes, you can do it directly from the view:

1. Click on a document that you want to modify.

2. Select Actions, Categorize, displaying the dialog box shown in Figure 8.6.

3. Select the new categories that you want from the list, deselect entries previously selected, and add new entries at the bottom. Your selections become the new values for the Categories field. These changes are immediately made in the database, so that other users instantly have access to your updates.

Figure 8.6

You can categorize documents directly from a view.

Here are some points to note about using this categorizing feature:

- You can set up the Categories field to be any type, but either the text or the keywords type is probably the most generally useful.

- If appropriate, set up the field to hold multiple values.

- Using the Actions, Categorize command, you can always add new items to the current list—even if you set up the Categories field as the keyword type but did not select the option Allow Values Not In List. On the other hand, if you open a document for editing and display the keyword list from there, you will not be able to add new values to the keyword list.

- You can use the Actions, Categorize command from any view that displays the documents containing the Categories field—even if that view that does not display a column for the values in the Categories field.

■ Displaying Response Documents

One of the most useful features of Notes views is the ability to display document hierarchies. In order to understand this feature, let's review the three basic types of documents you can create:

- *Main document.* If a database contains document hierarchies, the top of each hierarchy must be a main document.

- *Response document.* A response document is one that's created in direct response to a main document. For example, if you send a memo to someone, he or she could send you a reply in a response document. To create a response document, a user first clicks on the document being responded to and then creates the new document. Notes recognizes and stores the parent-child relationship between the two documents. Then, when you create the appropriate view, that relationship can be displayed.

- *Response-to-response document.* This is a document that's written as a response to a response document.

NOTE. *When you design a form, you select which type of documents are to be created with the form—either main documents, responses, or responses to responses.*

You can design a view that displays the document hierarchy: Each response to a main document is indented by three spaces. Each response to a response is indented another three spaces, and so on.

Figure 8.7 shows a view containing one level of document hierarchy. For example, there are two response documents listed under Laura Haskins.

Figure 8.7

This view displays document hierarchies.

Name	Phone #	City
Alan Brewer	(510) 555-0923	Berkeley
Alice Adams	(415) 555-4985	Oakland
Going on leave for 6 mo., starting in July		
Clark Kent	(415) 555-2346	San Ramon
Horace Manowitz	(510) 555-6652	Portland
Jane Aster	(818) 555-1239	Phoenix
Laura Haskins	(510) 555-2098	Tucson
Named Employee-of-the-month		
Taking vacation all of July		
Louise Young	(510) 555-1204	South San Francisc
Mary Lewis	(510) 555-4567	Portland
Needs to take maternity leave in August		
Noel Abercrombie	(510) 555-4991	Albany
Norman Albright	(510) 555-1045	San Francisco
Pete Pan	(510) 555-1234	Oakland

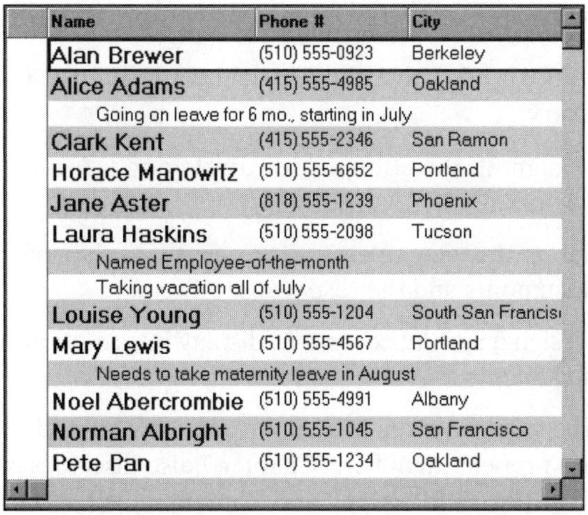

Example: An Employees Database

There are many ways in which you can create databases containing main documents and their responses. As a simple example, we describe the database for which the view in Figure 8.7 displays information.

This database contains two types of document:

- Main documents containing information about your employees; these documents are created by using a form called People.

- Documents containing notes that you keep about your employees. These documents are created by using a form called Comments, and each of them is created as a response to one of the main documents. In other words, to create a comment about a particular person, you first click on the main document for that person and then create the new comment document.

The following two lists show the fields for each of the forms.

Fields for the People form:

- Name
- City
- State
- Phone

Fields for the Comments form:

- Person
- Body
- From
- CreateDate

In order to create the view shown in Figure 8.7, several steps are necessary:

1. Design all the columns for displaying information from the main documents.

2. Set up the view selection formula to display information from both main documents and the responses to them.

3. Design a special column to display information only from the response documents.

The steps involved in creating a new view are described in Chapter 7, so we won't repeat them here. Chapter 7 also discusses how to design a new column. The details for steps 2 and 3 are discussed in the following sections.

Setting Up the View Selection Formula

To set up a view to display both the main documents and their responses, you must write a special view selection formula. There are a number of possible formulas, but here's the easiest one:

```
SELECT  (Form = "People") | @AllChildren
```

The term (Form = "People") indicates that only documents created with the form named People will be displayed as main documents. The term " | @AllChildren " has the following meaning: "display all the children documents for each main document that's displayed."

Notice that @AllChildren does not name a particular form for the response documents. Notes will display all response documents—regardless of the form used to create them.

Creating the Column for Response Document Information

In order to display information from response documents, you must use a special column—which you create with an option called Show Responses Only. In this example, it is the leftmost column in the view. The design of this column is summarized in the following illustration:

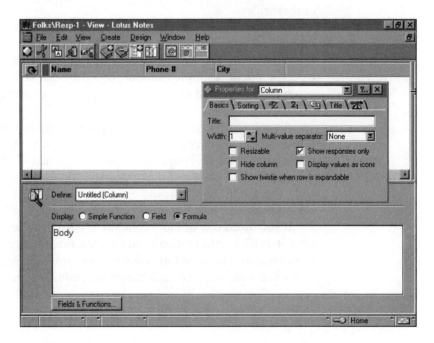

Here are some important points to note about this column design:

- *The Show Responses Only option.* Selecting this option sets up the column to display information only for response documents. This is the only column that displays information for response documents.

- *The Width option.* You can set the width to be 1—the smallest value allowed.

- *Column formula.* This formula displays the value of the Body field for each response document. (Note that instead of using Body in a formula, we could just as easily have selected the Field option and then selected Body from the field list.)

Because of the formula, this column will display only the contents of the Body field in response documents. (In a later example, we show how to expand on this simple column definition.)

Rules about Responses-Only Columns

Notes uses a special set of rules when handling a responses-only column. At first, those rules may seem somewhat arbitrary, but you'll get used to them after designing a few views that display hierarchies. Following is a summary of these rules.

Only one responses-only column can exist in a view; this column is designated by selecting the option Show Responses Only. The contents of this column are dictated by your selection in the Design pane: either the name of a field, a simple function, or a formula. The contents of this column are indented by three spaces under the corresponding main documents.

All columns *to the right* of the responses-only column display information only from main documents. For example, the view in Figure 8.7 displays information from the Name, Phone, and City fields—but only from the main documents. That is, even if the response documents contain the fields Name and City, those values will not be displayed—provided that the corresponding columns are placed to the right of the responses-only column.

If you insert one or more columns *to the left* of the responses-only column, it displays information from both the main and response documents. If these columns display information for the response documents, that information will not be indented underneath the main document.

Watching Column Positions

Because of Notes's rules for handling responses-only columns, you need to be very selective about inserting columns to the left of the responses-only column. You would do this, for example, when you wanted to categorize the information in a view: In this case, you insert the categorizing column(s) at the far left of the view.

You may also want to insert other special types of columns to the left of the responses-only column. For example, you can set up a column to display a special symbol when a row is expandable (that is, the document in that row has responses that are not currently displayed in the view).

Adding Other Information to a Responses-Only Column

In the prior example, the column displaying response-document information showed only the value of the Body field. However, a column can display more than just the contents of a single field. As an example, let's modify the design in the previous example so that the view displays the following:

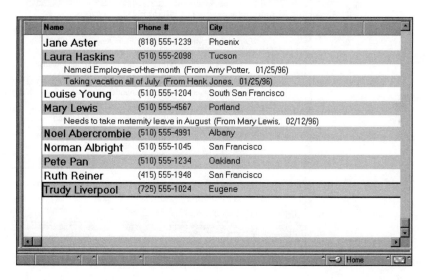

Here, the response-document rows display not only the contents of the Body field, but also the name of the author and the date on which the document was created.

To include this information, you must change the formula for the responses-only column to be the following:

```
Body + "  (From " + From + ",    " + CreateDate + ")"
```

Now, in addition to the contents of the Body field, the values of the fields From and CreateDate will be included, as well as some descriptive text.

Displaying Indicators for Documents Having Responses

If a database contains a large number of main documents, and if many of them also have several response documents, views that display this information can become quite unwieldy. To help deal with this potential problem, users can collapse a main document so that its responses are hidden.

To streamline the process of hiding and displaying response documents, you can assign a twistie marker to each main document having responses (see the example below). By clicking on the marker for a document, a user can hide or display the document's response documents. Also, the orientation of a twistie indicates whether or not a document's responses are hidden. This feature becomes more important when responses themselves can have responses.

Here's how to assign a twistie to main documents having responses:

1. Make sure that the view is open in edit mode.

2. Select the column to which you want to attach twisties. You can use any column you wish, but the most convenient one is usually the leftmost, because the twisties will be most visible there.

3. Display the Column InfoBox and then click the tab labeled Basics.

4. Select the option Show Twistie When Row Is Expandable.

TIP. *If a view displays documents having three or more levels of hierarchy (because responses may themselves have responses), you can assign the option Show Twistie When Row Is Expandable to the responses-only column. Then, a twistie will appear next to each response document that has its own responses.*

In addition to displaying twisties, you can also append a value to each column value for a main document, indicating the number of its response documents. Here's an example:

Name	Phone #	City
Alan Brewer	(510) 555-0923	Berkeley
Alice Adams(1)	(415) 555-4985	Oakland
Going on leave for 6 mo., starting in July		
Clark Kent	(415) 555-2346	San Ramon
Horace Manowitz	(510) 555-6652	Portland
Jane Aster	(818) 555-1239	Phoenix
Laura Haskins(2)	(510) 555-2098	Tucson
Named Employee-of-the-month		
Taking vacation all of July		
Louise Young	(510) 555-1204	South San Francisco
Mary Lewis(1)	(510) 555-4567	Portland
Needs to take maternity leave in August		
Noel Abercrombie	(510) 555-4991	Albany
Norman Albright	(510) 555-1045	San Francisco

Notice that numbers are attached only to main documents having responses. To include these numbers, use the following formula for the Name column:

```
LastName + @DocChildren(""; "(%)")
```

Here, LastName is the name of the field, and @DocChildren returns the number of immediate responses to each document. The first argument of @DocChildren indicates what to return if there are no response documents: Here, the null value ("") is returned. The second argument indicates what to return if a document has responses: The value here is (%): where the actual number for each document replaces the percent sign. Using these two different arguments is a handy way to call attention only to those documents that have responses.

TIP. *The function @DocChildren includes only* immediate *response documents—not responses to responses. If you want to display the* total *number of descendants of a document, use @DocDescendants instead of @DocChildren.*

You can also use the @DocChildren or @DocDescendants functions in a responses-only column to indicate the number of their children or descendants: Append the appropriate function to the end of the column formula, in a manner similar to that in the formula just shown.

■ Automating Views and Folders

An *action* is something that you create as a shortcut tool for users. Each action is attached either to one of Notes' built-in simple operations that you select, to a formula or script that you write, or to any combination of the two.

After creating a new action, you can make it available to users for point-and-click operation in two ways: as an action button on the action bar, or as an option in the Actions menu. The Action bar appears at the top of the view or folder, and the Actions menu automatically appears whenever you open a view or folder.

To perform an action, a user either clicks the appropriate action button or selects the corresponding option on the Actions menu. Here's an example of a view displaying an Action bar:

Action bar

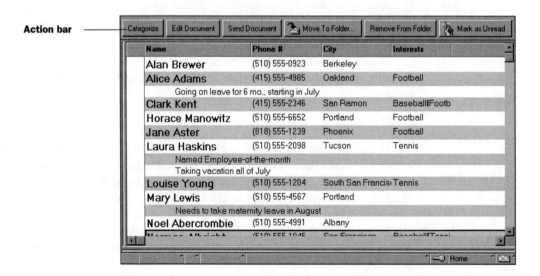

Because of the power of formulas and scripts, you can incorporate just about any collection of Notes operations into an action. Here are a few simple examples of the types of operations that you can make available to users via action buttons and the Actions menu:

- Delete a document

- Copy a document to a folder

- Mark a document as either read or unread

- Open a document in either edit mode or read mode

- Modify a specific field value of a selected document

- Change the value of a particular field in every document displayed in a view or folder

- Switch to another view or folder

Most actions either operate at the view (or folder) level or are specific to a particular document selected by a user. However, you can also use actions to affect every document in a view or folder.

Each action is specific to the view or folder in which you create it, but you can easily copy and paste an action from one view or folder to another. You can even copy and paste actions from folders to views and vice versa.

Displaying the Available Actions

To begin designing an action for a view or folder, you must first open that view or folder in edit mode. Then you can display the list of available actions:

1. Display the main display for the database, and make sure that the default navigator is displayed.

2. Pull down the list in the lower part of the navigator and then click on Views or Folders.

3. In the View pane, double-click on the name of the view or folder that you want to work with.

4. When the view appears in edit mode, display the list of available actions; to do this, select View, Action Pane.

Figure 8.8 shows how the Action pane appears in the right side of the window, listing the actions currently available.

Figure 8.8

The Action pane lists the
actions available for the
current view or folder.

Action pane ————

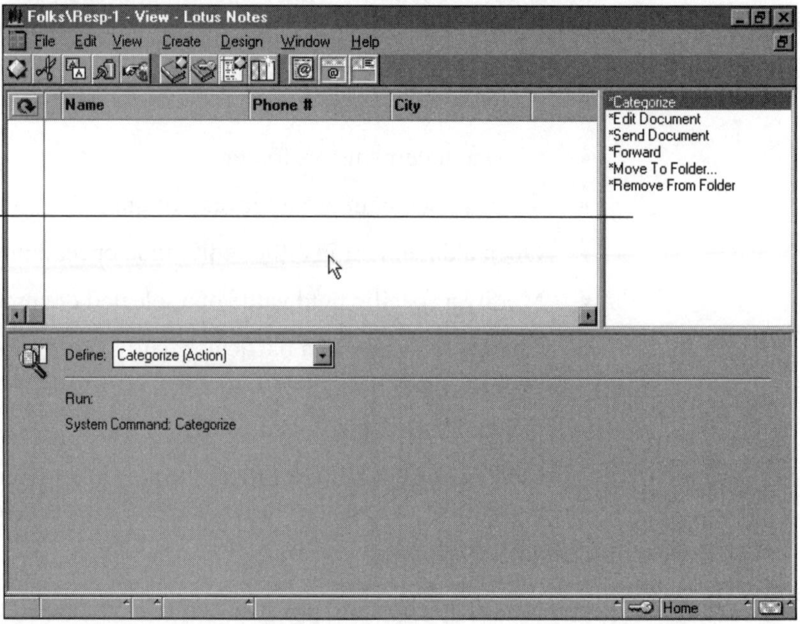

Using Notes's Built-In Actions

The Action pane (see Figure 8.8) displays the names of the actions available to
the current view or folder. The actions are preceded by an asterisk are automatically supplied by Notes to every new view and folder.

You can make any of the listed actions available to users as follows:

1. Double-click on the action that you want to make available, displaying
   the Actions InfoBox.

2. Make sure that the Basics InfoBox tab is selected.

3. Using the two options near the bottom of the InfoBox page, select
   where you want the action to appear: on the action bar, on the Actions
   menu, or both.

4. If you chose to display the action in the action bar, pull down the list of available icons and select the one that you want to associate with this action.

5. Unless you chose not to display the action in either the Actions menu or
   the action bar, choose the physical position of the action in the bar and/
   or menu.

Creating a New Action

When you create a new action, you can attach it either to one of Notes's built-in operations (which Notes unfortunately calls *actions*) or to a formula or script that you write.

To create a new action, select Create, Action, and you'll see the following (refer also to Figure 8.9):

- The Action InfoBox appears with the title (Untitled).

- A new action appears in the Action pane, called (Untitled).

- The edit box labeled Define—at the top of the Design pane—displays (Untitled) (Action), indicating that you're currently defining a new action, which is as yet untitled.

Figure 8.9

Use the bottom part of the window to define a new action.

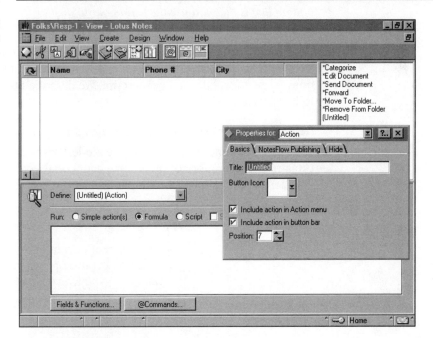

Customizing the Action

Using the Action InfoBox, you can assign a unique name to the action. And you can select whether the action is to appear on the action bar, the Actions menu, or on both:

1. Make sure that the Action InfoBox is displayed and that the Basics tab is selected, as shown in Figure 8.9.

2. Type in a descriptive name for the action.

3. Using the lower two options, select where you want to the action to appear: on the action bar, on the Actions menu, or both.

4. If you chose to display the action in the action bar, pull down the list of available icons and select the one that you want to associate with this action.

5. Unless you chose not to display the action in either the Actions menu or the action bar, choose the physical position of the action in the bar and/or menu.

NOTE. *If you try to fit too many actions on the action bar, the ones at the far right just won't be visible—with no warning from Notes. You can't improve things by reducing the size of the type displayed in the buttons, because you have no control over that size. The only variables that you can adjust are the number of buttons you want to display and the lengths of their titles. The bottom line is that you use the action bar to display the most commonly used actions.*

From here, you must design the exact operations that you want to attach to the action. You can either select one or more of Notes' built-in simple actions, write a formula, or write a script. We describe these possibilities in the following sections.

Attaching an Action to Built-In Notes Operations

Notes's set of built-in actions offers a modest array of routine tasks, and you can attach one or more of them to an action that you're creating.

Here's partial list of the simple actions you can use:

Simple Notes Action	Operation
Copy to Database	Copy the current document to the selected database (when you select this option, you must also select the database to which you want copy documents).
Delete from Database	Delete the current document from the database.
Mark Document Read	Mark the current document as read (remember that each document in a view is marked as either read or unread).
Modify Field	Change the value of the selected field to the specified value (when you select this option, you must select the field to be changed and also the new value).

Simple Notes Action	Operation
Run Agent	Run the specified agent (which you must also specify when you select this option).
Send Document	Mail the current document to the person listed in the SendTo field.
Remove from folder	Remove the current document from the specified folder.

NOTE. *Notes uses an unfortunate choice of terminology that can be extremely confusing: The term* simple action *refers to one of Notes' list of operations. On the other hand, an* action *is something that you create as part of a view or folder. You attach each action you create to either a formula, a script, or one or more simple Notes actions.*

To attach one or more simple Notes actions to an action that you're creating, follow these steps:

1. Click the radio button labeled Simple Action in the design pane.

2. Click the button Add Action, displaying the dialog box shown below.

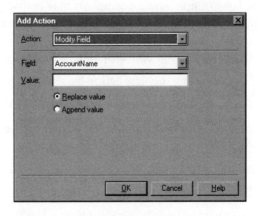

Note. For details about selecting a simple Notes action, see "Attaching a Simple Notes Action to an Action," in Chapter 5.

3. Select the operation that you want to attach to the action you're creating and then click OK to exit.

4. To attach other simple actions, repeat steps 2–3.

The action(s) that you select will appear in the Design pane, something like that shown below.

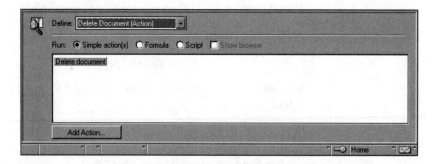

TIP. *The term* simple action *belies hidden power: One of Notes's so-called simple actions (see the preceding table) allows you to attach an existing agent to an action you're creating. The power comes from the fact that an agent can be either a formula or script, either of which can perform massive processing of the documents displayed in a view.*

Example: Marking Documents as Unread   Suppose you would like to be able to mark certain important documents as unread—even if you've read them. For example, some documents may be particularly significant, and you would like to keep them marked as unread so that you'll have a reminder of their importance.

Here's how to set up a new action to accomplish this:

1. Begin creating the new action by selecting Create, Action.

2. Assign the action a name, something like "Mark As Unread."

3. Assign the options to place the action on the action bar and/or the Actions menu.

4. In the Design pane, click the button labeled Simple Action.

5. Click the button Add Action, displaying the Add Action dialog box.

6. Display the top pull-down list box, select the option Mark Document Unread, and then click OK.

That's all there is to it. Whenever the view or folder is displayed, the new action will appear on the action bar and/or the Actions menu. Then, to mark a document as unread, click on it and then click the appropriate action button or menu option.

Writing a Formula or Script

When creating a new action, you can attach it to either a formula or script that you write: You click the appropriate radio button in the Design pane and then write the formula or script.

Here's how to assign a formula or script to an action that you're creating:

1. Begin creating the new action, as described earlier.

2. Make sure that the Design pane is displayed.

3. To assign the action to a formula, select the Formula radio button; or to assign a script, select Script.

4. In the Design pane, write the formula or script.

Later, whenever a user selects the action from the action bar or Action menu, Notes will run the corresponding formula or script.

Example: Opening Documents in Edit Mode   Suppose you want to create an action that will make it as simple as possible for a user to open a selected document in edit mode. To accomplish this, you'll need to create a new action, place it on the action bar, and write a simple formula. Here are the details:

1. Create a new action and assign it a descriptive label—something like "Edit Document."

2. Select the option on the Action InfoBox that will display this action on the action bar.

3. In the Design pane, click the radio button labeled Formula.

4. Type in the following formula in the Design pane:

```
@Command([EditDocument])
```

This formula, when executed, will open the document that's currently selected in the view and switch to edit mode.

Example: Processing all the Documents in a View   Most actions you create will operate only on the document that's currently selected by a user. However, by being a little sneaky, you can create an action that will process every document displayed either in the current view or in the entire database.

The trick consists of two parts: First, you can create an agent that processes all of the documents either in a view or in the entire database. Second, you create a new action and attach it to the "simple action" that runs the agent that you created. The result is an action that can process either all the documents displayed in a view, or all the documents in the entire database.

As an example, suppose that you would like to create an action that would perform the following convenient clean-up chore on the documents in one of your favorite views: rewrite the contents of the FullName field, making sure that the field values are correctly capitalized. Here's a brief outline of the steps to follow:

Note. For details about creating agents, see Chapter 10.

To begin, you create an agent to process all of the documents in a view. (Agents are usually not view-specific; they process the documents in whatever view happens to be displayed when the agent runs.) Assign the agent a meaningful name; let's say, FixUpNames.

As part of defining the agent, you specify the following options:

- The agent selects all the documents in the current view (that is, whatever view happens to be open when the agent runs).

- The agent runs manually from the Actions menu.

- For every document, the agent rewrites the value of the FullName field, so that its capitalization is correct (see the sample formula following this list).

5. Create a new action and then assign it a name, something like Clean Up Names. Assign options to display this action either on the action bar, the Actions menu, or both.

6. Select the option Run Simple Action and then click the button Add Action.

7. When the Add Action dialog box appears, select the action Run Agent and then choose the agent name FixUpNames.

Here's a formula that will work in the preceding agent, provided that names are originally entered in the format *{firstname lastname}*:

```
First := @Left(LastName; " ");
Last := @Right(LastName; " ");
NumFirst := @Length(First) - 1;
NumLast := @Length(Last) - 1;
FirstFirst := @UpperCase(@Left(First; 1));
RestFirst := @LowerCase(@Right(First; NumFirst));
FirstLast := @UpperCase(@Left(Last; 1));
RestLast := @LowerCase(@Right(Last; NumLast));
NewFirst := FirstFirst + RestFirst;
NewLast := FirstLast + RestLast;
@@SetField("LastName"; NewLast + ", " + NewFirst) ;
SELECT @All
```

In a more realistic situation, life wouldn't be so neat, and the formula would be much more complicated: It would need to figure out the format for the value in each document and then reformat accordingly.

TIP. *An action that operates on a large group of documents can be a potential weapon, because depending on the agent that's attached, a user can wipe out a lot of information. In fact, the scope of an agent is not necessarily limited to a particular view; it can be the entire database! Be very careful about the agents you make available to users—especially if those users have Editor access to the database.*

Hiding an Action

You can set up an action so that it is selectively hidden from the view or folder in which it is defined. To accomplish this, you write a formula that specifies the conditions under which the action is to be hidden.

Here's an outline of the steps involved:

1. Display the view or folder in edit mode.

2. Display the Action pane, showing the list of actions defined for this view or folder.

3. Select the action that you want to customize.

4. Display the View InfoBox and then click the tab labeled Hide, as follows:

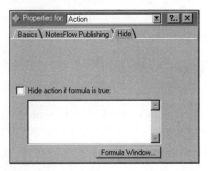

5. Select the option Hide Action If Formula Is True.

6. Click the button labeled Formula Window and then type in the formula. (See the following warning.)

WARNING! *In some Notes versions, there's a bug that prevents you from using the expanded formula window, which appears when you click the button Formula Window. You can tell if there's a problem, because the expanded window does not display an OK or Done button. If this is the case for your system, you can use either of two methods for writing a formula:*

- *Use the teeny window displayed on the Hide page of the InfoBox.*

- *Use any convenient text editor to write the formula, then copy and paste the formula into the InfoBox window. This is actually quite convenient if you have a text editor at your disposal, and it's worth the few extra steps in order to enjoy the convenience of using a full-size edit window.*

The formula that you write can be as long as you wish, but its final result must evaluate to True or False. If the result is True, then the action will be hidden; otherwise, it will not.

As an example, suppose that you have created a very convenient action, but that action is potentially dangerous if used by a careless person. You know of such a person, whose name is "John Smith," and you would like to hide the action whenever that person is logged on.

Here's a simple formula to accomplish this:

```
@If(@Name([CN]; @UserName) = "John Smith"; True; False)
```

If this formula returns the value True—because the user is John Smith—then the action will be hidden. Otherwise, the action will not be hidden.

■ Copying and Deleting Actions

When you create an action, it is defined only for the current view or folder. However, if you design a particularly useful action, you can copy it to other views or folders—even in different databases. You can also delete an action that's outlived its usefulness.

Copying an Action

To copy an action from one view or folder to another, follow these steps:

1. Select the view or folder containing the action that you want to copy; open that view or folder in edit mode.

2. Display the Action pane, by selecting View, Action Pane.

3. Click on the name of the action that you want to copy.

4. Copy the action to the Clipboard, by selecting Edit, Copy.

5. Now switch to the view or folder where you want to copy the action—either in the current database or another one.

6. Open the view or folder in edit mode.

7. Display the Action pane, by selecting View, Action Pane.

8. Paste the action into this view or folder, by selecting Edit, Paste.

The copy that you make will be identical to the original one: name, options, and so on. You can make whatever changes are needed. Your changes are confined to the new copy; the original remains untouched.

Deleting an Action

You can easily remove an action from a view or folder. Display that view or folder in edit mode, display the Action pane, highlight the action, and then either press Del or select Edit, Cut. Using Edit, Cut gives you a little bit of protection, in case you suddenly realize that you deleted the wrong action.

WARNING! *If you use the Del key to remove an action, it's irreversible. That is, you can't then use Edit, Undo to reverse your deletion.*

You can prevent tragedies from occurring by getting into the habit of always saving old actions. For instance, you can create a little database called Old Actions, create a simple view for it, and cut and paste all your old and unwanted actions to that view—just in case you someday decide that you would like to use that action in a new application.

■ Customizing the Action Bar

When you create one or more actions for a view or folder, you can optionally display some or all of those actions on the action bar. To a very limited extent, you can customize the appearance of this bar: You can select the background color of the bar, and you can draw a divider line beneath the action buttons. You can also select the style, length, and color of this line—although it usually winds up being fairly unobtrusive, no matter what you do to it.

Here's how to customize the action bar for a view or folder:

1. Open the view or folder in edit mode.

2. Display the action pane, by selecting View, Action Pane.

3. Click on any action in the pane.

4. Display the InfoBox (double-clicking on an action is a handy shortcut).

5. Pull down the list at the top of the InfoBox and then choose Action Bar, displaying the following options:

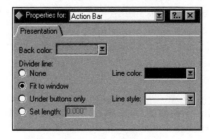

6. Make your customizing selections.

■ Views for Special Purposes

Some views are not designed to be seen by users. Instead, they are used for various internal purposes—particularly as part of an automated application. For instance, you can create a formula that pulls a specific value from a view, inserting that value into a field. In this example, the sole purpose of the view is to furnish values to the formula.

Using a View to Auto-Fill Forms

In some situations, you can use a view to help automate the process of filling in forms. To illustrate the process we'll go through an entire example.

Suppose that you maintain a database of documents containing basic personnel information. This database is called BasicData, and it resides on the server named Server1. Each document in this database contains the following information:

- Name
- ID number
- Phone number
- E-mail
- Fax
- Street
- City
- State
- Zip

Now, suppose that you also routinely fill in time-sheet information for the people in BasicData, using forms like the one shown in Figure 8.10.

Since most of the information on the time-sheet form is already stored in the BasicData database, you can automate filling in these forms. Here's how: When a user begins filling in a new form, the first data item that he or she enters is the employee's identification number. Then, using that number, Notes searches the BasicData database for the corresponding employee document and copies the relevant information into the new time-sheet form.

Here's how to accomplish this automation: First, you create the view called FindData, shown in Figure 8.11. This view, which accesses the information in the BasicData database, is used strictly for table-lookup, which we'll see shortly.

Figure 8.10

You can use a special
view to automate filling
out these forms.

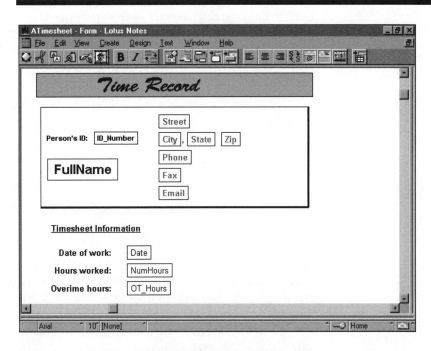

Figure 8.11

Use this view for
supplying automatic fill-in
information to new forms.

Next, you build the time-sheet form; for each field that you want Notes to fill in automatically, you write an appropriate formula. For instance, here's the formula for the Street field in the time-sheet form:

```
@If(ID_Number=""; ""; @DbLookup("";"Server1":"BasicData";
"FindData"; ID_Number; 3))
```

Here's a quick outline of what this formula accomplishes:

1. Notes searches the FindData view for the document whose ID value is ID_Number (this is the value entered by the user for the new time-sheet form).

2. When Notes finds the document, it reads the value in the Street field.

3. Notes copies that value back to the Street field in the new time-sheet form.

Now let's dissect the preceding formula, piece by piece.

The @If() function controls the entire calculation: If the current value of the field ID_Number is undefined ("")—because the user has not yet entered a value for this field—then @If() returns the value "" for the Street. However, if the user has input a value for the ID_Number field, then the @If function will return the value calculated by the DbLookup function.

The following table summarizes the meaning of each of the arguments within the @DbLookup function.

Argument	Meaning
""	Indicates the type of database being searched. A value of "" indicates a Notes database.
"Server1"	The name of the server containing the database being looked up.
"BasicData"	The name of the database being looked up.
"FindData"	The name of the view being searched within the specified database.
ID_Number	The value that's used to search the specified view. In this example, it's the value of the field named ID_Number.
3	The position number in the specified view of the column containing the value to be returned by the DbLookup function. In this example, column 3 contains Street values.

To help clarify the preceding discussion, let's go through the entire process, assuming that a user starts to create a new time-sheet document and begins by entering the value 5 for the ID_Number field. Notes then does a table lookup in the FindData view (within the BasicData database on the Server1 server) *in the first sorted column*, looking for the value 5. When it finds a document having that value, it reads the value in the third column and then copies that value to the Street field in the time-sheet document being created.

The DbLookup function is quite complex, and the preceding description has only scratched the surface of everything that you need to understand about it. Here is additional information about building the preceding application, which you may find useful:

- When creating the time-sheet form, select the option (on the Form InfoBox) Automatically Refresh Fields. This will ensure that whenever a user enters a value for the ID_Number field and then clicks on another field, Notes will recalculate the entire document, so that all the fill-in information is immediately displayed.

- When creating the FindData view, you must assign a Sorting option—either ascending or descending—to the column displaying the ID_Number values. Furthermore, that column must be the leftmost sorted column in the view. There can, however, be unsorted fields to the left of this column—although there's usually no reason for this.

- When entering a column number in the DbLookup function, you count from the left in the FindData view, assigning a value of 1 to the sorted column, and then count to the right. However, do not include in the count any columns that display only a constant value. For instance, if the formula for a column is "1," skip this column in the count.

- When counting columns, do not include any columns whose formula consists entirely of one of the following functions: @DocChildren, @Doc-Descendants, @DocLevel, @DocNumber, @DocParentNumber, @Doc-Siblings, @IsCategory, or @IsExpandable.

- If more than one document displayed in the FindData view has the identification number that Notes is looking for, the Street values for all of those documents are returned as a list (that is, the values are separated by colons).

PART

2

Advanced Application Development Features

- *Creating a Navigator*
- *Creating Navigator Objects*
- *Attaching an Action to an Object in a Navigator*
- *Working with Navigators*
- *Assigning the Default Database Navigator*

9

Designing Navigators

NOTES 4.0 INCLUDES A NEW FEATURE CALLED A *NAVIGATOR*, whose purpose is to simplify a user's work by presenting one or more menus. These menus help users find their way through different views and documents with a minimum of effort. Navigators also provide mouse-sensitive objects that act as buttons for performing common database operations.

The heart of each navigator is a group of mouse-sensitive objects, each of which is attached to a particular operation. When a user clicks on one of these objects, Notes performs the corresponding operation.

As an example, Figure 9.1 illustrates a relatively straightforward navigator. Each of the objects—except the top one—is mouse-sensitive; when a user clicks on an object, Notes displays the corresponding view.

Figure 9.1

This navigator helps users select different Notes views.

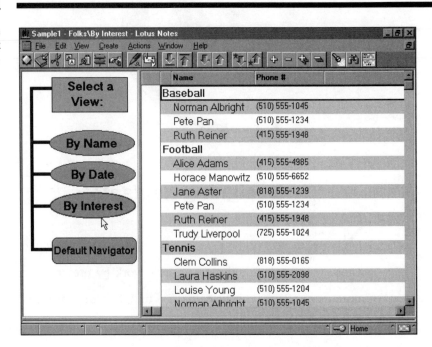

Each mouse-sensitive object in a navigator performs one of the following operations:

- Switches to particular view.

- Simulates the behavior of a particular folder: A user can click and drag documents to this object, and the documents then become part of the corresponding folder. A user can also click on this navigator object to open the corresponding folder.

- Displays another navigator.

- Switches to the document, view, or database that's linked to the navigator object.

- Runs the formula or script that's attached to the navigator object.

These options provide a powerful set of tools, which you can use to design a wide variety of user-friendly front ends. For example, the navigator in Figure 9.1 helps users to quickly and painlessly select a view.

You can create any number of navigators for a single database. You can also customize the database so that whenever it's opened, a particular navigator will be displayed. This can be extremely handy if you want a group of navigators to be the main tools by which users maneuver through the views and folders of a database. Each navigator is designed within a particular database and belongs exclusively to that database. However, you can easily copy-and-paste a navigator from one database to another.

Because you can use a mouse-sensitive object in one navigator to call another, you can design a group of navigators to act as a complete menu system for users. For example, you could set up a database so that each time a user opens it, the navigator shown in Figure 9.2 appears. Each item in this menu is attached to another navigator, and eventually some of these navigators lead the user to choose different database views.

Figure 9.2

This navigator acts as a menu.

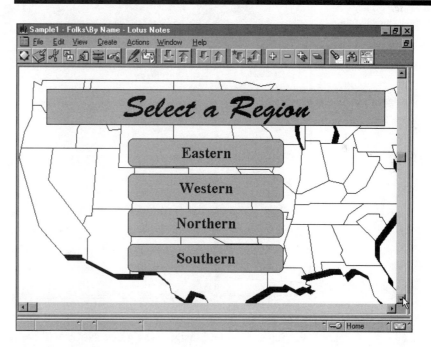

Each navigator you create is displayed in the Navigator pane. You can create a navigator so that it occupies the standard space reserved for the Navigator pane, as shown in Figure 9.1. Or you can customize a navigator so that it opens to include the entire window, as shown in Figure 9.2.

Notes provides a set of tools for drawing simple, mouse-sensitive objects, such as rectangles and ellipses. However, you can also import graphic objects from outside sources, such as drawing programs and clip art collections. This capability opens up a world of possibilities for creating attractive and easy-to-use navigators.

■ Creating a Navigator

To begin, you create a new, empty navigator. Next, you assign it various properties, such as name, background color, and so on. Finally, you add various design and mouse-sensitive objects to the navigator. To begin, follow these steps:

1. Display the default navigator for the database: Switch to the main database display and then select View, Design. The Navigator pane should then resemble that shown in Figure 9.3.

Figure 9.3

This window displays the default navigator for a database.

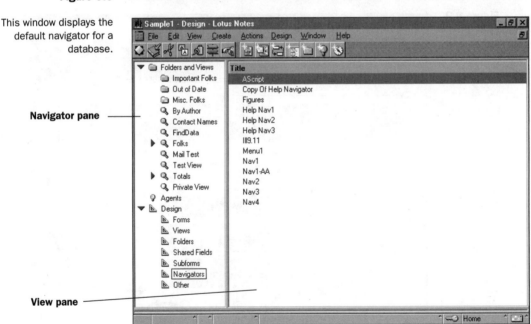

Navigator pane

View pane

2. Select Create, Design, Navigator. Notes will create a new navigator and display it in edit mode (see Figure 9.4), and you're ready to begin designing it.

Figure 9.4

Use this window to make
changes to a navigator.

Add objects to
this pane

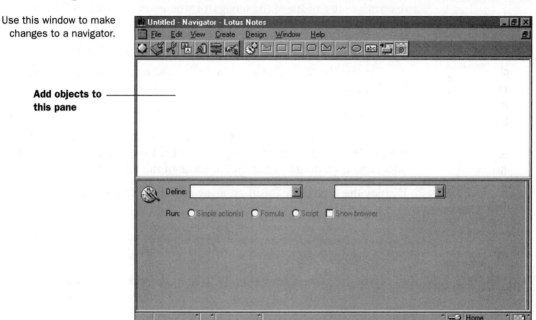

After creating a new, empty navigator, you can fill it with objects. These
can be either those you create by using the navigator's drawing tools, or objects that you paste into the navigator from other sources.

Customizing a Navigator's Properties

When designing a new navigator, you can customize it in the following ways:

- *Name*. You must assign a name to each navigator. Notes lets you assign
  duplicate names to two navigators in the same database, but this is a
  great way to create confusion. Make sure that each navigator has a name
  that's unique to this database.

- *Background color*. This is the color that will appear in the background of
  the navigator.

- *Initial view or folder*. This is the most important option you assign to a
  navigator, because it's the name of the view or folder that will be displayed in the View pane whenever this navigator is displayed in the Navigator pane. Note that if you're designing a navigator that will occupy the
  entire window width, your selection here is probably irrelevant, because
  the view or folder that you select won't be visible.

- *Setting the initial size of the Navigator pane.* You can set an option that determines the width of the navigator whenever it's opened. The two choices are

  - Do not change the current width of the navigator window.

  - Expand the navigator window so that the entire navigator width is displayed.

Here's how to set the options for a navigator:

1. Open the navigator in edit mode: Switch to the main database display; select View, Design; select Navigators in the lower part of the Navigator pane; and then double-click on the name of the navigator.

2. Display the Navigator InfoBox, using any of the following:

   - Select Design, Navigator Properties.

   - Right-button-click anywhere in the upper pane and then select Navigator Properties.

   - If the InfoBox is displayed, pull down the top list box and select Navigator.

3. Make sure that the Basics tab is selected (see below) and then select the options you want.

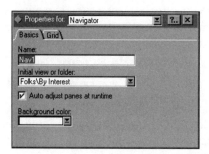

TIP. *If you select the option Auto Adjust Panes At Runtime, then whenever this navigator is opened (displayed in the Navigator pane), Notes will automatically expand the Navigator pane so that all the objects in the navigator are visible. Otherwise, whenever the navigator is opened, the width of the Navigator pane remains unchanged.*

■ Creating Navigator Objects

To add objects to a navigator, you must open it in edit mode, as described earlier. Referring to Figure 9.3, the top pane of this window is where you add new objects and modify or delete existing ones. This pane represents all of the available area for the navigator, and you can place objects anywhere within this space.

TIP. *When you're working out the placement of the various objects, you can maximize the design area by temporarily closing the bottom pane—the Design pane. To accomplish this, select View, then deselect the Design Pane option. Later, when you're ready to assign actions to the various objects, you can reselect this option to display the Design pane.*

Each navigator consists of one or more of the following items:

- Mouse-sensitive graphic objects

- Graphic objects for aesthetic enhancement

- Text labels for instructions and for identifying graphic objects

- A background graphic over which the other types of objects are distributed

When creating graphic objects, you can use three different types of sources: objects that you create with the built-in drawing tools, objects that you cut and paste from other navigators, and graphic images that you import from other software packages.

After inserting a new graphic object (regardless of its source), you can make it mouse-sensitive by attaching it to an *action*. The remainder of this section is devoted to the different ways in which you can create objects. Then you'll find out how to make an object mouse-sensitive (see "Attaching an Action to an Object in a Navigator").

If you do not attach an action to a graphic object, then it becomes simply a static object on the navigator. You would do this, for example, to enhance the appearance of a navigator.

Creating Graphic Objects within Notes

Table 9.1 shows the different types of objects you can create with Notes's built-in drawing tools. To create an object in the right-hand column, you begin by clicking on the corresponding SmartIcon tool in the left-hand column. Figure 9.5 shows an example of each of type of object.

TIP. *If you want an object to display a label that's longer than one line, use a text box. Otherwise, use a rectangle, rounded rectangle, or ellipse.*

To create an object, follow these steps:

1. Be sure that the navigator is open in edit mode.

2. Click on the tool corresponding to the type of object that you want to create.

3. Draw the object (see the following section for details).

Table 9.1

The objects you can create with Notes's built-in tools.

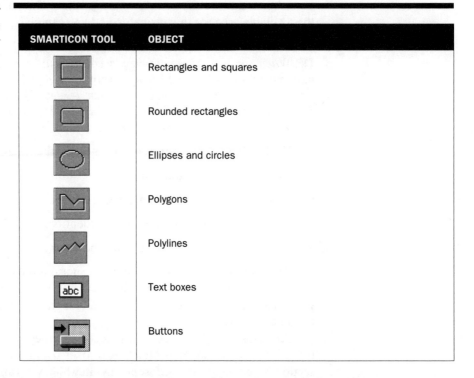

SMARTICON TOOL	OBJECT
	Rectangles and squares
	Rounded rectangles
	Ellipses and circles
	Polygons
	Polylines
	Text boxes
	Buttons

Figure 9.5

The various types of graphic objects you can create within Notes.

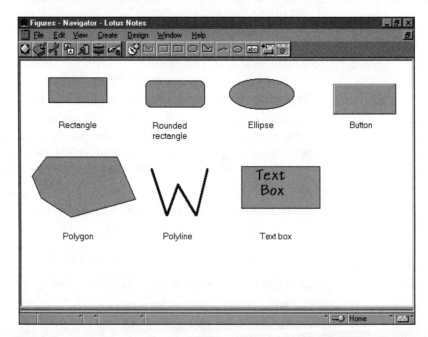

Rectangles, Rounded Rectangles, Ellipses, and Text Boxes

To draw rectangles, rounded rectangles, ellipses or text boxes: Click where you want to begin drawing, hold down the mouse button, drag the mouse to draw the object, and then release the mouse button when the object is the correct size. To draw a square or circle, hold down a Shift key as you draw the object.

Like other objects, a text box is empty until you create a label for it. See the later section "Assigning a Name and Caption" for details.

Polylines and Polygons

Here's how to draw either polylines or polygons:

1. Click on the starting position, hold down the mouse button, and draw the first line.

2. When you've finished the first line, release the mouse button.

3. To draw the next line, repeat steps 1 and 2.

4. When you've drawn the last line, double-click the mouse button.

Customizing a Graphic Object

After creating a new graphic object, you can customize it in various ways, including the following:

- Resize and reposition the object

- Assign a name and a caption to the object

- Select a background color and a border size and color

- Customize the way in which the object is sensitive to the mouse

To begin, display the InfoBox for the object that you want to customize (see Figure 9.6), doing any of the following:

- Double-click on the object

- Right-button-click on the object and then click on Object Properties

- Click on the object, then select Design, Object Properties

Changing Position and Size

To reposition an object, use the mouse to drag it from one position in the navigator to another. To resize an object, grab a handle and drag it in the appropriate direction. Polylines and polygons are special: By dragging one or more of their handles, you can change their basic shapes.

Figure 9.6

Use the InfoBox to
customize objects in
navigators.

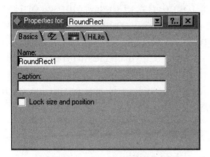

NOTE. *You can't resize a graphic object that you import from another software package.*

After you have sized and positioned an object exactly where you want it, you can prevent later mishaps by selecting the option Lock Size And Position on the Basics page of the InfoBox.

If you reduce the size of an object, part of its caption may disappear. To fix this, you can either enlarge the object or reduce the size of the text (for details about customizing text, see "Caption, Background, and Line Size and Color").

Using the Grid

Each navigator is equipped with an array of horizontal and vertical lines called the *grid*. You can't see this grid, but you can adjust its line spacing, and you can either activate or deactivate it. By default, the grid is inactive.

When you activate the grid for a navigator, each object that you create or resize will "snap to" the nearest grid line or intersection. This feature helps you to accurately size and position objects.

Here's how to activate and size the grid for the navigator that you're designing:

1. Display the Navigator InfoBox, using any of the following steps:

    • Select Design, Navigator Properties.

    • Right-click on any part of the design window and then select Navigator Properties.

    • If the InfoBox is already displayed, pull down the top list box and select Navigator.

2. Select the InfoBox tab labeled Grid, displaying the following options:

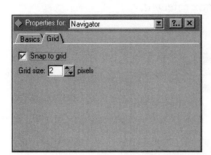

3. To turn on the grid, select the option Snap To Grid.

4. Select the grid spacing that you want, using any value between 1 and 16. These numbers are relative, so you'll need to experiment to find the value you find most comfortable to work with.

Assigning a Name and Caption

When you create a new object, Notes automatically assigns it a unique, generic name, such as RoundRect1, Ellipse2, and so on. If you wish, you can change this name. You can also assign a caption to an object; the caption appears across the object's face. To make either or both of these changes, click on the object and then enter the name and caption onto the Basics page of the InfoBox. Here are a few details to observe about captions:

- The caption that you enter will appear on the face of the object. For any object other than a text box, the caption will be centered.

- The caption must be short enough to fit in a single line within the object—except for text boxes, which can have multiple lines.

- A caption will automatically wrap around, within a text box. However, you can force a line break by using the Enter key.

- To center a line of text within a text box, you'll have to type in spaces.

- You can't assign a caption to a polyline or to an object that you import from another software package.

Caption, Background, and Line Size and Color

You can customize the caption of an object by adjusting its font, size, attributes, and color: Click the Fonts tab of the InfoBox (see below) and then make your selections. If you want your choices to apply to future objects of the same type that you create, click the bottom button, labeled Make Default

For Shapes or Make Default For TextBoxes depending on whether you have a shape or a text box selected.

You can assign a custom color to the background of an object, and you can also assign a width and color to the enclosing line. (In the case of a polyline, there is no background color.) To assign these features, display the Lines And Colors InfoBox tab (see below) and then make your selections.

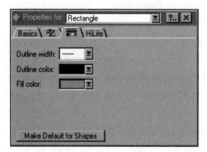

If you want your selections to apply to future objects of the same type that you create, click the bottom button labeled Make Default For Shapes or Make Default For TextBoxes depending on whether you've selected a shape or a text box.

Highlighting Options

Each object that you create is sensitive to the mouse: When a user clicks on the object, Notes will run the attached action.

You can customize a mouse-sensitive object so that it becomes highlighted under either or both of the following circumstances:

- When a user points the mouse at the object
- When a user clicks on the object

Using the first option is handy, because it alerts the user to the fact that he or she is pointing at a sensitive area on the navigator. On the other hand, using the second option is useful when the navigator will remain visible after the user clicks on it, because the highlighting serves as a reminder of which option has been most recently selected.

You can customize the nature of the highlighting for an object by choosing special colors for the object's background and outline.

To set up an object so that it will be highlighted either when pointed at or clicked on, display the InfoBox page labeled HiLite (see below) and then make your selections. Note that you can't select separate colors and line widths for the two highlighting options.

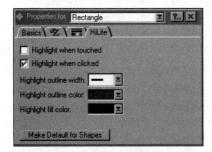

Working with Overlapping Objects

As part of a navigator design, you can overlap two or more objects to create special effects. For instance, you could combine a square and a circle to form a complex shape, as shown below.

When two or more objects overlap, you can select which parts of the various objects are hidden and which are visible, thereby creating different visual effects.

To move one of a stack of overlapping objects—either to the top or the bottom of the stack—click on that object, pull down the Design menu, and then select either Send To Back or Bring To Front.

Copying Objects from Other Navigators

If another navigator—in either the current database or another one—contains an object that you would like to use in the navigator you're building, you can copy and paste the object:

1. Switch to design mode for the navigator containing the object that you want to copy.

2. Click on the object and then select Edit, Copy.

3. Switch back to the navigator that you're designing and then select Edit, Paste.

After pasting the new object, you can modify it in any way you wish, using the methods described earlier.

Creating Text Labels

You can improve the appearance and usefulness of a navigator by including identifying labels for the various mouse-sensitive objects—unless, of course, they already display their own captions. For instance, if you paste in a graphic object created somewhere else, it may not be self-identifying. In this case, a label may be essential. You can use a label as general-information text for a navigator.

NOTE. *You can set up a text box in either of two ways: If you assign an action to the text box (see the later section "Attaching an Action to an Object in a Navigator" for details), it becomes a mouse-sensitive object. Otherwise, the text box remains simply an ordinary label.*

To create a label, you use a text box as follows:

1. Create the text box: Click the Text Box SmartIcon and then draw the box approximately where you want it.

2. Display the InfoBox for the label and then click the Basics tab.

3. In the edit box labeled Caption, type in the text. You can create multiple lines by using the Enter key.

4. Display the Fonts page of the InfoBox and then select the font, size, attributes, and color for the text.

5. Display the HiLite page of the InfoBox and then deselect both highlight options, if necessary.

6. *Do not* assign an action to this text box. It's just a label, right?

   If you want the label to be enclosed in a box go on with steps 7 and 8.

7. Select the Lines And Colors tab (third from the left).

8. Select an outline color and a fill color to match that of the background. These choices will allow the text to stand out naturally against the background, without displaying its enclosing box.

Importing Objects and Backgrounds

The objects you can create with Notes's drawing tools are limited to rectangles, circles, and whatever you're clever enough to dream up for polygons and polylines. However, if you have access either to a drawing package or a clip art collection, you can import graphic images that you either create or access. You can then assign an action to that object, just as you can to objects that you create with the built-in drawing tools. If you do not assign an action, the object remains as a decoration on the navigator.

Importing a Graphic Object

Note. Notes refers to this type of object as a *graphic button.*

Here's how to import a graphic object into a navigator:

1. If you're using a drawing program, create your masterpiece using any tools you wish.

2. If you're using a clip art collection, find the picture that you want to use.

3. Copy the finished image to your system Clipboard.

4. Return to the navigator that you're building.

5. Select either Edit, Paste or Create, Graphic Button. The object will then appear in the upper-left corner of the navigator.

You can't change the size or the colors of an imported object, but you can change its position by dragging with the mouse. You can also assign either of the highlighting options described earlier.

NOTE. *If you're using Windows, you can import objects in only one of two formats: either bitmapped or Windows Metafile. If you try other formats, such as TIFF, either the paste process won't work at all or the colors may not be reproduced properly.*

Importing a Graphic Background

A graphic background is different from a graphic object: The background is not mouse-sensitive, and you can't resize or reposition it within the navigator. In fact, a graphic background is just that: a background for the navigator, on top of which you draw all the other objects. You can obtain the graphic from any convenient source, such as a drawing program or a clip art file.

A navigator can have only one graphic background. When you paste a background into the navigator, its upper-left corner is placed at the upper-left corner of the navigator.

When creating a background in another software package, you must size it within that software to be as large as you want it to be for the navigator. You may need to do a bit of trial-and-error work before getting the size just right.

Here's an outline of the steps for inserting a graphic background into a navigator:

1. Using either a drawing program or a clip art collection, obtain the graphic image that you want.

2. Copy the finished image to your system Clipboard.

3. Return to the navigator that you're building.

4. Select Create, Graphic Background. The image will be inserted in the upper-left corner of the navigator.

5. If the background image is either too large or too small, return to the originating software, resize the image, and then repeat steps 2–4.

If you want to replace the existing background with another one, repeat steps 1–5 above. When you paste in a new background image, it automatically replaces the original.

To delete the current graphic background without replacing it with another one, select Design, Remove Graphic Background.

Creating Hotspots

A *hotspot* is a transparent object that you create within a navigator, and to which you attach a Notes action—making the hotspot mouse-sensitive. However, unlike the other types of mouse-sensitive objects, you use a hotspot not by itself, but in connection with other navigator objects that are not mouse-sensitive. For instance, typically you position a hotspot directly over a graphic image, a text label, or a combination of two or more of them. As an example, suppose that you import a little graphic image and then attach a label to it, as shown below:

 How do I...?

Now let's suppose that you want to make the entire area—both the graphic image and its label—into a single, mouse-sensitive object that's attached to a Notes action. The way to accomplish this is to insert a transparent hotspot directly over both the image and its label and then attach that hotspot to the Notes action. Remember: The hotspot is transparent so that users can see the underlying graphic and label.

You can create hotspots in two different shapes: rectangles and polygons. The former is quite easy to create, while the latter offers a high degree of flexibility in creating hotspots to cover weird shapes.

Here's how to create a hotspot:

1. Click on either of the two corresponding SmartIcons:

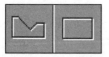

2. Draw the rectangle or polygon where you want it.

3. Reposition and resize the hotspot as needed—usually, to cover one or more other objects. (You may not be able to completely cover an object that has a complex curved shape, but you can usually come pretty close with a polygon hotspot.)

4. Select the highlight options for the hotspot and assign the highlight color (remember that these options are just that—optional): Display the Info-Box for the new hotspot, click the tab labeled HiLite, and then make your selections.

5. Assign an action to the hotspot (see "Attaching an Action to an Object in a Navigator" for details).

Example: The Notes Help Database

The Notes help database provides an excellent example of a set of navigators that use hotspot rectangles. To see how these work, select Help, Help Topics. When the first help window appears, the Navigator pane displays one of the custom navigators for this database. (The Notes help system consists of a single Notes database.)

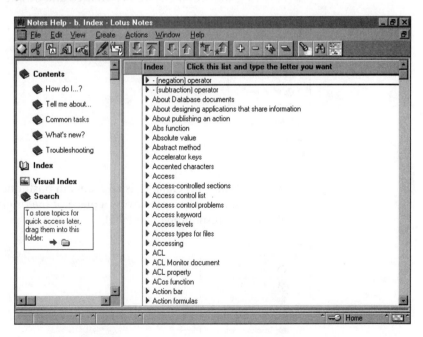

If you move the mouse cursor over each item listed under Contents in the Navigator pane, you'll see the different hotspots become highlighted. If you then click on one of those hotspots, Notes will run the associated action (most actions display different navigators and views).

Here's an outline of how the navigator shown in the preceding illustration is constructed:

1. To begin, the graphic image shown below is created with a drawing program and then pasted into the new navigator. This image is *not* assigned to a Notes action.

2. Next, a group of text labels are created and positioned as shown below:

3. A set of hotspot rectangles is created and positioned as shown below. Notice that each hotspot covers a piece of the original graphic image and also the corresponding text label.

4. Finally, each hotspot is attached to a different Notes action.

Design Tips

Here are a few ideas to bear in mind as you design a new navigator.

Keep the layout as clean as possible. If the navigator appears cluttered because of the number of objects on it, consider breaking up the navigator into two different ones—a menu and submenu situation.

For really attractive navigator designs, you'll probably want to use a decent drawing program to create the various graphic objects. Otherwise, you'll be limited to the few simple shapes that you can draw with the Notes drawing tools.

To create a label for a graphic object, use a text-box object, but do not attach an action to it, so that when a user clicks on the text nothing will happen.

Part of the planning process for a new navigator is to decide on its width. For instance, you may want a navigator to occupy only part of the total window. You would do this if you wanted users to be able to see both the navigator and the View pane at the same time, as shown in Figure 9.1. In this case, you must plan ahead when designing a navigator by using only the left-hand part of the upper pane for positioning objects. Notes doesn't provide a mechanism—such as a ruler—for helping you to limit the right-hand boundary of a navigator, so you may need to do a little experimenting in order to get the width the way you want it. On the other hand, if you want the navigator to occupy the entire window when it's displayed for a user, as shown in Figure 9.2, then you can use the entire pane-width for placing objects.

If you select the navigator option Auto Adjust Panes At Runtime, then whenever the navigator is opened, Notes will automatically expand the Navigator pane to display all the objects in the navigator. If you want to add a little extra space along the right-hand edge for appearance, insert a small, invisible object as far to the right as you want the Navigator pane to expand. You can make the object invisible by matching its background and outline colors to that of the navigator's own background color. Also, don't assign an action to this object.

■ Attaching an Action to an Object in a Navigator

Each navigator contains one or more mouse-sensitive objects, each of which is attached to an *action*; when a user clicks on one of these objects, Notes performs the associated action.

You can assign an action to the following types of mouse-sensitive objects in a navigator:

•   Graphic objects that you create with the built-in Notes drawing tools

- Graphic Objects that you paste from other applications
- Hotspot rectangles and hotspot polygons

Each action that you assign to a mouse-sensitive object can perform one of the following types of operations:

- Switch to another navigator
- Open another view
- Alias a folder
- Jump to a linked object—either a document, view, or another database
- Run a formula or script that you create

The ability to switch to another navigator is quite powerful, because you can create a set of integrated navigators that appear to the user as a set of menus. On the other hand, the ability to attach formulas and scripts offers a wealth of possibilities, because you can write formulas and scripts to perform just about any series of operations within Notes that you can dream up.

Here's how to attach an action to a mouse-sensitive object in the navigator:

1. Make sure that the Design pane is displayed, as shown in Figure 9.4 (the bottom half); if it isn't, select View, Design Pane, or click on the View Show/Hide Design Pane SmartIcon.

2. Click once on the object to which you want to assign an action.

3. In the Design pane, select the radio button corresponding to the type of action that you want to use: Simple Action, Formula, or Script.

4. Create the action (see the following section for details about each type of action).

Creating the Actions

After selecting the type of action you want to assign to a mouse-sensitive object in a navigator, you must then specify the details of the action. These details depend on the type of action that you have selected.

Attaching to a Simple Action

Notes provides a limited number of choices for simple actions. Each action can open another navigator or view, alias a folder, or open a link. To select the action that you want to use, pull down the list labeled Action; in the

Design pane (see below), select the type of action that you want; and then fill in the details, as described in the following sections.

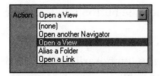

Open Another Navigator   When you select the option Open Another Navigator for the current action, you must then also select the name of the navigator that you want to be displayed whenever the action is executed. Your choice is limited to the navigators in the current database. (If you want to use a navigator in another database, you'll have to paste it into the current one before you can select it.)

Open A View   When you select the option Open A View for the current action, you must then select the name of the view that you want to be displayed in the View pane when the current action is executed. The view that you select must exist within the current database. Notice that unlike the previous option (above), the navigator is not replaced with another one.

Alias A Folder   When you select the option Alias A Folder for the current action, you must also select the name of a folder in the current database that you want to use. The attached mouse-sensitive area then behaves exactly as though it were the folder you selected: Users can drag documents into this object, and users can display the folder by clicking on the object. Again, the navigator is not replaced with another one.

Open A Link   Use the Open A Link option to create a link between the selected mouse-sensitive object and one of the following:

- Another database

- A view, either in the current database or another one

- A document, either in the current database or another one

After selecting the Open A Link option, your next steps depend on what you want to link to, as described next.

To link to a database:

1. Temporarily switch to your Notes workspace.

2. Click on the icon for the database for which you want to establish the link.

3. Select Edit, Copy As Link, Database Link.

4. Return to navigator that you're building.

5. In the Design pane, click the button labeled Paste Link.

   To link to a view:

1. Use the Window menu to temporarily switch to the main display of the database containing the view.

2. Select View, Design, if necessary.

3. Display the view by selecting it in the upper part of the Navigator pane.

4. Select Edit, Copy As Link, View Link.

5. Return to the navigator that you're building.

6. In the Design pane, click the button labeled Paste Link.

   To link to a particular document:

1. Temporarily switch to the main display of the database containing the document.

2. Select View, Design, if necessary.

3. Select a view that includes the document and then click once on that document.

4. Select Edit, Copy As Link, Document Link.

5. Return to the navigator that you're building.

6. In the Design pane, click the button labeled Paste Link.

Attaching to a Formula or Script

Attaching a mouse-sensitive object to a formula or script is a two-step process. First, you select the appropriate option in the Design pane—either Formula or Script. Then you create the formula or script in the Design pane.

As an example, Figure 9.7 shows a simple formula that opens another database. Note that *opening* a database is different from *linking* to another database.

For a set of complex operations that can't be handled by formulas, you'll need to write a script. As an example, here's a script that will display in turn the name of each database in the Notes data directory on the current computer (that is, the one running the script):

```
Sub Click(Source As Navigator)
    Dim directory As New NotesDbDirectory("")
    Dim db As NotesDatabase
    Set db = directory.GetFirstDatabase (DATABASE)
```

Figure 9.7

This formula will open the
BOOKS.NSF database.

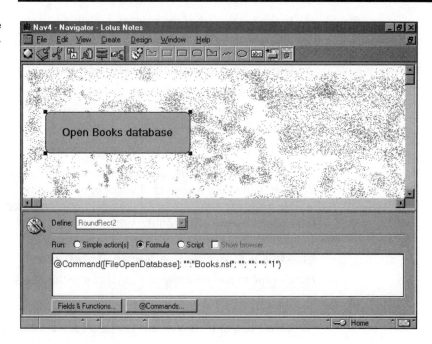

```
      While Not (DB Is Nothing)
            Messagebox db.Title
            Set db = directory.GetNextDatabase()
      Wend
      Messagebox "The End"
End Sub
```

■ Working with Navigators

You can copy a navigator from one database to another. You can also make
a copy of a navigator within a database. This can be extremely handy, for example, if you're creating a series of similar navigators. If a navigator has outlived its usefulness, you can delete it from a database.

Copying a Navigator to Another Database

When creating a new navigator for a database, you can copy one from another
database that contains features you can use. Then, you can modify the copy to
suit your needs. Here's how to copy a navigator from one database to another:

1. Open the main display of the database containing the navigator that you
   want to copy.

2. Make sure that the default navigator is displayed, by selecting View, Design.

3. In the lower part of the navigator, click on Navigators.

4. In the View pane, click on the name of the navigator that you want to copy.

5. Copy the navigator to the Clipboard, by selecting Edit, Copy.

6. Switch to the database where you want to make a copy of the navigator, display its main window, and then display the list of its current navigators in the View pane.

7. Paste a copy of the navigator, by selecting Edit, Paste.

The new copy will be identical to the original one—including its name. You can then make whatever changes you wish to the new copy. The original and the copy are completely independent of each other, so that changes to either one have no effect on the other.

Making a Copy in the Same Database

Here's how to make a copy of a navigator within the same database:

1. Follow steps 1–5 in the previous section.

2. To make a new copy of the navigator, select Edit, Paste.

3. The new copy will have the same name as the original, except for the additional prefix "Copy of." To change the name, and also to make any other modifications, open the navigator in edit mode (by double-clicking on it) and then make your changes.

Deleting a Navigator

Unfortunately, Notes makes it too easy to delete a navigator: Display the list of navigators in the View pane, select the one that you want, and then either press Del or select Edit, Cut.

This is a risky process, because you can't use Edit, Undo to recover your deletion. Unless you're 200 percent sure that you'll never use the navigator again—especially one that represents a lot of design effort—hedge your bets by storing a copy of the navigator somewhere safe. For example, one possibility is to maintain a "junkpile" database for storing old bits and pieces of other databases.

■ Assigning the Default Database Navigator

By default, each time that you open a database, Notes opens the default navigator named Folders. This default navigator is built into Notes, and it displays the names of all your views, folders, forms, and other database components. This navigator is what you see in the main database display when you select either View, Design or View, Show, Folders.

You can select as the default any navigator you create. This is the one that will appear in the Navigator pane whenever the database is opened. This is very handy, for example, if you are creating a set of navigators to use as a series of menus, and you want the main menu (one of the navigators) to appear whenever a user opens the database.

Here's how to assign a default navigator:

1. From wherever you happen to be in the database, display the InfoBox. Usually, you can accomplish this by pulling down the Design menu and then selecting *xxx* Properties, where *xxx* will depend on which window in the database is open.

2. Pull down the top list box in the InfoBox and then select Database. If you can't get the Database InfoBox to appear, click in another part of the database and then try again.

3. Click the InfoBox tab labeled Launch, displaying the following options:

4. Pull down the list box labeled Navigator and then select the navigator that you want as the default for this database.

- *Creating Formulas: An Overview*
- *Using Formulas with SmartIcons*
- *Using Formulas with Buttons and Hotspots*
- *Using Formulas with Actions*
- *Using Formulas with Fields*
- *New Functions in Notes, Release 4*
- *Using Agents*

10

Using Formulas and Agents

To be a successful notes designer you must be able to write formulas, because they exist in every nook and cranny of most database designs. In Notes, formulas come in all sizes. Some consist of a single word, while others may occupy several pages. Because of the basic simplicity of the formula language, the rules for writing formulas are quite simple—much simpler, for example, than the rules for LotusScript. With a little practice, you can learn enough to write simple formulas for various parts of your database designs; with extended practice, you can write much more complicated formulas.

Formulas in Notes 4.0 are backward compatible with those in Notes 3.0. However, Notes 4.0 formulas have many new features. For example, you can insert blanks and blank lines within a formula to improve readability. Also, @Commands now execute in the order in which they appear in formulas—instead of always being executed last. And Notes 4.0 contains a wide assortment of new functions, many of which are described in this chapter.

This chapter focuses on the following topics:

- How to write formulas

- A survey of where formulas can be used

- A partial list of the new formulas in Notes 4.0

- An introduction to writing formula-driven agents

■ Creating Formulas: An Overview

As with many other programming languages, Notes formulas contain the standard assortment of objects: variables, constants, operators, keywords, and built-in functions. Although the exact structure of a formula will depend on its context, the basic rules for creating formulas are always the same.

The Elements of a Formula

Each formula you write consists of one or more *statements*. When a statement is too long to fit on one line, Notes auto-wraps it to the next. A statement always terminates with a semicolon.

When creating a formula, you can insert blank lines and spaces between elements to improve readability. This feature is new to Notes 4.0; earlier releases discarded extra spaces and blank lines.

Each statement in a formula contains a combination of the following components:

- Keywords

- Variables

- Fields

- Constants

- Operators

- Built-in functions

- Comments

Here's a simple example of a formula that contains all of the above components. (For ease of discussion, the lines are numbered; an actual formula does not contain any line numbers:)

```
1. REM "This is a sample formula that outputs a person's full name";
2. TempName := FirstName + " " + LastName;
3. FullName := @ProperCase(TempName);
4. @Prompt([OK]; "The name is "; FullName);
```

NOTE. *Here are detailed descriptions for each of the elements in the preceding formula.*

- *Line 1: This statement consists of a remark, identified as such by the keyword REM. The remark is enclosed in double quotes, and like all other statements, it ends with a semicolon.*

- *Line 2: This statement combines the values of the fields FirstName and LastName and places the result in the variable TempName.*

- *Line 3: Here, the built-in function @ProperCase capitalizes the first letter of each word in TempName and stores the result in the variable FullName.*

- *Line 4: The built-in function @Prompt displays a message box containing the full name.*

Variables

Variables come in two flavors: *temporary variables* and *environment variables.* For simplicity, we refer to temporary variables simply as *variables,* because nearly all variables are temporary, but we use the full term *environment variables* for the other type.

Temporary variables—or *variables*—are locations in memory that contain values. These values exist only for the duration of the formula execution. When the formula ends, the values of those variables are lost. In contrast, an environment variable can also contain a value, but it is stored on the hard disk, so the value can be retained indefinitely.

Each variable has a name and contains either a single value or a list of values. To define a variable, you use the following type of statement:

```
VariableName := Expression;
```

Here, *Expression* can be any valid combination of variables, fields, constants, and operators—all of which combine to produce either a single value or a list of values. Notice that the operator := is used for assignment. The equal sign by itself (=) has another meaning.

Unlike stricter programming languages, value *types* in Notes formulas are handled rather casually—which makes it easier to write the formulas: the type of a variable is determined by the value assigned to it.

Here are a few examples:

```
(1) Price := UnitPrice * Quantity;
(2) Name := "John Q. Inglethorpe"
(3) DateOfPurchase: = [12/25/96]
(4) People := "Jane Austen" : "Lewis Caroll" : "Alice"
```

The type of the variable Price in the preceding line 1 is *numeric*. In line 2, the type of the variable Name is *text*, while in line 3 the type of DateOfPurchase is *time*. In line 4, the type of People is text, because it's assigned the set of values in a list, each of which is text type.

The formula language has one slightly annoying quirk: You can't assign the same variable two different values. For example, this little formula is illegal:

```
FullName := FirstName + " " +LastName;
FullName := @Uppercase(FullName)
```

Variables can take on any of the types allowed for fields: numeric, text, and so on. In addition, a variable can contain a logical (also called *Boolean*) value of either True or False—stored as the text values "1" and "0."

Most variables defined within a formula cease to exist when the formula terminates. However, environment variables, which are stored in the NOTES.INI file (the Notes Preferences file, on the Macintosh), retain their values unless a formula changes them. Usually, environment variables furnish the most convenient method by which different formulas can pass values to each other.

To define an environment variable, you use the keyword ENVIRONMENT. Here's an example:

```
ENVIRONMENT SpecialName := "Nancy Drew";
```

The variable SpecialName will be defined and saved in the NOTES.INI file. Later, another formula can retrieve that value by using the following syntax:

```
Person := @Environment("SpecialName")
```

The function @Environment retrieves the named variable from the NOTES.INI file and assigns the result to the variable named Person.

Variable Names

In creating a variable name, you can use letters, digits, the underscore, and most of the special characters that are not used as operators. However, each variable name must begin with either a letter or underscore character.

For your own convenience, you can capitalize names any way you wish. However, Notes ignores the capitalization. For example, suppose you name a variable MyVariable. When you refer to that variable in a formula, you can use any capitalization you want: Myvariable, MYVARIABLE, and so on.

Fields

Fields play an important part in formulas. A formula can use the values of one or more fields as part of a calculation, and to accomplish this, those values are referenced by their corresponding field names.

If a formula references a field name, that field must exist in the current document; otherwise, a runtime error will occur.

Constants

You can use constants as part of the formulas you write. There are four different types of constants:

- Numeric
- Text
- Time
- List

A *list* constant can contain several values of the same type.

The syntax for writing each type of constant is unique, so that there's no possible ambiguity when inserting constants into formulas. Here are examples of constants in formulas:

```
Value := 125
Name := "Joan  Lakes"
Deadline := [05/15/96 12:00 PM]
Guests := "John" : "Marcia" : "Alice" : "Joseph"
```

In the preceding examples, the types are numeric, text, time, and text list. The following sections describe each of these types.

Numeric Constants

You can write numeric constants in any of several different forms, including with or without decimal points and with or without plus or minus signs. You can also use scientific notation. Here are a few examples:

- 25.0
- +25.0
- –25.0
- 25.123
- 2.5E1
- 0.25
- 2.5E–1
- 1,250

You can also include commas—provided that you put them in the correct positions. For instance, if you type in the value 1,23 Notes will flag it as illegal. (Unfortunately, the error message you see will be something like "An operator or semicolon was expected but none was encountered.")

If you include a sign as part of a constant, make sure that there's no space between it and the rest of the number.

Text Constants

A *text constant* consists of any combination of characters enclosed by double quotes. You can include any character that you can find on your keyboard, including spaces and special characters. However, to include a double quote as part of a text string, you must precede it with a backslash, as follows:

```
"His name, \"Howard Jones\", was clearly phony."
```

Similarly, to include a backslash itself as part of a text constant, type two successive backslashes:

```
"The path is C:\\Myfiles"
```

Here are a couple of examples of how you can use text constants in formulas:

```
TotalAmount := @Text(Amount) + " dollars."
FullName := FirstName + " " LastName
```

In the first example, the built-in function @Text converts the numeric value of Amount (which could be either a field or a variable) to text. This text value is then combined with the text constant " dollars."

In the second example, the text constant " " —which consists of a single space—is inserted between the two values FirstName and LastName.

Time Constants

Time constants can contain either time values, date values, or both. To distinguish these values from other types, you enclose them in square brackets. Here's a set of examples, illustrating the different ways in which you can write time constants:

Constant Value	Interpreted As
5:00 am	5:00 AM
5:00	5:00 AM
5:00 AM	5:00 AM
5:00AM	5:00 AM
3:00 pm	3:00 PM
3:00 PM	3:00 PM
15:00	3:00 PM
3:05:25 am	3:05:25 AM
12/15/96	12/15/96
12/15	12/15/96[*]
12-15-96	12/15/96
12/15/96 3:00 PM	12/15/96 3:00 PM
3:00 PM 12/15/96	12/15/96 3:00 PM

[*] Defaults to the current year when the year is not included as part of the value

When writing time constants, here are a few points to keep in mind:

- You can use an optional space between the time value and "am"" or "pm," but "am" and "pm" must be written without spaces.

- If you use a 24-hour time, do not include either "am" or "pm."

- You can optionally include seconds as part of a time value.

- When writing date values, you can use either slashes or dashes as separators.

- When writing a compound value, you can put the time and date values in either order; but Notes reorders them so that the data is always displayed first.

List Constants

A *list constant* is a set of values, which can be either numbers, text values, or time values. The values in a list must all be the same type.

When writing a list, the values must be separated by colons, as in the following examples:

```
MyList := "Joe" : "Harriet" : "Roger" : "Alicia"
Values := 125 : 350 : 725 : 100
TimesRecorded := [1:15 am] : [2:25 am] : [1:15 pm]
```

In the first example, the variable MyList is assigned the list constant consisting of four text constants. Similarly, in the last example, the variable TimesRecorded is assigned the list of three time values.

Logical Constants

There's no formal type of value called *logical* in the formula language. Nevertheless, logical values are frequently used in formulas. Each logical value is written as a text constant—either "1" (the logical value True) or "0" (the logical value False).

Operators

Operators are the glue that bind together the other parts of formulas. Notes formulas can use a wide variety of operators for different purposes: numeric and text operations, logical comparisons, variable assignments, and list operations.

The following table lists the most commonly used operators, along with the type of information used by each one.

Operator	Operation	Used on Data Types
:=	Assignment	All
+	Addition, string concatenation	Numeric, text
-	Subtraction	Numeric, time
*	Multiplication	Numeric
/	Division	Numeric
=	Is equal to	Numeric, text, time
<	Is less than	Numeric, text, time

Operator	Operation	Used on Data Types
>	Is greater than	Numeric, text, time
<> or != or =!	Is not equal to	Numeric, text, time
<=	Is less than or equal to	Numeric, text, time
:	List concatenation	Numeric, text, time
&	Logical AND	Logical expressions
|	Logical OR	Logical expressions
!	Logical NOT	Logical expressions

Note. *Expressions* are described later on in this chapter.

Except for the first entry in the preceding table, all of the other operators are used for forming various combinations of variables, constants, fields, and functions; these combinations are called *expressions*. For instance, here are a couple of simple expressions:

```
LastName + FirstName
Salary * OvertimeRate
```

Order of Precedence

When evaluating an expression that contains more than one operator, Notes uses a set of internal rules to decide the order in which operations are to be evaluated. These rules are called the *order of precedence*. Following is listed a summary of this precedence order. The operations listed at the top are carried out before any others; then the next line of operations, and so on:

- Multiplication, division
- Addition, subtraction
- Logical comparisons (is equal to, is less than, and so on)
- Logical & (AND), | (OR), and ! (NOT)

    For example, consider the following formula:

```
MVal := 1 + 10*2 -3
```

Using the rules just given, Notes will calculate a result for MVal of 18 (multiplication before addition or subtraction).

Using Parentheses

Rather than depend on memorizing the rules of precedence, you can force Notes to evaluate expressions in the order that you want by using parentheses, because there's one additional precedence rule that comes first: *Anything inside a pair of parentheses is evaluated before anything outside.*

Using the preceding formula as an example, you could write it in two different ways, depending on how you wanted the calculation to be performed:

```
(1) Value := 1 + (10*2) -3      (result = 18)
(2)  Value := (1 + 10)*(2 -3)   (result = -11)
```

TIP. *If you get into the habit of using parentheses, you can forget about the other rules of precedence.*

Expressions

An *expression* is any combination of constants, fields, variables, and functions. Using the various operators, you can create a wide range of different expressions, which fall into the following categories:

- Numeric
- Text
- Time
- Logical
- List

Text and Numeric

Here are a few examples of text expressions:

```
FirstName
FirstName + " " + LastName
@UpperCase(FullName)
```

Numeric expressions can contain any combination of numeric values and operators, with parentheses thrown in when necessary to specify the order of calculations. Here are some examples:

```
UnitPrice*NumberOfItems*DiscountRate
TotalEstateValue/NumberOfDescendants
(GrossIncome-Deductions)*TaxRate
```

Time

There is only one type of simple time expression (not counting the many built-in functions for calculating time values): one value subtracted from another, and the result is expressed in seconds.

For example, consider the following formula:

```
Time1 := [04/10/96];
Time2 := [04/09/96];
```

```
NSeconds := (Time1 - Time2);
NDays := NSeconds/86400
```

The variable NSeconds is calculated as the time difference between Time1 and Time2—in seconds. NDays is then calculated as the difference in days (there are 86,400 seconds in one day).

Logical

In order to describe logical expressions, we must at the same time introduce the built-in function @If, which uses logical expressions. Here's a relatively simple example:

```
Result := @If(Age>=21; "Adult"; "Minor")
```

Here's how this formula works: First, the logical expression Age>=21 is evaluated: If the value of Age is greater than or equal to 21, the value of the expression is True; otherwise, the value is False. If the expression is True, then the function @If returns the value "Adult." If the expression is False, the value "Minor" is returned. The result—either "Adult" or "Minor"—is then assigned to the variable Result.

Here's the general form of the function @If:

```
@If(logical expression; Value1; Value2)
```

If the value of *logical expression* is True, then @If evaluates and returns the value *Value1*; otherwise, @If evaluates and returns the value *Value2*.

In technical terminology, @If uses three *parameters*, which are separated by semicolons. The first parameter, *logical expression*, always contains an expression whose value is either True or False. The other two parameters are the two possible values that @If can return.

Now that you have seen how logical expressions are used, we can describe how to build them. The simplest type of expression involves two values and a single *comparison operator*, which can be any of the following:

Comparison Operator	Meaning
=	Is equal to
<>, !=, =!	Is not equal to
<	Is less than
>	Is greater than
>=	Is less than or equal to
<=	Is greater than or equal to

Here are two examples of logical expressions:

Formula	**Meaning**
@If(SalesPrice<=Maximum; "Bargain";"No bargain")	If the value of SalesPrice is less than the value of Maximum, @If returns the value "Bargain"; otherwise, @If returns the value "No Bargain."
@If(DateOfSale>[06/30/96]; 95; 100)	If the date value in DateOfSale is later than June 30, 1996, @If returns the value 95; otherwise, @If returns the value 100.

You can combine simple logical expressions into more complicated ones by using the following three *logical operators*:

- & (logical AND)

- | (logical OR)

- ! (logical NOT)

Here are a couple of examples:

```
@If((Age>=21) & (Salary<20000); "Bonus"; "No bonus")
@If((LastName="Jones") & (FirstName="Peter"); "Yes"; "No")
```

In both of these examples, the two parts of each logical expression are separated by pairs of parentheses. These parentheses aren't actually needed, but they help to make complex expressions more readable.

Lists

A simple list consists of a group of components separated by semicolons. Here are a few examples:

```
"Alicia" : "Roberto" : "Pierre"
"Alicia" : FirstName : LastName : "Jones"
Salary : Bonus : Royalties
[1/1/97] : [3:15 PM 5/15/96 ] : [EndDate] : [StartDate]
```

The preceding examples illustrate several important points:

- List elements are separated by colons. Spaces next to the colons are optional.

- All the elements in a list must be the same type.

- A list can contain any mixture of constants, variables, and fields— provided they are all the same type.

A *list expression* involves two or more lists and suitable operators. When an expression involves two lists that are separated by an operator, that operator acts on corresponding pairs of values in the lists. When creating expressions involving lists, you can use any operator that could be used on the individual components of the lists.

Here's an example of a formula that involves two numeric lists:

```
List1 := 10 : 20 : 30;
List2 := 5 : 10: 15;
Product := List1 * List2
```

When this formula is executed, the variable Product will have the following value:

```
50 : 200 : 450
```

Keywords

A *keyword* is a reserved word that has a special meaning in formulas. Here are the keywords that you can use:

- REM

- SELECT

- DEFAULT

- FIELD

- ENVIRONMENT

A keyword must always be the first word in a statement.

The keyword REM indicates that the current statement is a remark. The text that follows must be enclosed in double quotes, followed by a semicolon. Here's an example:

```
REM "This is a remark";
```

SELECT is a special word that's used in selection formulas. For details, see "Formulas That Select Groups of Documents," later in this chapter.

The DEFAULT keyword is used to set a default value for a field when that field either has no current value or does not exist in the document. Here's an example:

```
DEFAULT Department := "Not available";
Title := "The current department is " + Department
```

When the second line is evaluated, the current value of the field Department will be used—if it exists. Otherwise, the default value of "Not available" will be used instead.

The FIELD keyword is used to assign a value to a field in a document. If the named field does not exist, Notes creates a field with that name. Here's an example:

```
FIELD Interests := "None"
```

If the field Interests exists in the current document, it is assigned the value "None." Otherwise, a new field named Interests is created for the document, and the value "None" is assigned to it.

The ENVIRONMENT keyword is used for defining environment variables. For a discussion of these types of variables, see the earlier section "Variables."

Types of Formulas

There are four basic types of formulas, each of which has specific uses within Notes:

- Formulas that calculate a single value and assign it to an object
- Formulas that perform a series of operations
- Formulas that select a subset of documents from a database
- Formulas that determine whether or not something occurs

It's important that you be able to recognize the situations in which each type of formula applies, so that you'll write the correct type for each particular circumstance.

Formulas That Return a Value

Some formulas return a value, which is then assigned to the object to which the formula is attached. This type of formula can be as long as needed. However, the very last line in the formula must calculate a single value—but not assign it to a variable. That value is assigned then to the attached object.

Here's a simple example of this type of formula:

```
FirstName := "Tom";
LastName := "Harrison";
FirstName + " " + LastName
```

If you're used to working with a standard programming language, the last line may seem to be incomplete—but it's not. It is simply calculating a value, which is then assigned to whatever object the formula is attached to.

For instance, the preceding example could be the default formula for a personal name field.

The following list gives the most common uses for this type of field. In each case, a formula supplies the final result for the object.

- Default formula for a field

- Field input-translation formula

- Field input-validation formula

- Formula for a computed field

- Column formula

- Window-title formula

- Standard-section-title formula

- Form formula

The following table gives a simple example of each type of formula.

Formula Type	Sample Formula	Meaning
Default-field value	@If(Age<21;"Minor"; "Adult")	Returns a default value for the field to which the formula is attached: either "Minor" or "Adult," depending on the value of the field Age.
Field input-translation formula	@ProperCase(FullName)	Converts the input value of the field to which the formula is attached (FullName) to proper capitalization.
Field input-validation formula	@If(Salary<10000; @Failure("Salary must be greater than $10,000"); @Success)	Will not allow input values for the Salary field to be less than $10,000.
Computed-field value	HourlyRate*NumHours	The value of the attached field is computed as the product of the two field values, HourlyRate and NumHours.

Formula Type	Sample Formula	Meaning
Column formula	LastName + ", " + FirstName	Displays the full name in the column attached to this formula.
Window-title formula	"Payroll information for " + FirstName + " " + LastName	For each document, displays the associated person's name.
Standard-section-title formula	"Information for " + FullName	Displays a custom title—including a person's name—for a standard section.
Form formula	"Special Form"	When documents are opened from the view to which this formula is attached, the form named Special Form will be used to display the documents.

Formulas That Perform a Set of Operations

Some formulas are used for performing specific sets of operations. The formula can be attached to any of the following types of Notes objects:

- SmartIcons
- Agents
- Actions
- Buttons
- Action hotspots

When a formula is attached to one of the above types of objects, you execute the formula by clicking on the object.

The scope of operations for this type of formula depends on the nature of the formula and how it is used; it could either be database-wide, limited to a particular document, or somewhere in between. For example, formulas attached to agents often act on either part or all of a database. On the other hand, a formula attached to a button in a document could change the value of a single field.

Here's an example of this type of formula; when executed, it switches from the current document to a specific view:

```
REM "This formula opens the view named Memos1";
@Command([ViewChange]; "Memos1")
```

The preceding formula could be attached to either a button, an action, an action hotspot, or a SmartIcon.

Formulas That Select Groups of Documents

A *selection formula* chooses a subset of documents from a database. What happens to those documents depends on the context of the formula. For instance, a selection formula in a view determines which documents are displayed in that view.

Here are the different circumstances in which selection formulas are used:

- View selection, to select which documents to display

- Replication selection, to select which documents to replicate

- As part of an agent, to select which documents to act on

A selection formula always involves the keyword SELECT, followed by an expression that specifies which documents are to be selected.

For example, here's a simple view-selection formula that chooses only those documents created by either of two forms:

```
SELECT Form = "Invoice" | Form = "Payroll"
```

Formulas That Specify Conditions

Some formulas determine whether or not something happens. Usually, the end result of each formula is a logical expression—which evaluates either to True or to False.

The following table lists the various circumstances in which these formulas can be used.

Circumstance	Purpose of Formula	Sample Formula
When hiding an object in a layout region or a paragraph in a form.	Determines under which circumstances the paragraph or object will not be displayed in documents.	$Username="Jill Standard": "Joe Jones"

Circumstance	Purpose of Formula	Sample Formula
When hiding an action.	Determines when an action will not be displayed either on the action bar or on the Actions menu.	Department != "Payroll"
When allowing edit access to a controlled-access section.	Determines the list of users who have edit access to the section.	"Clara Parton": "Horace Alger"

Functions

A *function* is a built-in set of operations that returns a result, which can be either a single value or a list. A formula may consist entirely of a single function, or a function can be part of a complex formula.

Most of the power of formulas comes from the wide array of built-in functions that are part of the formula language, and which cover an extremely wide range of topics. Functions can read, manipulate, alter, or otherwise work with many different types of objects, including the following:

- Numeric values
- Strings
- Environmental information (time, date, database name, and so on)
- Notes documents
- Document fields
- Notes databases
- Menu commands
- Status information
- Notes mail
- Interaction with users
- InterNotes access

NOTE. *Because of size constraints, a complete discussion of all of Notes 4.0's built-in functions is beyond the scope of this book. However, a later section in this chapter, "New Functions in Notes, Release 4," describes many of the new functions.*

Table 10.1 illustrates a few examples of functions.

Table 10.1

Function examples.

FUNCTION	RETURNED VALUE
@Right(Name; 5)	The rightmost five characters in Name (which could be a variable or a field).
@Month(HireDate)	The numerical value (between 1 and 12) of the month portion of HireDate.
@DocLength	The approximate size (in bytes) of the current document.
@IsDocBeingEdited	Returns the value True (1) if the current document is in edit mode; otherwise, it returns the value False (0).

Here are the main points about functions, which are illustrated in the examples in Table 10.1:

- Each function name begins with the @ sign.

- A function can have any number of *parameters*, which are values supplied *to the function*. For instance, the function in the first example in Table 10.1 requires two parameters, while the function in the last example has none.

- Parameters are separated with semicolons.

@Commands

A special subset of functions, @Commands, provide programmatic access to most of the commands available on menus—plus other operations as well. These commands can be extremely useful when building automated applications.

Here's an example of a short formula that uses a single @Command to open a new view:

```
REM "This formula opens the view named Memos1";
@Command([ViewChange]; "Memos1")
```

In earlier releases of Notes, @Commands embedded as part of a formula were always executed after everything else in the formula. This has changed, and, with a few exceptions, @Commands are now executed where they appear in the formula.

@PostedCommands

Release 4 of Notes also contains a special set of commands called @Posted-Commands, which behave like @Commands in earlier Notes versions: When a formula contains @PostedCommands, those commands are executed after everything else in the formula.

When you convert a formula from Notes 3.0 to Notes 4.0, every @Command is replaced by its corresponding @PostCommand; that way, the formula will run the same on Notes 4.0 as it did on Notes 3.0.

Parameters

Every @Command and @PostedCommand takes at least one *parameter*—the name of the command. For instance, @Command([EditClear]) has a single parameter—[EditClear]. (By the way, this command is the equivalent of the menu command Edit, Clear.)

Some @Commands take additional parameters. For example, @Command([EditDocument]; p) opens the current document either in view mode or edit mode, depending on whether the value of the second parameter p is 0 or 1.

■ Using Formulas with SmartIcons

Using SmartIcons is a handy way to run formulas—especially those that you or your staff use frequently. The scope of a formula attached to a SmartIcon is the user's local workstation—rather than being specific to a particular database, view, and so on. To put this another way: A SmartIcon is always visible in your Notes window, regardless of which database is currently selected.

As a simple example, you could use a SmartIcon to close the current database and then open another one—perhaps one you use on a regular basis.

Notes contains some custom SmartIcons to which you can attach formulas. However, there are only a few of these, so you may prefer to create your own SmartIcons and then assign formulas to them. In addition, many commercial sources are available, offering a wide range of icons that you can convert to SmartIcons.

Creating Custom SmartIcons

If you have access to an icon editor, you can easily create your own SmartIcons. You can attach formulas to those SmartIcons and then add those SmartIcons to the SmartIcon bar at the top of the Notes window.

To create a custom SmartIcon, you can use any handy icon editor. When creating the icon, make sure that its dimensions are no larger than 21 by 21 pixels. Then, save the icon in the appropriate subdirectory under the main Notes directory. For example, in Windows 95 the normal icon subdirectory is \ Data\W32. You can assign any name you wish to the SmartIcon file, but be sure to use the file-name extension .BMP. This SmartIcon will then appear on the list of available SmartIcons in Notes.

Assigning a Formula to a SmartIcon

You can assign a formula either to one of Notes's available SmartIcons or to one that you have created. Here are the steps to follow:

1. Select File, Tools, SmartIcons, displaying the dialog box shown in Figure 10.1.

2. Click the button labeled Edit icon, displaying the dialog box shown in Figure 10.2.

3. Scroll through the list of icons. When you find the one you want to use, click on it.

4. Type in a description for the icon. This description will appear whenever a user points to the icon on the SmartIcon bar.

5. To create a formula for the icon, click the Formula button and then write the formula in the formula box.

Figure 10.1

You can use this dialog box to drag an icon onto the current SmartIcon set.

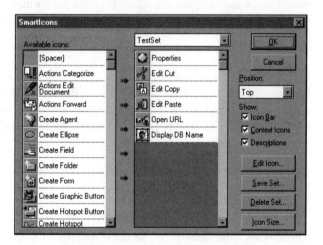

Figure 10.2

Use this dialog box to select the SmartIcon you want to use for a formula.

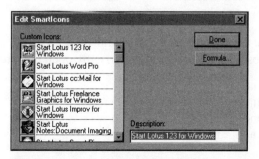

6. Exit back to the SmartIcons dialog box shown in Figure 10.1.

7. To add the customized icon to the current SmartIcon set, locate the icon in the left-hand list of icons and then drag it to the right-hand list of icons—which displays the current SmartIcon set.

8. Click on OK to close the SmartIcons dialog box.

Whenever a user clicks on the SmartIcon that you've created, the formula assigned to it will be executed.

Writing a SmartIcon Formula

Each formula that you write for a SmartIcon can perform any number of steps. Typically—but not always—the operations deal with managing databases, rather than working within specific views or documents. Consequently, these types of formulas make heavy use of the Notes @Commands.

Example: Opening a Database Navigator   Here's an example of a SmartIcon formula that you can attach to a SmartIcon. This formula opens the database stored in the file Sample1.nsf, which is on the server named Main1. When the databases opens, the navigator named Nav1 is displayed in the Navigator pane:

```
@Command([FileOpenDatabase]; "Main1":"Sample1.nsf"; "Nav1")
```

Example: Opening a Database View   The following formula opens the database stored in Sample1.nsf. It then opens the view named Folks\All By Name and selects the first document whose value displayed in the first sorted column of that view is "Harry Smith." Finally, the formula opens that document in edit mode and moves the focus down four rows:

```
@Command([FileOpenDatabase]; "":"Sample1.nsf"; "Folks\\All By Name"; "Clark
Kent");
@Command([EditDocument]; "1");
@Command([EditDown]; "4")
```

The first @Command opens the database, opens the selected view, and moves the focus to the document for Clark Kent. The second @Command then opens that document in edit mode, and the last @Command moves the focus down four lines.

Example: Closing Down   This formula—which could be attached to a SmartIcon—closes all of the windows currently open in Notes:

```
@Command([FileCloseWindow]);
@Command([FileCloseWindow]);
@Command([FileCloseWindow]);
@Command([FileCloseWindow]);
```

```
@Command([FileCloseWindow]);
@Command([FileCloseWindow]);
@Command([FileCloseWindow]);
@Command([FileCloseWindow]);
@Command([FileCloseWindow]);
```

Only nine copies of the above @Command are needed, because a maximum of nine windows can be open in Notes.

■ Using Formulas with Buttons and Hotspots

You can associate a formula with each button and hotspot that you create. Buttons and hotspots can occur in the following areas:

- Forms and subforms

- Layout regions within forms

- Navigators

- Rich text fields

The type of formula that you write depends on the object to which it will be attached:

- Formula pop-up hotspots. Each formula for this type of hotspot must return a single text value, which will be displayed when a user clicks the hotspot.

- Buttons and action hotspots. Each formula of this type can perform as many different operations as you wish. Typically—but not necessarily—the operations in a formula deal with the current database.

Note. For details about creating buttons and hotspots, see the section "Hotspots and Buttons" in Chapter 4.

To write a formula, you select the desired button or hotspot. Make sure that the Design pane is displayed, where you can then write the formula. As an example, if you're creating a formula for a button on a form, the Design pane would appear as follows:

Example: Displaying Current Information

Here's a simple formula that you could attach to a formula pop-up hotspot.
When a user clicks the hotspot, the formula displays the current date and the
title of the current database:

```
Title := "Database title: " + @DbTitle;
Date := "Current date/time: "+ @Text(@Now) ;
Title + @NewLine + Date
```

Here, the @Text function converts the value returned by the function
@Now. The function @NewLine forces the database title information to be
displayed underneath the date. Finally, @DbTitle returns the title of the
current database.

Notice that although the formula consists of three lines, the last line
returns a single text value—which is required for formula pop-up hotspots.

Example: Inserting a Special Field

Here's a formula that can be attached either to a button or to an action
hotspot. When it executes, the formula creates a new field in the current document—unless that field already exists. The field name is LastEditor, and the
value assigned is the name of the current user.

```
@Command([EditDocument]; "1");
FIELD LastEditor := @Name([CN];@UserName);
""
```

The first statement in this formula switches the current document into
edit mode. The reason for using this statement is that if the document is not
in edit mode, the operation in the second statement will have no effect on
the document.

The reason for the last statement—which consists of nothing but a pair
of double quotes—is a little obscure: Notes insists that the last statement of a
formula written for a button or an action hotspot must be a nonassignment
statement. That is, it cannot have the form *variable := value*. Putting in a simple pair of double quotes—which does absolutely nothing—is the easiest way
to satisfy this requirement.

Example: Closing a Document

The following formula saves and closes the current document. The formula
could be attached to a button that is conveniently located on a document, so
that a user can exit with a simple click.

```
@Command([FileSave]);
@Command([FileCloseWindow])
```

■ Using Formulas with Actions

Note. For information about creating actions, see Chapters 5 and 8.

You can attach a formula to an action that you create. Each action is associated with either a view or a form—and, therefore, to documents created with that form. Each formula that you write can perform any number of operations. To some extent, the type of operations you can write for this type of formula depends on the context. For instance, some operations that can be performed when a view is displayed cannot be performed from within a document.

To assign a formula to an action, you must first open the associated view or form in edit mode. Then display the Design pane, where you can create the formula.

Example: Selecting Values from a View

Suppose that a user is creating a set of documents created from the Products form. Each document will contain the name of a single product; it will also contain a field named Vendors, which holds the names of distributors who probably carry that product. You would like to automate the process as follows: When a user is creating a new Products document, he or she can automatically display a view similar to the one shown in Figure 10.3, which shows the names of all the current vendors that exist in the database named Sellers. The user clicks on the appropriate vendor names, which are then automatically inserted into the Vendors field on the current document.

Figure 10.3

A user can select a group of documents from this dialog box.

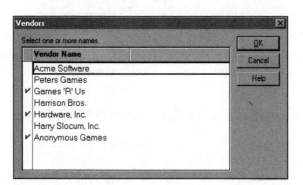

You can arrange this automation as follows: First, create a special view, Vendors, which displays only the documents containing the vendor names—similar to the view shown in Figure 10.3. Next, create an action on the Products form and then assign the following formula to that action:

```
FIELD Vendors := Vendors;
```

```
HoldNames := @PickList([Custom]; ""; "Sellers"; "Vendors"; "Select one or more
names"; 1);
@SetField("Vendors"; HoldNames)
```

The key to this function lies in the second statement, which uses the function @PickList—new to Notes 4.0. This function displays the named view (Vendors), from which the user can then pick selected documents. @PickList then returns the values in the specified column (the value of the last parameter, which is 1 here) for the documents selected by the user. Those values are stored in the temporary variable HoldNames. The last statement then assigns the values in HoldNames to the variable Vendors.

The first statement is the result of one of Notes's peculiarities, which requires that if a field name is used in a @SetField function, that field name must first appear in a FIELD statement—such as the first statement in this example.

Example: Switching to Another Navigator

In this example, we want to create an action that will allow a user to switch from the current navigator to another one, named Main. From the user's perspective, this navigator could be a main menu, similar to the one shown in Figure 10.4. To be as effective as possible, this action should probably be displayed on the action bar. This is a handy method that users can use for returning from anywhere back to the main navigator of a database.

Here's the formula for the action:

```
@Command([FileOpenDatabase]; ""; "Main")
```

When a user clicks the action button, Notes automatically closes the window that the user was viewing; Notes then displays the navigator named Main. The second parameter, "", specifies the current database.

■ Using Formulas with Fields

When you are creating a field—either on a form, a subform, or in a layout region—you can attach one or more formulas, which calculate field values under a variety of circumstances. The number of formulas you can attach to a field depends on the type of that field.

Fields fall into two broad categories: those that are editable and those that are computed. The latter fall into three subcategories: computed, computed-when-composed, and computed-for-display. Editable fields may or may not have formulas attached to them, but each computed field must always have an attached formula.

Figure 10.4

A navigator disguised as
a menu.

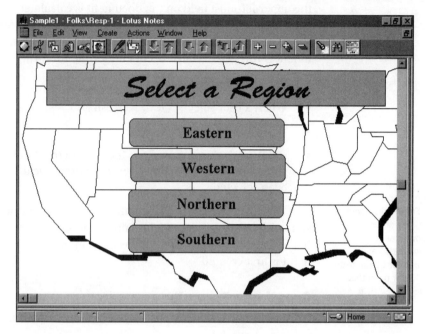

NOTE. *Field* formulas *are always created on a Notes form. On the other hand, field* values *occur in documents created with that form. To simplify the following discussions, we move freely between talking about field formulas (on a form) and field values (on documents created with that form).*

The formula for a field can be as long as needed. However, the final result must always be a calculated value—either a single value or a list. The type of the calculated result must be the same as the type assigned to the field: number, text, and so on.

NOTE. *Under some circumstances, Notes automatically transforms an incorrect value into the correct data type. However, you should not rely on this feature, because it is not completely predictable.*

When Field Formulas Are Calculated

As you become familiar with field formulas, and you begin to create complex sets of formulas for the fields on forms, you'll need to understand how and when Notes uses the field formulas to calculate values for those fields in a document.

Formulas in a document are always calculated in a particular order: First, the upper-leftmost field on the document is calculated, and then the others are calculated, working from top to bottom and from left to right on each line.

Notes recalculates most field formulas in a document whenever that document is refreshed, which occurs under the following circumstances:

- When a user presses the F9 key

- When a user selects View, Refresh

- When the document is saved

- Every time a user moves the focus from one field to another on the document—but only if the form option Automatically Refresh Fields has been selected

Note. For details about these types of formulas, see "Formulas for Editable Fields" and "Formulas for Computed Fields," later on in this chapter.

There are two types of formulas that are not recalculated as just described: default-value formulas and formulas for computed-when-composed fields. These two types of formulas are computed only once—when the document is first created.

Creating a Formula

Here's a broad outline of the steps to follow for writing a formula for a field:

1. To begin, open the form containing the field and then click the field that you want to work on.

2. Display the Design pane (see below) by selecting View, Design Pane.

3. Click the radio button labeled Formula.

4. Pull down the list box labeled Event and then select the type of formula that you want to write: Default Value, Input Translation, or Input Validation.

5. Write the formula.

Formulas for Editable Fields

If a field is editable, you can assign it one, two, or three formulas:

• A default-value formula

• An input-translation formula

• An input-validation formula

All of these formulas are optional.

Default-Value Formulas

You can write a formula that supplies a default value for an editable field. Whenever a new document is created, this value is automatically assigned to that field. Subsequently, the default-value formula is ignored for that field in the document.

If you don't supply a default value for a particular field, then the value of that field is null ("") until replaced with another value—either one that's entered by a user or one that's calculated by a formula somewhere else.

The following table lists a few examples of default values for editable fields.

Field Name	Field Type	Default Value
Department	Text	"Transportation"
CumHoursWorked	Number	0.00
State	Keywords	"California"
ValidAuthors	Authors	"Harry Chase": "Jill Jackson": "Henry Tudor"

Input-Translation Formulas

The purpose of an input-translation formula is to manipulate input values for a field, transforming them into other values. On occasion, you may also find it convenient to use an input-translation formula for one field to assign a value to another field.

Input-translation formulas are recalculated whenever a document is refreshed, guaranteeing that the current field values are always properly displayed.

As an example of an input-translation formula, suppose that you create a field named FullName for holding personal names, and you want to ensure that the values for this field are always properly capitalized. You also want to trim extra blanks from each input value. Here's a simple formula that will accomplish this:

```
@ProperCase((@Trim(FullName)))
```

Input-Validation Formulas

The purpose of an input-validation formula is to ensure that the values for a field conform to a particular set of rules. If an input value is acceptable to the formula, then the user can continue entering other data values. However, if the value fails to meet the rules written into the formula, Notes pauses with an error message to the user, explaining the nature of the error. Notes will not proceed until the user enters an acceptable value.

The input-validation formula for a field is recalculated whenever a document is refreshed—not just when a value is first entered.

As an example, the following input-validation formula checks values for a field named FirstWorkDay; the formula allows only days of the week:

```
ListDays :=
"Monday":"Tuesday":"Wednesday":"Thursday":"Friday":"Saturday":"Sunday";
@If(@IsNotMember(FirstWorkDay; ListDays);
@Failure("Please enter a valid day name"); @Success)
```

Here, the function @IsNotMember tests the current value for FirstWork-Day. If that value is a member of the variable named ListDays (to which the first statement assigns the names of the weekdays), then @Success is executed, allowing the user to continue. Otherwise, @Failure executes, displaying the following error message: "Please enter a valid day name." The user must then enter another value for the field.

As another example, suppose you want to ensure that the values for the field Salary are within company limits: $15,000 to $60,000. Here's a suitable input-validation formula:

```
@If( (Salary>=15000) & (Salary<=60000); @Success;
@Failure("Salary must be between $15,000 and $60,000. Please enter another
value"))
```

An input-validation formula can utilize on the values in other fields in a document. For instance, we could expand on the previous example, using different salary ranges for different departments according to the following table:

Department	Salary Range ($)
Personnel	25,000—45,000
Shipping	30,000—50,000
Programming	35,000—65,000

First, the user must enter a value for the Department field. Then the user enters a salary value, which is tested by the following input-validation formula:

```
Test1 := (Department= "Personnel") & (Salary>=25000) & (Salary<=45000);
Test2 := (Department= "Shipping") & (Salary>=30000) & (Salary<=50000);
```

```
Test3 := (Department= "Programming") & (Salary>=35000) & (Salary<=60000);
@If(Test1 | Test2 | Test3;  @Success;
@Failure("Salary is incorrect for this department. Please enter a valid value"))
```

The first three statements compute values for the three variables Test1, Test2, and Test3. Each value will be computed to be either 1 (True) or 0 (False), depending on the values of the Department and Salary fields. Then the @If function tests those three values; if any of them is True, then @Success is executed, and the user can continue entering other field values. Otherwise, @Failure displays the error message, and the user must then try again.

Formulas for Computed Fields

If a field is either computed, computed-when-composed, or computed-for-display, it must be assigned a formula, which calculates the field's value. Only one formula can be assigned to any of these three types of fields.

Neither input-translation formulas nor input-validation formulas are used. Instead, when you write the formula for a field you can incorporate whatever calculations are needed.

The formulas for computed fields and computed-for-display fields are recalculated whenever the document is refreshed. On the other hand, the formula for a computed-when-composed field is calculated only once—when the document is first created.

You can create a computed, computed-when-composed, or computed-for-display field whose value is calculated not by the formula in that field, but by a formula somewhere else—in another field, in a button, and so on. For this type of field, you assign it a formula consisting of its own name. That way, the field's own formula will not override the value for it that's assigned from elsewhere.

■ New Functions in Notes, Release 4

The current release of Notes contains approximately 50 new functions (not including new @Commands, which are too numerous to discuss in this chapter), covering a wide range of topics. Below is a list of these functions, divided into broad categories.

- Mathematical functions

    @Acos

    @Asin

    @Atan

@Atan2

@Cos

@Pi

@Random

@Sign

@Sin

@Sqrt

@Sum

@Tan

- Document-Related Functions

  @AllChildren

  @AllDescendants

  @DocFields

  @Docmark

  @DocumentUniqueID

  @GetDocField

  @InheritedDocumentUniqueID

  @IsDocBeingEdited

  @IsDocTruncated

  @IsValid

  @SetDocField

- Mail-Related Functions

  @MailEncryptSavedPreference

  @MailEncryptSendPreference

  @MailSavePreference

  @MailSignPreference

  @OptimizeMailAddress

- String and Text Functions

    @Abstract

    @Ascii

    @ReplaceSubstring

- InterNotes-Related Functions

    @URLGetHeader

    @URLHistory

    @URLOpen

- Miscellaneous Functions

    @Certificate

    @DbExists

    @DialogBox

    @GetPortsList

    @IsAgentEnabled

    @IsModalHelp

    @Like

    @PickList

    @UserAccess

    @UserRoles

    @Version

    @Zone

Mathematical functions

The following table includes a brief description of each new mathematical function.

Function	Calculates	Return Value
@Acos(*num*)	Inverse cosine of *num*	An angle in radians, having a value between 0 and pi (0° to 180°). The value of *num* must be between –1 and 1.

Function	Calculates	Return Value
@Asin(*num*)	Inverse sine of *num*	An angle in radians, having a value between –pi/2 and pi/2 (–90° to 90°). The value of *num* must be between –1 and 1.
@Atan(*num*)	Inverse tangent of *num*	An angle in radians, having a value between –pi/2 and pi/2 (–90° to 90°). *Num* can be any negative or positive value.
@Atan2(*x; y*)	Inverse tangent of the ratio *y/x*	An angle in radians, having a value between –pi and pi (–180° to 180°). *y/x* represents the ratio of two sides of a right triangle.
@Cos(*angle*)	Cosine of *angle*	A value between –1 and 1. *Angle* can be any value, expressed in radians.
@Pi	The value of pi	3.14159265358979
@Random	Random number generator	Generates a random number between 0 and 1.
@Sign(*num*)	Sign	Returns the sign of *num*—either –1 or 1. If *num* is 0, the value returned is 0.
@Sin(*angle*)	Sine of *angle*	A value between –1 and 1. *Angle* can be any value, expressed in radians.
@Sqrt(*num*)	Square root of *num*	The square root of *num,* which must be either zero or positive.
@Sum(*num1; num2; ..*)	Sum of parameters	The sum of all the parameters, which can be simple numbers or lists of numbers
@Tan(*angle*)	Tangent of *angle*	The tangent of *angle*, which must be expressed in radians.

Document-Related Functions

The following sections describe new functions that are related to documents.

@AllChildren

Function format: @AllChildren

Types of formulas used in: Selection

This function is designed to be a replacement to the earlier function @IsResponseDoc. It can be used in view- and replication-selection formulas. Here's an example of a view-selection formula:

```
SELECT Form="Memo"|@AllChildren
```

This formula will select all the documents created with the form Memo and their immediate-response documents.

The advantage of @AllChildren over the earlier @IsResponseDoc is that it selects only a main document's immediate-response documents, whereas @IsResponseDoc selects all the response documents.

@AllDescendants

Function format: @AllDescendants

Types of formulas used in: Selection

This function is used in view- and replication-selection formulas. Here's an example of a view-selection formula:

```
SELECT Form="Memo"|@AllDescendants
```

This formula will select both the documents created with the Memo form and also all of their descendant documents.

@DocFields

Function format: @DocFields.

Types of formulas used in: All, except selection, column, and navigator

This function returns a list of all the fields contained in the current document.

@Docmark

Function format: @Docmark([*parameter*])

Types of formulas used in: Agent

This function is used when writing agents for scanning and modifying a group of documents, but where you want to exclude particular documents from being modified. @Docmark determines whether the changes made to the current document should be saved or ignored. If the value of *parameter* is [Update], then changes to the document are saved. On the other hand, if the value of *parameter* is [NoUpdate], the changes are ignored.

For example, suppose that you write an agent that scans and modifies a selected group of documents, but you want to exclude the document belonging to Horatio Hornblower. You can accomplish this by including the following statement anywhere in the agent:

```
@If(FullName="Horatio Hornblower"; @Docmark([NoUpdate]); @Docmark([Update]))
```

@DocumentUniqueID

Function format: @DocumentUniqueID

Types of formulas used in: All, except navigator

This function returns the 32-character identification code that's unique to each document in a database. This identifier is unique to a document, and it remains part of a document throughout all replicas of a database.

You can display the ID code for a document as follows: Click on the document in any view, display its InfoBox, and then click on the Information tab. The third line from the bottom (labeled ID) contains the 32-character code— except for the character pairs OF and ON, which are not part of the code.

One of the main purposes of the @DocumentUniqueID function is to provide quick access from a response document to its parent document. To that end, each child document contains a field named $Ref, which contains the 32-character document ID of its parent.

There are two ways in which you can link to a document by using its unique document ID. First, you can create a view whose first column—which must be sorted—contains the formula @DocumentUniqueID. Then you can use the function @DbLookup to access any particular document by referencing its code as part of the @DbLookup call.

The second way in which you can access a document from its code is by using the functions @GetDocField or @SetDocField, described next.

@GetDocField

Function format: @GetDocField(*DocumentUniqueID, Field*)

Types of formulas used in: All, except selection, column, hotspot text pop-up, and navigator

This function first finds the document (in the current database only) whose unique 32-character code is *DocumentUniqueID*. The function then locates and returns the value of the field *Field* from that document. The primary use of this function is within child documents that refer to their parents.

Here's a sample:

```
FIELD Sender := @GetDocField($Ref; "FullName")
```

When this statement is executed, @GetDocField first finds the document whose 32-character code is the same as that contained in the field $Ref in the current document. Then the value of the field FullName in that document is returned and stored in the field named Sender of the current document. Note that the current document is probably a response document, because it contains the field $Ref.

@InheritedDocumentUniqueID

Function format: @InheritedDocumentUniqueID

Types of formulas used in: All, except navigator

This function returns the unique 32-character ID of the current document's parent document. It also creates a doclink to the parent document.

In order for @InheritedDocumentUniqueID to work properly, the following conditions must be true:

- The document containing the @InheritedDocumentUniqueID function is created as a response document, and it is set up to inherit values from its parent document.

- The function @InheritedDocumentUniqueID is the formula for a field that is set up as Text, Computed When Composed.

@IsDocBeingEdited

Function format: @IsDocBeingEdited

Types of formulas used in: All, except selection, column, agent, view-action, and navigator

This function returns a value of 1 (True) if the current document is open in edit mode. Otherwise, the function returns a value of 0 (False).

@IsDocTruncated

Function format: @IsDocTruncated

Types of formulas used in: All, except navigator

If the current document has been truncated (which occurs during replication), this function returns the value 1 (True). Otherwise, it returns 0 (False).

@IsValid

Function format: @IsValid

Types of formulas used in: All, except selection, column, scheduled-agent, hide-when, and window-title

When this function is executed, all the validation formulas in the current document are executed. If they all return values of True, the @IsValid returns the value of 1 (True). Otherwise, it returns 0 (False).

@SetDocField

Function format: @SetDocField(*DocumentUniqueID*, *field*, *value*)

Types of formulas used in: All, except selection, column, hotspot text pop-up, and navigator

This function first locates the document whose unique 32-bit ID code is *DocumentUniqueID*. Then the function assigns *value* to the field *field* in that document. The primary use of this function is within child documents that refer to their parents. Here's an example:

```
@SetDocField($Ref, "Person"; "Harriet Kornfeld")
```

Here's what happens when this function executes: First, it finds the document whose ID value is that contained in the field $Ref. Then it assigns the value of "Harriet Kornfeld" to the field named Person in that document.

Mail-Related Functions

The following sections describe the new functions dealing with Notes mail.

@MailEncryptSavedPreference

Function format: @MailEncryptSavedPreference

Types of formulas used in: All, except selection and column

This function returns a value of 1 (True) if a user has selected the option Encrypt Saved Mail in the User Preferences dialog box.

@MailEncryptSendPreference

Function format: @MailEncryptSendPreference

Types of formulas used in: All, except selection and column

This function returns a value of 1 (True) if a user has selected the option Encrypt Sent Mail in the User Preferences dialog box.

@MailSavePreference

Function format: @MailSavePreference

Types of formulas used in: All, except selection and column

The value returned by this function depends on a user's selection in the User Preferences dialog box. The following table shows the possibilities:

User's Selection	Value Returned
Don't Keep A Copy	0
Always Keep A Copy	1
Always Prompt	2

@MailSignPreference

Function format: @MailSignPreference

Types of formulas used in: All, except selection and column

This function returns a value of 1 (True) if a user has selected the option Sign Sent Mail in the User Preferences dialog box. Otherwise, a value of 0 (False) is returned.

@OptimizeMailAddress

Function format: @OptimizeMailAddress(*address*)

Types of formulas used in: All, except selection, column, and window-title

This function operates on the mailing address *address*, removing all the domains between any two identical domains—including the duplicate—that are part of the address.
    For example:

```
@OptimizeMailAddress("Sam Spade @Domain1 @Domain2 @Domain3 @Domain1 @Domain4")
```

When executed, this function returns the address "Sam Spade @Domain1 @Domain4."

String and Text Functions

The following sections describe the new functions related to text strings.

@Abstract

Function format: @Abstract(commands; size; introtext; fields)

Types of formulas used in: All, except selection, column, hide-when, section-editor, and navigator

This addition to Notes's arsenal of functions is probably the most complicated of all the functions. Its purpose is to condense or abbreviate the contents of selected fields, combining the abbreviated results into a single value. This function is useful in situations where a text value is too long and must be condensed.

The *commands* option represents one or more instructions that control the abbreviation process. You can supply any number of commands, although there are some restrictions on the order in which the commands can appear. Commands are executed in order, from left to right.

The *size* option is the maximum allowable size of the final result, in bytes; *introText* is a string—10 characters, maximum length—that will be added to the beginning of the text in the final result. The option *fields* represents the names of the fields—in quotes—to be condensed and combined into a single result.

Following are listed a few examples that demonstrate the various capabilities of @Abstract. In all examples, the field named Comment is used as the source of the text being processed.

Example: Trimming Blanks and Punctuation   Here's a simple example that abbreviates the value of the field Comment. It trims extra blanks between words, and it also deletes blanks surrounding punctuation:

```
@Abstract( [TrimWhite] : [DropVowels] : [Abbrev]; 1000; ""; Comment)
```

The command [TrimWhite] deletes extra spaces between words, and [TrimPunct] deletes all spaces surrounding punctuation marks. The command [Abbrev] must appear after [TrimWhite].

Example: Deleting Vowels   This example uses @Abstract to delete most of the vowels in each word:

```
@Abstract([DropVowels] :[Abbrev]; 1000; ""; Comment)
```

The command [DropVowels] deletes most vowels, while [Abbrev] is a general-purpose command that must be used with [DropVowels].

Example: Testing the Size   The following example uses the [TryFit] command to determine whether the current size of the text is less than the limit specified in the *Size* parameter. If so, @Abstract stops executing and returns the current text. Otherwise, @Abstract continues to execute.

```
@Abstract([TrimWhite] : [Abbrev] : [TryFit] : [DropVowels]; 1000; ""; Comment)
```

Using the commands [TrimWhite] and [Abbrev], @Abstract begins by trimming extra blanks from the value in the field Comment. Then the [TryFit] command compares the size of the text with 1,000: If it's less, then @Abstract stops executing. Otherwise, @Abstract continues executing, and the command [DropVowels] is performed, squeezing most vowels from words. If the final value is still longer than 1,000 characters, only the first 1,000 are returned by @Abstract.

You can insert as many [TryFit] commands as you wish when using the @Abstract function.

NOTE. *The @Abstract function can take a wide variety of different types of commands for condensing text. However, a full discussion of all possible options is beyond the scope of this book.*

@Ascii

Function format: @Ascii(*LMBCS string*) or @Ascii(*LMBCS string*; [AllInRange])

Types of formulas used in: All

Here, *LMBCS string* is any Lotus multibyte character set text string.

The @Ascii function converts each character in the original string to its equivalent standard ASCII code—a value between 32 and 127. If a character cannot be converted, a question mark is substituted instead.

If the optional parameter [AllInRange] is used, then @Ascii returns a null value if the output string contains any question marks.

@ReplaceSubstring

Function format: @Replace Substring(*OriginalList; FromList; ToList*)

Types of formulas used in: All

This function replaces specific values in a list with other values.

Here's a brief description of the options:

- *OriginalList*: Can be either a single text value or a list.

- *FromList*: The list of values to be searched for in *OriginalList*

- *ToList*: The list of replacement values, corresponding on an item-by-item basis to the items in *FromList*.

@ReplaceSubstring scans each item in *OriginalList*. If a value in *FromList* is found, the corresponding value in *ToList* is substituted.

If *FromList* contains more items than *ToList*, then the last item in *ToList* will be substituted for the remaining items in *FromList*. On the other hand, if *ToList* contains more items than *FromList*, the extra items are ignored.

Example 1   `@ReplaceSubstring("Now is the time"; "When" : "Now"; "Never" : "Then")`

The returned value is "Then is the time."

Example 2   `@ReplaceSubstring("Apples" : "Oranges"; "Pickles" : "Apples"; "Meatballs" : "Pears")`

The returned value is "Pears" : "Oranges."

InterNet-Related Functions

Types of formulas used in: SmartIcon, button, agent, window-title, field, and form.

Notes 4.0 contains three functions for performing various Internet-related operations. These functions can be used only in connection with the Web Navigator database.

The following table gives a brief summary of the three functions.

Function	Purpose
@URLGetHeader(*URLValue, HeaderString*)	Returns a variety of different types of information about specific Web pages. *URLValue* is the URL address of the Web site you want to access. *HeaderString* is the specific string that indicates which information you want returned.
@URLHistory([*command*])	Used for manipulating URL history lists. A wide variety of *commands* are available for different operations on history lists.
@URLOpen(*URLValue*)	Retrieves the specified WWW page.

Miscellaneous Functions

The following sections explain the new Release 4 functions that do not fit into any of the categories described in the previous sections.

@Certificate

Function format: @Certificate([*keyword*]; *CertificateField*)

Types of formulas used in: Column and field

This function returns selected information from the certified public key of servers and certificates documents in the Public Address Book. The format of the function is the following:

keyword specifies the exact information that you want to retrieve from the field *CertificateField* in the current document. The following table lists the possible values for *keyword*:

Value of Keyword Parameter	Information to Be Retrieved
Subject	Name of the certified person or server in the current document
Issuer	Name attached to the ID used to issue the current certificate
Expiration	Certificate expiration date and time (North American certificates only)
IntlExpiration	Certificate expiration date and time (International certificates only)

@DbExists

Function formats: @DbExists(*server:file*)
@DbExists(server; replicaID)

Types of formulas used in: All, except selection, column, scheduled-agent, and hotspot text pop-up.

This function returns the value 1 (True) if the specified database exists. Otherwise, it returns 0 (False). You can specify the name of the database in either of two ways: *server:file*, where *server* is the name of the server and *file* is the full path name of the database; or *server; replicaID*, where *replicaID* is the unique replica ID number of the database. To specify the current server, you can use the value " " for *server*.

Here's an example:

```
@If(@DbExists; "":"LocalCustomers.nsf"; "Database exists."; "Database does not
exist.")
```

If the database named LocalCustomers.nsf exists on the local machine, the function returns the text value "Database exists"; otherwise, it returns "Database does not exist."

@DialogBox

Function format: @DialogBox(*FormName*; [AutoHorzFit] : [AutoVertFit])

Types of formulas used in: All, except selection, column, field, and scheduled-agent

The purpose of this function is to provide a custom dialog box in which a user enters or edits selected values for the document.

When @DialogBox is executed, it displays a modal dialog box whose content is the form *FormName*. The two parameters [AutoHorzFit] and [AutoVertFit] are optional.

If *FormName* contains at least one layout region, and if both parameters [AutoHorzFit] and [AutoVertFit] are included, then the modal dialog box is scaled to fit just the first layout region in *FormName*; the remaining contents of *FormName* are not displayed in the dialog box. If only one of these two parameters is included in the @DialogBox call, then the dialog box is scaled only in that dimension.

Typically, the @DialogBox function is attached to a button, hotspot, or action. When a user creates or edits a document, he or she double-clicks the button, hotspot, or action, and the @DialogBox function executes, displaying the dialog box based on *FormName*. The user then fills out or edits the fields in this dialog box. Information passes back and forth between the original document and the dialog box as follows:

- If a field in the original document has the same name as a field in *FormName*, then its value is displayed in the corresponding field in the dialog box.

- Similarly, the value a user enters for that field in the dialog box will be copied to the corresponding field in the document, when the user exits normally from the dialog box.

- Information in rich text fields is not communicated between the document and the dialog box.

- If a user enters a value for a field in the dialog box, but the original document does not contain a corresponding field, Notes creates a corresponding field in the document and assigns it that value. Users can display that field value either by accessing the InfoBox for that document or by creating another form that contains that field.

Here are two possible uses for @DialogBox:

- Hidden fields. If documents contain a field that may hold long values not of general interest, you can hide that field by not including it on the form for creating those documents. Then, to create or view that field value in a document, users can click a button that executes @DialogBox, which in turn displays a special form containing that field.

- Increased automation. Use @DialogBox calls to help automate data entry by leading users through the fields to be filled out—in a specific order. For instance, a form could contain a series of buttons that users could click in turn, each of which would display a particular group of fields to be filled in.

As an example, Figure 10.5 shows a document that includes a button. The formula for this button is the following:

```
@DialogBox("Comments";[AutoVertFit]:[AutoHorzFit])
```

Figure 10.5

Clicking the button in this document will display the dialog box shown in Figure 10.6.

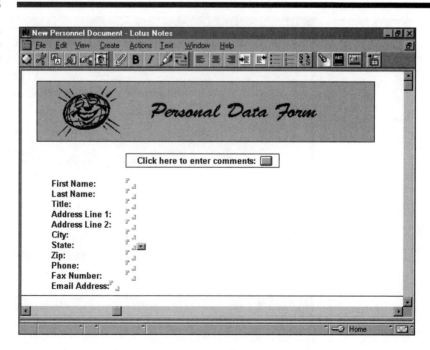

When a user clicks this button, the preceding formula executes, displaying the dialog box shown in Figure 10.6. The underlying form for this dialog box, named Comments, is shown in Figure 10.7.

Figure 10.6

This dialog box is based on the form shown in Figure 10.7.

Figure 10.7

The underlying form for the dialog box in Figure 10.6.

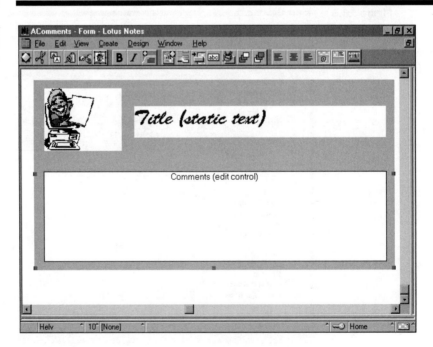

Here are some noteworthy points about this example:

- The entire Comments form consists of a single layout region.

- When the @DialogBox function executes, the layout region in Comments fills the entire dialog box.

- The layout region contains two text fields: One is named Comments and fills the bottom half of the layout region, and the other is named Title and has the following formula:

```
@If(Comments!="";"Please edit these comments"; "Please enter your comments")
```

This formula displays the title "Please enter your comments" if the Comments field is blank; otherwise, it displays "Please edit these comments."

@GetPortsList

Function format: @GetPortsList([*portType*])

Types of formulas used in: All

This function returns a list of the currently available ports of the type specified by *portType*, as follows:

- [Enabled]: Returns a list of enabled ports

- [Disabled]: Returns a list of disabled ports

@IsAgentEnabled

Function format: @IsAgentEnabled(*agentName*)

Types of formulas used in: All, except selection and column

If the agent named is *agentName* is currently enabled, then @IsAgent-Enabled returns a value of 1 (True); otherwise—if the named agent is not enabled, or if no agent with that name exists—the function returns 0 (False).

@IsModalHelp

Function format: @IsModalHelp

Types of formulas used in: All

This function returns a value of 1 (True) if the current document is a modal help document; otherwise, it returns 0 (False).

@Like

Function formats: @Like(*String*; *Pattern*)
                     @Like(String; Pattern; EscapeChar)

Types of formulas used in: All

This function compares *String* with *Pattern*. If they match, a value of 1 (True) is returned. Otherwise, 0 (False) is returned. *Pattern* can contain various wildcard characters. You use the parameter *EscapeChar* to indicate that you want to search for one of the wildcard characters itself.

In order for @Like to return a True result, *Pattern*—including any wildcard characters—must exactly match *String*.

@Like is similar to the older function @Matches, with the following differences:

- @Like supports fewer wildcard characters than does @Matches.

- @Like supports the NotesSQL™ ODBC driver; @Matches does not.

- @Like is case-sensitive; @Matches is not.

The following table lists the wildcards that you can use with @Like.

Wildcard Character	Meaning
_ (underscore)	Matches any single character
%	Matches any group of zero or more characters

To search for a string that includes one of the wildcard characters, you precede it with the escape character that you specify in the third parameter of @Like.

Here are a few examples:

Function Call	Result	Returned by @Matches	Reason
@Like("Now is the time"; "Now")	0		The pattern does not completely match the search string.
@Like("Now is the time;"Now%")	1		The % matches any number of characters.
@Like("now is the time; "Now%")	0		The case does not match exactly.
@Like("Now is the time; "%is%")	1		The two occurrences of % match the strings on each side of "is."

Function Call	Result	Returned by @Matches	Reason
@Like("Now is the time; "____is the time")	1		The four leading under-scores each match one character.
@Like("Rate is 15% less."; "Rate is __/% less"; "/")	1		The third parameter defines the slash character as the escape character, so the string "/%" is interpreted as the literal character "%."

@PickList

Function formats: @PickList([Name] : [Single])
　　　　　　　　@PickList([Custom]; Server:File; View; Title; Prompt; Column)

Types of formulas used in: All, except selection, column, scheduled, hide-when, window-title, hotspot text pop-up, and form

This function displays a modal window that contains either the Address Book dialog box or a view from which you select one or more items. We next describe each form of this function separately.

@PickList([Name] : [Single])　　Here, both [Name] and [Single] are key-words; including [Single] is optional. If you use both parameters, @PickList displays a dialog box, as shown in the illustration below. You can select from the available Address Books, choose a single name, and then exit. @PickList then returns the name that you choose as a text value.

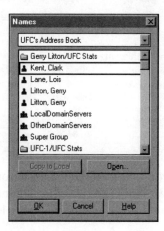

If you do not include the parameter [Single], @PickList displays the Address Book dialog box, but in a format that allows you to select several names, as shown in the following illustration. @PickList then returns these names as a list of text values.

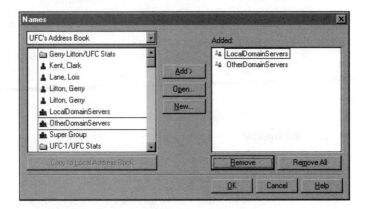

@PickList([Custom]; Server:File; View; Title; Prompt; Column)   This form of @PickList displays a modal dialog box showing the view named *View* from the database whose file name *File* is stored on *Server*. *Title* is the title displayed at the top of dialog box, with *Prompt* shown beneath it. *Column* is the number of the column whose values you want to be returned. Figure 10.8 shows an example of the type of dialog box that's displayed.

Figure 10.8

This dialog box is displayed by the @PickList function.

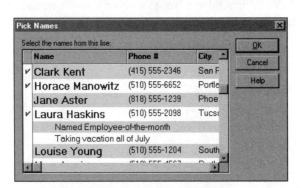

If you want to display a view from the current database, you can use " " for *Server:File*. When counting columns, use the view opened in edit mode and count every column, where the leftmost is numbered 1, and so on.

You can select as many documents as you wish from the displayed view, and the values in the column you specify in the @PickList function will be returned as a text list. For example, if you use the number 2 for the value of *Column*, then referring to Figure 10.8, the values in the column labeled Name for the three selected documents will be returned as a text list. (In Figure 10.8, the first column is used to display values for response documents.)

@UserAccess

Function format: @UserAccess(*ServerName:DatabaseFile*)

Types of formulas used in: All, except selection, column, hide-when, section-editor, and hotspot text pop-up

This function returns the current user's level of access in the database whose full path and file name is *DatabaseFile*, and which is stored on the server *ServerName*.

The returned value has the following format: *Level* : *Create* : *Delete*.

Create has a value of 1 if the user can create documents in the specified database; otherwise, the value is 0. The value of *Delete* is 1 if the user can delete documents; otherwise, the value is 0.

Level has a value between 1 and 6, according to the following table:

Value of *Level*	Access Level of User
1	Depositor
2	Reader
3	Author
4	Editor
5	Designer
6	Manager

@UserRoles

Function format: @UserRoles

Types of formulas used in: All, except selection and column

This function returns a text list, consisting of the roles of which the current user is a member for the current database.

@Version

Function format: @Version

Types of formulas used in: All

Restrictions: Does not work in scheduled agents, mail agents, or column or selection formulas

Return value: The build number of your Notes software

@Zone

Function formats: @Zone
                   @Zone(*TimeDate*).

Types of formulas used in: All

Return value: ZoneNumber.Flag

This function returns the time zone number of the current computer. *Flag* is equal to 1 if Daylight Savings time applies. Otherwise, *Flag* is not included as part of the return value.

If the format @Zone is used, then *Flag* indicates whether or not Daylight Savings time is currently in effect.

If the format @Zone(*TimeDate*) is used, *Flag* indicates whether or not Daylight Savings Time will be in effect on that particular date and time— again, for the computer's time zone. Both a date and a time must be included for *TimeDate*.

Time zones west of Greenwich Mean Time (GMT) are expressed as positive integers, while zones east of GMT are expressed as negative integers.

As an example, suppose that your computer is in time zone 8. Here are a few examples of values that will be returned by @Zone:

Function	Today's Date	Returned Value
@Zone	6/1/96	8.10
@Zone	3/1/96	8.00
@Zone(01/01/97 12:00AM)	Any date	8.00
@Zone(06/01/97 12:00AM)	Any date	8.10

■ Using Agents

Note. Earlier releases of Notes referred to agents as *macros*.

An *agent* is a set of steps that can be performed on one or more documents in a database. Each agent is specific to a particular database, although you can easily copy an agent from one database to another.

When you define an agent, you also define the documents on which it will operate. You can use agents to automate just about any group of database operations that you can think of.

Some agents process a group of documents, while others may operate on a single document. An agent's type determines which documents it can process.

Privileges and Agents

When you create a new agent, you can select whether it is to be private or shared (that is, *public*). A private agent is accessible only to the person who creates it, whereas a public agent is available to any database user with a sufficiently high database access level. Users with at least Reader access can create their own private agents.

When a user has at least Reader access to a database, he or she can run shared agents. Even though a particular user can run agents, that user's access level limits what those agents can do with documents. For example, suppose a particular agent deletes selected documents from a database. A user with Reader access can run that agent, but the agent won't be able to delete any documents.

Agent Types

Agents can be divided into two very broad categories:

- *Manual agents*. You create this type of agent to perform a particular type of operation—but one that is under your control. For example, you might create this type of agent for a once-only operation on a group of documents and then discard the agent.

- *Automatic agents*. These operate automatically—either on a regular schedule or in response to a particular type of event, such as the delivery of a document by mail. In a complex organization, agents may do an enormous amount of work behind the scenes: responding to mail, deleting or archiving old documents, and performing many other functions that keep the system working smoothly.

Manual agents and the various types of automatic agents are described next.

Manual Agent   Manual agents run by user action—usually from the Actions menu. As part of defining this type of agent, you select the group of documents to be processed by the agent. This could be any of the following:

- All the documents in the database

- All the documents in the view that's displayed when the agent is run

- Selected documents in the current view

- All unread documents in the current view

- All documents either created or modified since the last time the agent was run

Writing a manual agent is often a very convenient method for performing a one-time operation on a particular group of documents. For example, if you decide to add a new field to a selected group of documents, you can write a manual agent to accomplish this. Then, when you're finished you can delete the agent.

Mail Agent   Whenever a document arrives by mail, this type of agent automatically processes the document. Here are a few examples of the types of mail agents that you could write:

- An agent that replies to every piece of mail delivered to the current database. This could be useful, for example, for a special mail-in database created for a particular purpose.

- An agent that replies only to mail from a particular sender.

- An agent that customizes the reply, depending on the contents of the Subject field.

Create/Modify Agent   A create/modify agent runs against each new document, and also against every document that's modified. For example, you could use this type of agent to proofread specific fields in every document that you create of a certain type.

Paste Agent   Whenever a document is pasted into the database, a paste agent processes the document.

Scheduled Agent   A scheduled agent runs on a regular time interval—hourly, daily, and so on. You can set up this type of agent to run either on every document in the database, or just on those that have been created or modified since the last time the agent was run.

Scheduled agents are the hidden hands that can keep large databases functioning well. They can run checks on particular groups of documents, delete or archive out-of-date documents, and perform a great many different types of tasks.

Agent Names

You can use just about any combination of letters, digits, spaces, and special characters to create an agent name, whose maximum size is 64 bytes.

If an agent is going to be run from the Actions menu, you can assign a keyboard shortcut to its name (except with Macintoshes). By default, the shortcut for an agent is either the first letter of its name, or—if another agent name has the same first letter—the first letter of the name that's unique. For instance, if the Actions menu contains the agent names Delete Old Documents and Delete Other Documents, the default keyboard shortcuts for the two names would be Alt+D and Alt+T.

You can override the default keyboard shortcut for a name by preceding a letter in the name with an underscore. Alt + *that letter* then becomes the keyboard shortcut. For example, if you assign an agent the name Add N_ew Field, the keyboard shortcut is Alt+E.

If you intend to place a large number of agent names on the Actions menu, you may be able to minimize clutter and confusion by creating cascading names for the agents. These names then appear as one or more cascading menus on the Actions menu. For example, suppose you use the following agent names:

```
Documents\Delete Old
Documents\Archive Old
Documents\Update Fields
```

The Actions menu will then use a cascading menu for these names, as follows:

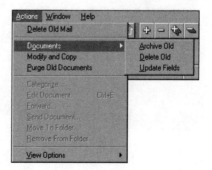

You can attach only one level of cascading to the name of an agent, and the maximum length for a cascading name is 127 bytes.

Creating an Agent

Creating an agent is a multistep process. Here's a brief outline of the steps:

1. Assign the new agent a name.

2. Select whether the agent is personal or shared.

3. Select the type of agent: manual, scheduled, and so on.

4. Select the group of database documents on which the agent will act.

5. Refine the selection by specifying search criteria based on specific field values.

6. Create the action, formula, or LotusScript program for the agent.

Here's a more detailed description of all of the preceding steps except the last one, which is covered in the next section:

1. To begin, select Create, Agent, displaying the dialog box shown in Figure 10.9.

2. Select a name for the agent.

3. To make this agent public, select the option Shared Agent. Otherwise, the agent will be private.

Figure 10.9

Use this dialog box to select the various options for an agent.

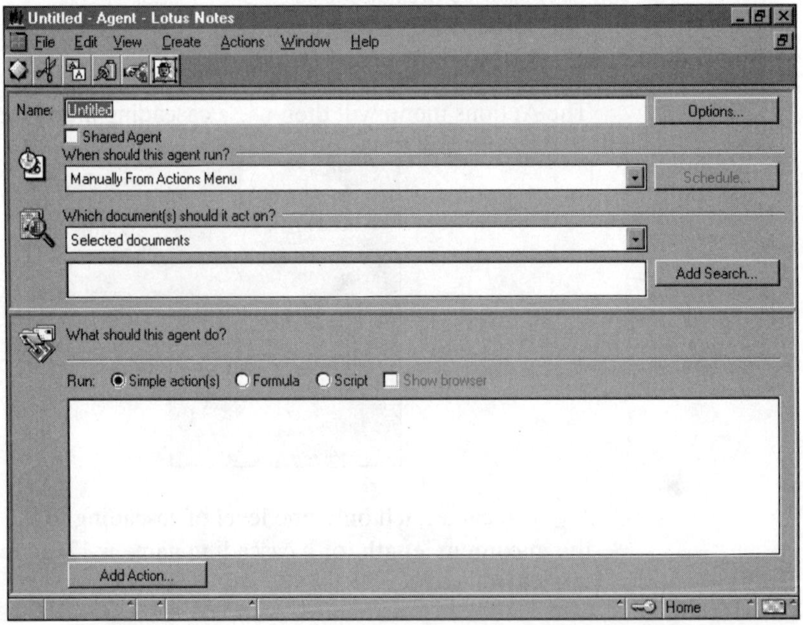

4. Select the type of agent that you're creating: Pull down the list box labeled When Should This Agent Run and then make your selection.

5. If you selected a scheduled agent in step 4, click the button labeled Schedule and then fill in the scheduling details.

6. In the list box labeled Which Documents Should It Act On, select the group of documents on which you want the agent to act. Note that for some types of agents, this option is preset and cannot be changed.

7. To further refine the group of documents on which the agent can operate, click the Add Search button. When the dialog box shown below appears, fill in the options for selecting documents that can be acted on by the agent. The selection criteria that you choose here will apply only to those documents specified in step 6.

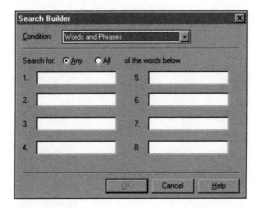

8. In the lower half of the Agent dialog box (Figure 10.9), create the action, formula, or script for the agent. (The next section describes choosing actions and writing formulas.)

Assigning a Task to an Agent

After creating a new agent, you must assign the task(s) it is to perform whenever it is run. You can select from three broad categories:

• Select a built-in Notes action

• Write a formula

• Write a LotusScript program

To make your choice, click the appropriate Run radio button in the lower half of the Agent dialog box (Figure 10.9).

    If at all possible, use one of the built-in Notes actions, because you can easily set up the agent by making selections from a list. These actions cover a fairly wide range of Notes operations, so you may benefit from studying the list of possibilities.

If the operations you want to use don't exist as a built-in Notes action, you'll probably need to create a formula for the agent. Formulas cover just about every aspect of Notes operation. For those few situations where formulas are inadequate to perform the operations that you want, you'll have to write a LotusScript program.

Assigning a Built-In Notes Action

Notes provides a wide range of built-in actions, any of which you can assign to an agent. The following table summarizes the types of operations available as built-in actions.

Action	Operation
Copy To Database	Copy the current document to the selected database (when you select this option, you must also select the database to which you want copy documents).
Delete From Database	Delete the current document from the database.
Copy To Folder	Copy the current document to a particular folder.
Mark Document Read	Mark the current document as read (remember that each document in a view is marked as either *read* or *unread*).
Mark Document Unread	Mark the current document as unread.
Modify Field	Change the value of the selected field to the specified value. When you select this action, you must select the field to be changed and also the new value.
Modify Fields By Form	Use a selected form to change values of selected fields. When you select this action, you must also choose a form and then fill in selected field values.
Move to Folder	Move the current document to a particular folder.
Remove From Folder	Remove the current document from a particular folder.
Reply To Sender	Mail a reply to the current document.

Action	Operation
Run Agent	Run another agent.
Send Document	Mail the current document.
Send Mail Message	Send a custom mail message.
Send Newsletter Summary	Send a summary of selected documents to selected recipients.

Remember that when an agent runs, the action you choose will operate on each of the documents selected for that agent. Consequently, the actions listed in the preceding table offer a wealth of possibilities for creating customized agents.

To assign a particular Notes action, follow these steps:

1. In the Actions dialog box, click the button labeled Add Action, displaying the dialog box shown in Figure 10.10.

2. Pull down the top list box, labeled Action (see below).

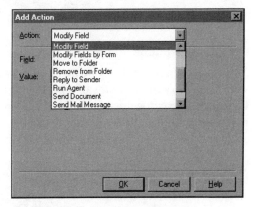

Figure 10.10

Use this dialog box to assign an action to an agent.

3. Select the type of action that you want.

4. If necessary, select the remaining options for the action.

5. Click on OK.

When you have finished assigning an action to an agent, the Design pane in the Agent dialog box will display a brief summary of the action, similar to the following:

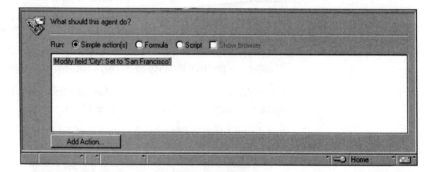

Combining Actions

You can assign more than one action to an agent. For example, you might want to modify the contents of a particular field on selected documents and then copy those documents to a folder, as indicated in the following illustration. To accomplish this, you simply use the steps described in the previous section twice—once for each action that you want to select.

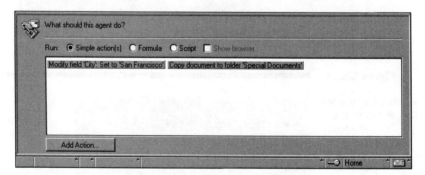

Formulas for Agents

To create a formula for an agent, you use the Design pane of the Agent dialog box (Figure 10.9). First select the radio button labeled Formula and then type in the formula.

A formula can be as long as needed, performing any number of steps. Remember that the formula will execute once for each document processed by the agent.

Every formula must include a SELECT statement, which for convenience should be at the top of the formula. This statement specifies which documents should be selected for processing by the formula. However, *this selection is limited to refining the group of documents selected as part of the agent's definition.*

For example, suppose that you're creating a manual agent, and for the option Which Documents Should It Act On, you select All Documents In View. Here, *view* refers to whatever view is selected when you run the agent. Say that you plan to use the view named Authors, which displays all the Author documents in your database. However, you want the agent to process only those documents for authors living in New York. To accomplish this, you would use the following SELECT statement as part of the agent you create:

```
SELECT State = "NY"
```

Example: Deleting a Particular Field

Suppose that you maintain a database of personnel information, including a group of documents created with the PersonalInformation form. You want to delete the field called EthnicBackground from these documents. To accomplish this, you can create an agent having the following options:

- Agent name: Delete Field (temporary)

- Shared/Private: Private

- When agent should run: Manually From Actions menu

- Which documents should it act on: All Documents In View

You make the action private because only you will be using it. Similarly, use a name that will clearly indicate both the agent's purpose and that the agent is temporary (so you'll remember to delete it when you have finished running it). When you run the agent, you'll need to be sure to select a view that displays at least all of the PersonalInformation documents.

Here's the formula for the agent:

```
SELECT Form = "PersonalInformation";
FIELD EthnicBackground := @DeleteField
```

Because of the SELECT statement, the view that you use when running the agent can display other documents as well, but they will not be modified.

Example: Creating a New Field

Using the same database described in the previous example, suppose you want to add a new field named CurrentJobDescription to the PersonalInformation documents. Here's a formula for a manual agent that will accomplish this:

```
SELECT Form = "PersonalInformation";
FIELD CurrentJobDescription := ""
```

When this agent runs, a new blank field will be added to each document that's processed. Later, you can either enter the new field values manually or possibly create another agent to enter the field values.

Example: Calculating Weekly Salary Values

You have a Personnel database containing Employee documents, and you want to create an agent that will run weekly to calculate the employees' salaries. Each employee's salary is based on the number of regular and overtime hours worked, and on his or her hourly rate. The clerical staff updates this information weekly on the Employee documents.

The Employee form contains the following fields: RegularHoursWorked, OvertimeHoursWorked, HourlyRate, and WeeklySalary.

Here are the options for the new agent:

- Agent name: Calculate Weekly Salary

- Shared/Private: Shared

- When the agent should run: Weekly

- Which documents should it act on: All Documents In Database

    Here's a formula for the agent that will calculate the weekly salaries:

```
SELECT Form := "Employee";
RegularSalary := RegularHoursWorked * HourlyRate;
OvertimeSalary := 1.5*(OvertimeHoursWorked* HourlyRate);
FIELD WeeklySalary := RegularSalary + OvertimeSalary
```

The SELECT statement limits the agent processing only to those documents created with the Employee form.

Example: Calculating Totals

The agent in the previous example calculated the weekly salary for a group of employees. Now we want to create an agent that calculates the total salary for all employees.

The solution that we present here uses two different agents, which are described in the following table.

Agent Name	Purpose
Set Total To Zero	Creates an environment variable named TotalPayroll and sets its value to zero.
Calculate Total Payroll	Processes every Employee document. For each document, the agent adds the value in the WeeklySalary field to the current total stored in the environment variable TotalPayroll.

The second agent in the preceding table uses the running total that's stored in the environment variable named TotalPayroll. Each time this agent processes an Employee document, it adds to the running total the value in the WeeklySalary field. Note that this total must be stored as an environment variable outside of the agent itself, because any variables defined as part of an agent's formula are lost each time the formula ends (remember that the formula will end once for each document it processes).

The sole purpose of the first agent listed in the previous table is to create that environment variable and set it to zero. This variable is then used as the starting point for the agent named Calculate Total Payroll.

In addition to creating the preceding two agents, the user must also create the following:

- A form named TotalPayroll, which is used to create a single document whose only purpose is to display the amount of the total payroll calculated by the agents. This document could have only a single field named Total with the following properties:

  - Field type: Number, Computed
  - Formula: @Environment("TotalPayroll")

  This formula guarantees that the field value will always display the current value stored in the environment variable named TotalPayroll.

- A view from which the preceding document can be displayed.

  Following are the listings of the two agents.

Agent: Set Total To Zero

When agent should run: Manually From Actions Menu

Which documents should it act on: Run Once (@Commands May Be Used).

Formula:

```
REM "This agent sets the environment variable TotalPayroll to zero";

@SetEnvironment("TotalPayroll"; "0")
```

Agent: Calculate Total Payroll

When the agent should run: Manually

Which documents should it act on: All Documents In Database

Formula:

```
REM "This agent process all the documents created with the form Salesperson";
REM "    It adds the value in the field WeeklySalary to the current total
stored in";
REM "    the environment variable TotalPayroll.";
SELECT Form = "Employee";
CurrentTotal := @TextToNumber(@Environment("TotalPayroll"));
REM "Add the weekly salary value for the current document to the current
total";
NewTotal := CurrentTotal + WeeklySalary;
REM "Save the current total";
@SetEnvironment("TotalPayroll"; @Text(CurrentTotal))
```

Most of this agent is concerned with converting text values to numbers, and vice versa. The reason is that an environment variable can contain only text, so a number must be converted to text before it can be stored.

Running the Agents   Having set up the agents described in the preceding sections, here's how a user could calculate the weekly payroll:

1. First, update all the Employee documents to reflect this week's salary information.

2. Run the agent Set Total To Zero.

3. Run the agent Calculate Total Payroll.

4. Display the TotalPayroll document, which would show the final value for the total payroll, stored in the environment variable.

- *Importing and Pasting Information*
- *Using File Attachments*
- *Linking Documents to External Information*
- *Embedding Information in Notes Documents*

11

User Tools for Integrating Other Information

IF YOU ROUTINELY CREATE NOTES DOCUMENTS, RELEASE 4 PROVIDES a wide variety of easy-to-use tools that allow you to include many different types of information with your creations.

NOTE. *Although primarily oriented toward users, the information contained in this chapter is also essential to database designers, who have to provide the forms with which users can create their documents.*

The oldest—but still effective—methods for incorporating information into Notes documents are importing documents and copying and pasting information. You can copy and paste diverse types of information into Notes documents, and on rare occasions, you might even want to import an entire document. Copying and pasting will almost always be successful, provided that the operating system can put the information into the Clipboard. Importing a file will work whenever Notes can manage to read the information.

Attaching files is, of course, old news, and you can continue to use this tried-and-tested technique for transmitting any type of file along with your documents. This technique is particularly powerful when used with Notes, because of Notes's information-sharing and workflow capabilities.

If an attached file happens to be a document, Notes provides convenient tools to help a recipient immediately launch and view the file's contents—provided the recipient has access to the parent software.

The latest version of the OLE standard—2.0—brings new ease and reliability to linking and embedding information from other sources, and Notes takes full advantage of these features to help you create documents with a mixture of diverse components.

To accomplish this wizardry, you can insert either linked or embedded OLE objects. The type of object you create depends on circumstances: If you want the Notes document to automatically reflect the latest information contained in a document stored somewhere else, you store an *OLE link* to that document. Then, whenever you open the document, Notes can easily update the linked object to display the current information in the linked file.

Instead of creating a link to an external file somewhere else, you can create an *embedded OLE object*. This type of object is actually part of the Notes document, and unlike a linked object, it has no attachment to any other document outside of Notes.

In order to create a linked or embedded object, you use an outside software package, called the *source application*. This application must be registered with your operating system as an OLE server; registration usually happens automatically when the software is installed. Many major software packages are now designed to act as OLE servers. For example, if you're running a relatively recent release of a software package on Windows 95, chances are very good that it's OLE-aware.

■ Importing and Pasting Information

Before describing the more exotic methods available to you for including various types of information as part of your Notes documents, let's first look at the more simple means at your disposal: importing entire documents and copying and pasting information from other documents.

These two methods have one important difference: You can import an entire document only into a rich text field, whereas when you paste information, the type of field you can use depends on the nature of the information.

Importing Documents

You can import a document into a rich text field, provided that Notes has a filter that can read the file. Here's a list of the major types of documents you can import:

- .BMP image

- .CGM image

- JPEG image

- Lotus .PIC image

- .PCX image

- .TIF image

- ASCII text

- Lotus 1-2-3 worksheet

- Microsoft Excel worksheet

- Multimate document

- Microsoft Word document

- WordPerfect document

This list may not be complete, because other filters probably will be added in the future.

Not all parts of all types of documents can be read with 100 percent accuracy. For instance, typically all of the text from a word processed document will be read accurately, but some formatting may be lost.

TIP. *If you want to retain all of the text formatting in a document, don't use importing. Instead, create either a linked or embedded OLE object in the Notes document.*

Also, do not try to import documents whose contents include both text and graphics, because typically only the text will survive. Again, use OLE objects for this purpose.

After importing, you can resize the information if it's a graphic image, or if it's text, you can edit it.

Here's how to import the contents of a file into a Notes document:

1. Make sure that the document is open in edit mode and that you have clicked on a rich text field. If the field contains other information, position the insertion point exactly where you want the new information to be placed.

2. Select File, Import. When the dialog box shown below appears, select the file that you want to import and then click the button labeled Import.

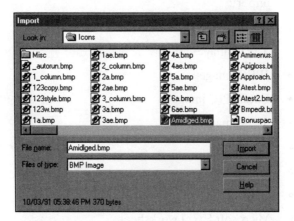

3. If the imported file contains a graphic image, you can resize it: Grab the handle in the lower-right corner of the image and drag it one way or the other.

4. If the imported file contains text, you can edit it any way you wish.

Copying and Pasting

You can copy and paste either text or graphics from other applications into a Notes document. If the information is entirely textual, you can paste it into any type of field. However, you can paste graphics only into rich text fields. If you can manage to copy both text and graphics to the Clipboard at the same time (yes, it's possible), only the text will survive the paste operation.

If you copy and paste a graphic image, you can then resize it within the Notes document. On the other hand, if the pasted information is text, you can edit it.

There are a couple of little tricks involved with copying and pasting, so let's briefly go through the steps:

1. Open the source document in the source application, select the information that you want, and copy it to the Clipboard.

2. Switch to the Notes document and click on the field that is to receive the information.

3. Pull down the Edit menu.

4. Select the Paste command. If the information pastes properly, you're done.

5. If the information does not paste properly, delete whatever did get pasted (if anything) and then select the Edit, Paste Special command.

6. Select the Paste option. Then, in the list box labeled As, select either Picture or Bitmap. *Do not select the top option.* Click OK to finish up.

If the pasted information is a graphic image, you can easily resize it: Grab the handle in the lower-right corner and then drag it in or out to resize the image.

If you can't successfully paste the information by using the preceding steps, you'll probably need to create an embedded OLE object. This process is described later in this chapter.

■ Using File Attachments

Attaching files is a standard technique for transmitting just about any type of computerized information. Because of Notes's information-sharing and workflow capabilities, attaching files is particularly powerful.

You can attach any file you want to a Notes document: worksheets, word-processed documents, binary data files, executable programs, and so on.

When you use file attaching, a copy of the original file is appended to the document. Whatever subsequently happens to this copy has no affect on the original.

In many ways, the easiest way to electronically transmit a file is to attach it to a Notes document and then send the document to the intended recipients. The attachment process is almost a no-brainer: You select the file by name and then click the mouse button once or twice.

The recipient of an attachment can use Notes' built-in viewer to investigate the attachment's contents. If the attachment is in a common format—a word-processed document, a spreadsheet, and so on—the recipient may also be able to launch the attachment directly from the Notes document, provided of course that the parent software is available.

NOTE. *With the development of embedded and linked OLE objects—and their inherent advantages—file attaching is not as critical as it once was. However, in some circumstances, attaching may be the only electronic way that you can transmit a file to someone else. This would be the case, for example, if the file were an executable, or if the file were a document whose source software did not support OLE embedding or linking.*

Setting Up a Form

The only requirement for file attaching is that it must be done within a rich text field. However, a document only needs to contain one rich text field, which can contain any number of attached files. Figure 11.1 illustrates a form containing a single rich text field.

Figure 11.1

This form contains a single rich text field for attaching files.

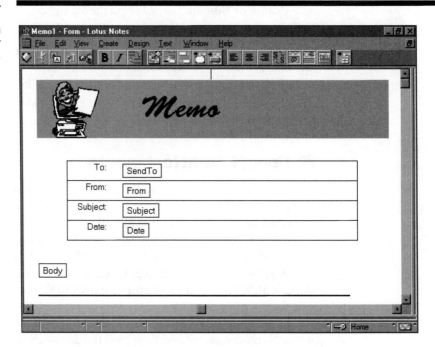

Attaching a File to a Document

The steps for attaching a file to a document are quite straightforward:

1. Using the appropriate form, begin creating a new document.

2. Click on the rich text field.

3. Select File, Attach, displaying the dialog box shown in Figure 11.2.

4. Be sure that the Compress option is selected—unless you have a special reason for doing otherwise.

5. Select the file that you want to attach and then click the Create button.

Figure 11.2

Use this dialog box to select the file you want to attach.

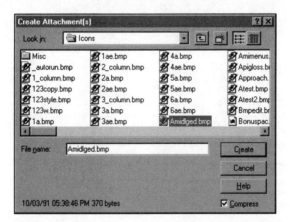

When you've finished, Notes will display an icon in the field, representing the attached file. If the software corresponding to the attached file is available to you, its own icon will be displayed. Otherwise, Notes uses a generic icon.

If you want to attach more than one file to the same rich text field:

1. Click again in the rich text field, if necessary.

2. Using the arrow keys, position the insertion point where you want to insert the icon for the attachment. Make sure that none of the icons is selected; otherwise, the File, Attach option will not be available.

3. Use the procedure described in steps 3 through 5 above to select the file you want to attach.

Figure 11.3 shows a document created with the form shown in Figure 11.1, containing several file attachments.

Using Attached Files

Once you have received a document containing an attached file, you can decide how to handle that file. You can

- Display information about the attachment

- View the attachment

- Detach the file

- Launch the file

Figure 11.3

This document contains
several file attachments.

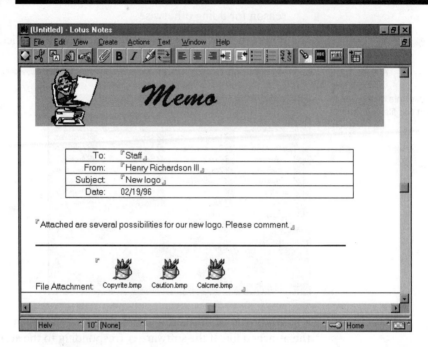

Viewing the Attachment

You can have Notes display the original name of a file attachment, and also
the date on which it was last modified. You can also use Notes's built-in
viewer to scan the contents of the attachment. Of course, this works only if
the viewer can recognize and interpret the file's contents, but amazingly
enough, there are very few files that the viewer can't interpret. For example,
if you try to view an .EXE file or a .COM file, the viewer will read and display any textual information stored in its header.

To view information about an attachment, double-click on it, and Notes
will display the Attachment InfoBox (see the following figure).

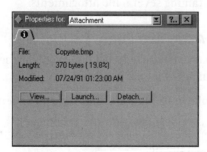

To view the contents of the attachment, first click on it; then either select Attachment, View or double-click on the attachment and click the View button on the Attachment InfoBox. If contents of the attachment are unrecognizable, the viewer will either do nothing or display a message to that effect.

Detaching a File

When you detach a file, Notes copies it to a new file on the directory that you select, and with the file name that you choose. After you detach the file, the original remains attached to the document. However, unless you have a compelling reason to do otherwise, remove the attachment in order to reduce the disk space needed by the document: Click on the icon for the attachment (if there's more than one icon, make sure that you click on the correct one) and then either press the Del key or select Edit, Cut.

Launching a File

If the parent application for an attached file is available, you can launch the file directly from the Notes document. For example, if the attachment is a Microsoft Word document, and if you have access to Word, you can let Notes do the launching work for you.

To launch an attachment from a document, click on the attachment and then do either of the following:

- Select Attachment, Launch.

- Double-click on the attachment and then click the Launch button.

After an attachment has been launched, you can use the parent software to edit it in whatever way you wish; and then save it to a new file.

NOTE. *Launching an attachment has no effect on the original, attached file. For example, you can launch an attachment, modify it, and then save it to a new file. The original file—which is still attached to the Notes document—remains unchanged.*

Auto-Launching a File

A database designer can set up a form so that each time you open a document created with that form, Notes will automatically launch the first attached file in the document. This would be handy, for example, if the main purpose of each Notes document is to send an attached document to a user and make it as easy as possible for the user to view that attachment.

When a form is set up with this option, there's one side effect that may or may not be desirable. You never have access to the rest of the Notes document that contains the attachment, because here's what happens: When you open a document, Notes immediately launches the source application for the attachment and loads the attachment, which you can then view and edit. When you exit from the software, Notes automatically closes the document and returns to the view from which the document was opened.

If you're a form designer, and if you're setting up a form to contain attachments, here's how to design the form to auto-launch the first attachment in each document:

1. Make sure that the form is opened for editing.

2. Display the Form InfoBox and then click on the Launch tab.

3. Select the option Auto Launch First Attachment.

Remember that this option works only for the first attachment in each document, and that the rest of the document will be unavailable to the user.

This doesn't mean that these documents are completely unavailable. On the contrary, a designer can create a special view for displaying the same documents. This view contains a form formula to specify that a different form be used for opening the document—a form in which the auto-launch option is *not* specified.

Customizing Views for Displaying Attachments

NOTE. *Unlike most of the chapter, which is oriented toward end-users, this section is specifically for database designers.*

You can set up views displaying special information for documents containing attachments. This information can include the following:

- An icon indicating the presence of one or more attachments

- The number of attachments

- The names and lengths of the attachments

To display this information in a view, you create special columns for that purpose. The formulas for these columns will use one or more of the Notes functions shown in Table 11.1.

Table 11.1

Notes Functions That Deal with Attachments.

FUNCTION NAME	VALUE RETURNED
@Attachments	The number of attachments for the current document
@AttachmentNames	The file name of each attachment
@AttachmentLengths	The length of each attachment

To illustrate how these functions work, Figure 11.4 illustrates a view displaying information about attachments. The little paper-clip icon indicates the presence of one or more attachments, while the right-hand columns display the attachment file names and sizes in bytes.

Figure 11.4

This view displays information about attachments.

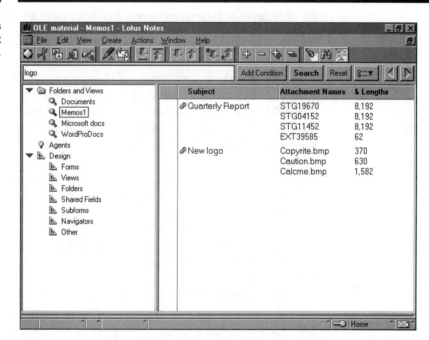

Table 11.2 lists the column formulas for the view shown in Figure 11.4.

Table 11.2

Column Formulas Used in Figure 11.4.

COLUMN	COLUMN FORMULA	SPECIAL COLUMN OPTIONS SELECTED
1	@If(@Attachments; 5; 0)	Display values as icons; Column cannot be resized
2	Subject	
3	@AttachmentNames	Multi-Value Separator = New Line
4	@AttachmentLengths	Multi-Value Separator = New Line

Here's a bit of explanation about the various entries in Table 11.2:

- Column 1. The @If function returns either the value 5 or 0. The option Display Values As Icons translates the number 5 into the Attachments icon—a paper clip. If the number 0 is returned, no icon is displayed.

- Columns 3 and 4. This New Line option forces each value to start on a new line in the view. For this option to work properly, you must also set the *view* options that allow multiple lines per row.

■ Linking Documents to External Information

The cutting edge of software technology contains powerful features for linking together diverse types of computerized information, and as a Notes end user, you can take full advantage of these resources. Using OLE linking, you can create Notes documents that reflect the latest information stored in many different types of application documents. You can create a link between a Notes document and part or all of an existing document created with a source application. The part of the document that's linked is called the *linked object.*

You can optionally set up a link to display either an icon or a visual duplicate of the original object. For instance, if you're linking to a tiny piece of a worksheet, you might want to display the actual information in the Notes document. On the other hand, if a linked object is too large to be displayed comfortably on the screen, you'll probably want to display an icon instead of the object itself. In any case, only the first page of a linked object appears in a Notes document.

When you open a Notes document containing an OLE link to another type of document, you can access the original source document by double-clicking on the image of the source document in the Notes document—provided that you have direct access to the source application. Notes will then launch that application and load the source document, and you can then make whatever changes are needed.

When you gain access to the source document, you can edit any part of it, not just the part that is directly linked to the Notes document.

On the other hand, if someone makes changes to the original source document—not from within Notes, but by direct access to the source application—those changes will automatically be reflected in the linked Notes document.

If the source file is moved from its original location, the OLE link to the Notes document is severed, and a new one will need to be established between the Notes document and the source document in its new location.

Pros and Cons of Using OLE

There are things you can do with OLE objects that you just can't dream of doing any other way. The most obvious one is that you can include a tremendous variety of different types of information in your Notes documents. Furthermore, linked OLE objects offer the additional advantage of displaying the latest information in Notes documents—all at the click of a mouse.

Using OLE objects is not all gravy, and in fact there are at least two significant disadvantages. First of all, using OLE objects can noticeably slow down your work—slower than you might wish. Just opening a Notes document containing OLE objects isn't the problem; the difficulty comes when you want to load a source application—or several of them—either to create objects in your documents or to make changes to them.

For instance, suppose you're creating a Notes document, and you decide to impress your boss by inserting a small Lotus 1-2-3 worksheet. In order to do this, you'll need to launch 1-2-3, and if your network happens to be busy, this could take quite a bit of time.

As another example, suppose that you open a Notes document containing three linked objects: part of a Microsoft Word document, a Lotus 1-2-3 chart, and a special graphic created with CorelDRAW. If you think that all of the source documents have been recently modified, you'll need to update all three links. If so, you'll probably have time to take a nice coffee break, because Notes will have to launch each of the three server packages in turn, let each one update its link, and then close that server when it's done.

Even with the fastest hardware now available, the newest releases of the major software packages are actually getting slower, because of all the features (read *baggage*) attached to them. The bottom line is that you'll need to be patient when creating or modifying OLE objects.

Note. For a detailed discussion of embedded OLE objects, see "Embedding Information in Notes Documents," later in this chapter.

The other downside to using OLE objects is that they can require a great deal of disk space, and this is true both for linked and embedded objects. It's impossible to give exact space requirements for OLE objects because the variation is huge, depending on the type of object you're creating, its size, and the way in which the source application creates the object.

Here are some guidelines to follow when using OLE objects:

- Linking to part of a document generally takes up less space than embedding the entire document.

- The minimum disk space requirements for an embedded object is always more than the space required by the same object when saved as a separate document in its native format. For example, embedding a copy of a 50K object could take anywhere from 50K to 200K. That's right—four times the original size!

- The minimum disk space requirement for a linked object is at least as much as the space taken up by the object within the linked file, and it can be several times greater.

Caveats

In order for OLE linking to be possible, the source application must support OLE. Unfortunately, there's no accurate way to list all of the different software packages that support OLE linking. If you can't find a reliable source of information about your system, and if you want to find out if you can create a particular type of linked object, go ahead and try using the method described here. If it doesn't work, then you'll know that your system doesn't support that particular type of OLE link.

Creating a Linked Object

To create a link between a Notes document and part of a document created by another software package, all of the following must be true:

- The Notes document must contain a rich text field. The field can be empty, or it can contain other objects.

- The source application must support OLE links.

- The linked object—the information to which you want to link—must be part of a document that has been saved to a disk file.

- You must have direct access to the source application.

  If all of the preceding are true, here's how you can proceed to create an OLE link:

1. Switch to the source application and then open the document containing the information to which you want to link.

2. Highlight all the material to be linked.

3. Copy the highlighted material to the Clipboard: To do this, select Edit, Copy. *Do not close the document.*

4. Return to the Notes document where you want to create the link.

5. Click on the rich text field that you want to use. If the field already contains other information, position the insertion point where you want to insert the linked information. If the field contains icons for file attachments or linked objects, be sure that none of them is selected.

Note. For a discussion of other options in the Paste Special dialog box, see "Other Paste Special Options," later in this chapter.

6. Select Edit, Paste Special, displaying the dialog box shown in Figure 11.5. If this option is not available, see the next section, "When Things Don't Work."

PERFECTION ISN'T HERE YET

WARNING! OLE linking and embedding represent relatively new technology, which is still evolving. Consequently, OLE may not always work exactly like it's supposed to. For instance, there are differences between OLE as implemented under 16-bit technology (Windows 3.*x,* for example) and under 32-bit systems (Windows 95 and Windows NT). Moreover, there may be differences between the 32-bit OLE implementations on different operating systems.

OLE may behave differently with different software packages, because it's up to each software developer to meet the current OLE standards. OLE is so complex that you're virtually guaranteed to find some bits and pieces of it that don't work 100 percent properly all of the time.

Because of all these differences, what you see on your particular system may not exactly correspond to the discussions presented in this chapter for OLE linking and embedding. If we state that a particular feature works in a particular way, then it will most likely be true for your system if it is running a 32-bit version of Notes. Otherwise, you can expect differences to arise.

So why use OLE at all? Because when it does work, it's a terrific tool for combining diverse types of information into a single location—a Notes document.

Bear in mind that all is not lost if you can't get OLE linking or embedding to work properly in a particular situation. You can always fall back on either importing files or copying and pasting information. If all else fails, you can always use the file-attachment feature, which although not as sophisticated as OLE, is still very powerful—and virtually bulletproof in all Notes environments.

7. Select the option Paste Link To Source. If this option is not available, see the section "When Things Don't Work."

8. To display the actual source object in the Notes document, select the display format in the list box labeled As (see the later section "Selecting the Display Format" for details). Click OK *and then skip the rest of the steps in this list.*

Figure 11.5

Use these options to
display linked and
embedded objects.

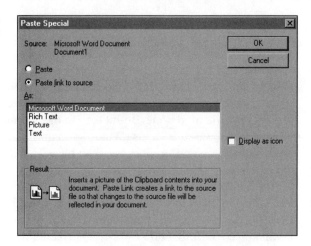

If the linked material is too voluminous to be displayed in the Notes document, you can instead display it as an icon, by performing the remaining steps:

9. Click the option Display As Icon. You'll then see the default icon for the source application.

10. If you're not satisfied either with the icon or with its label, you can change them: Click the button labeled Change Icon, displaying the following dialog box:

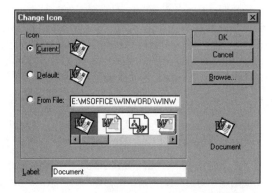

11. To change the label under the icon, type the new text in the Label edit box.

12. To select a different icon, you can either select one from the list (if any) that's displayed near the bottom of the dialog box, or you can use the

Browse button to select a different icon file and then choose the icon that you want.

If you selected a graphical type of display format for the object, you can resize it: Click on the object and then grab the handle in the lower-right corner and drag it in or out.

When Things Don't Work

If the Paste Special option is unavailable (dimmed), or if the option Paste Link To Source is unavailable in the Paste Special dialog box, then either you erred in the preceding steps, or—more likely—the source application does not support OLE linking. You can try using OLE embedding (see "Embedding Information in Notes Documents," later in this chapter), because some applications support object embedding but not linking.

If the application supports neither OLE linking nor embedding, you can try a number of alternate options:

- Copy and paste the object from the source document—not as an OLE object but as a regular one. This will probably work if the object is either all text or all graphics.

- Switch to another source application to create the source document. Of course, this may often be impractical, particularly if your organization is committed to one set of applications.

- Using the source application, create a new document that contains only the information you want to insert into Notes, save the document, and then attach it to the Notes document as an ordinary file attachment.

Selecting the Display Format

In the preceding step 8, you can select how you want the linked object to be displayed in the Notes document. Your available formats are displayed in the list box in the Paste Special dialog box. Your choices depend on the type of information that you're linking.

If you don't have any preference, select the top format, which will display the linked object just as it appears in the source document. Each of the other display formats presents an alternative way of displaying the linked object. The details of each format can't be predicted, because they will depend on how that particular format is implemented by the source application. You can easily try each one out, as follows:

1. Select one of the display options and then click OK, to return to the Notes document.

2. Click on the linked object in the document and then look on the menu bar for a new menu. For instance, if the linked object is from a Microsoft

Word document, the name of the menu will be Document. Or if the object is from an Excel worksheet, the menu name will be Worksheet. If you can't figure out which is the new menu, watch the menu bar as you click in and out of the linked object.

Note. For more information about this special menu, see "Using the Object Menu," further on.

3. Pull down the new menu and then select the option Display As, showing a list something like the following:

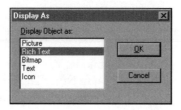

4. Select one of the display formats and then click OK. The linked object will then be redisplayed in the format that you've chosen.

5. To try the remaining display formats, repeat steps 3 and 4 for each one.

If you can't see much difference between some of the formats, it's not a cause for concern. What matters is that you can easily edit the linked object—no matter how it's displayed in the Notes document.

Other Paste Special Options

You can use the Paste Special dialog box (Figure 11.5) for purposes other than creating a link to an object. If you've copied material to the Clipboard from another application and then displayed this dialog box, here are your options:

- If you select the Paste option and also select the top option in the list box labeled As, the object will be copied into the Notes document as an embedded OLE object. (For more information about using embedded objects, see "Embedding Information in Notes Documents," later in this chapter.)

- If you select the Paste option and also select any display format except the top one, a copy of the Clipboard contents will be inserted into the Notes document—not as a linked object, but as ordinary text or graphics, depending on your selection. For example, if you select either Text or Rich Text, you can then modify the text using standard Notes editing tools.

Working with Linked Objects

When you open a Notes document containing one or more linked objects, you'll probably see the message shown below. If you select Yes, Notes will display the latest version of the source document in the Notes document.

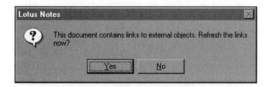

This process may take quite a while, because for each linked object in the document, the following steps take place: the corresponding source application is launched, the linked object is loaded, and the application is then closed.

If any of the original source documents has been moved or deleted, Notes will not be able to find it and will display a message to that effect. Notes will display the last version of the linked object in the document but will be unable to update it.

TIP. *If you know beforehand that you'll be using Notes documents containing OLE links to particular types of source documents, then before you begin editing your Notes work, open those applications* from within your operating system *and then minimize the applications. Later, when you open a Notes document containing OLE links, you can let Notes update all of the linked objects—without having to wait for each source application to be opened— because Notes will detect and use the applications that are already running.*

Also, when you double-click on an OLE object to edit it, Notes will use the running application—a lot quicker than waiting for the application to be loaded.

Using the Object Menu

Whenever you click on a linked object in a Notes document, a special menu appears on the Notes menu bar. The name of this menu will depend on the type of linked object. For example, if the object is part of a WordPro or Word document, the menu name will be Document. Or if the object is part of a Freelance presentation, the menu name will be Presentation.

You can use this menu to accomplish any of the following:

- Display the InfoBox for the object

- Change the display format of the object

- Launch the source application and open the object for editing

When you display the InfoBox for an object, it will appear something like that shown below. The options that you may find useful are related to formatting the "paragraph" containing the object. For instance, you can change the left margin, center the object between the left and right margins, and so on. You can also select options to hide the object either in view mode or edit mode.

If you select either of the object menu options Edit or Open, Notes launches the source application and loads the source document, which you can then edit. (These two options behave the same for linked objects, but they have different purposes when used with embedded OLE objects.)

Deleting a Linked Object

You can easily delete a linked object from a Notes document; this is an entirely different operation from deleting the linked object in the original source document. When you delete an object from a Notes document, the original object in the source document remains unchanged. However, if you delete the object from the source document, then when the link is subsequently updated, an empty space will be displayed for the the linked object in the Notes document. However, if the original source document still exists, you can launch it by double-clicking on that empty space.

To delete a linked object from a Notes document, open the document in edit mode. Then click on the object and either press Del or select Edit, Cut.

WARNING! *You can't reverse the act of deleting a linked object—even if you use Edit, Cut. However, accidentally deleting a linked object isn't a particularly serious crime, because you can recover by repeating the entire linking process.*

Editing a Linked Object

There are two ways to edit a linked object: from within the Notes document containing the link, or by launching the source application and then loading and editing the original source document. In both cases, the user is free to modify any part of the document—not just the linked object. In fact, when a user opens the source document from within the source application, he or she can't tell which part of the document is linked to a Notes document.

To edit a linked object from a Notes document, follow these steps:

1. Be sure that you have direct access to the source application for that object (otherwise, you don't have a link in the first place).

2. Open the Notes document containing the link.

3. Switch to edit mode: Pull down the Actions menu and make sure that the Edit Document option is selected (or press Ctrl+E).

4. Double-click anywhere on the linked object—whether it's an icon or a copy of the actual linked material. Notes will then either launch the source application or make it active if it's already running; that application will then load the source document containing the linked object.

5. Make whatever changes you want; you can edit any part of the source document—not just the part that's linked to the Notes document.

6. When you're finished editing, be sure to save the changes—usually, File, Save will do the job, but different software packages may have different equivalent commands.

7. Close the source document: File, Close is the most common command.

8. You can either close the source application or leave it running—depending on your intentions. For instance, if you plan to use it again later, leave it running.

9. Return to Notes.

NOTE. *Sometimes, when you return to the Notes document after making changes to a linked object, the changes will not appear. This will correct itself either the next time you edit the object or the next time you open the document and let Notes update the links; or, if you want to see the changes immediately, press F9.*

If your Notes document is open in read mode and you double-click on a linked object, Notes displays the following message, implying that you can't edit the object:

This message may or may not be true, depending on which flavor of
OLE you're running, and also on which source application is involved. Just
to be sure, switch to edit mode before attempting to edit a linked object.

Examples of Linking

You can create an OLE link to any document whose parent application supports that type of link. For instance, many of the major components of both
Microsoft Office and Lotus SmartSuite support OLE.

A Linked Table in Microsoft Word

Suppose your company has generated a quarterly earnings report, which naturally consists of several dozen pages. The report was created with Microsoft
Word, and luckily, the essence of the report is presented in a simple table
that shows the summary sales figures.

You can distribute a Notes memo that contains just that table as follows:
Open Microsoft Word, then open the Word document, select the entire table,
and copy it to the Clipboard. Switch to Notes, create a new memo, and create a link (in a rich text field) to the table. Figure 11.6 shows how the result
might appear.

Figure 11.6

This memo displays a
copy of a linked table in a
Microsoft Word document.

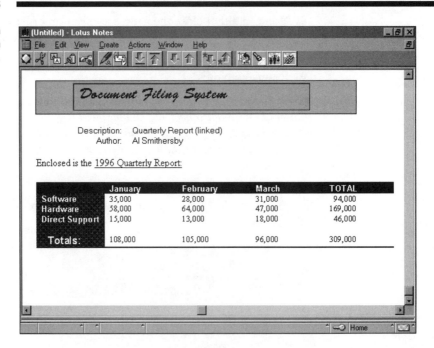

A Linked Freelance Presentation

Some presentation packages create objects that can be linked. For example, you can create a Notes document and insert a link to a part of a presentation created in Freelance Graphics. Figure 11.7 illustrates this type of document. To launch Freelance and load the presentation, double-click on the figure in the Notes document.

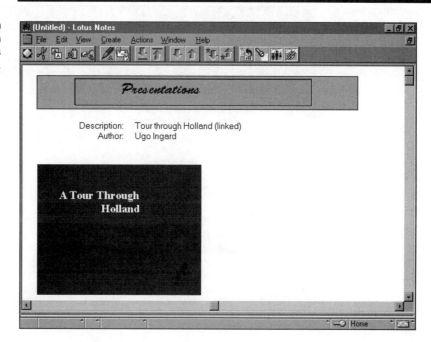

Here's a quick look at the steps you need to go through to create this type of link:

1. In Freelance Graphics, create the complete presentation. Be sure to save it to a file.

2. Select View, Page Sorter.

3. Click on the page that you want displayed in the Notes document.

4. Copy the page to the Clipboard.

5. Return to Notes and open the document where you want to create the link.

6. Click on the appropriate rich text field; select Edit, Paste Special; and then create the link.

7. Resize the image in the Notes document to suit the rest of the page.

A Linked Excel Chart

Figure 11.8 shows a Notes document that contains an image of a linked chart in a Microsoft Excel worksheet. Notice how the chart and its labels blend right in with the rest of the document. To the uninformed eyeball, the document appears to be an integrated whole!

Figure 11.8

This document contains a link to a Microsoft Excel chart.

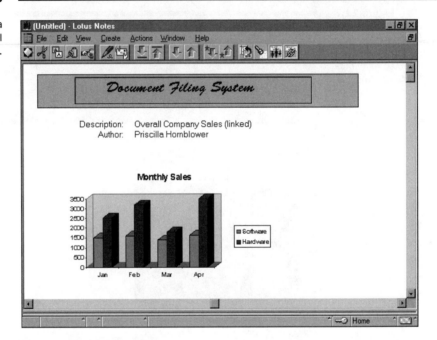

■ Embedding Information in Notes Documents

The latest incarnation of object linking and embedding has reached a high level of maturity. Using this technology, you can embed various types of OLE objects into your Notes documents. For instance, you can create a document that contains a copy of an Excel worksheet, a PowerPoint presentation, or a Microsoft Word document—or all three!

WARNING! *Embedding OLE objects doesn't always work exactly as it's supposed to. For details, see "Caveats," earlier in this chapter.*

Many software packages that support embedded OLE objects are now available—which means that you can embed objects created with that software in

Notes documents. Here's a sample—not meant by any means to be complete—of the types of objects that you can embed in Notes documents:

- Word processed documents (Microsoft Word and Lotus Word Pro)

- Worksheets (Lotus 1-2-3 and Microsoft Excel)

- Presentations (Lotus Freelance Graphics and Microsoft PowerPoint)

- Databases (Microsoft Access and Lotus Approach)

- Drawings (Microsoft Paint, CorelPHOTO-PAINT, Lotus Freelance, and many others)

- Charts (CorelCHART, Lotus Approach, Microsoft Excel)

- Forms (Lotus Word Pro, Microsoft Word)

- Sound clips and MIDI sequences

- Special notes (Lotus Annotator)

- Video clips

The only types of OLE objects that you'll be able to create are those for applications registered with your operating system as OLE object servers, and this registration occurs when the software is installed.

Here's how you can determine which types of linked OLE objects you can create: Open any Notes document that contains a rich text field and then click on that field. If the field contains any objects, make sure that none of them is selected. Select Create, Object, displaying the dialog box shown in Figure 11.9. The list shown in this dialog box displays all of the different types of linked OLE objects that you can create.

Figure 11.9

Use this dialog box to create an embedded object.

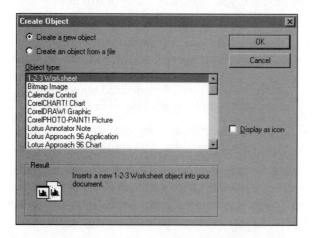

There are at least two very good reasons for embedding OLE objects in Notes documents:

- You can pull together diverse types of information into a single, integrated document. For instance, a document could contain a sound clip, an Excel worksheet, and a PowerPoint presentation.

- You can store many different types of information under the Notes umbrella. This offers all the advantages inherent in Notes: convenient views for sorting and displaying documents, built-in mailing facilities, and so on.

When you embed an OLE object, a copy of the original object is embedded in the Notes document. To edit an object, you double-click on it. Notes then launches the source application and loads the object into it, which you can then edit.

You can embed two types of objects: a copy of part or all of an existing document, or new information that you create from within Notes. When you embed a copy of an external document, the copy becomes part of the Notes document, and thereafter (unlike an OLE-*linked* object) the object has no connection to the original document.

To create a new embedded object within a Notes document, you first specify which type of object you want to create (an Excel worksheet, a sound clip, or whatever); Notes then loads the source application, where you create the object.

OLE 2.0 also allows you to create an embedded object by dragging and dropping it from the original source document into the Notes document. Alternatively, you can drag the object to your operating system's workspace and temporarily drop it there. Then, whenever convenient, you can drag and drop the object from the workspace into the Notes document.

The latest version of OLE—version 2—offers some other slick features. For example, you can select either of two modes in which to edit an OLE-embedded object:

- The Notes document continues to be displayed along with the object, but the top part of the Notes window changes to display the tools of the source application—including menus and icon bars. You can switch back and forth between the embedded object and other parts of the Notes document, simply by clicking where you want to edit.

- The source application becomes the active window, displaying the OLE object; the Notes document remains hidden in the background.

Each mode of editing has its advantages, depending on what you're doing. If an embedded object is small enough—such as a teeny worksheet—you can display it as an exact copy of the original object, and it can blend in quite naturally as part of the Notes document. However, if the object is too large

to be comfortably displayed, you can optionally choose to display an icon instead of the object itself.

Embedding a Complete Document

You can OLE-embed a copy of any document created by a software package
that supports embedded OLE objects. The new object becomes part of the
Notes document in which it's embedded and is completely unconnected from
the original document.

To embed a copy of an existing document as an OLE object, follow
these steps:

1. Create or open the Notes document that is to contain the embedded object.

2. Click on the rich text field where you want to embed the object. If the
   field already contains other information, position the insertion point
   where you want to insert the linked information. If the field contains
   icons for file attachments or linked objects, be sure that none of them is
   selected.

3. Select Create Object. When the Create Object dialog box appears, select
   the option Create An Object From A File, so that the dialog box appears as shown in Figure 11.10.

Figure 11.10

Use this dialog box to
begin selecting a
document to embed as
an OLE object.

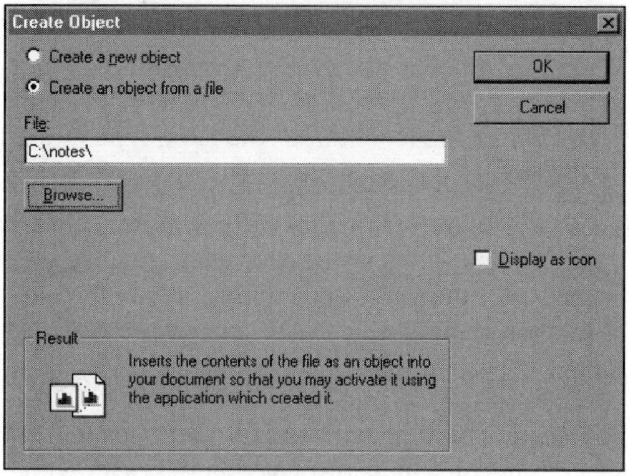

4. Click the Browse button, select the name of the document file that you
   want to embed, and then click OK.

5. When the Create Object dialog reappears, make sure that the correct
   file name appears there.

6. To display the actual object in the Notes document, make sure that the option Display As Icon is *deselected* and then click OK.

   TIP. *Unless you're absolutely sure that the object will be too big, start by displaying it in the document. If it's not attractive, you can easily replace it with an icon. Remember: Notes typically displays only the first page of an embedded object in a Notes document.*

   If you're positive that the object is too large to be displayed in the Notes document, you can display an icon instead, with the following steps.

7. Click the option Display As Icon.

8. If you're not satisfied either with the icon that appears or with its label, you can change either one: Click the button labeled Change Icon, displaying the following dialog box:

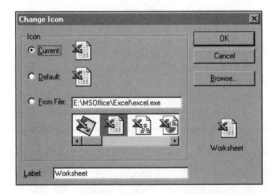

9. To change the label under the icon, type in the new text in the Label edit box.

10. To select a different icon, you can either select one from the list (if any) that's displayed near the bottom of the dialog box, or you can use the Browse button to select a different icon file and then choose the icon that you want.

11. Click on OK as many times as necessary to close all open dialog boxes.

    Depending on the options you have selected, either the embedded object or an icon will be displayed in the rich text field.

Embedding Part of a Document

You can select part of an existing document and embed it as a separate object within a Notes document. This can be part of a word-processed document, a worksheet, or any other document created by an OLE-compliant application.

After embedding, the object is no longer attached to the original file; you can make whatever changes you want to the object, and the original file remains oblivious.

You can embed part of a document in any of the following ways:

- Via the Clipboard

- By dragging and dropping via the operating system's workspace

- By direct dragging and dropping

Note. The last two options are available only on some operating systems—Windows 95, for example.

The last two of the preceding leading-edge methods seem particularly attractive—and they are indeed very impressive. However, in practice you'll probably find that unless you have a gigantic screen, it's a lot easier to use the old-fashioned Clipboard approach than it is to rearrange both the Notes and application software windows so that you can conveniently perform a drag-and-drop operation.

Having said that, we'll describe all of the preceding techniques—which, except for rearranging windows, are quite easy.

Setting Up

To begin setting up the Notes document to which you're going to insert an embedded OLE object, make sure that the document is open in edit mode and that there's an available rich text field. Next, switch to the source application and document from which you want to copy a piece as an OLE object. Highlight the portion of the document that you want to copy.

Now you're ready to use one of the following three methods to create the embedded object.

Using the Clipboard

Using the Clipboard is undoubtedly the fastest and easiest of the three methods. Here are the steps to follow:

1. Copy the object to the Clipboard.

2. Return to the Notes document.

3. Select Edit, Paste Special, displaying the dialog box shown in Figure 11.5.

4. Select the Paste option.

5. In the list box labeled As, select the top option, which describes the type of object you're pasting (Microsoft Word document, Microsoft Excel chart, and so on).

6. To display the object as an icon, select the corresponding check box.

7. To paste the object, click on OK.

Dragging and Dropping

If the drag-and-drop feature is available on your operating system, you can use it to insert an embedded OLE object in a Notes document as follows: Arrange the windows for Notes and the source application so that the parts containing the object (in the source application) and the rich text field (in the Notes application) are both visible on your screen. Then simply drag and drop the object from the application to the rich text field.

The dropped object becomes embedded in the Notes document—it's part of the document and is no longer associated with the source document.

Indirect Drag and Drop

Some operating systems include the OLE 2.0 feature that permits you to create a *scrap* by dragging and dropping an object from a source document to the system workspace. When this feature works, all you need to do is simultaneously display both the application and part of the workspace and then drag-and-drop the object from the document to the workspace.

For example, an object dropped onto a Windows 95 workspace looks something like the following:

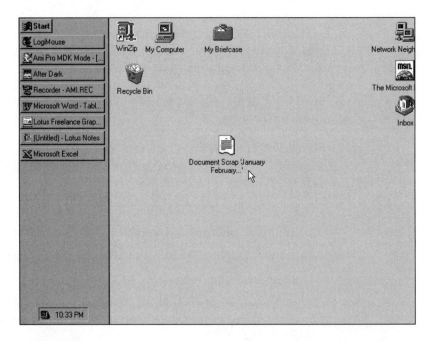

If you're not sure whether or not your system allows this slick operation, just try it. If it works, fine; otherwise, you'll need to use one of the other two methods described previously.

Embedding a New Object

OLE technology allows you to create a brand new embedded object from within a Notes document. This is different from creating an object by making a copy from an existing document: Here, you're starting from scratch.

To create a new embedded object, you specify the type that you want to build; Notes then temporarily opens the corresponding source application so that you can create your masterpiece. However, during this process *the Notes window remains visible*, but the top part of it is replaced by the standard menu bar (except for the File menu) and toolbars of the source document. Figure 11.11 illustrates how your window might appear.

Figure 11.11

Creating a new OLE object within a Notes document.

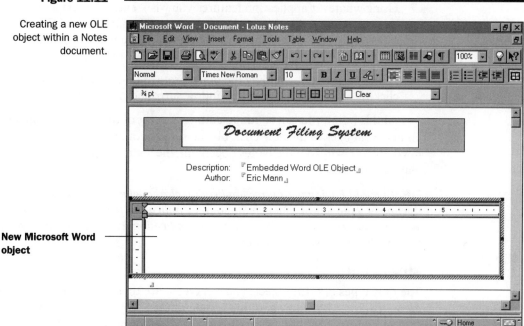

New Microsoft Word object

When you're done, you simply click outside of the new object to return to the Notes document. The object then appears as just another part of the document.

To create a new embedded object, follow these steps:

1. Create or open the Notes document where you want to build the new object.

2. Click on the rich text field where you want to embed the object. If the field already contains other information, position the insertion point where you want to insert the linked information. If the field contains icons for file attachments or other objects, be sure that none of them is selected.

11

3. Select Create, Object.

4. Scroll down the displayed list (see Figure 11.9) until you find the type of object you want to create, select the entry, and click OK. If you can't find what you want, then you're out of luck (see the next section, "Striking Out").

5. Notes will load the source application, displaying a new, empty object—which is surrounded by handles. You should still be able to see part of the Notes document as well, as shown in Figure 11.11.

6. If necessary, you can expand the new object by grabbing a top or bottom handle and dragging it outward.

7. Using whatever application features you wish, enter the text and graphics you want for the object—*but do not use File, Save or File, Close* because unlike the rest of the menu bar, the File menu belongs to Notes—not to the source application.

8. When you're done building the object, return to the Notes document by clicking anywhere outside the window surrounding the object.

At this point, you can continue editing the rest of the Notes document. To make changes to the new OLE object, simply double-click anywhere on it. When you exit from the Notes document, the source application will automatically be closed.

TIP. *To avoid having the source application closed when you exit from a Notes document, plan ahead: Launch the source application from your operating system—not from within Notes. Then the application will remain active when you exit from the Notes document.*

Striking Out

The only types of OLE objects you can create are those for applications that are registered with your operating system as OLE object servers. This registration occurs when the software is installed and forms the basis for the items displayed on the list in the Create Object dialog box. If the application you want to use isn't listed here, you may need to install a later version of it—if one exists.

Working with Embedded Objects

When you open a Notes document containing an embedded OLE object, the complete object will appear—unless one of the following is true:

• The object is longer than a page—in which case, usually only the first page appears.

- You elected to represent the object by an icon in the Notes document.

To illustrate the various options available for editing an embedded object, we use the Notes document shown in Figure 11.12, which contains an embedded Excel worksheet.

Figure 11.12

This Notes document contains an embedded worksheet.

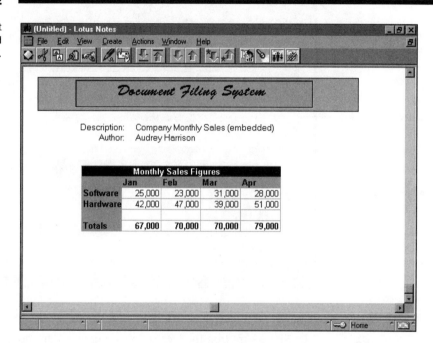

You can edit the embedded worksheet in either of two ways: in place, with the Notes document still in view; or separately in an Excel window, with the Notes document not shown.

Editing an Object in Place

Note. You can't use this mode of editing if the embedded object is displayed as an icon.

When you edit an object in place, you're utilizing some of the leading-edge OLE technology: The entire Notes document remains visible in the window, but the menus and other major tools of the source application appear at the top.

As an example, Figure 11.13 shows the same Notes document shown in Figure 11.12—but with the embedded Excel object ready for editing. Notice the following features:

- The standard Microsoft Excel menus and icon bars appear at the top of the window.

- The embedded object appears as an ordinary Excel worksheet—but within the Notes document!

- Although it's not obvious from the figure, the File menu remains that of Lotus Notes—not of Excel.

Figure 11.13

Editing an embedded OLE object.

Excel menus and icon bars

Notes document

Embedded object

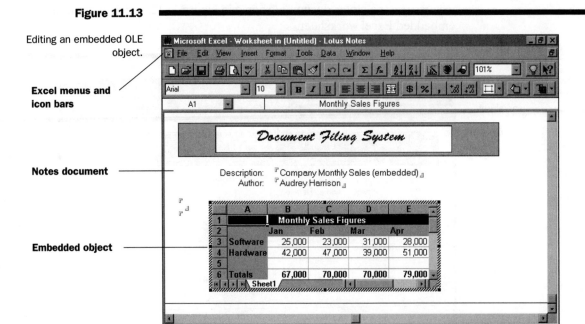

Here's how to use this mode of editing for an embedded object:

1. Make sure that the Notes document is in edit mode: Pull down the Actions menu and select the Edit Document option (or press Ctrl+E).

2. Double-click on the embedded object. Alternatively, you can select *MenuName*/Edit, where *MenuName* depends on the type of embedded object. For instance, if the object is a worksheet, *MenuName* will be *Worksheet*.

You can use all of the source application's features—except those that happen to reside on the File menu, because that menu is still that of Lotus Notes. If you need any of the server's File menu features, see the next section, "Editing an Object by Itself."

To edit any part of the Notes document other than the embedded object, simply click there. The standard Notes menus will reappear, and you can continue editing. When you want to return to editing the object, simply double-click on it.

When you're ready to save your changes, select File, Save. To exit from the document, select File, Close. If Notes displays an extraneous Save Changes dialog box, just select Yes and don't worry about it.

Editing an Object by Itself

Note. If the object is displayed as an icon, this is the only way in which you can edit the object.

If an embedded object is fairly large, you may want to edit it by itself, using a separate window. In this case, the Notes window is temporarily hidden, while the application window is brought to the front.

Here's how to edit an object in this mode:

1. Make sure that the Notes document is in edit mode.

Note. The menu name will depend on the type of embedded object.

2. Select *MenuName*/Open.

3. If necessary, you can maximize the server window.

4. Make whatever changes you want to the object.

5. Select File, Close.

6. If necessary, restore the Notes window.

Deleting an Embedded Object

To delete an embedded object from a Notes document, open the document in edit mode. Then click on the object and either press Del or select Edit, Cut.

WARNING! *You can't reverse the act of deleting an embedded object—even if you use Edit, Cut. Moreover, unless you happen to have a copy of the object lurking somewhere in a file, you won't have the option of easily restoring it— as you can with a linked object.*

Embedding Examples

As mentioned earlier, the types of embedded OLE objects you can create depends entirely on your system. To whet your appetite, this section presents a couple of examples.

Example: An Excel Chart

Worksheet charts are particularly nice to embed, because they can be made to be very attractive. As an example, suppose that you want to copy a chart from an existing Excel spreadsheet into a Notes document. You don't care about keeping the new copy up to date with the original document, but you might want to make changes to it within the Notes document. Consequently, you copy it as an embedded object.

Figure 11.14 displays a Notes document containing an embedded Excel chart. Of course, just by looking at the figure you can't tell whether the chart is embedded, linked, or simply pasted in as an inert object.

Figure 11.14

This Notes document contains an embedded Excel chart.

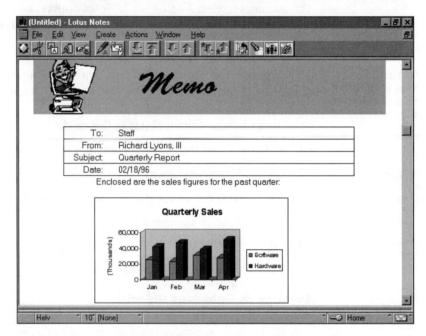

Example: Embedded Sound Clips

You can add a touch of class to a document by embedding a sound clip in it. This could be either a clip that you record or a prerecorded clip that's supplied with your sound software. As an example, the Notes document shown in Figure 11.15 contains an embedded sound clip. (It also contains an embedded slide show.) When a user double-clicks on the corresponding icon, the sound is played back.

The success of your effort to embed sound will depend on there being sound-producing software on your system. For instance, many software packages supply a variety of sound clips; some even allow you to record your own sounds.

Here's an outline of how to embed a sound clip—either one you previously recorded yourself, or one provided by the software:

1. Click on the rich text field where you want to embed the sound clip.

2. Select Create, Object, displaying the dialog box shown in Figure 11.9.

3. Scroll down until you see the type of sound object you want to embed. Double-click on that item to load the corresponding software.

Figure 11.15

This Notes document
contains an embedded
sound clip.

4. When the window for the sound software appears, select the name of the
   .WAV file (or other type of sound file) that you want to embed and then
   exit from the software.

The sound clip will now be embedded as an OLE object in the Notes
document, with a corresponding icon displayed in the rich text field. Subsequently, whenever a user opens that document, he or she can run the sound
clip by double-clicking on the icon.

The only downside to this otherwise slick operation is the following:
After the sound clip plays back, the sound software may leave its own window displayed. However, that window usually disappears as soon as the user
clicks anywhere on the document.

■ In Conclusion

Using OLE linked or embedded objects is fine under the right circumstances.
However, OLE can sometimes be overkill—when you can accomplish your
purpose in a more economical way. If you want to use information from another source as part of a Notes document, decide on how you plan to use the
information before you select a method.

When choosing a method, you can use Table 11.3 as a guide. The left-hand column describes how the information from another source will be treated in the Notes document; the right-hand column suggests the most appropriate method.

Table 11.3

A Summary of Methods.

NATURE OF THE INFORMATION TO BE COPIED INTO A NOTES DOCUMENT	BEST METHOD FOR COPYING THE INFORMATION
The information is an entire file, to be transmitted electronically to someone else.	Send the file as an attachment to a Notes document.
The information is an entire source document. Users will work with the file within its source application—not within Notes.	Send the file as an attachment to a Notes document.
The information is part of a source document. After being copied, the information will remain static—regardless of any changes to the original source document.	Copy and paste the information from the source document to the Notes document.
The information is part of a source document. After being copied, the information will remain static. However, the information contains both text and graphics.	Create a new source document containing just the parts you want. Then copy the entire document into the Notes document as an embedded object.
The information is part of a source document, and it contains only text. However, you want to retain the text and paragraph formatting exactly as it is in the original.	Copy the information to the Clipboard and then use Edit, Paste Special to copy it into the Notes document as an embedded OLE object.
The information is an entire source document consisting entirely of either text or graphics—but not both. After being copied, the information will remain static—regardless of any changes to the original source document.	Use File, Import to copy the file into the Notes document.
The information is part or all of a source document. After being copied, the information should reflect changes to the original source document. Also, users may want to modify the information from within the Notes document.	Copy the information from the source document to the Clipboard and then use Edit, Paste Special to paste the information as a linked OLE object.
The information is a copy of an entire source document. After being copied, the information should be independent of the original source document; however, users may want to modify the information.	Copy the information as an embedded OLE object. (Use Create, Object and then select the file to copy.)

Table 11.3

A Summary of Methods.
(Continued)

NATURE OF THE INFORMATION TO BE COPIED INTO A NOTES DOCUMENT	BEST METHOD FOR COPYING THE INFORMATION
The information is part of a source document. After being copied, the information should be independent of the original source document; however, users may want to modify the information.	Copy the information from the source document to the Clipboard and then use Edit, Paste Special to paste the information as an embedded OLE object.
The information does not exist in another document. It is to be created from within the Notes document, but another source application must be used.	Create a new embedded OLE object. (Use Create, Object and then select the server you want to use.)

This chapter has focused primarily on techniques available to users for including information from other sources in their Notes documents. Chapter 12 picks up where this one leaves off, concentrating on tools that are available to database designers to increase the ways in which end users can utilize data from diverse sources.

- *Using OLE Objects in Forms*
- *Using Field Exchange*
- *Importing Information into Notes*

C H A P T E R

12

Designer Tools for Integrating Other Information with Notes

THE DAY OF THE ISOLATED SOFTWARE PACKAGE SEEMS TO BE END-
ing. Integrated software systems such as Microsoft Office and
Lotus SmartSuite have a strong foothold in the business arena,
and just about every piece of major software now includes hooks
for importing information from outside sources—even direct
competitors.

Notes is no exception, and it offers a wide range of powerful features for accessing information from outside sources.

Chapter 11 described how users can utilize OLE (object linking and embedding) in their own documents. This chapter goes one step further, showing how database designers can integrate embedded OLE objects into the underlying database forms. This technique can be used to generate many types of sophisticated Notes applications. For example, by using OLE you can set up an application that seamlessly integrates and manages documents created from a wide variety of software packages.

Along with OLE, Notes utilizes another powerful information-sharing tool: *Field Exchange.* A relatively new technique, Field Exchange provides an automated method whereby information can be shared between Notes documents and other applications.

You can use Notes as a front end to manage information generated from many other sources. In fact, Notes can import any type of information that can find its way into tabular format in an ASCII file. Notes can also directly import selected parts of Lotus 1-2-3 worksheets. These features are particularly useful because they can smooth your path when converting to Notes from another information-management system.

■ Using OLE Objects in Forms

The previous chapter described how end users can insert OLE objects into Notes documents. Now we go one step further and show how you as a designer can insert linked and embedded objects into forms.

When you insert an OLE object in a form, every document created with that form will automatically contain a new copy of the original object. A user can access that copy for editing by double-clicking it.

Inserting an OLE object on a Notes form has many uses. For example, you can design forms that allow users to create Notes databases of documents created with other OLE-compliant software. In this type of application, Notes becomes a front end, managing diverse sets of documents.

As an example, suppose you want to use Notes to manage a group of loan applications, similar to the one shown in Figure 12.1—even though these applications are generated with Microsoft Excel.

To accomplish this, you can create a Notes form similar to the one shown in Figure 12.2. Then, each time a user wants to create a new loan application, he or she creates a new Notes document and then double-clicks on the embedded OLE object. Notes will launch Excel and load a copy of the application form, which the user can fill in.

Figure 12.1

A Microsoft Excel
worksheet for creating a
loan application.

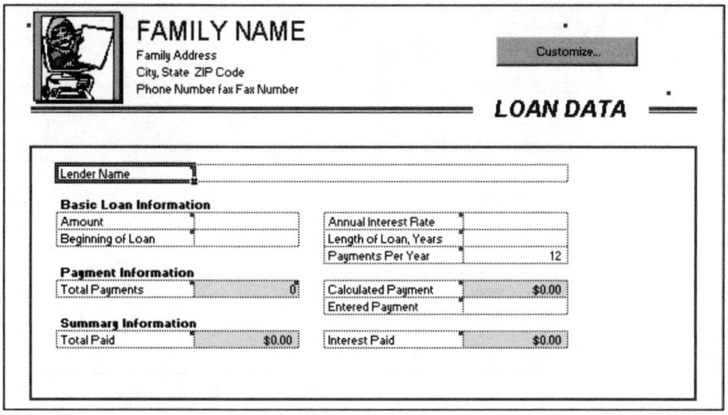

Figure 12.2

This form contains the
worksheet shown in
Figure 12.1, embedded
as an OLE object.

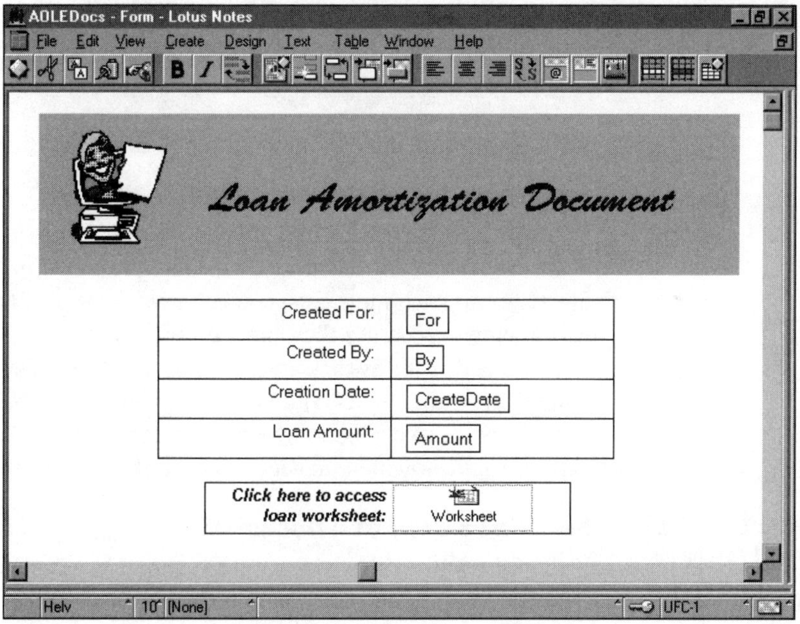

To help you manage these loan applications, you can create a Notes view that displays information from each loan document. Figure 12.3 shows one possible view.

Figure 12.3

This view displays a group of loan documents created by the form shown in Figure 12.2.

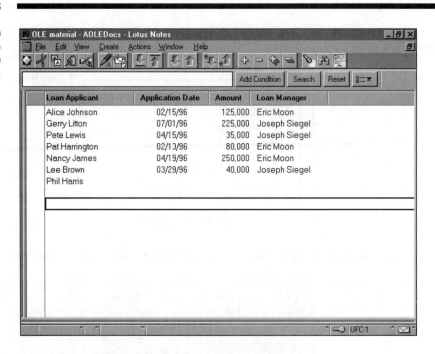

Inserting an Embedded OLE Object

You can embed an OLE object into a Notes form in either of two ways. First, if the object already exists as a separate file, you can embed a copy of that file. Or, if no such file exists, you can use the application software from within Notes to create the object directly on the form.

The end result is the same in both situations: The Notes form contains an embedded OLE object, and each document created with that form will contain a copy of that object, which users can manipulate with the source application. The following two sections describe each possibility.

Note. Notes provides a wide array of options for controlling how users see and work with documents containing embedded OLE objects. These options are discussed in the later section "Setting the Options for Embedded Objects."

Inserting a Copy of a Document

If the OLE object that you want to embed in a Notes form already exists as a separate document, here's how you can embed a copy of it:

1. Make sure that the form is open in edit mode.

2. Place the insertion point exactly where you want to insert the OLE object.

3. Select Create, Object.

4. When the Create Object dialog box appears, select the option Create An Object From A File, so that the dialog box appears as shown in Figure 12.4.

Figure 12.4

Enter the name of the file you want to copy as an embedded OLE object.

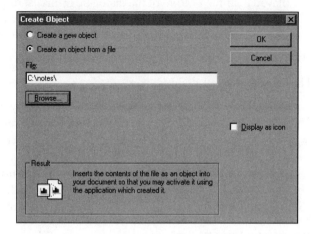

5. If you know the exact name (including path) of the file containing the document you want to copy, type it in. Otherwise, click the Browse button and then find and select the file.

6. To display the object as an icon, skip to step 7. Otherwise, to display the actual object in the Notes document, make sure that the option Display As Icon is *deselected* and then click OK.

If the object is too large to display directly in the Notes documents, you can display it as an icon by following the remaining steps:

Note. Remember that Notes typically displays only the first page of an embedded object. To see more, you'll need to double-click the object to launch it in its source server.

7. Select the option Display As Icon.

8. If you're not satisfied with either the icon or the label, you can change them: Click the button labeled Change Icon, displaying the dialog box shown in Figure 12.5.

Figure 12.5

Use this dialog box to select an icon and caption.

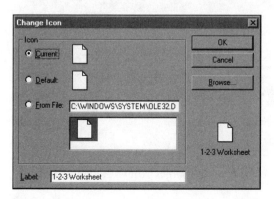

9. To select a different icon, you can either select one from the list that's displayed near the bottom of the dialog box (this list displays all the available icons in the source application's .EXE file), or you can use the Browse button to select a different icon file and then choose the icon that you want.

10. If you wish, change the text of the icon's label.

11. Close any open dialog boxes.

When you've finished, the Notes form will display either the embedded object or its corresponding icon, depending on your selections in the preceding steps. *This object is independent of the original document from which it was copied.*

You must now set the form options that will determine how the embedded object is handled in each new document created with the form. For details, see "Setting the Options for Embedded Objects," further on in this chapter.

Creating a New OLE Object

If the OLE object that you intend to insert into a Notes form does not yet exist, you can create and embed it from within that form. To accomplish this, you open the form and then select the type of object that you want to create. Notes will launch the appropriate application software, which you can then use to create the new object. When you're done, Notes embeds the object where you indicate in the form.

Here are the details:

1. Open the Notes form in edit mode.

2. Select Create, Object, displaying the dialog box shown below.

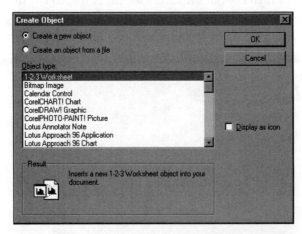

3. Select the type of object that you want to create.

4. Select whether or not you want to display the object as an icon. For details on customizing the icon, see the preceding section, "Inserting a Copy of a Document" (steps 7–10).

5. Click OK. Notes will launch the corresponding source application and load a new, blank object—*in place within the Notes form* (see the following section, "Building in Place").

6. Using the source application, create the new object.

7. When you're done creating the object, simply return to another part of the Notes form by clicking on it. Or, you can use your system hotkey commands to switch back to Notes (for example, the hotkey in Windows is Alt+Tab).

8. Continue working on the Notes form; when you're done, save it as usual.

Building in Place   When you create a new OLE object (the preceding steps 5 and 6), Notes displays both the original form and the new object. Here are some important points about this process:

- The new object is displayed on the Notes form where you previously placed the insertion point.

- Part of the form—or even most of it—may not be visible on the screen because of the size of the new object. To access other parts of the form, use the scroll bars.

- With the exception of the File menu, the entire menu bar is replaced with that belonging to the source application.

- The toolbars of the source application are also displayed.

- The original Notes File menu is retained.

- You can switch back and forth between the new object and any other part of the form: To switch out of the object, click anywhere else on the form; to reenter the object, double-click on it.

- When you click anywhere outside of the object and onto another part of the Notes form, the Notes menu bar reappears.

Setting the Options for Embedded Objects

Notes provides a wide array of form options that control how users see and work with documents containing embedded OLE objects. As part of designing a form, you must set these options, which include the following:

- *Opening mode.* Whenever a user opens a document, Notes puts it into either read or edit mode.

- *Displaying OLE objects.* You can choose how Notes displays each OLE object in a document: either by a picture of the actual object or by an icon. (You make this choice when embedding the object as part of the form, but you can later alter your choice.)

- *Version selection.* Whenever a user opens a document, Notes can display either the latest version of the embedded object or the original version stored in the underlying form.

- *AutoLaunch.* Whenever a user opens a document, Notes can optionally launch the source application and display the embedded OLE object—ready for editing. The form options that you select determine whether or not this occurs.

- *Method of launching objects.* When an OLE object is launched—either automatically (see the preceding option) or manually, by a user—it can be displayed either as part of the Notes document (*in place*) or in a window by itself (*out of place*). The form options that you select determine which occurs.

- *Hiding the Notes forms.* You can set options so that when a user opens a document containing an embedded OLE object, the document itself is hidden so that only the object is displayed. The form options also determine whether or not the Notes document is automatically closed when a user exits from the source application back to Notes.

The following sections describe the details of these options, most of which you can select from the Launch page of the Form InfoBox, shown in Figure 12.6.

Figure 12.6

Use these options to customize an OLE object on a form.

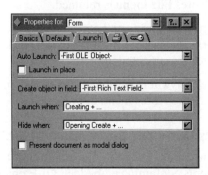

Setting the Opening Mode

Whenever a user opens an existing document, by default Notes puts the document into read mode. However, you can select a form option that changes this default, so that each document automatically opens in edit mode.

Here's how to accomplish this: Select the Defaults tab on the Form InfoBox and then select the option Automatically Enable Edit Mode.

TIP. *Select (or deselect) the option Automatically Enable Edit Mode before setting any of the other form options discussed next, because the value that you select for this option will affect some of the other choices you make.*

Displaying Objects as Themselves or as Icons

Depending on the size and content of an OLE object, you can either display a picture of it on the form (and consequently in each document created with the form) or as an icon. You make your choice when you first create the object (see "Inserting a Copy of a Document," earlier in this chapter).

However, you can change your original selection, displaying the actual object instead of its icon—or vice versa. Here are the steps:

1. Click on the OLE object (or its icon) in the form.

2. Pull down the special menu for the object. The name of this menu depends on the nature of the object. For example, if the object is a Microsoft Excel or Lotus 1-2-3 worksheet, the menu name will be Worksheet. If you're not sure which menu to use, watch the menu bar to see which one appears when you click on the object.

3. Select the option Display As and then choose whether you want the object to display either as a picture or an icon. If there are other options as well, you can try each one to see which shows the object to best advantage.

Displaying the Customized Version of an OLE Object

When a user creates a Notes document and customizes the embedded OLE object, Notes retains two copies of the object in the document: the one customized by the user and also the original one. Later, when a user opens the document, by default Notes displays the *original unmodified version of the object*. Usually, this won't be of much interest to the user, who will probably want to see only the customized version.

You can set up the underlying form so that users always see only the customized version of the OLE object in each document. Two extra design steps are required on the form: First, you insert a rich text field that will always display the customized version of the OLE object in the document; and second, you hide the original OLE object, so that it's invisible to users.

Here are the steps:

1. Open the form in design mode.

2. Insert a rich text field on the form, exactly where you want to display the customized version of the OLE object on each document.

3. Display the Launch page of the Form InfoBox.

4. Pull down the list labeled Auto Launch and then select First OLE Object. (See the next section for an explanation of this option, as well as explanations of the other options mentioned in the following steps.)

5. Pull down the list labeled Create Object In Field and then select the name of the rich text field that you created in step 2.

6. Pull down the list labeled Launch When and then select Creating. (You can also select other options on this list, which are discussed in the following section.)

The form now contains both the original OLE object—wherever you placed it on the form—and the rich text field for displaying the customized version of the object in each document.

The combination of steps 4, 5, and 6 has the following effect: Each time a user creates a new document, Notes creates a copy of the OLE object, inserts it in the rich text field specified in step 5, launches the source application for the object, and loads the object.

WARNING! *In order for the preceding steps to work, the OLE object must be nearer to the top of the form than any other OLE object.*

Now you must hide the *original* OLE object:

7. Click anywhere on the object on the form, and make sure that the top option on the InfoBox refers to the object. For example, if the object is a Microsoft Excel worksheet, then the top option should be Properties For Worksheet.

8. Select the Hide InfoBox tab (shaped like a window shade).

9. Select the following options: Previewed For Reading, Opened For Reading, and Opened For Editing.

The purpose of steps 8 and 9 is to hide the original OLE object on the documents, because users who open documents will want to see only the current OLE object. (If a user wants to see a copy of the original object, he or she can simply create a new document.)

Selecting the Launch Options

Whenever a user opens a document, Notes can either display the OLE object (or its corresponding icon) or it can automatically launch the embedded OLE object in its native source application; what Notes does depends on the options you have selected on the form. You can also select an option that specifies how the object appears when it is launched: either as part of the Notes document (in place) or in a window by itself (out of place). To select these options, make sure that the Form InfoBox is displayed.

Auto-Launching an Object   Here's how to set up a form so that the OLE object in a document will automatically be launched whenever the document is opened: Click the Launch InfoBox tab, pull down the list labeled Launch When, and then make your selections as follows:

- Leave the option Creating untouched, because you should have set it already (in step 6 of "Displaying the Customized Version of an OLE Object").

- If the documents will be opened in edit mode (see the earlier section "Setting the Opening Mode"), then click the option Editing.

- If the documents will be opened in read mode, click the option Reading.

If you select the Reading option, and if documents are automatically opened in read mode, then whenever a user opens a document, Notes will automatically launch the OLE object. However, because the document is in read mode, any changes that the user makes to the object will not be recorded in the Notes document. To inform the user of this, Notes displays the following message:

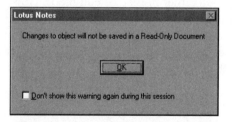

Launch Either in Place or out of Place   Whenever an OLE object is launched—either manually by a user or automatically by Notes—the way in which it appears depends on the particular form option you select: Either the object will appear by itself in a source-application window (called Out Of Place), or it will appear in place, as part of the Notes document.

To set the appropriate option, begin by clicking the Launch InfoBox tab. Then, to launch objects in place, select the option Launch In Place.

TIP. *Launching objects in place can often cause confusion for users, partially because of the superposition of the launched object onto the Notes document,* *and partially because of the way in which the video display jumps around during launching. If you expect this type of confusion to occur, deselect the option Launch In Place. Then, when an object is launched, its source application will appear in a separate window that's in front of the Notes window.*

Hiding Notes Documents

In some situations, you may wish to completely hide the Notes documents from users. Instead, when a user opens a document, you would like the embedded OLE object to be launched and ready for viewing and editing. Here are two possible scenarios you can arrange by selecting the appropriate form options:

- No user access to Notes documents. Here, you don't want users to have access to any part of the Notes documents other than the embedded OLE objects. When a user opens a document, Notes immediately launches the OLE object in its own application window and brings the focus to that window. Then, when the user closes that window, the Notes document is automatically closed. The user never sees the original Notes document—only its embedded object.

- Same as the above, but with one important difference: When the user closes the window displaying the OLE object, the original Notes document is then displayed for viewing and editing.

You can set up either of the preceding two scenarios when documents are opened either in read or edit mode. However, in read mode any changes a user makes to the OLE object are not saved in the Notes document.

Here's how to set up Notes documents for either of the preceding scenarios: First, display the Form InfoBox and select the Launch tab. Then pull down the list box labeled Hide When (see below) and make your selections.

The options that are available on this pull-down list will depend on your other option selections, as follows:

- If you select the Launch In Place option, then none of the Hide When options is available, because launching an object in place is incompatible with launching that object and simultaneously hiding the Notes document.

- The choices you make in the Launch When pull-down list determine which Hide When options are available. For instance, if you select only "Creating" for the Launch When option, then the only Hide When option available will be Opening Create.

■ Using Field Exchange

Field Exchange—also known as Notes/FX—is a method by which information can be exchanged between Notes documents and those generated by other source applications.

Because the use of Notes has become so widespread, and because as yet there are no competitive products, many software developers are adapting their applications to include Field Exchange technology. Then, users can utilize those applications to create embedded OLE objects in Notes documents, and information can flow freely between those documents and their embedded objects.

To illustrate how Field Exchange works, we use the following example: You want to use Lotus Word Pro to create a set of invoices, like the one shown in Figure 12.7. However, you want to use Notes to manage these documents; to accomplish this, you plan to embed each invoice as an OLE object within a Notes document, similar to the one shown in Figure 12.8.

To help you manage these documents, you could create various views. For example, the view shown in Figure 12.9 displays two fields from each Notes document: the vendor name and the amount of the invoice. Users can easily access any invoice from this view.

If you study Figures 12.7 and 12.8, you'll notice that various pieces of information—such as the vendor name and the invoice number—appear both in the Word Pro document and in the Notes document. This is very convenient, because it allows users to see critical information in either document. Moreover, by using Field Exchange a user can enter these pieces of information *in either place*, and Field Exchange automatically sends that information to the other document.

WARNING! *As of this writing, Field Exchange works reasonably well with some software—particularly that marketed by Lotus Development Corporation. However, Field Exchange is very complex, and there are still problems with it, and it doesn't always work exactly as specified by the software vendors. In fact, it doesn't work at all for some software that claims otherwise. Try it with your favorite software to see if it works.*

Figure 12.7

An invoice created by
Lotus Word Pro.

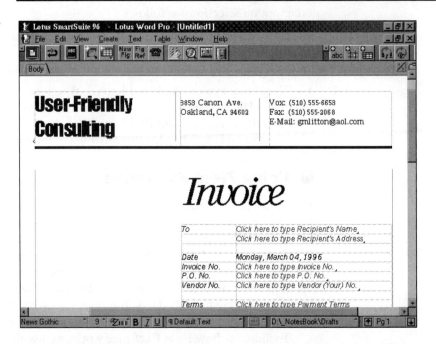

Figure 12.8

This Notes document
contains an embedded
Word Pro invoice.

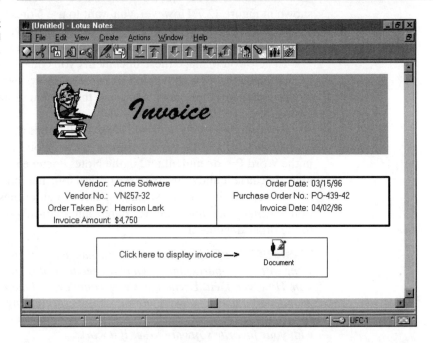

Figure 12.9

This view displays a
group of invoices, similar
to the one shown in
Figure 12.8.

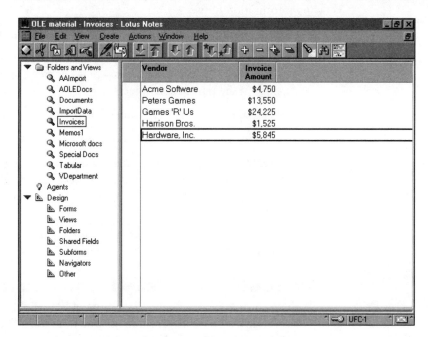

Which Information Can Be Exchanged

In general, you use Field Exchange by creating corresponding fields in a
Notes document and in its embedded OLE object. Information can then flow
freely between the two fields. The source application for an embedded object
determines which types of document information are available for Field
Exchange. Usually—but not always—the field names in the Notes document
and the OLE object are the same.

Currently, the Lotus SmartSuite applications have the largest numbers
and types of fields available for Field Exchange. These applications are Word
Pro, 1-2-3, Freelance Graphics, and Approach. Other software publishers—
notably, Microsoft—have promised to deliver Field Exchange capability with
their major software packages, such as Microsoft Word and Excel.

There are two types of Field Exchange fields: one-way and two-way.
With a two-way field, information can be exchanged in both directions—
from the Notes document to the embedded OLE object and vice versa.
However, information in a one-way field can be sent only from the embedded object to the Notes document.

Each application that supports Field Exchange must supply the following information to users:

- The names of the fields whose information can be exchanged.

- The names and types of the corresponding fields in the underlying Notes forms. Usually—but not always—these names are the same as the field names in the embedded objects.

- Which fields are one-way and which are two-way.

This information can usually be found in the application's online help.

NOTE. *Field Exchange has gone through several sets of changes, the latest of which is called FX 2.0 and which is supported by Notes 4.0. Earlier versions of Field Exchange—supported by many software packages—may not work with Notes 4.0.*

Also, there are different versions of FX 2.0 for 32-bit and 16-bit applications. OLE objects created by 16-bit applications do not work with the 32-bit version of Notes.

Field Exchange with Word Pro Documents

We'll use Lotus Word Pro as an example of how Field Exchange can work. However, it would be incorrect to assume that Word Pro is typical; in fact, it makes better use of Field Exchange than most other software packages. However, Word Pro does illustrate the possibilities that can exist with Field Exchange, and in the near future other software may become as flexible.

Within a Word Pro document, you can set up the following types of information for Field Exchange:

- Document information fields
- User-created fields
- Bookmarks
- Click Here blocks

Document Information

Each Word Pro document contains a large number of fields containing information about that document, such as file name, path name, document size, and much more. The following table lists the names of these fields, which you can use in Field Exchange. The first column in this table lists the Word Pro field names. The second and third columns list the corresponding field names and types that must be used by Notes documents. (In particular, remember that you can't use spaces in a Notes field name.) For example, if you wanted to use Field Exchange to work with the Word Pro field named Keywords, you would create a corresponding field named Categories in the Notes form.

Doc Info Field	Notes Field Name	Data Type
Filename	Filename	Text
Path	Path	Text
Document Description	Subject	Text
Keywords	Categories	Text
Date Created	DateCreated	Time
Date Last Revised	LastRevisionDate	Time
Total Editing Time	EditingTime	Number
Created by	DocumentCreatedBy	Text
Last Editor	DocumentLastEditedBy	Text
Other Editors	OtherDocumentEditors	Text
Number of Edits	NumberOfEdits	Number
SmartMaster	StyleSheet	Text
Document Class	DocumentClass	Text
Number of Pages	SizeInPages	Number
Number of Words	SizeInWords	Number
Number of Chars	SizeInCharacters	Number
Size of Document	SizeInK	Number
Document Category	DocumentCategories	Text
Version Created by	VersionCreatedBy	Text
Date Version Created	VersionCreationDate	Time
Version name	VersionName	Text
Date Version Last Edited	VersionLastEditDate	Time
Number of Versions	NumberOfVersions	Number
Other Editors for Versions	OtherVersionEditors	Text
All Version Names	AllVersionNames	Text
Version Remarks	VersionRemarks	Text
Version Last Edited by	VersionLastEditedBy	Text
Number of Revisions	NumberOfEdits	Number

NOTE. *In this section—and those that follow—we discuss Word Pro objects embedded in Notes documents. For simplicity, we use the term "Word Pro document" to refer to any embedded Word Pro object: either a copy of an existing document or an object that a user creates from within a new Notes document.*

When a Word Pro document is open, you can directly view the contents of any of the fields listed in the previous table, as follows: Select File, Document Properties, Document and then click the Fields tab, so that the dialog box shown in Figure 12.10 appears.

Figure 12.10

This Word Pro dialog box displays the fields for the current object.

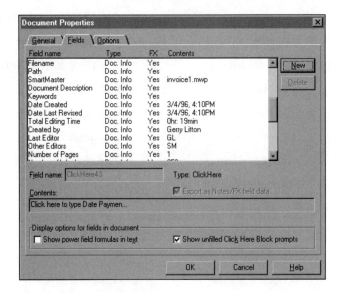

User-Created Fields

Word Pro allows users to create special information fields within a document. These do not appear in the main body of the document, but are instead available in the Document Information dialog box shown in Figure 12.10. After creating a special field, a user can type in a value for it.

As a designer, you can create special fields within the embedded Word Pro document on a form and then set up the fields for Field Exchange with corresponding fields on the form. Then, when users create documents, they can insert special values into these fields—either on the Notes document or in the embedded Word Pro document. Those values will then be accessible both within the Word Pro document and on the Notes document.

Here's how to insert a special field that utilizes Field Exchange:

1. Open the Notes form for editing.

2. Launch the embedded Word Pro document by double-clicking on it.

3. Select File, Document Properties, Document and then select the Fields tab, as shown in Figure 12.10.

4. Click the New button and then type in the new field name and contents.

5. Select the option Export As Notes/FX Field Data.

6. Return to the Notes form and then create a new field with the same name as the one you just created. To assign the field type, select Text, Editable.

Click Here blocks

A *Click Here block* is a special type of user-friendly object contained within a Word Pro document. Each Click Here block contains a built-in label that tells the user what to type in.

As part of an embedded Word Pro document on a form, you can create Click Here blocks. Then, by creating corresponding fields on the underlying Notes form, Field Exchange is enabled.

Later, when a user creates a Notes document and supplies a value to one of these fields—either in the Notes document itself or in the embedded Word Pro document, Field Exchange will supply that value to the corresponding field.

To create a Field Exchange–enabled Click Here block, follow these steps:

1. Open the Notes form for editing.

2. Launch the embedded Word Pro document by double-clicking on it.

3. Place the insertion point where you want to create the Click Here block.

4. Select Create, Click Here Block, displaying the following dialog box:

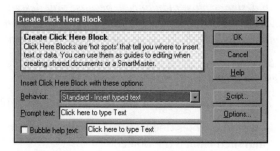

5. Fill in the options to create the Click Here block. Select a convenient name for the block.

6. Click the button labeled Options, displaying the following dialog box:

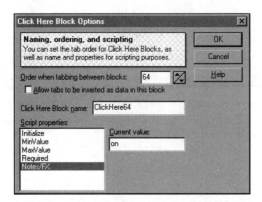

7. In the list box labeled Script Properties, select Notes/FX. Then, in the edit box labeled Current Value, type in the value On.

8. Exit back to the Word Pro document and then switch back to the Notes form.

9. Create a new field on the form, with the same name that you assigned to the new Click Here block. To assign the field type, select the Text option.

Bookmarks

Users can create bookmarks just about anywhere in a Word Pro document. If a bookmark consists of a text block, it can be used in Field Exchange. For this to be enabled, a Notes document must contain a field with the same name as the bookmark. Also, Field Exchange must be enabled for the bookmark.

NOTE. *Here, it's the users—not the form designer—who create the bookmarks. However, in order for a bookmark to work with Field Exchange, you as the form designer must plan ahead, because you design the underlying Notes form before users create the embedded Word Pro documents, and this form must contain a field with the same name as the bookmark.*

Subsequently, you will need to supply users with the names of the bookmarks they can create for Field Exchange.

Here's how a user can create a bookmark enabled for Field Exchange:

1. Open the Notes document containing the embedded Word Pro object and then launch the object.

2. Select the text to be used as a bookmark.

3. Select Create, Bookmark, displaying the following dialog box:

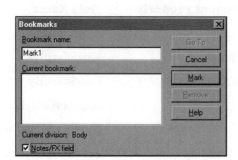

4. Enter a name for the new bookmark (no spaces are allowed).

5. Select the option Notes/FX Field and then click the button labeled Mark.

Field Exchange with Microsoft Word and Excel Documents

As of this writing, Field Exchange has not yet been successfully implemented either for Microsoft Word or Microsoft Excel, although that situation is expected to change in the near future.

According to current specifications, neither Microsoft Word nor Excel will be as tightly integrated with Notes as is Lotus Word Pro; in fact, only a fixed set of document information fields—which Microsoft calls *properties*—will be available for Field Exchange between a Notes document and its embedded Word or Excel object. The following table lists those document properties. The entries preceded by an asterisk will be two-way fields; others will be one-way.

Document Property	Lotus Notes Field Name	Lotus Notes Field Type
*Title	Title	Text
*Subject	Subject	Text
*Author	Author	Text
*Keywords	Keywords	Text
*Comments	Comments	Text
*Template	Template	Text
*Manager	Manager	Text
*Company	Company	Text
*Category	Category	Text

Document Property	Lotus Notes Field Name	Lotus Notes Field Type
Created	DateCreated	Time
Modified	LastSavedDate	Time
Last Saved By	LastSavedBy	Text
Size	NumberOfBytes	Text
Revision Number	NumberOfRevisions	Number
Total Editing Time	TotalEditingTime	Number
Printed	LastPrintedDate	Time
Pages	NumberOfPages	Number
Words	NumberOfWords	Number
Characters	NumberOfCharacters	Number
Paragraphs	NumberOfParagraphs	Number
Lines	NumberOfLines	Number
Security	Security	Number
Document Class	DocumentClass	Text
Name of application	NameOfApplication	Text
Custom Property name	Propertyname	Text
*Custom Value	Value	Text

■ Importing Information into Notes

You can import information from other software sources into a Notes database. You might do this, for example, if you decide that you want to use Notes to manage information that was created in a spreadsheet program or another type of software.

The imported information must be in columnar format. Each row will be imported as a separate Notes document, and each column will furnish the values for a single field in these documents.

The only types of information you can import are text and numbers. When information is imported, only the basic text is retained. Special formatting—font type and size, boldface, and so on—is not kept.

Notes can directly import only a few types of information, listed in the following table.

Type	File Extensions	File Description
Lotus 1-2-3 and Symphony	.WKS, .WK1, .WRK, .WR1, .WK3, .WK4	Either an entire worksheet or a named range
Tabular text	.TAB, .TXT, .PRN, .RPT	ASCII text arranged in rows and columns
Structured text	.LTR, .CGN, .STR	ASCII text that retains its structure in fields and values

When importing worksheet information, you can import the entire worksheet, a selected named range, or selected columns. When importing tabular or structured text, you must import the entire file.

Note. Notes also refers to a format file as a *column descriptor file.*

To import selected columns of a worksheet, or to import the other types of files listed in the preceding table, you'll need to create a *format file*, which supplies the descriptive information that Notes needs to import the data.

Although the types of information you can import seem extremely limited, this is not the case. In fact, you can import a wide variety of types of information, as follows: If you can't import a file directly into Notes, you may very likely be able to create an intermediate file of information in either 1-2-3 or ASCII format, either of which you can then import into Notes.

As an example, suppose you want to import a file of information that's in XYZ format—which Notes cannot directly import. Here are two possibilities for creating intermediate files:

First, if you can import the file into 1-2-3, you can then save the information as a standard 1-2-3 file. Notes can then directly read this file. 1-2-3 can directly read the following file formats:

- Microsoft Excel

- ANSI Metafile (CGM)

- dBASE

- Paradox

If you can't import the XYZ file into 1-2-3, you may be able to use the source application (the one that originally created the information that you want to import) to output that information in tabular format to an ASCII file. You can then import that file directly into Notes. The only catch to this is that you must have access to the source software, or to someone else who does.

Creating a Special Form and View

Before Notes can import any type of information, you must create a new form whose structure matches the imported information. You may also need to create a special view to display the imported information.

Here's why the form is essential: The imported information must be in tabular format, and each row will become a new Notes document. When importing the information, you must select the Notes form that will be used to create those documents.

When creating the new form, you can set up its structure in any way you prefer; however, you must create a separate field for each column of information to be imported. Also, the field order on the form (top to bottom, left to right) must match the order of the columns of the imported data. You can choose whatever field names you wish, but the field types must match those of the corresponding imported values. Field types will invariably be either text or number fields.

The form you create can have other fields as well, if you intend to supplement the imported information with additional values that you add later.

Usually, you'll also need to create one or more special Notes views to display imported information. When you create a new view, be sure to create a separate column for each column that's imported—corresponding to one of the fields that you create on the new form.

TIP. *Plan ahead. If you have a new view waiting in the wings, you can select it just before you import the information. Then, as soon as the import process is finished, Notes will display the new information in that view.*

Importing Lotus 1-2-3 Worksheets

When you import a Lotus 1-2-3 worksheet, you can import either the entire worksheet, a named range, or selected columns. When importing selected columns, you must first create a format file that specifies which columns are to be imported.

To import part or all of a worksheet, first create a corresponding Notes form and view, as described in the preceding section. Then, to import either the entire worksheet or a selected named range, see the next section, "Importing Either an Entire Worksheet or a Range." To import selected columns, see "Importing Selected Columns of a Worksheet," later in this chapter.

Importing Either an Entire Worksheet or a Range

If you intend for Notes to utilize all or nearly all of a worksheet, you can import the entire sheet and then delete the unwanted information. When you import an entire worksheet, Notes reads all the text it can find, converting worksheet rows into individual Notes documents. For example, Figure 12.11 shows a straightforward worksheet. You could import the entire sheet and then delete the top three rows—which would be imported as three documents—from within Notes.

Figure 12.11

A simple worksheet.

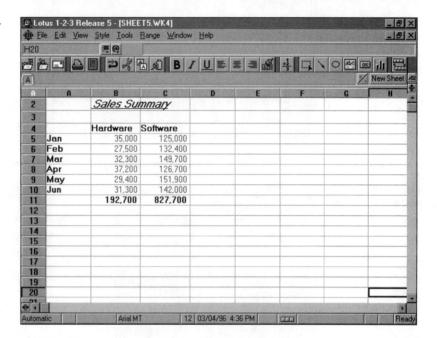

On the other hand, if you intend for Notes to use only a selected part of a worksheet, you may be able to save yourself a lot of work: If the information exists in the same part of the worksheet, highlight that information and then assign it to be a named range. Then you can import just that range into Notes.

To import either an entire worksheet or a named range, follow these steps:

1. Display the standard Notes navigator and then select the view that you plan to use to display the imported data. (This step is not essential, but it will make your work more efficient, because you can immediately see the results of the importing process.)

2. Select File, Import, displaying the dialog box shown in Figure 12.12.

3. In the pull-down list labeled Files Of Type, select Lotus 1-2-3 Worksheet.

4. Select the file that you want to import and then click the Import button. Notes then displays the dialog box shown in Figure 12.13.

Figure 12.12

Select the type of file that you plan to import.

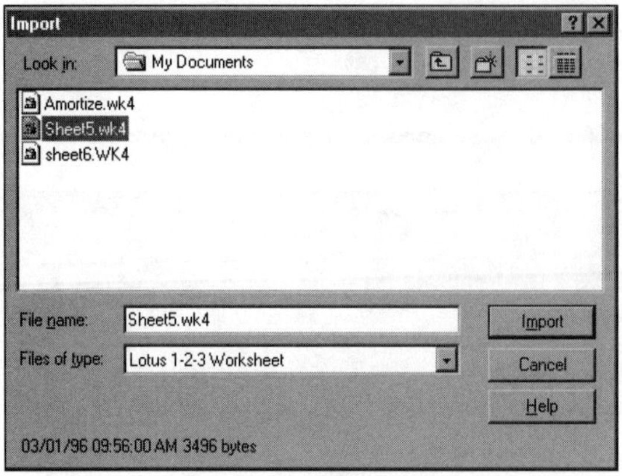

Figure 12.13

Select the options for importing part or all of a worksheet.

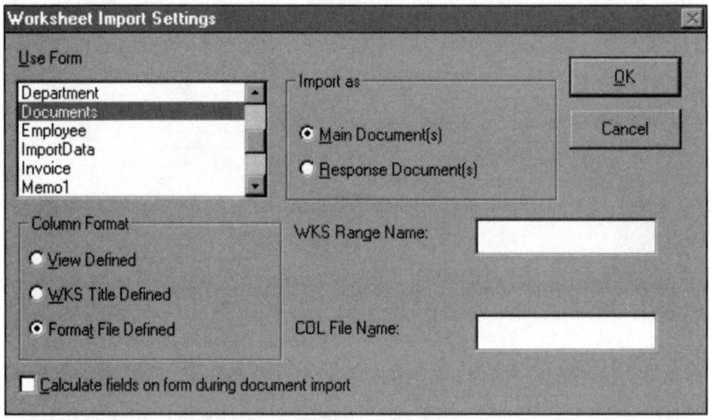

5. In the list box labeled Use Form, select the name of the special form that you previously created. *This step is essential.* If you have not yet created a form, abort the operation until you do.

6. If you want to import a particular named range within the worksheet, in the edit box labeled WKS Range Name, type in the name of the range. Otherwise, if you leave this edit box blank, the entire worksheet will be imported.

7. Click the two radio buttons labeled View Defined and Main Documents.

8. Be sure to *deselect* the option Calculate Fields On Form During Document Import.

9. Click OK to begin the import process.

TIP. *If some of the information does not import properly—most likely to happen for calculated cell values—then you'll need to try importing the information again, but this time, select the option "Calculate Fields On Form During Document Import." The import process will be much slower, but it may be more accurate.*

When importing has finished, the new documents should have been created, and they will be displayed on whatever view is selected at the time.

Importing Selected Columns of a Worksheet

Note. Notes also refers to a format file as a *column descriptor file*.

With a little bit of extra work, you can import a selected group of worksheet columns into Notes; the columns do not have to be contiguous. To accomplish this, you must create a format file that specifies the columns to be imported. The format file also assigns field names to the imported columns of information, and these names must match the names of the fields on the Notes form that you use when importing the data.

Creating a Format File   To create a format file, you can use any convenient text editor or word processor, as long as it can store the file in standard ASCII format.

As an example, suppose you want to import only the first three columns from the worksheet shown below.

Here are the contents of a format file that you could use to accomplish this:

```
; This file selects the first 3 columns from a worksheet.
; It assigns the following field names to them: Month, Software, and Hardware
;
Month: WKSCOL A
Software: WKSCOL B
Hardware: WKSCOL C
```

Any line in a format file that begins with a semicolon is a *comment line.* You can use comments to describe the purpose of the file and also to create informative notations throughout the file.

For each column that you want to import, create a separate line in the format file. The first part of the line names the field, and the last part of the line specifies which worksheet column to use. For example, consider the first line:

```
Month: WKSCOL A
```

The first part of the line supplies the name of the new field, followed by a colon. In the second part of the line, WKSCOL is a keyword indicating the name of the column in the worksheet. In this case, column A will supply values for the field named Month.

If the fields named in the format file do not match those on the form that you use to import the worksheet, the field information nevertheless will be imported, but you'll need to modify the field names in the form before you can display the information in the Notes documents.

You can skip the names of columns that you do not want to import. However, columns must be specified in ascending order (left to right), starting with the first one to be imported.

When you've finished creating the format file, save it as an ordinary ASCII file.

For additional information, see "Creating Format Files," later in this chapter.

TIP. *If you want to import different bits and pieces of a worksheet, you may often save time by importing each part in a separate operation—instead of trying to create a complicated format file to import everything at once.*

Importing the Worksheet Columns   After you've created a format file and saved it as an ASCII file, you can then import the worksheet information, as follows:

1. Display the standard Notes navigator and then select the view that you plan to use to display the imported data.

2. Select File, Import, displaying the dialog box shown in Figure 12.12.

3. In the pull-down list box labeled Files Of Type, select Lotus 1-2-3 Worksheet.

4. Select the file that you want to import and then click the Import button. Notes then displays the dialog box shown in Figure 12.13.

5. In the list box labeled Use Form, select the name of the special form that you previously created.

6. Click the radio button labeled Format File Defined.

7. In the edit box labeled COL File Name, enter the complete path and name of the format file that you created for importing this information.

8. Be sure to deselect the option Calculate Fields On Form During Document Import and then select the option Main Document(s).

9. Click OK to import the information.

Importing Tabular Text Files

You can import information stored in an ASCII file, provided that the data is tabular. Notes can import two types of tabular information: *delimited* and *fixed-length*.

Figure 12.14 shows the contents of a file containing delimited tabular information. Values are separated by commas, which are called the *delimiters*. Each row corresponds to a single record and ends with a hard return, and each row must contain the same number of values. Blank values are allowed; they are indicated by two successive delimiters.

Figure 12.14

A set of comma-delimited tabular information.

```
Gary Trudeau, Toronto, Canada
Nelson Barton, Boston, USA
Marie Clousseau, Paris, France
Jose Morello, Mexico City, Mexico
Anita Barraca, Toleo, Spain
Minnie Osawa, Kyoto, Japan
```

A tabular file can use any delimiter, which can be either a single character or a set of characters. Different delimiters can be used to separate different values, but the same delimiter must be used after the corresponding field values in each row. In Figure 12.14, for instance, each city value could be followed by a double quote instead of a comma.

Figure 12.15 shows the other type of tabular text file—fixed-length. Here, corresponding values in different rows have the same number of characters, with blanks filling in at the end of each value. Each row corresponds to a single record and ends with a hard return.

Figure 12.15

A set of fixed-length
tabular information.

```
Gary Trudeau        Toronto      Canada
Nelson Barton       Boston       USA
Marie Clousseau     Paris        France
Jose Morello        Mexico       City Mexico
Anita Barraca       Toledo       Spain
Minnie Osawa        Kyoto        Japan
```

You can think of either type of tabular text file as being arranged in a group of columns, which correspond to the columns in a Notes view where they will be displayed. Naturally, the columns are much easier to see when the information is arranged in fixed-length format.

If a tabular file is paginated, the import process can be set up to skip the headers and footers.

Creating Format Files

To import either type of tabular information, you must create a *format file*, which describes the exact structure of the information. It also assigns field names to the imported data. These names must correspond exactly to the field names on the form that you use to import the information (see "Creating a Special Form and View," earlier in this chapter.)

As described earlier for format files, comment lines begin with a semicolon, and the file must be saved in standard ASCII format.

Delimited Text Files   When a set of tabular information is delimited, the format file must specify the delimiters that are used, and also the field names.

Here's a sample format file that could be used for the information shown in Figure 12.14:

```
; This is a format file for a set of comma-delimited tabular information.
; The 3 fields are defined to be Name, City, and Country
;
Name: UNTIL ","
City: UNTIL ","
Country: UNTIL ""
```

Here's a summary of the important features of this type of format file:

- Each line corresponds to a single column of input information, and it also names the field for that column. This name must correspond to a field name on the form that you use to import the information.

- The first part of the line names the new Notes field corresponding to that column of values.

- The keyword UNTIL is always followed by the delimiter that ends the field values for that column. For instance, UNTIL "," indicates that each field value for this column terminates with a comma.

- The columns must be listed in the order in which they appear in the data file.

Fixed-Length Text Files In a set of fixed-length tabular data, corresponding field values in the different rows all have the same number of characters. If you use a monospaced font, then you can say that corresponding fields have the same length as well.

TIP. *When creating a fixed-length text file, use a monospaced font, such as Courier or Typewriter. Then you can easily line up columns of values on your screen.*

Here's a sample format file that could be used for the information shown in Figure 12.15:

```
; This is a format file for a file of fixed-length tabular information.
; The 3 fields are defined to be Name, City, and Country
;
Name: START 1 END 20
City: START 21 END 35
Country: START 36 END 50
```

Note the following points about the above format file:

- Each line corresponds to a single column of input information, and it also names the field for that column. This name must correspond to a field name on the form that you use to import the information.

- The keywords START and END indicate the first and last numerical positions for each column, counting from the beginning of a line.

- Instead of using the keyword END to indicate the final character number, you can use the keyword WIDTH, followed by the count of the number of characters in a field. For instance, instead of the three field lines in the preceding format file, you could substitute the following:

```
Name: START 1 WIDTH 20
City: START 21 WIDTH 15
Country: START 36 WIDTH 15
```

Importing a Data File

After you create a special Notes form, and after you create a format file, you're ready to import either type of tabular information. Here are the steps to follow:

1. Display the standard Notes navigator and then select the view that you plan to use to display the imported data. If you have not yet created a special view, skip this step.

2. Select File, Import, displaying the dialog box shown in Figure 12.12.

3. In the pull-down list labeled Files Of Type, select Tabular Text.

4. Select the file that you want to import and then click the Import button. Notes then displays the following dialog box:

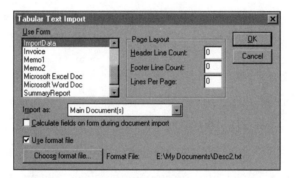

5. In the list box labeled Use Form, select the special Notes form that you created for importing this information. *This step is essential.* If you have not yet created a form, abort the operation until you do.

6. Click the button labeled Choose Format File and then type in the full path and name of the format file you previously created.

7. If the data file is paginated and contains either a header, a footer, or both, fill in the appropriate line counts in the boxes labeled Page Layout. Be sure to enter the exact counts for the header, footer, and page length. If the file contains neither a header nor a footer, you can leave all three values set to zero.

8. Select the option Import As Main Documents and then deselect the option Calculate Fields On Form During Document Import.

9. Click OK to import the data.

- *Lotus Approach: Basic Capabilities*
- *Opening a Notes Database in Approach*
- *How Approach Displays Information*
- *Creating Charts*
- *Creating Crosstabs*
- *Creating Reports*
- *Creating Mailing Labels*

CHAPTER

13

Using Lotus Approach and Lotus NotesReporter to Display Notes Information

As POWERFUL AND VERSATILE AS NOTES IS, IT HAS LIMITED ABILITY to display and analyze database information. For example, even though Notes is a natural tool for storing name and address information, it doesn't know how to generate mailing labels. And even if your databases contain volumes of statistical information, Notes can't create any type of graph or chart.

This shortcoming would seem to be a major flaw in Notes, except for one factor: The existence of Lotus Approach and Lotus NotesReporter is one of the major components of Lotus Smart-Suite, and NotesReporter is a custom software package whose sole purpose is to create reports, mailing labels, and other types of output from Notes database information. Both Approach and Notes are marketed by Lotus, so it's not too surprising to find a very strong link between them.

Using Lotus NotesReporter
The techniques described in this chapter apply equally well to Lotus NotesReporter and Lotus Approach, although the discussion and figures all focus on Approach. With respect to using Notes databases, the major difference between NotesReporter and Approach is that NotesReporter is a read-only package, which means that you can't use it to modify the contents of Notes databases.

■ Lotus Approach: Basic Capabilities

Lotus Approach has two strong features that dovetail nicely. First, Approach has built-in tools specially designed for reading selected parts of Notes databases. Secondly, Approach contains a variety of tools for analyzing information and generating different types of reports.

Taken together, these two capabilities provide you with a convenient mechanism for analyzing and reporting on information in your Notes databases.

For example, you can use Approach to read selected salary information from a Notes database and then generate various types of statistical output, including cross-tabulations; ordinary tabulations; bar, pie, and area charts; and line graphs. With similar ease, you can use Approach to read name and address information from a Notes database and then generate a set of mailing labels or form letters.

NOTE. *Approach by itself is a database software package. However, it is not a competitor to Notes, because Approach manages only highly structured information. By contrast, Notes can handle just about any type of information that can be digitized.*

Data Analysis and Display

Approach provides several powerful tools for analyzing information. Particularly powerful is its ability to generate a wide variety of *crosstab*s on a data set. The results of a crosstab calculation can be displayed either in tabular or graphical format. The latter include pie, bar, area, and line charts—in either two- or three-dimensional formats.

Reporting

Approach contains a reasonably flexible system for generating reports in a wide variety of formats. These reports can include a number of important features not found in Notes. For instance, a report can display information in tabular format. It can also contain a header and footer, which can include any combination of text and graphics. Moreover, field information in a report can automatically wrap, so that long values are conveniently displayed. (Notes views can also display headers and footers, and they can wrap field values, but these features are very limited.)

Figure 13.1 illustrates a sample report generated by Approach, using information from a Notes database. This report contains several noteworthy features: First, the report is basically columnar, and it contains a custom header that includes graphics. Also, the values in the last column automatically wrap around within the column boundaries; the amount of wrap is not limited to a maximum number of lines.

Figure 13.1

This report was
generated by Approach,
using information in a
Notes database.

Monthly Departmental Report

Department	Number of Employees	Primary Responsibilities
Billing	24	Responsible for sending out monthly invoices to all customers having outstanding balances. Also responsible for posting paid invoices and on-demand notices sent to customers.
Shipping	18	Ships completed orders to customers. Also responsible for handling returned merchandise.
Personnel	4	Hiring new employees. Furnishing monthly reports on employee problems and resolutions.
Accounting	15	All aspects of company financial information. Processes input from Payroll department. Prepares information for yearly audit and tax preparation.

Mailing Labels and Form Letters

Mailing labels and form letters are significant and useful features that are
completely missing from Notes but are native to Approach. For example,
using name and address information from a Notes database, Approach can
easily generate groups of mailing labels and form letters.

Information Combination

Approach contains a variety of tools for combining and manipulating information from different database sources. For example, you can use Approach
to perform complex joins, combining selected parts of a Notes database with
information from an Oracle, dBase, or SQL Server database.

■ Opening a Notes Database in Approach

You can easily read selected parts of a Notes database into Approach and then
use any of the preceding data analysis and reporting techniques. From within
Approach, you select the particular database that you want to open and then
choose either a particular view or form from that database. Your choice determines which documents from that database will be available to Approach.

When you open a Notes database in Approach, you can treat the information exactly as though it were a regular Approach database. Moreover,
if you modify a data value, your change will be made to the actual Notes
document—unless you opened the database in read-only mode, or unless
other read-only restrictions are in effect.

TIP. *Before using Approach to open a Notes database, decide which information you want Approach to manipulate. Then, if necessary, create a special Notes view that selects just the documents and fields that you plan to use. You can always add new fields while in Approach, but it's much easier to plan ahead in Notes.*

Notes Views

When you open a Notes view, Approach creates a single worksheet whose columns correspond to the columns in the view, and whose column titles match those in the Notes view. Approach also uses these titles as the names of the corresponding fields. For instance, if a Notes view contains a column labeled Salary, then Approach will treat the values in that column as if they belong to an Approach field named Salary. If a column in a Notes view has no title, Approach invents a unique field name for those column values.

Each row in the Approach worksheet displays the information from a single row in the Notes view—which corresponds to a single Notes document.

Approach can access all the documents displayed in the Notes view that you open. Furthermore, Approach has access to *all* the field information in these documents—not just the fields displayed in the view. (This is actually a bug that may eventually disappear.)

The illustration below illustrates a sample Approach worksheet.

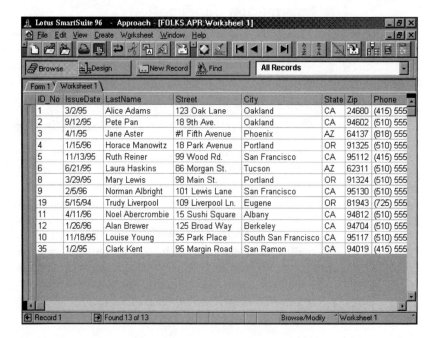

Notes Forms

When you open a Notes form—instead of a Notes view—Approach creates both a worksheet and a form for displaying the information. Only the first 16 fields of the Notes form are copied to the Approach form and worksheet. However, you can add the other fields manually, if necessary.

In creating a new form, Approach uses the same field names as the original Notes form. However, Approach does not attempt to match the structure of the Notes form. Fields on the Approach form will appear in approximately the same order as they appear on the Notes form—measuring top to bottom, left to right. Special design elements on the Notes form, such as layout regions, subforms, and sections, are not copied. Similarly, text on the Notes form is not copied.

The following illustration shows a typical Approach form:

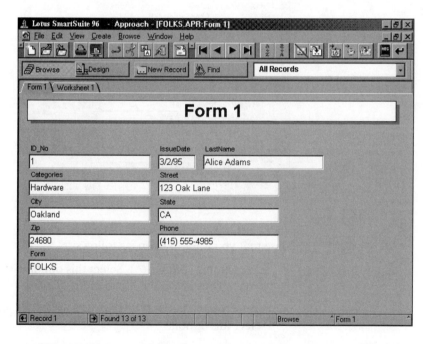

When you open a Notes form, Approach has access to all the documents whose Form field contains the name of the form you opened. (Every Notes document contains a field named Form.)

Opening a View or Form

Here are the steps for using Approach to open either a view or form from a Notes database:

1. If Notes is running on your machine, be sure that it is not accessing the database you plan to open in Approach. Otherwise, you might encounter access conflicts.

2. Make Approach the active window on your computer and then select File, Open, displaying the dialog box shown below:

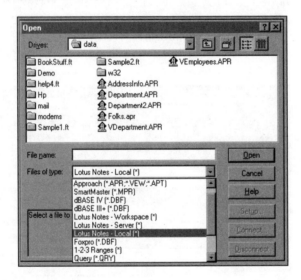

3. In the list box labeled Files Of Type, select the source for the Notes database that you want to open, as follows:

   - Lotus Notes - Server (*). Select this option if the database is on a server. Then select the name of the server.

   - Lotus Notes - Local (*). If the database is on your local workstation, select this option.

   Note. As of this writing, this option is inoperable.
   - Lotus Notes - Workspace (*). Select this option to display only the names of the databases on your current workspace.

4. Select the disk drive and directory containing the database that you want, select the name of the database file, and then click the Open button.

5. Select the name of the form or view you want to open.

■ How Approach Displays Information

Because of the extremely flexible way in which Notes deals with information, a great deal of the data in a Notes database cannot be properly displayed when you open it in Approach. This section describes how Approach displays Notes database information.

Field Types

Approach can display nearly all of the textual information stored in Notes databases. The following table summarizes the way in which different types of Notes fields are displayed in Approach, and it points out the types of information that Approach cannot display.

Notes Field Type	How Approach Displays This Information
Text	Displayed as a text field. Special attributes (bold, italic, and so on) are not displayed.
Number	Displayed as a numeric field.
Time	If the field values contain only time information, Approach creates a corresponding time field. Similarly, if the field values contain only date information, Approach creates a corresponding date field. However, if one or more of the field values contains both a time and a date, Approach creates two fields—one for the date values and the other for the time values.
Rich Text	Displayed as a text field. Although the text itself is displayed, attributes such as bold and italic are not. In some cases, formatted text may not be properly displayed. Embedded graphic images and other objects are ignored by Approach.
Keywords	Displayed as a text field.
Author Names	Displayed as a text field.
Reader Names	Displayed as a text field.
Names	Displayed as a text field.

Formulas

When the values of a Notes field are calculated from a formula, Approach displays the result of the calculations. The formula itself is not copied.

When the type of a Notes field is either Computed, Computed For Display, or Computed When Composed, Approach displays the calculated value in the corresponding field. However, that field is treated by Approach as read-only. By contrast, if the type of a Notes field is Editable, you can modify its values from within Approach.

If an editable Notes field contains a formula that calculates a default value, Approach will display that value for each document, unless a user has supplied another value.

If a Notes field has either an input translation formula or an input validation formula, then that formula will be applied to any value entered *from within Approach*. If a validation formula determines that a value is invalid, Approach will display a message to that effect.

■ Creating Charts

The ways in which you can use Approach to manipulate and display Notes databases are too numerous to describe fully in this book. However, if you're familiar with using Approach, most operations take only a few minutes—perhaps a bit longer if you want to be really fussy about details.

Here's an example of using Approach that describes how to create charts to represent Notes information; this example hints at the power Approach offers. Suppose you maintain a Notes database of company information, which includes statistical information about each department. Figure 13.2 shows one particular view that displays some of this information, including the total number of employees in each department.

Figure 13.2

This view displays selected departmental information within a database.

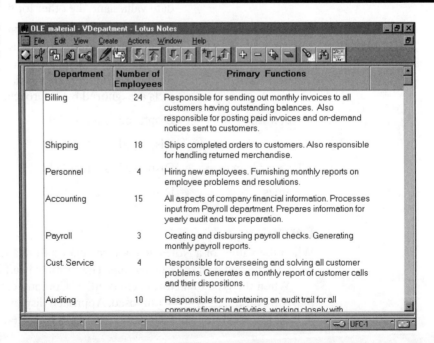

To present the information displayed in this view in a graphical format, you can use Approach to create various types of charts. Here's an outline of the steps to follow:

1. To begin, open the Notes database within Approach, selecting the view shown in Figure 13.2. Approach will open the Notes database and create the worksheet shown below:

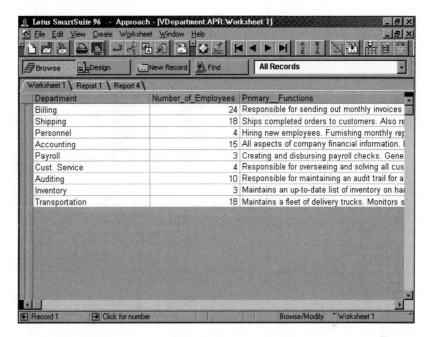

2. Select Create, Chart.

3. As the chart type, select Bar Chart. Then, for the x-axis, select the field Department; for the y-axis, select Number_Of_Employees.

4. When you're done, Approach will display the chart shown below:

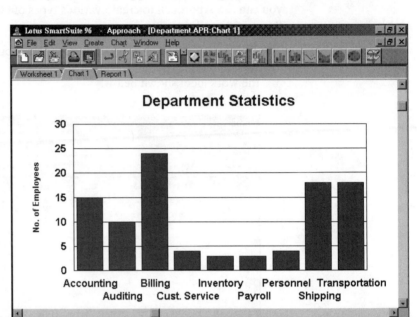

■ Creating Crosstabs

A *crosstab* is an information summary, displaying the results of some type of statistical calculation. Approach can display many different types of crosstab summaries for a given set of information, and these summaries can be presented either in tabular or graphical form.

As an example, suppose that you maintain a Notes database of employee information, part of which is shown in Figure 13.3. If you would like to summarize this information and display it in various ways, use the built-in tools in Approach. For instance, Figure 13.4 shows a crosstab summary of this information, calculated and displayed by Approach.

Approach can go one step further by displaying this information in graphical form: Figure 13.5 shows the results in bar-graph format, and Figure 13.6 shows the same information displayed as a pie chart.

To describe how to create crosstab information, we'll go through the steps for creating each of the displays shown in Figures 13.4 through 13.6, which are all based on the Notes database information shown in Figure 13.3.

Figure 13.3

This view displays selected employee information.

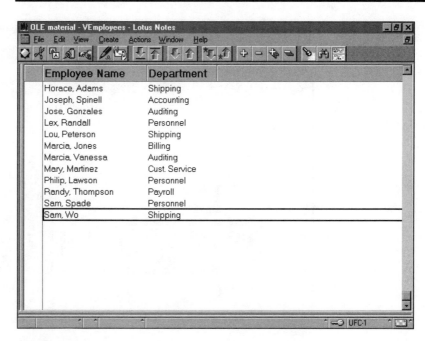

Figure 13.4

This crosstab summarizes the information shown in Figure 13.3.

Worksheet 1 / Crosstab 1 / Chart 1

	# Employees
Accounting	1
Auditing	2
Billing	1
Cust. Service	1
Payroll	1
Personnel	3
Shipping	3
Total	12

To begin, Approach must read in the data shown in the view in Figure 13.3 (as described earlier in this chapter, in "Opening a Notes Database in Approach"). Be sure to select the correct view, so that only the information you want to analyze is read in. Approach will create the two fields named Employee_Name and Department, which are copied from the column titles of the view.

Figure 13.5

The information shown in Figure 13.4 displayed graphically.

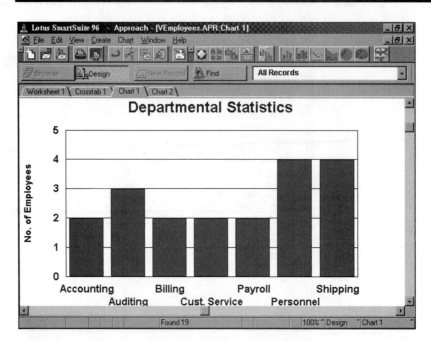

Figure 13.6

The information shown in Figure 13.4 displayed as a pie chart.

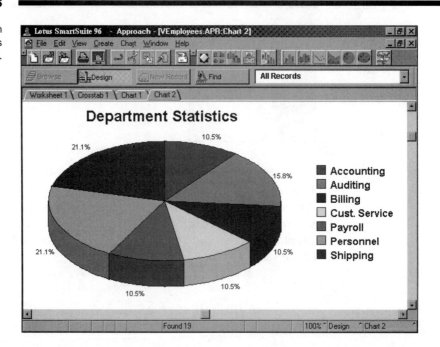

Creating the Basic Crosstab

After importing the employee information into Approach, you're ready to create the basic crosstab shown in Figure 13.4, as follows:

1. Select Create, Crosstab, and the Chart Assistant shown below will appear. Make sure that the tab labeled Rows is selected and then fill in the options as shown below:

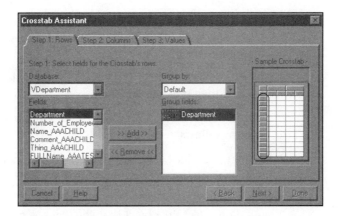

2. Click the tab labeled Values and then fill in the options as shown below:

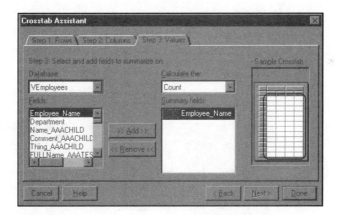

3. Click Done, and Approach will generate the crosstab shown in Figure 13.4.

NOTE. *Notes can create a great many different types of crosstabs for different types of information. However, a complete discussion of crosstabs is beyond the scope of this book.*

Charting Crosstab Information

When you have created the crosstab shown in Figure 13.4, you can then easily create a bar chart or pie chart to display the information.

Bar Chart

Creating the chart shown in Figure 13.5 is truly a no-brainer, once you have created the basic crosstab. Here are the steps:

1. Make sure that the crosstab is displayed on the screen.

2. Select Crosstab, Chart This Crosstab; Approach will automatically create the bar chart.

3. To modify either the top title or the y-axis title, double-click on either one and then type in your changes.

    You can also change the properties or contents of just about any part of the chart, as follows.

4. Display the Chart InfoBox: Click anywhere near the edge of the window, click on the chart, and then select Chart, Chart Properties.

5. When the InfoBox appears, pull down the top list labeled Properties For and then select the object that you want to modify.

6. Use the options on the InfoBox to make your changes to the object.

Pie Chart

A pie chart is a type of crosstab display, but you produce it directly from the original information—not from the crosstab summary. To create the pie chart shown in Figure 13.6, follow these steps:

1. Select Create, Chart, displaying the following dialog box:

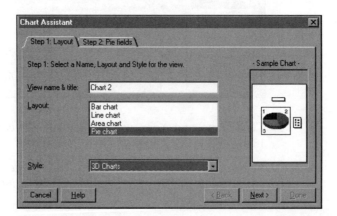

2. Select Pie Chart as the type, select a title for the chart, and also choose whether you want a two-dimensional or three-dimensional display.

3. Click the tab labeled Step 2 and then fill in the options as shown below:

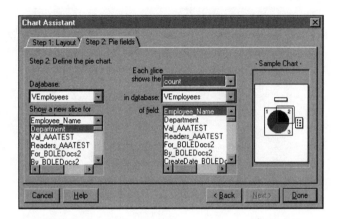

4. Click Done, and Approach will generate the chart.

5. You can customize various parts of the pie chart, using the options on the Chart InfoBox. See steps 4 and 5 in the preceding section, "Bar Chart."

■ Creating Reports

You can use Approach to create a wide variety of report types and styles. Reports can be either free-form or columnar. Headers and footers can optionally be included, and they can contain any arrangement of text and graphics (see Figure 13.1 for an example). Columnar reports can contain subtotals and grand totals.

When creating a report, you can select the fields to be included. You can also select from several different report styles. For example, the report shown below uses a style called Chisel2:

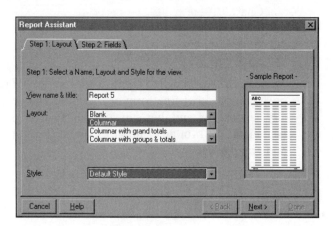

Here's a brief outline of the steps to follow for creating a report:

1. To begin, select Create, Report, displaying the Report Assistant shown below:

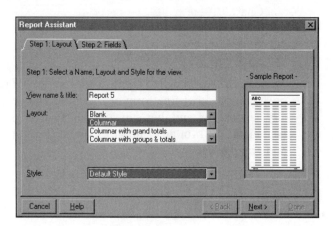

2. Select the report title (which you can later change), and the basic layout and style.

3. Click the tab labeled Step 2: Fields, displaying the following options:

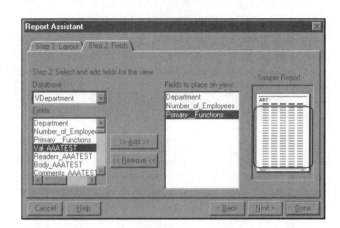

4. Select the fields that you want to include in the report.

5. Click the button labeled Done, and Approach will create the report.

6. To customize the various features of the report, display the Report In-fobox; to do this, select Report, Report Properties.

7. To customize a particular feature, pull down the top InfoBox list box, se-lect the feature that you want to modify, and then use the various In-foBox options to make your changes.

NOTE. *There are many ways in which you can modify an existing report to suit your particular needs. Regrettably, a full discussion is beyond the scope of this book.*

■ Creating Mailing Labels

You can use Approach to generate a group of mailing labels from name and address information in a Notes database. Approach can automatically print on just about any type of Avery labels, but can also customize the label size for other, non-Avery types.

As an example, we'll go through the steps to generate a group of labels from the Notes information shown in the following view:

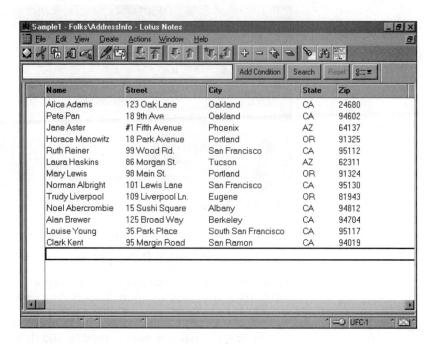

To generate the mailing labels:

1. To begin, create a Notes view that displays only the name and address information as shown above. Also, if you want to select a particular subset of documents, create a suitable view-selection formula.

2. Launch Approach and then open the Notes view that you created in step 1. Approach should then display a worksheet similar to the following:

Name	Street	City	State	Zip
Alice Adams	123 Oak Lane	Oakland	CA	24680
Pete Pan	18 9th Ave.	Oakland	CA	94602
Jane Aster	#1 Fifth Avenue	Phoenix	AZ	64137
Horace Manowitz	18 Park Avenue	Portland	OR	91325
Ruth Reiner	99 Wood Rd.	San Francisco	CA	95112
Laura Haskins	86 Morgan St.	Tucson	AZ	62311
Mary Lewis	98 Main St.	Portland	OR	91324
Norman Albright	101 Lewis Lane	San Francisco	CA	95130
Trudy Liverpool	109 Liverpool Ln.	Eugene	OR	81943
Noel Abercrombie	15 Sushi Square	Albany	CA	94812
Alan Brewer	125 Broad Way	Berkeley	CA	94704
Louise Young	35 Park Place	South San Francisco	CA	95117
Clark Kent	95 Margin Road	San Ramon	CA	94019

3. Select Create, Mailing Label, displaying the following dialog box:

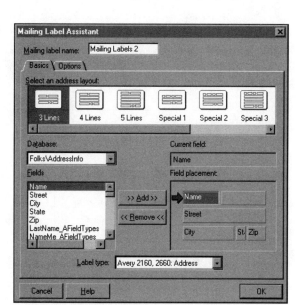

4. Select the type of address layout that you want for the labels.

5. In the lower part of the Mailing Label dialog box, select the placement of the various fields.

6. At the bottom of the dialog box, select the type of Avery label that you intend to use. If you're using a type other than Avery, just select the first one in the list. Later, you can modify the size to fit the labels you're using.

7. Click OK, and Approach will create a display similar to the following:

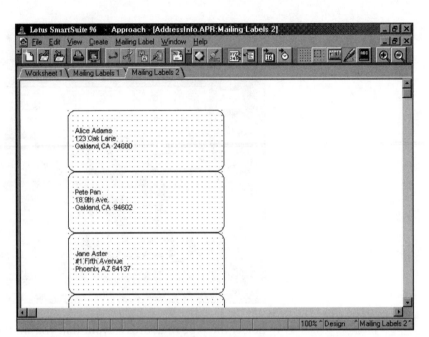

If you need to customize anything about the labels—size, margins, or whatever—go on with the following steps; otherwise, skip to step 14.

8. Click the top action button labeled Design. Then display the Mailing Labels InfoBox: Click anywhere except on a field, so that the Mailing Labels menu appears, and then select Mailing Label, Mailing Label Properties.

9. To change the margins, click the Margins tab on the InfoBox and then enter the new values.

10. To change the width of the labels, change the right margin setting.

11. To change the position of a field, click on it and then drag it to the new position. Or, to change the size of a field, drag one of the corner handles in the appropriate direction.

12. To change the font or other text characteristic of a field, click on the field, click the Font tab of the InfoBox, and then make your selections.

13. To change the vertical size of the labels, display the vertical ruler by selecting View, Show Rulers; click on the first label in the display—but not on any

field value—so that a surrounding box appears (as shown below); finally, drag the bottom line up to resize the labels, using the vertical ruler as a guide.

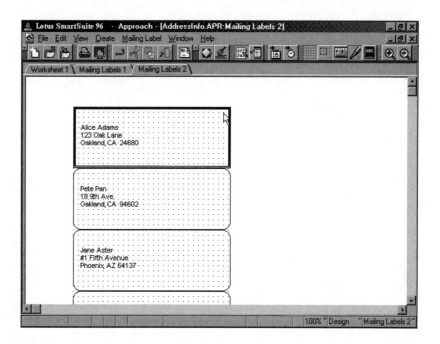

14. To print the labels, select File, Print.

TIP. *When you're creating mailing labels, always make a trial run using plain paper and a ruler. If you customized the label design in any way, you'll probably need to make a few trials—with subsequent changes to your design— before you get things just right. Plain paper is much less expensive than labels.*

If you make a complete mess of the mailing label design, probably your best course is to delete it and begin again. To delete it, be sure that the Design button is selected (near the top of the Approach window) and then select Edit, Delete Mailing Labels.

Notes Deployment

- *The Notes System*
- *Planning Your Notes Deployment*

14

The Notes Network:
Overview and Planning

THIS CHAPTER PROVIDES AN OVERVIEW OF THE NOTES 4.0 SYSTEM

for administrators who are new to *deploying*—or installing and set-

ting up—Notes. The information here will give you an overview of

features, functions, and tips so that you can quickly understand the

key components of this major release of Notes. In addition to gen-

eral information, you will find pointers to detailed information on

the subject. The planning information in this chapter will give you

guidelines for planning your Notes deployment.

■ The Notes System

The Notes system that you install will consist of a group of computers running either the Notes server software or Notes' workstation client software. These computers will share information. They do this by connecting via telephone lines and networks and then moving electronic documents from one place to another.

Notes uses, or "sits on top of," your existing computers, operating systems, and local/wide area networks. It uses the communications capabilities of these components to move documents from one computer to another so that the document can be easily accessed by users with the appropriate security privileges.

Like any network, a Notes network requires some care and feeding. Notes 4.0 has many new features that fall into one of the following categories:

- Ease of use for users

- Mobility

- Enhanced application development capabilities

- Scalability

- Internet integration

- Administration power and simplicity

In following chapters, we focus on those features that you as an administrator will need in order to set up the system for users, as well as those features that you will use in the management of your Notes network.

How the Pieces Fit Together

By first understanding key concepts and components of the Notes system, you will be able to make decisions that provide economy and performance to your Notes network.

The Notes *server* program has two main functions: moving documents from one server to another server—using routing or replication—and providing secure access to documents. The server program has many other tasks that keep it busy as well, and with Notes 4.0, many extensions that go beyond these capabilities, but the primary focus of the Notes server program is on moving and securing documents.

The Notes *client* (workstation) software provides an interface for users to create, find, and retrieve documents. The result of the client and server software working together is that users may have access to relevant information whenever they need it in a secure environment. The Note 4.0 workstation client is completely redesigned, making it far more functional and simpler to use than earlier versions. Figure 14.1 shows how a document may be created at a user workstation, once the Notes workstation software has contacted the server software and gains permission to store the document in the database on the server.

NOTE. *The user cannot create a document in a database that resides on a server unless he or she has the appropriate access to the database.*

Figure 14.1

A document created at a user workstation and saved on the server in a shared database.

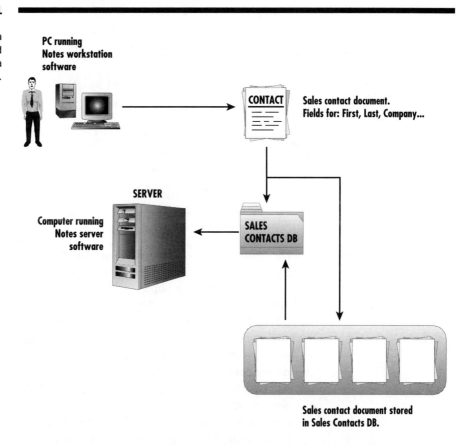

PC running
Notes workstation
software

CONTACT
Sales contact document.
Fields for: First, Last, Company...

SERVER

Computer running
Notes server
software

SALES
CONTACTS DB

Sales contact document stored
in Sales Contacts DB.

At the center of the Notes world is a *document.* A Notes document is similar to a record in a traditional database; it contains fields that are filled with information. Any type of data that can be created on a PC, Mac, or UNIX computer may be stored in a field of a Notes document. Figure 14.2 shows how information entered into fields on a form get stored in a document. Once information is in a Notes document, Notes knows how to move and secure that document. Notes 4.0 documents are enhanced in many ways, including field-level replication and better document/response referencing.

Figure 14.2

A Notes document with
fields to fill out.

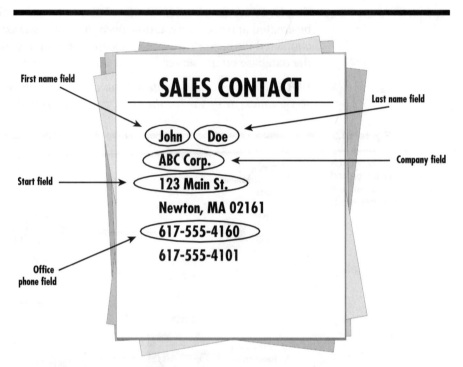

First name field

SALES CONTACT

Last name field

John   Doe

ABC Corp.   Company field

Start field   123 Main St.

Newton, MA 02161

617-555-4160

617-555-4101

Office
phone field

The Notes document lends itself well to the storage of knowledge and
narrative information. The anticipation of communicating (moving) documents is built into the document structure; that is, Notes documents have
qualities that make it easy to replicate (synchronize) and route the document
around the Notes network as necessary. For example, each Notes document
has a unique document ID number that Notes uses to track it. In addition,
fields may be signed and encrypted for security as the document travels
around the network. As a result, Notes is often used to create applications
that store unstructured information and group it logically, so that this information may be shared.

Views, folders, and *forms* are the mechanisms that Notes uses for displaying information to the user. Notes 4.0 *navigators* are a new design element
that provides a graphical interface for Notes database users. Navigators execute code to front-end views, folders, forms, and code. A view is similar to a
table of contents or a query in a traditional database; it may show all or a
subset of the documents in the database. Views list documents in a predefined (by the application developer) sort order and show data from particular fields. Users can find a document they like by using the view and then
double-click on the line item to see the entire document.

Folders are like views but are more dynamic, in that folders can be easily created by users and can store references to documents in views. A user looks in a folder just as he or she would look in a view, but the information is stored in a folder by dragging documents into it, rather than by a formula that is written by an application developer.

When users open a document, they see the data through a form. Forms are used in Notes for both data entry and data review. Different forms can be used to see the same document (data), to highlight different information, or to organize information differently for the user. As Figure 14.3 depicts, Notes separates the data itself from the way you look at the data (forms and views), so that you can place different forms on the data to see it represented in different ways.

Figure 14.3

A form with fields mapped to the Notes document.

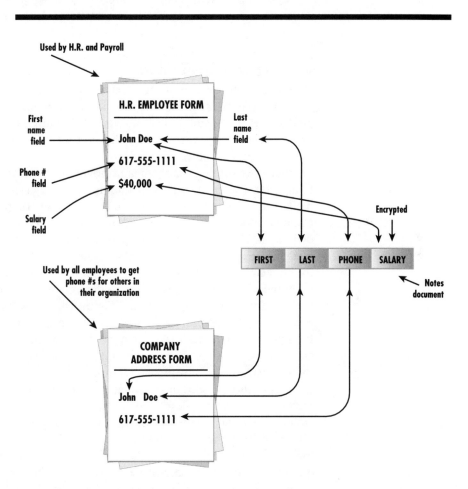

Documents, forms, views, and navigators are all stored in a single file that is the Notes database; this file has the extension .NSF. Unlike many traditional databases, the Notes database is flat file and contains all of the data, design, and security elements necessary to use and manage it. Among its many components are documents, forms, views, folders, indexes, access control lists, replication settings and agents, and more.

From a security perspective, having all these components in one place is helpful, in that it simplifies auditing and directs administrators to where to look for security breaches. On the downside, having all these components in a single (and replicated) file is a hindrance, in that users may have more access to the database structure than it is prudent to give them. High access to the database also gives users high access to all its design features.

In summary, we can define Lotus Notes as two programs that work together to move, secure, and provide a user interface to documents that store information.

Routing and Replicating

Notes can move documents in either of two ways: *routing* and *replicating*. These are the two key technologies that make Notes an information-sharing platform. Routing and replicating work differently from one another and have different purposes; together, they are the backbone of the Notes communication architecture.

In Notes, routing simply means moving a document from one location to another. The most common example of routing is in moving electronic mail. A user creates a mail message on his or her computer using the Notes client (workstation) software, and that message has the format of a Notes document. The user then sends the document to another user. Notes handles the moving of the electronic document from the sender's workstation to the recipient's mail database. If the sender elected to "save" the document before sending it, a copy of the document also remained in his or her mail database for future reference. Figure 14.4 shows the simplest form of routing—from one user's mail database to another user's mail database on the same server. Notes 4.0 has many enhancements to mail routing; especially noteworthy are the new user interface, the shared-mail databases, and the whizbang user-convenience features.

Replication synchronizes two files. For example, if a company has a contact database that its salespeople use, the company may have one copy of the contact file in the Boston office and another copy in the San Francisco office. Notes will keep these two copies of the database file synchronized by exchanging additions, deletions, and updates between the two file copies. If a contact is added in San Francisco, Notes will give that same update to the Boston copy of the file during the next replication event. If a telephone number is

Figure 14.4

A document is routed
from one mail database
to another mail database
on the same server and
is saved in both the
sender's and the
recipient's mail database.

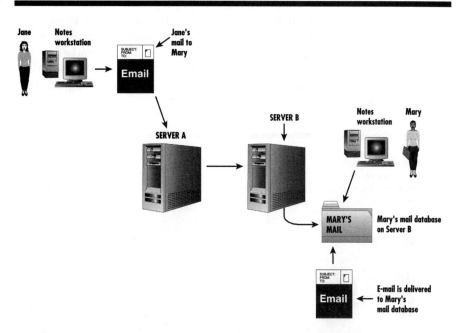

changed on one of the contacts in Boston copy of the file, the San Francisco
copy of the file receives that update during the next replication. Notes 4.0 can
replicate at the field level, which greatly reduces the amount of information
that must be exchanged during replication. In addition, user workstation replication has been beefed up and simplified from earlier versions.

Replication is important not only to distributing information for end users, but also for the management and security of the Notes network as a
whole. Notes, like any network, runs on the concept of membership. Each entity with any function on or access to the network must be known, so that appropriate rights and privileges can be granted to it. The common name for
such a membership list is a *directory*.

Notes has a directory called the Public Address Book (also often referred to as the NAB, for "name and address book"). Notes' Public Address
Book is a database that resides on each and every Notes server. This database has all the information about users, groups, servers, connections, and
more that Notes needs in order to stay up and running. All the servers in a
single Notes domain share a common Public Address Book. Figure 14.5
shows two servers with "replicas" of the same Public Address Book (in this
example, the organization's name is WorkGroup Systems, Inc., which is abbreviated to WGSI for the certifier, discussed later, and the domain name)
that is used to provide information to the servers as necessary for routing,
replication, and security.

A copy of your company's Public Address Book is replicated among all your company's servers. Thus, server A in Boston is looking at a directory that contains the same information as server B is looking at in San Francisco. This is a big distinction between Notes and other networks; a distributed directory changes the way we think about the security model. The Notes 4.0 Public Address Book has been greatly enhanced in its functionality, as well as its security.

Figure 14.5

Two servers with a Public Address Book that answers questions about mail database locations.

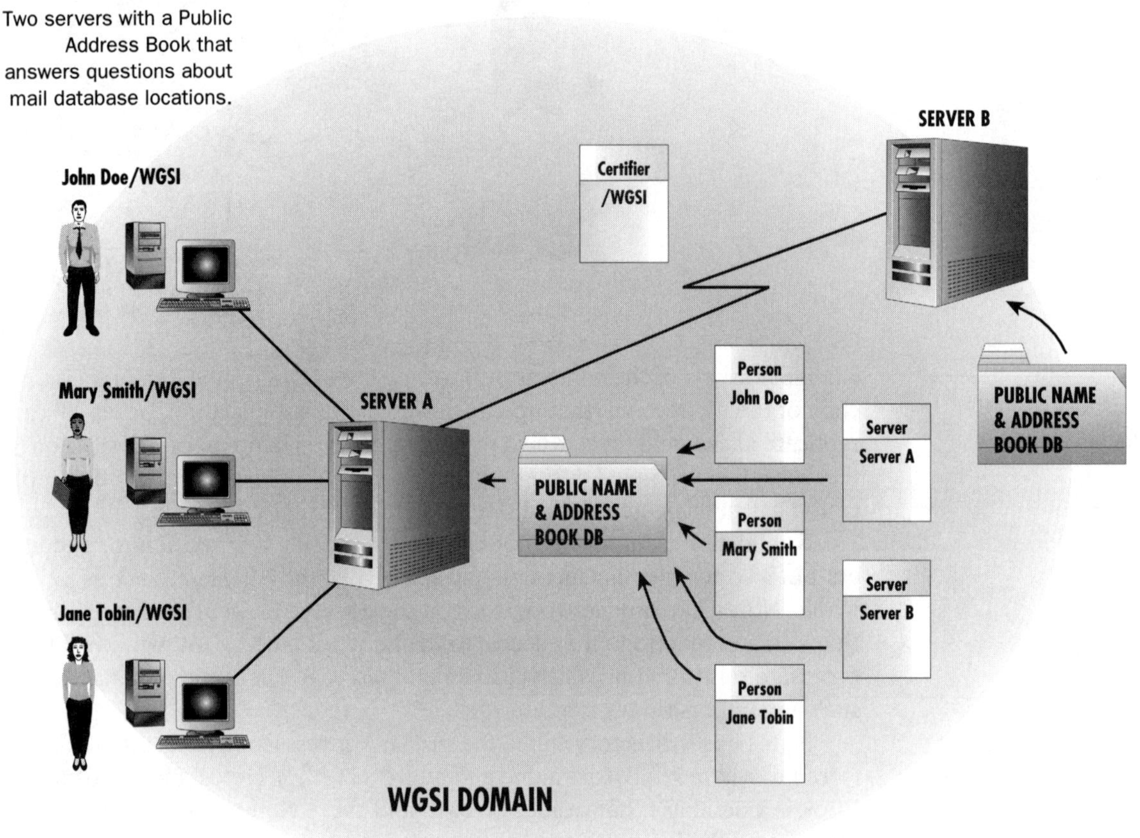

WGSI DOMAIN

To recap: We've established that Notes stores information in documents and uses forms, folders, and views to let users see the information. All the information necessary to store, use, and manage a Notes database is self-contained within that database. Notes uses one key database for management and as a directory: the Public Address Book. Replication is a service provided by the Notes server and is used to synchronize multiple copies of a database (as in the case of the Public Address Book, a system database that must reside on every server). Routing is another service provided by the Notes server and is used to move a document from one location to another, as in the case of electronic mail being sent by one user to another user's mail database.

The server program is the workhorse and watchdog of all the documents; it moves the documents using routing and replication, and it secures them. Any time that a Notes entity (a user computer or a server computer) requests access to a document, the Notes server program checks the access list (server and/or database) to see if that user has the privileges required.

Terms and Concepts

Familiarity with the following list of terms and concepts is key to understanding how Lotus Notes functions, as well as to designing your own Notes deployment.

- *Domain.* A Notes domain is a group of servers that share a common Public Address Book; in effect, the directory. This means that the servers all use the same Public Address Book and, as a result, can share and use each other's resources. For example, Samantha on Server A sending mail to John on Server B can be sure the mail will get to John, because Samantha's server has a copy of the Public Address Book with a "person" document telling Samantha's server where to send the message so that it will get to John's mail database.

- *Notes Named Network.* Notes Named Networks are groups of servers within your Notes domain that are physically connected (or bridged/ routed) and share a common network protocol such as TCP/IP or SPX. This means that these servers can communicate directly with each other. Understanding your physical topology as well as the network protocols running on top of the physical network will help you determine how to name your Notes Named Networks. For more information on Notes Named Networks, see Chapter 16, "Deploying Servers" and Chapter 26, "Managing the Network."

- *Security and ID files.* Overall, security in Notes 4.0 works similarly to that in earlier versions. Lotus has added enhancements for simplifying the use of security tools and caulked some holes in the old security model.

  ID files remain the lowest common denominator for security in Notes. There are still three kinds of ID files: *certifiers,* which are ID files that can create other IDs; *servers,* which are ID files used by computers running the Notes server software; and *user ID files,* which are used by computers that are running the Notes workstation software.

A certifier ID file is created when you run the setup program for your first Notes server. The setup program uses this ID file to create both the first server ID file and the user ID file for the initial Notes administrator. Using this same certifier, you may create *organizational unit certifiers* (see the later section, "Naming Hierarchies"), which in turn can also create organizational unit certifiers (up to four organization units are possible), as well as user and server ID files. Figure 14.6 shows how the certifier name is appended to the end of the "common name," and a hierarchy of certifiers can be created that matches an organization's structure.

ID files contain the same elements as those in previous versions of Notes, and each ID file still represents a single, unique entity on your Notes network. Each user and each server has a unique ID file that is used to prove to all other computers on the network that he, she, or it is who he, she, or it says. Once the identity is established, other controls are used to provide access privileges.

Some concerns about ID files remain with Notes 4.0. If an ID file is stolen and the password that encrypts it is discovered by the perpetrator, that person may still be able to pretend to be the user whose ID was stolen, although with Notes 4.0 this is now more difficult. Information that is encrypted with a lost or damaged ID file is still unrecoverable, unless a copy of the ID file can be restored. And finally, management of ID files is still somewhat cumbersome during distribution. Unlike systems that store their authentication mechanism at the server, Notes still distributes these files. This improves security in some ways but hinders it in others. Administrative control over ID files, although enhanced with some appealing tools, is still challenging in Notes 4.0.

What's New in Security for Administrators

The following Notes 4.0 features build on the security features and tools of earlier Notes versions. In general, these features either make managing security easier or close security holes of earlier versions of Notes.

- *Administration process*. Deleting, renaming, and recertifying users are now automated.

- *Administration server*. Database access controls are now updated automatically, based on changes in the Public Address Book, as part of the administration process.

- *Multiple passwords on ID files*. This requires multiple people to enter unique passwords before an ID can be used and is excellent added security for servers and certifier IDs.

Figure 14.6

The WGSI organization's naming hierarchy, with /Sales/West/WGSI the lowest certifier in the hierarchy.

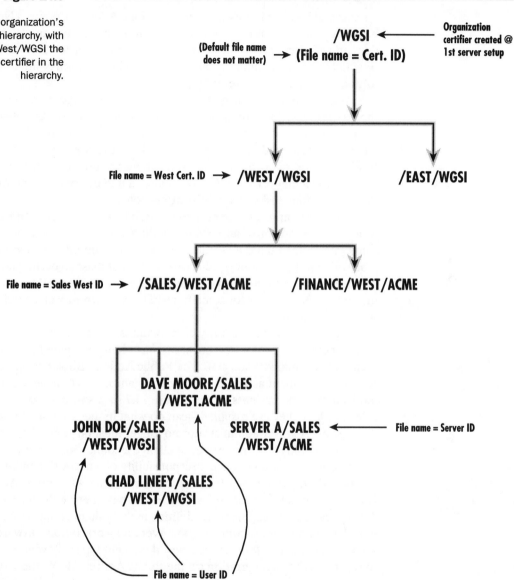

- *User types in database access controls.* Database managers can specify what kind of a Notes entity each entry is; the result is that it's more difficult to trick the system and bypass security.

The Public Address Book

As discussed earlier in this chapter, the Public Address Book is a Notes database that is used to store information about the Notes domain. It provides a domain-wide directory of key entities, as well as server-to-server communication and server program information. All this information is stored in the form of documents of different types.

As a result of the information it stores, the Public Address Book is still the key database that administrators use to manage the Notes network. In the past, many organizations customized their name and address books to implement security and other features. Thanks to the Notes 4.0 Public Address Book template, many of these customizations are no longer necessary. Notes 4.0 adds the Administration Control Panel, a unified control center that organizes the routine tasks of administrating Notes.

There are important changes to the Public Address Book, and all are welcome. First and most important, the Public Address Book template that ships with Notes 4.0 has a useful security model built in; this means that it is more difficult for unauthorized access to this database to occur, and it is easier to segregate administrative duties. The tools that are used to accomplish this have been in Notes for some time, but they are now well exercised in this critical database.

The key to this new security component is that Lotus has recognized that, as networks grow in size, most organizations segregate the duties of their Notes administration staff. The Public Address Book has implemented roles and document access lists to allow organizations to have the security model mirror the business model. Figure 14.7 shows who—based on the roles to which they are assigned—can do what in the Notes 4.0 Public Address Book. A server administrator no longer must be granted access privileges that would allow him or her to change a connection document, for example, if that document is the responsibility of a network administrator.

In addition to the security enhancements, Notes 4.0's Public Address Book has added functionality, as well. Forms have been enhanced with Notes 4.0 application development capabilities, making them easier to use. New options let administrators control new server and workstation software features such as enabling *passthru* servers. New document types allow administrators to control server configuration (in the Public Address Book, these documents are called Server Configuration documents) and standardize workstation program setup (these document types are called User Setup Profile documents). These additions extend the functionality of the Notes server and make it easier to remotely manage servers and more easily standardize user workstation installations.

Figure 14.7

The Public Address Book database with user roles represented.

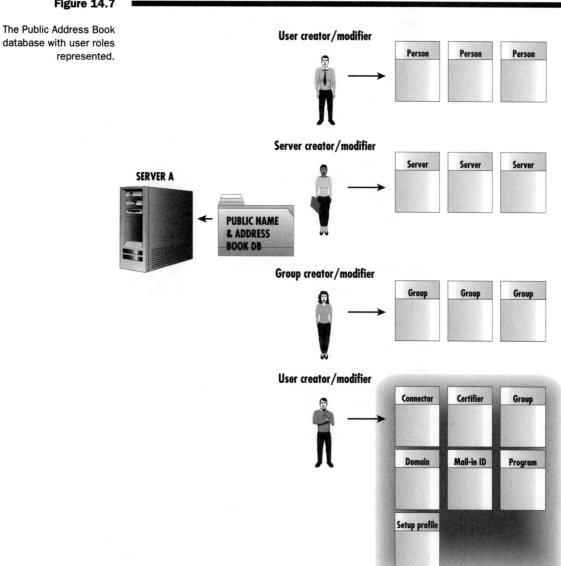

What's New in the Notes 4.0 Public Address Book

Notes 4.0 has a greatly enhanced Public Address Book. The enhancements serve purposes for the Notes 4.0 server program, as well as ease of use and security features for administrators. Following is a summary of new features:

- *Context-sensitive forms*. For example, selecting a COM port now offers choices relevant to modems.

- *Configuration documents*. These documents enable most changes to the NOTES.INI file, remotely and without restarting the server.

- *Security roles*. Security roles in Notes 4.0 enable organizations to protect the Public Address Book by segregating access to its views and documents.

- *User-Setup profiles*. These profiles let administrators standardize workstation setups.

Servers and Workstations

Notes is, of course, two programs that work together to help users share information. Both of these programs have been dramatically enhanced with Release 4, to provide additional functionality.

Servers

There are now two license types for the Notes server: a server license for single-processor computers and one for multiple-processor computers. This gives the administrator greater flexibility in designing a network of Notes servers. Because of Notes 4.0's ability to service an unlimited number of users when running SPX or TCP/IP, a multiple-processor server makes sense in many topologies.

For example, if you have a well-connected (networked) organization and have managed to keep costs down, you may want to run your entire organization on a single—or very few—multiple-processor server(s). Doing this will minimize hardware, software, and administrative costs.

On the other hand, you may want to take advantage of Notes' ability to distribute information and thus choose to have a server in each location that has a substantial number of users. In this case, you would use the single-processor license of Notes 4.0 and have multiple servers for different locations or business/server role functions.

The Notes 4.0 server has many new features that are either enhancements to what the server always did or provide new functionality. In terms of enhancements, the Notes 4.0 server program now supports an unlimited number of clients on popular network protocols such as TCP/IP and SPX. This means that you can have as many concurrent users on a single server as is practical, given connection and performance considerations. A new multiprocessor server program (for a higher price) lets you take advantage of computers running multiple processors and their respective operating systems, reducing the number of computers necessary to support the same number of users.

In addition, the Notes 4.0 server provides many long-awaited features such as *field-level replication,* which allows only the fields with changes—rather than entire documents—to be replicated. Notes 4.0 servers can provide *passthru service,* so that a user who is dialed in to one server may replicate with all the servers that he or she uses. New Notes 4.0 server processes simplify administration by improving the reporting and alerting capabilities of Notes with more features and simpler access.

What's New in the Notes 4.0 Server   The Notes 4.0 server has many enhancements to make it service more users, simplify management, tighten security, and improve performance. Following is a list of some of the important new features of the Notes 4.0 server:

- Unlimited concurrent sessions on TCP/IP and SPX, reducing the number of servers necessary

- Multiprocessor-server capability, reducing the number of servers necessary

- Field-level replication, minimizing time and connection costs

- Passthru capability, simplifying connections for end users and network managers

- Better reporting, allowing more information to be reported and improved event handling

- No limit on number of users (depending on the protocol that you run)

- New trace features for mail and ports

- Enhanced capabilities and more detailed restrictions in the Server document

- Database quotas, so the server automatically notifies users of databases growing beyond specified limits

Workstations

The Notes 4.0 workstation software is completely redesigned. It sports a new user interface that guides users to intuitively do what they need to do, and it hastens the process of getting routine tasks done.

Like the Notes 4.0 server license, the Notes 4.0 workstation license has more than one flavor. It can be one of three types: Lotus Notes Mail, Lotus

Notes Desktop, or Lotus Notes. The first two provide a subset of the functionality available in the third.

Lotus Notes Mail   The Lotus Notes Mail license of the workstation client software allows users to use Lotus Notes Mail as well as communication, collaboration, administrative, and documentation databases. These additional databases are limited in functionality and cannot be significantly customized. They include such applications as discussions, document libraries, and databases used by the Notes system itself. Custom databases that are created by application developers may not be used by Lotus Notes Mail licenses.

Lotus Notes Desktop   Lotus Notes Desktop provides complete access to any Notes database. These may include databases that are created by application developers, as well as those that ship with the Notes software. In addition, users of the Lotus Notes Desktop may create new databases from the templates included with it but will not be able to access the design features of Notes to edit the databases design elements, such as forms, views, navigators, and agents. The Lotus Notes Desktop license does not permit users to access the database design capabilities of Notes 4.0, nor does it allow users to access system administration features of Lotus Notes.

Lotus Notes   Lotus Notes is the full version of the client software license; it allows users to use, create, and modify databases—including the design of databases—as well as execute system administration functions.

What's New with the Notes 4.0 Workstation   Following are some of the new features for administrators in the Notes 4.0 workstation client software.

- *Administration Control Panel.* Provides one-stop shopping for most administrative functions. This pane has logically grouped buttons that let administrators do most administrative functions for all servers from a single workstation client.

- *Multipane user interface.* Simplifies accessing documents and navigating the screen and lets the user preview a document.

- *Workspace Replicator page.* A permanent tab on the workspace that allows users to schedule and manage replication and mail-routing activities. This simplifies using Notes remotely from many locations.

- *Folders.* Allow users to drag documents into the folders they create in order to organize their work. Folders may also be shared with others.

- *Action bars.* Persistent, context-sensitive buttons (menus) in forms and views used by application developers to give users quick access to features they build into the database.

- *Navigators.* Graphical regions that execute code used by Notes developers to build more intuitive interfaces to Notes, which guide users through the process of using the database.

- *Properties boxes.* Modeless (persistent) dialog boxes that provide one-stop shopping for all settings for a given element (database, document, field, and so on). Properties boxes limit fumbling through menus.

- *Agents and simple actions.* Macros that users can easily build. An *Agent Builder* helps users create the agents to execute routine tasks.

- *Context-sensitivity.* Main menu, SmartIcons, and right-mouse-button menus are context-sensitive, giving users relevant choices of what they can do based on where they are.

- *Workspace enhancements.* Add or remove workspace tabs and stack replica icons.

- *Better linking.* Users can now create graphical, hypertext links to databases and views, as well as documents. In addition, links can be created to World Wide Web pages.

- *User-customizable views.* Column widths and sorting can be done in the view by the user.

- *Better security.* Access control levels are enforced locally, and databases may be locally encrypted.

- *OLE 2.0.* Lets users work with objects created by OLE 2.0 servers.

■ Planning Your Notes Deployment

Installing and setting up your Notes network requires significantly more effort than should maintaining it, once the infrastructure is installed. Most Notes networks spring out of an application need, and they grow from there. If done properly, this is in fact a great way to start using Notes.

Regardless of who will be the initial users of the Notes network, it makes sense to have an understanding of the bigger picture before setting up. This way, you can avoid making decisions that need to be changed with great effort, down the road.

The installation and setup process can be broken down into five key areas:

- *Planning.* During the planning process, you determine physical and logical issues regarding the network, user base, support infrastructure, and purpose of your Notes domain. By thinking ahead and designing your domain around these issues, you will save time and aggravation later.

- *Installing software.* There are two software programs you will need to install, assuming that your computers are already set up and running with an operating system. The first is the Notes 4.0 server program, and the second is the Notes 4.0 workstation client. Both have simple installation programs that will enable you to easily copy the necessary files to your computer's hard disk. Additional software may be necessary for enhancing Notes 4.0 with gateways and add-ins, but for now, we focus on the basic Notes system components.

- *Setting up software.* Setting up involves running a program to configure the software once it is installed on a computer. The setup program will run automatically and determine if it should run a server or workstation setup for the computer, based on the software you installed. The setup program's primary purposes are to establish the identity of the new computer by locating (or creating) a user or server ID file for it; setting up the appropriate files, such as a public or personal name and address book and mail databases; and building the appropriate settings in the NOTES.INI file for that computer.

- *Setting up the network.* This process is less well defined than others. For our purposes here, you will need to "register" users and servers, establish how and when computers connect for mail routing and replication, and enter this information into the schedule of server tasks. You will also need to implement security guidelines to protect the system, as well as the data that resides on it.

- *Deploying Notes applications.* Rolling out Notes applications (databases) is the last step in getting users up and running. Notes mail automatically installs during the setup procedure and is actually a Notes application. However, applications developed to solve a particular organization process will determine the payoff for installing Notes. System administrators, application developers, and database managers must work in concert to get databases deployed to the user community.

Taking Stock

Planning involves many steps and processes and should be considered a complete project in and of itself. You need to take stock of what you have and what you will need in terms of computers, software, and network infrastructure. In addition, you need to plan who will roll out what components of the installation, as well as who will support the network once it is up and running.

Once you have gathered this information, you need to design your Notes domain: where the servers will reside, how they will communicate, what kind of security will be imposed on databases and servers, as well as how servers and users will be named.

The importance of planning cannot be overstated. A well-planned network will run and support users quickly and reliably. A poorly planned one may cost enormous amounts of time and money to reconstruct. It is well worth the time and money to invest in planning, up front.

It makes sense to have relevant people participate in the rollout process. Make sure that your rollout team is represented by people who understand your network, installing and maintaining hardware, installing and maintaining software, and supporting end users and the business units that will actually receive the technology. Bringing together representatives from different groups early on will greatly reduce the number of issues to iron out later.

Finally, it's important to have a goal for Notes from the beginning. Take a particular group and find out about their application needs. See how their business process can benefit from Notes, build an application for them, and deploy it to them as a pilot group. Use the opportunity to learn about Notes and how to support it before rolling it out to others. In some cases, you can say that the pilot application is electronic mail. Mail is, after all, just another Notes application.

We often recommend that the pilot group be a team within the information services department, because this group will greatly enhance its ability to support Notes if it uses Notes internally. There are many great applications that can be built in Notes for information services groups; for example, knowledge bases, support-tracking databases, and hardware/software-tracking databases, as well as more generic discussions and document libraries. Choose one and make it the pilot project.

The best way to plan your Notes network is to first think about your immediate deployment, then think about what you expect your long-term deployment to look like, and finally, fit your immediate deployment into the long-term vision that you have for your Notes network.

If you do not have another tool, we recommend buying a single notepad that will be your deployment journal. Keep all the information that you collect and create in this journal, so you know where to find the components you need as you plan. Start by considering where you are today. (If you have an electronic tool that can be available wherever you are in which to record information—such as a Notes database on a laptop—this will be even more useful, because the information will be easier to sort and share.)

A Physical and Logical Server Topology

Notes plays many roles; foremost, it is a communications product. Without communications, Notes has little purpose. For this reason, it is important to understand your existing communications infrastructure before planning how to deploy your Notes servers and workstations.

Notes 4.0 computers may connect with one another in three ways: always connected via LAN (local area network) or WAN (wide area network), sometimes connected via dial-up modem, or sometimes connected via remote LAN service. Notes computers connect with each other in order to access information, replicate information, and route information. Two types of server groupings are inherent in Notes. The domain and the Notes Named Network serve logical purposes in structuring your Notes system.

Establish how the servers and workstations may communicate and record this information in your journal. You will use it to design the logical organization of your Notes system:

1. Draw a diagram (map) of the places where users are located as well as the number of users. This diagram should show both the initial deployment group as well as the long-term plan for deployment, so you may want to use an existing organization chart. Both the physical location and the organization hierarchy will be important to have.

2. Add to this diagram representations of what kind of communications exist from location to location and from the location hub to the user workstation computers. Do they have an analog telephone line, a LAN connection, or a WAN connection to your organization's network? Include the bandwidth and availability of these connections.

3. Note the operating systems on user workstations as well as the network protocols that are running on these computers (see the Notes 4.0 documentation for system requirements). Figure 14.8 shows how you might diagram the hardware and software in your organization to prepare for the Notes 4.0 deployment. Notes 4.0 is certified with current operating systems, and Notes servers must run the same protocols as user workstations in order to share information (unless a passthru server is to be used).

4. Determine a place where you want to locate the Notes servers. This is an important decision, because the location that you choose must be able to support communication with the workstations, as well as be physically secure and convenient for administrative access. Notes 4.0 servers can service many users, so you will need to weigh the value of localizing information (having Notes servers located near the users), to limit WAN and phone costs, against the administrative time and cost savings of maintaining Notes servers centrally. If you can have your servers located in information services hub locations, where administrative support and physical requirements already exist, you can save significant time and money.

5. Think about how future additions to your Notes system will fit into the picture. For example, if you have laptop computer users, you may want to add dial-up capability to your server or add a server just for dial-in

Figure 14.8

Sample diagram of users, locations, servers, protocols, operating systems, and connections.

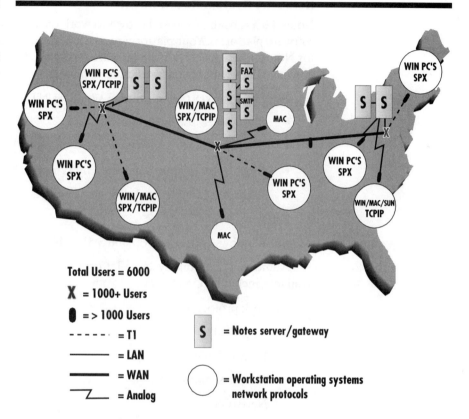

users. In addition, you may want to add other servers and server processes, such as passthru servers, fax servers, and mail-gateway servers. Where will these computers be located, and what communications will be available to them?

Once this basic information is compiled, refer to Chapter 26, "Managing the Network" to determine how you will have the computers connect with each other for replication and mail routing. You should also consider to which servers users will connect, LAN versus WAN, how many servers you will need, and the functions of the various servers in your organization. These numbers vary for each organization installing Notes, based on the number of users, the communication infrastructure that is in place, the performance of the computer hardware being used, and the volume and usage of the applications deployed.

Notes 4.0 System Requirements

Notes 4.0 has been tested and shown to work on a variety of hardware and software platforms. Your platform must meet certain requirements in order for Notes to run properly. Following are guidelines to help you ensure that you have the necessary infrastructure in place.

- Hardware, server (when running Windows NT)

  - 80486 processor or higher

  - 48MB of RAM

  - Any display adapter supported by Windows NT

  - 58MB of available hard-disk space (software only)

- Software, server

  - Windows NT server, version 3.51 or higher

Additional operating system platform versions of Notes will soon be available, including UNIX.

- Network protocols

  - AppleTalk

  - Banyan Vines

  - Novell Netware SPX

  - NetBIOS

  - TCP/IP

- Hardware, client

  - 80486 processor or higher

  - 6MB of RAM (with Windows 3.1 or 3.11)

  - 8MB of RAM (with Windows 95)

  - Any display adapter supported by Windows

  - 30MB of available hard-disk space (for workstations *not* running shared program software)

- Software, client

  - Windows 3.1

  - Windows for Workgroups 3.11

  - Windows 95

Additional operating system platform versions of Notes will soon be available, including Macintosh, OS/2, and UNIX.

- Network, client
  - Banyan Vines
  - Novell Netware SPX
  - NetBIOS/NetBEUI
  - TCP/IP

NOTE. *The workstation client software must run a protocol that also runs on the server computer. The client and server must have a protocol in common. For example, if the server runs only TCP/IP, the workstations must also run the TCP/IP protocol. Alternatively, you may add a protocol to the server so that it runs both TCP/IP and a protocol running on the workstations, such as SPX.*

Determining a Server's Role

Before installing and configuring your Notes system, clearly define how the system will work and the part each server will play. A Notes server can play many roles; defining those roles helps you name the server, select hardware, manage the server, determine how many servers you will need, and leverage your investment. Although you install and configure all Notes servers with the same procedures, it sometimes simplifies management of the servers to have them dedicated to certain tasks.

For example, with Notes 4.0's Internet capabilities, you can easily publish to the World Wide Web. You should probably have a special set of policies and people for managing and securing servers designated as InterNotes Web servers. (An InterNotes Web server is a server that allows users to browse the World Wide Web, using Notes.) In general, server roles may change significantly with Notes 4.0, as enhanced features make it possible to do more:

- "Anonymous" access list for making a Notes server open (good for Notes Net and the WWW or any other public network on which you may want to publish information, so that it can be easily found by those searching for it).

- InterNotes—for connecting with the World Wide Web—is included.

- Up to 500 concurrent sessions to support more users.

- Better replication and routing performance.

- "Passthru" to other Notes servers permits you to centralize remote services.

When determining the server role, consider the usage that the server will most likely receive. Notes 4.0 can support an unlimited number of concurrent users, depending on the network protocol that you install. When your network is running on TCP/IP and SPX protocols, there is no limit to the number of concurrent users. As a result, you may be able to realize some economic advantages by rethinking your topology and consolidating servers. For example, given these reduced restrictions, Notes hub servers can support far more "spokes." Consequently, you may be able to consolidate your network, saving significant administration time by caring for fewer servers and improving performance by limiting network traffic between servers.

Make sure that you plan the server with the resources it will need in order to be reliable and perform adequately for users. This means that you need to make the server fast, have plenty of room for storing data, and frequently back up the server. We usually recommend a minimum of 32MB RAM on Windows NT; 64MB RAM is desirable. Since most of the cost in Notes is in the deployment, processor, and management, you can in effect save money by adding memory and disk space; this makes the server better at performance, as well as more extensible—without greatly increasing per-user cost.

In addition, make sure that you have implemented a security strategy for that server that addresses the risk of data loss or interception. See Chapter 14, "The Notes Network: Overview and Planning" for more information on topology planning, and see Chapter 24, "Managing Security" for more information about Notes 4.0 security.

Workgroup Servers

Workgroup servers are servers that support both applications and mail. In larger Notes deployments, the mail function is often segregated from the application servers for reasons of performance, administration simplicity, and security. At small organizations or remote sites of large organizations, workgroup servers are usually set up to serve both mail and applications.

Because Notes servers running TCP/IP and SPX can support an unlimited number of concurrent users, and because the performance of replication and routing are dramatically improved with Notes 4.0, you may be able to consolidate server functions into one machine rather than two. In general, it is probably still a good practice to segregate mail databases to their own server(s).

Mail Servers

Mail servers are servers used specifically to store only mail databases and to route mail. You would designate a server as a mail server because doing so

1. Simplifies administration, by limiting the scope of server functions.

2. Reduces congestion on the LAN as more users can have mail files on one server, so that routing to another server on the LAN is less frequent.

3. Limits replication resources, because only the Public Address Book *needs* to be replicated.

4. Makes the Notes network expansion easier, as available resources are more easily measured.

5. Segregates server duties so that if an application server is down, mail can still be retrieved, and vice versa.

Hub Servers

Hub servers are used in a "hub and spoke" server topology to replicate databases and route documents. Hub servers are not accessed by users but rather serve as a physical and logical connecting point for the Notes domain.

Creating a hub and spoke topology of servers limits the number of "hops" that documents must make in order to get from the source server to the destination server. In most cases, a document will need to travel no farther than from the originating server—the hub server—to the receiving server. In addition, a hub and spoke topology is useful for simplifying the management of connection documents, especially since it minimizes the connections that are necessary. Many large organizations select hub and spoke topologies, because they can be easily adapted for system growth.

Application Servers

Application servers store Notes applications (databases). The range of applications stored on a server can vary from a simple discussion database to a mission-critical purchasing application. By segregating application servers, you can

- Expand your server network easily, without having to move user mail files and reconfigure person documents in the Public Address Book.

- Optimize server performance, by managing database usage and replication frequency without having to make accommodation for mail routing.

- Simplify administration by categorizing application servers for databases with high replication or security needs. This is a particularly useful strategy for storing "mission critical" applications, on which the organization lives and breathes. Servers storing these applications can replicate more frequently and have more restrictive access control lists.

- Simplify access for users by giving them "one-stop shopping" when they're looking for applications. If applications are located on many different servers, users may need to "surf" to find the applications they need. By locating only applications on some servers, users will have fewer servers to search, and fewer servers to which they must be granted access.

Remote-Access Servers

Remote-access servers allow users to dial in directly to a Notes server. By strategically placing remote servers, you can limit the connection costs. For example, a single remote-access server can store low-security databases and provide passthru services to other servers to which traveling users may need access. Remote-access servers are an excellent way to keep traveling laptop users connected and in the know. In addition, remote-access servers may store mail and/or applications. Remember that security is key to limiting risk when you make a server accessible via telephone line. See Chapter 24, "Managing Security," on Notes security, for more information about how you can protect information on remote-access servers.

Passthru Servers

Passthru is a great new feature of Notes 4.0. It enables one server to act as a bridge to other servers that are running different protocols. Using a server setup for passthru, a user who is dialed in to one server (the passthru server) may connect to other servers that run protocols other than the one running on the user's workstation.

For example, let's say that you have a mail server "A-MAIL-01" and an application server "A-APPS-01" and that you're traveling with a laptop. With earlier versions of Notes, you would need to make two calls to get access to both your mail and your applications. With Notes 4.0, you can call one server that is set up to allow passthru to the other server(s) and get your information in one telephone call. Servers designated specifically as passthru servers usually do not host applications, because the primary purpose of these servers is to provide connectivity to other servers. In some cases, a server with a different role may be set up to support passthru.

Passthru servers are also great for LAN workstation users, because passthru servers may enable users to connect to servers that run protocols to which these users previously had no access.

Establishing Naming Conventions

Naming conventions are insignificant when your Notes network is small, but they are extremely important when your network has grown large. By establishing early on how you will name Notes entities, you will simplify management of your Notes network, as well as provide better security and service. Renaming organizations or servers is time-consuming, even with the new Administration Process, so think this through carefully.

All entities on your Notes network are created as progeny of the certifier ID file that is created when you set up the first Notes server in your organization. Remember, each server and each user on the Notes network has a unique ID file that is used to determine who they are and what privileges they have. All organizational-unit certifier IDs, server IDs, and user IDs are descendants of the certifier ID. It is the Adam and Eve of all ID files (see Figure 14.6).

Naming Hierarchies

Notes lets you create hierarchies to break up your organization into logical groups, by creating *organizational-unit certifiers*. The structure is similar to standards such as X.500, an open standard that defines a customizable directory model for hierarchical naming. The advantage to creating hierarchies is that you can more easily distinguish users. For example, John Smith/West/WGSI and John Smith/East/WGSI are different entitites. Each of these names actually contains three entities (the user's common name, one organizational-unit certifier, and the organization certifier).

You can create a naming structure that mirrors your business hierarchy—simplifying administrative tasks—and enables you to distribute the task of adding and removing users from the system—certifying users and servers—in a secure way. Certifier ID files create organizational-unit certifier ID files, user ID files, and server ID files. Organizational-unit certifier ID files may also be used to create organizational-unit certifiers (up to four organization units, in total) and may also create user ID files and server ID files.

You may have up to four levels of organizational-unit certifiers. For example, you may have an organizational-unit certifier ID that has the name /Admin/Sales/West/DillDivision/WGSI. This organizational-unit certifier is a descendant of the organization certifier /WGSI. It is also a descendent of the organizational-unit certifier /DillDivision/WGSI. Users who are created (certified) with this organizational-unit certifier ID file would have names like Sam Relish/Admin/Sales/West/DillDivision/WGSI.

The following certifier ID files determine the names used in your organization hierarchy. You should create a nomenclature for these items that matches your organizational structure.

Organization   The organization name is the name that you give to your Notes network. Typically, it is the same name as your *domain* name. A domain, in Notes lingo, means a set of servers that share a common Public Address Book. Typically, in a hierarchical Notes system, users and servers that are listed in an organization's Public Address Book descend from a single certifier. Additional entities are "cross-certified," to let ID files—descending from other certifier ID files—"authenticate" with your system. The name that you determine will be appended to every user and server name (for example, John Smith/WGSI). The organization name should not exceed 31 characters and should be a single word. All the servers and users in your organization will be members of the organization name that you establish. It is usually a good idea to have this name match your Internet domain registration. This will be the progenitor of all other ID files. It will be stored on the first server with the *file name* (not organization name) CERT.ID.

Organizational Unit   Organizational units are subsets of the organization. You might, for example, create an organizational unit called /West/WGSI. In this case, users and servers that fall under this organizational-unit certifier would have names like Mary Chutney/West/WGSI. It's a good idea to have your organizational certifiers reflect location and/or business unit or function. These files are stored, by default, with the file name ORGUNIT.ID, where "orgunit" is the first eight characters of the name that you chose for this organizational-unit certifier name. If the "ou" is to be called "westcoast," the file will, by default, be saved as WESTCOAS.ID. The Notes hierarchical name contained within this ID file is, of course, westcoast/WGSI. This file may be given to a local administrator who will be able to create ID files that can be authenticated across the domain, but will always have the full organizational-unit name appended to them. This administrator, then, can create organizational units, servers, and users (provided that he or she is granted appropriate access to the Public Address Book) under the hierarchy /westcoast/WGSI. Examples would be the organizational-unit certifier /admin/westcoast/WGSI or Sally Sour/westcoast/WGSI.

Notes Entities

The following are the entities that you will name when building your Notes network. Give thought to the conventions you use to create these names, because if logically and consistently done, they can greatly simplify the management of your Notes network.

Servers   As your network of Notes servers grows, it is helpful to have a nomenclature for servers so that administrators can easily identify server locations and purposes. Notes 4.0 server names can consist of one or more words, up to a total of 79 characters. You can use any characters in the name except the following: (,) @ \ / = +.

NOTE. *You can use spaces in the names, but we advise against doing so because spaces can cause confusion and sometimes require enclosing a name within quotation marks.*

Some network protocol platforms require that the server name be unique within the first *x* characters:

Protocol	Number of Characters That Must Be Unique
NetBIOS	15.00
AppleTalk	32.00
SPX	47.00

Servers get their names from the ID files that they use. Hence, server names fall into the hierarchy that you give to your organization, as described previously. The *common name,* or the unique server name, that you give to each server should describe that server so that anyone familiar with the nomenclature can easily discern information about it.

For example, you might name a server P-WG-DIA-01, to indicate that it is a Pickles Inc. server, used for applications and mail near the Denver International Airport, and that it is the first server of this kind. Remember, the common name of the server will be appended with the complete hierarchy of its certifier ID file. Therefore, the fully distinguished name would be even more informative: P-WG-DIA-01/Admin/WestCoast/WGSI. Figure 14.9 shows the component breakdown of a fully distinguished server name. With this additional information from the certifier, an administrator can easily deduce the division and business group that is being serviced by this server.

Figure 14.9

The components of a server name.

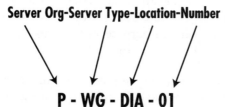

Server naming-"Common" name only

Server Org-Server Type-Location-Number

P - WG - DIA - 01

Since Notes allows for a broad array of server names, take advantage of this by making the name useful. Bear in mind that changing the name of a server requires recertifying the ID file and changing settings in many documents of the Public Address Book, as well as the access controls of other databases and servers.

Making these changes is easier with the Notes 4.0 Administration Process than in earlier versions of Notes. However, changing server names is still not something you want to do often. Because the server is treated much like a user by other servers, if its name changes, all of its security privileges throughout the system must be updated. It's best to choose a name that you are willing to stick with.

A simple and helpful way to name a server is to include information about it. Some good components of a server name are company indicator, location, role, and number. For example, if the company name is Acme and you are adding a Notes server for the Boston sales office, the server name might be A-BOS-WG-01, to indicate that this Notes server is for Acme Corporation; it is located near the Logan International Airport (BOS is the designator for Logan); it is a workgroup server (it acts as a server for both mail and applications); and it is the first of such servers at this location. If the Boston sales office has people who are out of the office and dialing in from laptops, it may also have a remote-access server named A-BOS-REM-01, to indicate that this is a server that is accessible remotely via telephone lines.

Notes administration can be organized in many ways. Regardless of how your support function is organized, having meaningful server names will save time in managing the Notes server network. If replication fails, a database manager can easily determine the location where the failure occurred if the server name includes the location.

If a Notes certifier administrator is determining how to expand the Notes system in order to meet growing user needs, he or she may need to know what roles the server in Boston is playing. If the server has a meaningful name, it will be easy for that administrator to distinguish a mail server from an application server. If the server is a workgroup server, serving both mail and application functions, another server in that location may be warranted as the user base grows. If the server is just an application server, perhaps the capital expenditure can be saved. It is always handy to have server names explain the server's purpose, rather than someone having to guess at it or contact a local administrator.

Users   User names require less preemptive thinking than do server names, because you do not need to determine an entire system of naming for them—they already have one, presumably. The real question with user names is which components of the users' names you should use.

Consider whether you will require or allow middle initials in the name stored in users' ID files, whether nicknames will be used, and so forth. Setting a standard here is important in order to make sure that mail is easily delivered to users' mail databases and so that database managers and server administrators will be able to assume—and be correct—about how a particular user should be listed in database and server access control lists. If the company standard is to not allow the use of middle initials and to use names as stated in the corporate address book, a database manager will know to list William Vinegar rather than William's nickname, Bill, in the database access control list. Notes 4.0 limits the risk of using the wrong name by letting database managers choose from a pick list of the users, groups, and servers listed in the name and address books that are available.

Notes Named Networks   In addition to naming entities on the Notes network, it is also important to develop a system of naming for the Notes Named Networks in your domain. *Notes Named Networks,* discussed in Chapter 26, "Managing the Network," are groups of servers that run the same protocol and are physically connected to each other so they can communicate directly. You could, by this definition, have one huge Notes Named Network for your entire organization, if, for example, all servers and workstations ran TCP/IP. However, it is usually a good idea to group your servers geographically, in order to lower communication costs and simplify access for users.

When a user selects File/Database/Open, he or she is given a list of servers from which to choose. This list includes all the servers in the Notes Named Network in which the user's mail file is located (the user's mail database is on one of these servers). As a result, you can limit the number of servers that a user sees when looking for a database, and you can simplify the searching process; at the same time, you are giving the user economical choices, because the servers will all be located in the same general area. It's good to include the type of network and the location in the name of a Notes Named Network. For example, you might choose EtherTcpBos for a group of servers on an Ethernet network running TCP/IP in the Boston area.

Once you have completed the planning process, read Chapter 16, "Deploying Servers" for information on installing and setting up your Notes domain.

Notes Server Connections

Server connections are logical rather than physical. This means that you can use "connection" documents that are stored in the Public Address Book to determine when, how, and for what purposes servers should connect. Obviously, these connections are a natural extension of your physical network topology. When servers connect, they use the *physical* connections available to them through network or telephone ports to execute scheduled routing, replication, and passthru services.

To plan connections, add to your diagram of what's in place additional lines that show which servers will connect with which other servers and for what purposes. Figure 14.8 shows how a typical network for a small organization may look. As guidelines, determine the following:

- What is your server topology?

- Will you use dial-in (remote-access) servers?

- Will you have passthru servers?

- Are you segregating mail and application servers?

- Do you need to have high-priority replications occur between certain servers?

Support Standards and Plans

You need a plan for supporting the following areas of your Notes 4.0 network: server issues, technical support, administrative tasks, and administrator and user training. Each of these areas represents an ongoing set of duties that will be necessary to keep the Notes 4.0 system and its users up and running.

As you make decisions about your Notes network, make notations in your deployment journal regarding which decisions will become policy and follow through with implementation plans for those policies.

Have a clear plan about how to set up a reliable Notes support infrastructure. By *reliable,* we mean that the system has a high availability rate, information stored on the system has integrity, and performance is adequate to meeting user needs. Users will put critical information into Notes, and they must know they can expect performance and reliability.

The Installation Support Spike

Initially, your Notes deployment will require a significant amount of time. This is because it will carry the unusual burden of setup and installation procedures, as well as limited knowledge of administrative staff until experience with Notes grows.

When planning the rollout, assign duties for the various aspects of the Notes deployment. Some people will need to install and set up the server and workstation software. Others will need to plan and create the ID files for users and servers. Still others can set up the connections for servers to connect with one another.

Notes is a large system with many discrete tasks. Providing your support staff with an overview of information about the entire procedure, as well as the detailed information that these people will need for their particular responsibilities, will make them more effective.

Segregating Duty

It's useful to break down the tasks of server issues and administration that are involved in maintaining your Notes system and then group these tasks within functional types of administrators. Table 14.1 describes these types, which match well the security roles provided in the Public Address Book.

The administrative roles outlined in Table 14.1 will be handled by different individuals in different organizations. For example, in smaller organizations, the segregation of duties described in the table may not be possible because of limited staffing and needs. In larger organizations, duties in some roles may overlap with others, such as LAN management, and thus be segregated differently.

Table 14.1

Administrative Roles and Tasks.

ADMINISTRATIVE ROLE	TASKS
Notes database manager	Manages Notes applications. Establishes database access controls, archives documents, checks replication, manages database size.
Notes server administrator	Installs and upgrades software and hardware, backs up databases, restarts server, resolves network (protocol, Network Interface Card) issues.
Notes network administrator	Determines and implements connection schedules, server access lists, passthru permissions, protocols, and Notes Named Networks.
Notes certifier	Adds and removes users from the Notes domain.
Network administration	Not a Notes function, but important, because Notes will use the infrastructure deployed by this group.

There are several reasons for breaking down the administrative duties described Table 14.1. First and most important is that each duty requires a specific set of skills, and these skills must be developed in such a way that expertise and proficiency are developed, too. The security advantage of segregating duties is also important; for example, by separating the function of managing databases from that of administrating servers, the risk of unauthorized access to data by a system administrator is greatly decreased.

In addition to proficiency and security issues, segregating duties as described in Table 14.1 will fit logically with the infrastructure of existing data systems. Server administrators, for example, already have knowledge of issues surrounding administration of servers. Similarly, the group responsible for creating users on the system (certifier managers or domain managers, in the Notes world) already have systems in place for adding and removing users as necessary from the system.

Training Requirements

Both administrators and users will benefit from training in Notes. Next to a useful set of applications with management support, there is little that is more critical to a successful deployment of Notes than training. If administrators are well trained, the system will be reliable and provide useful functionality. If users are well trained, they can take advantage of the tools Notes provides for them.

Administrators   Administrators should become familiar with the tasks for installing and maintaining the Notes system. The remaining chapters of this book break out the duties of administering the Notes system into two categories: deploying notes and managing notes, once it is deployed. Managing Notes is divided into chapters, based on the role each individual will play in the Notes system maintenance.

In addition to reading this book, administrators should practice installing and using a system. This experience is important, because having made a trial run, they can avert difficulties that may require significant time to rectify in the future. They can get hands-on experience in a Notes system administration training class or by going through the setup procedures outlined in this book and in the Notes manuals.

Users   Users can benefit from training to make them more productive. While this book is designed for administrators and application developers, there are a number of excellent materials available to users, including the manual that comes with the Notes documentation.

- *Installing and Setting Up the Domain— From Scratch*

- *Server Management Tools*

15

Notes Network Setup: A Quick Start

THIS CHAPTER GIVES AN OVERVIEW OF THE INSTALLATION AND setup process for new Notes networks. In this chapter, we assume that you have reviewed Chapter 14, "The Notes Network: Overview and Planning" and have developed a rollout plan.

■ Installing and Setting Up the Domain— From Scratch

Installing and setting up the domain is accomplished by running the setup program, after you've installed the first server software on the computer that will be your first Notes server. Use the information you developed in the planning process to enter choices in the setup procedure. In addition to making good use of planning exercises, it is also a good idea to start using some Notes 4.0 management tools right off, because these will help you run your network, as well as diagnose problems. For detailed information about setting up your domain, see Chapter 16, "Deploying Servers." Your procedure should look something like the following.

Install the Server Software

"Installing the first server" means using the Notes disks or CD to copy the program files to the file system of your new server. This process is automated by an install program described in Chapter 16, "Deploying Servers." The most significant part of installing the first server is running the setup program.

Run the First Server Setup Program

The first server setup program starts automatically when you run the workstation software and an incomplete NOTES.INI file is detected. Yes, you would think the *server* setup program would be started by running the *server* software program, but it is not. If you are creating a Notes network from scratch, you will select the option This Is The First Notes Server In Your Organization to kick off the process of creating a Notes domain.

When the server setup program runs and you tell it that this is the first server in your organization, the program will guide you through the steps to create a Notes domain. Some of the choices that you make during this setup will have long-term repercussions. Please read Chapter 16, "Deploying Servers," if you have never set up a Notes network before or if you want a refresher on what is actually happening with all the selections that you make during first server setup. Following are brief descriptions of the information you will need to provide to the setup program.

NOTE. *If you are installing only one server to begin with but are planning for your Notes network to grow, it is a good idea to create an appropriate organizational-unit certifier and to give names to the first server and initial users that are appropriate for the future hierarchy. In this way, you will not have to redo work such as naming users, moving mail files, and updating person documents. See Chapter 25, "Managing the Domain," for more information on registering organizational units.*

Server Name   This is the name that you want to identify the computer that's running the server software. Be thoughtful in creating a name for the server, because you may want it to provide useful information as your network of servers grows. We usually like to have the name offer some indication of location and purpose. For example, a server in San Francisco may be named ACME-SFO-WG-01, to indicate that this is an Acme Corporation server, it resides in a location near San Francisco International Airport (we often use airports, because their designators do not often change), it is a workgroup server (rather than a mail or remote-access server), and it is the first such server in this location.

Organization Name   This is the name you want to give to your certifier ID file. All ID files that are created with this certifier will have this name appended to the end of the fully distinguished name it contains. For example, if your name is John Smith, your user ID file may contain the fully distinguished name John Smith/Acme, if Acme is the name of your domain. By default, the domain is given the same name as the certifier.

Administrator's Last, First, and Middle Initial   This is the name of the first user in the network. This person is granted administrative rights to the server as well as the Public Address Book. Keep in mind that administrator ID files in Notes are identical to user ID files. Administrators can perform administrative tasks, because they have been granted privileges to do so. You may add other users to these privileges in the future.

Administration Password   This is the password that will be used to access the user ID created for the administrator and will also be used as the password for the certifier ID file. You may—and should—change the password of both these ID files, once they are created. In addition, Notes 4.0 allows ID files to have multiple passwords, so that multiple users must enter a password before the ID file can be used. This is an excellent security tool for server and certifier ID files. (See Chapter 27, "Managing Servers," for more information.)

Network Type   This field refers to the network protocol that the first Notes server will use to communicate with Notes users and other servers. Select one protocol here, and you may add additional protocols in the future. Notes has drivers to support all major protocols. You should choose the protocol that your organization uses to connect its computers. For example, if your organization uses SPX to share files and printers, this is probably the best choice on which to run Lotus Notes as well, because SPX is already running on all the computers on your network.

Serial Port   This is the modem port that Notes should answer for users and servers dialing in, as well as to call remote servers. Make sure to select the type of dialing necessary on the port (tone or pulse). If you have more than one modem on the server computer, you may add the additional modem later.

Modem Type This option allows you to select the type of modem in your computer, so that Notes can send it the right commands. If you do not see your modem listed, use the Generic All Speed modem choice. Modem files are text and can be edited through the File, Tools, User Preferences, Ports menu if you need to make adjustments in the future. Script files may also be specified.

Server Is Also Administrator's Personal Workstation This check box tells the workstation setup program to install the user ID file for the administrator and set up the local machine for workstation program use, as well as server program use. Notes will place the administrator's user ID file in the data directory rather than the Public Address Book, so that the user ID file may be used immediately by the administrator as a workstation on the same machine that runs the server software.

If you click the button labeled Advanced, you may change the following options or leave the default values.

Domain Name By default, this field is the same as the organization (certifier) name from the previous dialog box. A *Notes domain* is a group of servers that share the same Public Address Book. It is a good idea to have the domain name be the same as both your certifier name and your company's Internet domain registration.

Network Name Notes Named Networks are groups of Notes servers that run on the same protocol and are physically connected, so they can communicate directly. You may give the group of servers any network name you like. We like to use a name that will describe the location, protocol, and/or network type of that network. For example, SfoTcp might be a good network name for a Notes Named Network in San Francisco running the TCP/IP protocol. Using locations as part of the name is helpful, because this will limit the server options that users see when they select File, Database, Open. When issuing this command, Notes displays those servers that are in the same Notes Named Network. See Chapter 26, "Managing the Network," for more information about Notes Named Networks. If the location is part of the Notes Named Network name, users will get a list of servers in their geography—lowering connection costs and providing more relevant choices for users.

NOTE. *Notes Named Networks provide no inherent security features. A user on a server in one Notes Named Network may access a server outside his or her Notes Named Network if that user is running the same protocol as the second server, has a physical connection to the server, and is granted access to do so in the server's access control list.*

Organization Country Code   This entry will append the name of your certifier name with the country code that you enter and, as a result, will append the fully distinguished name of each ID file you create with that certifier. The country code should match the international standards country code for the country that you designate. We recommend that you leave the country code blank, because in the future, it may limit your ability to use this certifier for international domains.

Log Modem I/O   We usually check this box, to place a setting in the NOTES.INI file telling the server program to log all the information going to and coming from the modem when we start up the server. This information is very helpful for troubleshooting with the modem, because it shows the actual commands sent to and from the modem. If there is a problem, it is often due to an incorrect command that will appear in the log file as a result of checking this box. Later, when we establish that the modem works properly, we disable this feature.

Log All Replication Events   Checking this box will cause the server to record detailed information about replication events. This information takes space in the log but can be extremely useful in troubleshooting. If this option is chosen, the Notes server event task will record all replication sessions between servers. In addition, the log will detail when the replication took place, which server initiated the replication, how long it took to complete the replication, the number of documents exchanged (added, deleted, and updated) and the port used. This information is indispensable for troubleshooting replication problems.

Log All Client Session Events   Selecting this option will result in detailed information provided in the log file about the user activity on a server. This information is particularly useful when you're doing security audits and determining how to plan for server resources. It will give you information about which users are accessing the Notes server, when, for how long, and what databases they use.

Create Organization Certifier   Leaving this box checked will tell the setup program that it should create an organization certifier ID file that will be used to create all the other ID files in your organization. The only reason to uncheck this option would be that you have been given or previously created an organization certifier.

Create Server ID   Leaving this box checked will tell the setup program to create an ID file for the first server in the organization. This ID file will be necessary to run the server software program. The only reason to uncheck this option would be that you have created or plan to create manually the first server ID file for your organization.

Create Administrator ID   Leaving this box checked will tell the setup program to create an ID file for the first administrator of the system. This person may then use the certifier ID file to create other organizational-unit certifier ID files, server ID files, and user ID files. In Notes 4.0, an administrator is just like any other user, except that he or she is granted special administrative privileges in several areas of the Public Address Book.

Minimum Admin and Certifier Password Length   The number that you enter here will set the minimum length of the password that is required in order to use these ID files. Once you set this password length, you may not change it until you recertify the ID.

Start the Server

Your server is now ready to start working. You can run it by clicking on the Notes Server icon in the Program Manager of Windows NT. Once the server is running, you should check to see that it is operating as it should before you move on to complete your system setup.

Set Up Administrative and Security Groups

Groups are very helpful in using and managing a Notes network. For users, groups simplify the addressing of mail, as well as the process of securing documents, by minimizing the amount of information the users need to enter. For administrators, groups greatly reduce the amount of time required to manage the system's security.

Use the Notes 4.0 Administrative Control Panel button labeled Groups to create a group document in the Public Address Book. Table 15.1 lists access-type groups that you should consider adding immediately to your system. These groups will help you bring up Notes with adequate security while you're setting up systems that will reduce work in the future. Creating and implementing groups at this point in your setup will save a great deal of time later on.

NOTE. *The groups in Table 15.1 are examples of how you might think about segregating duties and granting access privileges to the Notes system. If you are planning a large deployment of Notes, you may want to further segregate duties to limit the privileges of any one of the groups described in Table 15.1. For example, if you will have three hubs where your Notes servers are located, you may want to have groups such as ServerAdminEast, ServerAdminCentral, and ServerAdminWest, so that the server documents and command consoles of servers are segregated by region. Only a small number of individuals, whether listed explicitly or via group, should have complete control of all documents in the Public Address Book. This group is usually a central Notes support organization, responsible for planning and strategy.*

Table 15.1

Groups and Purposes.

GROUP	PURPOSE
CanAccessServer	You may choose to use wildcard designators such as */WEST/WGSI to indicate all users (and servers) certified by /WEST/WGSI.
Terminations	List of all users and servers that should not have access to the server, especially those that previously had IDs (user accounts). Assign this group the "type" of Deny Access.
GlobalCreateDB	List of users who can put databases on the server.
GlobalCreateReplica	List of users who can put replicas on the server.
DomainAdmin	List of users who can create person and group documents in the Public Address Book.
NetworkAdmin	List of users who can create and edit connection documents in the Public Address Book.
LocationServerAdmin	Groups of local administrators who may edit the server documents for the locations they support.
ServerAdmin	List of users who can create and edit server documents in the Public Address Book.
NABAdmin	List of users who manage the Public Address Book.

Setting Access to the Public Address Book

The Public Address Book has had a face-lift since Release 3, and it looks great. In general, you will find the Public Address Book easier to use than in earlier versions of Notes, because it is better organized and now has context-sensitive forms. Centralized organizations may want to have a single group add, remove, and update documents in the Public Address Book. If this is the case for your organization, you can make Reader access the default access to the Public Address Book and then have your one administrative group entered into the various roles for creating and modifying different roles within the Public Address Book.

If your organization is more distributed—particularly if you have remote server administrators who will need access to server and server-configuration documents—you should create different types of administration groups (as described in Table 15.1) and enter that group name into the appropriate role in the access control list of the Public Address Book. For example, if you have a group of people who will be able to register new users, these users will have certifier—or, more likely, organizational-unit certifier—ID files and will need access to create person documents in the Public Address Book.

You might want to create a group called WestCoastCertifiers and add this group to the role UserCreator and UserModifier.

For extra security, you may want to encrypt the Public Address Book on every server, so that someone who gains physical access to the server cannot use local access to make changes to this critical database. Although doing this is only a precaution, Notes 4.0 user types will hamper attempts by someone who gains access to a server ID file from doing user tasks—such as creating documents—with that server ID. This means that even though the server ID file may have high-access privileges to a database, for example, it is less useful for unwarranted access by users.

The Public Address Book that resides on your new Notes server will also reside on every other Notes server in your domain. This database is critical to the functioning of the Notes system, because it contains all the information about whom and what is on the system, as well as many of those entities' access privileges. The Public Address Book does many other things as well, but the key point is that its integrity must be ensured if you are to provide a reliable Notes network.

To protect the Public Address Book, you should immediately set access rights for it. By default, the administrator who set up the first Notes server is granted Manager rights to this database; default access to this database is set to Author. The effect: A user not explicitly listed here or in a group listed here can edit his or her own person document but cannot create or edit any other documents in the Public Address Book, because that user is not listed in any roles. The new Notes 4.0 server that you set up is granted Manager rights, as is the group LocalDomainServers, which Notes creates during setup. The group OtherDomainServers is granted Reader access to the Public Address Book.

These access privileges may be fine for your organization. You may want to consider lowering the default access of this database to Reader, which will restrict a user's ability to change his or her person document. In addition, you may want to add some of the groups we created earlier to the access control list so that, as you add users to these groups, your Public Address Book access controls are kept in sync. For example, adding the group ServerAdmin to the access control list of the Public Address Book, granting that group Author privileges, and placing it in the roles ServerCreator and ServerModifier will relieve you from having to manually grant these privileges to each server administrator in the future. The people listed in this group will be able to create and modify server documents.

Set the Administration Server

Notes 4.0 has an administration process that updates databases and user ID files based on changes requested by administrators. For example, if a user is removed from the system, the administration process will automatically remove that user from all groups in the Public Address Book, as well as from all database access control lists that have an administration server designated. It is a good idea, therefore, to designate an administration server for the Public Address Book, so that changes resulting from additions and deletions of users will be updated to the access control list of only one replica and then replicated to all the other copies.

There are two ways to make the administration server designation. You may use the Administration Control Panel and select the Database button and the Database Administration Server option. Alternatively, you may select the icon for the database whose administration server you want to designate; choose File, Database, Access Control; and then select the Advanced icon.

Set Access Lists for the Server

The groups listed in Table 15.1 will be useful in many places. In addition to providing convenience and security for the Public Address Book access control list, you can use these groups in the appropriate fields of the server document for the first Notes server you have running, as well as future Notes servers. By entering these groups into the server document, you will limit access to the server.

The Restrictions sections of the server document allow you to control most of the access to the Notes server. Most of these fields are self-explanatory. For example, in the field Create New Databases, you would include the group called CanCreateDB. Enter the appropriate groups into the fields in this section.

In addition to inputting the correct groups, we recommend that you change a couple of defaults on the server document. The default for the field Compare Public Keys Against Those Stored In Address Book (located in the Security section of the server document) is No. We recommend changing this to Yes, because doing this will prevent users with a copy of a user ID file from authenticating with the server if the real user is given a new ID file with new public or private keys. If this server is for internal use only (not connecting with users or servers in another organization), we recommend changing the field Only Allow Server Access To Users Listed In This Address Book to Yes. This will add a layer of security against external infiltration.

Finally, at the bottom of all documents—in a section called Administration, in the Notes 4.0 Public Address Book—are the fields Owner and Administrator. These fields can have groups listed in them to control who can edit the document. By default, if a user is listed in a role of the Public Address Book, he or she will be granted access to appropriate forms of the Public Address Book—server documents, for example. If you want to grant Author access to a particular document, you may now do so without granting access to *all* such documents. Enter the person or group name in the

Administrator fields, to grant access to *only* this document. For example, in the Administrator field of a Server document, you may want to add the local administration group so that the local administrators will be able to edit the Server documents for the servers they administer, even though they did not create these Server documents and are not "Editors" of the database.

NOTE. *The user or group must have Author access to the database in order to edit the document, in addition to being entered in the Administrator field.*

Create System Databases

Notes uses its own database format to provide services and information, the most notable of which is the Public Address Book. Other system databases record information that will be useful to you in both the short and the long term. Following is a list of these databases, along with information about creating them.

- *Notes Log (LOG.NSF):* Automatically set up. The first time the Notes 4.0 server runs, it automatically creates a server log file from a template. You will use this log to see historical server events that help you troubleshoot, performance-tune, and plan for the future. The contents of this log—what the server chooses to record—are determined by settings in the NOTES.INI file. For additional information on the parameters of these settings, see Chapter 27, "Managing Servers."

NOTE. *The new Database Analyze feature on the Server Control Panel is useful with the log file, because this feature helps you search for information on a particular subject.*

- *Certification Log (CERTLOG.NSF):* Not automatically set up. The certification log lists all the entities that have been certified in your domain. This is a particularly important database to install if you wish to use the new Notes 4.0 administrative process, because it relies upon the certification log for information. You should create a certification log from the template that is provided, before adding additional users or servers. Have copies of the certification log on all servers that will run the Administration Process and on all servers on which administrators will register new users, servers, and certifiers.

- *Database Catalog (CATALOG.NSF):* Automatically set up. The database catalog lists all of the databases in an organization. The catalog is updated by the server task Catalog, which by default runs every day at 1 a.m. This task searches the server file system and records information about all the databases it finds, and then it stores this information in documents in the Database Catalog database. If you want users to have information about all the databases stored on all the servers in your organization, you use a single replica of the Database Catalog database, so that when servers connect and replicate, all documents about databases added to one server's database catalog get replicated to other catalogs.

NOTE. *Database managers can set databases to prevent the catalog program from publishing their existence to the database catalog. This is a security feature.*

- *Statistics and Events (EVENTS4.NSF):* Not automatically set up. The Statistics & Events database is used to tell the two server tasks, Event and Reporter, what events and statistics to gather and report. Like the Notes Log database, this database can be used on a single server, or it can have replicas on all servers in the domain, to provide information about all servers. This database is automatically created when—and if— you run the Event task for the first time. See the next section for information about the Event and Reporter tasks.

- *Statistics Reporting (STATREP.NSF):* Not automatically set up. The Statistics Reporting database is used to store information gathered by the Event and Reporter server tasks. Like the Notes Log database, this database can be used on a single server, or it can have replicas on all servers in the domain in order to provide information about all servers. This will be useful to you when you are centralizing administration. The Statistics Reporting database is created when, and if, you run the Reporter task for the first time. See the following section for more information about the Reporter task.

Set Up Event Monitoring and Statistics: The Event and Reporter Tasks

Notes 4.0 has the ability to monitor server and database events, as well as provide server statistics. These monitors and statistics provide extremely useful information for maintaining adequate service levels, planning connections, and troubleshooting. In Notes 4.0, monitoring and statistics work differently than in earlier versions. Here, we give you an overview of these tools; in Chapter 23, "Managing Overview and Management Tools," we give you detailed information on how to use them.

There are two programs—and, usually, two databases—involved in handling events and statistics in Notes 4.0: the Event task and the Reporter task. The Event task is the server process that reports server events. The Reporter task is the server task that checks statistics and mails a report on the statistics to a database.

The two key databases involved in event monitoring and statistics reporting are the Statistics & Events database (EVENTS4.NSF) and the Statistics Reporting database (STATREP.NSF). The Statistics & Events database is used to tell the two server tasks, Event and Reporter, what events and statistics to gather and report. The Statistics Reporting database is used to store information gathered by the Event and Reporter server tasks. The Event task creates a Statistics & Reporting database the first time the Event task runs. The Reporter task creates a Statistics Reporting database the first time the Reporter task runs.

NOTE. *Neither the Event task nor the Reporter task is set up to run by default. You must schedule these tasks to run in the NOTES.INI file, by adding them to the ServerTasks setting list.*

For starters, we recommend that early on, you set up some statistic and event monitors, to ensure that you have the information in place that will keep the first server up and performing. To do this, you use the Statistics & Events database and create *monitor documents*. These documents tell the Event and Reporter tasks what to check and report.

To begin with, set up an ACL Monitor for the Public Address Book and have the monitor mail an alert to you if a change is made to the access control list of this system-critical database. In addition, create a Replication Monitor to check replication of the Public Address Book, if you already have more than one server in your organization.

Create a Certifier Hierarchy: Register Organizational-Unit Certifiers

Before adding users and servers to your system, create the organizational-unit certifiers with which you will certify your users and servers. Use the naming plan that you created in Chapter 14, "The Notes Network: Overview and Planning", to create organizational-unit certifier ID files for the logical organizations that you mapped out.

Even if you do not yet have the support structure in place for all of these organizations, you should from the start register the users and servers in these organizations with the correct certifier. If you don't do this, in the future you will need to recertify the users and servers in order to give them the fully distinguished names that you want them to have. You can use the Certifiers button of the Administration Control Panel to create (register) organizational-unit certifiers. Remember to keep all certifier ID files safe by password-protecting them and removing them from the server file system, once they are created.

Set Up the Server for Using Shared Mail

Also before registering users, you may want to set up shared mail. *Shared-mail databases* are a new feature of Notes that allows mail messages with multiple recipients to be stored in one database. Messages stored here are still accessible to the user from his or her individual mail database and can be used in the same ways as other mail messages. Shared mail is *not* a default and must be configured by the system administrator.

Shared mail involves the use of two Notes databases that are automatically configured when you set up the server's router program to use shared mail. To enable shared mail at a server console, you issue the following command:

```
Tell router Use shared.nsf
```

where shared.nsf is the name that you want to give to the shared-mail database.

The router will then create the file that you specified and use it as the database in which to store mail that is addressed to more than one user. In addition, the router will create a database called MAILOBJ.NSF in the Note data directory and then set the NOTES.INI variable: Shared_mail=2. Shared mail will be enabled as soon as the server is restarted.

Add Users and Servers

Your rollout plan probably calls for a key group of users with a specific application to use as a pilot group. The next step, then, is to create accounts for these users. In Notes, this process is called *registering* users. It is during this procedure that you will use a certifier or organizational-unit certifier ID file to create user ID files.

Notes automatically places a document about each new user in the Public Address Book, so the person charged with registering new users must have appropriate access to the database. You may also need to add servers, if the pilot group is geographically or functionally dispersed and you have decided to have more than one server in your pilot.

When adding either users or servers, use the Administration Control Panel. The button labeled People and the button labeled Servers have options for registering these entities. Make sure that you use the correct organizational-unit certifier to register either the server or the user, so that the fully distinguished name falls correctly into the organizational hierarchy that you engineered.

NOTE. *When registering servers, use the common name that you think will be used by that server in the long run. For example, if your plan for naming servers calls for the local hub to be called WGSI-HUB-SFO-01, do not use this name, although you might think that a hub would be the first server you would create. If you use this name, you will need to move users' application and/or mail files off of this server when you later put the workgroup servers in place (hubs do not have users directly access them). Instead, if possible, call your first server by the name that it will use in the long term. To do this, you may* *want to bring up a mail server first and use it for both mail and applications and then later, move the applications off of it.*

Set Up Server Connections

If you have created more than one Notes server, you need to specify how the servers will connect in order to replicate databases and route mail. Even if users will not share databases across the servers, it is imperative that the servers have a replication schedule established, so that at least the Public Address Book gets replicated. This database must be kept synchronized on all servers within a domain.

If you have more than one Notes Named Network, or if you will send mail to domains other than your own, you need to create connections for mail routing, as well as replication. Remember that unlike replication connections, mail routing connections are a two-way street: There must be a connection document from Server A to Server B and from Server B to Server A, if you want users on both servers to be able to send documents to one another. Notes automatically routes documents *only* within the same Notes Named Network.

To create a replication schedule, review Chapter 14, "The Notes Network: Overview and Planning"; for information on how to create connection documents in the Public Address Book, see Chapter 26, "Managing the Network."

What's New in Connection Documents

Connection documents have many new options. Of immediate importance at this stage in your deployment are the following:

- *Connection types.* In addition to being network or remote types, connections may also be passthru, X.25, SMTP, X.400, cc:Mail, or remote LAN services. Right now, you are probably setting up replication and routing internally only, so you don't need to worry about the other types of servers until you are connecting your Notes system to other Notes systems.

- *Optional server addresses.* You may now specify physical addresses and aliases for host machines

- *Replication Type.* This specifies the directions in which replication will copy documents. The default is now pull/push. (In the past, it was pull/pull.) See Chapter 19, "Replication," for more information on the differences between pull, push, pull/push and pull/pull replication.

- *Files to replicate.* You may now specify that only certain files are to be replicated. You may, for example, want to have the Public Address Book replicated every hour to ensure that the terminations list is up to date. To do this, you could specify NAMES.NSF in this field.

- *Replication time limit.* You may now set the maximum amount of time that a connection will last.

- *Owners/administrators.* You may now specify a specific list of administrators who have Editor access to the connection document.

Set Up Security

Before bringing users up and putting information on the server, it is important to secure the server so that information on it will be safe. Different organizations rate the risk associated with information (databases) on the Notes server differently, but any organization can benefit from some moderate precautions. We have already discussed Public Address Book security, but here are some other precautions that should be taken immediately:

- *Security for physical servers:* Start by making sure that the server is physically secure and inaccessible to anyone except those chartered with monitoring it. Anyone with physical access has a much better chance of accessing data. Keep the Notes server in a locked room.

- *Security for certifier ID files:* Certifier ID files are particularly important, because they allow people to create entities on the Notes network. If someone were to create an ID file with a duplicate name as another user, there is the potential (although Notes 4.0 has closed some of these holes) for that person to access documents to which he or she was not granted access. Take certifier and organizational-unit certifier ID files off the server and keep them locked up, where only authorized people can access them.

NOTE. *Notes 4.0 allows you to put multiple passwords on ID files. With this feature, you may require, for example, that a certifier ID has three of its five passwords entered before that ID can be used. The advantage to this is that you can force the segregation of duties by requiring that three different people, with different passwords, enter their passwords before the ID file is useable. Multiple passwords on ID files should be implemented immediately for all certifiers and, perhaps, servers. You can create multiple passwords for an ID file in the Server Administration Console by selecting the Certifier button and then choosing the Edit Multiple Passwords option.*

Install User Workstations

Now it is time to install and configure user workstations. This is a two-step procedure. First, it involves running the Notes 4.0 install program in order to copy the correct files to the user's workstation computer. Then you have to run the workstation setup program, which will configure this user's computer properly for communication with the server, as well as locate and install the user's ID file, created during the registration process. See Chapter 17, "Deploying Clients," for more information on setting up user workstations.

Running the Installation Procedure for the Workstation Software

Running the installation procedure is similar to running any software installation program for the Windows platforms. The key points to plan for depend on the type of installation that you want to do. The installation program gives you the options of installing the software for use by a single machine; installing the software on a file server for shared use, so that a complete copy of the software resides only on the server's hard disk, and user workstations share this code; or installing the software for distribution so that users—laptop users, for example—may connect to the LAN and use the distribution code to install the software on their own systems without having to use disks or locate a CD-ROM.

Choose the type of installation that best suits your needs and then install the software so that the workstation is ready to run the setup program.

Running the Setup Program for Workstation Software

The workstation setup program, like the server setup program, runs when it detects a NOTES.INI file that is incomplete. The workstation setup program assumes that at least one Notes server is up and running and that the user for whom the software is being run has been registered on the Notes system. The workstation setup program will find the user's ID file that gives that user a unique identity on the Notes system (this is either in the Public Address Book or given to the user in a file, via disk or electronic mail), and the program will then configure the workstation for the way that that particular user will work.

If the user is connected to a LAN, the workstation setup program will enable the LAN port, add the appropriate database icons (such as the user's mail database) to the user's workspace, and then create a personal name and address book. If the user is a laptop (remote) user, the setup program will enable the modem port (and perhaps also a LAN port) to make a replica of the user's mail file for remote usage, create a local outgoing mailbox database, and add the appropriate icons to the user's workspace.

NOTE. *Most workstation setup problems occur for one of three reasons. First, the setup program is unable to communicate with the server in the way that you specified; in this case, try another port and make sure that the port works by testing it with another program. Second, the setup program has difficulty creating a file; in this case, make sure that you have local disk space and the template database files are available to the setup program. Third, the user-specific information cannot be located; in this case, make sure that the person*

*document is actually in the Public Address Book on the server on which you
are registering the user and that the user ID file is where you specified—on the
server or in a specific drive and directory.*

■ Server Management Tools

Following is an overview of the tools provided by Notes to help server administrators carry out their day-to-day tasks. Third-party tools also exist and can
greatly reduce the amount of time that is spent on any given task. See Chapter 23, "Managing Overview and Management Tools," for more information
on tools to help you manage Lotus Notes 4.0.

Administration Control Panel

The Notes 4.0 Administration Control Panel (see Figure 15.1) provides one-
stop shopping for many tasks performed regularly by the server administrator. This panel has eight buttons, each of which helps the server administrator execute routine tasks for a given part of the Notes system. Many of these
buttons create, edit, or view documents in the Public Address Book, because
this is where most administrative documents are located. Other buttons run
programs to do several tasks, such as registering a new server, which is a
choice from the Server button.

Figure 15.1

The Administration
Control Panel.

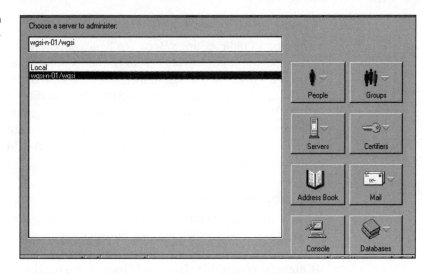

NOTE. *You can run the Administration Control Panel as a stand-alone program; for example, on the server. From Windows' Program Manager or Start menu, choose File, Run and enter* **Notes Admin YourServerName,** *where YourServerName is the name of the server that you want to administer.*

The Administration Process

The administration process helps Notes system administrators execute routine membership-related tasks, such as deleting, renaming, and recertifying entities in the Notes domain. The administration process, for example, will check the Public Address Book for deleted person documents and make sure that those names are removed from group and other documents, as well as remove those user names from the access control list of databases. This Notes 4.0 feature is a huge time-saver for administrators.

The administration process is a server task (NAdminP) that is set to run, by default, in the NOTES.INI file. It uses the Administration Requests database (admin4) to store requests that it will later execute.

The administration process works by having documents that request changes stored in the Administration Requests database. These documents are created automatically by Notes when administrators select actions in the Public Address Book. The administration process can also be used to make global name changes throughout a domain. See Chapter 23, "Managing Overview and Management Tools," for more information on the administration process.

Notes' Public Address Book

The Notes Public Address Book is a Notes database that stores all the information about users, servers, certifiers, connections, groups, and other settings that you will use to manage individuals, servers, and the network in its entirety.

Notes 4.0 has greatly enhanced the functionality, usability, and security of the Public Address Book. The results: There is greater functionality from Notes servers, administrative tasks are completed more quickly, and information stored in Notes is more secure. See Chapter 24, "Managing Security," for more information.

Database Libraries

A new feature of Notes called the *database library* is used to store information about databases, so that that information may be published to relevant users. Unlike the database catalog that is created and maintained by the Catalog server task, a database library is updated by people.

The benefit here is that users of a particular department or workgroup, for example, can have a library of the databases that they use and will need.

The databases they use may not be listed in the organization database catalog, for security reasons.

Server Commands

Server commands are commands that you issue to the server program, via the server console or the Remote Server Console tool. These commands let you tell the server program what to do, just as selecting a pull-down menu in the workstation client issues a command to that program.

You use server console commands to bring down a server, force routing and replication, and get status information on the server. You can issue server commands automatically by entering a program document in the Public Address Book.

Agent Manager

The *Agent Manager* is a Notes 4.0 task that runs agents on the server. In addition to running the agents within databases, the Agent Manager controls who is allowed to run server-based agents and when they can run these on each server. The Agent Manager is useful for controlling server load. If users created many server-based agents, the server might get bogged down, and performance would become unacceptable.

The access list for who can and cannot run agents on the server is set in the server document as one of the types of access to a server that users may be granted. This is a system administrator control; while database managers may or may not grant users the ability to create and store simple and Lotus-Script agents within the database, system administrators may or may not grant privileges to run agents on server replicas of databases.

See Chapter 27, "Managing the Server," for more information on the Agent Manager.

Troubleshooting Tools

Notes 4.0 provides two new tracing tools that help you troubleshoot problems with the routing of mail, as well as with port errors.

Mail Trace

Notes 4.0 has added a mail-trace feature that provides detailed information about the route a document takes. This helps administrators troubleshoot mail-routing problems.

To use the mail-trace feature, click on the Mail icon in the Administration Control Panel and then select Send Mail Trace. A test document will be sent to try the route and will return with detailed information.

NOTE. *Only Notes 4.0 servers will report information to the mail-trace document.*

Port Trace

Notes 4.0 lets you trace connections with its port-trace feature. To do this, select File, Tools, User Preferences and then choose the Ports icon. Click on the Trace button to send a trace via the selected port. Notes will report in the dialog box all the information coming to and going from the port.

- *Overview*

- *Setting Up the Domain*

- *Installing the Server Software*

- *Running the Server Setup Program for the First Server*

- *Running the Server Program*

- *Installing and Setting Up the Workstation Client Software*

- *Registering Users and Servers*

- *Adding Users*

- *Adding Servers*

16

Deploying Servers

IN THIS CHAPTER, WE TAKE YOU THROUGH THE INSTALLATION AND setup of your first server, as well as additional ones, and we provide information about the key choices you will need to make. In addition, we guide you through the multitude of options you can set up on any server and help you make sound decisions regarding which to choose.

If you have installed and set up earlier versions of Notes, the procedure will be quite familiar, and you may just want to review Chapter 15. If you have not previously installed Lotus Notes, read this chapter carefully so that you will know what is happening with each step. When you set up the first Notes server, you are setting up your Notes domain, so it is important to set up properly.

■ Overview

Deploying servers involves executing the plan discussed in Chapter 14. In the big picture, there are two types of servers that you may set up: the first, and all others. The first server is different from all others—as discussed in Chapter 15—because during the setup of the first server, the certifier ID file that will be at the top of the certification hierarchy for the organization is created. In addition, the Public Address Book for the domain is created from a template database and given a unique replication ID number. This Public Address Book, with its unique replication ID number, will reside on every Notes server within the domain.

Once the first server is set up—and the certifier ID file is created, as well as a server ID file and a user ID file for the administrator—other users, servers, and certifier ID files may be created. All additional servers will need to connect with an existing Notes server in order to obtain a replica of the Public Address Book. Furthermore, additional servers will need to receive the server ID file that contains their identities. This may be located in the Public Address Book, or it may be distributed separately. Figure 16.1 shows how a new Notes server connects to an existing server to obtain its server ID file and a replica of the Public Address Book.

Figure 16.1

New server getting Public Address Book and server ID from existing server.

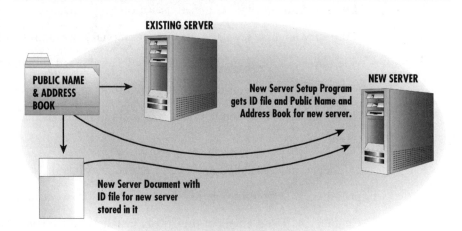

A Word about Security

Before moving on, it's important that you understand a few key elements about Notes security. While this subject is covered completely in Chapter 24, "Managing Security," a primer here will give you a clearer understanding of this chapter and others.

Notes ID files contain *identities*. That is to say that a single Notes ID file, whether it is a certifier, a server, or a user ID file, represents a single entity (certifier, server, or user). In the ID file are several pieces of information. The contents of the ID file are discussed in Chapter 24, but the important thing to understand now is that if two computers running either the Notes workstation client or the Notes server software are connected, they can verify who the other one is (note, though, that two Notes workstations never have cause to connect to one another. Once both computers verify who the other one is, access rights to all the resources on the Notes system can be granted or denied accordingly. Proving one another's identity is known as *authentication*. Figure 16.2 shows how Notes computers prove each other's identity before granting or denying any server access.

Figure 16.2

Notes computers shaking hands and authenticating.

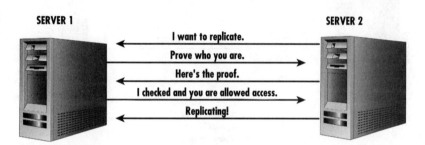

It is because of this need to authenticate that each computer running Notes software must have a unique ID file. The granddaddy of all the ID files on an organization's Notes system is the *certifier ID file*. From it, all other certifiers are created. It's like a family tree for computers: Because all the certifiers share a common ancestor—the certifier created when the first server was set up—they can all verify, or authenticate, each other.

How Notes Authenticates Users

It's important to understand how Notes security works, because much of what administrators do is to implement security or create the tools for others to do so. A Notes domain is very much like any other network. There are two programs running: a client program that is the software most frequently seen and used by end users and a server program that communicates and works in concert with the client (also known as the *workstation*) to provide access to information (documents).

For the client and server to grant document access to each other, Notes, like other networks, has a concept of membership. Anyone who wants to access a Notes server must have some kind of identity. That identity will then have access privileges associated with it, both in terms of what functions the person can perform on the server and what functions he or she can perform on a specific database. Figure 16.3 shows how employee Mary Pickle has access to a database but to only certain documents within the database.

Figure 16.3

A user with privileges to one database and ten documents in that database.

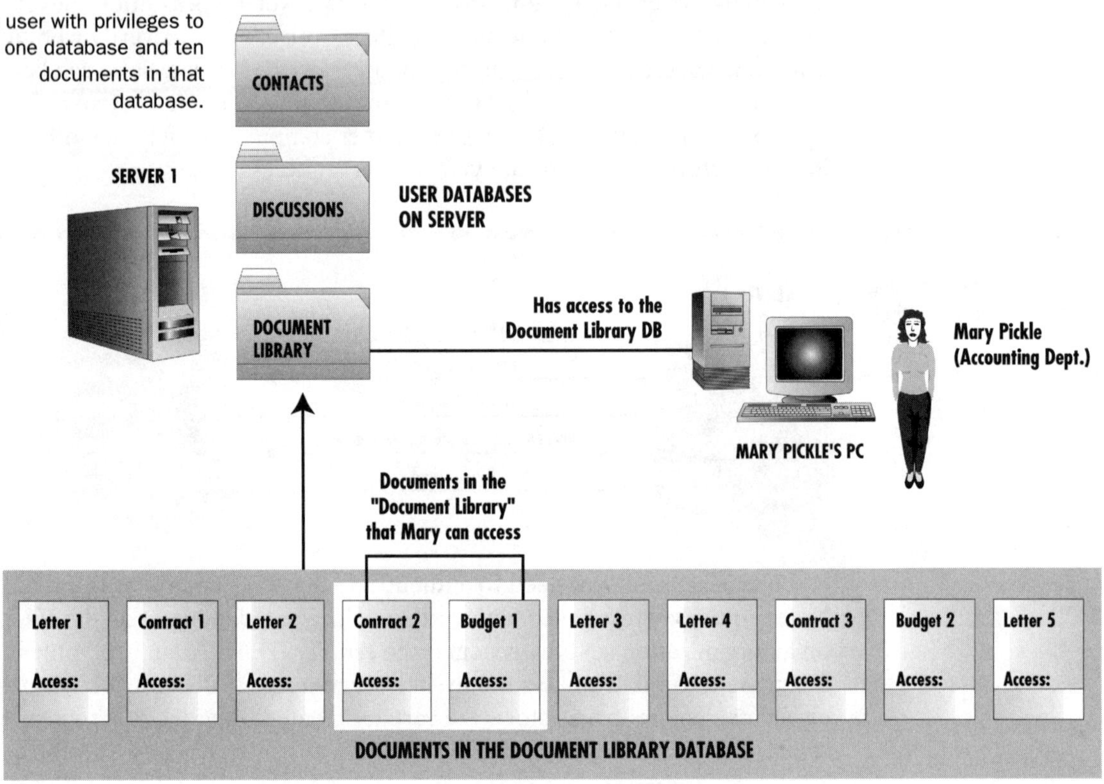

In Notes 4.0, it is possible to grant *anonymous access* to servers and databases. Anonymous access means that the user is granted access even though his, her, or its (in the case of a server or other program) identity is not authenticated, or proven. Anonymous access is useful for posting public information that you want users and servers of other organizations to see without having to cross-certify with your organization (see Chapter 27, "Managing Servers," for information about cross-certification). If anonymous access is set up, users and servers do not need to have a certificate in common with the server in order to access information. While an anonymous user's name may appear in fields that are designed to show such information, the name will be unverified.

Notes handles identity by using ID files (encrypted binary files) and a *challenge/response scenario* that is played out by the two Notes computers (client and server or server and server) when they connect. This scenario proves that the computers—and, therefore, the users of these computers who enter passwords—are who they say they are. Once this authenticity is established, the Notes servers refer to the access controls setup for the IDs (entities, users, servers) and grant access to servers, databases, and documents accordingly.

■ Setting Up the Domain

Many of the tasks for setting up a Notes domain are intended to deliver an ID file to a user in order to establish his or her identity or membership on the Notes network.

Initially, setting up a Notes domain may be broken down into a five-step process:

- Installing the server software

- Running the server setup program

- Registering servers

- Registering users

- Installing the workstation client software

- Setting up the workstation client software

■ Installing the Server Software

The server install program copies and (in most cases) decompresses files from the disks, CD-ROM, or network drive to the new file system. It then updates operating system files with information about Notes and creates a configuration file for Notes (the NOTES.INI file). When you run the server installation program, you get several options regarding how you want Notes installed on this system. These options allow you to choose where and how you want the software installed on the new file system.

The installation procedure can be customized to install files that are special for your organization; for example, modem files, database templates, SmartIcon macro files, and bitmap files, as well as the NOTES.INI file and the DESKTOP.DSK file.

The installation process is the same for first servers as it is for additional servers. Installing the server software involves using the installation program to copy and decompress files from the diskettes or CD-ROM to the file system that will be used by your server. The installation program offers three kinds of installation: Local installation, which installs the server or workstation software to the local file system for use only by the machine on which it is installed; Network Install, which installs software to one file system for use by many machines (used for workstation software only); and Network Distribution, which installs software to a file system that other computers may access in order to install their own copies of the software.

Besides offering choices for the type of installation you want to do, the installation program also lets you choose whether you want to install the workstation software or the server software onto a system; you would use the same installation program for either. If you choose to install the workstation client, the options provided to you will of course be different from those you would be given had you chosen the server.

NOTE. *It is always a good idea to disable screen savers, virus checkers, and any other software besides operating system software before the installation and setup procedures.*

Before running Install, if you are upgrading from an earlier version of Notes, you should back up your template (.NTF), modem (.MDM), and any other files that you have customized. We also recommend that you back up important data files, as well as the Public Address Book.

Take a Few Simple Steps

To run the installation program, perform the following steps:

1. From Windows NT, choose the Run command.

2. Choose the drive with the Notes media on it and run the file called INSTALL.EXE.

3. Enter your name and your company name, as prompted.

NOTE. *Do not check Install On A File Server unless you want this software installation to help other computers install the software from the network. That is, if you select this option, you are installing the software for one of two uses: First, as shared software for the workstations, so they do not have to load the entire Notes program on their local hard disks and will thereby conserve space. Second, as a distribution server to enable workstations—especially laptops—to copy the program files to their local hard disks so that the Notes program can be run when these computers are not connected to the LAN.*

4. Confirm your name and your company name.

5. Select Server Install.

6. Choose the drive and directory onto which you wish to install the Notes server software.

7. Choose the folder into which you want the installation program to put the Notes server icon, so that the server program can be easily started.

8. Select Begin Copying Files Now.

When the installation program successfully completes, you must run the appropriate setup program to set up and configure the software. In this chapter, we first give instructions for setting up the first server and then give instructions for setting up for additional servers.

Get Ready to Run Server Setup

Before running the server setup program, you need to think through a number of issues. If you read Chapter 14, "The Notes Network: Overview and Planning," you should have a notebook containing all the information you will need. Following is a brief overview of the considerations you should resolve before attempting to deploy either a first or additional server.

Have You Taken Stock?

Taking stock means checking all of your infrastructure to make certain that you have all the necessary components in place to run Notes. This includes checking your hardware to make sure that it meets the Notes and operating system specifications, checking the operating system to make sure it is a version that is supported with Notes, and checking the LAN/WAN hardware and software to make sure it is supported by Notes. If you plan to connect to the Notes server via a modem, you should make sure that the modem works and has an analog telephone line attached.

Have You Determined the Role of the Server and Server Topology?

A well-designed Notes server topology may include servers that have different roles in the network, such as mail versus application servers or mail-gateway servers. Make sure that you have thought through your server topology carefully before setting up Notes—an ounce of planning will be worth your while.

Do You Know How This Server Will Connect?

Consider how users and other servers will connect to the server that you are installing. In the case of servers, this means for the purposes of replication and mail routing—events that are scheduled in the Public Address Book and must be carefully planned. Even if you will have only one server in your organization, you will probably want to connect with outside organizations, and you should have the hardware, software, and logical schedule in mind for doing so before setting up your server. Know in advance what port and what schedule this computer will use to connect with other Notes computers. Question whether the ports available will be sufficient to support the amount of data and users that need to exchange information by using them. (Remember to refer back to Chapter 14 for more detailed information.)

Have You Established Naming Conventions?

How will you name your certifiers, servers, users, and Notes Named Networks? As discussed in Chapter 14, these are important decisions that should be carefully planned.

What Are Your Support Standards and Plans?

Resolve the questions regarding support: How will you support your users? Who will install and maintain your Notes servers and workstations? What guidelines will they use to do so? What roles will the different Notes administrators play? Will each administrator be responsible for all Notes-related activities in his or her respective location, or will duties be segregated? What standards do you have for configuring systems, troubleshooting, and resolving problems?

Have You Planned for the Installation Support Spike?

Buyer, beware: While Notes 4.0 is a stellar product with huge benefits to offer an organization, setting up your Notes network will require considerable time and effort. Plan on a *support spike,* while administrators learn Notes and deployment is in progress. Until Notes administration becomes routine, making the system run properly will require a good deal of time.

Have You Segregated Duties?

Will certain Notes administrators have special duties, such as registering users, servers, and certifiers? Segregating duties is key to a secure system, so you may want to consider in advance who will have what privileges.

Have You Trained Administrators and Users?

Training is critical to the proper use of a Notes system and an organization's benefiting from this usage. Administrators must be trained on Notes in order to properly install and maintain it. Notes is a network; like any other network, it must be cared for and fed. Without proper training, administrators will likely make errors more costly than the training itself.

Similarly, users must be trained on Notes and, perhaps, the applications they will be using; otherwise, they will not know how to use the system and are less likely to take advantage of it. Leveraging your investment in Notes depends on training.

■ Running the Server Setup Program for the First Server

There are actually two server-installation setup procedures: The first is for the first server in an organization, and the second is for all additional servers being added to that domain.

As mentioned, the certifier (granddaddy of all ID files) is created during the first server setup, as is a Public Address Book with a unique replication ID number; it is these two files that distinguish one domain from another and provide the basis for all security within the domain. Because all servers in a Notes domain share a common Public Address Book and probably descend from this certifier ID (though there are ways around this, such as cross-certifying), the additional server setup program locates the server's ID file and makes a replica on its own file system of the Public Address Book. As you can see, the job of the server setup program is entirely different for first servers than it is for all additional servers.

During the setup of your first server, several components critical to the functioning of your Notes network are created or assigned. The following descriptions of critical operations for first-time server setup will prepare you to provide information that the server setup program will ask for.

Critical Operations

The certifier ID file   This file is created and stored in your Notes data directory as CERT.ID. If you like, you may rename the file. Renaming the file does not rename the certifier name contained within the file (/WGSI, for example).

If you want to rename the information (certifier) contained within this file, you must create a new certifier ID. This may require recertifying all entities (users, servers, and organizational-unit certifiers) in your Notes domain. This is a big job if your network has grown to more than a few users, so it is important to create a name for the organization that you want to use going forward. It's best to get the name contained within the certifier ID file right before creating any additional ID files from it.

This *unique* ID file is used to create all other ID files within your organization. It is progenitor of all other organizational-unit IDs, server IDs, and user IDs in your Notes domain. Notes security is largely based on the assumption that one computer will be able to trust another computer because the two ID files used by these two computers are created from—and trust—the same certifier ID. Make sure that in the Notes setup dialog box, you thoughtfully name your certifier—preferably, with your organization's Internet mail domain name—and that you keep this certifier in a safe and locked place.

Public Address Book   In Notes 4.0, the Public Address Book is created from a template (.NTF) file called PUBNAMES.NTF. The Public Address Book is a Notes database that acts as the directory for the Notes network. All information necessary for the functioning of a Notes domain is stored in the Public Address Book and replicated to every server within the domain. This database replica with its unique ID number will reside on all the servers within your domain. Assign access controls carefully to this database: The system relies heavily upon it, so its integrity is critical. In Notes 4.0, the Public Address Book is by default stored in the Notes data directory and called NAMES.NSF.

Administrator's user ID file   Notes creates a user ID file for the first system administrator and a server ID file for the first server during the first server setup. As with earlier versions of Notes, these ID files should be protected early on, so that no unauthorized person gains access to them. Otherwise, that person can pretend to be the owner of the ID, with all that owner's privileges.

User, server, and certifier documents created in the Public Address Book Documents for the first user (the administrator), server, and certifier are placed in the Public Address Book. These documents are used by the server program in its routine tasks of moving and providing access to documents. The server program cannot function without the information about each entity in the domain being stored in the Public Address Book. As you add users and servers to the Notes domain, documents describing them will be placed in the Public Address Book.

Groups added to the Public Address Book   Notes creates the groups LocalDomainServers and OtherDomainServers. These groups are commonly used in database access control lists, so that all the servers in an organization have appropriate access to the database. Servers are automatically added to the LocalDomainServers group document when they are registered by the administrator as additional servers in the domain.

Notes Named Network created   The Notes Named Network is designated on the server document. This network refers specifically to groups of servers accessible on the same physical (or routed/bridged) network and running the same protocol. Network names may also be used for other purposes, but they always consist of servers running the same protocol on the same physical LAN, so that a server may connect to other servers in its Notes Named Network when sending or receiving information (documents).

Ports enabled   Notes enables network and serial ports as specified and can communicate via the modem port and network port that you choose. The setup dialog box allows for only one protocol and one modem. You may add more protocols and modems later by adding ports using File/Tools/User

Preferences on the server and adding the new port information to the server document.

Mail file created for administrator   A directory for storing mail files is created under the data directory, and a mail file (database) for the administrator is created.

Steps to Follow

The setup program will ask a number of questions, and your answers will provide all the information necessary to create a Notes domain consisting of one server and one administrator. From there, you can add additional resources and entities to the domain.

To run the setup program, follow these steps:

1. In the Program Manager, double-click on the icon labeled Lotus Notes. Your objective is to run the workstation client program in order to initiate the setup program, even though you are actually setting up server software.

NOTE. *Notes will detect that the information necessary to run the server has not yet been added to the NOTES.INI file and will run the setup program. If, in the future, you need to go through setup again, you can clear the NOTES.INI file of all information except the first three lines, which have the workstation client software initiate the setup program when it is loaded.*

2. When the Notes Server Setup dialog box appears, select This Is The First Notes Server.

3. Fill out all the fields as you are prompted to do so, providing the information necessary for the Notes setup program to create the domain.

Field Choices

To help you understand your choices and make good decisions about what to enter, the following descriptions tell you about each field that the server setup program will display:

Server Name   This is the name that you want to identify the computer running the server software. Be thoughtful in creating a name for the server, because you may want it to provide useful information as your network of servers grows. We usually like to have the name indicate location and purpose. For example, a server in San Francisco may be named ACME-SFO-WG-01, to indicate that this is an Acme Corporation server, it resides in a location near San Francisco International Airport (we often use airports, because their designators do not often change), it is a workgroup server (rather than a mail or remote-access server), and it is the first of such servers in this location.

Organization Name This is the name that you give to your certifier ID file. All ID files created with this certifier will have this name appended to the end of the fully distinguished name it contains. For example, if your name is John Smith and Acme is the name of your domain, your user ID file may contain the fully distinguished name John Smith/Acme. By default, the domain is given the same name as the certifier.

Administrator's Last, First, and Middle Initial This is the name of the first user in the network. This person is granted administrative rights to the server, as well as to the Public Address Book. Keep in mind that administrator ID files in Notes are identical to user ID files: Administrators can perform administrative tasks because they have been granted privileges to do so. In the future, you may grant other users these privileges.

Administration Password This is the password that will be used to access the user ID created for the administrator and as the password for the certifier ID file. You may—and should—change the password of both these ID files once they are created. In addition, Notes 4.0 allows ID files to have multiple passwords, so that multiple users must enter a password before the ID file can be used. This is an excellent security tool for server and certifier ID files. (See Chapter 27, "Managing Servers," for more information).

Network Type This field refers to the network protocol that the first Notes server will use to communicate with Notes users and other servers. Select one protocol here; in the future, you may add more. Notes has drivers to support all major protocols. You should choose the protocol that your organization uses to network its computers. For example, if your organization uses SPX to share files and printers, this is probably the best choice on which to run Lotus Notes as well, because it is already running on all the computers on your network.

Serial Port This is the modem port that Notes should answer for users and servers that are dialing in, as well as use to call remote servers. Make sure to select the type of dialing necessary on the port (tone or pulse). If you have more than one modem on the server computer, you may add it later by directly editing the NOTES.INI file or by using a server configuration document in the Public Address Book.

Modem Type This option allows you to select the type of modem that is in your computer, so that Notes can send it the right commands. If you do not see your modem listed, use the Generic All Speed modem choice. Modem files are text files; if you need to make adjustments in the future, you can edit them through the File, Tools, User Preferences, Ports menu. Script files may also be specified.

Server Is Also Administrator's Personal Workstation This check box tells the workstation setup program to install the user ID file for the administrator and set up the local machine for workstation program use, as well as server program use. Notes will place the administrator's user ID file in the data directory rather than in the Public Address Book. With this box checked, the computer is set up to act as a workstation for the administrator, as well as a server. It will run both Notes software programs (client and server), and the administrator can log on with his or her correct ID file, rather than using the server's ID file.

Notes servers are usually not used as workstations, too. Because they contain critical information and are accessed by many people and servers, it is a good idea to treat Notes servers as you would other mission-critical servers in your organization—by isolating them.

Before proceeding, you may want to click the button labeled Advanced.

Domain Name   By default, this field is the same as the organization (certifier) name from the previous dialog box. A Notes *domain* is a group of servers that share the same Public Address Book. It is a good idea to have the domain name be the same as your certifier name and also the same as your organization's Internet domain registration, if it has one.

Network Name   Notes Named Networks are groups of Notes servers that run on the same protocol so that they can communicate directly. You may give the group of servers any network name you like. We like to use a name that will describe the location, protocol, and/or network type of that network; for example, SfoTcp might be a good network name for a Notes Named Network in San Francisco running the TCP/IP protocol. When a user selects File, Database, Open, Notes displays those servers that are in the same Notes Named Network as the users home server. If the location is part of the Notes Named Network name, users will get a list of servers in their geographic area—lowering connection costs and providing more relevant choices for users.

NOTE. *Notes Named Networks provide no inherent security features. A user on a server in another Notes Named Network may access a server outside his or her Notes Named Network if that user is running the same protocol, has a physical connection to the server, and is granted access to do so in the server's Access server field.*

Organization Country Code   This entry will append the name of your certifier name with the country code that you enter, and as a result, it will append the fully distinguished name of each ID file you create with that certifier. The country code should match the International Standards Organization (ISO) country code for the country that you designate (per page 473 of Notes's *Administrator's Guide*). We recommend that you leave the country code blank; otherwise, it will limit your ability in the future to use this certifier for international domains.

Log Modem I/O   We usually check this box to place a setting in the NOTES.INI file telling the server program to log all the information going to and coming from the modem when we start up the server. This information is very helpful for troubleshooting with the modem, because it shows the actual commands sent to and from the modem. If there is a problem, it is often due to an incorrect command that will appear in the log file as a result of your checking this box. Later—after establishing that the modem works properly—we disable this feature.

Log All Replication Events   Checking this box will cause the server to record detailed information about replication events. This information takes space in the log, but it can be extremely useful in troubleshooting. If you choose this option, the Notes server's Event task will record all replication sessions between servers. In addition, the log will detail when the replication took place, which server initiated the replication, how long it took to complete the replication, the number of documents exchanged (added, deleted, and updated), and the port used—information that is indispensable for troubleshooting replication problems.

Log All Client Session Events   If you select this option, you will get detailed information in the log file about the user activity on a server. This information is particularly useful when you are doing security audits and determining how to plan for server resources. It tells you which users are accessing the Notes server, when, for how long, and what databases they use.

Create Organization Certifier   Leaving this option checked will tell the setup program that it should create an organization certifier ID file that will be used to create all the other ID files in your organization. The only reason to uncheck this option would be that you have been given or previously created an organization certifier.

Create Server ID   By leaving this box checked, you tell the setup program to create an ID file for the first server in the organization. This ID file will be necessary to run the server software program. The only reason to uncheck this option would be that you already have the id file on disk for the first server in your organization.

Create Administrator ID   When you leave this box checked, you tell the setup program to create an ID file for the first administrator of the system. This person may then use the certifier ID file to create other organizational-unit certifier ID files, server ID files, and user ID files. In Notes 4.0, an administrator is just like any other user, except that he or she is granted special administrative privileges in several areas of the Public Address Book.

Minimum Admin And Certifier Password Length   The number that you enter here will set the minimum length of the password that is required to use these ID files. Once you set this password length, you may not change it until you recertify the ID.

NOTE. *After you complete the information in the last two dialog boxes and click OK, Notes asks you to select a time zone and complete the setup procedure.*

Ready to Go

With the first server setup procedure complete, you have a Notes domain that includes a certifier ID file with which to create additional users, servers, and certifiers, as well as having a server ID and a user ID for the initial administrator of the system. In addition, you have a unique Public Address Book (directory), in which all the domain information for your new domain is stored. Three entities now exist in your Notes domain: the certifier, the server, and one user (the administrator).

Your Notes network is now ready to go. You can start the first server by double-clicking on its icon in the Windows NT Program Manager.

There are several critical components of your Notes system that have now been created. It is important to protect these early on. If these components (such as the ID files that are created) are accessed, the system could be compromised going forward, without your knowledge or ability to correct it. For more information about these components, please read Chapter 24, "Managing Security."

■ Running the Server Program

After server setup, you start the Notes server either by double-clicking on the icon labeled Notes Server in Windows NT's Program Manager. The Notes server then loads into a text window.

The Notes server is comprised of several programs, all of which will be started by the main program and which execute the different functions of the Notes server. Each program may be independently started and stopped; additional programs, such as Notes add-ins, may be run through the server as well. Once loaded, the server will present a text window that is called the "Server Console."

Check the Server Status from the Server Console

Most of Notes' setup and maintenance is done through the workstation client software when documents in system databases—such as the Public Address Book—are entered and modified. *Server-console commands* provide more direct access to some of the events that are typically scheduled using documents in the Public Address Book and settings in the NOTES.INI file (many of which can now be edited by using a server-configuration document).

Notes 4.0's Server Console window is useful for getting status information about the server, as well as for issuing commands to it. The server console has an expanded—though still limited—set of commands. To issue a command to the server, go to the Server Console window and, at the > prompt, type the command. You can issue these same commands using the Remote Console window. This tool lets you issue server commands while you're not physically at the server. You can access the Remote Console window by choosing File, Tools, Server Administration and then selecting the Console button.

To check the status of the server program, at the > prompt in the Server Console window, type **Show Tasks** and then press Enter.

The following table shows the server programs that, by default, run at all times.

Server Task	Program Name	What the Task Does
Database Server	Server	The Main Notes server program; checks access controls, grants access, runs other server tasks, listens for user and server connections, and executes commands issued to the server console.
Admin Process	Adminp	Performs global name changes and entity deletions. Also updates database ACLs with Public Address Book changes.
Agent Manager	Agmgr	Runs database agents.
Stats		Responds to the SHOW STAT command.
Indexer	Updall	Updates all changed views or full-text indexes for all databases.
Router	Route	Routes mail to other Notes servers.
Replicator	Replica	Replicates databases with other Notes servers.
Programs Not Always Running	Compact	Removes unused space.

Server Task	Program Name	What the Task Does
DB Fixup	Fixup	Finds and fixes corrupted databases by removing damaged documents.
Designer	Design	Updates databases with design changes from templates.
Event	Event	Reports on events occurring on the server, based on documents stored in the Statistics and Reporting Database.
Object Store Mgr	Object	Does several kinds of maintenance on databases (such as e-mail databases) that use shared mail.
DB Compactor	Compact	Compacts databases to remove white space.
Statistics	Statlog	Updates the log file (LOG.NSF) with server statistics.
DB Cataloger	Catalog	Searches the server file system for databases and updates the DB Catalog with the information it finds.
Collect	Collect	Purges messages from the shared mail database if all users have deleted the message from their personal mail database.
Chronos	Chronos	Updates full-text indexes that are scheduled to be updated hourly, daily, or weekly.

Check the Server Status from the Remote Console

Like earlier versions of Notes, Notes 4.0 lets you remotely issue commands to the server via the *remote-server console,* which is available from the workstation client. To access the remote-server console from the workstation client in Notes 4.0, follow these steps:

1. Select File, Tools, Server Administration.

2. Choose the server to which you want to send a command.

3. Click on the Console button.

4. In the field labeled Server Console Command, type **Show Tasks.**

5. Click Send.

The server response to your command will appear in the text box in the center of the screen.

■ Installing and Setting Up the Workstation Client Software

With the server setup program completed, the Notes workstation software must be installed on a machine for the administrator to use. Once the workstation client is installed, the administrator can use it to register additional users, servers, and certifiers, as well as to manage other aspects of the Notes system. Remember, most of the administration functions in Notes are done by entering information into Notes documents in a Notes system database, such as the Public Address Book—just as users enter information into documents in databases that support their business processes. Administrators, like users, use the workstation client software to create and edit documents.

Administrators' ID files are just like user ID files (with extra privileges granted in access lists throughout the system), so setting up an administrator's workstation is just the same as setting up a workstation for a user. You can install the software from floppy disks, a CD-ROM, or a network drive. You may install the software onto the local file system of each user's workstation, or you can use shared program files from a network file server.

NOTE. *If during the server setup procedure you selected Server Is Also Administrator's Personal Workstation, you may proceed directly—without first setting up the administrator's workstation—because the workstation is already set up on the same machine as the server.*

The workstation client setup program will find the administrator's user ID file, which contains the administrator's unique identity. The program next asks for a password, to make sure that the administrator is authorized to use that ID file (and to have all the privileges granted it on the system). Then the program connects to the server, to authenticate the user. Also during the workstation setup procedure, Notes configures the workstation to simplify future connections to the server.

To set up the administrator's workstation, you first install the Notes workstation client software on the hard disk. Then—just as with the server setup program—to start the setup program, you double-click on the Workstation Client Software icon. The setup program will ask for the user's (in this case, the administrator's) name; the server to which he or she will be connecting; and information about the port(s) that will be used, such as the LAN protocol and/or the modem port.

When entering this information, it's a good practice to enter the *fully distinguished* name for both the administrator and the server. For example, if you named your certifier /WGSI, you should enter the administrator's name as Sarah Jones/WGSI and the server's name as WGSI-CORP-01/WGSI. Entering information this way ensures that it is properly recorded in connection documents, if you are setting up on a laptop that may connect via dial-in telephone lines.

For detailed information about the Notes 4.0 workstation and setup programs, see Chapter 17, "Deploying Clients."

■ Registering Users and Servers

You have created the domain; now it's time to add users and servers to it. You must *register* users and servers before you can actually set up the machines to run the workstation client or server software.

During the first server setup, your user ID file is granted administrative privileges that enable you to do things that other users cannot; for example, you can use the Administration Control Panel to issue commands to the server and add users and servers. Later, you may grant these privileges to someone else (or a group of others). As administrator, you also have physical access to the certifier ID file that is used to certify all other ID files on the system.

NOTE. *If your workstation is a different machine than the server, you will need to go through the user workstation installation and setup procedures for yourself before adding users. This subject is covered completely in Chapter 17, "Deploying Clients."*

The process of adding users accomplishes two things. First, it creates an ID file with which the user presents his or her identity to other Notes computers; this ID file is of course unique and may be password-protected. Second, this process registers that user with the system, so that Notes servers can grant access and route mail to the user. You accomplish this by placing in the Public Address Book a person document that details information about the user, including name, mail-file location, public key (used for authentication), and so on.

■ Adding Users

To add users to your Notes domain, you must be working in the Notes workstation software, have access to the certifier ID created during first-server setup, and be able to connect to the Notes server. Then

1. While in the workstation client, choose File, Tools, Server Administration and then select the icon labeled People.

2. Choose Register Person.

3. When prompted for whether a license has been purchased, answer Yes.

4. Enter the certifier password.

NOTE. *In Chapter 14, "The Notes Network: Overview and Planning," we discussed creating an organizational hierarchy to assist you in managing your Notes network. You should create and use the appropriate organizational-unit certifier to register users and servers, so that they correctly fall into the organization you have planned. To create an organizational-unit certifier: From the Administration Control Panel, click on the Certifiers button and then select the button Register Organizational Unit. As an example, if you gave your certifier (CERT.ID) the name /WGSI, you could use this procedure to create child certifiers (organizational-unit certifiers) that would have names such as /West/WGSI. You could then use these organizational-unit certifiers to create other organizational-unit certifiers, such as /Sales/West/WGSI.*

5. Confirm that you have selected the correct registration server, so the person document that is created is placed in the correct replica of the Public Address Book. This ensures that this person document can be found by the workstation setup program.

6. Confirm that you have selected the correct certifier with which to certify the ID.

7. Confirm that you have selected the correct security type (North American is more secure but cannot be used outside the United States).

8. Confirm that the expiration date for the certificates that will be issued is acceptable. Notes makes this date two years in the future; we often change it to one year for employees and three months for contractors.

9. Choose Continue.

10. Enter the first name, last name, and password for the new user and then choose the license type (either Full Notes or the more limited Notes Desktop, which does not have administration and design capabilities).

11. If you have created user profiles to simplify workstation setup, choose the profile for this user.

NOTE. User-profile documents *are created in the Public Address Book; their purpose is to simplify the configuration of workstation clients. If a user-profile document is specified during workstation setup, the setup program will fill out a location form and include in it domain and passthru server information. For example, if a group of users with laptop computers in the San Francisco office will dial into the same passthru server, create a setup-profile document called SFDialIn. This setup-profile document might tell the workstation setup program to create a location document, and a connection document in the user's private address book, automating access to the passthru server. Note that each user can be associated with only one setup-profile document.*

12. Click on the Mail icon on the left-hand side of the Register User dialog box and then make sure that the Mail System, Mail File Name, and Home Server options are correct. The home server is the server on which the users mail file will reside and the server to which all other servers will send mail for this user. If the user will have a remote Notes server as his or her home server, you may want to click Create Files During Setup, to save time and communication costs.

13. Click the Other icon on the lower-left side of the dialog box and then enter a comment about, a location for, and the local administrator for this person. Direct Notes as to where it should put the ID file that will result from this registration (in the Public Address Book or in a file).

NOTE. *For security reasons, we strongly recommend storing the new ID file as a file on a disk (rather than as a file in a document in the Public Address Book) and physically or electronically mailing it to the user. If the ID file is stored in the Public Address Book, an unauthorized person could copy it and then use the copy to log in to the system as the designated user. Because Notes uses distributed files, it is very difficult to determine whether such a breach of security has occurred.*

Note as well that users may also be registered by importing from a text file. This is the best technique if you have large numbers of users to register. To do so, you will need a text file with the following format:

```
Lastname;Firstname;MiddleInitial;organization;password;IDFileDirectory;IDFilename;
HomeServerName;MailFileDirectory;MailFileName;Location;Comment;ForwardingAddress
```

To create new user IDs from a file, from the Administration Control Panel, perform the following steps:

1. Access the Administration Control Panel by selecting File, Tools, Server Administration.

2. Click on the button labeled People.

3. Select Register From File.

4. To indicate that you have purchased licenses for the users, click Yes.

5. Enter the password for the certifier ID file that you will use to register the users.

6. Choose the type of ID file that you want to create (North American or International).

7. Enter the name of the text file that contains the user information.

8. Enter the minimum password length for the user ID files.

9. Choose the type of license that was purchased (Notes or Notes Desktop).

10. Choose the type of electronic mail that the users will use.

11. Choose where Notes should store the user ID file until it is given to the user (in a file on disk or in a file in a document in the Public Address Book).

12. Enter the name of either the administrator for this user or a group name of administrators.

13. Click on Register.

■ Adding Servers

Adding servers to the domain allows you to extend your Notes network geographically, numerically (that is, the user base), and functionally. Notes servers can be geographically dispersed in order to localize user connections, improving performance and cost-effectiveness. Notes servers can also be added to the original location, increasing performance and the number of users who can access information, without undermining overall system performance. Finally, Notes servers can be added to provide greater functionality to your development platform; for example, Notes 4.0 servers make excellent World Wide Web servers, and Lotus Notes Document Imaging and Phone Notes extend the breadth of applications as well as the clients that can access them.

The process of adding servers to your Notes network is similar to that of adding users. First, an ID file is created from a certifier ID or organizational-unit certifier ID file. Then a document (in this case, a server document, rather than a person document) is added to the Public Address Book, to provide information about the server to other servers in the domain.

Registering the new server creates a server ID for that server, so it has a unique identity on the Notes network. The registration also causes a document for this server to be entered in the Public Address Book, and if you created a certification log, the registration causes an entry to be made in that log. Once the server identity is created, the setup program can retrieve the ID file and configure the server. You may then run the server and set it up to connect with users and other servers.

Preliminary Considerations

While the process for creating and installing a server is simple, its details have significant ramifications on how effectively you will be able to manage the server and the service that server will provide. The following sections tell you what to think through clearly before adding servers to your Notes domain.

Server Management

Notes servers are like any other application or file/print server: To run properly, they require care and feeding. If you already have a person or group assigned to managing a network server, this person or group is usually a good candidate for the role of Notes server administrator because familiarity with the important tasks and technical issues common to all types of networked servers already exists.

When the Notes domain is set up, policies should be put in place for how server ID files will be created: who will create them, how they will be named, the roles they will play, and what their topology will be. Just because a person or group manages the server, it does not automatically follow that this person or group has network administration privileges. One group of people may make sure that the server is up, running, backed up, and has plenty of disk space, while another group may add users and servers; yet another group may determine how servers connect for replication and mail routing.

We usually break Notes system administration into four categories and assign tasks accordingly, as shown in the following table. We have also noted a non-Notes job function, because this function is critical to running the Notes system. All the roles must interact in order to keep Notes up and running.

Administrative Role	Tasks
Notes database manager	Manages Notes applications: establishes database access controls, archives documents, checks replication, and manages database size.
Notes server administrator	Installs and upgrades software and hardware, backs up databases, restarts server, resolves network (such as protocol and NIC) issues.

Administrative Role	Tasks
Notes Network administrator	Determines and implements connection schedules, server access lists, passthru permissions, protocols, and Notes Named Networks.
Notes certifier	Adds and removes users from the Notes domain.
Network administration	Not a Notes function but important, because Notes will use the infrastructure deployed by this group.

The Infrastructure Plan

Be sure that you have a clear plan about how to set up a *reliable* Notes support infrastructure; that is, the system has a high availability rate, information stored on the system will have integrity, and performance will be adequate to meeting user needs. Remember that users will put critical information into Notes and will expect performance and reliability.

Naming Conventions

How you name your Notes servers and networks will play an important role in how easily they can be managed as your network grows. In general, it is a good idea to have your server names offer some indication of what role they play and where they are located. Notes Named Networks should indicate their location and the network protocol that they use. Please see the section "Establishing Naming Conventions," in Chapter 14, for more information on how to name Notes servers that you create.

An Organizational Hierarchy for Certifying Server Names

Hierarchical server names can enhance the server-naming conventions of an organization. For example, you can use an organizational-unit certifier to distinguish the location in which a server belongs. Our Boston sales server name A-WG-01 gives us more information when we look at its fully distinguished name: A-WG-01/Sales/BOS/WGSI, which tells us that this is an Acme server, located in the area near the Boston airport, used as a workgroup server, the first server of its kind, and serves the sales division.

Organizational hierarchies such as Sales/BOS/WGSI are established when ID files are created with an organizational-unit certifier; organizational-unit certifiers are created by organization certifiers, as children. The certifier /WGSI might create the organizational-unit certifier /West/WGSI, which in turn might create the organizational-unit certifier /Sales/West/WGSI. The advantage to using these hierarchies is that users and servers are more likely to have unique names, system management can be simplified, and the certification process may be distributed.

Server Connections

It's important to plan in advance how servers will connect. Think about the two purposes for which servers connect—replication and mail routing—and about the two contexts in which they connect— physical and logical. Remember that in general, the goal of defining a server topology is to limit the number of "hops" a document must make to get from one server to another. We like to have replication and routing share the physical and logical connections, to minimize administration and maximize efficiency.

Have as few connections as possible so that you do not have to manage many different communication events. For example, every time a server connects to replicate, it must have a Replicator task available to do so (Notes 4.0 lets server administrators simultaneously run multiple Replicator tasks on the same server), so if you are not careful with your connection schedule, you will have the same machine scheduled to replicate with more servers than it has replicators available at a given time. The result: Information will not replicate as expected. Issues such as this one compel us to create a system where connections are limited.

While minimizing administrative concerns, also consider LAN/WAN costs. For example, servers in the same Notes Named Network do not require a connection document in order to deliver mail; they communicate directly with each other and send mail immediately. If your Notes system runs on a WAN, you may not want all mail delivered to remote locations immediately, at a high cost. You can use Notes Named Networks and Connection documents to localize mail delivery and better manage mail connections that span large geographies.

NOTE. *Without connection documents, Server A in San Francisco immediately sends all mail to servers all over the country.*

By *physical connections,* we are referring to how the servers are physically connected to one another: Is Server A on the same LAN as Server B? If not, is the network protocol (SPX, for example) that is used by Server A routed to the LAN on which Server B resides? Does Server B use the same protocol as Server A? Answer these questions before installing additional Notes servers, and resolve them in conjunction with your network support team. Figure 16.4 shows two computers connecting via a LAN. They can do this because they run the same network protocol.

Logical connections are the connection documents put in the Public Address Book for the purpose of telling Notes servers when, with whom, and

Figure 16.4

Server A and Server B on the same LAN, running the same protocol (SPX or TCP/IP).

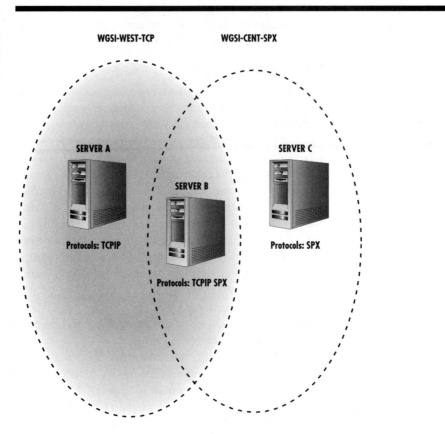

for what purpose to connect. You must fully understand how the physical network on which your servers will communicate works before setting up your logical connections.

Ports: The Physical Connection Before deploying a server, plan how it will connect to other servers in your Notes domain. It is critical that servers within the same domain can connect in some way, because they will need to replicate the Public Address Book. Even if a server does not need to replicate other databases—as in the case of a server designated as a mail-only server—Notes requires that all servers replicate the Public Address Book. You have two choices for how a server connects to other Notes servers: using a network port, running most popular protocols (see Table 16.1) and/or using a modem (COM) port. Figure 16.5 shows how a server designated for using electronic mail might have only the Public Address Book as well as the user-mail files. It would probably also have additional system databases.

Table 16.1

Notes Server Operating-
System Platforms with
Protocols Supported.

NOTES SERVER OS	PROTOCOLS SUPPORTED
Windows NT, version 3.51	SPX/SPXII, TCP/IP, VINES, NetBIOS, NetBEUI, AppleTalk
OS/2 Warp V3.*x*	SPX, TCP/IP, VINES, NetBIOS, NetBEUI, AppleTalk
Solaris 2.*x*	SPX/SPXII,TCP/IP
HP-UX	SPX/SPXII, TCP/IP

Figure 16.5

A Notes server with only
mail databases and the
Public Address Book on it.

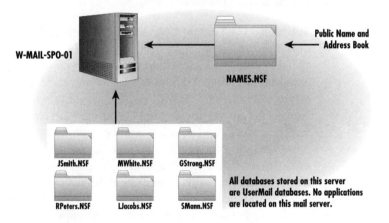

NAMES.NSF

Public Name and
Address Book

W-MAIL-SPO-01

JSmith.NSF   MWhite.NSF   GStrong.NSF

RPeters.NSF   LJacobs.NSF   SMann.NSF

All databases stored on this server
are UserMail databases. No applications
are located on this mail server.

NOTE. *Mail databases do not need to be replicated, but the server still must replicate with at least one other server in the domain in order to keep the Public Address Book synchronized.*

If you choose to connect via network port, you must ensure that the server with which you want to connect runs the same protocol as the existing one; also be sure that either the two servers are on the same physical LAN or that the protocol is routed between LANs. Notes servers can use multiple network protocols on the same machine, using the same—or separate—network interface cards so it is important that two servers share at least one protocol in common in order to connect.

Whatever port you choose, make sure that that port is functioning before you run the setup program on the new Notes server. A good way to do this is to test another application—one that you know works—with the two machines. If you are running TCP/IP, for example, you should be able to ping the machine (the existing Notes server) to which the additional server (the one that you are setting up) will connect during the setup procedure. If you cannot do this, you have a network problem that needs to be resolved before setting up the Notes servers.

During setup, the new server will connect to an existing Notes server, first to find information in the Public Address Book and then to copy the Public Address Book. The additional server setup program will need to use the port that you chose during setup in order to connect to the other server; in the future, just the Notes server program will need to do this.

If you chose to use a modem or COM port for connections to the other server(s), you must have a working modem on the new server as well as on the server to which the new server will connect. In addition, servers connecting via modem should have their own Notes Named Network (see Chapter 26, "Managing the Network").

Schedule: The Logical Connection   Notes servers connect for the purposes of routing and replication (see Chapter 19, "Replication," and Chapter 20, "Mail Routing"). To schedule these tasks, you must use *connection documents* in the Public Address Book. A connection document tells the Notes server when to connect with another server for routing and/or replication. Notes 4.0's connection documents have added features, to support both larger networks and passthru connections.

Scheduling connections in large Notes networks is a significant task to undertake. Most large Notes deployments have a group dedicated to this kind of Notes network management. Many variables come into play, and all must be weighed against one another.

Regardless of the size of your organization, ensure that at least one connection document exists for each server, so that the Notes server program will know how to route mail and replicate. Don't forget: The server *must* replicate the Public Address Book, if nothing else.

If you have a small Notes network, you probably have not segregated the duties of the server administrator and network manager. However, you should start thinking about a strategy for how and when Notes servers will connect as your network expands. If yours is a large organization, ensure that the group responsible for maintaining connection documents has at least one connection document for this new server to connect with another Notes server, so that the Notes server program will know how to route mail and replicate.

If a connection document does not exist to create a replication event with the new server and another server with which it can synchronize the Public Address Book, the system will not function properly when the Public Address Book is updated with new users, servers, and other information. If the new server is in a different Notes Named Network, or domain, than other servers to which users on the new server may send mail, mail will not be delivered without a connection document.

The Server's Role

Before adding a server, clearly define its purpose. A Notes server can play many roles; defining that role will help you name the server, select hardware for it, manage it, and leverage your investment in it. Although you install and configure all Notes servers with the same procedures, dedicating those servers to certain tasks simplifies their management.

For example, with Notes 4.0's Internet capabilities, you can easily publish to the World Wide Web. You should probably have a special set of policies and people for managing and securing any server that is designated as an InterNotes Web Server. In general, server roles may change significantly with Notes 4.0, because enhanced features such as the following make it possible for servers to do more:

- An *anonymous access list,* for making a Notes server open (good for both Notes Net and the WWW). This means that servers and users that are not cross-certified can access the server. In a future release of Notes 4.0 (version 4.2), the Notes server will be a native HTTP server, and WWW browsers will be able to access it if this setting is set to allow anonymous connections.

- InterNotes, which Notes 4.0 provides as a means to access files (documents) on the Internet's World Wide Web. The server can have the Web Navigator database on it, with the Web server task running to access HTTP, FTP, and gopher documents; convert them to Notes documents; and give users access to these documents. Using this feature lets you give access to the Internet without running TCP/IP on each workstation. You also get the benefits of Notes features and manageability for World Wide Web content.

- Up to 500 concurrent sessions, to support more users

- Better replication and routing performance

- Passthru to other Notes servers, permitting you to centralize remote services

When determining the server role, consider the usage it will most likely receive. Notes 4.0 can support an unlimited number of concurrent users, depending on the network protocol that you install. When Notes is running on TCP/IP and SPX protocols, there is no limit to the number of concurrent users. As a result, by rethinking your topology and consolidating servers, you may be able to realize some economies. For example, given these reduced restrictions, Notes *hub* servers can support far more *spokes*; as a result, you might consolidate your network, saving significant administration time by caring for fewer servers and improving performance by limiting network traffic between servers.

Make sure that you plan the server with the resources it will need in order to be reliable and perform adequately for users. This means make it fast, with plenty of room for storing data, and back it up frequently. We usually recommend a minimum of 32 megabytes of RAM on Windows NT; 64 megabytes is desirable. Since most of the cost in Notes is in the deployment, processor, and management, you can, in effect, save money by adding memory and disk space—to make the server better performing and more extensible, without greatly increasing per-user cost.

In addition, make sure you have implemented a security strategy for that server, one which addresses the risk of data loss or interception. For more information on topology planning, see Chapter 14, "The Notes Network: Overview and Planning"; for more information about Notes 4.0 security, see Chapter 24, "Managing Security."

The following sections describe common server types. These can be used to segregate the duties of servers, to improve performance and simplify management. In addition, segregation of server functions may be used to enhance security.

Workgroup Servers   *Workgroup servers* are servers that support both applications and mail. In larger Notes deployments, the mail servers are often segregated from the application servers for reasons of performance, administration simplicity, and security. Workgroup servers are usually set up for smaller organizations or remote sites of large organizations, to serve both mail and applications.

Because Notes servers running TCP/IP and SPX can support an unlimited number of concurrent users, and because the performance of replication and routing are dramatically improved with Notes 4.0, you may be able to consolidate server functions into one machine, rather than two. In general, it is probably still a good practice to segregate mail databases to their own server(s).

Mail Servers   *Mail servers* are servers used specifically to store only mail databases and to route mail. The reasons for designating a server as a mail server include the following:

• It simplifies administration, by limiting the scope of server functions.

• It reduces congestion on the LAN, because more users can have mail files on one server, making routing to another server on the LAN less frequent.

- It limits replication resources, because only the Public Address Book *needs* to be replicated.

- It makes the Notes network expansion easier, as available resources are more easily measured.

- It segregates server duties so that if an application server is down, mail can still be retrieved, and vice versa.

Hub Servers   *Hub servers* are used in a hub-and-spoke server topology, to replicate databases and route documents. Hub servers are not accessed by users but rather serve as a physical and logical connecting point for the Notes domain.

Creating a hub-and-spoke topology of servers limits the number of "hops" documents must make to get from the source server to the destination server. In most cases, a document needs to travel no farther than from the originating server—the hub server—to the receiving server. A hub and spoke topology is also useful for simplifying the management of connection documents, especially since this topology minimizes the connections that are necessary. Many large organizations select hub-and-spoke topologies because they can adapt easily to system growth.

Application Servers   *Application servers* store Notes applications (databases). The range of applications stored on a server can vary from a simple discussion database to a mission-critical purchasing application. By segregating application servers, you can

- Easily expand your server network, without having to move users' mail files and reconfigure person documents in the Public Address Book.

- Optimize server performance, by managing database usage and replication frequency without having to make accommodations for mail routing.

- Simplify administration, by categorizing application servers for databases with high replication or security needs. This is a particularly useful strategy for storing mission-critical applications—those on which the organization lives and breathes. Servers storing these applications can replicate more frequently and have a more restrictive access control list.

- Simplify access for users, by giving them one-stop shopping when they are looking for applications. If applications are located on many different servers, users may need to "surf" to find the ones they need; when applications are located on only certain servers, users have fewer servers to search—and fewer servers to which they must be granted access.

Remote-Access Servers *Remote-access servers* allow users to dial in directly to a Notes server. By strategically placing remote servers, you can limit the connection costs. For example, a single remote-access server can store low-security databases and also provide passthru services to other servers to which traveling users may need access. Remote-access servers provide an excellent means to keep traveling laptop users connected and in the know. These servers may store mail and/or applications.

One important thing to remember: Security is key to limiting risk when you make a server accessible via telephone line. See Chapter 24, "Managing Security," for more information about how you can protect information on remote-access servers.

Passthru Servers *Passthru* is a great new feature of Notes 4.0. It enables one server to act as a bridge to servers that are running different protocols: Using a server that's set up for passthru, a user who is dialed into one server (the passthru server) may connect to other servers that run protocols other than the one running on the user's workstation.

For example, say that you have a mail server called A-MAIL-01 and an application server called A-APPS-01. With earlier versions of Notes, if you were traveling with a laptop, you would have needed to make two calls in order to get access to both your mail and your applications. With Notes 4.0, you can call one server that is set up to allow passthru to the other server(s) and then get your information with one telephone call. Servers designated specifically as passthru servers usually do not host applications, because the primary purpose of these servers is to provide connectivity to other servers. In some cases, a server with a different role may be set up to support passthru.

Passthru servers are also great for LAN workstation users who run only one protocol on their systems. Using passthru, you can enable these users to connect to Notes servers that are running many other protocols, provided the server to which they connect runs the additional protocols. For more information on setting up a passthru server, see Chapter 26, "Managing the Network."

Gateway Servers A *gateway server* is any Notes server that runs a special process in order to convert Notes documents to the format of another system and then forward or receive documents from that system. For example, if you want your users to be able to send mail to the Internet using the Notes workstation client, you need to have an SMTP gateway that converts Notes documents to the SMTP format and then sends these documents to an SMTP host. Gateways convert documents to Notes format when they arrive at the Notes gateway server in another format. In general, it is a good idea to have a separate machine for running gateway and other connectivity software, because these servers often have high traffic, with the router using much of their resources. Some common connectivity software programs for Notes are: InterNotes, Lotus Notes Web Publisher, Lotus Notes SMTP Mail Transfer Agent, Lotus cc:Mail Mail Transfer Agent, Lotus Notes X.400 Mail Transfer Agent, and Lotus Notes FAX Gateway.

Backup Servers Replication features make it easy to create and keep synchronized, additional copies of applications (databases). You can set up and designate a server as a *backup server,* for use in the event that the primary Notes server goes down. If you set the server access list properly, users will then be able to access and enter information as easily as on the primary server.

The backup server should have sufficient RAM, disk space, and processing cycles to provide adequate support while the primary server is being serviced. To use the backup server, users need only be told to access databases on it via the File, Database, Open menu. Alternatively, you can quickly switch the backup server's name (provided that you are prepared to do so, with a copy of the primary server's ID file) to the name of the primary server, making the switch to the backup server entirely seamless for users.

NOTE. *Never depend on a Notes backup server as your only means of backup. You should have a tape backup of your Notes data, just as you would with any other system. If a database becomes corrupted or if documents are inadvertently deleted, Notes's replication will likely bring those changes to the backup server as well.*

The Server's Notes Named Network

Notes Named Networks are logical, rather than physical, groupings of Notes servers and are a subset of the Notes domain. A single Notes Named Network identifies a group of servers, all of which belong to the same Notes domain and are running the same protocol on the same LAN or on a bridged/routed WAN. The location of your servers and the protocols they run will dictate how you name your networks. The Notes Named Network to which a server belongs is determined by the entries in the Network Configuration section of the server document in the Public Address Book.

The key to remember: All servers in a given Notes Named Network must be able to communicate directly. For example, if the protocol on all the servers in a Notes Named Network called DallasEtherTcp (to indicate servers in Dallas running TCP/IP on an Ethernet) is TCP/IP, those servers should be able to ping one another, as well as share files. If they cannot directly communicate, they must be placed in different Notes Named Networks.

In addition to telling the Notes server program what other Notes servers it may directly communicate with, you can use Notes Named Networks to your administrative and financial benefit. By grouping servers regionally (placing them in regional Notes Named Networks), where connection costs are low, you minimize user access to servers that have a higher connection cost. When a user selects File, Database, Open, that user is presented with a list of Notes servers on which databases reside. This list is comprised of all the servers in the same Notes Named Network as the user's home server. If you have a WAN such that all Notes servers can be in the same Notes Named Network, you may still choose to break the servers into groups (Notes Named Networks) that indicate the location. This way, users will see only a list of servers in their geographic proximity, saving connection costs. If a user needs access outside that geographic location, he or she can simply type in the name of the server to which access is required.

Mail routing occurs automatically to servers in the same Notes Named Network; no connection document in the Public Address Book is necessary. Therefore, grouping servers into Notes Named Networks can simplify administration. Geographically close servers are clustered around a single Notes hub server, and they all send mail without the Notes network administrator having to manage connection documents for mail routing. Notes servers that are physically connected (or bridged/routed) and run more than one protocol may belong to more than one Notes Named Network.

Examples: Notes Named Networks   Say that you have a location called WestCoast and that all the servers run the same protocol; the servers can then all belong to the same Notes Named Network. Users who choose File, Database, Open will see a list of all the servers in the WestCoast Notes Named Network, even if the servers are running different operating systems. Remember, a protocol is like a language: If two or more servers run the same protocol, they speak the same language and can communicate directly.

As long as servers can directly connect using the LAN and the protocol, they can belong to the same Notes Named Network. A user whose home server is in this Notes Named Network can easily access any of the other servers in the same Notes Named Network, because those servers will be listed whenever the user chooses File, Database, Open.

If you have Notes servers in multiple locations and they are connected via WAN, you can have one large Notes Named Network that includes all of the Notes servers in your organization, regardless of whether the server is in Boston or Dallas. It's probably a better idea to break down the servers into logical groups (Notes Named Networks) that represent the location of the servers, or perhaps the business function served by the servers. Doing this will simplify administration in many ways and give users a more manageable list of servers from which to choose.

NOTE. *Access to any server is dependent upon two things: the protocol and the server access list (defined in the server document in the Public Address Book).*

This means that even if a user cannot see a particular server listed when he or she selects File, Database, Open—because the server is in a different Notes Named Network—if that user has a protocol in common between the workstation and the server and the user's workstation is physically connected to the server, the user may access the server by typing its name. It is the server's access list that determines whether and for what activities the user will be granted access to the server.

When to Set Up a New Notes Named Network   Notes Named Networks are assigned at the time the server is registered. Since a Notes Named Network designation is a logical one—a setting in a document in the Public Address Book—it may be changed at any time. When you register an additional server, Notes enters the Notes network name that you select into the server document. The Notes network name that you assign in the Register Servers dialog box (see the later section, "Registering Additional Servers") should be thought out in advance and should fit into your overall topology strategy.

Before you set up a new Notes Named Network, at least one Notes Named Network must already exist within your Notes domain. Your Notes domain name was created during the first server-setup procedure, and a Notes Named Network was assigned to the first server. You may add servers to this Notes Named Network and/or create additional Notes Named Networks. As described earlier, Notes Named Networks are groupings of servers.

The server setup program entered the name that you specified into the Notes Network field of the server document. If you did not specify a Notes Named Network name, the default of Network1 was entered into the server document. To change the name of the first Notes Named Network during the first server setup program, you would have selected the Advanced Settings dialog box and then entered the name you wanted for your Notes Named Network. To change the name of the Notes Named Network to which a server belongs after setting up the server, you can go to the server document in the Public Address Book for that server and edit the Notes Network field.

If you want to add a server to a Notes Named Network, you must do this: Specify the name as it already exists in other server documents into the Network Name field of the additional server's server document in the Public Address Book. If you ever want to change the name of a Notes Named Network, you must change the Network Name field in all of the server documents in which that Notes Named Network is entered.

How to Set Up a New Notes Named Network   To set up a new Notes Named Network: While registering the first server that will belong to this network, simply enter the name for the new network into the Register Servers dialog box. Notes then automatically enters this name into the correct field in the server document of the new server. If you want to move or add an existing server into a new Notes Named Network, you can make the change in its server document in the Public Address Book.

In addition to entering the name of the Notes Named Network, the setup procedure enables the appropriate network or modem port by entering the port into the NOTES.INI file; the server is then able to send and receive information from the enabled port. You may later enable additional ports for more modems or additional protocols.

Security Precautions

Security in Notes 4.0 is covered completely in Chapter 24, "Managing Security." Meanwhile, here are some important tips for ensuring that an early security breach does not cause problems for you down the road:

- Do not distribute server ID files (or user ID files, for that matter) in the Public Address Book. Although this is the default way for distributing ID files to new Notes entities, it is not secure: Anyone with access to the server (or person) document in the Public Address Book can make a copy of this file, work to break the password, and gain unauthorized access by using that password. Instead, have the server registration program store the new server ID file as a file on disk and then attach this file to a electronic mail message to the local server administrator. Alternatively, send a disk with the new server ID file to the local server administrator. Send the password for the file in a different message and do no use "standard" passwords—each one should be unique.

- Physically secure the server before bringing it on line. The best way to prevent unauthorized access to the ID files and Public Address Book is to prevent access to the physical machine from the moment it contains these files. Remember, because the Public Address Book is replicated to all servers in the domain, a server that is not physically secure (and, hence, its copy of the Pubic Address Book is not secure) poses a threat to the entire network. All the unauthorized changes made to that one copy will replicate throughout the organization.

- Check for viruses. If a virus infects a Notes server, the damage it causes will likely replicate to all other copies of the data it destroys.

- Change passwords for new servers immediately, even if each additional server is created with a unique password.

- Segregate duties. Set up your support function such that the people who manage the physical hardware and software installation do not also administer the Public Address Book, beyond the server(s) they support.

Procedures for Adding Servers to the Notes Domain

The following list gives the general procedures for adding servers to the Notes domain. In larger installations, where administrative roles are likely to be segregated, these tasks will probably be handled by different people.

- Registering the server (just as you would register a user)

- Installing the server program code on the new machine

- Running the server setup program

- Running and testing the server

- Scheduling connections to other servers

- Adding users and applications to the server

Registering Additional Servers

The registration process for Notes 4.0 servers is almost identical to that in Notes 3.0. The main difference is that you do the registration from the Administration Control Panel, rather than from the File menu. Also, the registration process fills out the administration ownership fields of the server document; this is to support the Notes 4.0 Public Address Book security features that limit the ability of administrators to change documents to those documents that pertain to the role that the administrator serves.

Remember, registering a server is the process of creating an identity (ID file) for the server and informing the rest of the network about the new entity (the server document in the Public Address Book). To register a server you must have access (a password) to the certifier ID file or an organizational certifier, and you must be authorized to create server documents in the Public Address Book.

There are two kinds of security, then, involved in creating a server. First, you must have either a certifier ID file that is the top-level certifier or an organizational certifier that falls within the hierarchy under the original certifier; you must also have the password for this binary, encrypted file. The second kind of security access is the appropriate access to the Public Address Book. This means that you have at least Author access in the database access control list and are listed in the role called ServerCreator. You must also be listed in the Administrators field in the server document on the server whose Public Address Book will first receive the new server document that is created during registration. This gives you the privilege of using the Server Control Panel and issuing commands on that server. Finally, you must be listed in the access control list of the server whose replica of the Public Address book will first receive the new server document.

What Happens When You Register a Server When you register a server, Notes uses the certifier ID or the organizational certifier ID file to create a unique ID file for the new server. This ID file has a genealogy that dates back to the certifier for your Notes domain; that way, other Notes computers in your organization will "trust" this ID file. Once the ID file is created, Notes stores it where you specify (we recommend not storing it in the Public Address Book) until the server setup program retrieves it for use by the new server. The registration program also adds a server document to the Public Address Book, to tell other servers and users in your Notes domain about this new server. To register an additional server, you must have the certifier ID file and the password to the certifier ID file and then "create" access to the server document form in the Public Address Book.

The Steps for Registering a New Server Follow these steps to register a new server:

1. Open the Notes workstation client software program.

2. Choose File, Tools, Server Administration.

3. Click on the tile labeled Servers.

4. Choose Register Server.

5. When alerted that you must purchase a license, answer Yes.

6. Enter the password for the certifier ID and then click OK.

NOTE. *The registration server is the server into whose Public Address Book the new server document will be placed. Remember that the Public Address Book is replicated to all servers in your domain, so the new server document will eventually reside in all replicas of the Public Address Book, one on each server. You cannot do the server setup procedure unless the server from which the new server will retrieve a replica of the Public Address Book already has a copy of the new server document. Bearing this in mind, choose your registration server carefully, so that it will either be the server to which the new server connects during setup or will replicate quickly to the server that the new server will connect to, so that the new server document is available before the new server setup program runs.*

7. Click the button labeled Registration Server and make sure that the server listed is the one that you want to first receive the server document.

8. Look at the text next to the button labeled Certifier ID and make sure that you have the correct certifier listed. The correct certifier is one that is part of your organization's hierarchy (see Chapter 24, "Managing Security").

NOTE. *Unless you are the person charged with certifying all entities throughout your organization, you probably will not have access to the top-level (/WGSI, for example) certifier and will use an organizational-unit certifier that was given to you (/WestCoast/WGSI, for example).*

9. Select the type of security that you want to use. If you select North American, the encryption will be more advanced, but the software cannot be used outside of the U.S. and you may have difficulty exchanging encrypted documents with users abroad. International security has a smaller encryption-key length but can be exported outside the U.S. If yours is a large organization with offices abroad that will eventually use Notes to communicate internally, we recommend that you choose the International option. This recommendation does not apply to financial institutions or other organizations with highly sensitive data. The following figure shows the initial server-registration dialog box, with a certifier ID file specified.

10. Choose continue.

11. In the field labeled Server Name, enter the name of the new server.

12. Enter a password for the server ID file that will be created.

13. Enter the minimum length of the password.

NOTE. *The minimum length of the password is the fewest characters that the ID file will accept for a password. When changing the password in the future, the server administrator will need to use at least this number of characters. See Chapter 24, "Managing Security," about using multiple passwords in Notes ID files.*

14. Check that the domain name that is listed is correct.

15. Enter the name of the person who will administer this server (the person listed as the owner of the server document in the Public Address Book). You may want to enter an administrative group name here.

NOTE. *To use Notes, the administrator must already be registered in the Public Address Book and have a valid ID file.*

16. In the upper-left corner of the dialog box, click on the icon labeled Other.

17. Enter a title for this server. (This information is placed in the server document for convenience only.)

18. In the field labeled Network, enter the Notes Named Network to which this server will belong.

19. Enter the name of the local administrator. (The local administrator has limited ability to modify the server document in the Public Address Book.) You may want to enter a group name here.

20. Choose the location where Notes should store the new server's ID file until the server setup program is run. Once again, for security reasons we recommend that before server setup, you store this ID in a file and mail it to the server administrator.

You have now completed the registration procedure. The server document created during this procedure will need to be in the Public Address Book of the server to which you connect when you go through the additional server setup procedure. This will be the case if you chose this server as the registration server and will occur naturally through replication, provided that all the replications have taken place that are necessary to get the document from the registration computer to the server to which you connect during setup.

Installing the Additional Notes Server Software

The server software installation procedure guides you through the steps to install the server program and configuration files on a file system that can be accessed by the processor that will run the server program. Once you answer questions about how and where you would like the files installed, the installation program will automatically decompress and copy them.

For more information about installing the Notes server software, refer back to the earlier section "Installing the Server Software."

The next step in setting up your additional server is to configure the new server, and the server setup program will help you do this. The setup program for the *server* software will run automatically when you start the Notes workstation *client* software.

Setting up the additional server software configures your system to work within the Notes domain. The setup program locates the new server ID file created for the particular server, based on information that you enter into the setup program. It then confirms that the user is authorized to set up this server, by requiring and then checking the ID-file password that is entered. Next, the server setup program contacts the server and checks to see that the new server is listed in the Public Address Book. Once these checks are complete, the setup program uses other information that is entered to configure the server and make a replica copy of the Public Address Book from the server to which it connected.

To run the setup program and configure the new server, first start the Notes workstation client from Windows NT, Windows 95, or OS/2.

NOTE. *The setup program will check the NOTES.INI file installed by the install program and see that this server has not yet been configured.*

Next, perform the following steps:

1. In the Server Setup dialog box, select the option An Additional Lotus Notes Server.

2. In the field labeled Server Name, enter the name of the new server that you are setting up.

NOTE. *It is a good idea to enter the server name exactly as it was entered into the Public Address Book of the server document on the registration server. Case-sensitivity is always a good idea, and using the fully distinguished name (for example, ServerA/Finance/WestCoast/WGSI) is most important. If you are unsure of the server name, look at the server document in the Public Address Book on any server that has this document. Ultimately, of course, the new server document will be in every copy of the Public Address Book, because this server was either the registration server or it received the document via replication.*

3. In the field labeled Get Domain Address Book From, enter the name of the Notes server to which you want to connect in order to validate the server setup and from which the Public Address Book will be copied.

4. Select the port that will be used to connect to the other (existing) server. The setup program will use this port to connect with the existing server during setup in order to copy the Public Address Book and will enable this port for future use in the new server document. You may later enable other ports. If you specified a serial port for the connection, enter the phone number to call the existing server.

5. Select the protocol that will be used to connect to the new server. If the protocol is already running, Notes should automatically detect it. If there is more than one protocol running, you must select the one that will be used for this initial connection.

6. If the new server will connect to the existing server via modem, select the COM port in the field labeled Serial Port.

7. Choose the modem type and the dial type. If your modem is not listed, you can select the Auto Detect option, which will work for most modems.

8. If the ID file for the new server has been supplied to you via electronic mail or disk, check the box labeled New Server's ID Supplied In A File. If this is not the case, the ID file should be stored in the new server document in the Public Address Book; the file will be copied to your machine during setup and then removed from the server document when setup is

complete. As discussed earlier, every Notes ID file is unique and represents a single entity in a single naming hierarchy. During setup, the new server must locate its ID and use that ID file, which must match the name and public key in the server document in the Public Address Book.

NOTE. *You have now entered all the information necessary to establish a connection and set up the new server. We recommend that you next select the button labeled Advanced Options and then select Log Modem I/O, Log All Replication Events, Log All Client Session Events. The information will be recorded in the Notes Log file and is useful for troubleshooting connection problems. You can turn off these logs in the future.*

9. Click OK.

10. Choose the correct time zone, check Observe Daylight Savings, and then click OK.

11. Notes will set up your server and prompt you when the setup is complete; when this happens, click OK.

Starting the Server Program

When you start the server program after server setup, the Notes server loads into a text window in Microsoft Windows NT or Windows 95. The Notes server is comprised of several programs, many of which will be started immediately by the main program. Other programs are loaded on a scheduled basis; these programs execute the different functions of the Notes server. Each program may be started and stopped independently, and additional programs, such as Notes add-ins, may also be run via the NOTES.INI file.

To start the Notes server program from the Program Manager in Windows, double-click on the icon labeled Notes Server; in Windows 95, select Notes Server from the Start menu. The server program will then load into a text window.

The Notes server console has a limited set of commands, because most of the server management is done via the Notes workstation client, by entering documents into the Public Address Book. The Server Console window, which comes up when you load the server program, is most useful for getting status information about the server. To issue a command to the server, you may go to the server console and then type the command at the > prompt. To check the status of the server program, do the following: At the > prompt, type **Show Tasks** and then press Enter.

Following is a table of the server programs that run at all times by default. For a complete list of server programs, see Chapter 27, "Managing Servers."

Server Task	Purpose
Database server	The main Notes server program; checks access controls, grants access, runs other server tasks, listens for user and server connections, and executes commands issued to the server console.
Admin Process	Performs global name changes and deletions.
Agent Manager	Runs database agents.
Stats	Responds to the SHOW STAT command.
Indexer	Updates all changed views or full-text indexes for all databases.
Router	Routes mail to other Notes servers.
Replicator	Replicates databases with other Notes servers.

Configuring the New Server

Now that the server is up and running, you need to make some important setting adjustments so that the server will run and be secured on the network. To make these adjustments, you must modify documents in the Public Address Book, and in some cases you must modify the NOTES.INI file. Several different documents in the Public Address Book pertain to the server so you must adjust different documents to change different settings (it is not one-stop shopping!). Right now, the primary concern is with settings stored in the server document for your new server in the Public Address Book.

NOTE. *Depending on how your organization structures its Notes administrative functions, you may or may not have the necessary access privileges to make changes in the Public Address Book. If your Public Address Book is centrally managed, you will need to work with the central organization in order to adjust the settings that follow.*

About the Public Address Book   The Notes 4.0 Public Address Book is designed with much better usability and security, right out of the box. Among the many enhancements is the addition of *roles* for the creation and maintenance of documents in the Public Address Book. With the use of roles, administrators can now be granted different levels of access to different documents. For example, it is now possible to give the local server administrator the ability to edit only documents related to servers that he or she manages, while still denying this user (administrator) the ability to delete these documents or look at documents belonging to other local server administrators.

Using roles provides for better segregation of duty within the Public Address Book. The following table lists the roles that you may assign within the Public Address Book, in order to provide more detailed control over who edits which documents.

Public Address Book Role	What Administrators in This Role Can Do
GroupCreator	Create new group documents.
GroupModifier	Edit or delete existing group documents.
NetCreator	Create all documents except person, group, and server documents.
NetModifier	Edit or delete all existing documents except person, group, and server documents.
ServerCreator	Create new server documents.
ServerModifier	Edit existing server documents.
UserCreator	Create new person documents.
UserModifier	Edit existing person documents.

NOTE. *Creator roles may be assigned to users with any access level assigned in the database access control list, but only users with Author access or above will actually be able to create a document. Modifier roles may be assigned to users with Author access and above to let these users edit the document types associated with that role.*

The Server Documents   Each Notes server in your organization has a server document in the Public Address Book of your domain. This server document controls configuration and security for that server, and it provides information about that server to other entities in the domain. The following is detailed information about the server document so you can easily determine what role each field plays in the operation of the server.

Server access controls   Server access controls detail what kind of access each user and other servers have to the server in question. Settings for access controls are in the server document of each server. Entries in the server document contain the following kinds of access to the server:

• Can Administer Server (use remote console and edit server document).

• Can Access Server.

- Cannot Access Server (explicitly not allowed to use this server; this applies to such people as terminated employees).

- Can Create Databases (for users who can create new databases on the server file system).

- Can Create Replicas (for users who can create replicas on the server file system).

- Can Passthru (there are several settings related to using this server to access other Notes servers).

These entries are usually represented either by using groups created in the Public Address Book or by using wildcards based on the hierarchical naming structure of the organization. For example, if a local administrator registers users (creates ID files and person documents in the Public Address Book), he or she might have an organizational certifier ID file with the name /WestCoast/Acme. This user's fully distinguished name might look like Margie Smith/WestCoast/Acme, because it was created with the organizational certifier.

TIP. *The server document can contain wildcards such as */WestCoast/WGSI to enable only those users created with that organizational certifier to access the server. */WGSI would enable all users created with the WGSI certifier to access a server.*

Note that access to a server is different from access to databases. Notes servers usually grant access privileges based on location, while database access controls are usually based on a user's job function.

Adding ports   You may need to add ports so that a server can communicate with additional users or servers. For example, if you were connected to a LAN during server setup, you may have enabled only the LAN port. As users are added to the system, it makes sense to let some of them dial in. To do this, you must enable a COM port with a modem attached to it. The Notes server program can then call and answer, using the modem. Port settings are stored in the NOTES.INI file and can be easily adjusted through the workstation client when you are sitting at the server. The enabled port should also be listed in the server document. The following steps describe how to enable a port:

1. In the workstation client software program, Select File, Tools, User Preferences and then select the Ports icon on the lower-left side of the dialog box.

2. Check the COM port that you want to enable.

3. Check the box labeled Enable Port.

You can designate the model number of the modem and other port settings by clicking on the button labeled COMx Options, where *x* is the number of the COM port that you are enabling. Port settings may also be changed by using a *server document.*

Server configuration document   Notes servers have three major functions: routing, replicating, and providing secure access to documents. In addition to these primary functions, the server program has many other tasks that execute regularly. The *server configuration document* is a new feature of the Public Address Book in Notes 4.0 that allows server administrators to make changes to the configuration (NOTES.INI file) of the server, without editing the NOTES.INI file and then restarting the server. This Notes 4.0 feature is an enormous benefit to server administrators, because it minimizes downtime when they are making changes to the server configuration and enables remote-configuration changes by anyone with proper access to the server configuration documents in the Public Address Book.

The Notes server checks the Public Address Book every five minutes for changes to configuration documents that pertain to it. If it finds a change, it edits its NOTES.INI file and puts into that file the change specified in the configuration document.

Because of this feature, it makes sense to create groups that detail the function of the server, as well as the hardware settings for the server. In this way, you can make a configuration change for a group of servers that meet a particular criteria. For example, by grouping all servers with similar hardware characteristics, you can make changes in the NOTES.INI file to all of the servers with a single configuration document.

Server connections   Server connections are set up using connection documents in the Public Address Book. These documents describe which servers should call which other servers, when they should call, and for what purpose (replication or routing). Connection documents are the cornerstone of all Notes networks, because they are the logical infrastructure on which documents will be moved (via replication or routing) from one server to another. Without connection documents, each server is an island, and its users cannot communicate with users on other servers.

See Chapter 26, "Managing the Network," for more information about connection documents.

- *How to Install the Workstation Software*
- *Setting Up the Workstation Software*
- *The Replication Workspace Page*
- *The Workstation Client Software and Security*

17

Deploying Clients

THE NOTES 4.0 WORKSTATION CLIENT SOFTWARE HAS BEEN COM-
pletely redesigned, and many new features and enhancements
have been added. For the system administrator, the best new feature of the workstation client is the *Administration Control Panel,*
which consolidates most of the commands necessary for a system
administrator into a single user interface. This greatly simplifies
the routine tasks of managing certification, server maintenance,
and Public Address Book maintenance, by limiting the number of
places a user must go to execute commands.

As with earlier versions of Notes, the workstation client software works in concert with the server software to let users create,
edit, and view documents stored in databases on the Notes server.

In addition, the Notes 4.0 workstation client now has more commands to let users manage communications with the server and control local and server database settings, and still other commands for administrators to manage the system.

■ How to Install the Workstation Software

Installing the workstation software is much like installing the server software, in that the install program decompresses and copies files so that they can be loaded into memory and run. There are two main differences between the two installation procedures. First, the software being decompressed and copied is different. Second, the workstation software may be installed in many different ways, to suit the system configuration of the user. For example, a laptop user will probably need to have the Notes workstation client software loaded on his or her machine so that when the laptop is not connected to a LAN, the user may still access the software. A user who has a workstation always connected to the LAN may use the program files located on the network file server, to conserve disk space.

NOTE. *The installation procedure has many options. The first and most important choice to make is whether the installation will be to a server to which users will connect to install their workstations or whether this is a stand-alone installation. If you have a file server and you want users to be able to download the software from it, or if you have a file server and you want users to load the program from this file server to conserve disk space on the local computers, select the Install On A File Server option in the Welcome To The Lotus Notes Install Program dialog box. If you check this option, the installation program assumes that you want to install only the workstation software and no server software. To change this setting, select Custom Install.*

Now that you have a server running and have added users to the Public Address Book, you need to install the workstation software so that users can access the system. To install the workstation software, perform the steps that follow, according to the type of installation you want to do.

Installing to a Workstation Drive

To install to a workstation drive, follow these steps:

1. From Windows, choose the Run command and then select the drive and directory that contains the Notes workstation software install program (this may be a floppy drive, a CD-ROM drive, or a network drive).

2. Select the Install (INSTALL.EXE) executable file as the one to run.

3. Enter your name and your company name in the fields provided. When prompted, confirm these entries. This information will be permanently recorded.

NOTE. *If you already have an earlier version of Notes on the PC, the install process will recommend that you install 4.0 in the same directory as the current version.*

To install the workstation software client and all its options as well as documentation on this workstation, choose Default Features; to select only the options that you want installed, choose Custom Features; Figure 17.1 shows the Dialog Box.

Figure 17.1

The Install Options
Dialog Box.

NOTE. *If this is a workstation for a Notes user, do not select Server Install.*

4. So that the program may be easily started, choose the folder into which you want Notes to place the program icon.

5. Confirm that you want the installation program to begin copying files.

6. When you receive the message that Notes has successfully installed the product, click Done.

Now skip to the section titled "Setting Up the Workstation Software."

Installing to a File Server for Shared-Program Use

To conserve disk space and simplify the upgrade process in the future, you may install a shared copy of the program code for multiple users to access. Choosing this install option means that although each user will have some unique files for his or her own use, such as the user ID file, they will load the software into memory from a common file system so each user does not need a local copy. This procedure is excellent for users who will always be connected via network to the file server. In addition the upgrade procedure is simplified because only one copy of new program code must be installed to upgrade all the users that access that code.

1. From Windows, choose the Run command and then select the drive and directory that contains the Notes workstation software install program (this may be a floppy drive, a CD-ROM drive, or a network drive).

2. Select the Install executable file (INSTALL.EXE) as the one to run.

3. Enter your name and your company name in the fields provided. This information will be permanently recorded.

4. Check the box labeled Install On File Server. This will give you options for installing the software to a file server, so that multiple users can access the software stored on this one file system.

5. When prompted, confirm your name and your company name.

6. To indicate that users will use shared program code stored on the file server, choose File Server Install.

7. Click Next.

NOTE. *Using the File Server Install option saves local hard-disk space, because workstations do not receive all of the Notes workstation program software; however, this option requires that when a user is using Notes, he or she must always be connected to the LAN. Figure 17.2 shows the installation types.*

Figure 17.2

The File Server Install or Network Distribution Dialog Box.

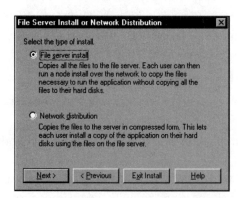

8. To make available all Notes features and documentation, select All Features; to choose only the components that you want to make available, select Customize Features.

9. Enter a drive and directory onto which to install the Notes software.

TIP. *Check with the LAN administrator to make sure that you have proper access to the file server in order to install software and that the drive to which you are installing will be available to all users who will run Notes.*

10. If you selected Customize Features, choose the features that you want installed. If you have sufficient disk space to do so, we recommend installing all the documentation databases, especially for file server installations.

11. When prompted that the installation is complete, click Done.

You have now successfully decompressed and copied the program files to a file server. Users will go through a Node Install procedure before moving on to the workstation setup procedure.

TIP. *Before instructing users to use the Node install procedure, test it by running through it on a typical workstation.*

Installing a Network-Distribution Copy

To install a copy of Notes 4.0 for network distribution, do the following:

1. From Windows, choose the Run command and then select the drive and directory that contains the Notes workstation software install program (this may be a floppy drive, a CD-ROM drive, or a network drive).

2. Select the Install executable file (INSTALL.EXE) as the one to run.

3. Enter your name and your company name in the fields provided. This information will be permanently recorded.

4. Check the box labeled Install on a file server. This will give you options for installing the software to a file server so that multiple users can access the software stored on this one file system.

5. When prompted, confirm your name and your company name.

6. To indicate that users will be able to install their own workstation software from the file server, choose Network Distribution.

7. Click Next.

NOTE. *This installation option uses more local hard-disk space but does not require that users be connected to the LAN when using Notes.*

8. Specify the drive and directory onto which the install program should install the software.

9. Choose to begin copying files.

NOTE. *Notes will copy the files in compressed form to this drive and use these files to install the software to the user's workstation. Users will not be loading shared program code from this drive; rather, they will be running the installation program from this drive, to install the executable code on their workstation's file system.*

10. When you receive the message that Notes has successfully installed the product, select Done.

You have now successfully copied the program files to a file server. Users must go through an Install procedure, to decompress and copy the files to their local machines before moving on to the workstation setup procedure.

TIP. *Test the user-installation procedure on a typical workstation before instructing users to use it.*

Testing the Lotus Notes Node Installer Procedure

The node-installation procedure will set up the Notes workstation to use shared program files that reside on the file server. Some files need to be copied to a drive that is particular to the individual user, to store his or her personal information and configuration. The following steps will guide you through the installation of the Notes software for shared use:

1. From Windows, run the Lotus Notes Node Installer procedure.

2. Enter your name. The Company Name field should be grayed out and inaccessible.

3. Confirm the name registration.

4. Select the drive onto which you want to install the user-specific files.

5. Select a folder into which the Install program should add the Notes icon, so the user can easily run Notes.

6. When prompted, choose Start Copying Files Now.

■ Setting Up the Workstation Software

Setting up the workstation software configures your system to work with the server and also sets up all the unique files for a particular user. When you set up the workstation software, Notes locates the user ID file created for the particular user, based on information entered into the setup program. Notes then confirms that the user is who he or she claims to be, by requiring and then checking the ID-file password that is entered. Next, the workstation setup program contacts the server and checks to see that the user is listed in the Public Address Book. Once these checks are complete, the setup program uses other information that is entered in order to configure the user's workstation to run Notes in the most convenient way, given the user's system configuration.

NOTE. *Notes 4.0 stores much more information in the personal name and address book than did earlier versions of Notes. This excellent new feature reduces the amount of information that must be kept in special text files and gives the user more options in how to work with Notes. For example, the new location documents in the personal name and address book permit multiple configurations to exist on one system. The user can easily switch from a home setup to an office setup. The Notes workstation client will know to switch from the modem port to the LAN port and to send outgoing mail directly to the server's MAIL.BOX file, rather than storing it in the local MAIL.BOX file. This is especially helpful to users of laptops, who are sometimes connected to the LAN and sometimes not.*

The first time the Notes workstation software is loaded and the Notes Workstation Program icon is clicked, the setup program runs automatically.

NOTE. *As with earlier versions of Notes, Release 4 checks the NOTES.INI file for complete settings to determine whether setup has been run before. If the NOTES.INI file is incomplete, setup will run. If you need to reconfigure a user workstation in the future, it is often simpler to return the NOTES.INI file to its incomplete state (first three lines only) than to manually change files.*

To run the setup program then, double-click on the Notes Workstation Program icon (in Windows 95, choose this icon from the Start menu) and then proceed with the following steps:

1. In the Notes Workstation Setup dialog box, select the kind of connection that this workstation will have to the Notes server (LAN, Remote, Both, or None). Notes will use this information to set up the workstation so that in the future it will be easy for the user to access the server.

2. If you have been given an ID file by the person charged with certifying (registering) users, check the box that says your Notes user ID has been supplied to you in a file, select the ID file to be used and, when prompted, enter the password. If you have not been given an ID file, the workstation setup program will assume that the ID file is stored in the person document in the Public Address Book and will extract the ID file from that document.

3. In the Network Workstation dialog box, enter the name of the person who will be using this workstation, and the name of that user's Home/ mail server. Also change the Network type if necessary. The user name

will be entered automatically if you are using an ID file that was distributed to you previously.

4. Select the correct time zone and then click OK.

NOTE. *If prior to running the setup program, the user ID file has been distributed to the user via disk or electronic mail, check the box marked Your Notes User ID Has Been Supplied To You In A File. We strongly recommend distributing the ID files via disk or e-mail. We also recommend that when you are entering the user name, you use the fully distinguished name of the user in order to ensure information is recorded completely and accurately. For example, if the user's name is Jane Sattle, her fully distinguished name might be Jane Sattle/Sales/West/Acme.*

Notes will find the listing for the user in the Public Address Book on the server. If the ID file was not supplied in a file, Notes finds the ID file on the server in the person document in the Public Address Book.

If an error occurs during the setup procedure, Notes will display an error message. The two most common types of error messages are file read/create errors or communications errors. If a file error occurs, check to see if the setup program can access a source (usually, a template) file it needs and that it can write files (for example, check the available disk space and for duplicate file names). During the setup procedure, Notes creates local files, such as the personal name and address book, by using templates. If these templates are not available for some reason, errors occur.

If the problem is a communication problem, test the NIC card or modem, using other software. If this works, there may be a problem on the server side or with the protocol selected. If the device is a modem, try selecting another modem command file. For example, if the workstation will communicate with the server via a TCP/IP network port, see if the user's computer can ping the Notes server, using other communications software. If the ping is successful, further Notes troubleshooting is necessary. If not, a physical or network software problem must be resolved before completing the Notes setup procedure. The following are suggestions that will help you diagnose and resolve problems that may arise as part of the setup procedure.

1. Check the ports, COM, or LAN and make sure that they work, by seeing if another program can use them. Make sure that you have the correct port specified in the Notes setup program and that you have the port configured with the correct modem file or network protocol.

2. Check destination drives and make sure that space is available and that files with the same names are not present and write-protected.

3. Check the source file locations and make certain that all the components you have specified to install (template files, for example) are available on the source drive.

Some of the most common user errors that occur during setup are:

- *Incorrectly spelling the user name.* Remember that the user name will probably include some suffix indicating the hierarchy of the organization that certified him or her. For example, a "fully distinguished" Notes user name may appear: Dave Moore/Finance/West/WGSI. The entire name should be used and spelled correctly.

- *Choosing a LAN connection when the server is not running.* If the server is not up and running when the setup procedure runs, a connection to the server cannot be established and the user will receive an error message. Ensure that the Notes server is up and running before setup runs.

- *Choosing the wrong connection type.* If the server is running TCP/IP and the user selects SPX during setup, the workstation and server will be speaking different languages and will not be able to communicate. Ensure that the user chooses the correct network protocol. If the connection to the server will be via a modem, ensure that the correct COM port is selected and that the correct server telephone number is entered.

- *Server information is incorrect.* During the setup procedure, the setup program will connect with a particular Notes server. It is imperative that the correct name of the server be entered.

- *Choosing "No Connection to Server" when other options fail.* If other options fail, users sometimes try to setup Notes without a server connection. This will cause the Notes setup program to create an ID file that is not part of the organizational hierarchy setup for the rest of your Notes network. If other options do not work, troubleshoot them and retry them rather than choosing this option, as it will not solve the problem.

- *Incorrectly entering the location of the Notes ID file.* If the ID file is supplied in a file, via electronic mail or disk, to the user, he or she must indicate this to the setup program. If not, the user must allow the setup program to search the public name and address book for the ID file, which it will do by default, telling the setup program that your Notes ID has been supplied in a file, when it hasn't or vice versa.

■ The Replication Workspace Page

Using the Replication Workspace page, you can have the workstation send and receive mail (a routing and replication process), replicate all databases, replicate some selected database, choose which of the documents in a database should be replicated, determine whether replication will be one-way or two, and schedule a replication event. Scheduling is especially useful in conjunction with Notes 4.0 passthru servers, allowing a user to replicate all databases on his or her remote computer with one telephone call—see Chapter 26 "Managing the Network" for more information on setting up passthru servers. This addition to Notes 4.0 greatly simplifies remotely using Notes. Coupled with the performance enhancements to Notes 4.0 replication, the Replication Workspace page makes the technology significantly more useful.

Settings on the Replication Workspace page are *location-sensitive*. This means that if you have more than one location document in your personal name and address book, you can have different locations replicate databases with different settings. By default, Notes sets up four different kinds of location documents for a user (detailed in the next section, "The Main Controls"). These may be added to, modified, or deleted.

For example, when at the office and connected to a high-speed LAN, a user may have his or her documents database set up to replicate completely in both directions. When the same user takes his or her machine home and is dialed in, the location that he or she selects is Home, rather than Office, and the Home location document has settings to use the modem port rather than the LAN port. The database settings when the location is set to Home may replicate only the first 40KB of each document, to save time and communications charges. Database replication settings are stored in the DESKTOP.DSK file. Communications settings are stored in the Connection and Location documents in the personal name and address book, and in the NOTES.INI file (editable through the Ports section of the User Preferences screen).

The location form stores information about the current location settings so that users can simply switch from one location, such as an office setup (set up on a network and set to replicate everything completely) to a hotel setup (set up to use a modem port and call a passthru server). The DESKTOP.DSK file stores users' preferences about what to replicate when set up for a given location, such as to replicate only some databases and to replicate those selectively.

The Notes workstation setup program will automatically set up the Replicator Workspace page. It may not be deleted and is always the last tab on the Notes workspace. The Replicator Workspace page provides a graphical environment using action buttons for communicating with a Notes server and allows you to adjust settings for these communications easily:

- The check box to the left of an entry is used to enable or disable that communication.

- The button to the right of each icon is used to specify details of that item.

- The text to the right of each button tells you the status of that icon.

- Clicking the right mouse button while pointing to an entry offers user preferences for that particular entry.

- Any item can be relocated by clicking and dragging it to a new location. The effect is that users can easily reorder the sequence of events during a communication event.

The Main Controls

At the top of the Replication Workspace page are four buttons that help users quickly execute the most common tasks.

Start

The Start button is used to initiate communication with a Notes server. Items will be executed during that communication event. The items that are checked are dependent on the location that is selected in the lower-right corner of the Notes Workstation screen. A policy database may be checked when the location is set to Office, where there is a LAN connection, but this database may be unchecked when the location is set to Travel, when dial-up connections are costly.

Send And Receive Mail

When the Send And Receive Mail button is used, it does just what it says: It takes messages that the user has created and stored in the MAIL.BOX file and sends them to the server, to be delivered to the recipient. Send And Receive Mail then replicates the user's mail file so that new messages that have arrived in the server copy of the user's mail file are copied to the local machine, so the user can read them off line.

Other Actions

The Other Actions button saves time for users by letting them execute only some of the communication components that they normally do. The choices under this button are

- *Replicate High-Priority Databases*, which tells the Notes workstation to call the server but to replicate only databases marked by the user as high-priority

- *Replicate With Server*, which lets the user change the default server that is called

- *Replicate Selected*, which is the same as checking Some Databases Only and selecting Start

- *Send Outgoing Mail*, which tells Notes to call the server and do nothing but send the outgoing mail to it

Help

The Help button brings context-sensitive help to the Workspace Replicator page.

Automatic Entries

The Notes 4 Workspace Replicator page will automatically set up the following types of entries when the workstation is set up:

Databases

An entry for each replica database on the workstation will automatically be placed on the Replicator page at the time the replica is first created. If the user is set up as a remote user, a replica of their mail database gets created during the setup process and the mail and outgoing mail databases are automatically added as entries to the Replicator page. Clicking on the button to the right of a database icon on the Workspace Replicator page will let the user determine the server with which to replicate and the direction to replicate (Receive documents from server is the default), as well as how much of each document should be replicated (truncating). Only users setup for remote access will have an outgoing mailbox on their system. Its file name is MAIL.BOX. When users send mail, the Notes workstation client uses a program called Mailer to take the mail document and store it in the Outgoing Mail database until the document is routed to the server. As with other icons on the Workspace Replicator page, this one can be set up by the user. The only options for the MAIL.BOX file are whether to send documents to the server or not.

Schedules

Schedules are cleverly stored in the personal name and address book in the location document. A schedule in the location document of the personal name and address book tells the Notes workstation client to call a Notes server and exchange information at a given time. The user can specify settings for routing electronic mail as well as replication in the Location document schedule.

NOTE. *For the schedule to be executed, the Start Replication At icon must be selected.*

Database Templates

As always, database templates may be updated using replication to the workstation client. With Notes 4.0, users can easily manage when and when not to update template files from the Notes server. Clicking on the button to the right of the Templates icon on the Workspace Replicator page will let the user determine the server with which to replicate and the direction to replicate (Receive documents from server is the default).

Selective Replication

Selective replication gives the database manager the ability to control what data and design elements are replicated during a replication event. The advantage of selective replication is that it minimizes the amount of information that is exchanged, saving disk space and communication costs. For example, if you have a large customer database and sales offices in 20 cities that need access to this information, by using selective replication, you may selectively replicate only the documents relevant to each sales office.

Notes 4.0 has greatly simplified the process of setting up a database for selective replication, by giving users with proper access the ability to easily limit the amount of information exchanged during replication events. The advantage is better use of time, disk space, and communications resources. Users may click on the Arrow button to the right of any database icon on the Workspace Replicator page to choose to receive complete documents, semi-truncated documents, or document headers only.

Personal Name and Address Books

Notes 4.0, unlike earlier versions, has a database template for personal name and address books that is different from that of the Public Address Book. The advantage is that users are not confused with documents (such as server documents) that are of no value on the workstation client. In addition, the new location document allows users to easily configure their machines for different operating (connection) environments.

For example, take a user who has a laptop computer and, when working in the office, is connected to the LAN. When working from home, the user is connected via a low-cost telephone line. When working from hotel rooms, the user is connected via high-cost telephone lines. This user can specify different databases to replicate from each of these locations. In addition, different connection (port) rules can apply. From the hotel rooms, Notes automatically dials 9 before dialing the server. Location documents are nice extensions to the passthru server options that allow a user to make a single telephone call in order to connect to multiple Notes servers.

The Administration Control Panel

The Notes 4.0 Administration Control Panel has eight buttons, each of which helps the server administrator execute routine tasks for a given part of the Notes system. Many of these buttons create, edit, or view documents in the Public Address Book, because this is where most administrative documents are located. Other buttons run programs to do several tasks, such as registering a new server, a choice found under the Server button menu.

NOTE. *You can run the Administration Control Panel as a stand-alone program; for example, on the server. From Windows' Program Manager or Start menu, choose File, Run and enter the following: "Notes Admin YourServerName," where ServerName is the name of the server that you want to administer.*

■ The Workstation Client Software and Security

Security is a big issue in every section of Notes 4.0. Good security tools have been added to enhance the functionality of the workstation client software. For more information on security and the tools introduced next, please see Chapter 24, "Managing Security."

Local Adherence to ACLs

The Notes 4.0 workstation client adheres to the access controls set in each database for the user. For example, if a user creates a replica copy of the company contacts database on his or her workstation at home and uses a modem to replicate with the server, that user will be able to do on the home (local) copy of the database only what he or she would be allowed to do if using the server copy. The access control level assigned to users is respected, even when the database is being locally accessed. This feature works only if the database manager has selected the option Enforce Access Controls Across All Replicas.

Local Database Encryption

Notes 4.0 databases can be encrypted locally. This means that Notes 4.0 clients or servers can encrypt and decrypt databases using the ID file associated with the particular user or server. The advantage to this for workstation users is that sensitive information can be protected. Even if a laptop were to be stolen, a password for the ID file on that laptop would be required in order to read the information stored in a database on that laptop. This is great news for servers, because it makes it more difficult for anyone gaining access to a Notes server to look at critical information without authorization.

Multiple Passwords on ID files

Although designed with segregation of duties and certifier ID files in mind, the multiple-password feature can be used on any ID file in Notes, including user IDs. For users with high access to the system or databases containing sensitive information, consider adding secondary passwords to ID files. This is a burden for users, but if the security risk warrants it, the extra time required to enter two or more passwords may be justified.

ID Type Checking for Server ID files

This feature prevents someone who gains access to a server ID from calling into a server and then pretending to be the server to whose ID file he or she gained access. This is a particularly helpful feature of the workstation client, because it limits infiltration of someone with access to the server ID file. Remember, to make complete replications possible, servers are typically granted very high access to the databases on Notes servers. Although not totally secure—because an add-in program can be built to use the server ID file as a user ID file—the different treatment of server ID files and user ID files by the workstation client greatly diminishes the threat of improper access by someone posing as a server.

User Types in Database Access Controls

A related feature on the server side allows database managers to list different user types within the database's access control list. The advantage of this is that a server receiving a request from another server to create a document can disallow such an activity, because another server would not create a document in this way.

- *The Role of the Database Manager versus the System Administrator*

- *Understanding Notes Databases*

- *Putting a Database into Production*

- *Setting Access Controls and Roles*

- *Putting the Database on the First Server*

- *Distributing Encryption Keys (Optional)*

- *Providing Key Information*

- *Creating Replicas*

- *Selective Replication*

- *Using Full Text Indexes*

- *Indexing Options*

- *Creating the Full Text Index*

18

Deploying Databases

IF YOU ARE NEW TO NOTES, YOU PROBABLY ARE NOT FAMILIAR WITH
the different components of the Notes system. In fact, Notes is
like two systems in one. It is a network of server and client machines that are managed much like a Novell NetWare or Microsoft
Windows NT network would be administered, and it is an application platform that is managed much like you manage access to database applications. Notes lets you divide administrative tasks into
several categories including, but not limited to: database manager,
server administrator, network administrator, and domain manager.

■ The Role of the Database Manager versus the System Administrator

The database manager is responsible for managing a specific database or set of databases. Database manager tasks include determining which users, groups, and servers may have access to a database, what level of access will be granted, managing database size, ensuring that database replication occurs, and many other routine housekeeping chores. Every Notes database must have at least one manager.

Notes servers use Notes databases to store and use important system information, such as when servers should connect to replicate databases, who is registered on the system, and how to route mail. System managers (people who manage the Notes server network) frequently act as database managers for these system databases that are used by Notes for system purposes (such as the public name and address book).

■ Understanding Notes Databases

Notes databases are *flat file* databases that are designed to communicate their documents to other Notes entities (workstations and servers). Unlike some other databases, Notes databases include all the data and design features and access controls in one file that has an .nsf file extension. These Notes database files are a proprietary file format with APIs available to get information in and out of the file format. Because all of the data, design, and security features of an application are stored in one file, the process of updating design or security features of the database to other replicas works the same way as the updating of data—using replication.

Forms are a key design element of the Notes database that are used to enter information into a document for storage in the database and then again to view the information. Forms are created by the application developer and may contain and define some of the security features the designer builds into the database. Users enter information into fields on forms. These fields on forms map directly to fields in the Notes documents in a database. They may be of many types (text, number, rich text, and date) and can be encrypted as well as signed to enhance security (see Chapter 24 for more information on security features of Notes). Notes 4.0 databases can replicate at the field level, rather than at the document level, while version 3 only allowed replication at the document level. This improves performance and minimizes replication conflicts.

Views sort and organize documents, similar to the way a query or report shows information in a traditional database. Not all views show all the documents in a database. Views can be thought of as a table of contents, a report, or a summary of documents that meet certain criteria. Since information in views can be organized in different ways and can show subsets of the documents in the database, most databases contain views that limit the amount of information a user must sort through to find what he or she needs. Notes 4.0 views have been greatly enhanced so that text can now wrap in columns, and an "action bar" at the top of the screen provides a way for developers to give users meaningful command buttons that allow the user to quickly navigate through the database. Personal views, folders, and agents created by users for their personal use may be stored in the desktop.dsk file in certain circumstances. For example, if a user does not have the appropriate access privileges to store these items in the server copy of a database he or she can store them in the desktop.dsk file of his or her computer.

Notes stores the indexes which display views (different from full text search indexes) in the database, along with everything else. These indexes are automatically created when the designer creates a view. This distinction is important because it can account for size differences in replica databases with the same documents. If one replica has had a view opened that the other has not, its file size will be larger.

NOTE. *Indexes for full text searching, if enabled, are the only components of a Notes database that are not stored in the database. These are separate files stored on the servers and are usually updated regularly by a server task.*

Navigators are a new graphical database element in Notes 4.0. They are areas on the screen where a user can click to execute code developed by the designer. Navigators act as a front end to forms and views to make using the database more intuitive.

Each replica copy of a database has many settings that control how it handles security, replication, and user preferences. These settings are all stored in the database itself, as mentioned earlier. Some of these settings replicate to other "replica" copies of the database, some do not. For example, the access control list (listing who can access the database and with what privileges) of a database may be different on two replicas because the database is used by two different organizations. Alternatively, Notes 4.0 allows the database manager to force a consistent access control list across all replicas if he or she wants to be sure who is accessing the database.

The data itself is stored as a document in Notes. A document is similar to a record in a traditional database in that it contains a set of fields of information. Documents in Notes may contain any kind of data and are all given a unique document ID number, by Notes, when they are created. This number is assigned by the system and used by the system to manage documents. It is not intended for use by users. In addition, Notes will automatically assign certain other fields of information to a document automatically, such as the dates of its revisions in the $Revisions field. This information is stored in the document permanently and may be seen by checking the document properties of any document. Notes 4.0 allows documents to replicate at the field level meaning that if two users change information on the same document on different replica copies of the database, as long as they do not change the same field, Notes will automatically merge the changes (the application developer sets this up when designing the form). Notes automatically performs the merge on Notes 4 databases if the fields that were changed are different. If both users changed the same field, Notes will accept the document with the most changes as the main document and the other document will become a response with a diamond in front of it to represent a conflict, just as it would a conflict in Notes 3. If a conflict does arise, it must be resolved by manually merging the data and removing unwanted information by a user with Editor or higher access to the database. The designer can use techniques such as the ACL, or Author access lists to stop multiple users from being able to edit the same fields. In addition, the form designer can use replication conflict fields to determine how conflicts will be handled.

Finally, Full Text Searching has been greatly enhanced in Notes 4.0 to allow for the searching of attached as well as embedded documents. You can now attach a document created in Microsoft Word or any other desktop application to a Notes document and Notes will search the Word document for matches. In addition, encrypted fields can now be searched and a thesaurus is provided to match words of the same meaning. The full text searching capability of Notes is dependent on an index that does not reside in the Notes database itself. The database manager creates this index and it may be automatically updated by a server task on a regular basis. The index is typically created on the server for all users' benefit, and can be placed on a local copy as well for a particular user's benefit. The decision to create a full text index is based on the user's need to search information. In some databases, it is very helpful to provide full text searching capability. In others, there is little benefit to users and not worth the disk space the full text index will consume. The server program Updall will update indexes on the server based on the settings chosen when the index was first created. These settings can be found in the properties of a database. If the index was created on a user's workstation, they must manually update the index in the properties info box for that database. Updall is scheduled to run on a regular basis by the server administrator.

■ Putting a Database into Production

There are several key steps to follow when putting a database into production. These are highly dependent on the particular deployment but can be categorized as follows: developing and testing the database, determining where replicas of this database will reside, planning for size management and archiving, filtering replication, creating a full text index and setting access controls. We assume here that the database you are going to deploy is already developed and that it is not yet in production on another server.

Before putting a database into production, you should find out if the database has any design features that require special treatment. For example,

- Does the database need to have special roles used to manage access to forms and documents? If so, must users and servers be maintained in these roles?

- Is the database designed to work with an encryption key that must be distributed to users?

- Is the database designed to work with other databases which should have their replica ID numbers listed in the access control list so they can access information in this database?

Discuss these issues with the application developer or person who gave you the database so you can fully understand all of the tools that have been implemented that you will need to manage.

■ Setting Access Controls and Roles

Setting the access controls is perhaps the most important factor in a successful deployment of a database. You must ensure that your fully distinguished name (Mary Ellert/AcctMgmt/WGSI) is listed in the access control list as a Manager. If you do not do this, you will not have the privileges you need to manage the database once it is on the server. Remember, the server will only let you do as much to the database as your access privileges permit. You need to be listed as manager in order to encrypt, create full text searches, or even add and remove users from the list of people who can access the database. At least one backup person should be designated as a manager of the database in case the primary manager is not available.

Access Level	Privileges
Manager	All privileges, including: change access levels of all users/servers, change database settings, encrypt for local security, all privileges of lower levels.
Designer	Can change database design (forms, views, formulas, agents, scripts), create full text indexes, all privileges of lower levels.

Access Level	Privileges
Editor	Can create and edit all documents in the database, including documents created by other users.
Author	Can create, edit, and read documents. Authors can only edit documents they create. This is a common default for databases with many contributors that will not modify the information entered by other contributors.
Reader	Can read documents in a database but cannot add documents to the database or edit documents in the database. Can create personal agents. This is a common access level default for policy databases.
Depositor	Can enter documents into the database but cannot edit, delete, or view documents in the database.
No Access	Cannot access the database. Use as a default for databases with any sensitive material.

The server(s) on which you put the database must also be granted appropriate access. This is critical for replication to work properly. For example, if you do not list the servers that store this database in the access control list, you may find that remote users do not receive documents from the server. This is because when the users create their replica copies, the access control list may have a default access of Reader. When they replicate, their workstation sees that the server is not explicitly listed in the access control list and it does not accept changes from the server because, by default, the server has only read privileges to the database.

Most organizations have a list of servers in a group (by default, it is called LocalDomainServers). If possible, use this group in the access control list as it will be updated by the Notes administrators. Usually, servers within your organization should be granted Manager access to the database. This enables one server to pass all changes—including access control changes, design changes, and document changes—to a replica on another server. If a server is not a Manager, a replica on another server will not, for example, accept changes to the access control list from the server not listed as Manager.

NOTE. *The sequence of replication is also important. If server A had connection documents such that it replicated directly with server B and server C, the access control change would have been passed to server C because server A is listed as a manager of the database in the replica that resides on server C. See Chapter 26, "Managing the Network," for more information on connection documents and server sequencing.*

■ Putting the Database on the First Server

The next step is to put the database on the server. You can put either a "replica" or nonreplica copy of the database on the first server. The best way to put a database on a server is by using Notes commands. If you want to put a "replica" (copy of the file that will synchronize with another replica when two Notes computers "replicate") on a server the best way to do it is with the File/Replication/New Replica command. Similarly, if you want to put a copy of a database on the server that will not replicate with another, you should use the Notes command File/Database/New Copy. If you want to put a new database on the server based on a template, you should use the command File/Database/New. By using these commands you ensure that you get replica and nonreplica copies where you want them.

If the database was ever copied using an operating system command or file utility command (such as File Manager) from another production database, you should not put this copy on the server even if its design has been altered because it may the same replication ID number as another database on the server. If you were to put this modified file on the server (and indeed there is another file with the same replica ID number), the changes you made to this new copy, such as deleting the old documents, changing the design and access controls, may replicate to the other replica.

When placing a database on the first server it is a good idea to start with a fresh replica ID number. To do this, put a copy of the database Icon on your workspace with the File/Database/Open command so that you can select the file that represents this database. You can use this file regardless of whether the application developer gave you the file on disk and it is stored on your local hard disk or whether it is on a Notes server already. Now select the icon for the database that is going into production and use the File/Database/New Copy command to make another copy of the database on the server you specify. Notes will create a new copy of the database and give it a new, unique, replica ID number.

If you have already adjusted the access control list, select the checkbox labeled Access Control List to copy the list into the new database you are creating. The most important consideration here is that you are listed in the database as manager in the access control list. If you are, then any modifications that need to be made can be done later. If you are not listed as the manager, the server will not grant you access to make changes above the access level you are assigned.

Consider the Access List for Users and Servers

Consider who should be allowed to access this database and with what privileges. Check the access control list in the original database to make sure you are listed as a database manager. If you are, you can select the "copy access control list" checkbox and make changes to the access controls later. If you are not listed as a database manager, uncheck this box and Notes will establish you and the server onto which you put this database as managers of the database.

NOTE. *You will only be able to change your access to Manager if you have a local copy of the database that you access without going through the server program. If you do not (you are using a database that is on a server) you can still make a replica or nonreplica copy of it but make sure that someone with access to the destination server where it is going to be placed is listed as Manager of the new replica or copy.*

You can add additional entries for users, servers, and groups later.

IMPORTANT. *You must be listed as the database manager in the access control list or you will not be able to make changes to it once the replica is on the server. Ensure that someone with access to the server has manager access to the database.*

Choose When to Populate the Replica

Consider whether you want to create the replica "immediately" or at the "next scheduled replication." If you choose "immediately," all the documents and design and access controls will be copied while you wait. If you are creating a replica of a database that has significant amounts of data stored, your machine will be unavailable for some time. Bear in mind that a new replica of a database that has large amounts of data will consume significant network resources while being populated. You may want to create such replicas and nonreplica copies at off peak times. Choosing "Next scheduled replication" will create a placeholder for the new replica. When the next replication occurs, all the design elements and data will be copied to the new replica.

Notes 4.0 allows you to force the access control list to be consistent across all replicas of this database. If there are replicas of this database, or will be in the future, you should decide whether you want the access control list to be consistent across all replicas. By selecting this option you prevent different replicas on different servers from having different access control lists. This is useful in situations where you want to ensure that replicas on other servers are not letting users other than those you specify have access to the database. In essence, it helps centralize the security settings of the database.

In addition to providing security on remote servers, this feature will force access controls to take effect on workstation replicas as well. This means that if a user opens a database that is located on his or her local workstation, he or she will have the same access to the database as he or she would if acting on the server copy.

NOTE. *Enforcing a consistent access control list on local replicas is not a security measure. A local user can create another copy of the database and change its access control list to gain access. Although changing the access on the local replica or nonreplica copy of the database will not change the user's ability to receive information from or send information to the server, it is sometimes confusing to users that their privileges are different on versus off the server. For local security, use database encryption described in the following section. Physical security and local encryption are the only tools to protect a Notes database on a local workstation.*

Will You Force Local Encryption?

Notes 4.0 allows you to encrypt databases so that users who gain access to the database without going through the server will still need the correct ID file and password to see the information. If you want to enable this local encryption to prevent users from looking at the database when they get physical access to the server, click the Encryption button and choose Simple, Medium, or Strong encryption.

Local Database Encryption scrambles the information in those fields based on the workstation or server ID file's private key. Only the same private key can unscramble the information. To use the private key of a user or server ID file, the ID file password must be entered.

Will You Encrypt Document Fields?

Fields in Notes documents can be encrypted. For this type of encryption to work, the application developer must have enabled the field for encryption when he or she designed the form. The designer may have set up the database to automatically encrypt document fields when the document is created. Alternatively, users may encrypt documents they wish to secure more rigorously. Since field encryption requires that any user who wants to view the field have the encryption key that encrypted the field, it is generally the responsibility of the database manager to distribute, and create, the encryption key for users. While document authors can create and use encryption keys if a field is properly enabled by the application developer, it makes most sense to have the person responsible for the entire data set (database manager) keep track and control of these encryption keys. Remember, if data is encrypted and the key used to encrypt it is lost, the data that is encrypted is also lost.

Consider How Much Server Disk Space Has Been Allotted

Consider placing a size limit on the database. If you want to force a maximum size for a database, click on the Size button and select a setting from 1 to 4 gigabytes.

Based on volume and content, determine whether the information in the database should be full text indexed. Full text indexes are the only component of a Notes database stored outside the .nsf file. They require extra disk space and processing power. If use of the database will be significantly enhanced by adding full text search capability to the database, click on the check box labeled "Create full text index for searching."

Determine What Database Components to Replicate

If the database you are putting on the server is a replica, determine what components of the database you want to replicate with other replicas. For example, if this replica is for use by a field sales office, it may make sense to use replication settings to limit the documents received by this copy of the database to a specific state or series of zip codes.

With What Priority Will This Database Replicate?

The Notes Network Administrators create "connection" documents in the public name and address book that tell servers when to connect and replicate. Connections can be designated as "High Priority" so that databases that need to be replicated frequently can replicate during these connections. Databases not designated as "High Priority" will not replicate during these connections, saving time so that "High Priority" databases will replicate faster.

If the database you are deploying needs to replicate frequently and your Notes Network administrator has created a connection document for "High Priority" databases, you can set this to be a "High Priority" database in the replication settings.

Will You List This Database in the Database Catalog and File Open Dialog Box?

Think about whether this database should be listed in the Notes database catalog and on the File/Database/Open menu. The Database Catalog database lists all the databases on the server or in the domain, helping users to find information. If the information is sensitive, you may want to keep the database unlisted. By default, all databases in a directory appear in a list when a user selects File/Database/Open. If you want to disable these listings, go to the Database Properties dialog box, select the Design tab and uncheck these options.

Make Sure You Are Configured to Replicate

Make sure there is a connection document specifying that the server on which you are placing the new replica will replicate with another server that has a copy of the database. Connections are created by Notes Network Administrators to tell servers to replicate with each other. If the server on which you are placing this database does not directly replicate with the destination server on which you want another replica to reside, you will need to place a replica on an intermediate server(s) that replicates with both.

Is This a Mail-In Database (Optional)?

If you manage a database that will have documents mailed into it, you will need to set up the database as a mail-in database or have someone with proper access to the public name and address book set it up for you. Mail-in databases work by having a document in the public name and address book that servers can look at and get all the information they need to locate the database and then send the document to that database. If the database has replicas on several servers, one of the servers is specified so that the mail-in document will be routed to the replica located on this server and then the document will then replicate via the normal sequence to other replicas.

■ Distributing Encryption Keys (Optional)

You may want to (or need to) distribute encryption keys to users of this database so that they can encrypt and decrypt documents. If the application developer constructed the database to be used with a particular encryption key, you will need to get or create a key with this name and distribute it to users of the database via electronic mail or on disk. You may want to distribute an encryption key for use with this database even if the designer did not force the use of one in the design. By doing so you will enable users to scramble documents with sensitive information in them. Other users who have the encryption key stored in their user ID file will be able to read the encrypted document without even knowing that it is scrambled. Notes will decrypt the document on the fly.

■ Providing Key Information

As the database manager you are the primary contact for issues and concerns regarding the database. You should change or have the database designer change the About This Database document to include key information about the database. In general you should publish your name and information about how to contact you in this document. In addition, it is a good idea to offer information about how the database is to be used and by whom.

Using Replica Databases

Replica databases are identical copies of Notes databases that share a common replica ID number. When Notes servers connect to replicate information, they search databases for common replica ID numbers and exchange documents between those files. Replica databases, as in earlier versions of Notes, are useful for localizing information so that a live connection to a single file is not necessary. You must consider the performance of your server, the cost of a LAN or WAN connection and the viability of having multiple copies of your database before creating a replica. Remember, some applications, such as ones with transaction-oriented data, usually must reside on only one server.

In general, it makes sense to create replica databases when you have significant user populations that need to access a database from a location where the connection is expensive. If they have a Notes server at their location, a replica copy of a database may save considerable connection costs. In addition, you may want to create a replica of a database if the database is getting significant usage and server performance is deteriorating. By placing a replica on another server, the load may be better balanced.

If the database is very large, you may want to limit the number of replicas you create so as not to use unnecessary amounts of server disk space. From a security perspective, each replica of a database represents an increased threat of data loss or misuse, so limit the number of replica databases you make if the information contained in that database is sensitive.

Notes 4.0 offers enhancements to the database file that improve security, such as the consistent database access list and forcing of local encryption. Database managers need to be fluent in the security features and functions of setting up replicas, as they may be the first line of support if users have difficulty.

■ Creating Replicas

For this section, we will assume that you have an icon on your workspace that represents a database on a server and you want to put it on another server so local users may start entering and using information. You have been granted the appropriate access to the other server by the server administrator.

To Put a Replica on a Server

The first step to enabling replication is to put a replica copy of a database on a server. When the server on which you place this replica replicates with another server that has a replica of this database, the two replicas will be synchronized.

NOTE. *You must have proper access to add a replica to a server. If you have not been granted the Can Create Replica access, see your server administrator. The list of users who can create replicas on the server is established in each server document. The server document for any server can be found in the public name and address book. In general, server managers are charged with adding databases to servers and it is these people who are granted access to do so in the Server documents by the database manager of the public name and address book.*

1. Add the database icon to your workspace.

2. Select the database icon and choose File/Replication/New Replica.

3. Click the down arrow in the server field and specify the server on which you want to place the new replica.

4. Check the database title and file name entries and confirm that they are as you want them to be (they will default to the same as the original database).

5. Choose the settings you want for Encryption, Size, and Replication.

6. Select "Copy access control list" if it has you entered as a manager.

7. Check "Create full text index for searching" if you want to enable this feature.

8. Select either "Now" or "Next scheduled replication" as the time to do the actual copying of database design and documents.

9. Choose OK.

Notes will create a replica copy of the database with the options you have set. The new database will appear on your workspace on top of the other replica icon.

NOTE. *If remote users will call this server to replicate local copies, it is also important that the server be explicitly listed as a manager so it can make changes to the users' local replica of the database. If the server is not listed, users may find that their local replica does not accept data and design changes to the database from the server in the future.*

■ Selective Replication

Selective replication limits the amount of information a server receives or sends during a replication event with another server. In most cases, it is a means of limiting the amount of information stored on a replica on a particular server. A database manager of a remote replica can change the replication settings for that replica, so it is important that a strategy around selective replication be developed if selective replication is to be used.

For example, if you have five field sales offices in addition to a headquarters office and you want to collect contact names centrally, you might use selective replication to minimize communications costs. You would set up selective replication such that each field sales office had a replica copy of the database that only received contact names for its geographical region (using a zip code or state field perhaps). The replica copy at the headquarters location would be setup to receive all documents. The result would be that users in each location would have the contact names they need and headquarters would have all of the names.

NOTE. *Selective replication should not be used if the intent is to prevent some locations from seeing certain information (contacts in this example). If limiting access is the goal, then document security should be used to prevent documents from traveling to servers in certain locations. Without a plan about who will change what selective replication settings, database managers may override each others' settings. Selective replication may also be managed centrally, but only certain features are available for central administration. If it is to be managed centrally, all the database managers must agree upon who will be the central administrator.*

Using selective replication you can have Notes 4.0 automatically remove (delete) documents when they reach a specified age during replication, receive only documents created after a certain date, truncate documents so that only header information (such as the subject and author) will be stored in the replica on which you make the setting, receive only certain documents that meet a specified criteria (this can be set up easily using views or more specifically with a formula), and limit what the replica on which you make the setting sends and receive only certain parts of the database design.

Bear in mind that selective replication is *not* a security measure. A local database manager can easily change the settings to receive or send more information to other replicas. The only way to secure the transfer of certain documents is with read access lists and encrypted fields.

■ Using Full Text Indexes

If you did not create a full text index at the time you initially created a replica of a Notes database, you can add one at any time. Remember, full text indexes may consume significant disk space. You can expect a database that has a large percentage of text to require an index that is about 30 percent of the size of the entire database. Databases with a medium or lower percentage of text will require an index that is 25 percent to 12 percent of the size of the entire database. To calculate the approximate size of the index, multiply the size of the database by one of these percentages. For example, if you have a database that is 100 megabytes and it has a large percentage of text, the index will be about 30 megabytes.

Index files are stored in a subdirectory under the one containing the database. Servers are generally set up to update full text indexes each night when users will not perceive a performance degradation. Like any server process, the updating of full text indexes can cause significant performance degradation, depending on many factors, especially the amount of new information that needs to be indexed.

When new documents are added to the database, users cannot search on them until they are indexed. Once an index has been created on a database you can set up an update frequency in the Database Properties InfoBox that determine when the full text index for that particular database will be updated, such as Immediate, hourly, daily or scheduled. If you set the frequency to Immediate, new documents will be indexed as soon as a user closes the database. This can affect the performance of the database by slowing down access time for users trying to access it. Another option is to set the frequency to hourly, or scheduled. Indexes stored on local file systems for use with locally stored databases must be updated manually for new documents to be indexed, and thus, found during a search.

■ Indexing Options

When you create a full text index you can specify what components should be indexed as well as how the index should be broken up for searching purposes.

Case-Sensitive Index

This option creates an index that you can use to match case. Selecting this option will limit the number of "hits" users receive when full text searching to case-sensitive matches. Think about the information stored in the database and how users will want to retrieve it. If case matching will be useful to them, select this option. Notes will index Computer and computer as two different occurrences if this option is selected. The size of the index may be as much as 10 percent larger with this option selected.

Index Attachments

Choosing this option will index documents that are stored as attachments to Notes documents as well as the Notes documents themselves. This option is useful if you have an application in which OLE cannot be used because some users do not have access to it. For example, if users work on different programs to create documents or if one of the programs they use does not support OLE, attaching documents as files is a better option than OLE embedding of them. The full text search index will be proportionately larger based on the number of attachments in the database.

Index Encrypted Fields

This option will index fields in documents that have been encrypted and will increase the size of the full text search index proportionately. You must have the encryption key used to encrypt the documents in your ID file to index encrypted fields. Users will also need the encryption key used to encrypt the documents to use the full text index and find matches on encrypted fields. If you do not have the correct encryption key to decrypt the data, the field is ignored during the search.

Exclude Words in Stop Word File

This option prevents Notes from indexing common words such as "and" and "or" to save space in the index—up to 20 percent. If you use a stop word file, users will not be able to search for words included in that file. If your stop word file included the word "of," users could not search for the phrase "nick of time." They could still, however, search on "nick" and "time." You can create your own stop word file to suit the vernacular of your organization or industry. The stop word file is located on every server and workstation and is called DEFAULT.STP. When the index is first created on the server copy of the database, and the exclude words in stop file is turned on, the DEFAULT.STP file on the server is used to create the index. All entries in that file at the time of creation are excluded from the index (meaning they will not be searchable), limiting hits for words such as "and." Anyone who has physical access to the Notes data directory on the server can change this file with any text editor, and changes will be used for future indexes that are created. If you are trying to allow users to search for numeric values, you will want to edit the DEFAULT.STP file and take out the line [0–9]+ before creating the index on the database. If the index is already created, you can edit the file, delete the index and recreate it to index with changes to the DEFAULT.STP file.

Word Breaks Only

This option will not allow users to limit their searches to one sentence or paragraph. This is the default option as it will find the occurrence of the word you are searching for regardless of where it lives in the document. Choosing "Word, Sentence, and Paragraph" will allow users to search for words within these break points but takes more index space. Word, Sentence, Paragraph allows the user to use a proximity operator in a query to find words close to each other. For example, if I want to find the words Notes, and Server together in the same sentence I can use "Notes Sentence Server" as my search criteria. The difference in size is approximately 25 percent greater with the "Word, Sentence, Paragraph" option.

NOTE. *You must have Manager or Designer access to a database to create or update full text indexes.*

■ Creating the Full Text Index

1. Select the database you want to full text index.

2. Select File/Database/Properties or click with the right mouse button and choose Database/Properties.

3. Select the tab labeled "Full Text."

4. Click the button labeled "Create Index."

5. Select which elements of the database you would like to index, whether you want to use a stop file, and how Notes should tag index breaks. Notes 4.0 lets you index attachments and encrypted fields.

6. Choose OK.

To set the frequency with which an index will be updated, select the Full text index tab on the Database Properties InfoBox.

19

Replication

REPLICATION IS THE PROCESS NOTES USES TO SYNCHRONIZE TWO identical files. These files may reside either on two computers that are running the Notes server software, or they can reside on one computer that's running the Notes server software and another computer that's running the Notes workstation software. If you have a database on one Notes server or workstation computer and an identical copy of that database on another Notes server computer, replication will keep changes to those files synchronized.

To illustrate, say that a user in the San Francisco office of an organization called WGSI is running the Notes workstation client software on Server B, and that user connects to Server A in Boston, which is running the Notes workstation server software. The user on Server B adds a new contact to the organization's sales contact database. Now, the next time Server A and Server B connect for a replication event, the addition made to the San Francisco replica of the database will be replicated to the Boston replica of the database.

The connection of Server A and Server B for the replication event is either scheduled by the Notes administration team using connection documents in the Public Address Book, or it is manually initiated by the Notes administration team using server-console commands. Figure 19.1 shows how a replication event can be scheduled by using a document in the Public Address Book. For information about using connection documents to schedule replication, see Chapter 26, "Managing the Network."

Figure 19.1

A connection document in the Public Address Book scheduling a replication event between servers in San Francisco and Boston.

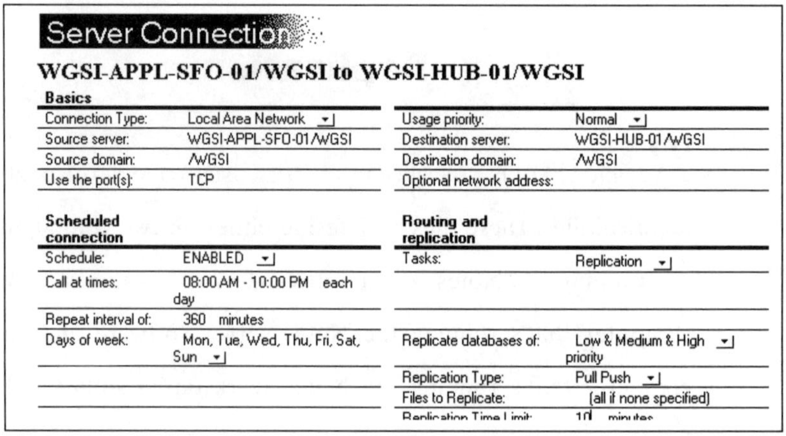

Server Connection

WGSI-APPL-SFO-01/WGSI to WGSI-HUB-01/WGSI

Basics			
Connection Type:	Local Area Network	Usage priority:	Normal
Source server:	WGSI-APPL-SFO-01/WGSI	Destination server:	WGSI-HUB-01/WGSI
Source domain:	/WGSI	Destination domain:	/WGSI
Use the port(s):	TCP	Optional network address:	

Scheduled connection		Routing and replication	
Schedule:	ENABLED	Tasks:	Replication
Call at times:	08:00 AM - 10:00 PM each day		
Repeat interval of:	360 minutes		
Days of week:	Mon, Tue, Wed, Thu, Fri, Sat, Sun	Replicate databases of:	Low & Medium & High priority
		Replication Type:	Pull Push
		Files to Replicate:	(all if none specified)
		Replication Time Limit:	10 minutes

In this chapter, we tell you all you need to know about replication. You will learn how computers connect to replicate, what is replicated, and the components of the Notes system that you must understand in order to manage replication.

■ Why Use Replication?

When replication occurs, Notes geographically and functionally distributes information around a network of computers. Users can look at and work on information locally on a LAN workstation, and they can use a disconnected laptop computer to share information. Through replication, the information that users create and store is distributed to all users of that database.

Notes also relies upon replication to synchronize its directory, the Public Address Book. The Public Address Book must be replicated to each server in an organization, so it is critical that replication be set up; otherwise, the information that Notes uses in order to run is not available to all the servers in the network. You must set up replication such that each and every server in your organization receives changes to the Public Address Book from the other servers in your organization.

Replication enables companies to conserve on connection costs and provide information access to users, even when it is difficult or impossible to connect those users to a LAN. For example, salespeople who carry laptops can keep a replica of their company's contact database and enter new contacts as they meet them. When these users connect to the LAN later on—or when they dial in—all their new entries are added to the server. From there, those entries are added to other users' computers and Notes servers when the entries replicate.

From the application development perspective, replication simplifies the deployment of applications, because design elements and access controls are replicated as well as data during a replication event. This means that as applications are added and updated, new software does not need to be installed. Figure 19.2 shows how Notes can be used to share documents within a workgroup.

NOTE. *In addition to exchanging data (documents), Notes replicates changes to the design and security of the application itself. Replicating design and security features of a database allows the distribution of applications without reinstalling software. This means that if your company uses a travel authorization application written in Notes to manage travel requests, your remote users will see updates to the preferred airline form, after replicating this database. The change to the form is made to the server replica copy of the database by a user with Designer access or above. Other users and servers get the update to the form as they connect with this server and replicate this database.*

■ How Connections Affect Replication

Computers running the Notes workstation software connect (establish communications) with a Notes server to do the following:

- Replicate databases
- Route documents
- Access information on the server

Figure 19.2

One user adds a document, and it is distributed to all other users via the server.

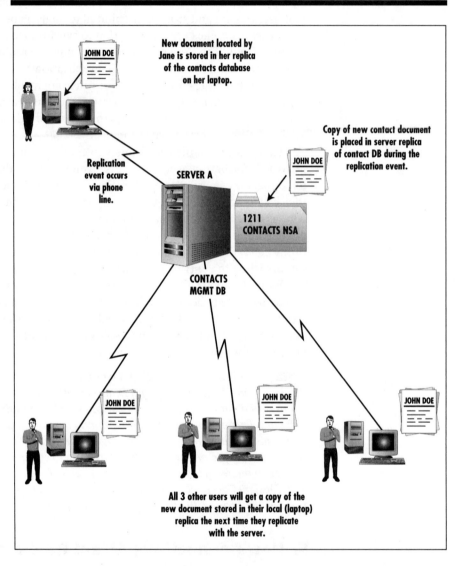

Computers running the Notes server software connect with another computer running the Notes server software to

- Replicate databases

- Route documents

Notes supports a wide array of connection types, including most popular LANs as well as telephone connections. Notes servers connect to replicate when an administrator manually initiates a connection using the server console command Replicate. More often, replication is a scheduled event that occurs as a result of a connection document in the Public Address Book. For more information, see Chapter 26, "Managing the Network."

Scheduling replication (and routing) is a key function of Notes system administration and is covered in Chapter 26. It is imperative that all servers are linked in a replication scheme that assures changes in a database on one server will get to all other servers with replicas of that same database. This is especially important because the Notes network itself relies on the Public Address Book to function. This Notes database is replicated to each Notes server in the domain. Figure 19.3 shows how information is commonly distributed using Notes.

Workstations use the Workspace Replication page to organize replication events between the user workstation and the Notes server. This page is accessed by clicking on the tab marked Replicator. Replication from a workstation is most often done by the user manually initiating it. However, in Release 4, Notes now has excellent tools for scheduling calls to a server so that, for example, remote users can replicate large numbers of documents at night, when costs are lower and the performance degradation caused by background replication is not a concern.

■ Replica ID Numbers

The *replica ID number* is critical for successful replication. After a connection is established, Notes determines which files are replica copies by comparing replica ID numbers. This number is encoded in every Notes database and is unique for each application.

For example, if you created a contacts database from one of the templates that comes with Notes, that database would be assigned a replica ID number when the database was created. If you wanted to put this database on other workstations and servers and use replication to keep all these replica copies synchronized, you would make replica copies of the database that contained the same replica ID number.

You can create these replicas by using operating system tools, such as Windows's File Manager, to do a file copy. Or you can use the Notes command File, Replication, New Replica to create a database with the same design attributes, the same data, and the same replica ID number. That way, when two computers with a replica of your contacts database connect and replicate, document changes in the contacts database are exchanged. Figure 19.4 shows how two computers running Notes software during a replication event look for database replicas that they share, so they can replicate them.

By contrast, you could have put the same database with different replica ID numbers on the server, to accomplish different tasks. For example, if you

Figure 19.3

A database replicating in a hub-and-spoke configuration to other servers.

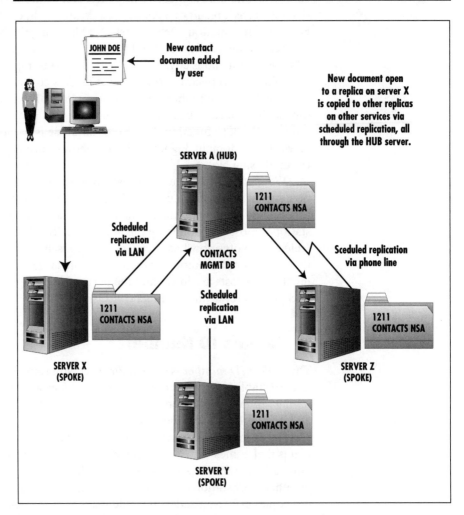

had a sales contacts database running with replica copies on several servers, you might want to make a nonreplica copy of this database to store a different set of data—vendors, perhaps. In that case, you would use the File, Database, New Copy commands to make a copy of the contacts database that is identical in structure but has a different replica ID number, and therefore will not replicate with the sales contacts database during replication events. Figure 19.5 shows how a database may have the same views, forms, title, and even data and may look identical on two computers, but the database does not replicate when computers connect because the replica ID numbers are different.

Figure 19.4

Two computers replicating and then checking and finding a replica ID number that they hold in common.

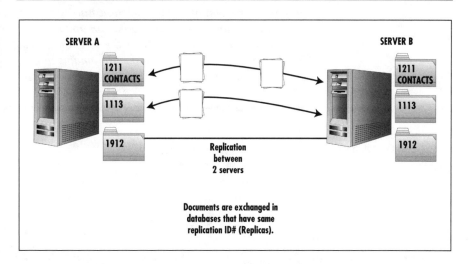

Figure 19.5

Two computers are replicating, but they do not replicate a database that looks identical on the two machines because on each machine that database has a different replica ID number.

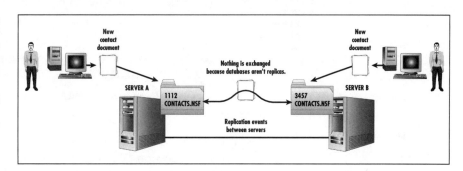

■ The Document ID Number

Every time a document is created in Notes, that document is assigned a *document ID number.* This number is used internally by Notes to track the changes and movement of each document in the database. If a document is deleted, the data is removed, and the document ID number stays in the database as a *deletion stub,* to note that the document was removed. If a document is updated, it is time- and author-stamped, to note that a change has been made. The document ID number never changes.

NOTE. *With multiple copies of a file being synchronized, deleting a document from one copy would be futile if that document were added the next time a replication event occurred. The copy of the database on which the document* *was not deleted would replace it in the copy with the deletion. Notes resolves this logical problem by having deletion stubs stay in the database, retaining the document ID number and noting that an update (deletion) of this document occurred. During replication, then, the deletion is treated much like an update. Figure 19.6 shows how a deletion stub remains in a database, to delete the document from other replicas during replication events.*

Figure 19.6

A deletion stub saved in the database.

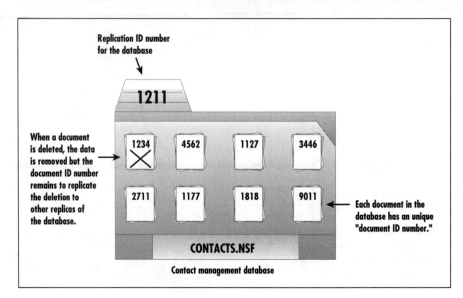

Document ID numbers are essential in the replication process, because the replicator asks the question "What changes have occurred since the last time these two computers replicated this database?" The answer is a list of documents (by document ID number) that have changed and thus need to be synchronized in the two replicas of the database. A change may include a new document, a modification to an existing document, or a deletion stub indicating that a document should be deleted.

■ Overview: What Happens during Replication

The following list outlines some of the procedures that two computers execute when replicating.

1. The two computers connect, so they can communicate directly with each other for the replication event.

2. The server that is called checks its access list to determine whether the calling user or server has appropriate access privileges to use the server that is called.

3. The two computers build a list of all the database files (based on replica ID numbers) that they have in common.

4. The calling computer checks the first database in common and *pulls*—or takes from the replica on the other computer—changes that occurred since the last replication of these two computers (as shown in the *Database Replication History*), including document additions, deletions, and updates. Database access controls are observed.

   NOTE. *The Database Replication History is a log that is stored in each copy of a Notes database and that shows the last successful replication events. Notes uses this log to see what changes need to be replicated. If the log shows a successful replication yesterday at 2:00 a.m., only documents that have been added, changed, or deleted since that time need to be replicated.*

   Notes 4.0 replicates at the field level, meaning that if only one field in a document changed since the last replication, only that field will be replicated, saving time and communication costs.

5. The calling computer then *pushes*—or sends from its replica to the replica on the other computer—changes that occurred in that database since the last replication from the called computer, including document additions, deletions, and changes. Database access controls are observed.

6. Replication history of both databases is updated to show a successful replication event.

Steps 4 through 6 are repeated for all the databases held in common on the two machines.

■ The Replication Process

By default, Notes 4.0 does pull/push replication, which is a change from earlier versions of Notes. In earlier versions, one server called the other server and initiated a replication event. Each server's replicator program then pulled changes from the other server.

In Notes 4.0, the default is to have the calling computer do all of the processing. In this default configuration, the calling server does a pull/push replication: The calling server pulls changes from the called server and then pushes its own changes to the called server. You can change this default push/pull replication either in the connection document in the Public Address Book or by replicating manually with server-console commands.

The advantage to having the calling computer do all of the processing (sends and receives) during a replication event is that this provides natural load management and enables hub servers to support more spoke servers. There is no longer the problem of replication events being queued by one server that has received more replication requests than it can handle at one time.

Because replication is now executed by one computer's processor, it is only that server's log file that shows the transaction record of the replication event. This means that you need to be sure to check the correct server log in order to see that you get all the results you're looking for.

■ Multiple Replicators

Notes 4.0 allows multiple replicator sessions to run on the Notes server. This is a huge advancement, because it makes the Notes server far more extensible. With multiple replicators running on the same machine—especially when used in conjunction with the new multiprocessor server software—a single Notes server can serve many more users and provide adequate frequency in the updates of replicated databases.

To enable multiple replicators on a Notes server, you can simply add additional replicator tasks to the NOTES.INI file in the ServerTasks setting. You can do this manually, by editing the NOTES.INI file, or use a configuration document (a better choice) in the Public Address Book and edit the Replicators setting.

In addition to setting the server to always run multiple replicator processes, you may at any time add a replicator process by using the server-console command. The syntax for adding another replicator task at the server console is

```
Load Replica (Servername)
```

Each time you issue this command, another replicator task is added to the server. You may specify a server with which to replicate by entering its name after the Load Replica command. This has the same effect as issuing the command Replicate Servername.

Finally, you may also run multiple replicator tasks directly from the operating system. To do this, you use a system prompt and issue the Replicate command, preceded by a platform-specific designator. The syntax of a command issued at the system prompt is

```
platform_designator replica [direction] servername
```

The designators are i for OS/2 and n for Windows 95 or Windows NT. By default, the replicator will do a pull/push replication. As the direction parameter, you may specify -p to do a one-way pull or -s to do a one-way push. You may also specify a particular server and/or a specific file name with which to replicate. An example of a system-prompt replicate command for a Notes server running on Windows NT might look like this:

```
"nreplica -p ServerA names.nsf"
```

This command would be issued at the system prompt (rather than at the server console) and would tell the replicator to do a pull/pull replication from ServerA on the file NAMES.NSF.

■ Replication and Security

Any time two Notes computers connect for any reason (replication, routing, or database access), the computers *authenticate* one another: Each computer verifies that the other computer is who it says it is. Then each computer uses server access lists, database access lists, and document Reader lists to determine what access the second computer has and does not have to the first computer's copy (replica) of the database being replicated.

NOTE. *The exception to the usual authentication process is with a Notes 4.0 server feature that's set in the server document in the Public Address Book. This feature allows anonymous connections to a Notes 4.0 server, enabling a server or user with whom the server does not share a certificate to access the server. Database access controls are still maintained for all databases, so you can make a server open: Any other Notes computer may access the server without being authenticated. Be sure to make the default of a database's access control list at least Reader, to let unidentified users find and use information in a given database. This server feature opens Notes to Internet-like functionality, where a Notes server can provide information to anyone, regardless of network. It is also great when used with InterNotes to provide WWW services.*

Security settings are important in the replication scheme, because if the access controls for both server and database access are not set properly for one server, replication may be thwarted for an entire organization. For example, say that you have a database replica on Servers A, B, and C and that Servers A and C are listed in the access control list of all these replicas as Manager—meaning that they have full access to all features of the database. Server B has Editor access to the database. If the connection documents in the Public Address Book have scheduled (sequenced) replication such that

Server A replicates with Server B and Server B replicates with Server C, will a change to the access control list on the Server A replica make its way to server C? The answer is no, because Server B does not have high enough access to change the access control list on the replica that resides on Server C. Figure 19.7 shows how the access control level that is assigned to a server in a database's access control list may affect replication.

Figure 19.7

Servers A, B, and C in an end-to-end replication scheme, with Server B having too low an ACL level to effect an ACL change in the replica on Server C.

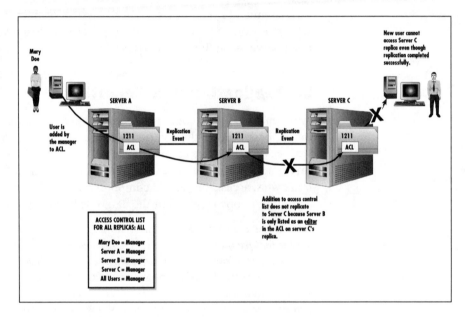

NOTE. *A new Notes security feature for databases allows the database manager to enforce a consistent access control list across all replicas of a database. This means that if an access control level is changed on one replica of the database, all copies of the database must receive the access-control-level change. Since access control levels are replicated during normal database replication, this feature is a great way to ensure that replicas at remote locations do not set up special privileges for some users without the primary database manager knowing about it. If a server does not have Manager access to change the access control level of a database that is set to have a uniform access control list across databases, the database will not replicate.*

For more information on how Notes security works, see Chapter 24, "Managing Security."

■ Replicating to Workstations

Replicating to the Notes workstation software accomplishes the same task as server-to-server replication, in that it synchronizes two copies of the same file. The real difference in replicating to workstation software is that one of the computers involved in the process is running the workstation client software and the other computer is running the Notes server software. Replication events between the workstation software and the server software are treated like client sessions rather than replication events in the server log, so they are more difficult to trace. The database history still shows successful replications on both replica copies and the computer with which the database successfully replicated.

Notes 4.0 has added the Workspace Replicator page, which greatly simplifies all workstation connections to the server. Users may now schedule replications with a server, select what they want replicated, and even preassign options such as the phone-dialing prefix for different calling locations (hotel versus home, for example).

■ Selective Replication

Selective replication gives the database manager the ability to control what data and design elements are replicated during a replication event. The advantage of selective replication is that it minimizes the amount of information that is exchanged, saving disk space and communication costs. For example, if you have a large customer database and sales offices in 20 cities that need access to its information, using selective replication, you may selectively replicate only the documents relevant to each sales office.

Notes 4.0 gives users with proper access the ability to limit the amount of information exchanged during replication events, thereby greatly simplifying the process of setting up a database for selective replication. The result: better use of time, disk space, and communications resources. See Chapter 18, "Deploying Databases," for more information on how to set up selective replication.

■ Setting Up Replication

There are two main components to accomplishing replication. The first is creating a replica copy of a database. As described in Chapter 18, "Deploying Databases," this is an exact copy of a Notes database and contains the same replica ID number—the key to successful replication of two files. The second component is making sure that the two computers on which the replicas will reside are capable and set up to communicate. In the case of two Notes servers, a connection document in the Public Address Book must be present to tell the two servers when and how to replicate.

Creating a replica of a database on a second Notes server can improve performance to users and provide locally relevant information. This will involve costs related to communications, disk space, and administration time. Before placing a replica on a server, be certain that doing this is the best way to achieve your goals. Following are some guidelines for when an additional replica is really necessary:

- Can users access the database in another way; via LAN, for example? If the answer is yes, you may want to hold off on adding a new replica. Unless server performance is not adequate, the speed and low communication costs of LAN access might indicate that you're best off using the existing database on its current server. If users would have to access this database via WAN or telephone line (costly connections), then it may make sense to place another replica on the user's server.

- Are there performance problems with the server on which this database is located? If the server has too many users, inadequate hardware specifications, or is running software, such as gateways, that slow it down, it may make sense to improve performance by making a replica, placing it on another server, and distributing the workload.

- Will replication meet the application needs of this database? Remember, replication does not occur in real time. As a result, a change on one database may not get to a replica of that database for minutes or hours. If the application requires that everyone always look at the most current information, you must have them look at a single file on a single server.

- Is the database approved for use? Your organization should have standards about what databases may be placed on Notes servers and should also have requirements about how those databases are built and secured. Make sure the replica that you want to place on a server follows these guidelines.

- Would a local replica on a Notes workstation client computer enable users to access the database while not connected to the LAN and provide benefit to the organization? If so, you may want to have the user create a database on his or her workstation.

- *New Mail Features*
- *How Mail Routing Works*
- *How Shared-Mail Databases Work*
- *How Connection Documents Affect Mail Routing*
- *Routing Costs*
- *Mail Routing and Security*

20

Mail Routing

In NOTES, MAIL ROUTING IS THE PROCESS BY WHICH A DOCUMENT moves from one machine to another, and it is entirely different from replication. In most cases, mail routing involves moving a document created by one user to another user's mail database.

Unlike replication, mail routing does not attempt to synchronize databases. This process accomplishes electronically what the postal service accomplishes with paper, trucks, and mail-delivery people. Figure 20.1 shows a comparison between mail routing and replication.

Figure 20.1

A mail document moving from one computer to another, compared to two databases being synchronized.

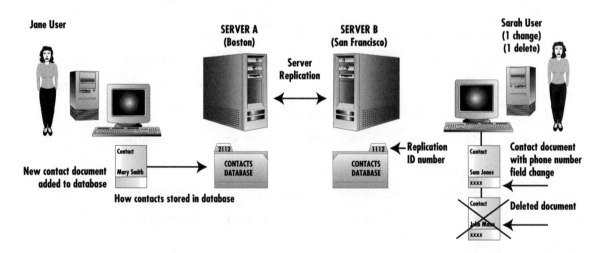

MAIL ROUTING:

Sender

Sender PC with Notes client running

Mail is sent to Server by workstation software.

SERVER A

The sender may have *saved* a *copy* of memo in his mailbox.

SENDER'S MAIL DATABASE

RECIPIENTS' MAIL DATABASE

Server's router program takes mail and delivers it to destination document.

Sender PC with Notes client running

Recipient

Recipient uses Notes client to ask server program for access to mail database. When granted, she sees new message.

REPLICATION:

Jane User

New contact document added to database

How contacts stored in database

CONTACTS DATABASE

SERVER A (Boston)

Server Replication

SERVER B (San Francisco)

CONTACTS DATABASE

Replication ID number

Sarah User (1 change) (1 delete)

Contact document with phone number field change

Deleted document

■ New Mail Features

Notes 4.0 has many new mail features that make it an even better platform than before for deploying mail. We like some of the following best:

- *Enhanced user interface.* The new Notes mail interface gives users excellent remote capabilities coupled with folders, a three-pane mail window, drag and drop, "type to match" to simplify addressing messages, and much more. In summary, Notes 4.0 provides a world-class e-mail client.

- *Shared-mail databases.* The shared-mail databases in Notes 4.0 greatly reduce the amount of disk space required to store user mail, because they store messages addressed to multiple users only once. This feature is a boon to disk-space-conservative administrators.

- *Internet document linking.* This feature allows users of Lotus Notes to link documents on the World Wide Web, as links in Notes mail messages; users who read the messsage can access the Internet document by double-clicking on it. See the chapter entitled "InterNotes" for more information on using documents on the World Wide Web.

- *Mood stamps and stationery.* Notes 4.0 mail lets users set the mood of their mail messages so that the messages convey more meaning. When users choose a mood stamp in Notes-4, the mail message will get a graphic to indicate how the author of the message is feeling. For example, when complaining about a co-worker, users may want to stamp their message with a "flame!" Users can also now personalize the mail they send, by creating custom stationary saying something such as "From the desk of."

- *Out of Office notifier.* This default feature in Notes mail is an agent that lets mail senders know if the mail recipient is away for a specified period of time. It's a simple but welcome enhancement.

- *Prevent copying.* If you've ever sent an e-mail message that came back to haunt you, this feature is for you. Notes 4.0 lets you prevent mail recipients from forwarding, copying to the Clipboard, or printing e-mails that were sent to them.

The purposes of mail routing are different from those of replication. Mail routing is perfect for one-on-one communication; for exchanging information without an organizational structure in place (such as a Notes application). Mail routing is often used to provide a private channel of communication for items not for common knowledge; and for alerts, as in the case of system alarms.

■ How Mail Routing Works

If mail routing is to move documents from one place to another, it must have a structured procuedure for managing this movement, just as replication has a structured procedure for synchronizing two databases. Figure 20.2 shows how a mail document moves from one location to another in a simple Notes server configuration.

Figure 20.2

Mail routing from one user on Server A to another user on Server B in the same Notes Named Network.

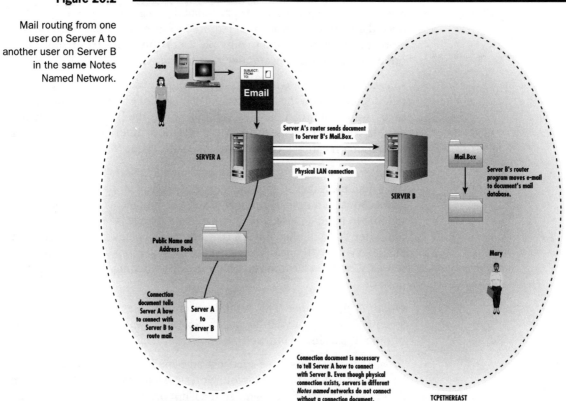

When Notes routes mail, the steps are very much like those used when the U.S. Postal Service routes a letter:

1. The user creates a mail message on his or her workstation and then selects Send.

2. The workstation verifies the message recipient and stores the message in the MAIL.BOX file on the recipient's server.

3. The Router program on the recipient's server looks at the message, determines that the recipient's mail database is on the same server, and moves the message to the recipient's mail database.

If the recipient's mail database is located on a different server, in other Notes Named Networks, or other Notes domains, then additional steps are taken. If the recipient's mail database is on the same server, the Router immediately delivers the message to the recipient's valid database.

If the recipient's mail database is on another server in the same Notes Named Network, the Router on the sender's server immediately delivers the message to the MAIL.BOX file on the server where the recipient's mail file is located. The Router program on that server picks up the message and delivers it to the recipient's mail database.

If the recipient's mail file is on a server in a different Notes Named Network, and there is a connection document specifying how and when to connect to that server, the mail Router waits to connect to the recipient's server, based on the information in that connection document. The Router delivers the message to the MAIL.BOX file on the server where the recipient's mail file is located. The Router program on that server picks up the message and delivers it to the recipient's mail database. As Figure 20.3 shows, servers deliver mail to each other based on rules set in Connection documents in the Public Name and Address book.

Figure 20.3

Server A delivers a mail message to Server B in another Notes network, based on information supplied by a connection document.

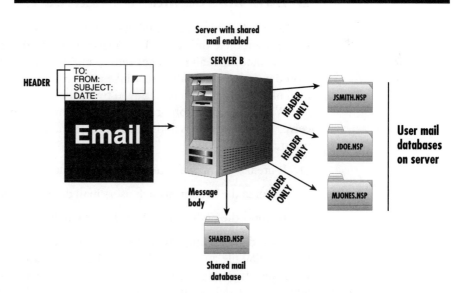

If the sender's server cannot directly communicate with the recipient's server because there is no connection document and/or because the two servers do not share a common protocol, the Router determines a route to the destination server and calculates all the servers that the mail message will have to pass through to get to the destination. The Router then delivers the message to the first server in that route and stores the message in the MAIL.BOX file of that server. This process is repeated at each server, or *hop,* until the document reaches its final destination server and is placed in the mail database of the recipient.

NOTE. *The Router always calculates the lowest cost route to the destination server and sends mail that way. This route is automatically adjusted, if the message becomes undeliverable, by adjusting to cost routing basis. See the later section "Routing Costs" for more information.*

As you can see, the key components in mail routing are the Router program that's running on the Notes server, the Public Address Book, and the MAIL.BOX file. Users' mail databases and shared-mail databases play a more static role. The Router program looks in the Public Address Book to find the person document of the recipient and determines where that user's personal mail database is located. The MAIL.BOX file stores messages that are waiting for the Router program to process them.

■ How Shared-Mail Databases Work

In Release 4, shared-mail databases enhance Notes mail. Administrators can save considerable disk space by using shared-mail databases. With shared mail enabled, all mail messages sent to multiple users on the same server are stored in one shared database. Links are then created to users' individual mail files, so users' mail is retrieved by a process identical to the normal one.

When the Router program on a shared-mail-enabled Notes server receives a message that is addressed to more than one person, here's what the program does:

1. It breaks the message into two parts: header and body.

2. It stores the header in each users mail database, with a link to the body.

3. It stores the body in the shared-mail database.

Shared mail is entirely transparent to users, because the header stored in a user's mail file automatically loads the body from the shared-mail database. Users may treat the shared-mail message just as they would any other. When all users have deleted the header from their mail files, the Collect task running on the server (at 2:00 a.m., by default) deletes messages from the shared databases that no longer have user links to them.

If shared mail is enabled on a server, the shared-mail database is kept open by the mail Router or by any user who is reading a shared-mail message. You may need to either shut down the server in order to make backups of the shared-mail database or use backup software that does not require files to be closed.

If a user receives encrypted mail or if the user's profile (in the person document of the Public Address Book) is set up to encrypt incoming mail, the encrypted mail documents are stored in the user's personal mail database.

Setting Up a Server for Shared Mail

Shared mail involves using two Notes databases that are automatically configured when you set up the server's Router program to use shared mail. To enable shared mail at a server console, you issue the following command:

```
Tell Router Use filenam.nsf
```

The Router will create the file you specified and use it as the database in which to store mail that is addressed to more than one user. In addition, the Router will create a database called MAILOBJ.NSF in the Notes data directory and set the NOTES.INI variable Shared_mail=2. The MAILOBJ.NSF database is used much like the MAIL.BOX file is used for messages addressed to one user. As long as the setting =1 or 2 is in the NOTES.INI file, the server will use shared mail whenever the server is restarted. A setting of =1 turns on shared mail for more than two recipients, a setting of =2 turns on shared mail for one or more recipients. A setting of 0 turns off shared mail for that server.

Adjusting Handling of Shared Mail

The NOTES.INI file contains a setting Shared_mail= that can be set to 0, 1, or 2. You may change this setting by editing the NOTES.INI file with a text editor or by using a server-configuration document in the Public Address Book.

0 tells the Router program not to share mail on this server. 1 tells the Router program to share mail only if a message has two or more addresses. 2 tells the Router program to share all mail that comes to that server for delivery.

Linking and Relinking Users' Mail Databases

When you've set up the server to use shared mail, Notes automatically links mail databases to the shared-mail database for messages that come in thereafter. If the server's and the users' mail files have been in use for some time, you may be able to save significant disk space by linking existing mail files to the shared-mail database.

To link a mail file or a directory containing mail files to a shared-mail database, enter the following command at the server console:

```
Load Object Link JDOEMAIL.NSF SHARED.NSF
```

where JDOEMAIL.NSF is the file name of a user-mail database and MAILOBJ.NSF is the name of the shared-mail database. You may specify an entire directory such as "mail," rather than just a single file, to link all the users' mail files to the shared-mail database.

When you issue the Link command, the server goes through each mail file, finds shared messages, stores the body in the shared database, and leaves the headers in the user-mail database with a link to the body. If a user's mail file has more than five documents linked to the shared-mail database, the Link process will also compact the user's mail database in order to reclaim unused space.

You may create additional shared-mail databases if you either want to keep the databases smaller in order to improve performance or if you want to link certain mail users to certain shared databases. To do this, you will still use only one shared-mail message store, MAILOBJ.NSF. However, you may add additional shared-mail databases to store messages that have already been delivered or that contain messages that have been manually linked to them.

To create additional shared-mail databases, issue the following command at the server console:

```
Load Object Create NEWMAIL.NSF
```

NEWMAIL.NSF can be any name that you wish to give the new shared-mail database. Once you have created the new mail database, use the Link and Relink commands to link mail files to the database.

If you create an additional shared-mail database, you may want to use the -Relink option to reassign links from one shared-mail database to another. To do so, you issue a command at the server console. The syntax is

```
Load Object Link -Relink JDOEMAIL.NSF SHARED.NSF
```

JDOEMAIL.NSF is the name of either the user's mail file or the directory containing all the mail files that you want to link to the new shared-mail database.

Getting Statistics for Shared Mail

By default, Notes 4.0 servers run the Collect task at 2:00 a.m. Among other functions, this task collects statistics about shared-mail databases running on the server. If you have set up the server to also run the Reporter task, you can view the results of the shared-mail statistics in the Stats and Events Reports database (STATREP.NSF) in the Shared Mail Statistics view of that database. You may get statistics on a shared-mail database on a server that is not running the Reporter task by issuing the following command at the server console:

```
Show Stat Object
```

The console will display statistics for every shared-mail database on the server.

■ How Connection Documents Affect Mail Routing

Connection documents are used by the Router program only to deliver mail to servers that are not part of the same Notes Named Network. This means that the recipient's mail database resides on a server that is part of another Notes Named Network within the domain or even on a server that is part of another domain. Connection documents are used by the server's Router program to build a "route" to the destination server and also to determine which ports will be used and when to establish the connection. The Router program uses information in the connection documents that build its routing table in order to determine the lowest-cost route for delivering mail.

The Notes 4.0 Connection document is greatly enhanced and provides more information, as well as more granular controls for managing the connections to connect servers.

■ Routing Costs

Routing is determined by the server's Router program, which retains, in memory, a *routing table*. This table determines the different possible routes a document might take in order to get from the sender's server to the recipient's. Routing cost bias is used only when a server is delivering mail to a server in another Notes Named Network; otherwise, it is ignored. Messages going to servers in the same Notes Named Network are always delivered immediately to the destination server. Each route to another Notes Named Network has a cost associated with it that is based on the kind of connection that will be involved. By default, a network connection via LAN has a cost of 1, and a telephone connection has a cost of 5. The Router will send mail via the lowest-cost route.

For example, say that a user on Server A wants to send a mail message to a user whose mail file is on Server X. If moving the mail message from Server A to Server X requires seven LAN connections (cost=7 connections * 1 for each connection), and another route is available that requires 1 LAN connection and one telephone call (cost=1 LAN connection (1) + 1 Telephone connection (5)), the Router program will choose the latter, because it is the lower-cost route.

How the Router Chooses a Route

The mail Router program is self-adjusting, to account for bumps on the road. If a message cannot be delivered by the lowest-cost route, the mail Router increases its assessment of cost for this route.

Here's the Router's process for deciding on a route:

1. Select the route that costs the least, based on the memory-resident routing tables built off the server, connection, and domain documents in the Public Address Book.

2. If the lowest-cost route fails, increase the cost of this route by 1.

3. Send mail by the lowest-cost route.

NOTE. *If there is another route that is equal to or lower in cost than the original lowest-cost route, the Router program uses this route. In the earlier example, one failed delivery would have changed the route, because there was a difference of only 1 in the original routing cost, meaning that once the routing cost was adjusted for that route, it became a more costly one than another route.*

Routing tables are built in memory when the server program starts. The cost bias is adjusted upward whenever a delivery failure occurs; for example, when a server cannot be reached. Routing tables are also adjusted when an incoming connection is received from a server that was previously unavailable. In that case, the cost bias is taken downward. Routing tables may always be reset by restarting the server. Routing tables are also dynamically reset at regularly scheduled intervals by the Indexer task running on the server. For dynamic routing tables to work, you must include "Update" in the ServerTasks setting in the NOTES.INI file to enable the Indexer. When an update is made by the Indexer, the Router can tell a change has ocurred by a view refresh date in the public name and address book and reads the new information, once a server comes back on line.

Overriding Routing Costs

You may override routing costs by adjusting the Routing Cost field in the connection document for a particular server connection with a number from 1 to 10. Be careful when adjusting the Routing Cost field, because you could inadvertently create routing loops, where mail messages loop continuously, or you could disable the correct selection of alternate paths. If you do decide to adjust the Routing Cost field, make sure you thoroughly test the impact of your changes.

Here's how to test your changes:

1. Make a list of all the servers to which the one you changed may potentially connect.

2. Make a list of all the servers that may connect to your server (and, hence, may route messages through your server). Then do one of the following:

   - Create mail messages that will test each connection and make sure that the messages are successfully delivered. If you enable delivery notification on these e-mails, you will receive information about the route that will help determine the cause of a mail-delivery failure.

   - Use the new Mail Trace option in the server console by selecting File, Tools, Server Administration; clicking on the Mail icon; and then selecting Send Mail Trace. Mail Trace is a Notes 4.0 feature that works only with Notes 4.0 servers and provides a report from either the last Router in a route or from all Routers in a route, detailing what the Router did and the results.

     `Server Administration Console is correct.`

   - Consult the Notes Log file to determine how often other servers are being contacted and which servers are being chosen first. You may want to do a database analysis on the Notes Log, as described in Chapter 27 "Managing Servers."

■ Mail Routing and Security

One of the great things about Notes mail is that it is just like any application built in Notes. It uses all the same tools and conforms to all the same requirements. With this in mind, take a look at a few security elements as they pertain to mail routing. Notice that the key components of running Notes mail are all Notes databases.

Server Access

As with any other application developed in Notes, in order to send or receive mail, a user must be granted access to a server. Since mail is sent out by the workstation software and then received in a database accessed via the workstation software, to receive mail, the user must be listed on an access list of his or her mail server. A user can send mail to any server to which he or she has access. Servers must also be listed on server access lists, to ensure that they can connect to send messages. If Server A has a message to send to Server B, it must be on Server B's access list in order to place the message into the MAIL.BOX file on Server B.

The Users Mail Database

The users mail database is a customized Notes application. The Notes 4.0 mail template is greatly enhanced and boasts many new features. It remains, however, a standard template that can be changed if an organization has special requirements. For example, an organization may require that all mail be marked with a level of confidentiality and be electronically signed. Using ordinary application development tools, an organization can customize the mail template to accommodate such requirements.

To access their own mail database and receive or save mail they have sent, users must be listed in the access control list of that database. A user's Notes server should also have access to that database, so that the server can deposit new messages into the database as the Router picks up messages for the user.

The MAIL.BOX File

The MAIL.BOX file is a holding tank for messages that are waiting for the Router program to pick them up and send them out. As a result, messages from many separate users are stored here. It makes sense, then, that the default access to this database is Depositor. Users and servers should both be granted Depositor access, so they may put messages in but not look at messages that are already stored there (just as with a U.S. Postal Service mailbox).

The Public Address Book

The Public Address Book is significant in relation to mail routing, because this is the database that the Router program looks to in order to find out where a recipient of a mail message has his or her mail database stored and how to connect to get to the recipient's mail-database server. In addition, groups that are defined to do so in the Public Address Book will grant access to important databases such as the MAIL.BOX file.

In addition to helping protect data with the use of groups, the Public Address Book stores the connection documents that tell servers when and how to communicate. These documents are largely what makes a bunch of servers a network. It is important that only authorized administrators have access to creating and editing the documents. A database's access control lists and a document's Reader and Author lists limit users' access to these documents.

Shared-Mail Databases

Shared-mail capability in Notes 4.0 is designed with security in mind, such that users are given access to only those messages to which they should have access. The following list highlights some security items regarding the use of shared mail.

- Shared-mail databases are encrypted with the server's public key, so that only the server ID file with the corresponding private key can decrypt the database.

- The shared database has only the server's name in it, so only that server can access it.

- The server is listed as a server in the User Type field of the access control list, so that a user with access to the server ID (such as an administrator) cannot use the Notes workstation client to access the database.

- Shared-mail databases contain no views, and none can be added to them.

- Users cannot add an icon for a shared-mail database to the desktop of a Notes workstation.

Mail Bombs

Mail bombs are not unique to Lotus Notes; they can be created with any system. A mail bomb is a message sent to a user, where that message contains code to subvert security. For example, a mail message might be sent that contains a button or file attachment that says "Click here." When the user clicks, code might be executed to mail that user's user ID file to another user, change the access control on databases of which he or she is manager, or install a virus.

The best defense against this possible intrusion is to educate users about it. Lotus is currently working on tools to help administrators minimize this threat.

- *About InterNotes*
- *Setting Up the Notes Web Navigator*
- *About InterNotes Web Publisher*

21

Deploying InterNotes and Web Publisher

THE LOTUS NOTES INTERNOTES WEB NAVIGATOR IS A SET OF features provided with Notes 4.0 that enables Notes 4.0 users to gain access to information stored on the World Wide Web. Inter-Notes can be used to access HTML, FTP, and gopher files via the Web.

InterNotes does not provide the ability to publish documents (such as a home page) onto the World Wide Web. Publishing capabilities are provided by the Notes Web Publisher, a separate add-in product. Web Publisher 4.0 is available for free on the Lotus home page (http://www.lotus.com) and will ship in the box with Notes 4.1.

■ About InterNotes

The Notes 4.0 server maintains a connection to the Internet directly or via proxy. A server task called WEB runs on the server just like any other task. This program retrieves documents that users request, converts them into a Notes 4.0 document file format, and stores them in the Web Navigator database. The Web Navigator database is a Notes 4.0 database that is designed to store and manage documents that are retrieved from the World Wide Web. This database stores all the Web documents for the given InterNotes server that are requested by users so that these documents may then be accessed with the Notes workstation client. Users then view the Notes document from the Notes workstation client. Figure 21.1 illustrates the process of retrieving a document from the World Wide Web.

Figure 21.1

Users accessing documents on the World Wide Web using the Notes workstation client and server programs.

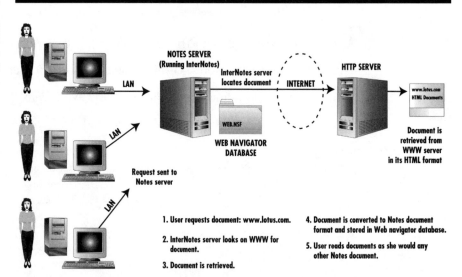

1. User requests document: www.lotus.com.
2. InterNotes server looks on WWW for document.
3. Document is retrieved.
4. Document is converted to Notes document format and stored in Web navigator database.
5. User reads documents as she would any other Notes document.

Why Use Notes Instead of a Web Browser?

By using a server to access documents and store the documents that are retrieved in a Notes database you get the best of both worlds. From the Internet you benefit from huge amounts of content. From Notes you get an easy-to-use client with content enhancing management tools and a simplified Internet connection, and data management with Notes server capabilities. For example, once the document is stored in the Notes database, the Notes 4.0 server can automatically refresh the document from the World Wide Web so that it is always kept current. As many documents on the WWW change frequently, this can save a great deal of time and communication charges for frequently accessed documents, as the server program automatically refreshes documents—if you tell it to—so that each individual user does not need to do the refresh while connected.

Another benefit of using Notes to access the WWW is the ability for disconnected use of WWW documents. Users may choose to create a replica of the Web Navigator database just as they would any other Notes database so that they can easily refer to WWW documents when they are not connected to the network. When the users replicate the database or a subset of it to their laptop, their local replica will be updated just as would any other local replica. They can then disconnect to review the documents using Notes views, full text search, and categories.

Finally, another of the many benefits of using Notes to access the Internet is that the Web Navigator database provides a simple means of developing an interface for users to find WWW documents. Because the documents users review are actually Notes documents that were created by translating HTML documents (Hypertext Markup Language), all the security and data manipulation features that are so easily accessible in Notes can be used on documents retrieved from the Web.

How Does a User Request a Document?

To access a document on the World Wide Web, a user specifies the document he or she wants to find by clicking on its URL link in an existing Notes document or by entering the URL (uniform resource locator). URLs are a standard means by which documents on the Internet are named so that they can be understood and retrieved by any program designed to retrieve such documents. The URL link is a text string that is stored in a Notes document. By double-clicking on the URL link, the user is issuing a command to access that particular document.

For example, if the URL link resides in a mail message and the user double-clicks on it to access the WWW page, the Notes workstation client will look first in the user's personal address book to see if an InterNotes server is specified in the user's current Location document. If an InterNotes server is specified in the personal Location document, the workstation client will contact the InterNotes server specified to request that the server obtain the document and store it in the Web Navigator database so that the user can access it.

If the user does not have an InterNotes server specified in the current Location document in his or her personal name and address book, the workstation client will look in the user's Location document for the home/mail server that is specified. It will then look in the Server document in the public name and address book to see if an InterNotes server is specified there. If an InterNotes server is specified in the Server document of the user's home/mail server, then the workstation client will contact that server and request the document. If no InterNotes server is specified in the Server document for the user's home/mail server, the user will receive an error message. Figure 21.2 shows the logic Notes will use to find an InterNotes server to access the document specified in the mail message.

Figure 21.2

How the workstation client determines to which server it should send requests for Internet documents.

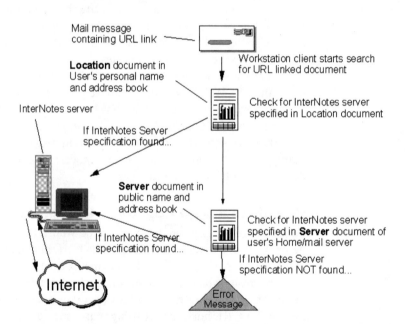

Instead of using the URL link in an existing document to open a document, Sally may open the URL directly. The InterNotes server will retrieve the document and store it in the Web Navigator database. Sally can open the URL by one of the following four methods:

- Clicking on the "Open URL" icon in the Notes Web Navigator database

- Selecting "Open URL" from the actions menu when in the Notes Web Navigator database

- Clicking "Open URL" when looking at a document in the Notes Web Navigator database

- Clicking the "Open URL" SmartIcon if she has added it to her Smart-Icon set

The Web Navigator database is a template that comes in the box with Notes 4.0. It provides a simple interface for users to locate and use documents stored on the World Wide Web. Because the documents are retrieved by the server and stored in this database, many features available only in Notes, such as views, action bars, and Notes' rich application development capabilities, make these documents easier to manage and secure. Figure 21.3 shows the opening screen in the Web Navigator database.

Figure 21.3

The Home Page of the InterNotes Web Navigator database provides a simple to use, customize, and understand, front-end to the World Wide Web.

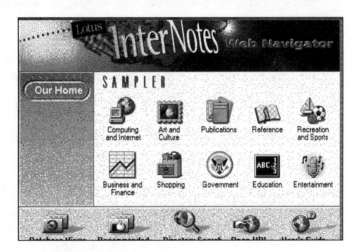

The Web Navigator adds ease of use and customizability to the World Wide Web. Documents can be accessed and managed with Notes icons, views, security, and programmability.

About Using the Web Navigator Database

The Web Navigator database offers several tools for managing documents. All of these, of course, are built on the rich set of Notes tools that is available to users, database managers, and developers. The following features are provided for both administrator and user convenience.

Automatic Refreshing of Documents

Documents stored on the Web are likely to be updated frequently. The Notes Web Navigator database comes with a "refresh" agent that will compare the date of the Web page in the database with the Web page on its Internet server. It will automatically update documents that are out of date.

Accessing and Organizing Web Pages

Users can sift through large quantities of data more easily when they are stored in a Notes database. In addition to storing documents in various categorized views, users can store documents in the "My Bookmarks" folder, in other private folders they create in the database, or by forwarding the documents with Notes mail to themselves, other users, or databases. These viewing capabilities of the InterNotes Web Navigator database make finding and using information much easier than it might be with a traditional Web browser.

To find a document, users may do one of the following:

- Select the Database Views icon from the home navigator and then choose a view that will provide the information in a helpful format.

- Click on one of the Sampler icons from the home navigator to get a listing of URLs they may want to access.

- Click on the Our Home button to go to their company's home page.

- Enter the URL of the document.

- Double-click on the URL link in a document they have on the screen.

To store a document in the "My Bookmarks" folder, the user simply opens the page he or she wants to store, and clicks on the Bookmarks button, or drags the document from the view into the My Bookmarks folder icon.

To store a document into another private folder, the user first creates the folder in the database by selecting Create/Folder, entering a name for the new folder, and clicking OK. The folder is now available when the user selects View/Show Folders. He or she may drag the document to the new folder.

To forward a document, a user simply selects the Forward button when viewing the document and enters his or her own name or another user's name as the recipient.

Security of Documents

Some Internet servers require authentication before granting access to documents. This is accomplished by having a user enter a name and a password. When the InterNotes server receives a document from such a server, it will encrypt the document with the user's public key and store it in a private folder after the user initially views the document. By so doing, the document is protected such that only the person who retrieved the document may actually read it.

Recommending and Sharing

The Web Navigator database provides a convenient means to recommend and share documents retrieved from the Internet. A user may click the Recommend button on any document he or she wants to recommend. The user then fills out the dialog box with a comment, a category, and a rating (1–5) of how he or she would rate the document. This recommendation is then stored in the Web Navigator database so that other users can click on the "Recommend" icon in the Web Navigator home screen. Users can see recommendations by Category, Recommended, Top Ten, or Web Navigator database view. This is a great way to help users sift through the enormous amount of data on the World Wide Web: Let them help each other.

Database Size Management

The Web Navigator database comes with a purge agent that can be set to automatically purge documents from the database. Since there are literally millions of documents stored on the World Wide Web today, your Web Navigator database could become quite large without good management tools. The Purge agent offers flexibility to purge documents based on different criteria. The InterNotes administrator can have the Purge agent remove documents that have been stored for a certain length of time, remove documents that have a certain expiration date, or remove documents that are larger than a specified size.

Using Web Forms

Internet documents often gather input from users with fill-out forms. These forms can be used for everything from registering customer information to taking orders, depending upon the complexity of the form that is created. The Notes Web Navigator database provides support for these forms automatically. When a user requests a document that contains a form, the InterNotes server will automatically create a Notes form to collect the information when the user opens that page. The information entered by the user is then converted back to HTML and submitted back to the Internet server. If the Internet server sends a response to the form that was filled out by the user, the document is stored in a private folder with the user's name within the Web Navigator database.

■ Setting Up the Notes Web Navigator

Setting up the Notes Web Navigator is a two-part process, just as is setting up Notes itself. You must first ready the server and then the workstation clients. Setting up the workstation clients individually may not be necessary, depending upon how you want them to connect to the InterNotes server. The following instructions will provide information to help you decide the best configuration for the Notes workstation client software.

System Requirements

The Web Navigator is a Notes database and the WEB program is a Notes server task. These are the two main components necessary to run InterNotes. Since they are both Notes 4.0 features, you need only meet the Notes 4.0 system requirements. In addition to the basic Notes 4.0 requirements, you will need to have a connection to the Internet. This must be either a leased-line connection to an Internet Service Provider or a network connection to a proxy Web server that connects to an Internet Service Provider. Furthermore, you must have the TCP/IP network protocol running on the InterNotes server.

NOTE. *The Web Navigator supports the CERN httpd and Netscape proxy servers.*

   Security Note: Anytime you connect a computer to the Internet by running TCP/IP on it, you open up the potential for others on the Internet to access computers within your organization. To properly defend against such intrusion, see the section "Securing InterNotes" later in this chapter.

   The following are some suggestions that will help you prepare for running InterNotes:

1. Have plenty of disk space. There is an enormous amount of content for users to collect, and you want to make sure the Notes Web Navigator database does not gobble up all of the available disk space on the server.

2. Have plenty of RAM (random access memory). Given the amount of information that is likely to be stored in the Web Navigator database, you will want to have the server optimized for speed. We recommend 48MB to 64MB of RAM.

3. Check your Internet connection before installing the Web Navigator. You should be able to send and receive messages to and from other computers on the Internet with the computer on which you will run InterNotes. For example, you should be able to successfully use a "ping" utility to see if another computer is responding.

Setting Up the Web Navigator

Once again, the Web Navigator requires the installation and setup of three main components:

- The WEB task that runs on the Notes server (InterNotes server).

- The Web Navigator database stored on the InterNotes server (based on the WEB.NTF database template).

- The Internet connection from your InterNotes server to the Internet. This is either a leased-line connection to a service provider or a network connection to a proxy server.

The only other requirement to run the system is that you configure the Web Navigator by completing a "Web Navigator Administration" document in the Web Navigator database. This document controls several features of the Web Navigator database, such as under what conditions to purge or refresh documents.

Simple Setup of the Web Navigator

Following are the steps you will need to take to get up and running with the Web Navigator immediately. Following later in this chapter are more detailed instructions on using the Web Navigator.

1. Start the WEB server task on the server you have designated to be the InterNotes server by entering the following command at the server console or remote console: **LOAD WEB**

2. Enter the fully distinguished name of the server you have selected to be your InterNotes server into the "InterNotes" field of the Server document(s) of the user's home/mail server. By entering the InterNotes server name in the Server document of the user's home/mail server, when users want a page from the World Wide Web, their workstation will know to use the correct server to request it. You will not need to modify the Location documents for each user who will use the Web Navigator. This saves an enormous amount of configuration time.

The Web Navigator is ready for use, presuming your connection to the Internet is up and running. You may tell users they can access the Internet by opening up the Web Navigator database with the File/Database/Open command.

NOTE. *When you entered the LOAD WEB command, the WEB task automatically created a Web Navigator database based on the template. It is named WEB.NSF and must retain this name, as the WEB task will not work properly if the database is named anything else. The default access to this database is Reader. The server administrator's name is granted Manager access* *and is entered into the "WebMaster" role so that he or she has proper editing rights to the Administration document that was also created when the WEB task loaded. In addition, the server name is also listed as a Manager. A Web Navigator Administration document is also created at this time. You may edit this Administration document to customize settings for your organization.*

Housekeeping

Now that you have installed the Web Navigator, there are some housekeeping issues to which you must attend to ensure that the Web Navigator functions properly in your organization. These may include

- Setting up the WEB task to run whenever the Notes server starts

- Setting up specific user workstations to automatically locate the InterNotes server if their home/mail server document does not specify an InterNotes server

- Enabling mail routing to the Internet

- Enabling or disabling the automatic creation of URL links

- Setting the Database Access Controls for the Web Navigator database

- Configuring the Web Navigator database

Setting Up the WEB Task to Run whenever the Notes Server Starts

In most cases you will want to configure the InterNotes server so that the WEB task runs whenever the server starts. This will simplify management of the server because you will not need to issue the LOAD WEB command each time the server loads.

To have the WEB task run automatically, simply add it to the NOTES.INI file ServerTasks= setting using the following steps:

1. Open the NOTES.INI file into any text editor such as Notepad.

2. Find the line that begins with ServerTasks=.

3. After the last entry in this line, enter a **,** (comma) and the word **WEB**.

4. Save the file and exit.

The next time you load the Notes server program on this machine, the WEB task will automatically run.

Setting Up User Workstations to Automatically Locate the InterNotes Server

The Notes workstation client will need to know which Notes server is acting as the InterNotes server so that it can direct requests for documents to this server. There are two ways of setting up workstations to know how they must connect to InterNotes. The first is to enter the name of the InterNotes server into the InterNotes field of the Server document of the server that acts as the home server. As described earlier, using this method, any user whose home server document specifies the InterNotes server name in the InterNotes field will automatically be able to access the InterNotes server.

Figure 21.4 shows the InterNotes server setting in a Server document. This field can be completed to give users who use this server as their home server access to the InterNotes server.

Figure 21.4

The InterNotes server setting in a Notes Server document.

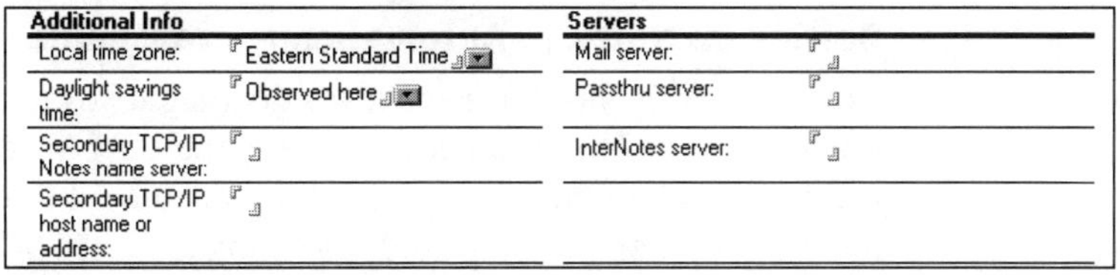

Alternatively, you may enter the name of the InterNotes server you want a particular user to access by entering its name into one or more of the Location documents in his or her personal name and address book. Using this method will require that each and every user who will access the InterNotes server have an InterNotes server specified in one or more Location documents in his or her personal name and address book, if no InterNotes server is specified in a user's home/mail server. While this process can be simplified by using Setup Documents in the public name and address book for use when setting up existing users, it will require a great deal of work if your installed user base is large. Furthermore, this method will require more maintenance if you ever change your server topology. In general, it is best to use this user-specific method only for traveling users who will access multiple InterNotes servers based on their location, or users whose home/mail server's Server document is not updated to include the name of an InterNotes server. This may be the case if you want to grant only some users access to the Web Navigator database.

NOTE. *The two setup methods are not mutually exclusive. The workstation client will first check its location document and then check the Server document. Therefore, you may enter the name of an InterNotes server in a Server document and enter another InterNotes server into particular users' Location documents.*

Enabling Mail Routing to the Internet

Some links in Web pages have a "mailto" URL link. When one of these links is encountered, the page expects a mail document to be created and mailed to a specific mail account. This technique is often used to facilitate electronic orders, registrations, and other online transactions. InterNotes depends upon Notes mail to support these links:

1. Make sure that Notes workstation clients are set up to use Notes mail.

2. Make sure that there is an SMTP MTA (mail transfer agent) or SMTP mail gateway connected to your Notes system that will enable electronic mail to be sent to an Internet address.

3. Configure the Administration document of the Web Navigator database by entering the domain name of your SMTP gateway into the SMTP domain field.

Setting Up Notes to Automatically Create URL Links

When the Web Navigator retrieves documents from a Web server, it creates hotspots in the Notes document where the URL links in the HTML document were. This enables readers of the document to jump from one document to another, as one would if looking at an HTML document with links to other HTML documents. In addition, the Notes workstation client automatically creates links out of URL text in documents stored in databases other than the Web Navigator database.

For example, if a user were to send a Notes mail user an electronic mail message and include a URL (http://www.microsoft.com, for example), that URL would be converted automatically to a hotspot in Notes, even though it is stored in the user's mail database, not the Web Navigator database. If the recipient (a Notes mail user, with the mail message stored in his or her Notes mail database) double-clicks on the hotspot—which will appear with green underlined text—a request will be sent to the InterNotes server to retrieve the document, convert it to Notes document format, store it in the Web Navigator database, and display it to the user.

If you wanted to tell someone who uses Notes mail to check out the Lotus home page, you could send that person an e-mail message with the Lotus home page URL in it. You would type something like:

```
Hi Sally,

Check out the Lotus home page: http://www.lotus.com. I think you'll like it!

Eric
```

When Sally reads the e-mail message using the Notes workstation client, it will automatically interpret the http://www.lotus.com as a link to a document on the World Wide Web. If Sally double-clicks on it, just as she would a link to another Notes document, Sally's InterNotes server will retrieve the document for her. The Notes workstation client creates links automatically for any URL that is in a Notes rich text field by interpreting the text and converting it to a link.

If you want to disable the automatic conversion of text representing the URL to the URL link:

1. Select File/Tools/User Preferences.

2. Click the Basics icon.

3. In the Advanced Options section, deselect "Make Internet URLs into Hotspots."

Setting the Database Access Controls for the Web Navigator Database

The Web Navigator database is the place users go to access information retrieved from the Web. By default, all users will be able to read documents that are stored in the database. Users to whom you grant Author access and above will be able to create Rating and Web Tour documents.

There are three types of documents that users may access in the Web Navigator database:

- *A Web Page document* is one in which information retrieved from an Internet server is stored in Notes format. Don't forget that when looking at Web pages using the Notes Web Navigator, you are actually looking at a translated copy of information that was stored in HTML (Hypertext Markup Language) on an Internet server. The Web Page document in the Web Navigator database may contain documents translated from HTML, FTP file attachments, or gopher menu lists. Web pages often contain URL links to other documents. These links enable users to jump to other Web pages. The Web Navigator database is primarily a storage place for Web Page documents.

- *Web Tour documents* contain historical lists of Web pages that have been previously opened using the InterNotes Web Navigator by a particular user. You can create Web Tours, save them in the Web Navigator database, and use them again later. You can also use Web Tours created by anyone else, just as they can use yours. Web Tour documents are created when a user clicks a button telling Notes to create a historical list of the pages accessed in the current session. This list may then be edited if the user so chooses. Web Tours are not administrative tools for tracking user access to documents. This functionality could, however, be added to the Web Navigator database using Notes 4.0 application development tools.

NOTE. *Web Tours are public documents. If a user creates a Web Tour, it may be accessed by anyone with access to the database.*

• *A Rating document* appears in one of the Recommended views. Rating documents are used to find out what Web Page documents have been recommended by other Notes Web Navigator users in your organization. Rating documents are a great way to help users sift through the enormous amount of content available on the Internet. They can reference what others in your organization felt were worthwhile. Using the Recommended view of the Web Navigator database will let users sort through the Web Page ratings by reviewer, category, popularity, and other simple criteria.

You must grant appropriate access to all users of the Web Navigator database. In general, all servers in your organization (usually listed in the group LocalDomainServers) should have Manager access to the database. In addition, at least two people should be designated as Database Managers (you and a backup) to handle the day-to-day chores of keeping the database running smoothly.

We recommend assigning the following access privileges to the database. Access controls for the Web Navigator database are set just as they would be in any other Notes database, by selecting File/Database/Access Control.

• All servers (usually the group LocalDomainServers) in your organization—Manager

• You and a backup Database Manager—Manager

• The fully distinguished name of the server which acts as the InterNotes server—Manager

• Default access to the database—Author

Configuring the Web Navigator Database and Server Task

As described above, the WEB server task automatically creates a Web Navigator database the first time the program loads. In addition, the WEB server task creates a "Web Navigator Administration" form. This document, stored in the Web Navigator database, is where all configuration information for the Web Navigator is set and stored. When the WEB server task initially creates the document, it enters default information that enables you to run the Web Navigator immediately (unless you connect to the Internet via a proxy server). You may want to customize settings in the Web Navigator Administration document to better serve your organization's particular needs.

Using the Web Navigator Administration document you can:

• Manage thresholds and services

- Automate document management

- Manage access (beyond what database access controls offer)

- Establish proxy server configurations

- Determine how information will be displayed in the Web Navigator database (fonts, icons, and so forth)

    To edit the Web Navigator Administration document:

1. Open the Web Navigator database.

2. Open the All documents View.

3. Select Actions/Administration.

4. Change settings as necessary.

    The following sections describe the settings that are available in the Web Navigator Administration document.

Managing Thresholds and Services

In the Basics section of the Web Navigator Document, you can adjust settings to manage settings that determine thresholds for users and database size as well as WEB program options. Figure 21.5 describes fields available in the Basics section of the Web Navigator Administration document.

Figure 21.5

The basics section of the Web Navigator Administration document.

Server Basics	
InterNotes Server name:	Your Server Name Here
Maximum database size:	500 MB
Maximum concurrent users:	25
Services:	HTTP, FTP, GOPHER
Server logging:	Off
SMTP Domain:	
Raw HTML save options:	Save in CD record

Here are explanations of each of the fields:

InterNotes Server Name   This field is case-sensitive and should be automatically completed when the WEB program creates the Web Navigator Administration document. If you change the name of the server running the InterNotes Web Navigator, you must change this field to include the "canonical" server name. This field is required. A canonical name specifies the components of the name before each component. For example, if the "common name" component of a server is acme-01, in the canonical name, this would be expressed as CN=acme-01. CN is an abbreviation for common name.

Maximum Database Size   Enter the maximum size (in megabytes) to which the Web Navigator database may grow. This will limit the amount of space the database can consume on the InterNotes server hard disk. The default is set to 500 megabytes by the WEB program when it initially sets up the Web Navigator Administration document.

Maximum Concurrent Users   Enter the maximum number of users that may access the Web Navigator database simultaneously. This field will help you manage server performance by limiting the number of requests that can be given to the server at one time. The default number set by the WEB program when the Web Navigator Administration document is created is 25. You should adjust this number based on the performance of your InterNotes server and the actual workload with which the server is taxed. For example, if most of the users accessing the Web Navigator are not searching for new documents, but rather accessing documents already stored in the Web Navigator database, you may want to increase this number significantly, as the server is not expending excessive processing cycles retrieving documents from the Internet. If the threshold is exceeded, the server will create a message telling additional users that they may not access the server at this time.

Maximum Documents per Private Folder

Enter the maximum number of documents a user may store in his or her private folder. This field helps you control a particular user's use of Web Navigator database space. Remember, Web pages that are retrieved from authenticated Internet servers are stored in private folders, so users who request such pages will need to have space available in which to store the documents they retrieve. The WEB program sets the default for this field to 200. You may want to increase or decrease the number of documents users can store in their private folder based on resources and user requirements.

Services   Enter the Internet services to which you want to provide access on this InterNotes server. The Web Navigator supports HTTP, FTP, and gopher. These services provide information from the different Internet protocols. HTTP is used for retrieving HTML documents. FTP is used to retrieve (download) binary files, and gopher is used to retrieve documents stored on gopher servers. The WEB program will set this field to provide access to all of these services by default. You may limit access to certain services if you like. The only real reason to do so is if you have limited server resources and need to maximize performance. For example, disabling FTP may save significant server resources, as users will not be able to download files. Since this process may take considerable processing for large files, overall server performance may be greatly improved.

Server Logging   Select On or Off to determine if the WEB program's activities will be logged to the InterNotes server log (LOG.NSF). The WEB program will set this field to Off by default. You may want to enable logging and have these messages sent to the server console for logging in the server log file when troubleshooting InterNotes server problems. Once a problem is resolved, you may once again disable logging. Logging set to On will show the beginning and end of InterNotes sessions.

SMTP Domain   Enter the name of your SMTP mail domain that your system uses to route mail to the Internet, if you have such a gateway. This field is used by the Web Navigator to know where it should send messages that are created as a result of a "mailto" link, discussed later in this chapter.

Raw HTML Save Options   Enter an option for saving the HTML source of pages retrieved. Remember, the Web Navigator retrieves pages from the Internet and converts them into Notes documents, which it then stores in the Web Navigator database. This field gives you the option of saving HTTP information in its original HTML format (coded text) in the Notes document. You may want to do this if you will use the information in its native format (HTML) for some other process. This will add significant size to each Notes document stored in the Web Navigator database. The default for this field is "Do Not Save HTML." The option "Save in CD record" is for a future feature.

Managing Documents and Controlling Database Size   In the Document Management section of the Web Navigator Administration database you control under what circumstances the InterNotes server will delete documents, and whether you want the WEB program to automatically refresh or update documents whose source has changed since it was stored in the Web Navigator database.

Since your Web Navigator database has the potential to become very large, you will need to fine-tune the settings in this section to control the size of your Web Navigator database while balancing performance considerations. For example, if you create settings that too frequently remove documents from the database, you may increase server load because users will re-request those documents. All document purging is executed by the Purge agent stored in the Web Navigator database. This agent uses the information you provide to determine what documents it will remove from the database. Figure 21.6 shows the Document Management section of the Web Navigator database.

Figure 21.6

The Document
Management section of
the Web Navigator
Administration document
allows you to determine
how documents will be
purged from the
database.

Purge Documents   Choose Yes or No to enable or disable the Purge agent.
The WEB program will set this field to Yes by default. If you select No, none
of the other settings in this section of the Web Navigator Administration document will have any effect on the database.

Delete Expired Documents   Choose Yes to have the Purge Agent remove
documents that are no longer available on their original Internet site. This is
a helpful way to manage content, as it relies upon the publishers of pages on
the Internet to determine the value of older documents. If the author of a
document has removed it from his or her Internet site, it is a good indication
that the document is outdated. If you select No, when documents are removed from their original location it will not trigger their removal from your
Web Navigator database. The default value for his field is Yes.

Expire Documents Older Than   Choose the criteria that suits your storage
requirements (30, 60, 90, 120 days or none). Documents will be removed
from the database once they reach the age you specify. If you select None,
documents will not be removed from the Web Navigator database based on
their age. The default for this field is 90 days.

Expire Documents Larger Than   Choose a size based upon which documents will be deleted. Documents larger than the size you select will be deleted when the Purge agent runs. The default is Over 256KB. This setting is
useful because it lets you remove documents that are very large. Once again,
you need to balance performance considerations. If large documents are

frequently used, then you may use more server resources by deleting these regularly, as users will repeatedly retrieve them.

Purge to What Percent of Maximum Database Size   Choose a percentage of maximum database size. The Purge agent will delete documents using the previous purge settings until the database is reduced to the percentage of total allowable size (based on Maximum database size setting in Basics section of Web Navigator Administration document). This is a great option as it gives you the flexibility to delete only as many documents as necessary to make adequate space available in the Web Navigator database.

Delete Private Documents   Check box to indicate Yes so that the Purge agent will delete documents that users store in their private folders. The default for this setting is unchecked, meaning do not delete documents that users have stored in their private folders. If a user has a local replica of the Web Navigator database on his or her computer, they may use access controls and filters to retain private documents after they have been purged from the server replica of the Web Navigator database. In addition, they can also move these documents to other relevant databases if the want to keep the information available.

Delete Recommendation Documents   Choose Yes to indicate that the Purge agent should delete rating documents. Once again, the setting you choose here is organization-specific. You may find that keeping Rating documents in the database actually reduces server load because it may limit the amount of documents users retrieve to find the content they want. Rating documents are not refreshed to indicate changes to the pages to which they refer.

Purge Rating Documents after How Many Days (Future Feature)   Choose the option to specify how frequently you want Rating documents removed from the database. Since pages stored on the Internet change frequently, it makes sense to remove Rating documents that refer to the Web documents frequently enough so that they do not encourage users to retrieve documents that no longer exist! The Purge agent will remove Rating documents that are older than the number of days you specify.

Refresh documents   Choose Enabled or Disabled to determine if the Refresh Agent should have the WEB program automatically refresh documents stored in the Web Navigator database to ensure that their content is up to date with the original Web page stored on the Internet server.

Setting Up the Purge and Refresh Agents

By default, the Purge agent will run each night at 1:00 a.m. and will purge documents based on the criteria you specify in the Web Navigator Administration document. The Purge Agent will use the following order when evaluating and then executing the criteria you have established:

1. Check the Expired header (if one exists) and delete the document in the Web Navigator if that page has expired. Since not all Web pages have Expired headers, do not rely exclusively upon this to manage the size of your database.

2. Check the creation date of the document for each document stored in the Web Navigator database and delete pages older than the number of days specified in the "Expire documents older than" field.

3. Check for documents larger than the size specified in the "Expire documents larger than" field and delete these documents

4. Check the "Delete Rating documents" field, and if "Yes" is specified, delete documents that are older than the date specified in "Purge Rating documents after how many days" field.

NOTE. *The Purge Agent will stop running when the database size specified in "Purge to what % of maximum database size" is reached. It will not delete additional documents, even if they meet the deletion criteria, once the database reaches the size specified.*

Server Document Settings to Run Web Navigator Agents

Notes servers provide controls for the types of agents that may be run on them and conditions for running them. The Web Navigator database relies heavily upon agents for managing documents, so it is important that the server settings allow these agents to execute their tasks. There are, by default, three agents in the Web Navigator database: Averaging, Purge, and Refresh. Each is set up with a schedule to run late at night when server load should be at its lowest. To set up the Server to allow the agents to run properly, you will edit the Server document for the Notes server that runs the InterNotes Web Navigator task and database according to the following steps:

1. Open the Server document for the Notes server with the Web Navigator running on it.

2. In the Agent Restrictions section, enter your name in the "Run restricted LotusScript agents" and "Run unrestricted LotusScript agents" fields.

3. In the Nighttime Parameters section, enter **3600** in the "Max LotusScript execution time" field.

4. In the Nighttime Parameters section, enter **80** in the "% of polling period before a delay" field.

5. Save your changes to the Server document and exit.

6. Enable the agents in the Web Navigator database by opening the database, choosing View/Design, and checking the box next to the agent you want to enable. Select or enter the name of your InterNotes server as the computer that will run the agent as shown in Figure 21.7.

Figure 21.7

Setting the server on which Web Navigator agents will run.

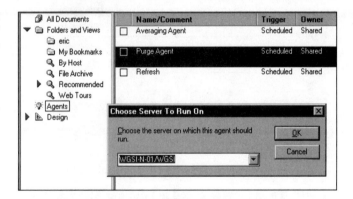

Even if the server settings are configured to allow agents to run, you may choose to run any agent manually rather than automatically. To run an agent manually:

1. Open the Web Navigator database.

2. Select View/Agents.

3. Highlight the agent you want to run.

4. Choose Actions/Run.

To change the time that any agent runs:

1. Open the Web Navigator database.

2. Select View/Agents.

3. Double-click on the agent whose schedule you wish to change.

4. Click on the Schedule button to change the time schedule for that agent.

Controlling Access to Web Sites

You can explicitly grant and deny access to specific Web sites using the Web Navigator Administration document. To do this you enter the names of the of the sites to which you wish to grant or deny access in the corresponding field(s) of the Access Control section of the Web Navigator Administration document. By entering names of sites into the Deny Access field, you prevent the user from accessing these sites because the server will not process the request to access that site. Figure 21.8 shows the Web Navigator Administration document fields you will use to set up access to Web sites.

Figure 21.8

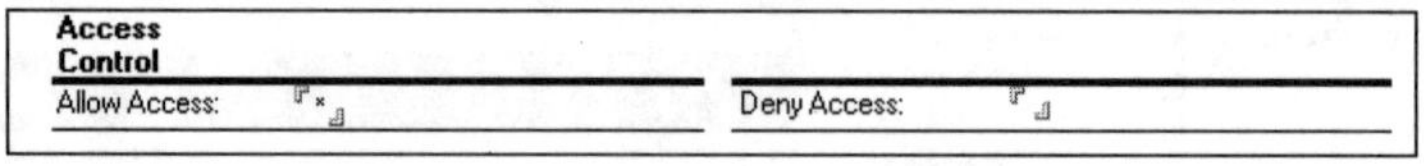

Allow and Deny Access
fields in the Web
Navigator Administration
document.

Here are some tips for controlling access to Web sites:

- By default, if the Allow Access and Deny Access fields are blank, all sites may be accessed by users.

- You may use one wild card in each field.

- If a site is referenced in both the Allow Access and Deny Access fields, the more specific reference will take precedence. For example, the site www.microsoft.com in either the Allow Access or Deny Access will take precedence over a *.com reference in the other field.

- If a site is referenced in both the Allow Access and Deny Access fields and both have the same level of specificity, the Allow Access takes precedence.

- You may use site names, such as www.lotus.com, or IP addresses to specify an Internet site in the Allow Access and Deny Access fields. InterNotes will do a DNS (domain name service) lookup to resolve names. If it is unable to resolve the name using DNS, access to the site will be denied.

Using Proxy Servers to Connect to the Internet

A proxy server is a computer that is used to provide access to information through a firewall. This common configuration is a security measure to ensure that your internal network is not available to external users or organizations. The InterNotes Web Navigator allows you to connect to the Internet using a proxy server. The Web Navigator supports CERN httpd and Netscape Proxy Server. Figure 21.9 shows the Web Navigator Administration document fields you will use to set up proxy servers.

Figure 21.9

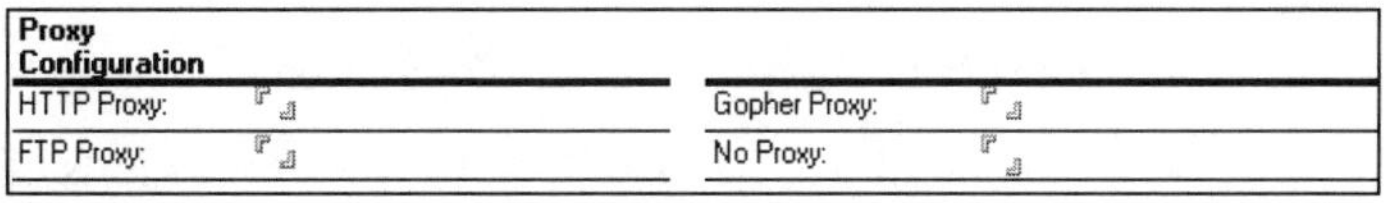

Proxy server fields for
different protocols in the
Web Navigator
Administration document.

Proxy Configuration		
HTTP Proxy:	Gopher Proxy:	
FTP Proxy:	No Proxy:	

To connect to the Internet using one of these proxy servers:

1. Open the Web Navigator Administration document.

2. Fill out the following fields in the Proxy Configuration section:

   • *HTTP Protocol Proxy*   Enter the Internet protocol, the name or the IP address of the proxy server through which you want to connect to the Internet. Include the port number at the end of the IP address. For example, if the proxy server's IP address was 111.222.33.444 and the port was 8080, you would enter http://111.222.33.444:8080 in the HTTP Proxy field. This will tell InterNotes how to access this computer to request documents on the other side of the firewall.

   • *FTP Protocol Proxy*   Enter the Internet protocol, the name or the IP address of the proxy server through which you want to connect to the Internet. Include the port number at the end of the IP address. For example, if the Proxy server's IP address was 111.222.33.444 and the port was 8080, you would enter ftp://111.222.33.444:8080 in the HTTP Proxy field. This will tell InterNotes how to access this computer to request documents on the other side of the firewall.

   • *Gopher Protocol Proxy*   Enter the Internet protocol, the name or the IP address of the proxy server through which you want to connect to the Internet. Include the port number at the end of the IP address. For example, if the proxy server's IP address was 111.222.33.444 and the port was 8080, you would enter gopher://111.222.33.444:8080 in the HTTP Proxy field. This will tell InterNotes how to access this computer to request documents on the other side of the firewall.

You may use the No Proxy field to enter the name of internal sites to which you want the InterNotes server to connect without going through the proxy server. This is useful for simplifying the availability of both internal and external Web sites.

Modifying the Way Information Is Displayed

You can control how Web pages will appear when accessed from the Web Navigator database. You do this by modifying the Presentation Preferences section of the Web Navigator Administration document. Figure 21.10 shows the setting fields for fonts and icons in the Web Navigator Administration document. You can modify the following attributes:

- Font face and size for Web page text
- Icons that will be displayed for different kinds of information and error conditions

Figure 21.10

The Presentation Preferences section of the Web Navigator Administration document.

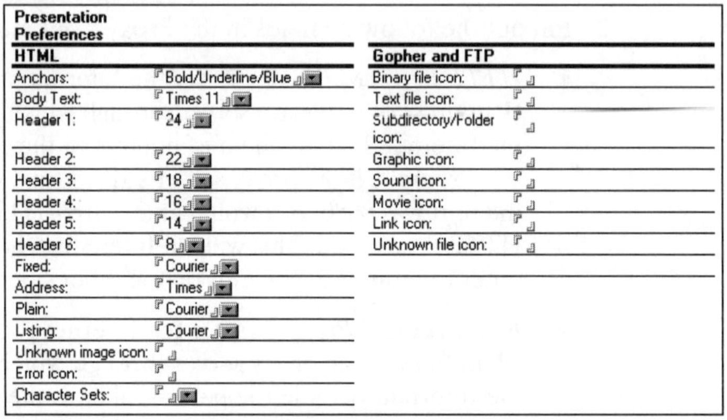

Presentation Preferences

HTML		Gopher and FTP	
Anchors:	Bold/Underline/Blue	Binary file icon:	
Body Text:	Times 11	Text file icon:	
Header 1:	24	Subdirectory/Folder icon:	
Header 2:	22	Graphic icon:	
Header 3:	18	Sound icon:	
Header 4:	16	Movie icon:	
Header 5:	14	Link icon:	
Header 6:	8	Unknown file icon:	
Fixed:	Courier		
Address:	Times		
Plain:	Courier		
Listing:	Courier		
Unknown image icon:			
Error icon:			
Character Sets:			

Font Sizes for Text of Web Pages Authors of Web pages use HTML to specify different elements of each document they create. For example, a Web page has the title, sections, and other elements distinguished so they can be better managed. The Presentation Preferences settings allow you to determine how you want the different elements of Web pages to appear in the Web Navigator. For example, you may want the body of the document to appear in 12 point Helvetica font. The Web Navigator supports Courier, Helvetica, and Times fonts.

To adjust how fonts appear, open the Web Navigator Administration document (View/Goto/All Documents, Actions/Administration) and fill out the following fields:

Field	Effect
Anchors	The colors in which URL Links will be displayed. The default for this is Bold/Underline/Blue.
Body Text	The font face and size for any element not explicitly defined elsewhere in the Presentation Preferences section of the Web Navigator Administration document. The default is Times font, 11 point.

Field	Effect
Header 1	The font size for text within the <H1> html tag. The default for this field is 26 point font.
Header 2	The font size for text within the <H2> html tag. The default for this field is 22 point font.
Header 3	The font size for text within the <H3> html tag. The default for this field is 18 point font.
Header 4	The font size for text within the <H4> html tag. The default for this field is 14 point font.
Header 5	The font size for text within the <H5> html tag. The default for this field is 12 point font.
Header 6	The font size for text within the <H6> html tag. The default for this field is 8 point font.
Fixed	Specifies the font and size for text within the <CODE>, <SAMPLE>,<KBD> and <TT> html tags. The default value for this field is Courier font, 10 points.
Address	Specifies the font and size for text within the <ADDRESS> html tag. The default value for this field is Helvetica font, 10 points.
Plain	Specifies the font and size for text within the <PLAINTEXT>,<PRE> and <EXAMPLE> html tags. The default value for this field is Courier font, 10 points.
Listing	Specifies the font and size for text within the <LISTING> html tag. The default value for this field is Courier font, 10 points.

Changing Icons   To change icons that appear under different circumstances, paste your own icons in the fields that specify different types of information.

You can replace icons for specific file types that are retrieved using FTP and gopher and also change the icons that will be displayed when the Web Navigator cannot determine the file type of a file it encounters. If you do replace the default icons with your own, you should make sure that they are 10 by 11 pixels for FTP and gopher icons and 32 by 32 pixels for Unknown Image types and Errors. This will ensure that the icons display properly.

Issuing Web Navigator Commands to the Server Console

There are only a few commands that the administrator needs to enter at the server console. These are used to manage the WEB program:

Command	Effect
LOAD WEB	Tells the server to load the WEB program, enabling users to access Internet documents.
TELL WEB HELP	Tells the WEB program to list all Web Navigator console commands.
TELL WEB QUIT	Shuts down the Web Navigator.
TELL WEB REFRESH	Updates the settings cached by the WEB program from the Web Navigator Administration document. This command lets you make changes you have made take effect without restarting the WEB task.

Securing InterNotes

Securing your InterNotes server is critical for preventing unauthorized users from accessing your internal environment. Notes 4.0, as described in the following chapters, has excellent tools for managing Notes-system and database (application) security. When you are connecting to the Internet, however, you must also concern yourself with network security. The InterNotes server will need to connect with external organizations so it is critical that it connect only in the manners in which you intend.

In general, there are three means by which you may defend against unwanted intrusion. These are listed below in order of the most secure to the least secure; however, any one is usually sufficient.

• Place the InterNotes server behind an Internet firewall server.

• Place the InterNotes server on an isolated LAN.

• Use the InterNotes server as a protocol gateway.

Using these methods it is possible to access the Internet and ensure that your organization's proprietary information is not at risk.

Defending against Intrusion with a Firewall Server

Using firewall servers to defend against intrusion is the best way to secure your InterNotes server. It is also a common mechanism for providing access to the Internet while preventing attack, so it does not require any unusual configurations to implement. The concept behind a firewall server is that packets (the data elements that are communicated over a network) can be filtered. Using a firewall server, you control which packets are allowed into your private network from the Internet and which packets are allowed out of your private network to the Internet. It is like having a security guard at the door of your organization who checks each piece of data to ensure it should be allowed to get in or out.

There are two technologies involved in any firewall server: hardware and software. Your solution may include one or both. In most cases, you will want to provide a solution that utilizes both of these tools to create the most secure environment possible. Since the firewall filters out information at the IP (Internet Protocol) packet level, you can only control data flow based on the seminal components of a packet, namely the source computer address, the destination computer address, and the port (service) to be used. Unfortunately, these components are not broken down in more useable categories such as critical data, public data, good guys, bad guys, big secrets, or marketing department only. Proxy servers make all packets coming from your network appear to come from the same computer address, making it difficult for external entities to learn about your network from the requests you make to other servers on the Internet.

To access the Internet through a firewall server you must do both of the folowing items:

1. Set up a firewall server. You can purchase complete solutions or build your own hardware and software solutions with components from many vendors. Part of your firewall will contain a proxy server.

2. Set up the Web Navigator to use the proxy server by specifying port addresses (services such as http, ftp, gopher) as described earlier. You will need to know the port numbers for the services you will use.

Figure 21.11 shows how a passthru server may be used to help secure your connection to the Internet.

Defending against Intrusion by Isolating the InterNotes Server

If setting up a firewall server is not possible, you can use a similar concept that requires less administration and installation costs. The idea is to create a LAN on which only the InterNotes server resides, making it impossible for packets to pass through to other computers on your organization's internal network.

To do this, you will run multiple protocols on your InterNotes server. You will need TCP/IP to run the TCP/IP protocol to access the Internet, so that is one of the protocols needed. In addition, you will run another protocol supported by Notes 4.0. For this example, we'll assume you have a Novell

Figure 21.11

An InterNotes server
connected to the Internet
via a passthru server.

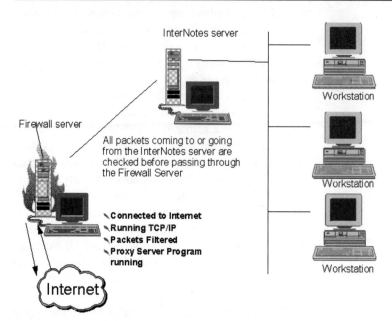

LAN and will use the SPX protocol to connect your other Notes computers
to your InterNotes server.

You will connect the InterNotes server to the rest of your network by
using a Notes passthru connection. This means that when a Notes workstation client makes a request to the InterNotes server, it is actually passing that
request through another Notes server that will then pass the request on to
the InterNotes server. Because the workstation clients do not directly connect with the InterNotes server—and because the Notes passthru server connects to the InterNotes server using a different protocol than the InterNotes
server uses to communicate with the Internet—you have effectively filtered
the packets that can be introduced to your LAN or sent to the Internet. Figure 21.12 shows how you might use an isolated LAN to defend against intrusion from the Internet.

Using an InterNotes Server as a Protocol Gateway

This approach is not recommended. I do not believe it adequately secures
your organization from external intrusion. However, based on the information you need to protect and your necessity for accessing the Internet, this
may serve as a simple solution.

This method entails installing two Network Adapter Cards (NICs) on
your InterNotes server. One of these cards will run your internal network

Figure 21.12

An InterNotes server on
an isolated LAN.

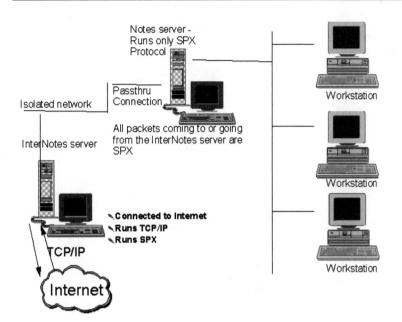

protocol (such as SPX) and the other will run TCP/IP. Provided that the computers on your internal network are not running TCP/IP so that packets cannot be exchanged through the InterNotes server to the Internet, you will block intruders from accessing your organization's proprietary information.

It is possible to have both of the Network Adapter Cards running TCP/IP if your organization uses this as its internal network protocol. If you do this, ensure that you do not route protocols between the two cards so that packets from the Internet (handled by one NIC) cannot be exchanged with your internal network (handled by the other NIC). Also ensure that you use access controls in Notes to verify that the correct ports (NICs) are in use by the correct computers. Figure 21.13 shows how a single computer with two Network Interface Cards can limit the flow of data in and out of your organization.

Customizing the Web Navigator Database

One of the nice features of InterNotes is the simplicity with which you can customize it to meet the particular needs of your organization. This is possible, of course, because the documents retrieved from the Internet are stored in a Notes database. The following information is designed to stimulate thought about how you might want to customize the Web Navigator database. It is best to have a knowledgeable Notes application developer make

Figure 21.13

An InterNotes server with two NIC cards limiting packet flow to and from the Internet.

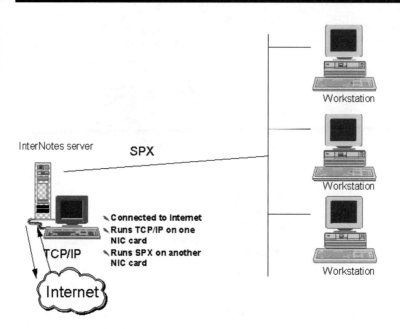

any changes that involve altering or enhancing the functionality of the database. If the change requires only that the URL be changed, you can easily do it without concern.

The following suggestions should always be followed when making changes to the Web Navigator database:

- Never change the name of the database. It must always be called WEB.NSF. You can use a database pointer to move the database out of the Notes 4.0 data directory (see Chapter 27, "Managing Servers," for more information about database links.

- Never change the names of existing design elements (forms, views, navigators, or agents), as the WEB program uses these to perform its routine functions.

- Keep a backup copy of the Web Navigator database template (WEB.NTF) so that you can revert to this if changes you make do not work out as planned.

Make your changes to the Web Navigator template (WEB.NTF) so that your changes are not overwritten by the DESIGN task. The design task runs on a schedule determined by the server manager or network manager and updates the design features of databases with those stored in templates. The design task simplifies the distribution of new Notes database features but could, if not used properly, overwrite your enhancements with older versions of your Notes database. See Chapter 28 for more information.

You can use standard Notes programming techniques to customize the Web Navigator database. Several Notes 4.0 @functions and LotusScript methods are available specifically for the purpose of enhancing the functionality of using Notes 4.0 with Internet data.

The following list contains some suggestions for enhancing the Web Navigator database to better suit your organization's needs. You may consult an application developer or the application development section of this book for instructions on how to modify the database design.

- Change the look of the Home navigator to include your organization's logo.

- Change the links that are available from the Home navigator. For example, you may want to have the Home button open your organization's home page. In addition, you may want to remove some of the links, like the one opened by the Shopping icon, and instead have icons and links to more relevant information.

- Create actions for users to easily incorporate the content they find on the Internet into other business applications. For example, you might create an action bar button to take a document and move it into your organization's competitor tracking Notes application.

- Create agents that will automate routine tasks for users. If users routinely look (surf) for the same information, you may create an agent that will regularly check for the information that interests them (perhaps using full text searching) and then send a Notes mail message to them that provides links to those documents.

- Finally, you may want to create additional views in the Web Navigator database that will help users of the database sift through information more effectively.

This is by no means a comprehensive list of the modifications you may want to consider making on the Web Navigator database. Be creative and take advantage of the simplicity with which you can provide Internet tools to users because you have the Notes 4.0 environment driving the process. Finally, check out the Lotus Web site, as it provides updates to the Web Navigator template (http://www.lotus.com/webnav.htm).

■ About InterNotes Web Publisher

InterNotes Web Publisher enables you to use Notes 4.0 as a publishing system for the World Wide Web. At the time of this writing, InterNotes Web Publisher may be downloaded, free of charge, from www.internotes.lotus.com. Notes 4.1 will ship with InterNotes Web Publishing features in the box, and Notes 4.2 will provide even greater integration with the Internet.

How It Works

InterNotes Web Publisher exports information stored in Notes databases and stores it in HTML files on a Web server. The Web server then provides Web browsers with access to these files as it would any other HTML files. The WebMaster can set up the schedule when exporting of a particular database will take place. This ensures that changes to the Notes database are reflected on the Web server with changes to the HTML documents. Therefore, Web browsers that access the server will receive updated information. The WEB-PUB 4.0 Notes 4.0 add-in supports the exporting process.

InterNotes Web Publisher also lets users of Web browsers interact with the Notes server for such activities as submitting information (like an information request form) and full text searching. Interactive activities are supported by the INOTES CGI program and the INOTES 4.0 Notes 4.0 add-in program (part of the Web Publisher add-in task). These programs take information from the Web server (that originates from a user submitting the request or information to a Web browser) and pass the information back to the WEBPUB program, which creates a document in the Notes database. In essence, the INOTES CGI and INOTES add-in make it possible to reverse the publishing process by taking WEB information and creating Notes documents from it, interactively. Figure 21.14 shows how the different InterNotes Web Publisher programs work together to provide interactive Web support to Notes 4.0.

The Web Navigator, Web Publisher, and Web Server should be run on a single computer. All the configuration information that is necessary for the Web Publisher as a whole, as well as the configuration information for each database that you want to publish to the Web, is stored in a single database: the InterNotes Configuration database. The two document types the Web Master will use in this database are the WebMaster Options document and the Database Publishing Record document. The WebMaster Options document is used for setting up the Web Publisher as a whole. The Database Publishing Record document enables and configures publication of each database you wish to make available on the World Wide Web.

Figure 21.14

The Notes server,
InterNotes Web Publisher,
and Web server
exchanging information.

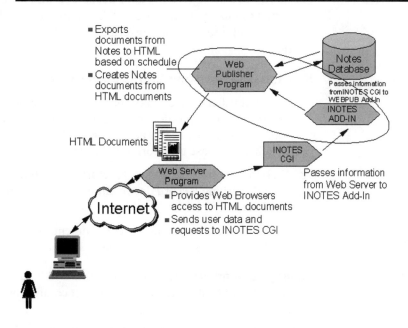

- Exports documents from Notes to HTML based on schedule
- Creates Notes documents from HTML documents

Web Publisher Program

Notes Database

Passes information from INOTES CGI to WEBPUB Add-In

INOTES ADD-IN

HTML Documents

INOTES CGI

Passes information from Web Server to INOTES Add-In

Web Server Program

Internet

- Provides Web Browsers access to HTML documents
- Sends user data and requests to INOTES CGI

How Documents and Views Are Published on the Web

The Notes Web Publisher converts all documents and views (that you specify) in a Notes database to the Web as individual HTML pages. Documents or views that would be too large to be stored in a single HTML document are stored in multiple ones.

Usually, each Notes document in a database becomes a single file on the HTTP server, probably with an .htm extension (or whatever extension you specify). The Notes database "About Database" document becomes the home page for the database. Links to all the published views in the database are stored on the home page. Views are also stored as HTML documents on the HTTP server. Views stored as HTML documents converted with links to Notes documents referred to in that view.

The benefit of publishing views in this way is that it minimizes the amount of manual linking from one Web page to another that you are required to do. As long as you are publishing views that reference all the documents you want available on the Web, there will be a link to make that document easily accessible to users.

If you want to create additional links from one page to another, you can easily do this by adding a standard Notes link from one document to another. These links will be converted to URLs (links) when the Notes documents are converted to HTML documents. In addition, because Notes 4.0

allows you to store URLs in Notes documents and have these automatically converted to links, you can enter URL text into the Body field of any Notes document and it too will be converted to a link from one Web page to another.

How the Web Publisher Stores Documents

1. Web Publisher creates an output HTML directory (as specified in the WebMaster Options document) if one does not already exist. This is the top level directory that is accessible by the Web server and under which all other database directories will be created.

2. Web Publisher creates a subdirectory for each database that has a Database Publishing Record document in the Web Publisher Configuration database.

3. Web Publisher translates Notes documents and views into HTML and stores the results in the subdirectory for that database.

Naming Conventions   The following table and Figure 21.15 demonstrate how the Web Publisher will store the files it creates for the Web server program to access:

Notes Element	Output HTML File Name
Site Home Page Document (About document of database that is designated as the home page database)	DEFAULT.HTM (or whatever you specified as the home page file name and HTML file extension fields in the WebMaster Options document). File stored in output HTML directory (top level of HTTP server directory).
Database Home Page Document	DEFAULT.HTM (or whatever you specified in the database). File stored in database directory under output HTML directory.
About Database Document	POLICY.HTM File stored in database directory under output HTML directory.
Database Help Document	HELP.HTM File stored in database directory under output HTML directory.
View	A unique name or synonym for the view name with the extension you specified in the WebMaster Options document. File is stored in the database directory under the output HTML directory.

Figure 21.15

The structure of output files from the Web Publisher program.

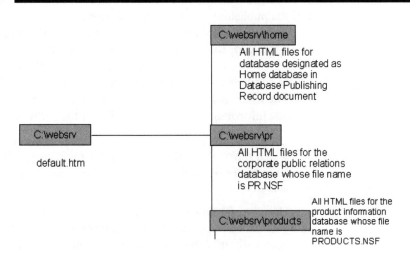

Setting Up the InterNotes Web Publisher

The following instructions will guide you through setting up the InterNotes Web Publisher. Please note that we do not, here, describe how to modify Notes databases to enhance their functionality for use on the World Wide Web.

Overview of the Installation and Configuration Process

The following is an overview of how the process of installing and configuring the InterNotes Web Publisher works.

1. Set up Notes server and Web server on a computer that will act as Inter-Notes Web Publisher server.

2. Establish a connection to the Internet such that Web browsers on the Internet can access the Web server you have set up.

3. Install the InterNotes Web Publisher software.

4. Modify the WebMaster Options document that is stored in the Web Publisher Configuration database to suit the needs of your particular setup.

5. Run the InterNotes Web Publisher software.

6. Create a Database Publishing Record document for each Notes database you want to publish to the Web.

Modifying the WebMaster Options Document   The WebMaster options document is used to tell the Web Publisher programs where to store files, with what names to store files, and where other files will be stored. This document controls the Web site as a whole. Database Publishing Record documents control the publishing of each individual database.

A default WebMaster Options document will be in the database when you open it for the first time. Only one of these documents may reside in the database or you will get erratic results from the Web Publisher. Do not create an additional WebMaster Options document; modify the existing one.

The following descriptions of fields in the WebMaster Options database provide information about how to fill out the form to suit your site's needs.

- Output directory for HTML files—Enter the name of the directory to which the Web Publisher program should store HTML files it creates from Notes documents. This directory must be accessible to the HTTP server.

- Home page file name—Enter the name for the file you want to act as your home page file. Your HTTP server will use this as the default file to access when Web browsers access your Web site. You must choose the name that your particular HTTP server will recognize. Most HTTP servers expect DEFAULT.HTM, DEFAULT.HTML, INDEX.HTM, or INDEX.HTML as the name of the file that will act as the home page. Check your HTTP server documentation to find the correct name to specify in this field. If you do not specify the correct name for this file, users will have to explicitly list the name of the file when accessing your Web site. For example, if you choose the name DEFAULT.HTM and your HTTP server uses INDEX.HTML as the name of the home page, a user accessing your Web site with a Web browser will not be able to enter http://www.sitename.com and get your home page. The user would need to enter http://www.sitename.com/default.htm.

- HTML file extension—Enter the file extension you want the Web Publisher to use when it creates HTML files. Your HTTP server may require a specific file extension such as .htm or .html and you must correctly specify the extension here for your HTTP server to be able to access the files created by the Web Publisher.

- Mapped path to INotes CGI file—Enter the relative path to the INOTES.EXE program. This file is used to take information from the Web Server and communicate it to the Web Publisher add-in programs. The path you enter here is relative to the HTTP server's program directory. If the INOTES.EXE program is stored in a directory called c:\websrv\cgi-bin, you would enter \cgi-bin in this field.

- Mapped path to output directory—Enter the directory where you want the Web Publisher program to put the HTML files it creates if they are not to be stored in the root directory of the HTTP server. For example, if your HTTP server's directory is c:\websrv and you want the files to be stored in c:\websrv\notesweb, you would enter that relative directory in this field.

- Publishing enabled—Press the space bar to select enabled or disabled. If you choose disabled, no Notes databases will be published. If you select enabled, all Notes databases that are set up to be published with Database Publishing Record documents will be published.

- Purge logfile entries after—Enter the amount of time you want to elapse before entries in the Web Publisher log database are deleted. This option is used primarily to minimize disk space consumption.

- Notes server console messages—Check the appropriate boxes to have information about the starting and ending of the publishing process displayed on the Notes server console. These entries will also appear in the Notes server log database.

Bear in mind that all settings stored in the WebMaster options document are read by the Web Publisher program when it starts. If you make changes to this document, you will need to reload the Web Publisher processes to have the changes take effect.

Publishing Databases with the InterNotes Web Publisher   Publishing databases with the InterNotes Web Publisher is quite simple once the Web Publisher is installed and configured. The only task for the WebMaster is to create a Database Publishing Record document in the InterNotes Web Publisher Configuration database for each database you wish to publish. To publish a database, follow the steps below.

1. Open the InterNotes Web Publisher Configuration Database.

2. Choose Create/Database Publishing Record.

3. Enter the appropriate information into the following field:

   - Notes server name—The name of the Notes server where the database you plan to publish is located. If you do not enter anything in this field, the Web Publisher program assumes that the database is located on the same server as the Web Publisher is running.

   - Database name—Enter the name of the database you want to publish. If the database is not located in the Notes server's data directory, enter the relative directory where it is located. For example, if the database is actually located in c:\notes\data\corpcomm and the Notes server's data directory is c:\notes\data, you would enter \corpcomm in this field.

- Publish Now (button)—Publishes the database immediately, even if the schedule is set for another time. This is useful for first time publishing and for testing the results without waiting for the schedule to kick in. If you do not click this button, the Web Publisher will publish the database at its next scheduled time.

- Publishing status—Enter Updates Only, All Documents, Disable, or Remove from Web Site by pressing the spacebar. Usually it is best to select Updates Only as this will only publish documents if a change has occurred in the Notes database. If you have a database that has information that may need to be presented differently, even if the data itself has not changed, then select All Documents. For example, if you have a view in the database, that will be translated into a page on your Web site that is called "What's Happening Today" in which documents that are relevant to the current date are listed, you would choose All Documents to ensure that this page is updated each day, even though the documents to which it will provide links may be the same as they were the last time the database published. Disable allows you to turn off publication of this particular database while others continue to be published—you do not need to shut down the entire Web Publisher program. Remove from Web Site will delete any HTML files associated with the specified database from the output HTML directory. This means that no one who accesses your Web site will be able to access the information stored in that database, as the files which they would access are no longer available.

- How often to publish—Enter the frequency with which you want this database to be published. Enter a number in the first field and use the spacebar to choose Hours, Days, or Weeks in the second field.

- Allowed publishing times—Enter the range of times during which you want the database to be published. For example, if you get a great deal of activity on your Web site, you might only want to publish during off-peak hours. In this case you could specify a time range in the middle of the night. The format for entering the time range is 12:00 a.m.–6:00 a.m.

- Allowed publishing days—Press Enter to select the days of the week on which you want publishing to occur.

- Most recent publishing time—This information will automatically appear if the Web Publisher has previously published the database.

- Next scheduled publishing time—This information will automatically appear if the Web Publisher has previously published the database.

- Logging level—Check this box if you would like detailed information about the publication of this database to be stored in the Web Publisher log database. Deselect this checkbox if you do not require detailed information. In general, this option is useful if you need to troubleshoot the publication of a database.

- View layout—Select how you want information from Notes database views to be presented in an HTML document. Check Preformatted to display the links to the HTML documents in a fixed pitch font and preserve the line and space breaks that were originally in the Notes database view. Check Tables to store the links in a structured tabular format. In general, Tables is easier for users to read but is supported only in newer browsers (Netscape Navigator 1.2 and above, for example).

- Font mappings—Use these fields to have the Web Publisher place information with certain HTML tags so that Web browsers can apply the fonts selected by a user. You can assign heading levels available in HTML documents (Heading 1 to Heading 7) by font size or style name. For example, if you use Notes styles when creating Notes documents in the database, you might say that any text that uses the Notes style "Subhead" will receive the tag Heading 2 when it is converted to an HTML document. Alternatively, you may say that any text that is 20 point font in the Notes document will be tagged as Heading 2 when converted to HTML. Web browsers allow users to specify how they want these different levels to display on their systems.

- Is this the home page database—Select Yes or No. If this database will create the document that will be used as the default or home page document for your Web site, select Yes. This means that when a user accessing your Web server with a Web browser enters your site location (host computer name) such as www.lotus.com, the information stored in this database will be used to create the DEFAULT.HTM file (or whatever name your HTTP server requires) so that users accessing your Web site will not need to know a specific document name to get information initially. This means they will not have to specify a document to access your site (http://www.lotus.com/index.htm), for example.

- Views to publish—Enter the names of the views you want published into HTML documents with links to the documents in those views.

The view names you enter in this field must be identical to the names in the Notes database itself. For example, if a view is hidden, include parentheses around its name. If a view includes an underscore character, omit it. If you do not enter anything in this field, all views in the Notes database will be published. If you enter any view names in this field, only those that you enter will be published.

- Manager—Enter the name of the manager of the Notes database. This field is optional.

- Comments—Enter any comments about the database. This field is optional.

You have now set up a database to be published to the World Wide Web. You may take advantage of Notes document collaboration capabilities to simplify the creation and management of content. The Web Publisher automatically make your content available to millions of people with Web browsers!

- *Key Migration Tips*
- *Migration Overview*
- *Planning*

CHAPTER

22

Migration

MIGRATION IS THE PROCESS OF UPGRADING AN EXISTING NOTES network to a newer version of the software. In this case, we'll be describing the process of migrating from Notes 3.0 to Notes 4.0. Migration involves a large number of tasks that switch over the system while keeping users productive on the system. The migration to Notes 4.0 is somewhat more complicated than an upgrade to a desktop application such as Lotus 1-2-3 or Microsoft Excel. This is because there are two software programs that need to be upgraded—the client and the server—and because unlike a desktop application, Notes almost always involves the sharing of information. As a result, we must consider the impact on all users with each step of the migration.

It's a good idea to break down the migration process into discrete tasks that can be independently planned and managed. The following is a guideline that we recommend when planning the migration.

■ Key Migration Tips

As noted above, there are a number of critical steps in the migration process. The following are some overview concepts which we have broken out to better explain them. Later in this chapter you will see them again and they will be described in detail and make more sense.

Upgrading the Software

Upgrading the software involves installing the new Notes 4.0 software on clients and servers. In general, you will want to upgrade from the top of your organizational hierarchy down. By this I mean start by upgrading servers—hub servers first if possible, application servers second, and mail servers third—then upgrade workstations. All of these software upgrades should be done by workgroup if possible (the accounting department or all the people involved in sales, for example). If it's not possible to upgrade by workgroup, schedule them by location and then workgroups within the location. You will not need to run the setup program unless you install Notes 4.0 in a different directory than Notes 3.0. The install program will use existing settings (such as where to look for the desktop.dsk file and the user.id file) and will append the notes.ini file with any new settings that Notes 4.0 requires.

Upgrading the Name and Address Book

This is of course the most important database on your Notes system. The Notes 4.0 Public Name and Address Book has changed significantly from the Notes 3.0 version of the database. Many new features have been added that make it easier to use and more secure. Upgrading the Public Name and Address Book involves several steps.

You may upgrade the Public Name and Address Book on Notes 4.0 servers and it will work without a problem when replicated to Notes 3.0 servers. You first upgrade the design of the database to the Notes 4.0 design by using the template "pubnames.ntf." Then you add roles to the database and assign people to the roles you add. An agent that comes with the new database design will do this for you automatically with the message "Add Admin Roles to Access Control List."

NOTE. *If you do not add roles and assign people to those roles, no one will be able to create new documents in the Public Name and Address Book because* *of the new security features. You must then update existing documents so they can be modified and deleted by administrators. Another agent is provided for this purpose (Apply Delegation to All Entries). If you do not complete this step, you will not be able to modify or remove existing documents in the Public Name and Address Book.*

Upgrading Databases—The Basics

Upgrading the file format lets you take advantage of Notes 4.0 specific features such as changing size limit to 4 gigabytes, using field level replication, and using new Access Control List features. Some of these features, like field level replication, will automatically work with databases once they are converted to the Notes 4.0 file format. The design will be upgraded by the Notes 4.0 server's compact program. The compact program can also be used to convert databases back to the Notes 3.0 file format by using the -r switch.

Upgrading the design of a database means enhancing the design with Notes 4.0 features and taking advantage of the Notes 4.0 user interface. Upgrading documents means adding or modifying the data in documents to support new design enhancements. Upgrading views and full text search indexes lets you take advantage of server caching for better view performance and full text searching of encrypted fields and attached documents.

Upgrading Mail Databases In Particular

Mail is a tricky issue. To use Notes 4.0 mail you must upgrade the design of the database to the new design (StdR4Mail - Mail4.ntf) and then update existing documents so they take advantage of the new design. There is a server utility that will do both of these tasks for you, or they may be done manually by the user with menu commands and an agent provided in the new mail design.

The most important things to remember here are that you should only update the primary mail database (the one listed in the user's Person Document) and let other changes occur by normal replication. Do not convert more than one replica of a user's mail database, or you may get replication conflicts and erratic results. If a user has a mail database replica that will continue to reside on a Notes 3.0 server or client, make sure that database *does not* replicate the new design of the database. You may do this by using replication settings or lowering the server with which this database replicates to "Editor" in the replica's access control list.

Mixed Software Version Matrix

In general, you can have mixed versions of Notes 3.0 and Notes 4.0 running together and users will have access to all the information they would if they were on the same platform. The following are some areas where this otherwise harmonious integration becomes discordant:

- Notes 3.0 clients and servers work with Notes 4.0 clients and servers seamlessly for all Notes 3.0 functionality. Notes 4.0 functions, such as field level replication and databases larger than 1 gigabyte, do not work when using a Notes 3.0 client or server with a Notes 3.0 client or server.

- Databases using the Notes 4.0 file format do not work when accessed by Notes 3.0 clients *directly,* such as on a local machine. They *do* work when accessed via a Notes 4.0 server.

- Databases using the Notes 4.0 file format cannot reside on Notes 3.0 servers. With normal operation—even when using a Notes 4.0 client to create a database on the server—this situation should not occur unless you use file system commands to copy a Notes 4.0 database onto the Notes 3.0 server. If you create a database with a Notes 4.0 client and save it to a Notes 3.0 server, the 4.0 client will automatically convert the database to Notes 3.0 format so that the Notes 3.0 server can use it. Simply put, if you use standard Notes 4.0 commands to place databases on either a client or server (such as File/Database/New Copy or File/Replication/New Replica) Notes 4.0 will ensure that a Notes 4.0 file format database will not be placed on a client or server running Notes 3.0.

- Databases using Notes 4.0 features in the design may run on Notes 3.0 clients and servers, but those design features will not be available. Make sure that no critical database components are available only through Notes 4.0 clients and servers, as Notes 3.0 users will not be able to access them.

NOTE. *A database saved on a Notes 4.0 server with the file extension ".ns3" will automatically be saved as a Notes 3.0 file format. When the compact utility runs, it will not convert this file to a Notes 4.0 database file format. In almost all cases, it is all right for a database to be converted to a Notes 4.0 file format on Notes 4.0 servers. It will not interfere with Notes 3.0 computers accessing the information stored in it. Figure 22.1 shows where Notes 3.0 and Notes 4.0 file format databases may reside.*

■ Migration Overview

The following is the basic outline you should follow in your migration to Notes 4.0. Many factors, of course, play into this outline, so each organization must adjust it to meet their specific needs.

Figure 22.1

Where Notes 3.0 and
Notes 4.0 file format
databases may reside.

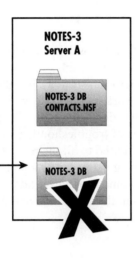

**NOTES-3
Server A**

NOTES-3 DB
CONTACTS.NSF

NOTES-3 DB

A Notes-4
database cannot
reside on a
Notes-3 server.
Notes-4 clients and
servers will convert
a database to Notes-3
format automatically
when saving to a
Notes-3 server. Do
not use file system
commands to copy
Notes-4 databases
to Notes-3 servers.

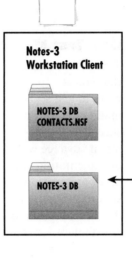

**Notes-3
Workstation Client**

NOTES-3 DB
CONTACTS.NSF

NOTES-3 DB

A Notes-3 workstation
cannot have a Notes-4
file format database on
it. If you use Notes "File"
menu commands to create
databases and replicas,
even databases in Notes-4
format on a Notes-4
server will be auto-
matically connected to
Notes-3 format for
storage on the Notes-3
workstation.

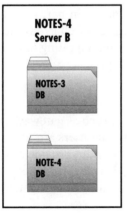

**NOTES-4
Server B**

NOTES-3
DB

NOTE-4
DB

A Notes-4 server
can have both
Notes-3 and
Notes-4 format
databases on it.

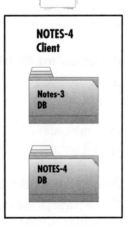

**NOTES-4
Client**

Notes-3
DB

NOTES-4
DB

Who Will Be Involved?

Compile a list of all the people who will need to be involved in the migration to Notes 4.0. Also consider who will play what role in the migration. Each task should have a project manager assigned as well as implementers.

Do a Test Migration

There is nothing like experience. If at all possible we strongly recommend that you set up a test environment that resembles your production environment to test and document your migration strategy. It is the only real way to make sure your plans are going to work on schedule while also helping to ensure a level of service while the migration takes place. Testing and documenting in advance will save many hours of troubleshooting later, especially if the documentation you provide is distributed to all the people relevant to the migration. Remember, the cost of having many server administrators troubleshooting many servers, all with the same problems, and the cost of the user downtime, is far more expensive than the small time and dollar investment in a test migration lab.

System Requirements

Don't forget system requirements. Plan your hardware, operating system software, and network software upgrades well in advance. You may need to order and install these upgrades before migrating to Notes 4.0. See the new system requirements later in this chapter.

Companion Products

If you are using companion products, such as gateways, develop a strategy for providing the same functionality that users are now accustomed to. When you move to Notes 4.0, you will not want to provide any less functionality from the system. In the short term, this may mean keeping a Notes 3.0 server up and running with a gateway on it until the new gateway is available.

Prioritize and Schedule the Migration

This is perhaps the most challenging task, as it brings into play so many variables. Plan which machines will receive new hardware and then software, and then configurations, and in what order. Break down the schedule into digestible projects, either by location or workgroup. In large installations, this will require significant communication and organizational efforts. It will, however, provide a solid foundation on which to base your time and cost estimates. Make sure you schedule time to test and troubleshoot during a migration as well as after one.

Upgrade Hardware and Operating Systems

Determine what, if any, upgrades to equipment and software will be necessary to run Notes 4.0. While many of the same platforms are supported, check and make sure that you have the right components in place to support the new version. For example, older versions of OS/2, Windows NT, and Windows 3.1 are not supported for certain server products. Make sure you don't find out about this the day the new Notes software is to be installed. Notes 4.0 caches much more information than earlier versions to improve performance. The message: Your best investment is in lots of memory for your Notes servers.

Upgrading the Software on Servers and Clients

Install the new Notes software on the machines. This should be a no-brainer, but we've all heard that before! If you tested the installation process in your test environment, make sure that anyone installing software gets a cheat sheet with general instructions as well as special tips for your particular environment.

Update the Public Name and Address Book

Ouch. To anyone with experience with Notes, this one sends a chill up the spine. The Public Name and Address Book is critical to the functioning of Notes. This is not one that you want to go awry, so practice doing it in advance and make sure you do it on servers that will replicate the changes appropriately.

Update Mail Databases

Here is another one that can have a seasoned Notes administrator sweating in his or her sleep. Mail is integral to Notes and is also a much relied upon user service. The tools provided with Notes for this upgrade are good and the process is clear. Make sure those who are doing the upgrade understand these and have good documentation.

Update Application Databases

Updating applications has many meanings, as described earlier. The most important one to remember is that design enhancements that use Notes 4.0 features cannot be used by Notes 3.0 clients, so make sure that everyone has migrated to Notes 4.0 or that the database is still useable without those features. For example, if you add an action bar to a view in Notes that gives users an option such as creating a document, make sure there is another way to create that document that will be accessible by Notes 3.0 users. The Notes

4.0 server will make Notes 4.0 databases accessible to Notes 3.0 clients automatically. It will not make Notes 4.0 design elements work on a Notes 3.0 client in so doing, however.

Also, be certain to add databases to servers and clients using the menu commands in Notes. This will prevent a Notes 4.0 database file format from ending up on a file system that is accessed by Notes 3.0 clients and servers. Once again, the Notes 4.0 server will make accessible Notes 4.0 databases to Notes 3.0 clients and servers, but Notes 3.0 clients and servers cannot (on their own) understand the new file format.

Implement New Features

Notes 4.0 has lots of great new features for administrators. In particular, setting up new monitoring tools and the Administration Process can help administrators maintain high levels of service with Notes 4.0. We recommend that you set up these new utilities after stabilizing the new platform.

Testing

A reminder: Testing in advance is important to develop the best practices for your migration. Testing during the migration process is critical. Once you have everything up and running, make sure it really is up and running. There are many test procedures to use; some simple ones will be trying out critical databases on all platforms on which they will run (such as Notes 4.0 and Notes 3.0 platforms if your environment will be temporarily mixed), as well as using the new Mail Trace feature to make sure that e-mail arrives where it is intended. Plan your migration schedule to allow for a little time after the migration to ensure that everything is up and running.

Training

I know, I know. You've heard it before, and no one has the time, no one has the budget. But training is important. System administrators must be briefed on the new features and procedures of Notes, and users should get some information on how to take advantage of new features. You can pay now or pay later with training. If you pay now, you will probably save money overall in time saved and productivity gained.

■ Planning

Planning is a favorite word and an unpopular activity. It is, however, a critical component of the migration process. If you do not adequately plan the migration, users may not get the service they need from the Notes system.

Depending upon how heavily an organization relies upon Notes, this can be a very costly result. The following components of your migration should be thought out and documented. As with an initial rollout, we recommend keeping a journal of information to help you plan. If you are migrating, it means you are on Notes already and a simple discussion database is an excellent tool to help you gather and share information with others who will be involved.

Planning a migration is as important—if not more important—than planning an initial deployment of Notes 4.0. If you are migrating, you have users who depend on Notes and are accustomed to using Notes in their day-to-day activities. Limiting the interruption of service during migration is critical if you are to gain the benefits of Notes 4.0 without experiencing reduced productivity. This chapter will help you with planning and then implementing the migration process.

Putting Together a Plan

The planning process can be broken down in many different ways. The key is to make sure you have covered all of the significant (and seemingly insignificant) components of the migration. Regardless of how you organize your migration plan, make sure you document it well and publish it along with other documentation on the process so that others can "be on the same page."

Assembling the Interested Parties

You will need to start out by assigning project management roles to individuals and making them responsible for certain tasks. In addition, you may need to assign others to work with these project leaders to help them in their assigned duties. It would not, for example, make sense to have a project leader responsible for all the server upgrades in a large organization with many Notes servers located around the country.

Plan on a project manager and some kind of a project team for each of the following areas of the Notes migration project. Of course smaller organizations may have smaller teams (in some cases just one person, the Notes administrator).

Project Management

This group will plan and oversee the project from beginning to end. This team (or person) will define the resources that will be necessary to roll out the Notes 4.0 system and will manage the staffing of the project. People in this group will also act as backup support when server and workstation issues need to be resolved. By centralizing this function, a solid body of knowledge may be built. It is a good idea for this group in particular to keep knowledge databases of information learned at each location to help other locations better deploy the new platform.

Members of this team should be equipped to address the following questions:

- What should the server platform be, including hardware, operating system, and network software?

- What training will be delivered and by whom?

- What new security and application development standards should be put in place immediately and over time?

In addition to managing the technical components of the rollout, the planning team must coordinate the logistical processes, such as determining what computers will be upgraded in what order, what hardware and software upgrades will be necessary to complete before the Notes migration, and then plan and execute ordering the hardware and software. Distribution of the software also falls into the domain of the project management team.

Network Managers

Notes 4.0 brings with it some significant enhancements in performance as well as some new replication, routing, server access, and server configuration options. It is important that the central staff who will be responsible for the Notes network is made aware of the new features and start to plan for them.

The tasks for this group will include, but are not limited to:

- Creating a new replication scheme to take advantage of new server capacity and pull/push replication.

- Considering how to leverage passthru servers to lower communications costs and simplify access, particularly for dial-in users.

- Developing standards for server notes.ini files and planning the new configuration documents that adjust those.

Server Administrators

The job of upgrading the system and the workstation clients and servers at each location should normally go to the people who have the most familiarity with the system. This means that your Notes server administrators will play a key role in the deployment of Notes 4.0. As much as Notes 4.0 has changed from Notes 3.0, much has remained the same. The current Notes administrators have excellent resources in their existing knowledge of the system. With the help of the project management team and detailed documentation on how to roll out the new platform, Notes server administrators will be the most adept at getting the new system up and running quickly.

Particularly at smaller or remote sites, Notes server administrators are often local network file server administrators as well. This dual function is useful in the Notes migration because it is helpful to understand networking and protocol issues when installing the new Notes software. Many installation difficulties arise from networking and protocol issues rather than Notes issues, particularly on new or upgraded computers. If the person installing these systems is familiar with Notes as well as the network, installations will go more smoothly.

NOTE. *Some organizations break down tasks, with one team installing clients while another team is installing servers. Other organizations have one group of people doing installations and another group doing configuration. While these logical breakdowns may work well, I recommend having a smaller group of people with a higher level of knowledge. As a result, a the local Notes server administrator is my first choice for client* and *server software installation* and *configuration.*

Remote Location Administrators

In most organizations there are remote sites that do not have on-site staffing but will need installation and configuration support for Notes workstation clients. For these locations we suggest enlisting the support of a computer-savvy end-user who can follow the detailed documentation you provide for installing Notes clients. If servers are located at these smaller, remote locations, you will need to send a Notes Server Administrator to upgrade the server.

NOTE. *Notes 4.0 servers have more bandwidth than earlier versions. As a result, you may be able to better centralize your servers so there is less need for remote servers in locations where having support staff is not feasible. Alternatively, you may have some server administrators responsible for an entire region, such as the Northwest, who manage all of the Notes servers— and perhaps network file servers—within that region.*

Database Managers

Database managers in Notes range from systems administrators to end-users within any work group. When planning the migration you will need to plan the migration of key databases to the Notes 4.0 file format, and you may also want or need to plan on enhancing the database with Notes 4.0 features. It is usually the database manager who initiates and coordinates these tasks. As a result, you will need to communicate the issues surrounding a database upgrade to these database managers. In addition, you should develop a set of guidelines to determine if an application can benefit from an upgrade as well as what the organizational benefit of such an upgrade will yield.

It is also critical for database managers to understand the components of a database upgrade so they can support their user base. Most important, a database manager needs to understand that Notes 4.0 design features will not work in Notes 3.0 and to follow the guidelines that you establish for implementing Notes 4.0 design features. Database managers should also be advised to use Notes 3.0 and Notes 4.0 features for adding and removing databases from file systems. If they do, Notes will automatically avert any incidences of Notes 4.0 format databases ending up on hard disks that are accessed by Notes 3.0 workstations or clients.

An information update for database managers might include the following information, entitled "Initial Notes 4.0 Policy and Procedures for Database Managers."

Mixed Client and Server Version Period

During the migration period, we will have mixed versions of Lotus Notes running in our environment. Notes 3.0 clients will access both Notes 3.0 and Notes 4.0 servers, and Notes 3.0 servers will access and be accessed by Notes 4.0 servers.

Notes can work effectively in this manner until all computers are upgraded. It is important to ensure that computers running Notes 3.0 software (client or server) do not have databases in the Notes 4.0 file format stored on them. To avert this, please do not use file system commands to load new databases or database replicas onto computers. By using the Notes menu commands such as the Notes 4.0 commands File/Database/New Copy and File/Replication/New Replica, or the Notes 3.0 commands File/Database/Copy and File/New Replica, the Notes 4.0 software will always ensure the proper file format conversion occurs when the destination is a Notes 3.0 computer.

In addition to ensuring that Notes 3.0 clients and servers have access to the correct database file format, it is important that databases that will be accessed by Notes 3.0 clients and servers do not have Notes 4.0 features enabled that will cause incompatibilities or preclude the use of critical database functionality. For example, database size must not be set to exceed 1 gigabyte if that database is to be accessed by a Notes 3.0 client or server. Similarly, Notes 3.0 cannot take advantage of Notes 4.0 design features, although they can use databases that contain Notes 4.0 design features. It is important, therefore, to make sure that if Notes 4.0 features are added to the database, such as action bars or navigators, that the functionality provided in these new design features be included via Notes 3.0 design objects if they are critical to use of the database.

Security

Notes 4.0 security features must be implemented to better protect corporate data. A complete outline of the new security policies will be published in the (*your policy's database name here*) database. Initially, we suggest using the Notes 4.0 local encryption of databases feature on all laptop computers running Notes 4.0 software as well as all databases containing sensitive information if they are located on a computer running Notes 4.0 workstation client or server software.

In addition to encryption, user types should be assigned to all entities listed in the access control list of any database for all databases located on a Notes 4.0 computer (client or server). This will prevent the misuse of ID files as well as group documents to gain access to a database without authorization. The Notes 4.0 workstation client will automatically look up and assign user types in the Public Name and Address Book for you.

Specify an administration server for all databases residing on Notes 4.0 servers. Only one administration server should be specified for a database. Replicas of the database will receive changes made by the administration server through normal replication to other Notes 4.0 servers and clients. The administration server will automate the removal and name change procedures based on changes that occur in the Public Name and Address Book. You will no longer need to remove names from an access control list, for example, if a user leaves the organization.

Finally, a consistent access control list should be forced across all replicas of a database to ensure that other servers have not granted access to unauthorized users or servers. This security feature, like the others, should be implemented at the hub server if possible.

Feature Enhancements and File Format Upgrades

A complete policy regarding upgrading database features will follow in the (*your policy and procedures database here*) database. During the transition to Notes 4.0 we recommend the following:

1. Limit database feature enhancements to those that make Notes 3.0 databases useable in Notes 4.0 where they are not now (adjusting colors and view columns, for example). Invest in redesigning applications once the migration to Notes 4.0 is complete so that all users can benefit from the improved application and the design specification is not limited by the need to support Notes 3.0 clients.

2. Enhance database functionality first and foremost where productivity, reliability, and security gains are apparent and measurable.

3. Target key applications for major enhancements when the migration to Notes 4.0 is complete.

4. Convert to the Notes 4.0 file format as soon as possible to take advantage of automatic new features, such as field level replication.

Training

Larger organizations often have in-house training resources. Others do not. In either case, involve the group you will use to train Notes administrators and users early in the process and help them identify key issues that will need to be addressed in the Notes training. It is particularly useful to have the training group participate in the scheduling component of your planning phase so they can be prepared to meet that schedule.

Scheduling the Migration

This is a tough one. You need to gather all the information about your environment and then provide a plan for migrating each component of the environment. It is important that all of the different components of the migration are in place at the right time as some will be dependent on others. As a result, the more accurate your schedule, the less chance of interrupting service during migration. The simple progression of the migration should be servers, then workstation clients, and then applications. Unfortunately there are many details and roadblocks to such a simplistic approach.

Ideally you will migrate servers and clients by workgroup so that all the users in a given workgroup will be running the new Notes 4.0 software at or around the same time. The advantage of this is that the Notes databases they share can be enhanced with Notes 4.0 features and converted to the Notes 4.0 file format. If a workgroup spans multiple locations, this may not be possible. It may not be feasible to have users at five locations that represent a small percentage of the Notes user base upgraded simultaneously. Given geographical considerations, it makes sense to organize first by location and then strive to migrate logical workgroups within a given location.

Start the scheduling process by doing a map that details the clients and server computers that will need to receive an upgrade to Notes 4.0 by location. On your map, tag the machines that will need hardware upgrades and also tag those machines that will need non-Notes software upgrades. Code the hardware and non-Notes software upgrades differently so they are easily distinguished. Also code the map to indicate the role it plays in the Notes system. Is it a workstation client? A hub server? Is it an application server? Mail server? Gateway or backup server? You will want to upgrade the computers based on the function they serve as well as the location and workgroup they service.

When Is a Non-Notes Hardware or Software Upgrade Necessary?

You need to upgrade your computers' hardware or software when it does not meet the minimum Notes 4.0 system requirements or when you want to improve the performance of your system.

Platform	Notes 4.0 Client	Notes 4.0 Server
Windows 95	Yes	
Windows 3.1	Yes	
Windows for Workgroups 3.11	Yes	
Windows NT 3.5.1		Yes
OS/2 Warp 3.0		Yes
OS/2 Warp Connect 3.0		Yes
HP-UX 10.01		Yes
Sun Solaris 2.4		Yes
IBM AIX 4.1.3		Yes

The following platforms are no longer certified for use with Notes:

- Windows NT 3.5
- OS/2 2.0
- OS/2 2.11 (supported, but not certified)

Assuming you are organizing your migration by location, prioritize the upgrades of Notes software in the following way:

1. Hub Servers—Replication
2. Hub Servers—Mail

NOTE. *By upgrading hub servers first, user service is not disrupted, as they do not directly connect with hub servers.*

3. Application Servers

NOTE. *By upgrading application servers you can start to take advantage of Notes 4.0 features (both administrative and end user) immediately, even if you are not yet prepared to migrate servers designated for mail only.*

4. Mail Servers

NOTE. *Mail is a heavily used application in most organizations. Be sure you schedule adequate time to troubleshoot and revert to Notes 3.0 if problems arise.*

5. End User Workstations

NOTE. *Ideally you upgrade these by workgroup so that users creating documents with Notes 4.0 features are sharing documents with users who can also use these features. In addition to this criteria, choose "Technology Leaders" as the first to receive Notes 4.0 upgrades. These users generally learn quickly and can help test, troubleshoot, and provide information to other users in their departments and locations.*

6. Backup, Gateway, and Companion Product Servers

NOTE. *Leave backup servers for last as you may want to rely upon them to quickly revert to Notes 3.0 should problems arise. Gateway and companion product servers should be upgraded as soon as these products are available for the new platform. Since these are often not native Notes servers (although some gateways are now native Mail Transfer Agents (MTAs), it makes sense to thoroughly test these products before putting them into service.*

Review the map with your knowledge of the resources you have to execute these upgrades. If you are part of a large organization that has regional sites with support staff, for example, it makes sense to schedule the migration with the local staff at each site.

A database such as the following (easily developed in Notes) may help you schedule and disseminate information to others. By sorting in different ways, you can see logical sequences for the migration. You may also want to use a tool such as Microsoft Project to assist in the scheduling process. Remember, the first goal of the migration is to limit the disruption of service. Once the platform is stable, then seek to add functionality.

Location or Site	Workgroup Serviced	Computer	Role	Hardw- Softw Upgrade Req?	Time Est.	Time Sched.	Technician	Doc - Disks - Train	Comments & Dependents
NYC	All	acme-nyc-hub-01	Hub server	Yes - 32 meg RAM	3hrs total	6/5/96 - 4:30p.m.	NYC Server Admin	Sent Sent Attended	
NYC	All	acme-nyc-wg-01	Workgroup Server	Yes - 1 gigabyte Disk	3hrs total	6/6/96 - 4:30p.m.	NYC Server Admin	Sent Sent Attended	
NYC	Acctg	John Doe/ Acctg/ Acme	Technology Leader User	No	1hr total	6/7/96 - 4:30p.m.	End User will install	Sent On Serv. n/a	
NYC	Acctg	Sarah Simms/ Acctg/ Acme	Technology Leader User	Yes - 8meg RAM	3hrs total	6/7/96 - 2:30p.m.	NYC Server Admin will install	Sent On Serv. n/a	
NYC	Acctg	PhoneNotes/ Acme	Companion Product Server	No	2hrs total	6/7/96 - 4:30p.m.	End User will install	Sent On Serv. n/a	

Location or Site	Workgroup Serviced	Computer	Role	Hardw-Softw Upgrade Req?	Time Est.	Time Sched.	Technician	Doc - Disks - Train	Comments & Dependents
NYC	All	PhoneNotes/ Acme	Companion Product Server	No	1hr total	6/9/96 - 4:30p.m.	NYC Server Admin	Sent On Serv. yes	Still testing, install not confirmed
SFO	All	acme-sfo-hub-01	Hub server	Yes - 32 meg RAM	3hrs total	6/5/96 - 4:30p.m.	SFO Server Admin	Sent Sent Attended	

Migration Crew Issues

Before casting the schedule in stone, address the following issues for the team:

- Make sure you have everyone available and in agreement with the tasks that have been set out for them.

- Make certain all people involved in the migration are clear about their role, even if it only involves ordering hardware upgrades. They must understand the schedule so they can work within its guidelines.

- Create and distribute (on Notes perhaps!) clear documentation for each significant role in the migration. This will be particularly important for people doing software upgrades, acting as project managers, and updating the Notes system databases.

The Server Software Upgrade

Once you have upgraded hardware and non-Notes software it is time to install and configure the Notes 4.0 software. There are several components to the actual upgrade. The following is an overview; your own processes and documentation may include additional steps to support your environment.

- Back up the server before upgrading.

- Upgrade the server's hardware and non-Notes software.

- Install the new version of Notes.

- Update the Public Name and Address Book.

  You may also want to complete the following:

- Modify the replication scheme to leverage Notes 4.0' few features.

- Update mail.

- Set up monitoring tools.

Backing Up the Server

You should back up the server before upgrading the hardware or software, whether it's Notes or any other hardware or software. To back up the server you will probably need to bring down the server unless your backup software will back up open files.

You may choose to back up the entire server file system or a subset of it. If you can easily restore the operating system, network, and Notes server software, it is best to back up just the unique files you will need to restore the server in the event that difficulties arise during the upgrade procedures.

The key files that must be backed up are:

- notes.ini

- server.id (the server's Notes ID file)

- names.nsf (the Public Name and Address Book)

- desktop.dsk

- log.nsf

- certlog.nsf (if it exists)

- All Directory Link (.dir files)

- Any template files that have been customized (.ntf files)

- All Notes databases that contain your organization's information (.nsf files)

NOTE. *If the administrator's user ID files or certifier ID files (cert.id, for example) reside on the server, these too should be backed up. In general,* don't leave these files on the server anyway!

If the above files are safely backed up, you can easily restore your server in the event of a hard-disk failure. Be careful to prevent these backup files from getting into unauthorized hands. Together they make up the identity of the server as well as containing the data that is protected by that server. These backup files falling into the wrong hands represents a significant security threat.

Installing the Server Software

To install the server software you will need to bring down the server if it is not still down from the backup procedures. The server software installation program will install the software and will make modifications to the notes.ini file to include new settings that are necessary for the Notes 4.0 server program. Install the Notes 4.0 server software to the same directories as Notes 3.0 was installed. In this way, the installation program will properly configure, by adding some and writing over other files.

If you are going to upgrade the hardware or software, it should be done and tested before installing the Notes 4.0 software. It is especially important to test communications as Notes relies so heavily upon them. Make sure you can connect to your network using the physical port (NIC card) and protocol you want Notes 4.0 to use. In addition, make sure that the computer's modem works if you plan to use this server for dial-in or dial-out capability. Do these tests by using other software, such as Terminal in Windows NT 3.5.1 before installing Notes 4.0.

To do the installation you will need to shut down the Notes server. Given that service will be disrupted, it is best to schedule this during a low usage time, such as a weekend or night. Bear in mind that when you do the installation, Notes will overwrite some Notes 3.0 files, especially template (.ntf) files. If you have customized any of these files, you may want to make an easy-to-access backup version of them so that you can copy the customizations to the new template files. Alternatively, you can customize the new template files before running the installation program. It is important that you NOT overwrite the new templates with the Notes 3.0 ones, even if you did customizations. Notes 4.0 relies on certain design aspects of these templates. You will need to add your customizations to the Notes 4.0 templates.

Make sure to install the server into the same directories as the old Notes software. In this way, the installation program will find the necessary information to complete the setup for you. Additionally, you do not want to have more than one version of Notes on the system (except in special cases) as there is an opportunity for files to get mixed and matched when the program is running.

Upgrading the Public Name and Address Book

There are several components to upgrading the Public Name and Address Book. Not all of these steps must be taken immediately. Some are required to run the Notes 4.0 server. Some organizations modified their Notes 3.0 Public Name and Address Book to do things that the new Public Name and Address Book does. It is strongly recommended that you make no changes to the Notes 4.0 Public Name and Address Book. If you must modify it, make certain the changes do not affect any of the fields, views, or documents that are in the new template, as Notes 4.0 relies upon these.

The steps you need to take to upgrade your Public Name and Address Book are listed below. Following the list, they will be described in more detail.

1. Upgrade the design of the Notes 4.0 Public Name and Address Book. This is required, and the installation program will automatically prompt you and take you through this process.

2. Change the name of the Public Name and Address Book design template. The installation program will automatically prompt you and do this for you.

3. Add roles to the database and assign users to these roles. This is required, but it is not automatic. An agent in the new Public Name and Address Book is provided do this for you.

4. Add users to the list of editors of a document. This is required but not automatic. An agent in the new Public Name and Address Book is provided to do this for you.

5. Lower administrator's privileges in the access control list of the Public Name and Address Book. This is not required, but administrators will have complete access to documents in the Public Name and Address Book, just as they did in Notes 3.0, unless you lower them to Author with create rights and assign them to a role.

6. Upgrade the database format to Notes 4.0. The Compact server task can do this for you.

7. Upgrade the database views indexes. The Updall server task will do this automatically when the server program is started, or it runs at 2 a.m. according to the Notes.ini file. However, you may want to run Updall starting the server program and can do so by typing Load Updall at the command prompt.

8. Change the replication to pull/push.

9. Move monitoring documents to Statistics & Events database. The Event and Report tasks will do this automatically when loaded. These server tasks are not loaded by default.

As discussed earlier, there is upgrading and there is upgrading! As outlined above, only some of the steps above are actually required. You do not need, for example, to upgrade the file format of the Public Name and Address Book. You may leave this in a Notes 3.0 format if you choose. There is no harm in upgrading the file format to Notes 4.0, as this database (names.nsf) will now reside on a Notes 4.0 computer that can understand the Notes 4.0 database file format. In general, you will want to complete all of the tasks described above to take full advantage of Notes 4.0.

You *do* need to upgrade the design of the Public Name and Address Book. The server is greatly enhanced in Notes 4.0, and it looks to new components of the Notes 4.0 Public Name and Address Book to execute these enhancements. After you upgrade the Public Name and Address Book, the server can still replicate with Notes 3.0 servers. When replicating with Notes

3.0 servers, the new design features of the Public Name and Address Book will not cause a problem in running the Notes 3.0 servers.

Notes 4.0 has different templates for personal and Public Name and Address Books. The Public Address Book template has the filename "pubnames.ntf." It has the design template name "StdR4PublicAddressBook." The file name of the Public Name and Address Book database that is on a server will still, by default, be called "names.nsf."

Now we'll go into more detail on the steps listed above.

Upgrade the Design of the Notes 4.0 Public Name and Address Book (Required)   The Notes installation program will automatically prompt you and take you through this process. When completed, the Public Name and Address Book will have the same replication ID number it did when running with Notes 3.0, will have the new design features of a Notes 4.0 Public Name and Address Book, and will have the new design template name (StdR4AddressBook) listed as its design template.

Add Roles to the Database and Assign Users to These Roles   This is an important step. If you do not do this, the Public Name and Address Book will work fine on your server, but you will not be able to add any new documents to it. The Notes 4.0 Public Address Book relies heavily upon document level access controls. It uses roles and author names fields to implement this security. The advantage is that some administrators will have access to some documents while others will have access to other documents. In other words, you may now have segregated duties with security.

The first step is to add the roles that will be used to the database and to assign users to these roles so that they will have the authority to create the documents they need to create. For example, a person charged with registering users cannot complete this task unless he or she has been assigned to the role that grants him or her the ability to create Person Documents.

After it is upgraded, the Notes 4.0 Public Name and Address Book will contain an agent that will automatically create the roles that will be used to segregate duties and will add the users listed in your Public Name and Address Book access control list to these roles based on their access level to the database.

Anyone in the Public Name and Address Book's access control list with Author and Create Document access, or higher, will be added to the following roles:

- *Group Creator*—Can create new Group Documents

- *NetCreator*—Can create any document except Person, Group, or Server Documents

- *ServerCreator*—Can create new Server Documents

- *UserCreator*—Can create new Person Documents

Anyone listed in the Public Name and Address Book access control list with Editor access or above will be added to the following *additional* roles:

- *GroupModifier*—Can modify and delete existing Group Documents

- *NetModifier*—Can modify and delete all existing Documents except for Person, Group, and Server Documents

- *ServerModifier*—Can modify and delete existing Server Documents

- *UserModifier*—Can modify and delete existing Person Documents

In summary, if you had Author and Create access in the old Public Name and Address Book, you will have the ability to create new documents of all types in the database, although this should be modified later to grant access to those types of documents you are required to create. If you had Editor or above access in the old Public Name and Address Book, you will be able to create and modify all new documents added to the Public Name and Address Book. This too should be modified based on a user's actual need to modify specific types of documents.

Add Users to the List of Editors of a Document   Once roles are added to the database and to the documents in the database, it is important to make sure that these roles are entered into existing documents in the database so that the appropriate users (administrators) can update the existing documents in the database. To do this, use the "Apply Delegation to All Entries" agent. If you do not run this agent, no one will be able to modify the documents that already exist in the Public Name and Address Book.

Lower Administrator's Privileges in the Access Control List of the Public Name and Address Book   Now that you have better controls in the Public Name and Address Book for who can do what, you should implement these by making sure that administrators are listed with Author and Create document access and are listed in the roles that are necessary to support the tasks for which they are responsible. Remember, anyone with Editor access or higher to the Public Name and Address Book has the ability to modify all documents in the database.

Set Up Administration Groups   While the new roles in the Public Name and Address Book give you the ability to define which users can create and modify particular types of documents, the "Administrators" field lets you assign individual users and/or groups to have editor rights to particular documents.

For example, you may want to give users the ability to modify their Person Document in the Public Address Book so they can enter telephone numbers and other information (Note: I don't like to let users edit their Person documents because they might make changes that prevent things (like mail) from working properly. I think it is asking for trouble; some organizations like to live on the edge though).

By entering the user's name into the administration field, that user will be able to edit only his or her Person Document. Another example is if you have several sites with local server administration in each site. You may want to create a group called WestCoastAdmin and add this group to the Administrator's field of all the Server Documents for servers that are located on the West Coast. In this way, you do not have to enter these server administrators into a role that would give them access to all the server documents, rather you can limit their access to the Server Documents that are relevant to their jobs.

Upgrade the Database Format to Notes 4.0   The Public Name and Address Book will work fine without having the file format upgraded. By doing the upgrade though, you will be able to take advantage of features available in Notes 4.0.

For example, Notes 4.0 will automatically start replicating at the field level rather than at the document level. This will save time and communication charges, and reduce replication conflicts. In addition, by upgrading to the Notes 4.0 file format you will be able to take advantage of new security features such as User Types.

To upgrade the Public Name and Address Book file format before starting the server you may type the following at the Notes program directory prompt:

ncompact names.nsf—for a Windows NT server

icompact names.nsf—for an OS/2server

compact names.nsf—for a UNIX server

To upgrade the file format you need only to run the server's Compact task on the database. The Notes 4.0 version of this task will automatically upgrade the file format. If necessary, the Compact program may be used with the -r switch to regress to the Notes 3.0 file format. Databases with a .ns3 extension that are Notes 3.0 file format databases will not be updated to the new file format by the Compact task.

Upgrade the Database Views Indexes   You do not need to manually upgrade the view indexes in the Public Name and Address Book as the server will do this upon loading.

You will save time by running the Updall task manually from the command line. This is mostly useful for Public Name and Address Books that have thousands of entries. To run the Updall task from the command line in the Notes program directory (C:\NOTES) in Windows NT type:

nupdall names.nsf

iupdall names.nsf—for an OS/2 server

updall names.nsf—for a UNIX server

Steps to Upgrade the Public Address Book

1. Make sure you have backup copies of the files as described in the section "Backing Up the Server."

2. Document any customizations to your Public Name and Address Book so they may be added to the upgraded Public Name and Address Book if necessary (remember, customization of the Public Name and Address Book is *not* recommended in Notes 4.0).

3. Start the Notes workstation client program.

4. Select "Yes" when prompted if you want to upgrade the Public Name and Address Book.

NOTE. *This will add the Notes 4.0 design features to the Public Name and Address Book.*

5. Select the Public Name and Address Book icon on the desktop.

6. Choose Action/Add Admin roles to Access Control List.

NOTE. *This will add roles to the database and add the users listed in the access control list to those roles, based on their level of access to the Public Name and Address Book. By running this agent, you give anyone who had Author and Create access to the database the ability to create documents in the database and anyone who had Editor access to the database the ability to edit new documents that are created in the database going forward.* You should adjust these access settings as the agent has a very limited set of criteria on which it bases its assignments. *The Notes 4.0 address book offers a great deal of granular control that you may want to leverage by modifying the default access this agent assigns.*

Lower user's access (usually this is the default access) in the Public Name and Address Book access control list to Author or Reader. If you are willing to take the risk of letting users modify their own Person Documents, you can set it to Author. If not, you can reduce user access to the Public Name and Address Book to Reader and if changes to a user's Person Document are necessary, have a systems administrator with appropriate access do it.

7. Open the Public Name and Address Book.

8. Select a set of documents that may need to be modified in the short term.

NOTE. *This may include Server Documents and Connection Documents if you are going to implement Notes 4.0 feature enhancements immediately, for example. Bear in mind that this agent takes time to run. In a large organization with many documents in the Public Name and Address Book, it makes sense to run this agent in stages by selecting documents that need to be modified in the order they will need to be modified. In general, start by updating Server Documents and then Connection Documents so that you will be able to make necessary changes to your configuration. Thereafter, update Group and Person Documents, followed by all others.*

9. Choose Actions/Apply Delegation to All Entries.

NOTE. *By running this agent you will give the entries in the access control list who have been granted the modifier privileges to edit existing documents in the database. Although the server will run without a problem if you do not run this agent, a user with Author access and all appropriate modifier roles will not be able to modify existing documents until this agent is run.*

NOTE. *If the notes.ini file was modified to include the setting ServerPushReplication=1 to override the pull/pull replication used in Notes 3.0 you will need to modify the Connection Documents in the Public Name and Address Book to pull/push replication. The notes.ini setting will be overridden by the Notes 4.0 Connection Document setting "Replication Type." Because the Notes 3.0 Connection documents did not let you specify a type of replication, they all default to pull/pull replication.*

10. Exit from the Notes Workstation Client.

NOTE. *Before loading the server program you may want to run the Compact and Updall utilities from the operating system prompt to convert the Public Name and Address Book to the Notes 4.0 file format, and to update the view indexes so this does not have to be done when the server is loading other programs at the same time.*

Notes 4.0 statistics and events monitor documents are not stored in the Public Name and Address Book. Instead, they are stored in the Statistics and Events database. Leave the monitor documents in your Public Name and Address Book until you have upgraded all servers to the Notes 4.0 Public Name and Address Book and enabled the statistics and events server tasks on each server. The first time you run these server tasks (they are not set to run by default, you must manually start them and/or add them to the ServerTasks setting in the NOTES.INI file, the statistic and events tasks in the Public Name and Address Book will be removed and place in the new Statistics and Events database.

To run the compact task in Windows NT type:

```
C:\NOTES> Ncompact names.nsf
```

To run the Updall task in Windows NT type:

```
C:\NOTES> Nupdall names.nsf
```

If you are running an OS/2 server the commands are iupdall and icompact, and if you are running a UNIX server the commands are updall and compact.

You may run both of these tasks simultaneously if you want by typing:

```
C:\NOTES>nupdall names.nsf & ncompact names.nsf & notes server
```

You may now run the Notes 4.0 server by clicking on the Notes Server icon in the Program Manager of Windows NT.

Updating Monitoring of Statistics and Events

Statistics and Events are handled differently in Notes 4.0 than in Notes 3.0. Monitor documents are no longer stored in the Public Name and Address Book. Instead, they are stored in the Statistics & Events database.

There are two programs and, usually, two databases involved in handling events and statistics in Notes 4.0. The two programs are the Event task and the Reporter task. The Event task is the server process that reports server events. The Reporter task is the server task that checks statistics and mails a report on the statistics to a database.

NOTE. *Neither the Event task nor the Reporter task is set up to run by default. You must schedule these to run in the notes.ini file by adding them to the ServerTasks setting list.*

The two key databases involved in Event Monitoring and Statistics Reporting are the Statistics & Events database (EVENTS4.NSF) and the Statistics Reporting database (STATREP.NSF). The Statistics & Events database is used to tell the two server tasks, Events and Reporter, what events and statistics to gather and report. The Statistics Reporting database is used to store information gathered by the Event and Reporter server tasks. The Events task will create a Statistics & Reporting database the first time it (the Event task) runs. The Reporter task will create a Statistics Reporting database the first time it runs.

When you load either the Event or Report task for the first time, the task will do the following to migrate your monitoring documents:

- Create a Statistics & Events database (EVENTS2.NSF) in the Notes data directory. If you load the Report task, it will also create a Statistics Reporting database (STATREP.NSF).

- Assign Manager access to the server administrator (based on the entry in the server document field "Administrator"), the server, and to the group LocalDomainServers. The default access to the database will be reader and the group OtherDomainServers will have No Access.

- Copy the Notes 3.0 server and event monitoring documents from the Public Name and Address Book to the Statistics & Events database where the Event task will look for its settings.

NOTE. *Notes will leave a copy of the statistics and events monitoring documents in the Public Name and Address Book. You should remove these after* all servers are upgraded (and therefore Public Name and Address Books are upgraded) to Notes 4.0.

By default, Notes sends the statistics reports to the Notes server administrator via electronic mail rather than to the Alarm Tracking database.

Setting Up the New Events and Statistics Monitoring

To set up the Events and Statistics Monitoring Tools for Notes 4.0, type the following at the server console prompt:

```
Load Event
Load Report
```

After loading these two programs, your notes.ini file will be modified to include them in the ServerTasks setting of the notes.ini file so you will not need to run them manually in the future.

NOTE. *You may delete the database EVTTYPES.NMF that was used by Notes 3.0 to store information about the events on which Notes could report. This information is now stored in the Statistics & Events database (EVENTS4.NSF).*

For more information about using statistics and events, please see Chapter 27, "Managing Servers."

Following Up on Upgraded Servers

The following are some guidelines you may want to consider after upgrading a server to Notes 4.0. Remember, the server may be a critical part of user's effective functioning. Performance degradation and down time are expensive. Keeping the server up and performing optimally is critical and easily done.

Watch the Obvious

Especially after an upgrade, make sure you are monitoring server statistics and events frequently to see that all necessary functions are performing as expected. To do this:

- Check the Notes Log (LOG.NSF) daily for problems. The Routing Events and Replication Events views and documents can be easily scanned to check for communications, access control, and server errors. In addition, you can check the Usage views to see if the activity level is above or below what you anticipated so you can plan accordingly.

- Use the new Database Analyze feature on the Administration Control Panel to create a database that provides lots of information from the Notes Log. LOG.NSF is easily full-text searched for particular items.

- Check the outgoing mail database (MAIL.BOX) daily and make sure there are no undeliverable messages.

- Use the server console commands Show Tasks and Show Stats to check for dead mail and see how the server is performing.

- Enable statistics and events monitors in the Statistics & Events Database to alert you to key failures (see Chapter 27, "Managing Servers," for more information).

- Provide a means for users to provide you with feedback. This can be a hotline number that is used during the migration or on an ongoing basis. In some cases, you may wish to provide a service feedback form and/or trouble ticket form in the user's mail database to automate the process of reporting problems.

Neat New Features of Notes 4.0

- Consider using shared mail to save disk space.

- Try using the Notes 4.0 passthru feature to simplify access to databases for users, reduce the number of servers on which replicas of a database must reside, and provide one server for remote users to call in to for mail and all the applications they want to replicate or access.

- Migrate to the Notes 4.0 file format as soon as possible. If the database resides on a server, Notes 3.0 clients can still access it without a problem as the server will convert it on the fly for them, and Notes 4.0 clients and servers will immediately be able to take advantage of Notes 4.0 database features.

- Enhance security with local encryption of databases on servers and workstations, enforcing a consistent access control list, using the Notes

4.0 user type assignment in database access controls, and using multiple passwords on critical ID files (such as certifier IDs).

- Change your Notes topology to leverage Notes 4.0 features. Notes 4.0 servers handle more users, bigger databases, multiprocessor computers, passthru connections to other servers, native Internet access, and more. Consider how you might use these features to save money on communications costs, simplify access for users, limit the number of computers that must be administered, improve performance, and provide an all-around better computing environment for users and administrators. See Chapter 26, "Managing the Network," for more information.

- Implement and use new administration tools to shorten the time necessary to manage the Notes network and provide higher quality of servers. The administration process, events task, and report task can help you do this. See Chapter 27, "Managing Servers," for more information.

Upgrading Notes Workstation Clients

Now that the Notes 4.0 server is up and running, it is time to upgrade Notes workstations. Upgrading the workstation clients is important because until you do, you cannot take advantage of key Notes features such as field level replication with workstation clients and, more important, you cannot upgrade to the Notes 4.0 mail template or use shared mail.

In summary, upgrading the workstation will involve some or all of the following activities:

- Backing up the workstation clients.

- Installing the Notes 4.0 software.

- Upgrading Notes mail to the Notes 4.0 template (optional).

- Using shared mail (optional).

- Converting databases to the Notes 4.0 file format will automatically make local replicas of databases take advantage of Notes 4.0 features, such as field level replication and local adherence to database access controls. Select the database you want to convert and select File/Database/ Properties, Information Tab, and click on the Compact button to convert the database to Notes 4.0 file format.

Backing Up the Notes Workstation Client

As with backing up the server, you may back up the entire Notes program directory and the notes.ini file, or you may back up a subset to expedite the backup process. Back up just the important files if you have easy access to the Notes 3.0 software in the event it needs to be reinstalled. The files that must be backed up before installing the new Notes 4.0 software are:

- user.id (or whatever it is called)
- notes.ini
- desktop.dsk
- names.nsf (the user *Personal* Name and Address Book)
- Any Notes 3.0 templates that have been customized (.ntf files)
- Any local Notes 3.0 databases (.nsf files)

If something goes wrong during the upgrade procedure, you will need these files to restore the system to its pre-upgrade state.

Upgrading Non-Notes Hardware and Software

Make sure you check the specifications (see the table earlier in this chapter or your Notes documentation) to make certain you have the correct hardware, operating system software, and network software to run Notes 4.0. Backup procedures should be followed prior to upgrading these non-Notes items. If the non-Notes items will be installed on a different schedule from the Notes software, you will need to go through the backup procedures before each of the installations.

What Happens When You Upgrade

When you run the Notes 4.0 installation program, the Notes 4.0 program files will be copied to your computer. You should install the Notes 4.0 program to the same directory that Notes 3.0 was installed on so that the installation program can automatically set up the software. Some files, such as program files and template files, *will* be overridden. In addition, the installation program will make the following modifications to your system:

- Update notes.ini file with new settings used by the Notes 4.0 workstation client.
- Upgrade the Personal Name and Address Book with the Notes 4.0 Personal Name and Address Book template (pernames.ntf).
- Upgrade the Mail.box file to the updated Notes 4.0 mail.box file.

NOTE. *The installation program does not update the desktop.dsk file to the Notes 4.0 file format. You will need to do this manually by compacting the desktop to take advantage of Notes 4.0 capabilities such as adding workspace pages.*

Installing the Software

To install the Notes 4.0 software, run the installation program on the disks, CD-ROM, or network drive that contains the file install.exe. If you select the same directory to which your earlier version of Notes is installed, the installation program will not require any setup information.

To enable users to add workspace pages and be able to compact the desktop.dsk file, you will need to convert the desktop.dsk file to the Notes 4.0 file format. To do the conversion:

1. Click on a blank area on the workspace.

2. Choose Edit/Properties.

3. Click on Compact.

Upgrading Notes Mail

Upgrading Notes mail has several components to it. If your goal is to improve the quality of the Notes mail experience for users, you need to:

- Upgrade mail databases to the Notes 4.0 template design.

- Convert existing mail documents to suit the Notes 4.0 mail template.

NOTE. *Both utilities provided change the "Inherit design from" setting in the database information infobox to "StdR4Mail" automatically.*

Options to Consider

You may also want to implement shared mail. Shared mail is, as described later in this chapter, a new feature of the Notes server that saves server disk space by storing only one copy of mail messages that are addressed to multiple users. All addressees can access the mail message documents and it is not removed from the storage database until all users delete their pointer to it.

You may also want to change the file format of the mail database to the Notes 4.0 file format to improve system performance and enable the use of new security features. Local encryption of mail databases is particularly useful for laptop users. You can change the file format of the mail database by running the server Compact task on the database(s).

What Happens When You Upgrade Notes Mail

When you upgrade to Notes 4.0 mail you are really replacing the design elements of the mail database to ones that take advantage of Notes 4.0 design capabilities and make using mail easier and more versatile for users. After upgrading the mail database's design elements, the documents that are already in the database (including sent, received, and draft mail) must be updated to include elements that the new design requires to display and store these documents properly. The data contained in the Notes 4.0 mail documents will not be disturbed.

Because part of the mail database upgrade includes modifying documents in the database, you should only upgrade the primary mail database, not replicas of the mail database if the user has replicas of his or her mail database on their workstation. The primary mail database is the one that is listed in the user's person document and the one to which mail documents are initially delivered. If more than one replica were to be converted, documents would be altered in more than one replica, at the same time causing replication conflicts. The design of replicas of the primary mail database may receive the upgraded mail database design through normal replication.

NOTE. *If a user will still have a Notes 3.0 workstation client running, the replica on that client should have access controls set to not allow the design of the database to replicate, or should have replication settings set to not allow replication of the design elements of the database. Notes 3.0 clients will not be able to use the Notes 4.0 mail database design elements.*

How to Upgrade Notes Mail

There are two ways to upgrade to the Notes 4.0 mail database design. The first, and recommended, is to use the mail conversion utility on the server. The alternative is to manually replace the design of the mail database (or have users do their own) and then run the "Convert Categories to Folders" agent. Both methods achieve the same goals. The conversion utility is faster, enables you to automate the process for users, and has options that may come in handy.

Using the Conversion Utility to Upgrade Mail

The server-based mail conversion utility will do the following:

- Upgrade the mail database design template to the Notes 4.0 design.

- Change the design template name specified in the database to StdR4Mail.

- Create folders for categories and subcategories and put documents into these folders.

- Place uncategorized (received) documents into the InBox.

    The server based mail conversion utility will NOT do the following:

- Change read and unread marks on documents.

- Change the file format of the database to a Notes 4.0 file format.

A few rules to keep in mind when upgrading Notes mail:

- Do not upgrade the mail database until the server and workstation client have been upgraded.

- Do not upgrade more than one replica of a user's mail database.

- Set replicas residing on Notes 3.0 workstation clients and servers to not replicate the design changes. You may do this with access controls or replication settings.

To use the convert process to upgrade mail:

1. Make sure that the Notes user's workstation clients are upgraded to the Notes 4.0 software.

2. Alert users to copy their customized forms, views, and macros to a holding database. They can do this by choosing File/Database/New Copy in Notes 4.0 and giving the database a name other than the name of their mail database. It will also have a different replication ID number.

3. Shut down the router by issuing the command Tell Router Exit. (Note: When you complete the conversion you will need to reload the router program by issuing the command: Load Router.)

4. Issue the command Load Convert [-1] [-r] [-f] [-i] [-d] [-n] DRIVE:\ DIRECTORY\MAILFILE [oldtemplatename newtemplatename]. (Switches in brackets are optional; -1 and -f may *not* be used simultaneously.)

The following table lists and describes the available switches.

Switch	Description	Example
-1	This switch creates a text file of all the primary Notes mail databases on the server. You may then use this text file with the -f switch to determine which mail databases to upgrade. You must have upgraded the Public Name and Address Book for this argument to work properly.	load convert -1 c:\notes\ PrimMail.txt

Switch	Description	Example
-f	This switch upgrades only the mail database files specified in the text file you list. For example, if you have upgraded the accounting department workstations to Notes 4.0, you may list those mail databases in a text file called Acctg.txt and upgrade only those mail databases.	load convert -f c:\notes\ PrimMail.txt
-r	Searches the directory you specify and all of its subdirectories for mail databases	load convert -r mail*.nsf stdnotesmail mail4.ntf
-d	Replaces the design template of the mail databases with a template you specify. If this switch is used the conversion utility *does not* create folders and add categorized documents to them.	load convert -d mail*.nsf StdNotesMail mail4.ntf
-i	Ignores the maximum folder limit of 200. If you try to upgrade a mail database with more than 200 categories you will receive an error message. This is because Notes 3.0 workstation clients will not be able to access the database when converted. Use the -i switch to indicate that it is okay to convert the database and all of its categories or subcategories to folders.	load convert -i mail*.nsf stdnotesmail mail4.ntf
-n	This switch is used to test which files will be upgraded. It will display a list of databases on which the convert program will run.	load convert -n mail*.nsf stdnotesmail mail4.ntf

Manually Upgrading a Mail Database

The manual process for upgrading a mail database has the same effect but is less automated than the server convert process. The same rules, however, apply.

- Do not upgrade the mail database until the server and workstation client have been upgraded.

- Do not upgrade more than one replica of a user's mail database.

- Set replicas residing on Notes 3.0 workstation clients and servers to not replicate the design changes. You may do this with access controls or replication settings.

    To upgrade a mail database manually:

1. Run the Notes workstation client program.

2. Copy customized forms, views, and macros to a holding database. You may do this by selecting File/Database/New Copy in Notes 4.0 to create a database with a different file name and replication ID number than the primary Notes mail database for the user.

3. Select the mail database on the Notes workspace.

4. Select File/Database/Replace Design.

5. Choose the design template Mail(R4) (MAIL4.NTF).

6. Click Replace.

7. Click Yes if you already copied (backed up) your custom forms, views, and macros when you are alerted that the forms, views, and macros will be overwritten.

8. Choose View/Go To Agents.

9. Select (Convert Categories to Folders).

10. Select Actions/Run.

11. Copy customized forms into the upgraded mail database. Make sure the elements you copy into the newly upgraded database do not have the same name as your custom elements.

NOTE. *This process, although simple, will take longer to run than the conversion process on the server. It is probably most applicable to "technology leaders" who have early access to the Notes 4.0 client and want to use the new mail database. When mass migration is taking place, the conversion utility is a better tool.*

Upgrading Database Files to Notes 4.0 Format

The advantage of upgrading databases to the Notes 4.0 file format is that you can take advantage of Notes 4.0 features such as:

- Enhanced security (local encryption and forcing a consistent access control list)

- Setting a limit on the database size to control the amount of disk space that the mail database occupies on the server

- Replicating at the field level to lower communications costs

- New @ functions such as @AllChildren and @AllDescendants to replicate only response documents that are children of main documents that are selected to replicate

To upgrade to the Notes 4.0 file format use the Compact server task.

NOTE. *You need to have enough disk space for a full copy of the database to reside temporarily on the disk. The Compact server task will delete the second (copy) of the database when it is done with the compacting process.*

By default, Notes sets the maximum default size of the database to 1 gigabyte—the Notes 3.0 limit. This ensures that the database can still replicate to Notes 3.0 servers. If you want to exceed this limitation, you must create a new replica of the database and specify a limit of up to 4 gigabytes.

P A R T

Notes Management

- *Roles of Administrators*

- *The Notes 4.0 Public Name and Address Book*

- *Administration Control Panel*

- *The Administration Process*

- *Agent Manager*

- *Notes.ini File*

- *Tools*

- *Server Console Commands*

- *System Databases Overview (Other Than Public Name and Address Book)*

23

Managing Overview and Management Tools

Mᴀɴᴀɢɪɴɢ ᴀ ɴᴏᴛᴇꜱ 4.0 ꜱʏꜱᴛᴇᴍ ɪꜱ ᴀ ʟᴀʀɢᴇ ᴀɴᴅ ᴄᴏᴍᴘʟɪᴄᴀᴛᴇᴅ charter. It involves many tasks and an understanding of many subjects, some quite technical. In addition, managing the Notes 4.0 system will require technical resources in many locations for large organizations with a disparate user base and interaction with related groups such as the physical wiring and software protocol managers of your organization's network. For these reasons and to further enhance security by segregating duties, it makes sense to break down the job of managing the Notes system into discrete tasks.

■ Roles of Administrators

Generally, the larger the organization and Notes installation is, the more important (and feasible) greater segregation of duty becomes. In smaller organizations, there may be only one Notes administrator who is charged with managing the entire network.

Larger organizations have segregated the duties of managing the Notes system for some time. The Notes 4.0 Public Address Book now supports such segregation out of the box with the inclusion of roles into which administrators may be placed, and document Author fields to supplement access to documents in the Public Name and Address Book.

Most organizations with large Notes deployments think about managing their Notes system in four functions. These are, of course, logical breakdowns, so the actual tasks of any one function may vary from organization to organization. The four types of administration typically are:

- Domain Managers (Certifiers)

- Network Managers

- Server Administrators

- Database Managers

The following are some guidelines you may wish to use to organize the ongoing support of your Notes system. The suggestions here will need to be modified to suit the specific environment to which they are being applied.

Domain Managers (Certifiers)

In general it makes sense to have a central Notes team that is responsible for the overall Notes deployment. This team will make decisions about how all the Notes system administration tasks are divided. The team will also make decisions about how to manage the security and policy surrounding Notes implementation and usage.

Specifically, individuals in the domain manager's team will have Manager access to the Public Name and Address Book, will be in all the roles of the access control list to the Public Name and Address Book, and will possess the organization (top level) certifier ID file. By having Manager access to the Public Name and Address Book and by having control of the top level certifier, this group owns and can dispense other system administration privileges. Like any secure network, Notes requires a clear hierarchy and someone or group must be at the top of it.

What Tasks Are Domain Managers Responsible For?

The domain management team is responsible for the entire Notes system. This includes the strategic planning around what resources will execute which tasks. For example, the planning objectives of this team will probably include resources for installation, training, server administration, workstation installation and maintenance, technical support, security, and all policy guidelines and procedures. While planning is a big task during the initial deployment of Notes, it should become more manageable as the systems become routine. Migrations will always require a spike in time spent on planning, but as the knowledge base of Notes information grows internally, this too may be minimized.

The issues of support, training, and general administration are some basic categories that the domain management team should address directly or assign to other groups to address. It is important to clearly communicate and document all the procedures and processes this group develops, as these procedures will be the benchmark for administering Notes system service.

Support   Support is a tricky issue. End users will need assistance in accessing software, making changes and resolving other issues including errors and lower-end configuration problems. A good strategy is to have a help desk—preferably integrated with your organization's other help desk services—as the primary or first-level contact for end-users. A local server administrator is often a good person to resolve technical issues if the problem cannot be solved via a telephone conversation with the end user. The following are key support issues for which there must be a set of procedures in place to address:

- End-user help desk

- Server support strategy. (**Note:** Given the considerable cost of lost productivity of a down server, this process should have a concise escalation procedure to ensure that problems are resolved quickly.)

Training   Training is a key component to a successful deployment of Notes 4.0. It is important that some form of training be planned even if a comprehensive program is not feasible. In general, system administration training is the most critical because the effectiveness of users and application developers hinges on the integrity of the platform. The following items outline important training issues for which there should be policies and procedures in place:

- End-user training

- Application Developer training

- System Administration training

General Administration

In addition to support and training, the domain management team must develop the strategy for the following administrative issues:

- Security guidelines for workstations in addition to servers.

- Management of administrative requests (how to receive, track, and assign jobs).

- Physical server locations (central with single location, central with different locations, distributed with workgroups).

- Resources to tap. (What existing resources may be tapped to handle Notes related tasks. For example, it often makes sense to have a local network file server administrator serve as a Notes server administrator in a small organization.)

In addition to the planning functions described above, the domain management group will:

- Audit security, including the controls set in the Public Name and Address Book, the distribution and protection of ID files, database access controls and encryption as well as properly segregating administrative duties within the Notes environment to ensure that data is secure.

- Register users

- Register servers

- Register organizational unit certifiers

- Plan service extensions (gateways and processes)

- Manage the Public Name and Address Book

These functions are important because they represent the security aspects of the Notes system. While tasks within these functions may be delegated, the domain management group must assume overall responsibility for these tasks. For example, domain managers may delegate to local administrators an organizational unit certifier ID file to distribute the registration function. Similarly, for delegation purposes, domain managers may grant editor access to the Public Name and Address Book so certain administrators (typically network managers) can adjust settings to any document as necessary. While some of these tasks may be delegated, the ultimate responsibility for the certification process and for the security of the Public Name and Address Book belongs with the domain management group.

Using the roles created in the Public Name and Address Book as a guideline, you might assign the domain managers group into the following roles:

- GroupCreator can create new Group Documents.

- GroupModifier can edit or delete existing Group documents.

- ServerCreator can create new Server Documents.

- UserCreator can create new Person Documents.

- NetCreator can create all documents except Group, Server, and Person documents. (This would include certifier documents.)

By so doing you will give them the authority to create new users, servers and certifiers, as well as all other required documents in the Public Name and Address Book.

Network Managers

Network managers are responsible for just that—the network! This group is focused on delivering the communications and configurations plans for all servers in your organization's Notes network. Some of the tasks you might expect this group to routinely undertake are

- Designing a connection strategy between all servers within and outside a domain that will need to communicate

- Creating and modifying connection documents

- Establishing standards for server configuration so that servers will be equipped to support the connections that are setup for them

- Creating and modifying Notes named networks

- Instituting installation and migration policy and procedures for Notes software upgrades

- Implementing and managing gateways and integrated products

Using roles created in the Public Name and Address Book you can assign the network managers group Author access to the PAB, assign them the roles of NetCreator, NetModifier and ServerModifier to allow them to create and edit the documents they need to maintain in the PAB. You may want to divide the responsibilities of the network managers by creating additional roles and adding specific network managers to each role, then placing the new role into the Administrators field of specific documents in the PAB. By doing so you will give only those roles listed in the Administrators field authority to edit those documents, creating a segregation of duty and thus, better security. For example, you may want one group of network managers the responsibility of setting up and maintaining connection documents and another group of Network Managers will maintain server configurations and Notes Named Networks.

Server Administrators

The following are processes that will regularly need to be handled at the server level. In larger organizations, tasks related to these issues will probably be handled by the server administration group in each location.

- Implement installation and migration policies and procedures.

- Define backup/restore policies and procedures.

- Define procedures for adding databases to servers.

- Define server configuration standards.

- Using the roles created in the Public Name and Address Book as a guideline, you might assign the server administrators group into the NetModifier and ServerModifier groups. By so doing you will give them the authority to edit Server Documents as well as Program Documents in the PAB.

  This will also give them the authority to edit additional documents in the PAB that you may not want them to edit. For this reason you can create new roles in the PAB and assign the server administrators to these new roles and place these roles in the Administrators field of only those documents in the PAB that you want them to edit.

  For example, you may want to create a role called WestCoastServerAdmin and place this role in the Administrators field of all documents pertaining to West Coast servers. In this way, server administrators on the West Coast will be able to edit documents for servers they administer, but will not be able to edit documents pertaining to servers they do not administer.

Generally, it is best for security and efficiency to maintain and administer servers in a central location for each of the organization's sites. Security is enhanced because you can create a single, secure, and monitored environment for servers. In addition, having a single location limits the amount of hopping from one place to another for administration staff.

NOTE. *In addition to paying attention to the physical location of the servers, it makes sense to organize your support for them to best leverage support staff. For example, regardless of where the servers are located, you may want to have all server monitoring sent to a single database and monitored by one person or group. In this way, you get the benefit of organized server monitoring without adding to the task list of* all *the administrators' daily chores.*

However you manage the daily routine of maintaining servers, make certain that you have a plan, that it is documented, and that the people responsible for executing it are trained and capable. The servers in your network are critical to the service levels you can deliver. A strong support team and plan is the only way to deliver consistently high service.

Database Managers

Database management may not require as much experience or technical knowledge as a domain, network, or server manager may require but it does require a good understanding of the Notes 4.0 software. The role of database manager is often delegated to the end-user community so that they may manage the databases they use. Because database managers will be responsible for updating the ACL for their respective databases, as well as the design of these databases, it is important for these managers to understand the implications of the changes they will make. For example, if a database manager changes the ACL for a database that resides on Server A by changing Server B's access to that database from Manager to Reader, all changes that are made on Server B will not get replicated to Server A.

The primary responsibility for the domain management team in database management is around database policy, what can go on servers, and what security tools must be implemented as well as an archiving strategy. The following items should be addressed as part of the database management policy that the domain management team creates or has created:

- Risk rating system for databases

- Security tools to implement or not implement for each risk rating

- Routine tasks for database managers (replication, size, compact)

Using the roles created in the Public Name and Address Book as a guideline, you might assign the database managers group into the following groups. By so doing you will give them the authority to manage the data for their location or business function while minimizing the resources that are necessary:

System database management—These people may be responsible for managing specific system databases. In this case, it makes sense to have a server manager or other system administrator fill this role, especially if the security provided by segregation of duty will not be impaired by doing so.

Specific Locations—These people may be responsible for managing all the databases in specific geographic locations. By organizing database management in this way, you limit the number of people who must learn the nuances of managing databases but still get the advantage (security) of having databases managed by a person not affiliated with the system administration of Notes.

Business Function—By having specific people within different business groups responsible for managing the databases used by that business group, you get the benefit of keeping the data exclusive to the business group (say the executive staff, or marketing department) while limiting the number of people who need to have the training and privileges associated with being a database manager.

■ The Notes 4.0 Public Name and Address Book

The Public Name and Address Book contains the definition of resources for the Notes system. It is also the primary resource for the Notes administration team to find and administer the resources in the Notes domain.

This Notes 4.0 database is the key repository for information about users, servers, connections between servers, Notes-initiated programs, groups, certifiers, and public keys. Each of these entities has a form that may be used to create and edit the associated document that is stored in the Public Name and Address Book.

All of the forms that were in earlier versions of Notes have been updated to include new functionality in Notes 4.0.

Access Controls

Access controls are the same as they are in other databases. In the Notes 4.0 Public Address Book, you will want to grant most administrators with Author and Create privileges so that they may create documents for the roles they support (see the section on roles later in this chapter) and so they may edit certain documents they create. Administrators will have to be granted Editor access to all documents of a certain type, such as Server Documents, by being added to a role, or they must be granted Editing rights to specific documents by being entered into the Administrators field.

In general, having Editor access to the Public Name and Address Book is a high level access as it permits that user to edit any document in the Public Name and Address Book. Because there are Author fields and no Reader fields in the database, there is no way to limit what an editor of the database can control. As a result, use the Editor access level with discretion. It should usually be granted to a limited set of users, often in the domain management team. Other administrators will be able to edit select documents even if they have only Author access because they will be listed in roles or Administrators fields on the document. Once again, to limit the access of specific administrators to only the specific documents they should be able to edit, you must enter their name in the administrator field for those documents or enter their name in a role and enter the role into the administrator field for those documents. The roles provided in the template name and address book apply to types of documents, and therefore will not limit a given administrator to just the documents in his or her geographic region, for example.

By default, all users in the Notes network will have Author access to the Name and Address book. However, because all of the forms in the Name and Address Book have Author fields set up, no user will be able to create a document in the Public Name and Address Book unless he or she is entered into one or more roles.

With Author access, users *will* be able to replicate the Public Name and Address Book down to a local machine. This means all of the user, server, certifier, connection, and other information is easily downloadable in electronic format because there are no reader names fields on documents in the Public Name and Address Book, by default.

The standard Notes 4.0 Public Name and Address Book offers more inherent security than did earlier versions of the Public Name and Address Book. In Notes 4.0 there are a total of three security tools that can be used to limit access to the name and address book. These are:

- Access control list and options

- Roles

- Administrator fields

In Notes 4.0, the Public Name and Address Book provides these tools so that each organization may customize access. To adequately protect against assault, it is important to understand clearly how each of these components controls access so that they may be correctly used. Here are some summary suggestions on how to use these tools:

- Grant Author access to the Public Address Book for all system administrators and users. Some system administrators will also need create privileges so they may create certain document types (such as connection or server).

- Grant document creation and edit privileges to administrators using roles. Be careful with roles as a user (administrator) in a role can, for example, edit *all* documents of a specific type (connection documents, for example).

- Grant editing rights to a *particular* document using a role placed in the Administrators field. This is useful, for example, to grant the group West-CoastAdmin edit capabilities *only* to the Server Documents for West Coast servers.

With these three controls to choose from, the Notes 4.0 Public Address Book can be secure and functional. Each organization will have to make its own determination as to what specific access levels users and administrators will fall into. In addition, each organization will have to consider how to segregate administrative duties.

How to Assign Access

In summary, some administrators, such as the domain management group, should have Editor or higher access (depending on their function) to the Public Address Book. Others should be given Author access and listed in the roles appropriate for their job functions. Because the roles are established with access to documents by type, they are able to edit certain *types* of documents. For example, you may want to list network administrators in the NetModifier and ServerModifier roles so they can create and modify all documents necessary to set up and continually optimize the network. To do this they will need to modify server, connection, and configuration documents. In addition, you may create groups containing specific administrators and then enter these group names into *selected* documents to grant edit rights for the group to these documents.

Servers must be listed in the access control list of the Public Name and Address Book with editor or higher access so that changes to the databases can replicate. The same restrictions to replication that apply to all other databases apply to the Public Name and Address Book as well. A server listed in the Public Name and Address Book can access control lists with Designer access and may pass design features as well as document changes. A server listed in the Public Name and Address Book access control list with Manager access may exchange any kind of change to other replicas of the Public Name and Address Book, including security, design and document.

If you have a clear hub and spoke topology whereby only hub servers replicate directly with spokes, it makes sense to grant Manager access to the hubs and Reader access to the spokes. Under this scenario, you will not create group documents or register users or servers on a spoke server, as the new documents will not replicate back to the hub. If registration and group documents will be created on the spokes, you can raise the access to Author and still have a secure environment. It is especially important to limit the access to the Public Name and Address Book where remote (spoke) servers are more susceptible to attack than are the centrally managed or headquarters servers that can be better secured.

Documents

All documents in the Public Name and Address Book have been enhanced to enable settings for new features as well as to improve useability and security. Included are:

- Administrators (Author fields) to provide greater control over who can edit documents

- Collapsing sections to make forms easier to navigate

- Context-sensitive choices to offer relevant choices based on field values entered into other fields

- Change request fields used by the Administration Process to automate routine processes

Person Documents

Every user in the Notes domain has a Person Document in the Public Name and Address Book. This document contains information necessary for the user to send and receive mail, as well as to sign and encrypt mail. Additional information such as location and telephone number may also be stored in this document.

Server Documents Each server in the Notes domain must have an associated Server Document in the Public Name and Address Book. This document has information about the server such as name, active ports, and the Notes Named Network to which it belongs. In addition, security information such as the list of those authorized to access this server and those authorized to create databases and add replicas to this server is stored here.

Group Documents

Groups are lists of users and servers. Groups are primarily used for setting access controls to servers and databases. In addition, they may also be used to send mail to multiple recipients. Notes 4.0 introduces group "types" which improve security by limiting the kind of activities for which a group may be used. For example, if you assign a group the type "Deny List only" and use this group in the Server document to deny access to the users in this group (such as terminated employees whom you no longer want to have access to the server), you would not want the Administration Process to remove that user's name from the group when the user's Person document is removed from the Public Name and Address Book (because he or she is terminated and you no longer want him or her in your system). The new "type" attribute of Group Documents prevents this because the Administration Process checks the type before removing names from groups and does not delete names from groups that have the type "Deny List Only."

Certifier Documents

A list of organization certifiers is maintained in the Public Address Book, each with its own document. It describes the name (and lineage in the case of organizational unit certifiers) of the certifier. The certifier's public key is also listed in this document.

Domain Documents

This document defines domains, other than the domain (group of servers that use the same, replicated Public Name and Address Book) in which the server belongs. The Domain document is used for routing information between your domain (group of servers) and servers that belong to a "foreign" domain.

Connection Documents

Connection Documents specify when and for what purposes servers will connect. These definitions are contained in connection documents. Mail routing and replication—as well as passthru services—are dependent on Connection Documents. Connections are critical to the Notes system as it is these documents that manage the movement of documents throughout the system. Typically network managers are responsible for maintaining Connection Documents.

Program Documents

The Notes 4.0 server, as with earlier servers, can be configured to execute other programs on a schedule. Program Documents may be used to schedule backups, batch programs, other Notes server tasks, and add-in products.

Mail-In-Database Documents

Mail-In-Database Documents are used to route documents to specific applications. Similar to Person Documents, they tell the Notes 4.0 server's router program where to send documents, meaning on which server and into which database on that server. Mail-In-Databases are used when many users or applications need to send information into a database automatically or for a specific business function.

Cross Certificate Documents

Cross Certificate Documents stored in the Public Name and Address Book allow an ID file created by a hierarchical certifier to be validated and authenticated by an ID file that does not descend from the same hierarchical certifer. In essence, a Cross Certificate Document in your Public Name and Address Book contains the public key of the ID from another certifier. Your organization certifier issues a certificate to this public key and stores that in the Public Name and Address Book where all users and servers in your organization will be able to access it to authenticate the other ID file. Cross Certificate Documents are created by using the Administration Control Panel and issuing one of the cross certify commands.

Configuration Documents—New in Notes 4.0

Configuration Documents allow administrators to make notes.ini settings without using a text editor or accessing that server directly. For example, an administrator in Boston may, with appropriate access to the Public Name and Address Book, create a Configuration Document that will turn on replication logging for those servers on the West Coast (the notes.ini setting "Log_Replication=" will be changed from the value 0 to the value 1).

Location Documents—New in Notes 4.0

Location Documents in the Public Name and Address Book serve no purpose. They are designed for mobile users who may have different types of connections used to access the server based on different physical configurations. For example, a user with a notebook computer may access the server from home using a modem but will connect via LAN to the server while at the office. Location documents on the user's laptop simplify his or her switching from one configuration to the other.

Setup Profile Documents—New in Notes 4.0

Used during the workstation client setup program, these documents determine what Connection Documents will be placed in a user's Personal Name and Address Book so that he or she may easily connect to a server. These documents serve no system purpose. They only simplify the setup procedure for workstations.

Public Name and Address BookSecurity Documents

Protecting the Public Name and Address Book against intrusion is critical to the integrity of the Notes system. Since Notes itself relies entirely upon this database for determining server access privileges as well as communications, a breach of the NAB database could be catastrophic.

As with other databases, database access controls represent the first and primary control against attack. By managing the access control list, and roles within the access control list, the Public Name and Address Book will remain safe. In addition, creating administration groups will simplify the process of granting and removing access to documents within the Name and Address Book.

Roles

The default roles available in the Public Address Book are listed below. Entering a user (administrator) into one of these roles gives that user Create or Modify rights to all documents of a given type (or types in the case of Net-Modifier & NetCreator). Limit access to roles to those administrators who really need to have this much control over system documents.

- *GroupCreator* can create new Group Documents.

- *GroupModifier* can edit or delete existing Group Documents.

- *NetCreator* can create any document except: Group, Person, and Server documents.

- *NetModifier* can edit or delete any existing documents except Group, Person, and Server Documents.

- *UserCreator* can create new Person Documents.

- *UserModifier* can edit existing Person Documents.

- *ServerCreator* can create new Server Documents.

- *ServerModifier* can edit existing Server Documents.

Assigning a user to a particular role in the name and address book gives them the right to create or modify certain types of documents. In some cases they should not be able to edit certain types, but rather certain documents, in which case an administration group is the best way to solve the problem.

Roles beginning with Creator must be assigned to any user who will need privileges to use a form to create a document that the role allows. "Modifier" roles need only be assigned to users with Author access because any user with Edit access or above will automatically have editing capabilities for all documents in the database.

New Roles   You may create additional roles in the Public Name and Address Book just as you would in another database and then use the role names in security components of the database. For example, if you wanted to give all server administrators the authority to edit Configuration Documents without giving them authority to adjust settings in Server Documents, you may want to create a role called ConfigModifier and place this role in the Administrators field of the Configurations Document. This would give the administrators assigned to this role the access necessary to edit Configuration Documents without giving them access to edit all the other documents that NetModifier would have granted them. Segregating duties and access privileges in this way is the best way to provide a secure environment. Notes 4.0

does provide the tools necessary to sufficiently segregate duties such that data is never at risk, even from an administrator.

Administrators Fields

Administrators fields further refine access to the Public Name and Address Book. Unlike access controls, which grant general access to the databases and roles that grant access to create or edit all documents of certain types (all Server Documents for example), Administrators fields have been added to all documents in the Public Name and Address Book.

Administrators fields are actually Author fields. Names entered in this field will have complete editing rights to the document into whose Administrator's field they are entered. For example, you may have a group of West Coast server administrators to whom you would like to grant access only to those servers that they administer. If you entered them into the ServerModifier role, they would have access to all the Server Documents in the database. Instead, you could enter this group name into the Administrators field in each Server Document to which this group should have access and they will be able to edit only those documents. Users and servers with Edit access and above to the Public Name and Address Book do not need to be listed in either roles or Administrator fields to edit documents. Their high access to the database will give them Edit privileges to all documents, although they will not be able to create documents unless they are entered into the create roles.

Remember, servers are treated just as users in the Notes replication scheme. As a result, servers must have the same access privileges as would a user if changes are to replicate from one server to another. Since there are no Reader fields (by default) in Public Name and Address Book documents, and because servers typically have high (Editor or above) access to the Public Name and Address Book, changes made on one server to a document will replicate throughout an organization as they should to update all the replicas with that change. Be careful, this means that if a single server is vulnerable to attack, especially by someone who might gain direct access to the file system where the Public Name and Address Book resides, a change could be made to the Public Name and Address Book that would replicate throughout the organization. This threat is another good reason to consider one or more of the following: keep servers physically secure, do not store the Notes workstation software on server computers, lower the access privileges of non-hub servers so they could not replicate changes made to documents throughout the organization, protect server ID files with two passwords, and encrypt the Public Name and Address Book on all replicas.

Groups

As described above, groups are lists of Notes entities (users and servers) that save time. By using groups, a user can send e-mail to ten people without typing ten names and an administrator can remove access from a user from three servers by taking the user's name out of one group.

Notes 4.0 introduces the notion of categorizing groups to provide additional security. By creating different types of groups, their purpose and scope can be more securely defined. There are four types of group documents (stored in the Public Name and Address Book) in Notes 4.0:

- Mailing List

- Access List

- Deny Access List

- Multi-Purpose

Creating Groups

To create a group you must have Author access to the Public Name and Address Book and you must be entered into the role GroupCreator. With this access you may open the Public Name and Address Book and choose Create/Group. A group form will appear. Enter a name for the group, enter a type (see below) for the group, and enter a description so others will know the purpose of this group. Next, enter a list of the users or servers you want in this group. If you select the down arrow, you will be able to choose from a list in the Public Address Book. Finally, at the bottom of the form you may enter the names of users or groups you wish to be able to edit this group document.

Groups For Administering Notes

Groups offer a means of centrally managing security elements. By creating a group such as WestCostServerAdmin, we can grant access to many parts of the system to this group rather than individuals. By so doing, we simplify the addition and removal of users (administrators) from these access privileges because by removing the person from the group, they are removed from all the privileges granted to that group.

For example, let's say we want to grant Server access, Create Replica access, Create Database access, and Administrator access to the group "West-CoastServerAdmin" in the Server Documents of all the servers on the West Coast (let's say there are six). This means we will enter the group four times in each Server Document, multiplied by six Server Documents. We will make 24 additions to add this privilege. Going forward, however, we need only to add or remove a user (administrator) once from the group "WestCoastServerAdmin" to add or remove all 24 privileges.

You should consider adding the following groups to simplify administration of your system. These groups can be placed in the corresponding fields in Server Documents to manage the access to a Notes server(s). Furthermore, some of these groups may be useful for adding users to roles in the Public Name and Address Book. For example, perhaps server administrators should be able to create group documents so they would be added to the GroupCreator role.

In larger organizations with distributed management of the Notes environment, you may wish to add a Group Document of administrators for the following categories for each *geographic* support team as well. In this way, you can distribute responsibility by location rather than granting blanket responsibility for a given privilege:

- ServerAdminWest

  ServerAdminEast (add a group for East and West if necessary)

- CanAccessServerWest

  CanAccessScrverEast

- Terminations

- CanCreateDb

- CanCreateReplica

  New features for Notes 4.0 are

- Access this server (passthru)

- Route through (passthru)

- Cause Calling (passthru)

- Destinations Allowed (passthru)

- Run Personal Agents

- Run Restricted LotusScript Agents

- Run UnRestricted LotusScript Agents

All of the above groups should have the type Access Control List Only. By creating these groups you can delegate the responsibility for maintaining these groups and simplify the management of these server access privileges.

By default the Notes setup program adds two multipurpose groups to the Public Name and Address Book to assist in administering the system.

These are LocalDomainServers and OtherDomainServers. Whenever a
server is created in your domain, the registration process will add the server
to the group LocalDomainServers automatically. It is convenient to use this
group because you typically want all servers in your organization to have
high access to user databases (and probably *not* to the Public Name and Address Book) so that by listing this one group it is easy to replicate changes in
the database all the way through the organization to all replicas on any
server without granting this high access to sensitive databases, such as the
Public Name and Address Book.

OtherDomainServers is a helpful group for granting limited access to
servers outside your organization with whom you want to share information.
Vendor servers, for example, can be entered into this group and this group
can then be given read access to databases that are designed to provide information to outside organizations. While you want to exchange information
with these outside organizations, you probably do not want to give them unlimited access to your internal documents! Hence, having one group of servers that is internal and one group of servers that is external makes it easy to
distinguish which servers are internal and external and easily grant appropriate access for each.

Types of Groups

The following are the types of groups that Notes 4.0 lets us define. Each one
has a specific purpose and, especially when using the Administration Process
(below) it is important to correctly assign group types to prevent unauthorized access.

Access Control List Only   Groups of this type, "Access Control List Only,"
may be used only to grant access to a server or database privilege. It may not
be used for sending mail (the mailer program will not look up names in it)
and it should not be used to deny any kind of access as the Administration
Process will remove users from it when those users are removed from the
Public Name and Address Book.

Mail Only   Use these groups to provide a convenient way for users to address mail messages to multiple users without having to type each name individually.

Deny List Only   Use this type of group to explicitly deny access. For example, if a user leaves the organization, he or she should be listed in a Terminations group of the type Deny List only. It is important that the type is Deny
List only as the Administration Process does not search and remove users
from this type of group (as it does other group types in the Public Name and
Address Book) when a user is removed from the system.

Multi-purpose   Use multi-purpose groups when you want to use it for granting access to a server or database and sending mail. For example, you may want the group WestCoastServerAdmin to be a multipurpose group so that it can be granted Administrator privileges to servers and also be used by the Report task for sending mail to all administrators notifying them of a server event.

Actions Everywhere!

In addition to the definitions and security tools described above, the Public Name and Address Book contains actions to help administrators execute routine tasks. These actions supplement the automation provided in the Administration Control Panel.

For example, if an administrator is looking at the People view in the Public Name and Address Book, the Action menu will have actions available to add users, remove users, edit users, recertify users, and rename users. Similar actions are available in all of the views in the Public Name and Address Book to simplify the Administration Process and guide administrators through all the necessary steps of an operation.

■ Administration Control Panel

The Administration Control Panel is a single-user interface for many of the administrative tasks associated with maintaining Lotus Notes. It acts as a shell to logically organize the menu commands—and Public Name and Address Book document editing tasks—involved with managing a Notes network.

To access the Administration Control Panel, select File/Tools/Server Administration. You will be presented with a window on the left and eight buttons on the right, as illustrated back in Figure 15.1. The window lets you choose the sever you wish to monitor. The buttons represent administrative tasks logically grouped.

People Button

Use this button to register new users or go to the People view of the Public Name and Address Book on the server you have selected. Once in the People view, you may add, edit, or delete Person Documents and rename and recertify user ID files using actions in the action menu.

Servers Button

Use this button to configure servers, register servers, log analysis, and view servers. The configure servers option actually takes you to the configurations view of the Public Name and Address Book where actions will assist you in adding server configuration documents to automate changes to the notes.ini file for any Notes 4.0 server in the domain. Registering servers is similar to registering users in that a server ID file and a Server Document (to reside in the Public Name and Address Book) will be created. Log analysis uses the new database analyze feature (see Database button below) to provide detailed information on the server log file. And accessing the server view of the Public Name and Address Book will provide actions to add, delete, and edit Server Documents as well as recertify server ID files and convert server ID files to hierarchical certificates.

Address Book Button

This button simply opens the Public Name and Address Book to the last view that you had open.

Console Button

The console button opens a new window with a remote server console. You may issue commands to a server as if you were working directly on the console window on the server itself. Notes 4.0 adds new commands to the server console as detailed in Chapter 27, "Managing Servers."

NOTE. *If any name entered as a parameter for a command contains a space character, enclose the name in quotation marks.*

Groups

This option lets you create a new group or go to the groups view in the Public Name and Address Book so you can edit or delete an existing one.

Certifiers

This button gives you access to all the tasks related to certification, except registering users and servers. Using this button you may do the following:

- Certify an ID file.

- *Cross-Certify an ID file*—Add a document to the Public Name and Address Book that will enable servers to authenticate ID files that do not have a common ancestral certifier.

- *Cross-Certify a Key*—Same as above but does not require a "safe" ID that stores the public key.

- *Edit Multiple Passwords*—Add, edit or delete multiple passwords in (to) a Notes ID file.

- *Open the Certification Log*—Lets you review certificates that have been issued.

- *Register Organizational Unit*—Create an organizational unit certifier that falls beneath another certifier in a hierarchy.

- *Register Organization*—Create a new top-level certifier ID file.

- *Register Nonhierarchical*—Create a nonhierarchical certifier ID file.

Mail

This option helps you troubleshoot mail routing. You may open the outgoing mail database (mail.box) or send a mail trace to get detailed information about the route a mail message takes to get to the recipient destination.

Database Button

This button lets you open system databases—including log, catalog, statistics, and administration requests databases—so that you may review information stored there by the Notes 4.0 server programs. In addition, you may open the Statistics & Events database to configure server statistics reporting. Finally, you can take action on any database stored on the server you are accessing such as:

- *Analyze*—Create a database analysis of a database (see database management chapter).

- *Compact*—Remove white (unused) space from an existing database. (Remember, the compact utility will convert a database to Notes 4.0 file format. See Chapter 22, "Migration.")

- *Full Text*—Create, update, and delete full text indexes.

- *Quotas*—Set a disk space quota for a database so that the server will not permit it to grow beyond a specified size on disk.

- *Administration Server*—Set the Administration Server for a database (same effect as this option in the Advanced Icon in Access Control dialog box).

■ The Administration Process

The Administration Process is a server task that can (and does by default) run on every Notes 4.0 server. It performs the following tasks:

- Renaming users and servers

- Recertifying user and server ID files

- Upgrading to hierarchical ID file
- Updating access control lists in databases
- Updating Group documents in the Public Name and Address Book

The advantage of the Administrative Process is that it eliminates many steps in dealing with certification issues as well as access control and group document changes. Because Notes ID files are distributed, many of these tasks have required several steps from both users and administrators in the past. If you do not already use hierarchical ID files in your organization, you should use the Administration Process to assist in the conversion process. Hierarchical ID files offer much more security and the Administration Process can be used on them once converted, minimizing administrative duties. The following is an explanation of how the Administration Process works.

The Administration Process (AdminP) task runs on all Notes 4.0 servers. It is added, by default, to the ServerTasks notes.ini setting when Notes 4.0 is installed or upgraded. This server process is responsible for executing the procedures necessary to rename, recertify, upgrade to hierarchical, or remove an entity from the system.

Three system databases are critical to the functioning of the Administration Process:

- The Administration Requests database
- The Certification Log File database
- The Public Name and Address Book database

The Administration Requests database stores the tasks the Administration Process is to execute, the certification log file that is updated to reflect certification activities, and the Public Name and Address Book that stores many of the changes to certificates. For certification activities, then, the Administration Requests database stores the request and documentation of what occurred, the certification log receives notifications regarding certificates issued, and the Public Name and Address Book stores the certificates that will be taken by the server or workstation client and placed into the ID file itself.

NOTE. *Many Administration Process tasks are dependent on the certification log. This database is* not *created by default. You will need to create this database before doing certification actions such as renaming a user with the Administration Process. Furthermore, you should replicate this database to all servers involved in the certification process.*

When a Notes administrator makes a request by selecting an action in the Public Name and Address Book, a request to complete a set of tasks is stored in the Administration Requests database. This database (ADMIN4.NSF) is created automatically the first time the Administration Process runs on the server. The documents stored in this database are designed to tell the Administration Process what actions to take as well as to document the status of a task assigned to the Administration Process. As the Administration Process executes tasks, it places response documents into the Administration Requests database to document the steps taken.

Different servers will need to execute Administration Requests. Therefore, replicas of the Administration Request database must reside on all Notes 4.0 servers that will have the Administration Process running so that each server may periodically check to see if there are administration requests (see Figure 23.1) pending that it is supposed to execute.

NOTE. *For most tasks, the Administration Process requires that ID files it works with be hierarchical. While the Administration Process can upgrade flat certificate ID files to hierarchical, it cannot work with flat certificate ID files to rename or recertify them.*

For example, if an administrator were to select Actions/Recertify Server while in the Servers view of the Public Name and Address Book, here is how the procedure might look:

1. User selects Actions/Recertify Server.

2. User (administrator) enters certifier ID to issue certificate.

3. Notes posts an Initiate Recertify Address Book document into the Administration Requests database (ADMIN4.NSF) on the server where the request was initiated. This document contains the new certificate issued by the certifier.

4. Notes posts an entry into the Certification Log (CERTLOG.NSF) on the same server where the administrator initiated the request to document the certification.

5. The Administration Requests database replicates with the server that acts as the "Administration Server" for the Public Name and Address Book. (This server is designated in the access controls of the Public Name and Address Book.) The Recertify Server in Address Book document now resides in the Administration Requests replica that is on the same server that acts as the Administration Server for the Public Name and Address Book.

6. The Administration Process, running on the server designated as the Public Name and Address Books Administration Server, looks in the Administration Requests database for actions it should take. It sees the RecertifyServer in Address Book request, verifies the electronic signature on it, and updates the appropriate Server Document.

Figure 23.1

A recertification request
is made by an
administrator.

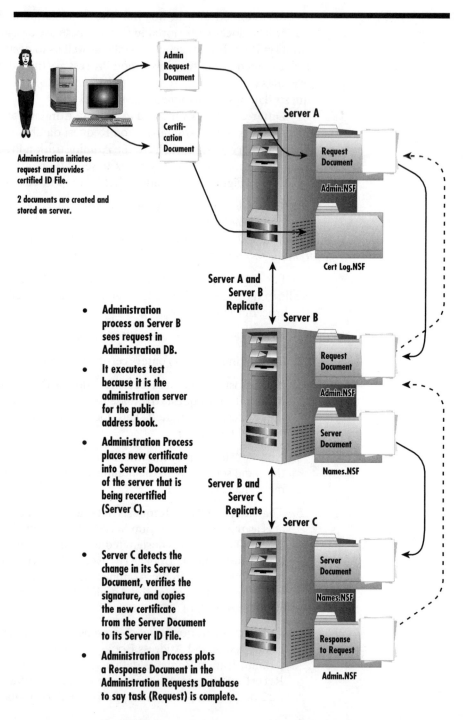

Administration initiates
request and provides
certified ID File.

2 documents are created and
stored on server.

- **Administration
  process on Server B
  sees request in
  Administration DB.**

- **It executes test
  because it is the
  administration server
  for the public
  address book.**

- **Administration Process
  places new certificate
  into Server Document
  of the server that is
  being recertified
  (Server C).**

- **Server C detects the
  change in its Server
  Document, verifies the
  signature, and copies
  the new certificate
  from the Server Document
  to its Server ID File.**

- **Administration Process plots
  a Response Document in the
  Administration Requests Database
  to say task (Request) is complete.**

7. When the server that is being recertified detects (during a regular refresh of its Public Address Book and notes.ini cache) the new certificate in its Server Document residing in the Public Name and Address Book, the server verifies the change by checking the digital signature and copying the new certificate to the server ID file.

Functions

Following are the different kinds of tasks the Administration Process automates. The general process of creating a Request Document in the Administration Requests database and then having the servers throughout the organization check this database for requests it is designated to execute apply to all of the tasks the Administration Process automates.

Renaming

You may use the Administration Process to rename users. When you do, the Administration Process will also replace all entries of the user's old name and replace it with the new one in database access controls as well as Group documents in the Public Name and Address Book. The Administration Process automates this procedure such that an administrator makes one request and no additional steps (other than to confirm the change as it is being made) are required.

Recertifying

On a periodic basis, Notes server and user ID files need to be recertified. The date for when they need to be recertified depends upon what date their certificate was set to expire when their ID file was created or last certified. Just like a license from the Department of Motor Vehicles, Notes IDs must be issued a new stamp of authenticity from the certifying authority (certifier ID file). The Administration Process automates this procedure such that an administrator makes one request and need not take any additional steps other than to confirm the change as it is being made.

Upgrading to Hierarchical

The upgrade to hierarchical ID files is important to provide security in your Notes network. This upgrade has been painful in the past because so many ID files needed to be recertified at the same time. The Administration Process will help with this task by requiring that only one server be upgraded manually. All additional servers (and then users) may be automated with the Administration Process.

Updating Access Control Lists in Databases

By specifying one Administration Server for each database, the change is made on the replica that resides on that server and the change it makes replicates to all other replicas in the organization. Any time a user or server ID file is changed due to a name change or recertification as a hierarchical ID file, or when a user is removed from the system, the Administration Process will make a corresponding change to any database that has an Administration Server specified. An Administration Server designation simply determines which server will make administrative changes automatically to the database. If all servers running the Administration Process made all such changes (for example, if every server's Administration Process deleted a user from every replica's access control list) replication conflicts would occur.

Administration Server

NOTE. *The Administration Servers rely upon replication to spread changes to all other replicas, so it makes sense to make hub servers act as Administration Servers as well. This is an efficient means of distributing such changes and generally is supported by high access control levels for hub servers to other servers and databases.*

Updating Group Documents in the Public Name and Address Book

Changes to user names and deletion of user names will also be reflected in group documents, provided an Administration Server is specified for the Public Name and Address Book. For example, if an administrator removes a user from the system by choosing Actions/Delete Person in the People view of the Public Name and Address Book, the Administration Server will also remove that user's name from all group documents in the Public Name and Address Book *with the exception of groups that have the type "Deny Access."* This means that if a user is removed, his or her access to servers and databases that is granted via group documents will be removed. The explicit denial of access that comes from groups such as Terminations will not be removed. This means that if a user leaves the organization and is removed (by the Administration Process) from the access lists for the server and databases that used to grant him access, he or she will not be removed from the Terminations group to which he or she should have been added to explicitly deny access to the server and databases.

Setting It Up

Running the Administration Process requires the following:

- Notes Servers running Notes 4.0 software

- A certification log replica on all servers

- The AdminP program included in the ServerTasks notes.ini setting

- An Administration Server designated for the Public Name and Address Book

- A replica of the administration requests database on each server

- Access control to the Public Name and Address Book, certification log and administration request databases of Author with Create privileges

NOTE. *In addition to the items listed above, you will need hierarchical ID files for users and servers. If you do not already have these, the Administration Process can assist in converting your existing flat ID files. You will need to determine a hierarchical naming scheme before employing the Administration Process to help with this task.*

Converting from Flat to Hierarchical ID Files

The Administration Process can assist in the hierarchical certification process. The key to using the administration process is to first upgrade a single server to hierarchical ID file manually so that it may initiate additional upgrades. Once you have this single server upgraded to hierarchical, you may select it as the Administration server for the Public Name and Address book (which was upgraded during the migration to Notes 4.0). The hierarchically certified server that you manually upgraded, can now be used to upgrade other servers and then workstation clients to hierarchical certificates by choosing the Server or Person Document you wish to update and choosing the appropriate action from the menu in the Public Name and Address Book.(Actions/ Upgrade Server to Hierarchical or Actions/Recertify Person.)

■ Agent Manager

Agents in Notes 4.0 automate tasks similar to the way Macros automated tasks in Notes 3.0. Notes 4.0 ships with a number of agents that users can take advantage of immediately, such as an agent to alert senders of e-mail that a user is on vacation. In addition to these predefined (pre-built) agents, users can create their own (personal) agents to automate tasks. To do this, they must have appropriate access to the database (Reader in the access control list) and server (specified in the Server Document in the Public Name and Address Book) where they want the agent to run, or they must store the agent locally in their DESKTOP.DSK file. Notes 4.0 provides the Agent Builder to create simple agents, formula agents, or LotusScript agents. If users want to create an agent that can be used by others, they must have Designer access to the database on which they want this agent to run.

The agent manager controls who can use agents and when the agents may run on each server. This control helps maximize server efficiency by only letting users who need to have the privilege of running agents use the server resources to do so. In addition, by providing controls for the types of agents a user may run as well as the times and conditions under which agents may run, server resources may be well planned.

Agents, like other design elements, reside in a database. There are two kinds of agents: public and private. A public agent is one that may be used by anyone with the appropriate privilege in the database and the appropriate access to the server on which the agent resides. A private agent may only be used by the user associated with it and is still beholden to the database and server access controls that will let the user run it. Public agents may be created by anyone who has Designer access to the database. Personal agents may be created by any user who has Reader and Create Personal Agents privileges to the database.

There are two overall kinds of restrictions for the use of agents: Database and Server. Database access control list privileges must be granted for a user to access an agent. Server access controls—found in the Server Document for the server on which the agent will run—may override database access controls to limit who may and may not use agents on the server.

How Agent Manager Works

The agent manager is a server process that is always running (the installation program adds it to the ServerTasks notes.ini setting). It references field values that are specified in the Server Document to determine who may run different kinds of agents, when, and under what circumstances. Certain types of agents can have enormous power over the server to execute tasks outside the realm of database functionality. As a result, each agent in a database is digitally signed to ensure that an authorized user did in fact approve the agent for use. This signature is checked before an agent runs. Restrictions listed in the Server Document for the server on which the agent will run are also checked before an agent will run.

Run Private Agents

Users granted this privilege will be able to run agents they create in the database. They may use formulas or the Notes 4.0 agent builder to create the agents, provided they have Reader and Create Personal Agents privileges to the database.

Run Restricted LotusScript Agents

Users listed in this field may run agents with a limited set of features. The purpose here is to grant greater flexibility by allowing the use of LotusScript in the creation of the agent while at the same time protecting the security of the server by preventing certain LotusScript functions that would give users control of the file system, operating system, and other areas not necessary for most database functionality.

Run Unrestricted LotusScript Agents

Users listed in this field may run agents with the full set of LotusScript features. This privilege gives users very high authority, as they may be able to create agents that access such things as the server's ID file and execute tasks using the servers—rather than their own—authority to do so. The point is, the Agent Manager lets administrators segregate what agent processing privilege different users should have. As a result, administrators can put the power of agents in the hands of those they trust to respect security and the limited processing cycles of the server.

Daytime and Nighttime

These columns determine the time periods and settings for running agents. For example, you may want to limit the use of agents to evenings when server resources are more abundant. You may set the resources separately for both daytime and nighttime such that you control the amount or resource devoted to agents in either of these time periods.

Start/Stop

These fields determine the specific day and night times when agents may run. For example, you may want to prohibit the use of agents from 8:00 a.m. until 10:00 a.m. when large numbers of users are first accessing the server to check their mail.

Number of Concurrent Sessions

The entry in this field determines how many agents may run at the same time on a server. While only one agent can run on a single database at a time, multiple agents can be running on multiple databases simultaneously.

Maximum Agent Execution Time

This field limits the amount of time an agent may take to complete. If an agent runs for more than the amount of time specified here, the agent manager will terminate it.

Percent of Polling Time

This field determines the amount of the processing capability agents may demand without being delayed. During daytime hours, you probably want to have a lower number specified here so that other server processes, such as user access to databases, do not get delayed too long. At night you may want a higher number as there are few if any users requesting server processing time.

■ Notes.ini File

The notes.ini file contains all the information the server needs to set when it loads. Each time a Notes 4.0 server starts, it reads the notes.ini file to determine how different settings that affect the Notes environment should be set. For example, the notes.ini file contains the list of programs that should be loaded at startup (ServerTasks) as well as a list of programs that should run at different specified times (ServerTasksAt1).

You may control the contents of the notes.ini (and thus the Notes environment) by:

- Using a configuration Document in the Public Name and Address Book to change settings in the notes.ini file for any server in the domain

- Editing the notes.ini file with a text editor

- Using a set configuration command at the server console or remote console

The notes.ini file is in different locations on different operating system platforms. The following table indicates where to find the NOTES.INI file on different server operating system platforms.

Platform	Location
OS/2	Notes data directory
Windows (any version)	Windows directory or Notes data directory
UNIX	Notes directory
Macintosh	Preferences stored in preferences folder in the system folder
NetWare	Notes directory

Improving Server Performance

The following notes.ini settings may be adjusted to fine-tune server performance for your organization's particular needs.

notes.ini Setting	What It Does
MailMaxThreads	Determines the maximum number of threads that the mail router can create to perform its mail transfers efficiently. Without this variable, the default is one thread per server port.

notes.ini Setting	What It Does
Memory_Quota	Determines the maximum number of megabytes of virtual memory that Notes is permitted to allocate. Administrators gain more control over the growth of the swap file.
MinNewMailPoll	Determines how often workstations can contact the server to see if new mail has arrived for the user. This setting overrides the user's selection in the Mail Setup dialog box. No default is set during server setup.
NSF_Buffer_Pool_Size	Sets the size of the NSF buffer pool, a section of memory used for buffering I/O transfers between the NSF and NIF indexing functions and disk storage. The default value is usually sufficient, but if users get an error telling them to increase the value of this variable, increase the value a few megabytes at a time. You can use a performance monitor to find out if a larger value is causing too much swapping or paging.
ServerTasks	Controls the tasks that the server runs. These tasks start automatically at server startup and continue until the server is shut down. Improve performance by removing tasks that aren't appropriate to the server if it is a specialized server. Do not remove the update task from a server. If you do so, the public address book will not update.

Settings That Cannot Be Specified with a Server Configuration Document

While Server Configuration Documents offer administrators greater flexibility and simplify the process of updating the notes.ini file, there are some settings that might jeopardize server security if they were to be changed with configuration documents. Remember, the NetModifier Role in the Public Name and Address Book lets anyone in that role change Server Configuration Documents but it does not grant privileges to modify Server Documents.

For security purposes, the following notes.ini settings cannot be changed with a Server Configuration Document, they should be made in the Server Document itself:

- ServerName
- Server_Title
- Domain
- MailServer
- MailFile
- Type
- Allow_Passthru_Access
- Allow_Passthru_Targets
- Allow_Passthru_Clients
- Allow_Passthru_Callers
- Form
- Names
- Allow_Access
- Deny_Access
- Create_File_Access
- Create_Replica_Access
- Admin_Access
- Ports
- KitType
- Server_Console_Password

NOTE. *You must use the console to specify the Server_Console_Password setting.*

■ Tools

The following tools may be used by the server manager to get information, force server tasks, and monitor information about the Notes system. As users become dependent upon the Notes applications that are deployed, maintaining high quality, reliable Notes server availability becomes increasingly important. The following tools help you by letting you force tasks at the server command that would normally be scheduled (so you can override schedules), allowing you to find out information about the system, and alerting you if thresholds are met (so you can avert a problem before it happens), reporting failures, and keeping track of the system on the whole to help you provide the best service possible.

■ Server Console Commands

Server console commands are the means by which administrators may communicate directly with the server program. The command console itself is a text interface with no menus and only the limited set of commands that follow which may be issued. Most commands to the server are issued via documents in the Public Name and Address Book or settings in the notes.ini file. The server console commands, however, allow administrators to issue commands directly to the server program. The administrator may sit at the physical machine where the server is located and type at the server console or use the remote console feature to send server console commands to the server program while sitting at a Notes workstation computer. The following is a complete list of the commands.

Command	What It Does
Broadcast	Sends a message to users on the server.
Drop	Closes one or more server sessions.
Exit	Shuts down the Notes 4.0 server program.
Help	Gets information about commands you may issue to the console.
Load	Runs a server program.
Pull	Pulls (without a scheduled connection) changes from a replica on another server.
Push	Sends changes from one server to another server without a scheduled connection.
Quit	Shuts down the server.
Replicate	Exchanges changes between two servers without a scheduled connection.
Route	Sends mail from one server to its next location without a scheduled connection.

Command	What It Does
Set Configuration	Adds or resets a setting in the Notes.ini file.
Set Secure	Password protects the command console.
Set Statistics	Resets the numeric-additive statistics.
Show Configuration	Lists the current notes.ini settings for this server.
Show Directory	Lists all Notes databases in the Notes data directory. Similar to DOS command "dir."
Show Diskspace	Shows the available disk space on volume, drive, or file system or on the specified volume, drive, or file system.
Show Memory	Displays virtual memory, including: RAM and the boot drive's swapping memory.
Show Port	Shows traffic and error statistics for the port specified.
Show Schedule	Shows the next time that a server or program, is scheduled to run.
Show Sessions	Displays information about current Notes sessions.
Show Statistics	Shows server statistics.
Show Tasks	Shows the status of all active server tasks.
Show Transactions	Displays the transaction statistics for the server.
Show Users	Lists all users who are currently accessing the server and the databases they're using.
Tell	Issues a command to a running server program.

Events and Reporting Tasks

Notes 4.0 has the ability to monitor server and database events as well as provide server statistics. These monitors and statistics provide extremely useful information for maintaining adequate service levels, planning connections and troubleshooting. Notes 4.0 monitoring and statistics work differently than earlier versions.

There are two programs and, usually, two databases involved in handling events and statistics in Notes 4.0. The two programs are the Event task and the Reporter task. The Event task is the server process that records server events. The reporter task is the server task that collects and delivers server statistic information. The event task will deliver information for both events and statistics via posting in database, e-mail message, snmp message, or other vehicle (usually determined by an add-in program).

You may establish event monitors on the following types of event categories. Each of these has many events in six different severity categories it will check.

- Comm/Net

- Replication

- Resource

- Server

- Mail

- Misc

- Statistic

- Security

    The severity categories are:

- Fatal

- Failure

- Warning(high)

- Warning(low)

- Normal

- All Severities

The two key databases involved in Event Monitoring and Statistics Reporting are the Statistics & Events Database (EVENTS4.NSF) and the Statistics Reporting Database (STATREP.NSF). The Statistics & Events Database is used to tell the two server tasks, Events and Reporter, what events and statistics to gather and report. The Statistics Reporting database is used to store information gathered by the Event and Reporter server tasks.

Neither the Event task nor the Reporter task runs by default. You must schedule these to run by adding them to the ServerTasks setting list in the notes.ini file. The Events task will create a Statistics & Reporting database the first time the Event task runs. The Reporter task will create a Statistics Reporting Database the first time it runs.

To schedule Event or Database monitors or to create a Statistics monitor, you use the Statistics & Events database. In this database you create documents that describe the events and statistics you want to monitor. For example, if you want to monitor security, you might put an Event Monitor Document into the Statistics & Events database that tells the Events task to monitor Security type messages of the Severity "Warning(high)" and report those by sending an e-mail to the server administrator and the security department.

About Severity Levels and Types of Events

Monitor documents stored in the Statistics and Events database determine what events will cause a report as well as how that event will be reported. In addition, you can further refine what events are reported by their severity.

In addition to storing monitor documents, the Statistics and Events database also stores the definitions of all of the messages, definitions, thresholds and methods on which the Event server task can report. Each of these documents describes an individual event, has a message for that event and an associated severity level for the event. You may change any of these components by editing the appropriate document.

■ System Databases Overview (Other Than Public Name and Address Book)

Notes relies heavily upon its own database format for storing, securing, and moving system information. The most important of these databases is, of course, the Public Name and Address Book. In addition, there are several other Notes databases that are used by Notes servers as well as by Notes administrators to keep the system up and running. The following descriptions will introduce you to these databases and their functions.

Automatically Established Files

Some of the sysem databases described above are automatically created by the server program if they do not already exist. For example, the setup program will automatically create a Public Name and Address Book or find one on another server when a new server is installed. Similarly, a Log database is created by the server when it first starts if one does not already exist. The following databases are created automatically by the system.

Administration Requests (ADMIN4.NSF)

This database stores the Request Documents that are created when an administrator selects an action that is to be executed by the Administration Process. The document goes into the replica of this database on the server where the command was issued. It, the document, then replicates to all other replicas of the Administration Requests database. When the server that is designated (on the request document) to carry out the procedure finds the Request Document in its replica of the Administration Requests database, it executes the procedure(s) and places a response document in the Administrative Requests database to document what has occurred. This database is created by the Administration Process the first time it runs. It is set up to run each time the server loads in the ServerTasks field of the NOTES.INI file when you install Notes 4.0.

Database Catalog (CATALOG.NSF)

The database catalog lists all of the databases in an organization. The catalog is updated by the server task catalog which, by default, runs every day at 1:00 a.m. This task searches the server file system and records information about all the databases it finds and stores this information in documents in the Database Catalog database. If you want users to have information about all the databases stored on all the servers in your organization, you use a single replica of the catalog database so that when servers connect and replicated, all documents about databases added to one server's Database Catalog get replicated to other catalogs. This database is created by the Catalog server task. This task is setup to run automatically each time the server runs in the ServerTasks field of the NOTES.INI file.

NOTE. *Database managers can set databases to prevent the catalog program from publishing their existence to the Database Catalog. This is a security feature.*

Notes (server) Log (LOG.NSF)

The Notes 4.0 server will automatically create a server log file from a template the first time it runs. You will use this log to see historical server events that help you troubleshoot, performance tune, and plan for the future. The contents of this log, what the server chooses to record, are determined by settings in the notes.ini file. The settings in the notes.ini file control what gets recorded in the Notes Log. For additional information on the parameters of these settings, see Chapter 27, "Managing Servers." This database is created by the server program when it loads, if a LOG.NSF file does not already exist.

NOTE. *The new Log Analysis feature on the Server Control Panel is useful for use on the Log file as it helps you search for information on a particular subject. You may enter text for which you would like to search (such as a server name or particular error) and the Log Analysis feature will create a database that shows the results of the search.*

Files Not Automatically Established

The following files are not automatically created by the system either because they are not created by an automatically loaded server task or the server task that creates them is not setup to run automatically by Notes, you must configure it to do so.

Certification Log (CERTLOG.NSF)

The certification log lists all the entities that have been certified in your domain. This is a particularly important database to install if you wish to use the new Notes 4.0 Administration Process as it relies upon the certification log for information. You should create a certification log from the template that is provided before adding additional users or servers. You will want to have copies of the certification log on all servers that will run the Administration Process and on which administrators will register new users, servers and certifiers. You should definitely create and use a Certification Log as it is the best means to record all of the certified ID files in your hierarchy. Because ID files can authenticate on your system until their certificate expires, the Certification Log will help you maintain an accurate count of what IDs are capable of authenticating on your system.

Statistics & Events (EVENTS4.NSF)

The Statistics and Events database is used to tell the two server tasks, Events and Reporter, what events and statistics to gather and report. Like the Notes Log, this database can be used on a single server or can have replicas on all servers in the domain to provide information about all servers. This database is automatically created when, and if, you run the Event task for the first time.

Statistics Reporting (STATREP.NSF)

The Statistics Reporting database is used to store information gathered by the Event and Reporter server tasks. Like the Notes Log, this database can be used on a single server or can have replicas on all servers in the domain to provide information about all servers. This is useful when centralizing administration. This database is created when, and if, you run the Reporter task for the first time.

- *What's New in Notes 4.0 Security*

- *Everything You Ever Wanted to Know about ID Files (and More)*

- *Fully Distinguished Naming of ID Files*

- *What Is Encryption?*

- *What's New in Notes 4.0 ID Files*

- *How Notes Authenticates Users*

- *Physical Security*

- *Server Access*

- *Database Access*

- *Document and Form Access*

- *Field Encryption*

- *Electronic Signatures*

- *How Do Electronic Signatures Work?*

- *Notes Security Policy*

CHAPTER

24

Managing Security

Notes 4.0 offers significant enhancements in security. This chapter will explain how security works in Notes and highlights the important new features you may want to implement. Then we will look at the means by which the new security tools can make Notes 4.0 a more secure environment. To start with, let's discuss the new features of Notes 4.0 security.

In general, we assume that your system is or will be a hierarchical one, meaning that there is a tree-like structure to the identities on your system. Older versions of Notes (ending with version 2) did not have the capacity to create a hierarchical system into the ID files, so it was up to the organization to build it with "trust" relationships. In Notes 3.0 and Notes 4.0 if you use hierarchical ID files (strongly recommended) the trust relationship between one ID file and another is inherent if they share a common ancestry.

Using the security tools in Notes 4.0 you may limit access to servers, databases, forms, documents, and even fields within documents. You can also determine which users may use features such as agents and replication.

There is an 80 percent–20 percent rule that applies to Notes security: 80 percent of the security in your system probably results from 20 percent of your efforts. The following is a quick list of things to do to ensure that your Notes 4.0 environment is a secure one:

- Keep all machines that run Notes software and have a Notes ID file on them physically secure such that an attacker may not gain access to local databases or the Notes ID file.

- Keep the server default of "Allow Anonymous Access" set to "No" unless you have an isolated server that is designed for public accessibility (and that does not contain databases with sensitive information).

- Limit user and administrator access to servers by using settings in the server document of the public name and address book. These include who can use the server, for what purposes and by what types of connections.

- Segregate administrative duties such that no administrator has too much system access. In general this means assigning some people the privileges to create users and servers (certification administrators), others the rights to manage servers (server administrators) and yet others the rights to manage databases (database managers).

- Keep database access controls up to date to specify which users have what level of access to a database.

- Use author name and reader name fields in the design of databases to limit which users have access to which components of the database.

- Sign and encrypt mail documents (although this one may slow down the system).

- Encrypt databases locally on all machines, especially laptops, including in some cases, server databases—make sure you have backup and recovery tools in place. Local encryption is critical to providing a system with appropriate segregation of duty.

- Encrypt network traffic (ports are easy to encrypt in Notes 4.0 by selecting the following in the workstation client: File/Tools/User Preferences, Ports and checking the Encrypt Network Data checkbox).

Notes 4.0 Security is designed to address the following issues:

- *Authentication* This step (and the one that comes just before it: validation) are the steps where a Notes server and another Notes computer (workstation client or server) prove their identities to each other. It is like providing a driver's license to show that they are, in fact, who they claim to be and they can prove it. All other security features in Notes are predicated on the notion that who a computer is has been verified during this step (which is unnoticeable to users).

- *Server Access* Set in the Server document for each server in the public name and address book. There are different types of access that can be granted to a server. For example, users will be allowed to use the server, but may not be allowed to add new databases to the server, a privilege reserved for system administrators.

- *Database Access* Determines the access a user will have to a particular database on a Notes server. Can they add information to the database, read information in the database, edit information in the database...?

- *Document Access* Determines what specific documents a user may read and edit. It is dependent upon the higher level database access that has been set.

- *Confidentiality* Refers to the secret key encryption of fields in a document. Only users who have been given copies of the secret key may decrypt, and thus read, the information. It is a means of adding security to particular fields in particular documents in the database.

- *Source Verification* Source verification enables the reader of information in a database to verify that the creator of the information was, in fact, who he or she claimed to be and that the information has not changed since the author signed it.

■ What's New in Notes 4.0 Security

Notes security works very much like earlier versions in most respects. The security enhancements in Notes 4.0 are designed to tighten security rather than change the security model. Notes 4.0 still relies, fortunately, upon public/private key encryption to prove identities as well as encrypt and sign mail. It also still relies upon access controls for servers, databases and documents to grant access based on the name that is proven in the authentication process.

Finally, fields are still encryptable using secret keys created by users and stored in their ID files. What has changed is the tools we have to manage these capabilities, and a few feature enhancements. The following are the new features that will help you make your Notes environment more secure.

Multiple Passwords for ID Files

Notes 4.0 allows the person charged with certifying ID files to specify that an ID file have multiple passwords. Furthermore, he or she can specify that a certain number of these passwords must be used to access the ID file. For example, Notes can be set to require five of eight passwords to open this ID file. This feature is available with all ID files and is especially useful for the Certifier ID. Enabling this security feature requires the cooperation of several individuals to use the ID file.

NOTE. *Multiple passwords should be immediately added to an ID file after it is generated to prevent someone from intercepting and copying the ID before it is protected with the additional passwords.*

Public Key Verification

Notes server managers can specify that Notes 4.0 servers not grant access to the server to any entity whose public key (which is sent during the authentication process described below) is different than that of the public key listed in the Person document in the public name and address book. This protects against lost/stolen/compromised IDs from being used after a new ID is generated with a new public key and private key.

Enforcing Consistent Access Control Lists

Managers of Notes 4.0 databases can have the access controls forced to synchronize across all replicas. This makes it more difficult for replicas, in remote sites for example, to provide access to unwarranted entities, and protects against unauthorized access to a database going undetected. If a database manager has specified that a database enforce a consistent access control list across all replicas, any replica on a server that does not grant sufficient access for a change to be made to the access control list by another server will be unable to replicate the database. Simply put, if a local administrator were to change the access control of a database and prevent that database from replicating with other replicas so that the access control change would not be overwritten, the entire database (documents and design) will not replicate. Normal replication monitoring alarms such as those set in the Statistics and Events database with Replication monitors will cause attention to be raised.

Local Database Encryption

Perhaps the best enhancement to security in Notes 4.0, the local database encryption feature enables the encryption of a database using the user or server public key. The database cannot be opened without the ID file that encrypted it and, of course, the password to open that ID file. In other words, a database manager may check a box that says this database should be encrypted and any replica that is made of this database will be encrypted with the public key of the ID file that is being used to create the replica. The advantage is that even if an intruder gains access to the file system, he or she will not be able to decrypt the database without having the ID file whose public key encrypted it. He or she will also need the password to that ID file. This is an excellent security measure to require for users storing information on laptops and unprotected workstations, such as those found in home offices.

Local Database Adherence to ACL

Although not really a security feature because there are means of circumventing it, local Notes 4.0 databases now limit users' activities to those they would be able to execute when working through the server. For any Notes 4.0 database, the database manager can select the command File/Database/Access Control, choose the Advanced icon and check "Enforce a consistent access control list" to enable local adherence to a database access control as well as server adherence. This makes circumventing security more cumbersome and makes using local replicas less confusing for users because their access to the database functions the same way locally as it does when working on the server replica.

Tighter Server and Database Access Controls

Server access controls can now be set to include entities that may and may not use agents of different types, servers that may be accessed anonymously, and servers that may and may not use and/or be accessed by passthru servers. Database access controls now include a user "type" designation for all entities in a database access control list to limit fraudulent use of groups and server ID files to gain access. In addition, Notes 4.0 databases have new security options for each level within the database access control list, such as who may and may not run agents of different types. This security feature would be used for databases located physically on the server but that can be accessed from any authorized user's workstation.

Access Control List Logging

Notes 4.0 databases log all changes to the access control list of a database. This tool is excellent to use with forced access control lists so the database manager can see who changed the ACL on any replica of a database. Because this logging is based on a user's authenticated public key and associated name, this information is highly reliable.

Administrative Process

The administrative process, although not a security feature in itself, helps administrators keep the house in order, thereby helping maintain a secure environment. The administrative process assists in the management of user and server names. It will rename users and servers, recertify users and servers, remove deleted users and servers from group documents in the public name and address book, and will remove user and server names from access control lists for all databases that have an administration server specified. The risk that results from oversight is reduced by automating these tasks.

■ Everything You Ever Wanted to Know about ID Files (and More)

Notes ID files are probably the most important feature of the Notes system. Security privileges in Notes are derived from these ID files. Every entity in the Notes world has an identity based on an ID file. The only exception to this is the new Anonymous server access feature that allows access to a server by an entity with no verifiable identity on the system.

What Is an ID File?

A Notes ID file is a binary file that can have any name. Every computer in the Notes system uses an ID file when communicating with other Notes computers. By default the name is user.id for a user's ID file, server.id for a server ID file, cert.id for a certifier ID file, and unitname.id for an organizational unit certifier ID file name (where unitname is the name of the organizational unit such as SalesWes.id).

The ID file for any of the entities mentioned above contains that entity's *identity* on the system as well as the components that entity will use to prove its identity to other computers on the Notes system. This is important because it is based on this identity that all access rights on the system are granted. For example, if a user has an ID file with the name Samantha Boxer as the common name and the fully distinguished name Samantha Boxer/Sales/West/WGSI, when she accesses servers and databases her access will be that which the administrators have granted to Samantha Boxer/Sales/West/WGSI. An ID file contains the full name of the user, their password, license number (to indicate a North American or International license), Public and Private keys, encryption keys, and certificate information. Therefore, Samantha Boxer/Sales/West/WGSI is a different person as well as a different ID file from Samantha Boxer/Sales/East/WSGI because the OU (organizational unit) certificates are different in each ID.

Each ID file has one or more passwords that must be entered to use it. If a user has an ID file and enters the correct password for that ID file, Notes will then use that ID file to "authenticate" with other Notes computers. Therefore, if a user enters the correct password for an ID file, the system assumes that the user is the person whose name is stored in the ID file and will grant access to the user as if he or she were that user.

Where Do ID Files Come From?

A stork carries an ID file over the hard disk. Just wanted to make sure you were paying attention. ID files are created by administrators who have two special privileges. First, the administrator must have create privileges for Person documents in the public name and address book. This means simply that the administrator has been granted the right to create these documents in the public name and address book just as any user would be granted rights to create documents of a certain type in any database. In addition, the administrator must have a certifier ID or organizational unit certifier ID file to which he or she has the password(s).

The administrator uses his or her access to the certifier ID file and the public name and address book to register a user, server, or organizational unit certifier ID file. The administrator does this by issuing a command in the workstation client's Administration Control Panel.

During the registration process a public/private key pair is created. The public key and user name are then certified by the certifier ID file. Also, in the case of registering a person, a Person document is created for the user and his or her new ID file's public key is listed in it. The ID file itself is created so it may then be given to the user or server (or administrator in the case of an organizational unit certifier). The ID file can now be used for authenticating a user (for more information about what's in a Notes user ID, read on).

About the Certifier ID File

The certifier ID (don't get confused here, there are *certifier ID files* and *organizational unit certifier ID files* that are the children and grandchildren of certifier ID files) is a Notes ID that has a unique identity just like any other ID file in the Notes 4.0 world. The certifier has a name, such as /WGSI, as well as a public and private key pair. The certifier ID is used to vouch for or assert that a specific public key and a specific entity (person, server, or organizational unit certifier) are bound together. If Jane Smith claims that her public key is 1234, the rest of the entities on the Notes 4.0 network will not trust this association unless there is a certificate that they trust that attests to it.

The certifier ID file is a special ID file that is used to create all other IDs (entities) in the Notes system. All other ID files created within a Notes domain (servers using the same public name and address book) are children of the certifier ID. Because all server and user ID files in your organization have this common ancestor, they can *validate* and then *authenticate* (both will be described later) each other. The certifier ID should be given to a limited set of people, stored on floppy disk only, and password protected, as it can be used to create false identities. The certifier ID itself is not used to gain access to servers or databases.

By stamping each new ID with a *certificate* the certifier ID tells other Notes entities that the name, license, and public key are correctly associated and together represent a single, unique identity in the system. The certificate is like the Registrar of Motor Vehicles stamp. It states that the picture, name, and number on the license go together and that the registrar attests to them. Other entities (in this example, the police department and liquor stores) agree to trust anything that has the seal of the Registrar of Motor Vehicles. In the Notes world the Registrar of Motor vehicles would be called a certifying authority, or certifier, and the seal would be called a certificate.

What's This "Certificate" Thing?

The *certificate* is a digital document that attests to the binding of a public key to an entity name (such as a person, server, or organizational unit certifier). It allows verification of the claim that a public key belongs to a particular entity. The most important component of a certificate is the digital signature from the certifying authority (certifier). This means that any other ID on the system can check and ensure that the trusted certifying authority really did attest to the binding of the particular name and public key and that the information (in this case a public key and a name) have not changed since the information was digitally signed (certified). A certificate is issued by the certifier (or organizational unit certifier) ID file and signed with its (the certifier's) private key. Because every ID file in the system inherently trusts the certifier (in our examples /WGSI) and can discern its digital signature (by using the certifier's public key), all entities on the Notes 4.0 network can authenticate each other. If you do not clearly understand what a digital signature is, skip ahead and read that section. In essence, a digital signature proves the authenticity of the signer and the information signed. In this case, the information being signed is the association of a name and a public key.

What's in a Notes 4.0 ID File?

Each unique ID file contains a name, license number, private key, public key, password(s), certificate (in flat file systems an ID may contain more than one), and encryption keys (optional).

Name is the given name of a fully distinguished Notes entity. This means that in a hierarchical system, the name of the user, Marge Fleischer, for example, is appended by the name of the certifier to create a *fully distinguished* name such as Marge Fleischer/Sales/WGSI. The name of the server, WGSI-APP-SFO-01, might be certified by the organizational unit certifier /Sales/ WGSI, in which case its name would appear as WGSI-APP-SF0-01/Sales/ WGSI.

A Private Key is a very long number held only by the user or server in his/her/its ID file that is used for encryption. This key is located ONLY in the ID file so that only the user or server may access it. It bears a mathematical relationship to the public key such that information encrypted with one may be decrypted with the other.

The Public Key is a very long number with a mathematical relationship to the private key such that information encrypted with one may be decrypted with the other. A copy of the public key is in the public name and address book where all computers on the network can access it.

Encryption keys are very long numbers, stored in the ID file and used to encrypt information. These keys, unlike the public/private key pair, are created and distributed by users to encrypt documents and fields. Users may distribute keys via Notes mail or diskette and can specify if the recipient is allowed to distribute a key he or she receives to others or not.

Finally, ID files may contain up to eight passwords. Passwords are user changeable. An ID file is not useable unless a user enters a password. Once he or she enters the password, that user may use the Notes software to connect with other computers and gain the access to the Notes system. The user of an ID file is granted access to the system based on which privileges have been set up for that user's name.

■ Fully Distinguished Naming of ID Files

Fully distinguished names in Notes 4.0 enable the certifying authority (Notes administrator with access to the certifier and create privileges for Person documents in the public name and address book) to create a greater number of unique entities on the Notes system. In addition, they simplify the management of the Notes network by creating logical groups.

In essence, a fully distinguished name of a person or server is really just that person's or server's name (let's say the name is Marsha Brady) appended with a hierarchy or organizational certifiers.

Because certifier ID files may create organizational unit certifiers, an ID file may belong to a hierarchy of certifiers. For example, the certifier /WGSI may create the organizational unit certifier /WestCoast/WGSI. This organizational unit certifier might create another organizational unit certifier called / Sales/WestCoast/WGSI. A user created with this organizational unit certifier would then have the fully distinguished name of something like Marsha Brady/Sales/WestCoast/WGSI. The user inherits the rights assigned at other levels of the name. The administrator does not have to totally rethink security for each new user.

The advantage of such a hierarchy is of course that users can more easily be distinguished from one another, management is simplified, and the job of certification may be distributed (different organizations can have their own organizational unit certifier allowing them to create entities under but not above it in the hierarchy). All these benefits are possible because of the digitally signed certificate by the top level certifier. All entities that descend from this certifier can verify its digital signature and therefore validate public keys of entities falling beneath it in the hierarchy.

■ What Is Encryption?

Encryption is the scrambling of information using a string of numbers called a key. Only users with the correct string of numbers can unscramble the information. In Notes 4.0, encryption is used for two purposes: The first is for authentication; the second is for data access (privacy). Authentication may occur because each entity (Notes ID file) has a unique private key associated with a public key. Information that is encrypted with a private key may be decrypted with the associated public key and vice versa. As a result, if a client or server encrypts information with a public key, the associated private key should be able to decrypt the information and vice versa.

- A *private key* is a very long number held only by the user or server in his/her/its ID file that is used for encryption. This key is located only in the ID file so that only the user or server may access it. It bears a mathematical relationship to the public key such that information encrypted with one may be decrypted with the other.

- The *public key* is a very long number with a mathematical relationship to the private key such that information encrypted with one may be decrypted with the other. A copy of the public key is in the public name and address book where all computers on the network can access it.

Authentication is used in several areas of Notes. One example of this is when one Notes computer connects to another Notes computer to ensure that the two computers know who the other one is, and then can assign access rights accordingly. In addition, the public/private key encryption is used for electronic signatures and port encryption. If the sender encrypts information with his or her private key, the recipient may decrypt it with the sender's public key and the source as well as data is ensured.

Encryption is used for data access (privacy). Users create encryption keys to scramble fields of data. These encryption keys (secret key encryption rather than public/private key encryption discussed earlier) created by the user in the File/Tools/User ID, Encryption dialog box are given a name by the user and then stored in the user's ID file by Notes 4.0. Users do not need to generate a number or go through special steps to store them. A user simply creates a name and Notes creates and stores the key in his or her ID file. They may then distribute these keys to other users so that these other users may encrypt and decrypt the fields of information using the same key. In this scenario, the same key is used to encrypt and decrypt information; no public/private key relationship is necessary.

■ What's New in Notes 4.0 ID Files

The only significant change to Notes 4.0 ID files is the ability to store more than one password that must be used to access it. This is extremely useful for ID files that will grant significant system privileges, as it enables an organization to require that more than one person be present to access an ID file.

Up to eight passwords may be stored in an ID file and any number less than or equal to the number stored may be required to access the ID file. For example, you may assign five passwords to the organization certifier and you may specify that three of these passwords are necessary to access this ID file. When an administrator wants to register a user, server, or organizational unit using this certifier, at least two other users (administrators) will need to enter their passwords to make the ID file accessible. This technique is useful for storing backup copies of user and server ID files safely.

One concern about ID files is that if lost, stolen or corrupted, there is no way to recover them. However, neither should a copy of user ID files be kept that only requires one password to access the ID file because this places too much power in one individual's control. Using multiple passwords on a dummy ID can help resolve this situation. By registering the dummy user, a copy of each user ID file can be sent to the dummy user's e-mail database as a central storage place for copies. If a user loses his or her ID file, more than one administrator must enter passwords to access the dummy user's ID file and mail database. A copy of the lost ID file can then be sent to the user. Bear in mind, with the new Administration Process in Notes 4.0, storing backup copies of ID files on behalf of users is less necessary as reissuing them is greatly simplified.

■ How Notes Authenticates Users

Now that we have discussed some basic security elements, it is important to understand how these are used. A Notes domain is very much like any other network. There are two programs running: a workstation client program that is the software most frequently seen and used by end users, and a server program that communicates with the client to provide access to information (documents).

Whenever a client (workstation software or server software) connects with a server to access a database, route, or replicate, validation and authentication procedures will automatically occur to establish the validity of the computer's identity. Validation means ensuring that the public key the computer claims to be its own can be trusted by the computer that is called. This is accomplished by verifying the certifier of the public key. Authentication, the second process, means verifying that the computer whose authorized public key is presented (and is now trusted because of the validation step) has the associated private key to prove that he or she is the rightful owner of the public key.

For the client and server to grant access to documents to each other, Notes, like other networks, has a concept of membership. This means every entity that will connect to another entity has access privileges of some level to a server(s), a database(s), and document(s) within the database. The system grants access based on these privileges that are set by different administrators, such as the server administrator(s) and the database manager(s) for various servers and databases.

Before it can grant any access, however, the two computers must verify each other. This means that they must prove to each other that they are who they claim to be. This process is called *authentication*. Authentication, as described above, is based upon the concept of trust in a common certifying authority. In the Notes world, this Certifying Authority is called the certifier. Because all computers in the network agree to trust the certifier, and because they can verify the digital signature of the certifier, and because they agree to trust ID files that are certified by the certifier, entities on the Notes network can authenticate each other.

NOTE. *When two servers communicate there is a client/server relationship even though the programs are called servers.*

Anyone who wants to access a Notes server must have some kind of identity. Their identity will then have access privileges associated with it, both in terms of what functions they can perform on the server as well as what functions they can perform on a specific database.

Notes 4.0 allows anonymous access to server and database access controls. *Anonymous access* means that the user is granted access even though his or her or its (in the case of a server or other program) identity is not authenticated, or proven. Anonymous access is useful for posting public information that you want users and servers of other organizations to see without having to cross certify with your organization (see Chapter 27, "Managing Servers," for information about cross certification). If anonymous access is set up, users and servers do not need to have a certificate in common with your server to access information because they do not need to prove their identity to each other. While an anonymous user's name may appear in fields that are designed to show such information, the name will be unverified. To clarify, when two Notes computers connect for any reason they attempt to verify each others identity using validation and authentication. Once they prove each others identity, or are unable to prove each others identity, Notes will grant access to servers and databases based on the identity it has proven. In some cases, Notes servers may be setup to allow "anonymous" access. This means that the server will let other Notes computers access it even if it cannot successfully validate and authenticate those computers.

Notes handles identity by using ID files (encrypted binary files) that store the name of a user or server and all the security tools necessary to prove that the identity claimed by an ID file was created by a trusted certifying authority. To do this, a "challenge/response" scenario that is played out by the two Notes computers (client and server or server and server) when they connect. This scenario proves that the ID files (and therefore the users of these computers who entered passwords to the ID files) are who they say they are. One computer can authenticate another computer because of the identification tools provided in ID files. Once their authenticity is established, the Notes servers refer to the access controls setup for the IDs (entities: users, servers) and grant access to the server itself, databases that reside on the server and documents in the databases accordingly.

The validation process by which trust is established is based on some rules:

- Trust the public key of any of your ancestors in the hierarchical name tree because you have a copy of their public key in your own ID file.

- Trust any public key that is certified by any ancestor in your hierarchical tree.

- Trust any public key that is certified by any trusted certifier that belongs to one of the certifier's descendants.

Here is one example of how and when a typical validation and authentication scenario might be played out. A user has the Notes workstation client software open and double clicks on a database that physically resides on the server. The server software and the client software play out the challenge response scenario before the server program will grant the user access to the server itself, then the database, and then documents within the database. We have two entities in this scenario, Peter Moore/Sales/WGSI and Server1/Corp/WGSI.

NOTE. *In the following examples,* verify *means decrypt to test the validity of the signature.*

1. The workstation software sends information (name, certifier name) to the server: Peter Moore/Sales/WGSI.

2. The server looks at its own ID file and finds the certifier /WGSI's public key. Let's say the certifier's public key is 2222.

3. The server now reads Peter's ID file and looks for the /Sales certificate that was issued to the /Sales/WGSI organizational unit certifier by /WGSI. The server uses /WGSI's public key (2222) to verify that the /Sales certificate is valid. If the certificate is valid, the server now trusts the /Sales public key. Let's say the /Sales public key is 3333.

4. The server reads Peter's ID file to verify that the certificate issued to Peter from /Sales is valid. The server verifies the certificate by using the /Sales public key (3333) which it (now) trusts. The server now trusts Peter's public key (let's call it 4444).

The server now trusts that the public key of the user is in fact associated with the name in the user ID. Now the server will attempt to authenticate the user.

1. The server generates a random number (let's say 1155) and sends it back to the workstation software.

2. The workstation software scrambles the number with its private key and sends the scrambled (encrypted) number back to the server software.

3. The server descrambles (decrypts) the encrypted number using Peter's public key (4444) and gets the same number it sent to Peter initially (1155).

Peter has proved who he is because he must have had the correct private key associated with the trusted public key to scramble the random number sent by the server such that the server could decrypt it with Peter's public key. The scenario is now reversed so that the server proves its identity to the client workstation. Having proven their identities, the computers then use access controls set for the server, databases, and documents to grant each other access as appropriate. This process is extremely fast so the users are unlikely to notice it. If authentication takes a lot of time, LAN performance is usually more the cause of delay than the processing by either computer.

All Notes security is based on this challenge/response mechanism for ensuring that an entity on the network is who it says it is. Identity is critical not only when users try to see the databases on a server, open those databases and open documents within those databases, but also when servers contact (connect) with each other to exchange documents. Remember, the Notes server program is constantly moving documents via replication or routing to get them from one server and database to another. As a result, the servers must check each others' identity and access rights to databases and documents before exchanging documents just as they would check a users' rights.

All Notes access privileges are predicated on the notion that each entity may be authenticated by other entities on the system. Public and private key encryption is a tool that is used to produce a digital signature that is used in the authentication process to verify that an entity that is trusted (the certifier) attests to the fact that the public key presented belongs to and is bound to the name that is presented.

■ Physical Security

Physical security of Notes servers is a premise upon which all other security tools and features are built. Notes servers must be in a locked and supervised room so that the file systems that reside on them cannot be directly accessed. Although new tools in Notes such as multiple password ID files and local database encryption are useful in protecting against attack, physical security remains the cornerstone of a Notes 4.0 system's integrity.

If an ID file is easily copied from the server, the assailant has the opportunity to break the password and then access servers and databases as if he or she were the server. The Notes 4.0 security features are only as good as the physical security that protects them.

■ Server Access

Controlling access to the server is achieved through the server access list. This list is contained on the Server document in the public name and address book. It may also be contained in the notes.ini file. The notes.ini file is overridden by the information in the server document at server startup, so it is always recommended that the Server document has the correct information as this is the information that will be used by the server when granting access. All Notes entities that connect to the server for database access, routing, and replication, must be listed in the server access list or the server will deny access.

In addition to granting access to the server, fields in the server document (and lines in the notes.ini) allow us to control other server privileges. These other controls include specifying a server administrator (someone who can edit the server document and send console commands to the server), denying access to the server, creating replica copies of databases, creating new databases, allowing "anonymous" (unauthenticated) access to the server, and checking public keys against those stored in the public name and address book. Additional controls determine what "passthru" privileges exist for the user and server and what rights to run agents a user has on a given server.

A server administrator's name is entered into the Administrators field when the server is initially brought up. All documents in the Notes 4.0 public address book have Owners and Administrators fields (this one is named LocalAdmin internally). These fields add flexibility in managing the server document and the server. Additional names or groups may be added in the future. The defaults for the other fields are as follows:

- Can Access Server—Default is Everyone unless something is entered, in which case only those entered.

- Deny Access To Server—Default is No one (meaning everyone can access) unless something is entered, in which case that explicit user, server, or group may not access the server.

- Can Create Databases—Default is Everyone can create databases unless an entity or group is specified, in which case only that group or entity can create databases.

- Can Create Replica Copies—Default is No one can create replicas except those users, servers, and groups explicitly listed.

- Access to Port—Default is Everyone can access all enabled ports unless a specific entity or group is entered. This setting is available only in the Notes.ini file. Uses public/private key. If either party has an encrypted port, the two will create a one-time encryption key. A random number is generated and used for that session only. The public key is used to pass this random number from generator to the other entity.

What's New in Notes 4.0:

Setting	Default
Compare Public Keys	Default is No (meaning a connecting person or server will not have the public key he or she presents compared to the public key that is stored in the public name and address book).
Allow Anonymous Connections	Default is No (meaning all connecting entities must be authenticated and therefore must be certified by the trusted certifier or have a cross certificate from the trusted certifier).
Only Allow Server Access to Users Listed in the Public Name and Address Book	Default is No (meaning users that are not listed in the public name and address book can be granted access). This situation could occur in two circumstances: 1. The server is set to allow anonymous access, or 2. A certifier from another organization is cross-certified, which means that ID files certified by it could be authenticated. These entities, however, would not be listed explicitly in your organization's public name and address book.
Access this server (passthru)	Default is empty (meaning no one may access this server via a passthru connection).
Route through (passthru)	Default is empty (meaning no one is allowed to use this server to "passthru" or route to another server).
Cause Calling (passthru)	Default is empty (meaning no one connected to this server may initiate the calling of another server to route to it).
Destinations Allowed (passthru)	Default is empty (meaning this server may route to any other server to which it can connect).
Run Personal Agents	Default is empty (meaning anyone can run personal agents that are stored in a database that resides on the server and use the server processor to do so).

Setting	Default
Run Restricted LotusScript Agents	Default is empty (meaning no one can run restricted LotusScript agents that are stored in a database that resides on the server and use the server processor to do so).
Run UnRestricted LotusScript Agents	Default is empty (meaning no one can run restricted LotusScript agents that are stored in a database that resides on the server and use the server processor to do so).

■ Database Access

As we discussed earlier, every Notes database is self-contained. It has all of the security, design, and data elements stored in a single file. One of the key security components is the access control list. This list applies only to this particular database and it grants the different levels of privilege to users and servers.

The seven levels of access that can be granted to a database are manager, designer, editor, author, reader, depositor, and no access. A *depositor* can add documents to the database but cannot see or read documents. A *reader* can look at documents but cannot edit or create documents. An *author* can create documents and edit the documents that he or she creates. *Editors* can read and create documents and can also edit documents created by others. *Designers* can do everything that editors can do and they can change the design (forms, views, macros) of the database. *Managers* can change access controls and delete the database. Every database must have at least one manager designated and an access set for default.

In addition to the seven levels of database access, database managers can specify which users may create and delete documents, create personal agents, create personal folders and views, create shared folders and views, and create LotusScript Agents. See Chapter 18 "Deploying Databases" for more information.

In addition to access controls, the same dialog box found with the File, Database, and Access Control menus allows for the creation of roles. Roles are groups built from the access control list. Roles are used to quickly add and remove users and servers from different types of privileges within the given database.

■ Document and Form Access

Document and form access determine the level of access a user has to a particular form (forms are used to enter and view information in documents) or document (a document is where the data is actually stored). Security may be added to particular documents that will require privileges in addition to those specified in the database access control list. In general, we recommend using these additional privileges to make certain that users have access *only* to the information they need. Every database should be rated with regard to the risk potential of having the information contained within it leaving the organization. With this risk rating in mind, document access tools should be implemented to limit user access.

The most useful tool available to prevent users who must see some but not all documents in a database are *read access fields*. These fields, set up by the application developer, contain a list of names of users and servers that can read the particular document. In a database with 2,000 documents, a user may only be able to see 200 of these documents. Read access fields can be filled in programmatically or manually. The application developer should adhere to the organization's policy for securing documents in a database with a given risk rating. For example, if a database is a high risk, your organization may require that each document have a list of authorized readers and that certain types of fields (salary for example) be encrypted. If so, the application developer should design the database to include these security features.

In addition to read access, the application developer can enable forms to limit access for creating and editing a document. A field that determines who may edit the document is called an Author field. Settings on forms control who may and may not access forms. This technique is useful in limiting the access users have to creating and reading information using the forms that have Author and Reader lists created in them. When the structure of a system is easily disseminated, the security components are more easily circumvented.

At the document level read and author fields determine who may access a document for reading and editing rights. Privileges specified in these fields that are lower than those specified in the Access control list take precedence over the privileges in the access control list. For example, if a person named Virginia is listed as an author in the database but is not listed in the read access list of a document (if a read access list has been assigned) then she will not be able to see the document. A designer of the database may see all documents in the database by default, but will not be able to see documents that have a read access list on which he or she is not listed. Document Read Access lists and Author Access lists, then, refine the access controls set at the database level.

■ Field Encryption

A layer below document read and author access in the security picture is field encryption. *Field encryption* enables a user to encrypt (scramble) a field of information in a document based on a key (long number) such that readers of the document must have the same key to read the information in that field. Unlike the public and private key encryption and decryption used elsewhere in Notes, field encryption uses a single key to encrypt and decrypt information. All users who want to share encrypted fields must share an encryption key.

Using encryption requires significant system resources in saving and reading documents because of the added processing required to encrypt and decrypt information and adds significant administrative burden, because the keys must be distributed to all the readers and creators of documents. Notes uses the RSA "Cryptosystem" for its encryption technology. The U.S. version of Notes has a significantly longer encryption key than does the international English version of Notes. If your organization will be exchanging information overseas, you may want to make sure that ALL ID files are created as International English so that encryption can be used across continents.

To use field encryption, the designer of the database must enable a field (or fields) on a form for encryption. A user must then create an encryption key (File/Tools/User ID in the encryption icon) that will be used to encrypt information. The user then encrypts the document before saving the document using the key. This option is found in the Document Properties box in the security tab. The user then can easily distribute the key (using Notes mail or disk) to other users who will import this encryption key into their personal ID file. Documents will be automatically decrypted as users with the correct key open the document.

WARNING. *If users lose their ID files with the encryption key stored in it, there is no way to recover the data. If there are other copies of the key stored in other user ID files the data is recoverable and the key may be (or may not be) exportable to another user ID file. The point is that using encryption is a powerful way of limiting access at the field level but it comes with significant administrative burden and some risk of data loss.*

This book does not discuss mail encryption at length. However, be aware that if mail encryption is enabled and a user loses his or her ID file, the mail cannot be recovered because the server encrypts the user's incoming mail with the user's public key so it cannot be read without the associated private key. There is no recovery for the data in the mail file unless a backup ID file exists.

■ Electronic Signatures

Electronic signatures are a critical security feature of Notes because they are used to ensure the source of information as well as to verify that the content of the information has not changed since it was signed. More important, electronic signatures are used in the authentication process that ensures that a user or server is who he/she/it claims to be every time server access is attempted. Electronic signatures are made possible by the public key encryption capabilities of Notes.

Electronic signatures are used by Notes 4.0 in two ways. First, they are used by the system to authenticate users, servers, and certifiers. On the other side of security, electronic signatures provide readers of documents with the assurance that the creator of the document is who he or she claims to be.

The signature is a piece of data that cannot be forged that asserts that a named person wrote or agreed to the data which is signed and to which the signature is attached. The recipient of the signed message and third parties can verify both that the document did indeed come from the person whose signature is attached to the data and that the data has not been altered since the signature was placed on it. Electronic signatures can not be repudiated later by the signer because a claim cannot be made that the document was forged (as the data is linked with the signature itself).

Importantly, the certificate, found in every Notes ID file, that attests to a user name being correctly associated with a public key is actually an electronic signature with the result of a hash algorithm run on source data (the user name and public key). As you can see, electronic signatures, then, are another security tool upon which all security in Notes relies.

■ How Do Electronic Signatures Work?

Signatures are similar to encryption in that they involve the scrambling and descrambling of information in a field. In electronic signatures, there are two kinds of scrambling that take place. Here's how they work.

Notes creates a *fingerprint* based on the data stored in the field marked for signature. This fingerprint is actually a *hash value* of the data in that field. A *hash* is a computation that takes a variable size input (like the data a user enters into, say, the Body field of a document) and returns a fixed size string known as the hash value. If the hash function is a one-way function (meaning difficult to invert) it is also called a *message-digest* function and the result is called a *message digest*. Hashes are a critical component of an electronic signature.

In Notes 4.0 the message digest (the result of the hash computation) is 128 bits. If a single bit of source data is changed, almost 50 percent of the message digest that results from the hash function will change. This means that if a user enters something into a signed field and the information in the field changes even slightly, it will produce a dramatically different result if the hash function is again run on it. This is important because when a reader opens a document, the signature is automatically checked and the message digest (or fingerprint or hash value, whatever you want to call it) is compared to the data in the field to ensure that it still matches.

This ratio of bit-change to fingerprint-change and the size of the fingerprint make it very unlikely that source data can be composed in such a way that it will create a duplicate fingerprint. As a result, forgeries of electronic signatures made by appending an old signature to a new one are difficult to imagine, unlike paper signatures which are easily reproduced.

Okay, so now we have this message digest of the data. This message digest is then encrypted using the private key of the signer. Only the public key of the signer (that is mathematically related to the private key of the signer) can decrypt the message digest. Appended to the encrypted message digest is the certificate the signer holds in his or her ID file and his or her public key.

When the recipient opens the message, Notes 4.0 automatically checks the certificate list to find a common (trusted) ancestor (certifier). Once it finds a certifier it trusts, Notes 4.0 uses the public key of the signer (which it now trusts because it was certified by a trusted certifier) and uses it to decrypt the message digest. If the message digest can be reproduced by running the hash again on the source data, the data has not changed. The signer's identity is proven because he or she must have had the private key necessary to encrypt the data such that the public key could decrypt it.

NOTE. *If Notes 4.0 cannot verify a signature it means one of three things, that:*

- *The signer did not have a trusted certificate in common or from an ancestor the recipient trusts.*
- *The signer did not use the correct private key to encrypt the message digest (forgery).*
- *The data changed since it was signed.*

To enable electronic signatures in Notes 4.0 the application developer must enable fields for signature when designing the form. When a field on a form is so enabled, Notes will "sign" a document with a stamp of the author's upon which other Notes entities can rely. Fields enabled for signature in Notes are signed when a document is mailed or when a document is saved (if the signature enabled field is within a section on the form).

When reading a signed document in the Notes 4.0 workstation client, the recipient will receive a message in the Notes client (workstation) software either verifying or failing to verify the signature when the document is opened.

■ Notes Security Policy

In addition to the tools available to secure information in Lotus Notes, policy plays an important role in managing risk. Remember two key points about how access to Notes data is obtained.

1. Direct file system access, such as a drive mapping to a directory where Notes databases reside gives the intruder full access to the database unless it or fields within it are encrypted.

2. False identity (using the ID file of another user or of a server) can give intruders access to information they should not have.

Any time a user can gain access to the file system where Notes data is stored, they can easily look at the data with a Notes client (or add-in). In addition, Notes cannot protect information from intruders who can pretend to be a person or server who has been granted access to information.

Since Notes databases are easily replicated by anyone with appropriate access, to the extent that they have this access, you must implement policies about what kinds of data can be replicated to unsecured machines—especially laptops.

All access controls in Notes are based on the users' or servers' authenticated identity. This identity is determined by a challenge/response scenario played out by two Notes computers, each using a Notes ID file. The Notes ID file is a distributed file. Each user and server has its own. Make sure that no copies, other than backup, of this ID file are obtained illicitly. A user who got an ID file of another user (and got the password) could pretend to be that user. A user (perhaps system administrator) who gets hold of a Notes server ID can pretend to be that server, and servers usually have very broad access to databases.

Finally, have a policy that requires someone to consider the data that is being stored in any Notes database. Think about the data as if it were paper and consider how that document would be marked with regard to internal security. Consider the database with the same risk factor and establish server, database, and document access list policies to adequately protect the information. Furthermore, have application development policies that require the developer to implement security tools such as read access lists, signatures, and encryption based on the risk rating of the data to be stored. We often do not think the notes we took in a meeting are a security threat because they are ours. When we put them online, the risk is exponential.

Security Top Priorities

Here are some security tips you can use to make your system trustworthy from its inception. By implementing these ideas, you will protect your data without the cost of redoing procedures later on.

• *Control file access to databases*. This means that no user or administrator should be able to access a server copy of a Notes database directly, without going through the server program. Notes is a client/server program where the Notes client asks the server program to give it a document. It is the server that checks different access controls to see if it should grant the request. If this process is subverted by directly accessing the database from the workstation client because the database could be accessed directly through the file system, such as a mapped drive, all controls other than encryption are bypassed.

• *Control ID files from the start*. The Notes ID files are intended for use by a single user or server. They contain a "private" key that is designed to be just that—private! If another user or an administrator gets hold of an ID file for a user, server or certifier, that person can bypass system security by pretending to be someone they are not. This is a particularly difficult riddle to solve in Notes because an ID file can so easily be copied without any audit trail. For example, if the president of your company were to get Notes and an administrator were to make a copy of the president's ID file before giving it to her, the administrator could use that ID file to pretend to be the president even after the administrator left the company.

Notes 4.0 offers some good tools for addressing this problem, but they are not foolproof. Unlike other systems, Notes does provide a system whereby administrators cannot have access to all the information. This is accomplished by public/private key encryption. To make this reliable, however, you must ensure that the ID file is never copied or given to anyone but its intended owner. This is why it is generally not a good idea to maintain backup copies of Notes ID files for users. These backups provide little benefit over regenerating an ID file from scratch and open your organization to the potential misuse of ID files.

• *Limit access to the public name and address book*. The public name and address book is a critical system database on which the Notes system runs. It is imperative that this database not be manipulated by anyone who is not appropriately authorized. In general, there should be very few people listed with Editor access or above. Anyone who can change the content of group documents or Server documents can gain access to parts of the system you may not intend. Carefully monitor who has access and to what level they have access to the public name and address book. Usually users should have Reader access, server managers should have Author access with Editor (administrator field) privileges to the specific servers they manage and only the domain and network management staff should have editor access to a broad range of public name and address book documents.

- *Segregate duties.* Notes 4.0 provides excellent tools to segregate duties within the system management functions. Use segregation of duty to ensure that no one user or administrator has more access to the system or data than is appropriate. Ideally, we would have the Security department of an organization responsible for Manager access to the public name and address book as well as the certification of users, servers and organizational unit certifiers. They can delegate some authority as necessary for different administrators to perform job functions.

  For example, the domain and network management groups may be granted Editor access to the public name and address book to do their jobs, and server managers in remote locations may get an organizational unit certifier to register users remotely, if distribution of ID files is very difficult otherwise. Also worth noting is that managing a database is relatively easy to do and should be done by a person who owns the data. For example, if a database is created and used for marketing purposes, it makes sense to have the manager of the database be someone within the marketing department. This lightens the load of the administration team and provides better security for the data. There is no good reason to have Notes system administrators be listed in every database access control list.

- *Formalize policies and procedures.* Like any other system, good security flows naturally from good policies and their execution. Determine a good way to create and distribute ID files, a good way to manage the public name and address book, a good way to delineate different system maintenance activities such that you have good segregation of duty. If you then follow these policies and procedures, you will have a much more secure environment.

- *Security Policies*
- *Network Management Policies*
- *Server Administration Policies*
- *Database Management Policies*
- *Support Policies*
- *Domain Management Activities*

25

Managing the Domain

THE DOMAIN MANAGEMENT TEAM IS RESPONSIBLE FOR THE ENTIRE Notes system. This includes strategic planning for what resources will execute what tasks. Planning, procedures, and security administration are the most important objectives of the domain management group. Planning objectives of this team will include resources for installation, training, server administration, workstation installation and maintenance, technical support, security, and all policy and procedures. Planning an initial Notes deployment or large Notes migration (from one version to another) will require significant resources and should be well staffed. Future deployments and migrations can leverage the strategies of earlier ones. As administrators (and users) become more familiar with Notes, the time required to administer the system diminishes.

In this chapter, we refer to the domain management team as if it were an entire department. In most cases, this is unlikely. A more likely scenario is that there is a central Notes administration team that is segregated into different groups for the different administrative roles necessary to run a Notes domain. In reality, then, the domain management team is probably one or two people who have the organization's top-level Certifier and Retain Manager access to the Public Name and Address Book. This team is charged with instructing and or managing the rest of the Notes administration support functions.

The domain management team should address the following issues or or assign other groups to address them. The policies, procedures, and processes this group develops must be well documented and well communicated to the groups that will use them. They will be the benchmark for delivering service in the Notes system.

■ Security Policies

An entire book could be devoted to security. We have addressed technical security issues in Chapter 24. In general, the following categories should be addressed in security policies issued by the domain management group:

Servers

- Privileges for direct access to servers

- Privileges for remote, passthru, and external organization access

- Privileges to create databases and replicas

- Privileges to run agents

- Policy about having server allow access only to public keys stored in the address book

- Policy about anonymous access to the server

Workstations and Users

- Adding and removing users from the system

- Policy for minimum Notes password length

- Policy for what kinds of databases (risk level) may be replicated to workstations

- Policy for local encryption of some or all databases?

Databases

- Policy regarding using encryption

- Policy regarding using electronic signatures

- Policy and procedures for development of databases

- Policy about risk rating databases and matching security elements of a database design to its risk level

- Policy and procedures for approving a database for server use and how the database will receive the approval

Many of the security features of Notes that address these categories are handled from documents within the Public Name and Address Book. The domain management team should establish policies and procedures that reflect the necessary security controls. In particular, the Server Document provides all of the security and privilege granting capability for a Notes 4.0 server.

The database access control list and the Encryption button in the database properties InfoBox provides the majority of the security for a database. The domain management team must establish policies for each of the settings that are important to the particular Notes environment, such as how to determine if a database should be marked as high priority for replication. Another example would be risk rating a database to determine the needs for reader fields and/or field encryption. The guidelines created for implementing security features in the development of the database and the guidelines on using the security features of a database will be critical to providing a secure environment.

Creating and Maintaining a Secure Notes Environment

Perhaps the most important functions of the domain manager are to determine a security policy and establish procedures that support the security policy. The security policy must clearly outline who is responsible for the security components of the Lotus Notes environment.

Certifier Security

The security of the certifier ID file and, secondarily, organizational unit certifiers are critical to ensuring a secure Notes environment. The responsibility for the safety of the certifier ID file should be assigned to the domain manager. Organizational unit certifiers, in some cases, are distributed and their security must be delegated in these instances to whomever has been given the organizational unit certifier. All certifier ID files should be password protected. Multiple passwords are desirable for certifier ID files so that multiple users (administrators) will need to enter passwords before the certifier may be used. For example, you can assign five passwords to the certifier ID file but only require three to be entered when needed. In this way, even if an administrator is on vacation or unavailable, the ID file may still be used by getting a different group of three to enter their password. In addition to being password protected, certifier ID files should be stored only on a lockable file system. A backup of the certifier, equally secured, is critical. If the certifier ID file is lost, stolen or damaged, another one with its private key *cannot* be created. Such circumstances would require the creation of another certifier and then the recertification of all entities on the network.

Server Security

Typically this responsibility is delegated to the server administration group as discussed in Chapter 23. The server should be physically secure, have password protection on the console and server ID file (preferably multiple passwords on the ID file if possible), be regularly backed up, have an uninterruptible power supply, and have all databases of strategic importance locally encrypted using the Notes 4.0 local encryption function. In addition, it makes sense to have backup servers available in the event of a major failure such that service can be restored quickly by switching ID files (using the ID file of the down server on the backup server so it takes on the identity of the down server) and bringing the alternate computer online. This eliminates the need to backup from tape, providing faster restoration of service. In this way, users can seamlessly access their databases without having unexpected interruption of service or error messages (such as "server not responding").

As you might expect, having multiple passwords on server ID files might inhibit your ability to quickly restore service to users. Each organization must weigh the value of security against the value of uninterrupted service to users. This is never a simple formula, but a policy should be established, plans made around this policy, and then procedures created and followed to implement it.

Database Security

Database security is typically the responsibility of the database manager. Databases should be risk rated. Appropriate access controls should be set for the entire database as well as the documents in the database based on the risk rating of the database. The application security may need to be enhanced by a database designer based on the risk rating of the data it will store. For example, if the database contains very sensitive information, your policy may state that it must contain Reader and Author fields to control access to specific documents. The database designer can program the database so that individual users will automatically have access to documents they need to perform their job functions and be prevented from accessing documents that do not pertain to their scope of duties.

In addition, the database manager should require that the access control be enforced on all replica copies of the database to ensure that local security procedures do not open the database to attack. Since enforcement of access controls is not a default on all databases, the policies and procedures laid out for database managers should address this issue. If the database has a significant risk rating, local encryption of all replicas should be required. Local encryption is the only way to protect workstation copies of databases from unauthorized access, especially in the case of laptop computers which are easily stolen.

Further, using local encryption on servers provides excellent segregation of duty because it prevents server administrators from accessing a database without the server ID file (whose private key is necessary to decrypt the database). If this ID file is protected with multiple passwords, it makes it difficult even for someone with physical access to the server to see what is in a Notes 4.0 database. Do not worry; if you encrypt a server copy of a database, clients can still see the data in it even though they do not have the server's private key. Remember, clients use the server to gain access to the database and at that point the server will be kind enough to decrypt the data before giving it to the authorized client!

User ID Security

It is the responsibility of each user to secure his or her own ID file. The significance of this file cannot be overstated. Especially if encryption of databases, encryption of fields, or electronic signatures are being used, an ID file that is not adequately defended can cause huge problems. Notes 4.0 does not provide tools such as expiration of passwords, so the domain management group and those designated by this group must set policy and procedures and manage enforcement of password changes and user backup of ID files. Some organizations find it useful to have a regular, automated electronic mail message reminding users to change their password and back up their ID file if new encryption keys have been added since the last notice. Other organizations have created LotusScripts and macros to force regular password changes and backups.

Whatever your organization deems appropriate, make sure that a method for ensuring password change and backup of ID files is in place and is followed. Bear in mind, proper segregation of duty is not possible if the systems administrators maintain copies of user ID files. It is critical that the ID file remain the exclusive property of the user.

Public Name and Address Book Security

For a complete discussion on security in the Public Name and Address Book, see Chapter 23, "Managing Overview and Management Tools." In general, use the three levels of database security provided in the Public Name and

Address Book to grant only the access a given administrator needs to this critical database. You may assign an access control level (usually Author with Create rights is adequate for most administrators), a role (bear in mind that assigning a user to a role gives them the privilege to create or modify *all* documents of a given type, such as Server or Configuration Documents) and you may assign administrators to specific documents (ideally you have groups established for this purpose, but in either case this will give you the ability to let certain administrators modify only certain documents, such as Server Documents for servers in their location).

Using the roles created in the Public Name and Address Book as a guideline, you might assign different users in the domain managers group into all of the Create roles in the Public Name and Address Book. It makes sense to segregate which users in the domain managers group have this access so that no one user (with the exception of the Public Name and Address Book managers) have all the privileges for all the documents. Remember that anyone listed as an Editor or above to the Public Name and Address Book may edit any document in the Public Name and Address Book, they do not need to be assigned to Modifier roles. In general, however, you should grant Edit and above access to the Public Name and Address Book judiciously. It is best to grant Author access with Create rights and then enter users (administrators in this case) into the appropriate roles and administrative groups to let them modify the documents necessary to execute their job functions.

■ Network Management Policies

The domain management group should institute guidelines by which network managers design the Notes network. These guidelines should include service requirements (reliability and availability of the system) as well as efficiency requirements (how much are we willing to spend to get the reliability and availability we want).

When establishing policies and procedures for the network management team, remember that the connections and configurations this group creates will be the backbone of your Notes network. Included in your policies should be the following:

- *Replication Policies*—How frequently replication must occur, how many different priorities will be available.

- *Routing Policies*—The amount of time acceptable for a message to travel from the sender to the recipient, the amount of downtime that is acceptable (if any).

- *Remote and Passthru Support*—What is the policy on the availability and usage of remote dial-in and passthru access to your Notes network? You need to establish a policy so that the network manager(s) can design the network to support it.

- *Connecting to External Organizations*—While the cross-certification function is the job of domain manager(s), connecting to cross-certified organizations is tasked to the network manager(s). How often, and for what reasons will connections be established? A policy should be put in place to guide network managers.

- *Server Support*—How will configuration settings be determined and implemented? Both network managers and server managers will need to play some role in the ongoing maintenance of servers. Who will create and edit Connection and Configuration Documents?

- *Change Order Approval*—How will the network plans (Connection and Configuration Documents) be tested and approved? What will be the procedure for implementing approved network plans? Remember, once your Notes system is running with mail and applications, you do not want any unexpected problems causing unavailability.

■ Server Administration Policies

Server administration policies will help your server administrators ensure reliability and security of the Notes system. Physical access to the server and proximity to the day-to-day use of Notes by end users makes the server managers important success or failure elements in the administration of the Notes system. It is important, then, that policies and procedures help server managers maintain the system such that it meets the needs of users and complements the other system administration functions, especially network management. In particular, policies for the following must be established and conveyed to server managers:

- *Server Security*—Who may physically access the server, for what reasons, and with what monitoring. Which managers will have access to the server ID file and how many will need to enter passwords to use it. What file access (local or network) to Notes databases will be made, and for what reasons (usually, there is not a good reason for file access to Notes databases).

- *Server Backup*—How often the server will be backed up, how many historical backups will be kept, how the server will be backed up, and who will have access to the backups.

- *Server Maintenance*—How the server will be upgraded and fixed when new functionality is needed or problems need to be resolved. How service will be delivered to users while maintenance occurs.

■ Database Management Policies

Database management policies are important to document. In Notes, many different users throughout the population may be managers of databases, but many of these people may not have data systems backgrounds. As a result, it is imperative to document and train anyone who will manage a database so that the data stored is protected.

For example, have your policy require that database managers use fully distinguished names in access controls. To the typical user the importance of this may not be apparent. Using a fully distinguished name will prevent unauthorized access by someone not intended to access the database who has the same common name as a user who does have access to the database. For example, if an administrator has access to the /Sales/West/WGSI organizational unit certifier, he or she could create a user named Sarah Jones/Sales/West/WGSI. If there is a user in the payroll department named Sarah Jones/Payroll/Corp/WGSI, a fully distinguished name in the database access control list can prevent the wrong Sarah Jones from gaining access to the database.

Make a clear and concise policy for database managers about how access to database requests is approved and implemented, how databases are backed up, data is archived, and database managers are trained. In addition, develop policies for support responsibilities as well as problem escalation procedure policies.

In general, your policies for database managers should cover the following:

- *Database Manager Qualities*—To establish proper management of data (the reason we have Notes!), database managers should posess certain qualities. In particular, they should have an interest in the data, and be trustworthy and competent in the key tasks for which they will be responsible. In general, system managers should not be database managers of end user databases, as this undermines segregation of duty. System managers may be managers of system and system related databases. In many cases, it makes sense to train a nonsystems person in various locations to manage multiple databases from different end user communities. In other scenarios, each group within your organization should designate a person(s) to manage databases.

- *Database Archiving*—The database manager should develop a strategy around the archiving of information so that as much information as should be kept available, in some way, is available. If necessary, the database manager should create or have created an automated means of archiving data.

- *Managing Size*—The database manager will need to manage the overall size of the database so that it does not exceed the amount allotted to it. There are several techniques for doing this, and each database manager must determine the best plan based on the data and the needs of the organization that will access that data.

- *Managing Replication*—The database manager must ensure that replicas reside wherever users need to access them and that replication is occurring regularly.

■ Support Policies

Support is a tricky issue here. End-users will need assistance in accessing software, making changes, and resolving other issues including bugs and lower-end configuration problems. A good strategy is to have a help desk, preferably integrated with your organization's other help desk services, as the primary or first level contact for end-users. A local server administrator is often a good person to resolve technical issues if the problem cannot be solved via a telephone conversation with the end-user.

End-User Help Desk Policy

Who will answer end-user questions on Notes 4.0 and Notes 4.0 applications? If a problem cannot be resolved via the telephone, who will support the user locally? In most organizations, a set of procedures exists for addressing problems and escalating them if necessary. Wherever possible, make your Notes support policies consistent with the support to other systems (such as network support) and use existing resources to minimize costs, if possible.

Training Policies

Training is a key component to a successful deployment of Notes 4.0. It is important that some form of training is implemented, even if a comprehensive program is not feasible. In general, system administration training is the most critical because the effectiveness of users and application developers hinges on the integrity of the platform. Some organizations have been very successful with video training and computer-based training, especially for end-users. In general, the domain management group should plan on (at a minimum) these categories of training:

- System administration training

- Application developer training

- End-user training

General Administration Policies

Notes 4.0 is a large and complicated system with many nuances. It is important to clearly define roles and responsibilities before deploying Notes. Roles and responsibilities should be further defined once the system is up and running and you have an understanding of how your organization uses Notes. The following are some tips you may want to consider:

- Management of administrative requests (how to receive, track, and assign jobs).

- Server topology concerns (central with single location, central with different locations, distributed with workgroups). What will be the deciding factors in designing the topology?

- Hardware requirements for servers and clients. Determine what your minimum and ideal hardware platforms are for computers with different tasks.

- Installation instructions for each platform (including directory contents).

- Application installation policies and instructions for how applications will be deployed, as well as what criteria they must meet before going onto a production server.

- Ongoing system enhancement. Who will manage the process of evolving the system so it continues to meet your organization's needs? What resources will be available for these tasks and how will these plans be converted to reality?

■ Domain Management Activities

In addition to the planning and policy functions described above, the domain management group will have specific tasks to execute as well. They are

- Registering users (as well as developing naming conventions)

- Registering servers (as well as developing naming conventions)

- Registering organizational unit certifiers (as well as developing naming conventions)

- Adding domains

- Removing users

- Removing servers

- Removing certifiers

- Cross-certifying

- Recertifying users/servers

- Renaming users/servers

- Changing hierarchy for users/servers

- Converting users and servers from flat to hierarchical certificates
- Auditing security

One must hold a certifier ID to execute the registration functions. The higher the certifier is in the certification hierarchy, the more potential risk there is in giving out that certifier. ID file Because certifier ID files can create an ID on the system, giving a certifier ID file to someone is allows them significant responsibility. Make sure that certifiers are kept with trusted administrators.

Registering Users

Adding and removing users is done through the Administration Control Panel. During the procedure of registering a user, a private and public key pair will be generated for the user and then certified by the certifier ID file.

All of this information will then be stored in an ID file for the user. In addition, a Person Document will be created and stored in the Public Name and Address Book so that information about the user will be available on every server, mostly for electronic mail purposes.

In general, users should be added by using an organizational unit certifier ID file so that they fall into logical hierarchies that represent the structure of your organization. While this may not be necessary in smaller organizations, it is critical to larger organizations to simplify administration and to ensure unique user names.

Procedures for Registering Users Manually

1. Choose File/Tools/Server Administration.
2. Click the People button.
3. Choose Register Person.
4. Click Yes when prompted regarding the purchase of a license.
5. Enter the password for the certifier ID file.
6. Ensure that the correct certifier ID file and registration server are selected.
7. Enter the type of license you wish to register and the date the certificate should expire.

NOTE. *North American licenses may not be exported from the United States. In addition, encrypted documents with a North American ID file cannot be decrypted with an international ID file.*

8. Enter the name and password for the new user.

9. Choose the license type (Lotus Notes or Lotus Notes Desktop).

10. If there is a connection profile in your organization's Public Name and Address Book that you want set up to use when configuring the workstation, select it.

11. Enter the number of characters this ID file will require for passwords.

12. Choose the Mail icon.

13. Enter the type of mail the user will use (preferably Lotus Notes mail).

14. (Optional) Change the name of the user's mail file if you do not like the default.

15. Select the time that the mail file should be created.

NOTE. *If the user will use a remote server as his or her home server, you may want to select "Create files during setup" to avoid delays.*

16. Choose the server that will be the user's home server.

17. Choose the Other icon.

18. (Optional) Enter a comment to appear on the user's Person Document.

19. (Optional) Enter the location of the user's server.

20. (Optional) Enter the name of the local administration group for the user.

21. (Optional) Select "In File" to store the ID file that is created in a file on the file system rather than in the Public Name and Address Book. *This is recommended for security purposes.*

22. Select Next to add an additional user to register.

23. Select Register when you have entered all the users you with to register.

Procedures for Registering Users from a File

Users may also be registered by importing from a text file. This is the best technique if you have large numbers of users to register. To do so, you will need a text file with the following format:

```
Lastname;Firstname;MiddleInitial;organization;password;IDFileDirectory;IDFilename;
HomeServerName;MailFileDirectory;MailFileName;Location;Comment;ForwardingAddress
```

To register users from a file, follow the steps below:

1. Select File/Tools/Server Administration to access the Administration Control Panel.

2. Choose the People button.

3. Select Register from File.

4. Click Yes to indicate you have purchased licenses for the users.

5. Enter the password for the certifier ID file you will use to register the users.

6. Choose the type of ID file to create (North American or International).

7. Enter the name of the text file with the user information in it.

8. Enter the minimum password length for the user ID files.

9. Choose the type of license that was purchased (Notes or Notes Desktop).

10. Choose the type of electronic mail to be used.

11. Choose where Notes should store the user ID file until it is given to the user (file or Public Name and Address Book).

12. Enter the name of the administrator for this user, or a group name of administrators.

13. Click Register.

Security Concerns When Adding Users

The user name will need to be entered into the appropriate field on the Server Document to ensure that he or she has access to the server that will be used for setup and any additional servers that the user will need to access. The best way of doing this is to enter the user in a group that will provide such access. For example, if the user works in the Los Angeles field sales office, you might enter him or her into a group called LAXUsers if that group is already listed in the Server Document in the appropriate Access Control fields for the Los Angeles server.

Ensure that the user has access to the appropriate public databases, either through default access privileges, being explicitly listed in the access control list of these databases, or being entered into a group that is listed in the Access Control list. The user will need access to the Public Name and Address Book, the database catalog, and database libraries, as well as policy and other databases.

While the actual setup will probably be done by a user or local administrator, the domain management group should have a clear set of policies about who will do user setup and with what set of instructions. In addition, it makes sense for larger organizations to create profile documents to hasten the setup procedure by telling the setup program how to configure the workstation to communicate with the server under different circumstances. While the addition of setup profile documents to the Public Name and Address Book is probably the job of the network administration group, the policy is the responsibility of the domain manager.

Registering Servers

Registering servers is much like adding users. Notes treats users and servers alike in many respects, so it makes sense that the two procedures have similar effects. Servers are added from the Administration Control Panel. When you register a new server the server's public and private key pair will be created, certified, and stored in an ID file. In addition, a Server Document will be created and stored in the Public Name and Address Book. This document provides information the server needs at startup and information other servers need for communication purposes.

Procedures for Adding Servers

1. Select File/Tools/Server Administration.

2. Choose the Servers button.

3. Select Register Server.

4. Click on Yes when prompted regarding a license.

5. Enter the password for the certifier ID file.

6. Ensure that the correct certifier ID file and Registration Server are selected.

7. Enter the security type (North American or International), bearing in mind that documents encrypted with the North American license cannot be decrypted with the international ID.

8. (Optional) Change the date the certificate for this ID file will expire.

9. Choose Continue.

10. Enter the name of the new server.

11. Enter the password and minimum password length.

12. Enter the domain and administrator's name.

13. (Optional) Enter a title to appear on the Server Document.

14. Enter the name of the Notes Named Network to which this server will belong.

15. Enter the name of the local administrator for this server.

16. Choose where the ID file will be stored (in Public Name and Address Book or in a file—*it will be more secure in a file*).

17. Choose Register.

Security Concerns for Adding Servers

Now is the time to institute server security by limiting access to the server ID file and setting up access control fields in the Server Document. These may need to be fine-tuned in the future, but by starting now, you can defend against attack better.

In particular, do not store server ID files in the Server Document. While it simplifies the setup procedure, it is not a secure method of delivering the ID file. In addition, by storing it in a file from the start, you give yourself time to implement other worthwhile security options, such as mailing the ID file to a secured (encrypted) mail system to which only multiple administrators acting together have access (for backup purposes) and also adding multiple passwords so that it will require multiple users to access a server ID file.

While the domain management team will probably not be responsible for the setup of the Notes 4.0 server, they should develop the policy and procedures necessary to do so. These include the physical specifications for the hardware, the software, the location requirements of a Notes server, the names of directories that will store Notes software and data, how the computer will be backed up as well as any other operational procedures necessary to keep the server up and running as well as defended against attack and catastrophe.

Registering Organizational Unit Certifiers

The purpose of adding organizational unit certifiers is to create a hierarchy that will provide a better environment for managing your Notes system by allowing for wild card referencing and distributed registration. In addition, hierarchical naming provides for a greater number of unique names in your organization. See the Chapter 14 for more information on hierarchical naming.

Creating an organizational unit certifier means that you use the certifier (let's say that its name is /WGSI) and instead of certifying a user or server ID with it, you certify another certifier ID file. The result is a concatenated name and a traceable lineage of certificates. For example, you may have an organizational unit certifier such as /West/WGSI that is used to certify all users and servers on the West Coast. A user named John Smith that is certified with this certifier would have the fully distinguished name John Smith/West/WGSI.

Registering Organizational Unit Procedure

Organizational unit certifier ID files are Notes ID files that have been created with the organization certifier ID file (the parent of all IDs in your domain) and have the ability to create other ID files below them in the hierarchy. Chapter 14, "The Notes Network: Overview and Planning," describes the use of naming hierarchies in your organization. To create an organizational unit certifier:

1. Select File/Tools/Server Administration.

2. Click the Certifiers button.

3. Select Register Organizational Unit.

4. Enter the password for the Certifier ID file.

5. Enter the name of the organizational unit.

NOTE. *Notes will automatically append the certifier's name to the end of the organizational unit, so you do not need to enter it here. For example, if you are using the organizational certifier with the name /WGSI, and you want to add an organizational unit called /WestCoast/WGSI that you can give to the system administrator for the West Coast to register users and servers, simply type WestCoast and Notes will append /WGSI.*

6. Enter a password to be used with this organizational unit certifier ID.

7. Enter the name of an administrator for this certifier to whom requests for new certificates will be mailed.

NOTE. *You may want to enter the name of an administrative group that exists in your name and address book and will be kept current so that mail is not sent to administrators who have left the company or are no longer in that role.*

8. Select Other Certifier Settings, change the license type, add comments that will go into the certifier document in the Public Name and Address Book, or change the length of the password that will be required for the ID file (default is eight characters).

9. Choose Register.

Figure 25.1 shows the dialog box you will use to register organizational unit certifiers.

Figure 25.1

The Organizational Unit registration dialog box.

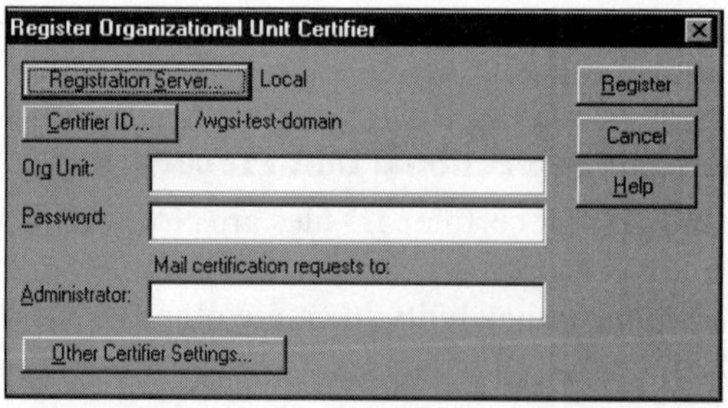

Notes will create an organizational unit certifier ID file. This certifier may be used to create additional organizational units (provided there are not yet four in the hierarchy) as well as users and servers. To use the ID file, an administrator must have its password and appropriate access to the Public Name and Address Book. If more than one password has been added to this ID file, the administrator must have others enter their passwords before commencing with the certification process. See Chapter 14 for more information about setting access to the Name and Address Book and Chapter 24, "Managing Security," for more information about assigning multiple passwords to an ID file.

Distributing Organizational Unit Certifiers

The organizational unit certifier you create may be distributed to local administrators who will need to create server and user ID files. These administrators will need Author and Create privileges to the Public Name and Address Book and will need to be entered into the CreateUser and CreateServer roles if they are to create such ID files.

If possible, we generally prefer to hold all organizational unit certifiers as well as the top level organization certifier in the domain management group and do all certification centrally. This limits the number of people who have access to the critical ID files and also limits the threat of attack while transporting a certifier ID file to a remote administrator.

Adding Domains

You may want to add domains to your Notes system to add a secure "firewall" that will enable your organization to safely communicate with other organizations. In addition, you may want to have multiple domains if you want to distribute the responsibility for managing the resources on a system. Large companies with international locations will often create multiple domains, manage them separately, and integrate the two so users can seamlessly exchange mail and replicate databases.

Domain documents in the Notes 4.0 Public Name and Address Book are used for mail routing. In Notes 4.0 they tell your servers how to route mail outside your Notes domain to other domains (Notes and non-Notes). In addition, they provide security by limiting which domains may send mail into your domain.

To create another domain, such as a firewall domain, you can go through the first server setup procedure and build an entirely new network. You can then cross-certify this new domain and even store both Public Name and Address Books on all servers in both domains to simplify sending mail and replication. You will still have the benefit of being able to manage each domain independently.

Removing Users

Removing users from the system involves several steps. It can be done manually as with earlier versions of Notes or with the Notes 4.0 Administration Process. In general, the goal of removing a Notes user from the system is to remove his or her access privileges. Because the ID file he or she had can be authenticated with another Notes ID file that was created with common ancestry, it is important that access restrictions be used to remove all of such a user's privileges. In general, users should not be able to take their ID files with them when they leave an organization, any more than they would take a badge. Because ID files are easily and frequently copied, you will need to defend against potential assault by implementing explicit access denials.

What Needs to Be Done

The following are the key goals (from a security perspective) to removing a Notes user from the system:

- Prevent the user from accessing the server by explicitly listing him or her as an entity that may not access the server.

- Prevent the user from accessing any database on the system to prevent the theft or tampering of data.

- Remove the user's Person Document from the Public Name and Address Book in case any processes key off of this database.

  The simplest way to achieve these goals is with two steps:

1. List the user in the Deny Access group you have created and listed in all Server Documents to explicitly deny access to server (most organizations call it the "Terminations" list).

2. Use the Administration Process to remove the user from the system.

  In addition, you will want to reclaim server space by deleting the user's mail database. If the user is using shared mail, you will need first to unlink his or her mail database from the shared mail database (see Chapter 27, "Managing Servers") and then delete the user's private mail database.

Procedures for Removing a User from the System

1. Choose File/Tools/Server Administration.

2. Click the People button.

3. Choose People view.

4. Select Actions/Delete Person.

5. Confirm that you wish to delete the person by clicking on Yes.

6. (Optional) Unlink the user's mail database from the shared mail database by typing **Load Object Unlink MAILDB.NSF** at the server console or server remote console (where MAILDB.NSF is the user's mail database). (This is probably the responsibility of the server administrator.)

7. Delete the mail database. (This is probably be the responsibility of the server administrator.)

8. Add the user to the Terminations group.

Security Issues When Removing Users

The Administration Process will remove the user's name from database access control lists for all databases that have an Administration Server specified. In addition, the Administration Process will remove the user's name from all group documents in the Public Name and Address Book that are not of the type "Deny access." Provided you granted the user's privileges by entering his or her name into a group in the Public Name and Address Book (the group then being entered into the appropriate field on the Server Document), the user's privileges will be removed when he or she is removed from the group.

Since access control changes are stored in databases (Server Document in Public Name and Address Book for server access, access control lists for database access), and the Administration Process is kicked off by the Administration Requests database, it is important that the Administration Requests database and the Public Name and Address Book replicate quickly around the organization so that a user deletion actually occurs quickly. It makes sense, then, to mark these databases as high priority so they replicate on the high priority, schedule or even use the Notes 4.0 database specific replication feature to schedule replication of these two databases frequently.

Using a hub server as the server on which you issue the command is also likely to hasten the process of getting these changes replicated around the organization. While you could force a replication between two servers manually each time a user was removed from the system, this is inefficient and, in some cases, impossible to effect for any organization with a considerable user base and large number of servers. For example, if you have 40 servers supporting 10,000 users you would need to force 40 replications for each user you remove from the system. It is best, then, to set up a general replication schedule that supports the timely replication of system databases as well as other critical databases.

NOTE. *As part of your security policy you may want to enable the Notes 4.0 "Only allow server access to users listed in this address book" field. This will further prevent a user whose Person Document has been deleted from accessing the system.*

Removing Servers

The process for removing servers is similar to that of removing users. The main differences are that you must check to make sure that all data is backed up, that users are migrated to another server, and that there is no mail database for the server that will need to be removed.

Procedures for Removing Servers from the System

The same security precautions that are implemented with users should be implemented with servers to defend against unauthorized access to other Notes 4.0 servers and databases.

1. Select File/Tools/Server Administration.

2. Click the Servers button.

3. Select Server View.

4. Choose Actions/Delete Server.

5. Confirm that you wish to delete the server.

Security Issues When Removing Servers

The Administration Process will remove the Server Document from the Public Name and Address Book as well as remove the server from access control lists of all databases that have Administration Servers specified. Furthermore, the server's name will removed from all group documents in the Public Name and Address Book.

These precautions are important so that a server ID file cannot be used by an unauthorized person to replicate data. Just like a user ID file, a server ID file can be authenticated if it has the same ancestry. As a result, specifically removing access privileges granted to the server and explicitly denying access are the only way to defend against unwarranted use of the server ID file.

Removing Certifiers

In some cases, you may need to remove organizational unit certifiers from your system. This need might arise because you have reorganized and no longer need that hierarchy or because a business unit associated with a hierarchy has been dismantled, sold, or dispersed. To delete a certifier:

1. Open the Public Name and Address Book.

2. Select View Certificates.

3. Choose Actions/Delete Certifier.

The certifier will be deleted. Bear in mind that ID files created with it can still be authenticated if they share a common ancestry. It is important, then, to make sure that a copy of the ID file is not obtained by unauthorized users. In addition, you may explicitly remove access to ID files created with this certifier.

For example, let's say you change your organizational structure and want to exclude the use of the organizational unit certifier /Sales/West/WGSI. Enter the following in a group that denies access to a server (like "terminations"):

```
*/Sales/West/WGSI.
```

Cross-certifying

Cross-certifying ID files enables your system to authenticate with an ID file that was not created using a certifier anywhere in your organization's hierarchy. Since the two ID files (such as two server IDs) share no common ancestry, they could not under normal circumstances authenticate each other.

Cross-certifying basically takes the name and public key of another system's ID file and places a certificate on it just as it would an ID file in your system. Instead of storing the certificate in the ID file itself, however, it stores the certificate in the Public Name and Address Book where all the servers in your system will be able to find it to authenticate if necessary.

How Cross-certification Is Used

Cross certification is often used to allow sharing of information between two organizations. For example, let's say you have a product information database that is frequently updated. You may want to share this database with your distribution channel that also uses Notes. For security reasons it is imprudent to give them an ID file from your system as they might gain too much privilege to proprietary information.

Instead, you cross-certify a server in their Notes system with one in your Notes system. This will enable the two servers to authenticate. You then place a replica of the database you want to share on each of the servers and set up a connection between the two servers to have them replicate. In this way you will exchange information but limit the access the other organization has to your Notes system.

NOTE. *When cross-certifying with other organizations it makes sense to have a "firewall" server to protect your information. This means that you create a small Notes domain (one server) and cross-certify a server in your main domain with this external domain. You then cross-certify all external organizations with the external "firewall" domain you created. In this way, no external organization will gain access to your internal production servers or Public Name and Address Book.*

Types of Cross-certification

There are essentially two types of cross-certification that you can do. The first is to cross-certify a certifier from another organization. If you do this, you will enable all the ID files created under this certifier in the hierarchy to validate and then authenticate with all of the ID files under the certifier that was cross-certified from your system.

826 Chapter 25: Managing the Domain

NOTE. *We recommend using this type of cross-certification only for internal certification purposes. For example, if your organization's international Notes domain uses a different certifier(s) you may want to cross-certify at the certifier (or organizational unit certifier) level to simplify communication between the two internal organizations. We* do not *recommend this type of cross-certification for connecting with outside organizations because it grants more opportunity to the other organization to authenticate than is necessary.*

Another kind of cross-certification (although the procedures for doing it are the same as the first type mentioned) is to cross-certify specific users or servers. This procedure is best for allowing external users (consultants, vendors, or customers) to access your system without giving license to their entire organization.

NOTE. *We recommend using this type of cross-certification for allowing external entities to connect with your organization to share information. For example, you might cross-certify one Notes server in your organization (preferably in an isolated domain—see Figure 25.2) with one server in your vendor's domain. By so doing, you can replicate databases and exchange mail securely. No outside organization will be able to see your internal Public Name and Address Book or access an internal production server.*

Cross-certification Procedures

To cross-certify another ID file the domain manager needs to create a document in the Public Name and Address Book that attests to the fact that the public key and the name that are in that ID are in fact valid. There are two procedures that will do this for you: a safe ID and a public key.

NOTE. *An ID file from your organization (such as the server ID of the server that is to communicate with the other organization) will need to be cross-certified on their system.* Never send an ID file to another organization: Send only "safe" ID files. *These do not have the user's private key and can therefore not be used to gain unauthorized access to your Notes system.*

A safe ID file is one that contains the name and public key but does not contain the password or private key. It is therefore "safe" to distribute this ID file to provide information in the cross-certification process. Notes 4.0 will automatically pull the information it needs from this ID file to simplify the process of cross-certifying the other ID file.

How to Cross-certify ID Files

The following steps detail how you cross-certify an ID file that was not created as part of the same hierarchy as the ID files in your organization.

1. Choose File/Tools/Server Administration.

2. Click on the Certifiers button.

Figure 25.2

Cross-certification allows ID files that are not part of the same hierarchy to authenticate with each other.

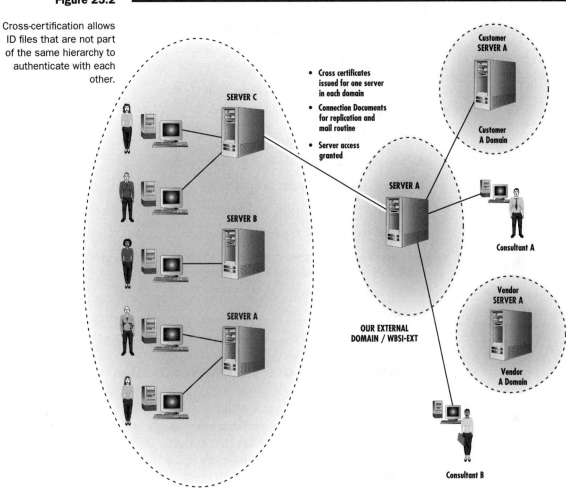

- Cross certificates issued for one server in each domain
- Connection Documents for replication and mail routine
- Server access granted

SERVER C

SERVER B

SERVER A

OUR EXTERNAL DOMAIN / WBSI-EXT

OUR DOMAIN (IWGSI)

Customer SERVER A

Customer A Domain

SERVER A

Consultant A

Vendor SERVER A

Vendor A Domain

Consultant B

3. Choose Cross-Certify ID file.

4. Select the certifier that you wish to issue the certificate.

5. Enter the password for the certifier.

6. Select the safe ID file that contains the other entity's public key and name.

7. Ensure that the certifier and registration server specified are correct.

8. (Optional) Change the expiration date of the certificate you are about to issue.

9. Select Cross-Certify.

The effect of issuing the cross-certificate in this way is the same. The difference is that this option allows you to cross-certify without having received a safe copy of the ID you are cross-certifying. Instead you need to have the user name and key associated with that ID file. The following steps detail how you can cross-certify another organization using only a public key rather than a "safe ID" file.

1. Choose File/Tools/Server Administration.

2. Click on the Certifiers button.

3. Choose Cross-Certify Key.

4. Select the certifier you wish to issue the certificate.

5. Enter the password for the certifier.

6. Ensure that the certifier and registration server information are correct.

7. Enter the name of the entity you wish to cross-certify.

8. Enter the public key of the entity you wish to cross-certify. This will be found when you choose File/Tools/User ID.

9. (Optional) Change the expiration date of the certificate you are about to issue.

10. Select Cross-Certify.

Recertification of User and Server ID Files

Recertifying ID files is the process of issuing an updated certificate to a Notes ID file so that it can successfully authenticate with other Notes ID files on your system. Remember, certificates are stamps of authenticity that all ID files on your system have. They say that a trusted entity (the certifier ID file) has verified that the name and public key in the ID file that is requesting to authenticate are correctly associated (create one entity).

When an ID file receives a certificate, the certificate has with it an expiration date entered by the administrator who used the certifier ID file to create (and certify) the ID file initially. Notes ID files check the expiration date of certificates during the validation process and will not validate an ID file that has an expired certificate.

NOTE. *You can set an event monitor in the Events and Statistics Monitoring database to alert you to an expired ID file, server, or user. It is a better policy to regularly check the Certification Log (By Expiration Date view) and issue new certificates* before *they expire so as not to disrupt service.*

The Administration Process automates many of the steps necessary to re-certify an ID file. The Administration Process must be running on all Notes 4.0 servers involved in the recertification.

What Happens during Recertification

During recertification, an ID file (user, server, or organizational unit certifier) receives a new certificate (stamp of approval) with a new expiration date. In essence, recertification is the Notes equivalent of having your driver's license renewed.

Procedures for Recertifying User ID Files

The following instructions detail the steps you must take to recertify a user's ID file to renew its certificate.

1. Choose File/Tools/Server Administration.

2. Click the People button.

3. Choose People view.

4. Select all of the users you want to recertify by clicking next to their name.

5. Choose Actions/Recertify Person.

6. Choose the certifier with which you wish to recertify the user (should be the same as the one originally used).

7. Enter the password for the certifier.

8. (Optional) Change the date the new certificate will expire (default is two years).

9. (Optional) Enter a date for recertifying ID files (ID files whose certificates expire *after* this date will not be recertified at this time).

10. Click Certify.

11. Select No to indicate you are finished recertifying users.

Procedures for Recertifying a Server ID File

Server ID files, like user ID files, need to be recertified periodically. When an ID file is created, the certificate that is included in it has an expiration date. Other ID files will not authenticate with that ID file once the expiration date passes. Notes ID files check the expiration date of certificates during the validation process and will not validate an ID file that has an expired certificate.

NOTE. *You can set an event monitor in the Events and Statistics Monitoring database to alert you to an expired ID file, server, or user. It is a better policy to regularly check the Certification Log (By expiration date view) and issue new certificates* before *they expire so as not to disrupt service.*

The following instructions detail the steps you must take to recertify a server ID file.

1. Choose File/Tools/Server Administration.

2. Click the Server button.

3. Select Servers view.

4. Select the server(s) you wish to recertify.

5. Choose Actions/Recertify Server.

6. Select a certifier ID file to certify the server ID file.

7. Enter the new certificate expiration date (or leave the default).

8. (Optional) Enter a date indicating to indicate which certificates should be recertified. Server ID files with certificates expiring after this date will not be recertified.

The Administration Process will automate the update of the certificate in the server ID file.

Renaming Users

Renaming a user is similar to recertifying in that you need to recertify the ID file after making a change to one of its components. In this case, you are changing the common name (rather than just the expiration date) that is stored in the ID file. For example, if a user gets married and requests a name change from Mary Jones to Mary Burke, only the common name portion needs to change so the new fully distinguished name will still reflect the same certifier or organizational unit certifier. The user will stay in the same hierarchy.

For example, Mary Jones/Sales/West/WGSI will become Mary Burke/Sales/West/WGSI. The key to remember here is that the same certifier that was originally used to certify Mary must be used to place her in the same hierarchy.

Procedures for Renaming a User

The following instructions detail the steps you must take to rename a user.

1. Open the Public Name and Address Book.

2. Choose View/People.

3. Select the user's Person Document.

4. Choose Actions/Rename Person.

5. Choose Change Common Name.

6. Select the certifier that was used to originally certify this user's ID file (for example /Sales/West/WGSI).

7. Enter the password for the certifier.

8. (Optional) Change the expiration date of the certificate.

9. Enter the user's new common name.

10. (Optional) Enter a name to distinguish this user from another that was certified with the same certifier (for example, a department may have two users named John Smith). You can enter a user unique organization that will appear between the user's common name and the certifier's name.

11. Click Rename.

The Administration Process will automatically recertify the user without further intervention from the Notes administrator. The user will be asked to confirm the name change before the new name replaces the old one in the user's ID file.

Renaming Servers

Notes 4.0 does not specifically provide a tool for renaming servers. The key objectives when renaming a server are to ensure that:

- The old server ID file cannot be used to access information.

- The new server ID file has all the privileges necessary to access other servers and user workstations.

- Connections to and from the old server are transferred to the new server.

Procedures to Rename a Server

1. Back up the server.

2. Follow instructions below for moving user mail accounts (if the mail accounts will stay on this computer and the computer will simply be renamed, you need only change location information in the Public Name and Address Book).

3. Alert users that the server will no longer be available.

4. Follow instructions above for registering a new server.

5. Follow the instructions in Chapter 16, "Deploying Servers" to bring up the computer as if it were a first time installation.

6. Set up server access control lists.

7. Set up connection schedules (Network Management Group).

Moving Users Elsewhere in the Hierarchy

Moving a user to somewhere else in the naming hierarchy means that you are using a different organizational unit certifier to issue the certificate that is stored in the user's ID file. The certificate, once again, is the component of the ID file that allows it to validate itself (prove a common, trusted, ancestor) with other ID files so that it can then go through the authentication process.

Procedures for Moving Users Elsewhere in the Hierarchy

The following instructions detail the steps you must take to change the hierarchy to which a user ID file belongs.

1. Choose File/Tools/Server Administration.

2. Click the People button.

3. Choose People view.

4. Select Actions/Rename Person.

5. Click Request Move to New Certifier.

6. Select the Original Certifier used to certify this ID file.

7. Choose OK.

Switching User and Server ID Files from Flat to Hierarchical Certificates

Hierarchical names are an important component of securing your Notes network. Notes 2.02 and earlier versions did not permit the use of hierarchical names and some organizations are still using ID files with "flat" names. Notes 4.0 makes the task of migrating users and servers to hierarchical names much simpler with the assistance of the Administration Process.

To upgrade names from flat to hierarchical using the Administration Process, you will need to:

- Upgrade clients and servers to Notes 4.0.

- Have the Administration Process running on each Notes 4.0 server.

- Replicate the Administration Requests and Certification Log databases to each server.

- Manually upgrade the first server to a hierarchical ID file.

- Upgrade other server ID files before upgrading workstation client ID files.

How the Administration Process Upgrades Names from Flat to Hierarchical Names

The procedure for converting to hierarchical names is similar to renaming a user, or recertifying a user or server. An administrator uses an Action in the Public Name and Address Book to request the upgrade to hierarchical.

1. Request goes into Administration Request database that replicates to each server.

2. Certified User document goes into Certification log that replicates to each server.

3. Administration Process on the "Administration Server" for the Public Name and Address Book changes the name field in the Person Document or Server Document in the Public Name and Address Book.

4. Administration Process on the "Administration Server" for the Public Name and Address Book adds the hierarchical certificate that will ultimately go into the ID file to the Person or Server Document.

5. Administration Process on the "Administration Server" for the Public Name and Address Book adds a change request field to the Person or Server Document.

6. Administration Process creates a Response Document to the Request Document in the Administration Request database describing the change it made to the Person or Server Document

7. The Public Name and Address Book replicates to the user or server computer that will be receiving the changed name.

    • For Users—When the user connects to the server the name in his or her ID file is compared with the information in the Person Document, the change is detected, and the user is prompted to approve the change.

    • For Servers—The server periodically checks the Server Document and detects that its name has been changed by comparing the name in its ID file with the name in the Change Request field of the Server Document. If they do not match, the server updates its own ID file with the hierarchical name in the change request field.

8. A Rename User or Server Document is posted to the administration requests database by the workstation or server program. This document tells the Administration Server for the Public Name and Address Book to update to the new name all other occurrences of the user's or server's old name.

9. The Administration Process posts a Response Document to the rename user or Server Document describing the changes it made to the Public Name and Address Book (such as changing the user or server name in all group documents)

10. The Administration Process posts a Rename in Access control list document that tells all administration servers for all databases that have an Administration Server specified to change the user or server name to the new hierarchical name in the access control list of all databases for which it is the Administration Server.

Procedures for Upgrading ID Files to Hierarchical Names

If you have ID files that contain flat certificates you will want to use the Administration Process to upgrade these certificates to hierarchical format. The following steps will guide you through the process.

1. Upgrade all workstations and servers to Notes 4.0.

2. Ensure that the Administration Process is running on all servers (see Chapter 27, "Managing Servers").

3. Create hierarchical certifier ID files using the Administration Control Panel, choosing the Certifiers button and selecting Register Organization.

4. Manually convert the first server (the Administration Server for the Public Name and Address Book) to a hierarchical ID file.

Steps to Take

The following steps will guide you through the process of upgrading the first server to a hierarchically certified ID file. Once this procedure is complete, you may use the Administration Process to upgrade other server and user ID files to hierarchical certificates automatically.

1. Open the Public Name and Address Book.

2. Select the first server to be upgraded.

3. Choose Actions/Upgrade Server to Hierarchical.

4. Choose the certifier to be used.

5. Enter the certifier's password.

6. Enter the date when the server's certificate will expire.

7. Click Upgrade.

8. Choose OK when the procedure has completed.

9. Shut down the Notes server and open the Public Name and Address Book using the workstation client with local access.

10. Open the Server Document of the first server to convert.

11. Delete the contents of the Certified Public Key field.

12. Open the Administration Requests Database.

13. Open the Initiate Rename in Address Book Request Document.

14. Copy the contents of the Certified Public Key field to the Certified Public Key field of the Server Document in the Public Name and Address Book.

NOTE. *You are manually giving the server a new certified public key just as the Administration Process will give all future servers a new certified public key.*

15. Copy the contents of the Change Request field in the Administration Request Document to the Change Request field in the Server Document.

16. Save the Server Document.

17. Start the Notes server.

NOTE. *You now have your first hierarchical server. Now it is time to let the Administration Process upgrade other servers and then users.*

Upgrading Additional Servers and Users to Hierarchical Certificates

Follow these instructions to upgrade additional servers and users to hierarchical certificates with the help of the Administration Process.

1. Open the Public Name and Address Book.

2. Select View/Server/Servers.

3. Select the servers you want to upgrade to hierarchical names.

4. Choose Actions/Upgrade Server to Hierarchical.

5. Choose the hierarchical certifier with whose certificate you want the servers you selected to stamped.

6. Enter the password for the certifier.

7. Enter an expiration date for the certificate that will be issued to these servers.

8. Click Upgrade.

9. Click OK when the procedure is complete.

NOTE. *The Administration Process will use the steps described above to upgrade the servers you selected to a hierarchical name using the common name they already have. For example, if the server name was WGSI-APP-SFO-01 and you used the organizational unit certifier /Sales/WestCoast/WGSI,* *the server will now have the fully distinguished name WGSI-APP-SFO-01/ Sales/WestCoast/WGSI.*

Once the changes in the Public Name and Address Book have replicated to all the servers that are to be upgraded, you can use those servers to upgrade user ID files for the users that connect to them. Use the following steps to do this:

1. Open the Public Name and Address Book.

2. Select View/People.

3. Choose the name(s) you want to upgrade to hierarchical names.

4. Select Actions/Rename Person.

5. Choose Upgrade to Hierarchical.

6. Choose the hierarchical certifier with whose certificate you want the ID files(s) to be stamped.

7. Enter the password for the certifier.

8. Enter the date for the certificate(s) you are issuing to expire.

9. Click Upgrade.

10. Click OK when the procedure is complete.

NOTE. *The Administration Process will upgrade flat user names you specified to hierarchical names based on the certifier you used to issue the certificates. For example, a user named Mary Stevens that is upgraded with the organizational unit certifier /Finance/WestCoast/WGSI will have the fully distinguished name Mary Stevens/Finance/WestCoast/WGSI.*

Auditing Security

Since security is the responsibility of the domain management group and is such an important task, we recommend that you set up an internal review program to regularly check key security controls and ensure that your Notes system is adequately protected from attack. The following list will give you an idea of the system components you should review. Because each organization supports the system in a different way and has a different set of priorities, you need to make sure that your review program checks the system and ensures compliance with the policies you have set.

- Database access controls for system databases, especially the Public Name and Address Book to ensure only appropriate people can access this critical system database.

- Server Documents (all) in the Public Name and Address Book to ensure server access is appropriately set and only correct users and servers can gain access.

- Connection Documents (all) in the Public Name and Address Book to ensure the system is efficient and reliable.

- Group Documents (all) in the Public Name and Address Book to ensure that now entities are incorrectly listed in groups that might give unauthorized access to servers or databases.

- Certifier and Organizational Certifier Security to ensure that these ID files are stored in a locked drawer and encrypted with multiple passwords so that multiple users must enter passwords to use them.

- Database file security to ensure that databases cannot be accessed directly via local access to the server or through a network connection to the file system where the databases are stored.

While this is by no means a comprehensive list of the security items that your policies and procedures should address, it should guide you in the development of a regular program to monitor security. A little work in advance and on a regular basis can save a great deal of work later with respect to security in Notes.

- *Replication Connections*

- *Planning Your Connections*

- *Setting Up Replication Schedules*

- *New Notes 4.0 Connection Document Options for Customizing Replication*

- *Mail Routing Connections*

- *Monitoring the Network*

- *Setting Up Servers to Use Passthru Servers*

26

Managing the Network

N ETWORK MANAGERS FOCUS ON DELIVERING THE COMMUNICATION and configuration plans for your organization's Notes network. This group is not concerned (specifically) with maintaining the security elements of the Notes system, although they will develop a topology that can be well secured.

Network managers design a strategy for how servers will connect to replicate, route, provide passthru services, and access the Internet. Once the design is in place, network managers will create Connection Documents in the Public Name and Address Book to schedule the connections they designed. Once the network is up and running, network managers modify the Connection Documents to improve performance of or expand the functionality of the Notes system.

Connection schedules are dependent on the ability of each server that is scheduled to execute the tasks (many of them connections) laid out for it. As a result, network managers are also involved in determining the configuration (hardware, software, and settings) of servers. In this way a network manager can be sure that the server he or she wishes to schedule for two simultaneous replication events has two replicator tasks running on it to support that plan.

In addition to ensuring that the server has the resources to execute schedules in a Connection Document, Notes network managers must make sure the server is capable of connecting to other servers. Part of enabling connections involves the installation of hardware and software (usually done by server managers) to network managers' specifications. Another component to enabling communication is designing Notes Named Networks (groups of servers that can directly connect) to balance mail performance and delivery cost.

Finally, network managers may need to schedule regular server activities (such as backup, application APIs and monitoring programs), manage hub servers, and plan/implement gateways to other systems.

To accomplish these goals, the network management team must have access to create and modify Connection Documents, Configuration Documents, Mail-in Database Documents, Program Documents, and Setup Profile Documents. Network managers do not need access to security settings in the Server Document although they may need to access these documents to make changes to server network configurations (such as Notes Named Networks).

The tasks of the network management group are well suited to the Net-Modifier role in the Public Name and Address Book. While this role grants some access that is not directly relevant for the tasks of most network management groups, it is mostly appropriate and does not offer a security threat to assign members of the network management team to this role.

A network management group will improve the performance and reliability of any Notes system with a significant number of servers. Having a single, central organization that is responsible for maintaining connections, establishing server configurations, and managing connections to outside organizations is imperative to ensure reliable and efficient communications.

Roles into which the network manager(s) should probably be placed in are NetCreator, NetModifier, and ServerModifier.

Designing a Connection Strategy

In Chapter 14 we discussed server topology and naming conventions.

These concepts tie in logically to how servers connect within a domain and to external computers. The network management group is responsible for creating this overall plan (specified by the domain management group), and then implementing it.

When designing the connection strategy, we want to provide as much connection as possible to ensure the timely routing and replication of documents. At the same time we must balance the cost of frequent connections in both communication expense and server resource depletion. In other words, designing the connection strategy is a delicate balance between performance and cost. While considering these issues, we must also make sure the schedule is "clean," meaning without any overlap that might confuse the server and cause unpredictable results.

Designing a Connection Strategy

In developing the connection strategy, you have to weigh several variables to deliver the level of service necessary to support users. Notes 4.0 provides new alternatives for connecting computers that add to this list of variables.

Ensure That All Servers in the Notes Domain Replicate

All servers in your domain must be included in the replication schedule. Even if you do not have any cross-organizational applications for users, the system databases, particularly the Public Name and Address Book, must replicate. Make sure that all Notes servers in your organization are in the replication scheme. Carefully consider the frequency of replication of system databases. Since the security and Administration Processes features key off of these databases, the speed with which they replicate across your organization largely determines how quickly you will close security threats and how quickly other changes such as user name change requests will execute. In addition, users of Notes applications often rely heavily upon them. You want to ensure that replication of key applications can occur frequently so users have up-to-date information with which to work.

Make Connections Inexpensive and Easy

When planning your connection scheme, you should also keep in mind cost and convenience. Cost is a function of how much data must move from one place to another and how much it costs to move each chunk (bit, byte, megabyte—however you choose to measure) from one place to another. Convenience comes in two forms: how easy it is for users to get the information they need and how easy it is for system administrators to manage the system.

In general, it's best to make user convenience the priority as this will provide the best return on investment (and minimize some support calls). To simplify connecting for users, limit the number of servers they must access when connected to the LAN and limit the number of servers they must dial into when accessing Notes remotely. The new passthru feature is a great way to give users a single number they must dial to access all of their mail and application databases when not connected to the LAN.

High Priority Replications

High priority replication connections are useful for hastening the replication of important databases. By designating a connection to be a "high" priority, you tell Notes 4.0 to replicate only those databases that are marked as high priority. It is like creating a high speed lane on a highway for important databases. As a result, you replicate less information and can efficiently synchronize important information without using all of the server resource and communication resources that would be necessary to synchronize all the information stored in all the databases.

In general, it is the responsibility of the database manager to designate a database as high priority. This should be done judiciously so as not to have every database traveling in the fast lane. In general, the domain management group will issue a policy dictating the type of information that can be designated as high priority. Many organizations will have high priority connections that enable the replication of high priority databases to occur within one hour.

Database Specific

Usually reserved for system databases such as the Public Name and Address Book, Notes 4.0 Connection Documents can be used to schedule the replication of specific databases. This extends the prioritizing of databases by allowing the network management team (which has access to create Connection Documents) to specify critical databases for regular replication without forcing the replication of all databases of a particular type.

In some organizations, this may be useful only for the Public Name and Address Book to ensure that updates to it are rapidly replicated throughout the domain to all servers. In addition, this new feature will help to provide a consistent and predictable schedule on which to replicate applications that users depend on.

General Databases

Of course some general use databases will probably need to be replicated across more than one server and connections must exist to service this "normal" priority need. In most organizations, databases that are not critical are replicated about three times each day. In the case of some lower priority databases, this may be once a day or even less often.

Limit Connections

Limiting connections means that you structure connections to maximize efficiency. By developing a clean replication and routing schedule you can maximize resources. Every connection you do not make is more server resource for other purposes. Therefore, it makes sense that you must carefully weigh the benefits of adding a connection against the communication cost savings and server availability of not creating a connection. The following guidelines should be kept in mind when creating your connection documents:

- *Limit Time of Connections*—By entering a specific amount of time a connection may last in the Connection Document you will better control the environment to ensure that all of your connections can be achieved. Keep your eye on the log files and adjust time limits if connections are frequently being cut short.

- *Lower Overall Costs*—Wherever possible, use the lowest cost connection. For example, if you have LAN connections that are inexpensive and can develop a replication scheme that will involve slightly more lag time between updates but will be significantly less costly than creating a dialup connection, do so. As users fill up their applications and mail with data, the cost of moving that data becomes significant.

- *Remote Connections*—Develop a plan that enables users to easily connect when they need to dial into the system. For example, by having a server dedicated to remote access and establishing it as a passthru server that may access mail and application servers you will save time and aggravation for users as well as connection costs because the user will not need to dial multiple servers to get the data he or she neeeds.

- *Extension of the Platform*—It is tempting to put many types of gateways to other systems onto Notes. They are easy to add and provide great convenience. When making your plans, think about what other systems you really must connect to and how often you really must connect to them. The more connections and gateways you must maintain to external organizations, the more connection and administrative costs you will incur.

  Consider limiting remote connections and gateways to a single vendor, and having all of the external organizations and systems you need to exchange information with go through this vendor. Limit mail gateways such as these are seldom simple connections and it is better to do one well (such as SMTP) rather than many poorly!

NOTE. *Don't run unnecessary programs on servers.*

Hub servers do not need to have the Updall, update, or agent manager tasks running in most cases. Similarly, hub servers do not need full text indexes running on them as no users will connect to a hub server to do a full text search. The Administration Process can run less frequently on hub servers than on spoke servers. Most of its functionality will be used on user ID files, and users attach to spoke servers, not hubs. Similarly, most spoke servers do not need to have Notes 4.0 add-in products running—as these should usually be relegated to dedicated servers so that performance for users will not be impacted.

Creating Connections

When you schedule a connection for one Notes server to contact another, or when a Notes client contacts a Notes 4.0 server, there are two steps involved in making the connection. The first step is finding a path to the server. The second step is making the actual connection. Notes 4.0 uses the Connection Documents you create in the Public Name and Address Book (or the Connection Documents that are stored in the Personal Name and Address Book for workstations) to determine the route to the server; as soon as the path is found the additional steps are abandoned and the connection to the server is made. The following list identifies the steps Notes computers make to find the path to a server.

1. The server looks for normal priority Connection Documents to find the path to a server. If the calling computer is a workstation, the Connection Document must be for the currently selected location.

2. If multiple connections exist for connecting to the same server, use the following order of preference: local area network, remote LAN service, dialup modem, and passthru server.

3. Use Connection Documents where servers are explicitly named before using servers that meet a wildcard criteria. For example, if two Connection Documents exist—one for WGSI-APPL-SFO-01/West/WGSI and one for *-SFO-01/West/WGSI—the connection specified in the Connection Document with WGSI-APPL-SFO-01/West/WGSI will be used.

4. If the connection is to be made via a passthru server, two Connection Documents must exist. One Connection Document must be to the destination server and one Connection Document must be to the passthru server.

5. Use the information stored in the Public Name and Address Book to get the address for a Notes server.

6. If a workstation is making the connection, it attempts to get the path first from the user's home server or a secondary name server before attempting a direct connection to the destination server.

7. If no home or secondary server is available to provide address information, use the protocol driver to determine the path to connect directly to the server.

NOTE. *This procedure may be more time consuming than if the Notes 4.0 home server provides the information directly from the information it stores in memory from the Public Name and Address Book as the protocol driver will have to search the network to find the server.*

8. If the server cannot be found using the normal priority Connection Documents or by using the protocol driver, use low priority Connection Documents to find the server.

9. If the server still cannot be found, an error message will appear.

10. Make the connection.

11. If the connection must go through one or more passthru servers, connect to the first passthru server and then make a routing request to connect to the next passthru server.

Troubleshooting Server Connections

Use the Notes 4.0 trace capability (File/Tools/User Preferences, Ports Icon, Trace Connection Button) to determine how the Notes client is attempting to connect to the server. The Trace feature will describe in the dialog box the steps it takes to connect to the server and the results it received from the steps it took. By looking at this information you can determine if the setup information the workstation client is using to connect is correct or if there is a problem with the connection itself.

You can use this same technique at the server workstation client to see how servers connect. The Notes 4.0 log file also provides information about how connections are made.

■ Replication Connections

You may schedule replication so that it occurs at specific times (2:00 a.m. for example), for a list of times (2:00 a.m., 10:00 a.m., and 3:00 p.m. for example), or for a range of times with a predetermined repeat interval (every 20 minutes between 12:00 a.m. and 6:00 p.m. for example). You can use these different types of schedules to fine-tune your connections so that they meet the specific replication needs of your organization.

Replication for a Call At Times Range without a Repeat Interval

Scheduling replication to occur at a specific Call At Time means that you tell a Notes server to contact another server at a specific time. This is useful for replicating low priority databases that you may want to replicate at a low cost time, such as in the middle of the night. Specific times are also useful when you are certain that the connection will be successful after only a few attempts. When issuing a specific time connection, do not enter a repeat interval into the Connection Document. The Notes server will make the call at the specified time and retry for up to one hour. If the call is not successful, the server will not make additional attempts until the next scheduled call.

Scheduling Replication for Specific Times

You can specify in a Connection Document that a server connect to another server at specific times such as 7:00 a.m., 12:00 p.m., and 3:00 p.m. This option is useful for schedules to replicate low and medium priority databases. As with using a Connection Document that specifies a single specific connect time, these connections are best used when you are certain the connection is likely to be successful. The Notes server will only retry each specified time for one hour. If it cannot connect during this time, the replication event will not take place until the next scheduled replication.

Scheduling Replication within a Call At Times Range Using Repeat Intervals

Scheduling server connections within a time range and using a repeat interval means that the server will start calling at the first time specified. It will continue calling until it successfully connects and replicates with the other server. If retries are necessary to connect, the server will gradually increase the time between recall attempts.

Once the server successfully connects and replicates it will wait for the specified Repeat Interval and then call the destination server again. Using a Connection Document with a Call At Times range and Repeat Intervals is useful for high, medium, and low priority databases. By creating Connection Documents with different priorities that have different time ranges and repeat intervals, you can have high priority databases replicating frequently, and medium and low priority databases replicating less frequently.

For example, let's say you have a high priority Connection Document specifying that Server A call Server B over the LAN to replicate every 60 minutes starting at 7:00 a.m. Server A starts calling Server B at 7:00 but does not successfully connect until 7:15. It completes the replication at 7:30 a.m. In this situation, Server A will call Server B to replicate again at 8:30 a.m. (60 minutes after the last replication successfully completed). Because this is a high priority connection, no medium or low priority databases will replicate during this schedule.

Scheduling Replication for a Call At Times Range without a Repeat Interval

Scheduling replication for a range of times without a repeat interval is useful if you only want the replication event to occur once during the day and anticipate that many retries may be necessary to connect with the destination server. If you create a Connection Document with a Call At Times Range and no Repeat Interval, the Notes server will start calling the destination Notes server at the beginning of the Call At Times range and will continue trying until it successfully connects and replicates. It will not call again until the next scheduled Call At Times range begins. If a call is unsuccessful, the server will continue to try to contact the destination server but will increase the time in between retries with each unsuccessful attempt.

■ Planning Your Connections

Planning your connections can be complicated depending upon the number of servers, users, and the underlying communications (transport) that will be used. Use a diagram of the servers in your network to start the planning process and color code the diagram with additions that you plan to make to your Notes system. For example, if you will be adding a server to send and receive SMTP mail, access World Wide Web documents, or send faxes, you should show these computers in your diagram and code them so you can easily see they are future additions to connect to external systems.

Once you have your physical servers drawn, add the connections you need to make to the drawing. In the process of drawing the connections, it will be helpful for you to use different types of lines to indicate different types of connections. For example, you will want to differentiate the types of connections: replication connections, Notes routing connections, and non-Notes routing connections (smtp, cc:Mail, and x.400). In addition, determine a means of signifying the priority of replication connections, if only certain database(s) are being replicated during a particular replication.

When developing your connection scheme, it is often a good plan to differentiate connections for mail routing from connections for replication. Since the two processes serve different purposes it makes sense to plan and manage them separately. This gives the network managers the opportunity to fine-tune the network for each function.

Notes Named Networks

Notes Named Networks are logical, rather than physical, groupings of Notes servers—and are a subset of the Notes domain. A single Notes Named Network identifies a group of servers, all of which belong to the same Notes domain, running the same protocol on the same LAN or a bridged/routed WAN. The location of your servers and the protocols they run will dictate how you name your networks. The Notes Named Networks to which a server belongs is determined by the entries in the Network Configuration section of the Server Document in the Public Name and Address Book.

The key thing to remember is that all servers in a given Notes Named Network must be able to communicate (connect) directly. For example, if the protocol on all the servers in a Notes Named Network called "DallasEtherTcp" (to indicate servers in Dallas running TCP/IP on an ethernet) is TCP/IP they should be able to "ping" one another as well as share files.

If they cannot directly communicate, they must be placed in different Notes Named Networks.

In addition to telling the Notes server program what other Notes servers it may directly communicate with, you can use Notes Named Networks to your administrative and financial benefit. By grouping servers regionally (placing them in regional Notes Named Networks) where connection costs are low, you minimize user access to servers that have a higher connection cost. When a user selects File/Database/Open, he or she is presented with a list of Notes servers on which databases reside. This list comprises all the servers in the same Notes Named Network as that user's home server. If you have a WAN such that all Notes servers could be in the same Notes Named Network, you may still choose to break them into groups (Notes Named Networks) that indicate the location. This way, users would only see a list of servers in their geographic proximity, saving connection costs. If the user needed access outside the geographic location, he or she could simply type in the name of the server to which access was required.

Notes Named Networks Example

If you have a location (let's call it WestCoast) and all the servers run the same protocol, they could all belong to the same Notes Named Network. Users who choose File/Database/Open would see a list of all the servers in the WestCoast Notes Named Network, even if the servers were running different operating systems. Remember, a protocol is like a language. If two or more servers run the same protocol, they speak the same language and can communicate directly.

As long as they can directly connect using the LAN and the protocol, they can belong to the same Notes Named network. Users whose home server is in this Notes Named Network can access any of these servers easily

Note. Mail routing occurs automatically to servers in the same Notes Named Network; no Connection Document in the Public Name and Address Book is necessary. Therefore, grouping servers into Notes Named Networks can simplify administration. Geographically close servers are clustered around a single Notes hub server and they all send mail without the Notes network administrator having to manage Connection Documents for mail routing. In this example, a hub and all of its spoke servers represent a single Notes Named Network. Notes servers that are physically connected (or bridged/routed) and run more than one protocol may belong to more than one Notes Named Network.

because they will see all the servers in their Notes Named Network listed when they choose File/Database/Open.

If you have Notes servers in multiple locations and they are connected via a WAN, you could have one large Notes Named Network that included all of the Notes servers in your organization, regardless of whether the server was in Boston or Dallas. A better idea would be to break down the servers into logical groups (Notes Named Networks) that represent the location of the servers or perhaps the business function served by the servers. This will simplify administration in many ways and will give users a more manageable list of servers from which to choose.

NOTE. *Access to any server is dependent upon two issues: protocol and the access list. This means that even if a user cannot see a server because it is in a different Notes Named Network, he or she may access it by typing its name if he or she has a protocol in common between the workstation and the server. It is the server's access list that determines if the user will be granted access to the server and for what activities.*

When to Set Up a New Notes Named Network

Notes Named Networks are assigned at the time the server is registered. Since a Notes Named Network designation is a logical one—a setting in a document in the Public Name and Address Book—it may be changed at any time. When registering an additional server, Notes will enter the Notes Network Name you select into the Server Document for you. The Notes Network Name assignation you make in the Register Servers dialog box (see the section on registering additional servers) should be thought out in advance and fit into your overall topology strategy.

At least one Notes Named Network must exist within your Notes domain and must therefore already exist. During the first server setup procedure when your Notes domain is created a Notes Named Network was assigned to the first server. This is done by the setup program which enters the name you specify, default is "Network1," into the "Notes Network" field of the Server Document. This default may be changed during the first server setup procedure by going into the advanced settings dialog box within the first server setup program. The name of this Notes Named Network can be found by looking at the Server Document for the existing server within your organization.

If you want to add a server into the same Notes Named Network, you must specify the same name as it already exists so it is entered into the Network Name field of the additional server's Server Document in the Public Name and Address Book. If you ever want to change the name of a Notes Named Network you must change the "Network Name" field in all of the Server Documents to the new Notes Named Network name.

How to Set Up a New Notes Named Network

To set up a new Notes Named Network you simply enter the name you would like to give this new network into the Register Servers dialog box while registering the first server that will belong to this network. Notes will automatically enter this name into the correct field in the Server Document of the new server. If you want to move or add an existing server into a new Notes Named Network you can make the change in its Server Document in the Public Name and Address Book.

In addition to entering the name of the Notes Named Network, the setup procedure will also enable the appropriate network or modem port by entering the port into the notes.ini file so that the server will be able to send and receive information from it. You may enable additional ports for more modems or additional protocols later.

NOTE. *Don't put hub servers in the same Notes Named Network as any other servers. They do not need to participate in mail routing and they should not appear in a user's File/Database/Open dialog box.*

■ Setting Up Replication Schedules

Developing a replication strategy is usually an iterative process. As organizations store more and more information in Lotus Notes, the replication needs of the organization change. As a result, it is usually a good plan to think about replication in at least two stages. The first is a basic replication schedule that guarantees all servers will receive updates to the Public Name and Address Book and will also exchange updates to user databases.

The second stage involves looking at the types of databases, the amount of data being replicated, the locations where data is being replicated, and the connections (physical) to those locations. Using this information we can derive a replication schedule that serves our cost containment as well as security and performance goals.

As you move into the second stage of managing and fine-tuning connections, bear in mind that the way you schedule replication has a significant impact on the performance of your Notes 4.0 system. By tailoring your replication schedule to your physical infrastructure as well as the data flow (usage) patterns, you can prevent servers and networks from being bogged down. The following are some suggestions for using Connection Documents and Configuration Documents to fine-tune your Notes system:

• Run multiple replicators

• Use selective replication

• Limit connection time

- Keep the replication path short (where possible)
- Put complete replicas on hub servers
- Watch out for overlaps of all kinds
- Replicate during off-peak times
- Use only one Connection document for replication events
- Base replication schedules on needs
- Remember the order of operations
- Choose a port
- Stagger replication schedules

Run Multiple Replicators

Notes 4.0 allows multiple replicator tasks to run on a single machine. This means we have more flexibility in scheduling replication, as a replication request will not have to queue up on a single machine. For example, use multiple replicators on a hub server to have it replicate to multiple spokes simultaneously. This will use the hub server's processing capacity (if the replication connection uses the new pull/push default replication) and may improve the frequency with which you can replicate to spokes. Some organizations may still want to have spoke servers contact the hub to place the performance degradation while replicating onto the spoke.

Selective Replication

Replicate only the information that needs to be replicated. Selective replication is easier with new replication settings that do not necessitate the use of formulas to limit the documents that replicate during each replication event. In addition, you may use security to limit the documents that replicate (if your application uses Reader fields) so that only relevant documents are exchanged. If the San Francisco sales office needs to replicate only the sales figures for the West Coast, why waste the connection and processing time to replicate East Coast sales figure documents?

Limit Connection Time

Certain connections may overlap with other connections if they run for too long. If you know, for example, that a high priority replication must take place shortly after you anticipate a normal priority replication to take place you may want to use the Notes 4.0 Server Document to limit the amount of time a replication event may take. The Notes 4.0 server will terminate the replication if the event takes too long. Documents that do not get replicated because the event was cut short will be replicated during the next scheduled replication. This will ensure that high priority information is not hampered by lower priority information.

Keep the Replication Path Short When Possible

Notes 4.0 servers support much larger user bases than did earlier versions of Notes. As a result, you can have more users on a server, which translates into fewer hubs and fewer spokes. Thus, if a database has replicas across the country, the goal should be to limit the number of "hops" from one server to another to three or less, meaning that there need be no more than four replicas of the database. This will improve performance so that changes are replicated in a more timely fashion, limit communications costs because fewer connections are being made, and improve security as fewer replicas need exist to replicate the application across the country.

Put Complete Replicas on Hub Servers

If a database is to be replicated via a hub server, make sure that the replica on the hub is a complete copy with no security or selective replication restrictions. If the hub cannot replicate all changes, spokes replicating from the hub will not be able to receive those changes that did not replicate to the hub.

Watch Out for Overlaps of All Kinds

Make sure that if Server A is scheduled to call Server B starting at 10:00 p.m. that you do not schedule Server A to call Server C at the same time, unless you have multiple replicators running. In addition, make sure you do not have a server A calling another server B on the port LAN0 and the port COM1 at the same time. You will get erratic results that may be difficult to troubleshoot.

Replicate during Off-Peak Times

Replication moves lots of information and may take significant Notes server and LAN resources. To improve performance, replicate as much as possible during nights and weekends. During the day, take advantage of lunch hour to replicate. Take advantages of time differences between the East and West Coasts as well as international time zones. Make sure you do not replicate a database with very large document changes during the West Coast "log on and check mail" period in the morning.

Use Only One Connection Document for Replication Events

Replication by definition is a two-way exchange (unless you specify otherwise). If Server A is to replicate with Server B, starting at 3:00, you need specify this with only one Connection Document. One server will initiate (and by default execute) the replication of data to and from both servers. This is different than how Connection Documents handle mail routing where each server needs a Connection Document to deliver mail to a server in another Notes Named Network. This *does not* mean that you should not have more than one Connection Document between servers for other purposes such as prioritizing replications (high, medium, and low) or replicating specific databases.

Base Replication Schedules on Needs

In general, connection schedules for daytime, nights, and weekends should be different to ensure that information is delivered in a timely way during the day without degrading performance and making sure that unnecessary connections are not made during low usage times when no user benefit will be gained by frequently updating replicas. For example, medium priority databases probably do not need to replicate every three hours during weekends, especially if the connection is a costly one via a modem port.

Remember the Order of Operations

Notes 4.0 replicates servers alphabetically if connections overlap. Server WGSI-APPL-SFO-01 will replicate before WGSI-APPL-SFO-02 if the connections overlap. It is important to use connections that are staggered so that confusion does not arise. In general, do a sequential set of replications: hub-spoke1, then hub-spoke2. Because replication events take different amounts of time to complete, you will have a difficult time and you'll complicate the replication schedule if you try to ensure that certain data elements get replicated up to a hub and then down to other spokes using cleverly timed connection schedules. Instead, keep it simple, sequential, and organized. Use multiple replicators if it is necessary to move data very quickly.

Choose a Port

In general, it is a good idea to enter the port you want the Notes server to use into the Connection Document. This helps you control and track how connections are made and will assist you in scheduling connections. In some cases, for example, if you have more than one port that can be used and you have multiple events occurring and one of them may take longer than anticipated, you may leave the port field empty and the Notes 4.0 server will use information from the Server Document's enabled ports fields to choose a port for you.

Stagger Replication Schedules

While you can use multiple replicators on a Notes 4.0 server and replicate with multiple servers simultaneously, you may want—for performance reasons—to simply stagger the replication schedule such that the hub server starts calling Server A at 7:00 a.m., starts calling Server B at 7:05 a.m., and so on.

Using Multiple Replicators

If you set up Connection Documents that have a single server scheduled to do multiple replications with different destination servers at the same time, you need to configure the server to have multiple replicators running. This will ensure that the server program will not get confused and will enable you to shorten replication cycles by communicating with more than one server at the same time.

The Replica task is enabled in the notes.ini file and can be configured using a Configuration Document in the Public Name and Address Book. When you have more than one Replica task running, each one can handle a single replication session at a time. Therefore, if Server A is scheduled using Connection Documents to replicate at 2:00 p.m. with Server B and with Server C, one replicator will handle the replication with Server B and the other replicator will handle the replication with Server C. Do not attempt to have multiple replicators replicate with a single destination server (two replicators on Server A should not both attempt to replicate with Server B at the same time).

Using multiple replicators will give you more service out of your hardware. For example, a single hub server with multiple replicators can now have a much larger number of spoke servers attached. Use multiple replicators to shorten the time required to complete a replication cycle enabling you to increase the number of replication cycles or add additional resources to the same number of servers.

See the section "Configuration Documents in Detail" later in this chapter for more information about running multiple replicators.

■ New Notes 4.0 Connection Document Options for Customizing Replication

Connection Documents in Notes 4.0 have many new features to give you greater flexibility in customizing replication.

- Use the Replication Time Limit field to specify the maximum amount of time a connection can take before being terminated.

- Specify Files to Replicate to have a particular connection and replicate only those files rather than all files in common on the server.

- Specify which port a server is to use when contacting another server to better plan traffic and communication time.

- Determine the Replication Type to better define server workload: pull/push (new default), pull/pull, pull only, or push only.

- Create Passthru servers so that one server can let other servers and workstations connect to servers through it.

Replicating Databases by Priority

Notes databases must have a replication priority assigned to them. By default, a database has "normal" priority assigned. The database manager can change this setting to "high" or "low" to indicate the importance of replicating this particular database. The domain manager usually establishes guidelines for what conditions are appropriate for setting a database to "high" priority.

It is the charter, then, of the network manager(s) to ensure that connections exist to rapidly replicate those databases that are deemed high priority. By creating connections that specify only high priority databases be replicated, we limit communication costs and server workload by frequently replicating only those databases that need to be replicated often. Other databases may replicate less frequently on the "normal" or "low" priority schedule we determine.

For example, if your company has a critical database that is used to process time sheets nationwide, you may choose to make this a high priority database and have Connection Documents that ensure that it—along with other high priority databases—replicates hourly so that a change in San Francisco is seen in Boston within that time frame. The Public Name and Address Book is often set to high priority as it contains critical information to run Notes. If a person is added to a Terminations list so they cannot access servers anymore, we want that change to replicate across the country to all servers as quickly as possible.

To replicate databases by priority, edit the "Replicate databases of" field in the Connection Document. By default, Connection Documents are set to "Low & Medium & High." This means that Notes will replicate all databases that two servers have in common, of any priority setting. By creating replication documents specifically for different priority level databases, you can maximize your server resource and provide more frequent updates for the databases that really need it.

NOTE. *If two replicas have different priorities assigned, Notes will use the priority specified on the replica of the server that initiates the replication event.*

Limiting Replication Time

Limiting the time a server has to replicate with another server reduces the cost of replication with servers in other locations and helps you better plan server connections to avoid overlapping schedules. For example, if replication from Boston to San Francisco requires a long-distance phone call and the database takes a long time to replicate, you may want to limit how long the replication period may last. More important, if you have a server with a limited number of replicators running on it and you need to ensure that all of its scheduled connections occur within a short period of time, you can limit the amount of time any particular replication may take. It is especially effective if you limit the amount of time lower priority connections can take.

Remember, if the database does not have time to replicate completely, replication terminates upon reaching the time limit and the database will not have completely replicated. A message is reported in the Notes Log, indicating that termination has occurred but that the *replication was successful*. This is a little misleading. However, the database replication history is not updated so that the next time the two computers connect for a replication event, the documents that did not get exchanged before will be exchanged.

How to Limit Time of Replication Events

For a specific connection you can set the Replication Time Limit field in the Connection Document. This is useful because you may have some replications (especially high priority ones or specific database ones) that you want to complete regardless of how much time they take.

More generically you can change the notes.ini file to include the setting:

```
ReplicationTimeLimit=
```

Bear in mind that you cannot use a Configuration Document to set the ReplicationTimeLimit setting.

Also remember, when the Replication Time Limit field (in the Connection Document) is blank the Notes server will take as much time as necessary to complete the replication event which could make the replicator unavailable for another scheduled replication event.

■ Mail Routing Connections

Mail routing is a critical component of the Notes server. It is also among the most used components of the Notes system. It is imperative, therefore, that your mail routing be reliable and efficient. If you are not already familiar with how mail routing works in Notes 4.0, read Chapter 20, "Mail Routing" to understand it in greater detail.

Simply put, the Notes server has a router program that moves documents from one location (workstation or database) to a destination database (usually a user mail database on a Notes server). To do this, the Notes server reads information out of the Public Name and Address Book to find out how it may deliver the message (document) to the recipient. It looks in the Person Document to find out if the person is part of the Notes domain as well as which server his/her mail database is on and also how to route to that server if it is not the same server that is doing the lookup. The router then moves the document into the recipient's mail database or moves it to the next server in the route to get to the destination server on which the user's mail database is stored (the user's home server).

The following are tips to help you better manage your mail routing connections.

You do not need Connection Documents to route mail to servers in the same Notes Named Network. These servers can connect directly with each other and will automatically route mail to each other.

You do need Connection Documents to route mail to servers in different Notes Named Networks and to Notes servers in different domains.

If a Connection Document is needed (because servers are in different Notes Named Networks or different domains and you want these two servers to exchange mail) a Connection Document will be needed for each direction. For example, if Server A and Server X are in different Notes Named Networks, you need one Connection Document from Server A to Server X and one Connection Document from Server X to Server A.

Designate one server in each Notes Named Network to route mail to servers in other Notes Named Networks or other domains. This will simplify your routing connections. Notes servers within the same Notes Named Network will see the connection to the other Notes Named Networks or domains and will route mail intended for servers outside their Notes Named Network or domain to the server in their Notes Named Network that has the connection to the server(s) in other Notes Named Network(s) or domain(s).

Keep the Public Name and Address Book updated on all servers. All Notes server functions depend on the Public Name and Address Book, including the mail router. Server, Person, and Domain Documents must be up-to-date for routing to work properly. Make sure the Public Name and Address Book replicates frequently.

Do not have more than one Connection Document for mail routing with the same source and destination servers of the same type (LAN, Dialup Modem, and so forth). This may confuse the router program.

For mail to route between two servers in adjacent domains (meaning a server in one domain can connect directly with a server in the other domain) place a Connection Document in the Public Name and Address Book of each domain.

For mail to route to a nonadjacent domain (no server in your domain can connect directly with a server in the recipient's domain and the message must therefore go through a domain that connects to both your domain and the recipient's domain) create a Connection Document to the adjacent domain and a nonadjacent Domain Document in the Public Name and Address Book. The message will be routed first to a server in the adjacent domain and then to a server in the nonadjacent domain where a server will deliver it to the recipient. If you do not create the non-adjacent Domain Document, every user needs to enter the full delivery path for mail going to a nonadjacent domain.

For mail to route from a Notes server to a non-Notes server in a foreign domain, such as an Internet address, create a Connection Document and a Foreign Domain Document in the Public Address Book of your domain. Mail will be delivered to the server in your Notes domain that has the connection to the external mail system. Notes 4.0 servers can have native Mail Transfer Agents (MTAs) for SMTP, X.400, and cc:Mail.

You can use a passthru server as a "stepping stone" for mail routing. When you set up a passthru server, a remote workstation or server can access multiple servers by making a single phone call to the passthru server. The remote workstation or server connects to the passthru server and uses the passthru server to make a connection to other servers without having to connect to each one directly. In addition, you can set up a passthru server to establish a connection on a LAN between a workstation and a server or between two servers that don't share a common network protocol.

Messages such as "No route found to Domain A from Server B" usually mean that a connection from one server in domain A to a server in the other domain could not be found. Make sure a Connection Document from your domain to a server in the other domain exists and that the sender's home server can route to the server in your domain that has the connection (based on the rules above).

Draw pictures (no, not those kinds of pictures). Look at the Server/Connections view in the Public Name and Address Book. Draw a line starting at the calling server with an arrow to the destination server that represents each connection you find in this view. No two servers should have only one document connecting them unless it is between domains (or for replication). If you add all servers to your artwork and draw the Notes Named Networks, you should be able to find the route any message will take to any destination server. Edit your Connection Documents if you find inconsistencies, overlaps, or servers that will not be able to route mail.

Use Shared Mail (see Chapter 27, "Managing Servers" for information on setting up) to save server disk space. Some people argue that storing mail in individual mail files is more reliable than in a shared database and that mail is such a critical function that increased reliability is worth the additional disk space requirement. While this theory is not proven, you need to judge the value of reliability of individual mail files against the cost of shared mail.

Use the Mail Trace feature (File/Tools/Server Administration, select Mail button and then "send trace" to have each Notes 4.0 server show complete routing information of how the mail message was routed and where failure occurred.

Remember, if you create a Connection Document to another domain you will need to cross-certify at least one server in each domain so they can communicate or allow anonymous connections to the Notes 4.0 servers.

When Do I Need a Connection Document for Mail Routing?

For detailed information about mail routing, see Chapter 20 "Mail Routing." Following are basic rules for mail routing upon which we will expand:

Mail Routing Do's

You *do need* a Connection Document if the router program will not be able to determine a route that will get a message from Server A to Server X if the servers are in different Notes Named Networks (for example, if you have a hub and spoke topology with three hubs, each of which has spokes with which it replicates). Each hub and its spokes represent a different Notes Named Network (TCPEast, IPXCentral, and TCPWest are the Notes Network names). Since none of the servers in any of the Notes Named Networks are in a second network, the router program will not be able to determine a route to get the document from one server to another. In this case, you will need to have a Connection Document specifying how at least one server in each Notes Named Network will connect with at least one server in another Notes Named Network to route the message across the country.

You *do need* a Connection Document if the recipient's server is in another domain, as the router program will not be able to determine a route to the other domain without one.

Mail Routing Don't's

You *do not need* a Connection Document if the sender's server and the recipients server are in the same Notes Named Network.

You *do not need* a Connection Document if the sender's server and the recipient's server are in different Notes Named Networks but there is a server(s) (even if it is neither the sender or receiver's server) that is in

BOTH the sender server's and the receiver server's Notes Named Network. The sender's server will see that the intermediary server(s) can route mail to the other Notes Named Network and route the message to it so the intermediary server may forward it to the destination server(s).

This "route" is determined as the message lands on each server before being forwarded based on the information the server has from the Server Documents (which servers are in which Notes Named Networks) and Connection Documents. If more than one route will get the message to the destination server, the router program at each server will compute the lowest cost route to get to the destination and forward the message to the next stop in that lowest cost route.

The Connection Document in Detail

You will use Connection Documents to configure several components of your Notes system. Because the settings in these documents have domain-wide implications, you should coordinate settings in Connection Documents with settings in Configuration Documents. For example, if you set up a schedule using Connection Documents that may have the same server replicating with two other servers at the same time, use a Configuration Document to enable additional replicators on the server that will have the overlapping schedules. Connection Documents serve three main functions:

• Schedule Replication Events

• Schedule Routing Events (to Notes or non-Notes system)

• Enable passthru use of the server

Fields options that come later in the connection form will change based on the entries you place in the fields that come earlier—they are context-sensitive. The following table outlines the key fields on the Connection Document and describes the information you need to enter. Not all of the fields below will be available at all times because of the choices you make in other fields.

Field Name	What It Does
Connection Type	The type of connection that will be used to access the destination server.
Source Server	The common name of the server that will initiate the routing or replication or passthru activity.
Source Server Domain	The name of the organization certifier for the server that will initiate the routing or replication or passthru activity.

Field Name	What It Does
Use Passthru Server	The name of the server that will be used to access the destination server. For example, if Server A will connect to Server B to connect to Server C, enter Server B in this field.
Usage Priority	The priority that should be given to this Connection Document if other Connection Documents also provide a route to the destination server.
Destination Server	The name of the server with which you ultimately want the Source Server to connect.
Destination Domain	The name of the organization certifier for the destination server (the top level certifier of that organization).
Use Ports	The port(s) you want the source server to use to initiate this connection. More than one can be specified. If you do not specify one, Notes will choose one that is capable of making the connection.
Optional Network Address	The network address of the destination server. For example, if you use TCPIP and your DNS server is not available to provide the computer's alias, the IP address entered here will be used.
Login Script File Name	(Modem connections only.) The name of the text file to run once the modem connects with the remote computer.
Login Script Arguments	The arguments to pass as requested by the remote computer while the login script runs. Account name and password, for example.
Schedule	Whether schedule is enabled or disabled. You may want to have a schedule even if it is disabled to ensure that connections can be forced if necessary.
Call Times	The times to call. You can enter specific time(s) or a range of times. (8:00, 11:00, or 8:00 a.m.—6:00 p.m.).
Repeat Interval of	How soon (in minutes) you want the connection to occur again after it successfully completes.

Field Name	What It Does
Days of Week	The days of the week that this schedule should be used on.
Tasks	What you want the server to do once the connection occurs. In general this means replication or routing. If you have additional Notes 4.0 MTAs, you may also indicate non-Notes routing such as x.400.
Route at Once If	The number of MAIL messages that must be waiting to force the use of this Connection Document even if the repeat interval has not been reached. For example, if 3 is selected here, the server will route mail messages even if the start time for the schedule has not yet come, but three mail messages are waiting to be routed.
Routing Cost	Notes uses this number when it is calculating the least cost route for sending messages. In general it is best to leave the default value (1 for LAN connection, 5 for dial-up) as changing these may cause endless loops as the router cannot find a least-cost route.
Replicate Databases of [Low_&/ Medium_&/ High_&] priority.	Priority of databases to replicate during this connection. Use this field to create different "lanes" so that high priority databases replicate more frequently by using different (or additional) connections that are not used by normal and low priority databases.
Replication Type	How you want documents to be exchanged: pull from destination server and then push to destination server, pull from destination server while destination server pulls from source, push changes only, or pull changes only.
Files to replicate	Specific files to replicate during this connection. For example, you may determine that the Public Name and Address Book is your highest priority database and create a Connection Document that replicates it only four times per hour.
Replication Time Limit	The maximum amount of time this connection may take if it is for replication before being terminated.

NOTE. *If you select a Connection type to a non-Notes system you will get options for connecting to that system that are not listed here. See the remote system documentation for more information on the configuration choices it will need to allow the Notes server to connect.*

To Create a Connection Document

Creating Connection Documents is a simple task. Spend time thinking about what purpose the Connection Document will serve and what setting it will need to have to accomplish that purpose before creating one. To create a new Connection Document all you need to do is:

1. Open the Public Name and Address Book.
2. Choose View/Server/Connections.
3. Click the button Add Connection.
4. Fill out the fields.
5. Press Escape.
6. Click "Yes" to save the document.

Testing Mail Connections

Make sure that in addition to drawing and reviewing your Connection Documents, you test them as well. Some tips follow that you can use to test your mail routing connections:

- Send a message and use the console (or remote console) to review the console display as the router program sends the message.
- Use the Mail Trace command in the Server Administration Console to send a test message and review the information that returns about how it routed to the destination.
- Review the Notes Log and check for abnormal mail routing events. For example, by checking the log you may see that a server was not responding when the router program attempted to call it. Alternatively, you may notice an unusually large amount of mail routing taxing one server and decide to add resource to improve performance. To record additional information about mail routing in the Notes Log, use a server configuration document to edit the notes.ini Log_MailRouting setting (see below).

Configuration Documents in Detail

The Configuration Document is used to modify the notes.ini file on a server. It is an extremely useful Notes feature that enables network managers to effect changes on servers that are not nearby. It also averts much of the need to use a text editor to make changes to a Notes server's configuration.

The Notes server periodically checks for Configuration Documents that impact it and updates its own notes.ini file with the changes that it finds in the Configuration Document. This means that a remote network manager who adds a Connection Document that will create two replication events simultaneously on the same server can also create a Configuration Document that will enable an additional replicator task to handle the added replication event. Changes made by a Configuration Document occur almost immediately once the document replicates to a server that it affects.

Wildcards can be used when creating Configuration Documents so that you can create one Configuration Document that affects a single server, a group of servers, or all servers in the domain, (every one to which the Configuration Document replicates). Because more than one Configuration Document may apply to a specific server, Notes' servers follow an order of priority:

1. Configuration Documents that are specific to a server take first priority.

2. Configuration Documents that are specific to a group take second priority.

3. Configuration Documents that apply to the entire domain take third priority.

Notes.ini Setting	Impact on Notes Log
Log	Controls the name of the Notes Log. Also determines if information is logged to the server console and how frequently information is automatically deleted from the Notes Log.
Log_MailRouting	Controls how much detail is recorded in the log for mail routing events.
Log Replications	Determines if the beginning and end of replication sessions are included in the Notes Log.
Log_Sessions	Determines if user sessions are recorded in the Notes Log.
Log_Tasks	Determines if the status of server tasks is recorded in the Notes Log.
Log_View_Events	Determines whether or not to log messages generated when view indexes are rebuilt.

Notes.ini Setting	Impact on Notes Log
Mail_Log_To_MiscEvent	Determines if mail routing events are in only the Miscellaneous Events view or divided between it and the Mail Routing View.

You can configure servers by creating groups and referring to those groups in the Configuration Documents. This is helpful as you may want to create different configurations for servers of different functions or with different hardware. For example, you might create Configuration Documents that improve performance for servers with more than 48 megabytes of RAM. You can create a group with these server names in it and enter this group name into the Configuration Document that will performance-tune these servers.

Creating Configuration Documents

To create a Configuration Document in the Public Name and Address Book that will adjust settings in NOTES.INI file(s) follow the steps below. Remember, Configuration Documents are generally a better way to make changes to a NOTES.INI file than editing it directly because the change is easily seen by anyone with Public Name and Address Book Access.

1. Open the Public Name and Address Book.

2. Choose Create/Server/Configuration.

3. Enter the name of a server (or group or wildcard such as */West/WGSI). Note: If you specify "*" in the Server Name field this becomes the default configuration for all servers in the domain. You may only have one Configuration Document that specifies "*" in the Server Name field. This Configuration Document will take the lowest precedence of all Configuration Documents.

4. Click Set/Modify Parameters button.

5. Select a Parameter to modify in the top box or

6. Press the arrow next to the Item field to create a new parameter.

7. Enter a value for the setting in the field labeled "value."

8. Choose Next to enter the value

9. (Optional.) Choose another parameter to set or modify.

10. Choose OK to confirm the settings.

11. Press Escape and click "Yes" to save the document.

To see the meanings of different settings in the Configuration Document, see the complete list of notes.ini settings in Chapter 27, "Managing Servers."

■ Monitoring the Network

Although it is also the responsibility of the server administrator, monitoring the network is an important function of the network manager because he or she determines and manages all of the connections (and probably server configurations) in most organizations. By monitoring system events you can:

- Plan connections better to fine-tune them.

- Respond more quickly to problems.

- Improve security by seeing all errors that occur.

- Improve efficiency, as only one person needs to look at the log and reports rather than each server manager having that responsibility.

Server Logs

Each Notes 4.0 server will create a log file when the server starts if one does not already exist. The log file will be a recording of different events that occur on the server. You can have the server record additional information in the log file by changing settings in the notes.ini file.

To get the most out of the Notes Log you can use the Log Analysis feature to create an easily searchable database with information from the Notes Log.

1. Open the Server Administration Console.

2. Select the server whose log file you want to search.

3. Click the Server button.

4. Select Log Analysis.

5. Click the Results Database button.

6. Enter the location and name for the new database that will be created.

7. Select OK.

8. Enter the number of days of activity you want included in the database analysis.

9. Enter keywords, separated by commas, for words you want to search for.

10. Click Start or Start and Open (this will open the results database as soon as it is created).

Statistics Reporting Database

For more information about statistics and events reporting, see Chapter 23. You may want to have a single Statistics Reporting database to which all servers report information. This will serve as the centralized location for all statistic and event information so that the network manager(s) can easily see activity on all servers. The Event and Reporter tasks must be running on each server that will report to make this work.

To set up centralized monitoring you will have a Statistics Reporting database on a single server that receives all information via Notes mail. To do this, create Monitor Documents on each server in the Statistics and Events database to specify the information you want recorded and specify the Notification Method as "Relay to other server" and the Notification Destination as the name of the server on which the central database resides. The only exception to this setup will be the server on which the database resides which should have the Notification Method set to "Log to Database" and the Notification Destination set to "statrep.nsf" so that it records information without using mail.

Using Passthru Servers

Setting up passthru servers involves two main steps. The first is editing the appropriate Server Documents and the second is editing the appropriate Connection Documents. You do this to create passthru servers and destination servers. Passthru servers are the servers that will be used as a routing agent for workstation clients and servers that want to access a destination server. Destination servers, obviously, are the servers that the workstation client or server needs to access. The overall process of setting up for passthru servers looks like this:

1. *Set up servers to be used as passthru servers*—Setting up the passthru server determines which destination servers the passthru server can access and which users and servers can use the server for passthru services.

2. *Set up destination servers to allow passthru servers to access them*—Setting up destination servers means specifying which users and servers can access a destination server via a passthru server.

3. *Set up workstation clients and servers to access destination servers through passthru servers*—Setting up workstations and servers means designating which passthru servers the workstation client or server will use by default as well as how it will connect to other passthru servers if it will use more than one. To set up workstations, you will specify a default passthru server for the workstation to use. In addition, you may use

Connection Documents if the user will need to access more than one passthru server.

To set up servers for passthru, you designate a Connection Document for each destination server that must be accessed. You can also designate a default passthru connection for servers to use if a Connection Document specifying a passthru server to use to connect to a destination server does not exist.

You will use the Server Documents of the servers involved as well as create Connection Documents to enable passthru.

Plan a Passthru Server Topology

Just as you plan your overall Notes server topology, you must plan your strategy for how passthru servers will be used in your organization. This means determining which servers may be accessed by one computer through another computer (destination server), which computers will act as the middle (or passthru servers) and which users and servers will have access to use the destination and passthru servers. Start by referring to your diagram of the servers in your organization like the one in Figure 14.8 in Chapter 14.

Use this diagram to draw in how passthru services will be implemented and used. The following are some tips for creating your plan.

Use dedicated passthru servers if you anticipate high volumes of passthru activity. Just like any other service on your Notes network (such as mail), if it will be a significant part of your infrastructure you will want to segregate it out so that you can manage it more effectively. Depict dedicated passthru servers in your diagram.

Make sure you anticipate the number of passthru users (and servers) and designate on your diagram a default passthru server for each workstation client and server that will use a passthru server.

Make sure the hardware on the server meets your organization's needs. For example, if the server is to be a dedicated passthru server, it probably does not need much disk space as few databases are likely to be stored on it. Instead, you may want to put a large bank of modems on the server so users can call in and use the dedicated passthru server to access multiple application and mail servers.

Check your protocols! Passthru servers must be able to communicate with the other computers involved in the passthru activity. This means that if the destination server is running only the SPX protocol and the Workstation client is running only the TCPIP protocol, the passthru server must run both of these protocols.

Clarify what servers you want to be accessed via passthru servers. In general, you want to think carefully about this decision as passthru servers are often used to connect remote users. This means that if you grant a passthru server access to a destination server, you have in effect put a modem on the destination server itself.

Think about how many "hops" are reasonable for passthru connections. Both workstation clients and servers can reach a destination server by hopping multiple passthru servers. This capability adds enormous flexibility, but if too many hops are required, connections become very expensive and performance degrades.

By using restrictions on passthru servers, you can actually improve security by providing different levels of filtering out who can access the progressive passthru hops. While this does complicate the security model, it may also provide the flexibility necessary to provide, for example dial in service, to restricted access servers.

In addition to granting passthru privileges, review your overall security strategy to ensure that passthru access does not subvert it.

Set Up Servers to Be Used as Passthru Servers

To set up a server for passthru use, follow these steps:

1. Open the Public Name and Address Book to the Server's view.

2. Open the Server Document of the server you want to become a passthru server.

3. Click on the Restrictions section.

4. In the Route Through field enter the names of users, servers, and groups who can use this server to access another (destination) server.

5. (Optional.) In the Cause Calling field enter the names of users, servers, and groups that can force the passthru server to call a destination (or another passthru) server to complete the connection.

6. In the Destinations Allowed field enter the names of the destination servers that this passthru server can be used to access.

7. Press Escape and click "Yes" to save the changes to the Server Document.

The server may now be used as a passthru server to access destination servers.

NOTE. *You will need to create a Connection Document specifying the new passthru server as the source server and the destination server as the destination server for any destination servers that are not physically connected on the same LAN. For example, if the passthru server will need to use a modem to connect to the destination server or if the destination server is in* *another Notes Named Network that must be accessed by yet another intermediary passthru server, create a Connection Document detailing how the passthru server will access the next server in the route to the destination server.*

Set Up Destination Servers

Remember, configuring a server to act as a passthru server is only part of the setup procedure required to enable passthru. The destination server must also request passthru requests from the server that is doing the passthru. Follow these instructions to enable a destination server for passthru use:

1. Open the Public Name and Address Book.

2. Choose View/Server/Servers.

3. Open the document of the server you want to become a destination server.

4. Click on the Restrictions section.

5. In the Access This Server field, enter the names of users, servers, and groups who should be able to access this server via a passthru server. You may use the "*" to indicate all users and servers.

6. Press Escape.

7. Choose "Yes" to save the changes to the Server document.

The server is now set up to act as a destination server and accept connections from users and servers via the passthru servers you specified.

Setting Up Workstations to Use Passthru Servers

When a user attempts to access a server for which he or she has no connection defined in a given location, Notes will use the passthru server specified in the workstation client Location Document that is stored in the user's Personal Name and Address Book. If the user will need to access multiple passthru servers, you must create Connection Documents in the user's personal Name and Address Book for each passthru server the user will need to access. These Connection Documents tell Notes to use a specific passthru server (other than the default passthru server specified in the user's location document) when accessing a particular destination server.

Connection Documents specifying a passthru server will take precedence over the passthru server specified in the Location Document. If the user travels frequently and will dial into different passthru servers, you may instead want to create additional Location Documents. The user will need to switch to the different Location Documents for different locations, but this is simple to do and will simplify the user's setup by minimizing Connection Documents.

If the user is not connected to the LAN on which the passthru server resided, he or she will also need to create a Connection Document to tell Notes how to connect to the passthru server. The passthru server specified as the default in the Location Document and in the Connection Documents determine which passthru server will be used. You need additional Connection Documents to tell the workstation client how to connect with the passthru server by providing the path. This second Connection Document will specify how to connect with the passthru server.

For example, if you create a Location Document that specifies Server A as the default passthru server and then you create a Connection Document that specifies Server X as the destination server and to use Server A as the passthru server to access Server X, you will also need to create a Connection Document that specifies how the workstation client will access Server A (the passthru server). This may be LAN, dial-up-modem, remote LAN service (such as Microsoft RAS), or even another passthru server.

NOTE. *Location and Connection Documents for passthru servers can be automatically created for users during the workstation client setup procedure by using a Setup Profile Document in the Public Name and Address Book and specifying that Setup Profile Document during the workstation client setup procedure.*

Steps to Set Up the Default Passthru Server in the Location Document

1. Choose File/Mobile/Locations. (This will open the Locations View in the personal Name and Address Book on the workstation client.)

2. Open the Location Document to which you want to add a default passthru server.

3. In the Passthru Server field, enter the name of the server to be used as the default passthru server.

4. Press Escape and click "Yes" to save the changes to the Location Document.

■ Setting Up Servers to Use Passthru Servers

Servers use Connection Documents in the Public Name and Address Book to determine whether or not they should use a passthru server to connect with a destination server. The Connection Document tells the server to use a particular passthru server whenever it wants to communicate with a particular destination server.

In addition to using Connection Documents, you can define a default passthru server for a server by editing the server's Server Document in the Public Name and Address Book. The Server Location section of the Server Document allows you to enter a default passthru server name that will be used if the server needs to replicate or route or provide passthru service to a server and no other specific connection is defined.

Like the workstation client program, if the server is not connected directly via the LAN to the passthru server it will use, you must create an additional Connection Document to define how the server will connect to the passthru server.

- *Maintaining the Server*

- *Server Task Monitoring*

- *Support Tasks*

- *Configuring Servers*

- *The Server Document in Detail*

- *Configuring the Server with the Notes.ini File*

- *Notes.ini Settings*

- *Making Backups*

- *Creating and Managing Directory and Database Links*

- *Managing User Mail Files*

- *Checking to See if a Mail File Is Linked*

- *Unlinking Mail Files*

- *Using the Administration Process*

- *Setting Up the Administration Process*

- *Events and Statistics Guidelines*

- *Server Events*

- *Setting Up Event Monitoring*

- *Server Statistics*

- *About Statistics Reporting*

- *Setting Up Statistics Alarms*

- *Setting Up ACL and Replication Monitors*

- *Routine Server Administration Tasks*

27

Managing Servers

Server administration can be managed by one person or a group when server monitoring data is sent to a single database. This means you get the benefit of organized server monitoring without adding the task to all administrators' daily chores. Make certain that you have a documented plan for managing the daily maintenance of servers. The people responsible for executing daily maintenance must be trained and capable since the servers in your network are critical to the service levels you can deliver. A strong support team and plan are the only ways to deliver consistently high service.

The domain manager is concerned with overall system planning, policy, and security. The network manager is concerned with the connection between Notes computers (mostly servers) and developing configuration strategies to support these connections. The Notes 4.0 server administrator is responsible for the routine maintenance of the Notes 4.0 server. It is the server administrator (manager) who has hands-on interaction with the server and is the first line of defense when users have difficulty accessing a server. The server manager may also be involved in helping install and troubleshoot workstation clients if the location or your organization is not large enough to break down workstation tasks into a different function. Server administrator duties include the following.

■ Maintaining the Server

The task of maintaining the server will involve the following duties:

- Backing up the server
- Reviewing backup logs
- Managing disk space (removing obsolete files, compacting files)
- Updating hardware and software (upgrades and service extensions)
- Managing local server security

■ Server Task Monitoring

The tasks involved in server task monitoring include the following:

- Checking server for "dead" mail
- Examining the local Public Name and Address Book for corruption/ replication conflicts
- Checking the server log for replication and routing errors
- Escalating replication, routing, and passthru errors to Notes network management group

■ Support Tasks

Support tasks include:

- Adding databases to server as requested by users
- Replicating new global databases from hub servers

- Supporting local end-users
- Documenting, tracking, and reporting all administrative requests
- Managing local groups
- Providing local Notes guidance to database managers and users

To execute these tasks, the server manager should have the following access to the Public Name and Address Book:

Kind of Access	Access Granted
Access Control List	Author with Create privileges
Roles	GroupCreator
Administrator Access to Specific Documents	Server Documents for which he or she is a manager or backup manager, Group Documents for local groups, Configuration Documents for servers he or she manages

Of course every organization manages its Notes servers differently based on various conditions such as the number of Notes servers in the organization, their location, and staffing/organizational issues. For example, some organizations have a technical services group that is responsible for all workstation client installations and maintenance, so the Notes server administrator does not need to address workstation client issues. In other organizations the Notes server administrator is responsible for the server and all of the clients that connect to it. Some organizations have excellent WAN connectivity and can house all servers in data centers; others use telephone lines to connect servers at many different sites. The result is that how your people and technology are organized will dictate how you manage your Notes installation. The suggestions above are meant as guidelines for an organization that plans to have a dedicated group of server administrators. Regardless of whether or not this specific group exists in your organization, all of these tasks should be addressed.

In addition to the access to the Public Name and Address book listed above, you may want to further distribute certain management tasks to the server administrator's group. For example, currently the task of creating user setup profiles for registering new users will fall back to the NetCreator group. Since server administrators will not be listed as members of this group and you would like the task of creating the setup profiles to be given to the server administrators, you may want to edit the design of the Setup Profile form in the Public Name and Address Book. You can enter a server management (administration) group into the "Who can create documents with this form" properties setting for the Setup Profile form. This will provide the server managers with the ability to create Setup Profile Documents that are relevant to their local configuration. Because the access is granted only to these specific documents, these server managers will not have the ability to create all of the documents someone in the NetCreator role would be able to create.

■ Configuring Servers

Configuring servers is the responsibility of both the network managers and the server administrators. Organizations segregate these duties along different lines depending upon how their system's support is structured. Many of the tasks involved in configuring servers, however, will undoubtedly fall to the person(s) responsible for the day-to-day maintenance of the server.

Managing the Server Document

Each server has a unique document related to it in the Public Name and Address Book. This document is used by the server to gather security and configuration information. Much of the information in the Server Document is written to the notes.ini file and read during server startup. The server also refers to the Server Document to communicate with other Notes servers.

The server administrators are usually listed as Authors for the Server Documents they manage. This access gives them the ability to edit the Server Document and affect how the server works. Their changes usually pertain to the following areas:

- Security and access controls (who can do what on this server)

- Server functions (can it be used for passthru, X.400 routing, or Inter-Notes)

- Communications (how this server communicates with others and the network)

Server administrators generally coordinate changes to the Server Document server with the domain management and network management teams, as most changes must be integrated with changes occurring on the Notes system. For example, if new security groups are being created by the domain management team, the server administrator may be responsible for updating fields in the Server Document to reflect the new group names. If the network manager is adding servers running a new protocol with which a server must communicate, the server administrator will add port and network information to the Server Document after upgrading the server to support the new protocol.

■ The Server Document in Detail

The Server Document is broken down into logical sections. Each section contains fields relevant to a particular aspect of server configuration. For example, the Network Configuration section provides information to all servers on the network—including the server for which the document is created—about how to communicate with the server over the network. The Restrictions section of the Server Document provides fields for granting and limiting access to different server functions (for example, who can create databases on this server and who can use this server to passthru to other servers). The following table describes the fields on the Server Document that the server administrator will need to enter or edit on an ongoing basis.

Field Name	What It Does
Cluster Name	Reserved for a future feature.
Server Build Number	Shows the software program build number for the server. Information in this field is kept current by the Administration Process.
Routing Tasks	This field tells the server which Mail Transfer Agents it may use when routing mail. The Notes 4.0 server has add-in products to make it a native MTA for SMTP, X.400, and cc:Mail routing.
Server's Phone Number	This information is not used by the server, it is informational only.
Secondary TCP/IP Notes Server Name	Notes will use this server to build a list of servers for a workstation to access when the user's mail server is down, or not running TCP/IP. You can specify the name of the secondary TCP/IP Notes server here in the user's Location Document.
Secondary TCP/IP host name or address	Notes will use this server to build a list of servers for a workstation to access when the user's mail server is down, or not running TCP/IP. You can specify the name of the secondary TCP/IP host name or address here in the user's Location Document.
Mail Server	If a user is unable to contact his or her home server base, the server in this field will be used as a backup.

Field Name	**What It Does**
Passthru Server	Default server to use for passthru access to other servers if no connection document is found. This server will also act as the passthru server for users who use the server in whose Server Document this information is located as the default passthru server (if they do not have one explicitly specified in the Location Document on the workstation).
InterNotes Server	Default server to use for access to the Internet using the Notes Web Navigator for all users who have this server as their home server.
Port	The name of a port that is enabled (for example: COM1, SPX, TCP, or LAN0). It is recorded in the notes.ini file as "Ports=LAN0,TCP."
Notes Network	The name of the Notes Name Network of which this server is a member. Servers in the same Notes Named Network must be physically connected and run the same protocol so if this server is running TCP do not enter an NNN for a group of servers running only SPX.
Net Address	This field determines the address other servers will use to communicate with this server. Notes enters a default net address if you leave this field blank. You may enter the name of the server or a more specific (as allowed by the protocol) address in this field. For example, servers running TCPIP may have their IP address here.
Enabled	Determines if this port is active or not.
Compare public keys against those stored in the address book	A Notes 4.0 security option that will compare the public key of a connecting server or workstation against the public key stored in the server or Person Document. Prevents old ID files that have been replaced from being used (a user who receives a new ID file will have that new ID file's public key listed in his or her Person Document).

Field Name	What It Does
Allow Anonymous Connections	Lets users and servers that have no certificates in common with the server's ID file (certified by another organization, for example) access this server. An excellent option for posting public information so anyone with a Notes workstation client may access it.
Can Access Server	Default is Everyone unless something is entered in which case only those entered will have access.
Deny Access To Server	Default is No one (meaning everyone can access) unless something is entered in which case that explicit user, server, or group may not access the server.
Can Create Databases	Default is Everyone can create databases unless an entity or group is specified, in which case only that group or entity can create databases.
Can Create Replica Copies	Default is No one can create replicas except those users, servers, and groups explicitly listed.
Only Allow Server Access to Users Listed in the Public Name and Address Book	Default is No, meaning users that are not listed in the Public Name and Address Book can be granted access. This situation could occur if the server is set to allow anonymous access, or a certifier from another organization is cross-certified which means that an ID file certified by it could be authenticated. These entities would not be listed explicitly in your organization's Public Name and Address Book.
Access this server (passthru)	Default is empty, meaning no one may access this server via a passthru connection if nothing is entered in this field.
Route through (passthru)	Default is empty, meaning no one is allowed to use this server to passthru or route to another server.
Cause Calling (passthru)	Default is empty, meaning no one connected to this server may initiate the calling of another server to route to it.

Field Name	**What It Does**
Destinations Allowed (passthru)	Default is empty, meaning this server may route to any other server to which it can connect.
Run Personal Agents	Default is empty, meaning anyone can run personal agents that are stored in a database that resides on the server and use the server processor to do so.
Run Restricted LotusScript Agents	Default is empty, meaning no one can run restricted LotusScript agents that are stored in a database that resides on the server and use the server processor to do so.
Run UnRestricted LotusScript Agents	Default is empty, meaning no one can run unrestricted LotusScript agents that are stored in a database that resides on the server and use the server processor to do so.
Refresh Agent Cache	The time that the Agent Manager's cache is refreshed so that changes to the fields above will be obeyed by the Agent Manager. The default is 12:00 a.m.
Start Time/End Time	Time period for running agents with the specified configurations. For example, you may limit the number of agents that may run simultaneously during daytime (peak usage) hours. You can have one daytime and one nighttime set of parameters. The default start and end times for daytime parameters are 8:00 a.m. (start) and 8:00 p.m. (end). For nighttime, the default start is 8:00 p.m. and the end time is 8:00 a.m.
Max Concurrent Agents	How many agents may run at the same time on a server.
Max LotusScript Execution Time	The most amount of time a single LotusScript will be allowed to run before being terminated.

Field Name	What It Does
Max % busy before delay	The amount of the processing capability agents may demand without being delayed. For example, 50% means that the Agent Manager may use up to 50% of the computer's processing cabability before it will be delayed to let other programs run.
Owner/Administrator	An Author field enabling you to enter specific people or groups that may edit this document, such as the local server administration team's group. (Owner/Administrator are two separate fields.)
Certified Public Key	The server's public key. This is used if "Compare public keys" is enabled. Public key is updated by the administration agent if servers ID file is recertified.
Change Request	A field used by the Administration Process for changes that are to be made to the servers ID file or server document. Administrators should not need to change this field.

NOTE. *Only important fields and those which are not simple to understand are covered here. For example, we skipped the Server Name field assuming that our readers could guess its purpose! In addition, the fields described here are addressed sequentially as they appear in the Server Document itself.*

■ Configuring the Server with the Notes.ini File

The notes.ini file is read by the Notes server whenever it starts. Many important settings are determined in this file, including ones that affect security, communications, and server operations. The notes.ini file can be updated in many ways: text file editor (no longer recommended for most changes because they can be made within Notes 4.0 dialog boxes or Configuration Documents), server console command, or Configuration or Server Document in the Public Name and Address Book.

Organizations with a strong central management group for Notes will want to use Configuration and Server Documents controlled primarily by the network management group to configure servers. By using these documents, servers in remote locations can still be centrally configured. Central management of configurations ensures integration with other network plans (such as new connection schedules) and will enhance security (local servers adhere to central policies).

However, many organizations do not have such centralized control over their environments—and even those that do will always have exception conditions that require local server administrators to make changes that will improve performance or provide functionality. For example, if the network manager has added a replication connection to a server, the server administrator may need to update the Server Document to add a replicator task if the network manager did not make this change.

■ Notes.ini Settings

Most notes.ini settings can be made using Configuration Documents in the Public Name and Address Book. See Chapter 26, "Managing the Network," for more information on Configuration Documents. A complete listing of all notes.ini settings may be found in the documentation for Notes 4.0, specifically Appendix A of the Administrator's Guide.

The Set Configuration Server Console Command

Using the Set Configuration server command to specify settings actually changes the Configuration Document that applies to the server or creates one that will apply to the server. When you issue a Set Configuration command, Notes checks the Public Name and Address Book to see if the setting exists in a Server Configuration Document. If it does, Notes updates this Server Configuration Document with the new setting.

If a server-specific Server Configuration Document does not exist for the server and the setting was set using an "*" to indicate all servers or by using a group name, Notes creates a new, specific, Server Configuration Document for the server with the new setting. By so doing, the setting specified using the Set Configuration command will not be lost as a result of a change to a more generally defined setting in the Server Configuration Document as it would if the change were simply made to the notes.ini file. To set a server configuration by using the server console, follow the steps below:

1. Access the server console window or remote console window (with the server whose notes.ini file you want to change selected).

2. Use the Show Config command to review the current setting for the item you want to change (for example, type: "Show Config Server Tasks").

3. Enter the Set Configuration command to specify a new setting. (For example, Set Config ServerTasks=Router,Update,Stats,Replica,Replica to have two replicators running on this server).

The notes.ini file will be updated when the server reads the Server Configuration Document in the Public Name and Address Book.

NOTE. *If you make changes to any of the following settings, you will need to restart the server before they take effect.*

- *ServerTasksAt*
- *Ports*
- *ServerTasks*
- *Domain*
- *NSF_Buffer_Pool_Size*
- *ModemFileDirectory*
- *ServerKeyFileName*

Set Configuration Command Exclusions

The following notes.ini settings may not be changed by a Server Configuration Document and therefore cannot be changed with Set Configuration command. This limitation is established for security reasons. You must either modify the notes.ini file manually or use a Server Document (preferred method) to change the following settings. Remember, the Notes server will not use settings changed in the notes.ini file that have conflicting values in the Server Document. It will use the information in the Server Document.

- All settings that begin with $
- Type
- Form
- KitType
- Names
- Allow_Access
- Deny_Access
- ServerName
- Server_Title
- Create_File_Access
- Create_Replica_Access
- Admin_Access

- Ports

- Domain

- MailServer

- MailFile

- Allow_Passthru_Access

- Allow_Passthru_Targets

- Allow_Passthru_Clients

- Allow_Passthru_Callers

- Server_Console_Password (the server console must be used to specify the Server_Console_Password setting).

Routine Tasks

The following tasks are the day-to-day duties of the server administrator. Since every organization has a different set of tasks set out for the server administrator, use this list as a starting place when establishing the exact roles of your server administrator positions.

Monitoring Server Functions

The following server functions should be monitored on a daily basis to ensure that information is correctly traveling to and from the server. If any problems are detected, they must be documented, escalated if necessary, and resolved. Event and Statistic Monitor Documents can be created in the Statistics and Events database to assist in the monitoring of servers. Many of these monitoring functions can be automated through the use of alerts set up in the Statistics and Events database. These documents will then mail reports to an administrator or database to report on different events on the server.

Monitoring and Maintenance Tasks to Establish Immediately

Just as every organization has different roles for different administrators, organizations have different monitoring needs. For example, if your organization bills the cost of supporting the Notes system back to the users of the system by the amount of resource they use, you will probably need detailed information about connect to server time and disk usage. Other organizations do not bill back to end user departments, but do keep tight security monitoring procedures in place to see what data is flowing to whom. The following monitoring suggestions are general and should be implemented shortly after setting up your system to make sure you get all the information you need from the start!

- *Monitor Mail Routing Events*—Monitor mail routing events as mail is one of the most relied upon services by users. Check daily if you have these reports sent to a database. You can create a Statistics Monitor Document in the Statistics and Events database to obtain this information.

- *Monitor Replication Events*—Like mail routing, monitoring replication will ensure that users have the correct information with which to work in a timely fashion. You can create a Replication Monitor Document in the Statistics and Events database to obtain this information.

- *Monitor Disk Space*—Set up a Statistics Monitor document to alert you if disk space is running low. You may also create an event monitor that will send an e-mail message to an administrator if the statistic monitor reports an alarm like this. You can create a Statistics Monitor Document in the Statistics and Events database to obtain this information.

- *Monitor Database Usage*—Use the User Activity information stored in each database (File/Database Properties, Information, User Activity) in conjunction with the Usage By User view of the server log to plan load for the server. You may also want to take note of unusual amounts of usage by any user or server to correct communication problems and prevent security breeches. You can check this information in each database with the command described above. In particular, you should check this information in the Public Name and Address book to ensure authorized usage.

- *Monitoring the Server Log*—Several views of this system database are helpful. For starters, frequently check the Miscellaneous Events view as it will help you determine what is and what is not functioning properly on your server. For example, you may use information in this view to help troubleshoot the commands going to a modem that is not performing properly.

- *Mail.box Database*—Check for dead mail daily in this system database. Dead mail refers to a message that cannot be delivered to the intended recipient, nor can it be returned to the sender. It can occur for a variety of reasons, including a server that is not responding, or a missing connection document or documents that will tell a server how to return a mail message from where it came. In any case, the server administrator must check daily to ensure that no messages are stuck in this way. If dead mail resides in the mail.box file, select Actions/Release Dead Messages to resend the messages. If the problem persists, use the mail trace feature to trace the problem and report it to the network manager for correction.

- *Monitoring the Public Name and Address Book*—Review the Replication History, User Activity (both can be found in the File/Database/ Properties InfoBox) and the Access Control List log (located in the File/ Database/Access Control InfoBox) to ensure successful replication, access by appropriate users, and quickly see changes to the access control list. In addition, you may want to have an Access Control Monitor Document set up to alert you of changes to the Access Control List in the Public Name and Address book. This can be set up in the Statistics and Events database. Also, force a consistent Access Control List on this critical database by selecting File/Database/Access Control and using the setting located in the Advanced section of the InfoBox. Finally, set up this critical database with an Administration Server so that the Administration Process will be able to process requests (File/Database/ Access Control in the Advanced section).

- *Virus Scanning*—Different organizations have different strategies about scanning for viruses. Notes 4.0 servers should be incorporated into this plan. If a server becomes infected, the consequences can be very costly. In particular, new LotusScript capabilities grant access to the server file system (to those authorized to create and run these agents) making the server more vulnerable to viruses than before. Ensure that the server file system and boot strap are checked for viruses on a daily basis. Also make certain that the server memory is checked for viruses. As new viruses may infect a machine, be certain to update the virus checking software on a regular basis. In general, a virus check should occur before a backup so that infected data is not backed up.

■ Making Backups

In general we recommend two kinds of backup be performed on the Notes servers at each location. The first is an incremental backup. This should be done daily and will back up all changes that have occurred since the last backup. These backups should be saved for three full days. If a file becomes corrupted, the maximum amount of data can be restored quickly and easily.

In addition to daily incremental backups, we recommend doing a complete (entire Notes file system) backup on a weekly and monthly basis. These backups should be kept for three consecutive intervals as well. In addition to restoring lost data, they can provide useful information about the status of a database at a particular point in time. For example, since many Notes databases are set to purge documents when they reach a certain age, without three months for historical data (backups) it may be impossible to reclaim data that is more than 90 days old (a common interval for purging documents).

Dealing with Open Files

There are some logistical issues that complicate backing up Notes 4.0 servers. Open files cannot be verified. If a user or server is using a database, then it cannot be verified. Some system databases are always open while the server is running. The result is that if you want to verify your backup (highly recommended) you must take down the server or create a second copy of these databases to do so.

Downing the server is not an option for most organizations, even late at night, so we recommend creating a replica of the database with a Notes 4.0 File/Replication/New Replica command and storing it on a file system that can be used for backup purposes. Alternatively, you can use an operating system command to create a binary copy of the file. For databases that have users or servers connected, you can either create a copy of the database that is in use or use the server console command Drop to disconnect a user temporarily from the server. You may also investigate backup programs that reliably backup open files, even though they probably will not be verifiable.

Automating Backup

Most organizations automate the backup process. This can be done by using a Notes 4.0 program document in the Public Name and Address Book. In addition to running the backup utility program, you can create other scripts that will set up the server to be backed up. For example, you may create a script that copies system files that will remain open to another directory so that they may be backed up and verified.

Storing and Testing Backups

As with other systems, it is important that backups be properly stored and tested. Proper storage of a backup file includes making sure that it is safe from damage as well as attack. This usually means storing it off-site in a locked and supervised location. In addition, your backup procedure should provide plans to restore lost data as well as restore the system to its previous condition at a given place in time. For example, if documentation about how a discussion evolved in a discussion database was important, you may need to have a backup from several months before to produce the information and confirm that it had not been altered since that date. It is for this reason that we recommend keeping three consecutive backups for each backup interval.

In addition to storage policy, it is important to test backups on a regular basis. This ensures that your hardware and procedures do as they are intended. A quarterly restoration of one of each type of backup (daily, weekly, and monthly) will ensure that your drive, tapes, storage location, and procedures produce the expected results.

All of your Notes backup procedures should comply with your organization's standard policies and procedures for backing up and recovering any data system. When verifying the integrity of your Notes backups, like any backup, you should not do so on a production machine. Once again, backup is an important component of supporting Notes, and a solid set of policies and procedures on how backups are created, tested, and restored is critical to providing a safe computing environment.

Ongoing Tasks

As you use and expand your Notes system, you will need to take advantage of additional Notes features to simplify managment of servers, improve performance, and extend capacity. The following features of Notes 4.0 let you extend your system using configurations to expand the system, rather than hardware.

■ Creating and Managing Directory and Database Links

Linked files, whether a directory link or a database link, are simply text files that allow the Notes server to access and store Notes data in other directories and other physical drives. Directory links point to all files in a directory. File links point to only one specific Notes database.

Directory and file links are often used when a physical drive is added to a server, constituting another file system, or when a network drive is used for additional disk space or simplified backup. For example, if you have backup procedures in place for NetWare, it may be easier to store Notes databases on a NetWare file system, using directory links, and do standard NetWare backups to that file system. The Notes server must have access to the file system that is specified.

NOTE. *If you use directory or database links to store databases on a network drive, it implies that the server is logged into the network. It is critical that users not be able to access, via the network, the Notes program and data directories, regardless of where they are (on the Notes server or on the network file system). This means that neither users nor administrators should have direct file access to the Notes server or the directory on a network file server where the Notes databases are stored. This requirement poses a dilemma in many instances because most network operating systems have administrators who have complete access to all system resources, including all directories. The best advice we can offer is to endeavor to limit the extent of any one administrator's (Notes or network) privileges such that he or she cannot easily access data to which he or she has not been granted access.*

The following are the contents of a directory link file called ADMIN.DIR.

```
N:\Data\NotesDBs\
Administrators
```

The result of creating such a directory link is that when users select File/ Database/Open and look at the server files, they will see a directory called ADMIN even though the databases in this directory are actually stored on the N drive (network file server) because the directory link (ADMIN.DIR) makes the directory on the network file server appear as if it resides on the Notes server. It is because of the extension and placement in the Notes data directory that the Notes server treats it as a directory link (pointer).

The first line specifies the destination of the link (N:\Data\NotesDBs\). The second line specifies the users and groups that have access to this directory (administrators). As you can see, directory links are a nice way to limit access to entire directories so that unauthorized users cannot even see what databases are in these directories. Any user trying to open this directory to see the databases in it would have to be a member of the administrators group.

■ Managing User Mail Files

When users leave the organization or move to a different group within the organization, the user's mail file will need to be deleted or moved. Before deleting a mail file completely or after copying it to a new server, it must be unlinked if shared mail is being used on the server. If you do not unlink files before deleting or moving them, the Collect task that runs on the server will not be able to purge messages to which this mail database is linked.

■ Checking to See if a Mail File Is Linked

To see if a mail file is linked to a shared mail database, issue the following command at the server console.

```
Load Object Info MAILFILE.NSF
```

MAILFILE.NSF is the name of the user mail file or the name of the directory containing mail files you want to see if linked. Information about the link status of the file(s) will be returned.

■ Unlinking Mail Files

Periodically, for a variety of reasons, you will need to unlink mail databases from the shared mail database. Unlinking a mail file causes messages addressed to the user to be stored entirely in his or her mail database. It is important to unlink mail databases before deleting them from the server (either because the user has terminated or because he or she is moving to another server for mail) because messages addressed to this user cannot be deleted from the shared mail database—manually or by the Collect task—if the user's mail database is still linked to them. In the following example, SHARED.NSF is the name of the shared mail database. To unlink all the mail files from a shared mail database, use the following console command:

```
Load Object Unlink SHARED.NSF
```

The Notes Server will unlink each mail message document in the shared mail database and store a complete copy of it in each recipient's mail database.

Moving a User's Mail File

Once you have unlinked a user's mail database, you may move it to another server. You may need to do this if the user is switching departments or if you are segregating server duties such that some servers will service only mail databases and others will service applications. To move a user's mail database after unlinking it:

1. Create a replica of the mail database on the new server. You can use File/Replication/New Replica (preferred) or an operating system copy command if you do not have direct access to the new server).

2. Make sure that access controls are properly set for the new location.

3. Delete the old mail database from the previous mail server.

4. Edit the user's Person Document in the Public Name and Address Book to reflect the new server name and, if necessary, mail database directory. All routers in the domain look to this document when delivering mail to the user.

5. Have the user edit Location and Connection Documents in his or her personal Name and Address Book to specify the new home (mail) server name.

Server Console Commands

Server console commands are the Server Manager's means of communicating directly with the server program. In many cases, the Server Manager uses settings in Public Name and Address Book documents to schedule server tasks. In some cases, however, we need to issue a command directly to the server. The following commands may be issued at the command console on the server at a > prompt. They may also be issued using the remote console feature of the Administration Control Panel (File/Tools/Server Administration, Console button).

Server Console Command	Function	Example
Broadcast message [users]	Sends a message to users of this server. Specifying user names is optional. Group names as entered into Group documents in the public name and address book may also be used. Message will be displayed in the Notes workstation client status bar.	Broadcast "Server going down for maintenance in 10 minutes."
Drop	Closes one or more user/ server sessions.	Drop "Dave Sing" "Ralph Tobin-Moore"
Exit	Shuts down the server.	Exit
Help	Displays the list of server commands.	Help
Load	Runs a program on the server. See server tasks for list of server programs to run.	Load Fixup
Pull	Forces an unscheduled "pull" replication from the destination server to the current server.	Pull WGSI-N-01/WGSI
Push	Forces an unscheduled "push" replication from the current server to the destination server.	Push WGSI-N-01/ WGSI
Quit	Shuts down the server.	Quit
Replicate	Forces an unscheduled replication.	Replicate WGSI-N-01/ WGSI

Server Console Command	Function	Example
Route	Forces an unscheduled routing of mail from the current server to the server specified.	Route WGSI-N-01/ WGSI
Set Configuration	Creates or resets a setting in the notes.ini file by creating/ modifying a Configuration document.	Set Configuration ServerTasksAt2= Compact, Collect
Set Secure	Password protects the server console.	Set Secure DontTell
Set Statistics	Resets the numeric-additive statistics in statistics reports.	Set Stat NET-BIOS.LAN0.* 0
Show Configuration	Shows the notes.ini value for the specified setting.	Show Configuration ServerTasks
Show Directory	Lists all Notes databases ONLY in the Notes data directory.	Show Directory
Show Diskspace	Shows the disk space available on the specified file system.	Show Diskspace D
Show Memory	Displays available RAM, plus the boot drive's swapping memory.	Show Memory
Show Port	Shows traffic and error statistics for the specified port.	Show Port Com1
Show Schedule [server/ program/ location]	Shows the next time that a program will run on a given server or location.	Show Schedule Fixup
Show Sessions	Displays information about current Notes sessions.	Show Sessions

Server Console Command	**Function**	**Example**
Show Statistics [statname]	Shows all or only specified server statistics.	Show Stat NETBIOS.*
Show Tasks	Shows the status of all active server tasks (programs).	Show Tasks
Show Transactions	Displays transaction statistics for the current server.	Show Transactions
Show Users	Lists users who are currently accessing the server and the databases they are using.	Show Users
Tell	Issues a command to a running server task.	Tell Replicator Quit

Setting Up the Administration Process

The Administration Process relies upon three Notes databases to assist administrators by automatically renaming users and servers, recertifying users and servers, and updating access control lists and group documents with changes and deletions related to users and servers. The three databases it uses are the Administration Requests database, the Public Name and Address Book, and the Certification Log. Replicas of all of these databases should be on all servers that will run the Administration Process.

NOTE. (TO ADMINISTRATORS OF SYSTEMS USING FLAT ID FILES) *In addition to the presence of these databases, the administration process must be started by a server with a hierarchical ID file. This means that the first server to execute Administration Process tasks must be hierarchically certified. As a result, you will have to create a naming scheme (nomenclature), create the first hierarchical server ID, and upgrade the server that will use this ID manually. You can then set up this server as the administration server for the Public Name and Address Book so that other Notes 4.0 servers running the Administration Process can be upgraded to hierarchical ID files automatically. You should have a hierarchical naming scheme planned in advance of creating the ID files. See Chapter 14 for more information about hierarchical ID files.*

■ Using the Administration Process

Once it is set up and configured, you use the Administration Process by choosing Actions in the Public Name and Address Book. For example, if you want to automatically rename a user, you would select the user's Person Document in the People view of the Public Name and Address Book and choose Actions/Rename Person. This action will automatically create a request in the Administration Requests database and will modify necessary fields in the user's Person Document. The user's ID file will be updated with the new name and the name will be changed in all group documents in the Public Name and Address Book and will also be changed in any database access control list (provided the database has an administration server specified). Similar actions are available in other views of the Public Name and Address Book for renaming and removing servers and users.

■ Setting Up the Administration Process

The Administration Process will greatly simplify the day-to-day maintenance of your Notes system. By automating some of the tasks that required direct interaction with users or servers in earlier versions of Notes—such as recertifying ID files and changing NOTES.INI files on servers—Notes 4.0 enables you to better centralize the management of these tasks. Before you can use the Administration Process, you must set it up as described below.

1. Upgrade all servers to Notes Release 4.

2. Create the Certification Log database using the Notes 4.0 design template. If you already have a certification log, upgrade the design to the Notes 4.0 template using File/Database/Replace Design. Be sure the file name for this database is CERTLOG.NSF.

3. Create the hierarchical IDs based on the hierarchical name scheme you created.

4. Ensure that the Adminp server program is listed in the ServerTasks setting of the notes.ini file. This setting should occur automatically when installing or upgrading to the Notes 4.0 software.

5. Start the Notes server program.

6. Start the Notes workstation program on the server computer

7. Add the Administration Requests database (ADMIN4.NSF) to the workspace. This database will be created automatically by the Adminp program the first time it runs.

8. Ensure that administrators who will create requests for the Administration Process to execute have proper access to the Public Name and Address Books. They must have at least Author and Delete access and should be in the appropriate roles for whatever activities they will perform. Remember, the access control list must replicate to all Public Address Books in the domain.

9. Add the names or group name(s) of Notes administrators who will perform actions that are processed by the Administration Process to the Administration Requests database. These administrators should have least Author access to this database. The access control list will replicate to all Administration Requests replicas in the domain.

10. Specify an administration server for the Public Name and Address Book. An administration server is the name of the server on which the Administration Process will execute a request.

    For example, the Public Name and Address Book database is, by necessity, replicated on every server in the Notes domain. You must designate only one of these servers as the administration server. The updates this server makes will be replicated to other replicas of the database through normal replication. The command to specify an administration server for a database (Public Name and Address Book or other) is File/Database/ Access Control, Advanced Icon, Administration Server.

    If you use a hub and spoke server topology, it is best to specify a hub server to perform all administration requests so that changes made by the Administration Process replicate quickly to other servers in the domain.

Using Events and Statistics

Events and statistics monitoring are among the most useful tools a server manager has at his or her disposal. By monitoring these two types of information, the server manager can avoid problems by staying informed of important server thresholds and be alerted immediately if problems occur. Events and statistics are created and reported by two server tasks: the Event task and the Reporter task. The event task determines what is to be reported by looking for monitor documents in the Statistics and Events database and then comparing it to the known events and statistics that are also stored in the Statistics and Events database. The Reporter task creates and delivers reports to the Statistics Reporting database.

NOTE. *It is important to realize that neither of these processes are set up to run by default. You must enter them into the "ServerTasks" setting in the notes.ini file. However, both the Statistics and Events database and the Statistics Reporting database are created automatically when either the Event or Reporter task is run for the first time.*

■ Events and Statistics Guidelines

Following are some suggestions about how to best use Events and Statistics monitoring to your advantage:

- Always use ACL (access control list) and Replication monitors to alert you to changes to critical databases. The Public Name and Address Book, as well as other databases containing sensitive information should have the benefit of this added security.

- Establish procedures for how events and statistics that are reported get handled. These procedures should include how they will be logged into your trouble ticket system, who will address them, and how they may be escalated if necessary.

- If possible, centralize the monitoring procedure to reduce the number of tasks required by an administrator. If you are reporting information to the Statistics Reporting database, you can have one copy of this database to which all server statistics and events are reported. Only one administrator will need to review this database and can take appropriate action by communicating findings to others.

- Standardize the statistics and events to be monitored. All server administrators should be aware of and trained to handle a core set of events. You may have more than one set of events and statistics to monitor based on different hardware and software platforms. Included in this list of standards should be the thresholds your organization wishes to use for different statistics reports.

- Minimize server log monitoring duties by creating events and statistic monitors to report this information. This will reduce the amount of work for each server manager.

- Periodically review the information reported in Statistics Reporting databases to plan for the future. The information stored here can be well used for performance planning and proactive troubleshooting.

■ Server Events

Server Events are errors and alarms occurring on a server that is being monitored. Statistics track information about the status of the server in critical areas. Server events are categorized into key types of system errors. You can choose what type of events you want reported. To do this, you create Event Monitor documents in the Statistics and Events database to indicate which category of event you wish to monitor. In addition to specifying the category, you indicate a severity level that is associated with this type of event.

For example, you may choose to monitor Comm/Net events that have the severity Failure. You may have Comm/Net events of Failure severity notify the server manager via electronic mail. In addition to this monitor, you may have another Comm/Net Event Monitor document that specifies that Comm/Net events of severity Normal are recorded in the Statistics Reporting database. In this way, only high priority issues, such as the failure to connect with another server ("Could not establish dialog with remote system") will notify the server manager via electronic mail while lower priority errors will be easy to track using the Statistics Reporting database.

Following are the types of events for which an Event Monitor document may be created. Within each category are subcategories of different severity. Within these subcategories are the events that can be monitored.

The events that can be monitored are stored in the Statistics and Events database as Message to Event Mapping documents and may be modified to suit specific organizational needs. For example, you may want to change an event message and customize it for your organization. If a disk is full, you might enter a message that tells the administrator receiving the message the name of the internal organization to call if a new disk needs to be ordered.

- Comm/Net
- Security
- Mail
- Replication
- Resource
- Misc
- Server
- Statistic
- Update

■ Setting Up Event Monitoring

To determine which events a server will monitor and where it should place the reports (Statistics Reporting database or e-mail to administrator are most common) you create an Event Monitor document in the Statistics and Events database. You create one Event monitor for each type of event (as listed above) that you want to monitor at a given severity level.

1. Open the Statistics and Events Database.
2. Choose Create/Monitors/Event Monitor.

3. In the Event type field press Enter to choose from a list the type of event you wish to monitor (see list above).

4. In the Notification Method field choose how you want this event to be reported (Log to Database, Mail, Send to Another Server, SNMP Trap).

5. In the Server Name(s) field enter a name, group, or wildcard to indicate the server that you wish to monitor this event.

You must use a replica of the Statistics and Events database to have this monitor document affect more than one server. To make this happen, follow the steps below.

1. In the Event Severity field enter the severity level at or above which you want to be reported. For example, you may not want to receive messages for low severity events.

2. In the Notification destination field enter the location where the report is to be delivered (this field will change based on the choice selected in the Notification Method field).

3. Press F9 to update the form and confirm that you have selected the options you want by reading the description field at the bottom of the form.

NOTE. *Event reporting has little impact on server performance, so setting up additional event monitors will not significantly degrade server performance.*

■ Server Statistics

The Reporter task reports statistics to the Statistic Reporting database. By default, the statistics will be reported to The Statistics Reporting database (STATREP.NSF) which is based on the template included with Notes 4.0. This database will automatically be created when the Reporter or Event task is started. You can specify another database as the recipient of the reports in the notes.ini file. The reporter task delivers statistics on the following server functions to help you assess the status of the server and preempt problems of any kind.

- Communication

- Database

- Disk

- Mail, including shared mail

- Replication

- Server load

- Server configuration

- Session

The statistics reported are the same ones that are available from the server console by issuing the command Show Stat.

In some cases, you will want to keep statistic monitors in the Statistics and Events database indefinitely. These monitors will produce alarms for conditions that you will always need to address, such as low memory, disk space, or failed replication attempts. You may also use Statistic Monitor documents to help troubleshoot problems. For example, if a server is not replicating and you suspect it is due to a connection problem, you might create a Statistic Monitor to alert you if a given number of Netbios transmissions are aborted. When the Reporter task reports a statistic alarm, it stores it in the Statistics Reporting database. If the same alarm goes off again, the Report Count field is incremented by 1 in the existing document.

You can compose documents in the Statistics Reporting database to produce Alarm Trouble tickets and Event Trouble tickets. You may use the documents to create reports of problems on the server that can then be mailed and logged to the appropriate manager. For example, if a network connection fails because new users are on the system and more data is being replicated than before, and an alarm goes off, you could create an Alarm Trouble ticket to notify the network manager of the problem so that he or she can adjust the connection schedule as necessary.

■ About Statistics Reporting

You set up statistics reporting by creating Statistic Monitor documents in the Statistics and Events database. These documents tell the Notes server what statistics to monitor and when what thresholds are met to sound an alarm. For example, you may want to create a statistics monitor to alert the server manager if the server is running low on disk space. In this case you would create a statistic monitor that checked the disk space on a specified drive and enter the threshold (number) under which an alarm should be created. The alarm will be sent to an administrator or database so that the low disk space situation can be corrected before service to users is disrupted.

NOTE. *To use a central repository (Statistic Reporting database) for all servers in a domain, you will need to place a Mail-In database document in the Public Address Book that points to the Statistics Reporting database so that servers without direct protocol access to that server can use the mail router to mail reports to the server that stores the database.*

Statistics are reported to the Statistics Reporting database based on the frequency specified in the "Server to Monitor" document in the Statistics and Events database. This document provides information to the Reporter task as to how deliver the reports.

■ Setting Up Statistics Alarms

Statistics alarms are set up in the Statistics and Events database just like other monitors. To set up the system to alert you if certain thresholds are met:

1. Open the Statistics and Events database.

2. Choose Create/Monitors/Statistics Monitor.

3. In the "EnabledDisable" field accept the default STATISTIC MONITOR ENABLED.

4. In the Statistic Name field click the arrow and choose the statistic you want to monitor.

5. In the Threshold Value field leave the default value or enter a new one (Note: If you want to change this default, you may do so by editing the Statistic Description document in the Statistic Names view of the Statistics and Events database.)

6. In the Server Name field enter the name of the server for which you want this monitor to report statistics. You may enter group names or use wildcards such as "*."

7. In the Threshold Operator field click on the arrow and choose whether you want the report triggered by a less than, greater than, or multiple conditions.

8. In the Event Severity field enter the level of severity you want to associate with this statistic monitor.

9. In the Comment field enter text that suggests what action should be taken to correct the alarm condition.

You can report alarms as events by creating an Event Monitor. Enter the Event type as Statistic and indicate which alarms to generate as events. You do this by specifying an Event severity level. Each Statistic Monitor document that is assigned to the severity level you assigned in the Event Monitor document is reported as an event.

Sample Statistics Alarms

The following statistic alarms are often set by server administrators to help them monitor the servers for which they are responsible. By setting these alarms, you will be able to minimize down time by taking action on issues before they prevent the server from functioning properly.

Statistic	What It Does and What It Means
Comm.NumOld SessionsClosed	This statistic returns a number that represents the sessions that it closed to allow new users onto the server. Server is closing sessions to accommodate new users. Set the threshold to a number that will indicate to you that users are not logging off properly or that server usage has grown (especially at peak time) such that you need to do load planning.
Disk.n.free	This statistic returns the amount of disk space available on the specified drive. Use this statistic to alert you to remove and compact databases or add disk storage space. Usually the threshold should be <10,000,000. Remember, servers with large numbers of users can use disk space quickly.
Disk.Swap-disk.Free	This statistic reports the amount (in bytes) of disk space that is available for virtual memory swapping. This statistic is important because if the server runs out of swap space, it is essentially out of memory and will become unstable and unreliable. Correct the problem by making more disk space available and increasing RAM if the problem persists. If your server is using a great deal of swap space, performance is probably suffering from all of the disk access.
MAIL.Dead	This statistic reports the number of (undeliverable) messages in MAIL.BOX. Open this database and use the Release Dead Mail action to resend the messages. If the messages come back again, use the trace feature to locate the problem and report it to the network manager for correction. Depending on the importance your organization places on mail delivery, you may want to set this to >0.

Statistic	What It Does and What It Means
MAIL.Transfer Failures	This statistic reports the number of mail messages that the router program could not transfer. Frequent reports may indicate an unreliable port or connection. Correct and/or report the problem. A common threshold for this statistic is >10.
MAIL.Waiting	This statistic reports the number of mail messages currently waiting in the mail.box file to be transferred by the router program. You might set this threshold to >12. If the number of messages exceeds this, there may be a problem with the router program or the connection documents it uses.
Mem.Free	This statistic indicates the amount of free memory available to the server. Once again, servers become unreliable in low memory situations, so set this threshold to not less than <1,000,000 to give you time to correct the problem before data and time are lost.
Mem.Swap-File.Size	This statistic reports the size (in bytes) of the server's swap file. If the swap file becomes too large performance is probably suffering as the server uses disk space when it runs out of RAM. Set the threshold to >20,000,000 to alert you before the performance gets too bad.
Replica.Failed	This statistic returns the number of attempted replications that returned some kind of error. Use it to help alert you to databases that are not being kept in sync with the replicas on other servers so that you can make sure users have current information with which to work. Set the threshold to >3.
Server.Sessions.Dropped	This statistic returns the number of sessions dropped in mid-transaction. It often indicates that server performance is so slow that other servers timed out or users aborted a transaction after waiting too long. You may set the threshold to >5 to indicate that a load review should be performed.

Once again, using statistics alarms is the best way to proactively manage Notes servers. It is the only way, using built-in tools, to ensure that the various components of a Notes server are within the boundaries you set for normal operation.

◼ Setting Up ACL and Replication Monitors

Setting up ACL and Replication monitors is done in the Statistics and Events database using a Replication or ACL Monitor Document. For information on how to set up these useful tools for managing databases, see Chapter 28, "Managing Notes Databases."

◼ Routine Server Administration Tasks

The table below shows a sample of server administrator tasks, the recommended frequency to perform the tasks, and a few comments on issues concerning each task. Each organization is different and has a different set of requirements about how servers should be managed. You may, however, want to use the following table as a starting point when establishing your policies and procedures for managing Notes servers.

Task	Frequency	Comment
Virus Scanning	Daily	Ensure that Notes server is virus free by scanning file system and memory with an updated virus scanning program.
Backup Databases	Daily	A daily incremental backup of all Notes databases should be performed. Note: It is especially important to back up critical data such as that kept in the shared mail database if shared mail is used.
Examine Backup Logs	Daily	Ensure that backup successfully completed.
Examine Local Server Log	Daily	Check for mail, replication, and communication errors. Also check phone log for problems and long connections (suggest better connection if recurrent). Check usage by user and date and report suggestions for performance planning as appropriate. Resolve and/or report findings as necessary.
Examine Mail.box	Daily	Check for dead mail and pending mail that is overdue. Resolve as necessary.

Task	Frequency	Comment
Check server disk space	Daily	Ensure adequate space for anticipated growth; usually a minimum of 40 megabytes should be free or corrective action (deleting obsolete files, adding disk space) should be taken.
Compact Databases	Weekly	Run the compact utility to recover disk space. Some administrators run this task nightly, but this may interfere with other programs (such as backup).
Reboot Server	Weekly	Cold boot to improve stability.
Create Replicas	Weekly	Check database catalog for new general availability databases and create local replicas as necessary.
Check notes.ini	Weekly	Ensure no Configuration Documents have inappropriately changed settings.
Database Backup	Weekly	Full Notes (generational) backup should be performed of entire Notes file system. Maintain three generations of backups, secure and off-site.
Database Backup	Monthly	Full Notes (generational) backup should be performed on entire Notes file system. Maintain three generations of backups, secure and off-site.
Test Backups	Quarterly	Test restoration of backed up data should be performed to verify system works as planned.
Troubleshoot Workstation Failures	Ongoing	Document (and resolve if appropriate) all user workstation and communication failures. Record information necessary to troubleshoot and prevent in future.

Task	Frequency	Comment
Create and manage database and Directory links	Ongoing	Directory links enable a Notes server to access databases not stored in one of the program subdirectories. It is a simple text file that must be created as necessary to point to other file systems, such as a new physical drive or a network file system.
Restore Server	Ongoing	Restore crashed servers. Check which databases get checked for consistency (these were open during crash). Run fixup utility on these databases. Check server file system for errors. Ensure server is functioning properly.
Manage System/General Availability Db Replicas	Ongoing	Manage access control lists, reset replication history as necessary, force replication for system databases and general availability databases that server administrator manages. (For example, Public Name and Address Book, database catalog, Notes log, mail.box, statistics and events, statistics reporting.)
Manage Local Groups	Ongoing	Local server managers may assist local workgroups by creating and updating local groups that may be useful for electronic mail and database access control lists.
Security Checks	Ongoing	Ensure server lockdown, users encrypt sensitive databases and maintenance of local "terminations" list to prevent server access by recently terminated employees.
Report User Requests	Ongoing	Inform domain management and network management of user service requests (for example, improving performance or adding gateways).

Task	Frequency	Comment
Create new databases	Ongoing	As requested by user groups in conjunction with application developer.
Change passwords	Monthly	Change administrator, server, and (if appropriate) certifier ID file passwords. Send e-mail messages requesting that users change user ID passwords.

Depending upon how your organization is set up to support Notes, you may need to add or subtract from the above list. The main purpose of having such a list, however, cannot be understated. Many security breaches and system failures result from inadequate planning of policies and procedures. By creating and using a list such as the one above, you greatly reduce the opportunity for oversight and improve the quality of Notes service as a result.

- *Notes 4.0 Database Management and Security Features*

- *Using Access Controls*

- *Managing Database Size*

- *Checking Replication*

- *Using Replica Databases*

- *Using Full Text Indexes*

- *Deleting Databases*

- *Monitoring Usage*

- *Analyzing the Database*

28

Managing Notes Databases

Notes divides administrative tasks into several categories. The database manager is responsible for managing a specific database or set of databases. Database manager tasks include
determining which users, groups, and servers may have access to a
database, what level of access will be granted, managing database
size, ensuring that database replication occurs, and many other daily
or weekly tasks. Every Notes database must have at least one manager. System managers (people who manage the Notes server network) frequently act as database managers for databases used by
Notes for system purposes (such as the name and address book).

This chapter describes the tasks of a database manager and
the steps necessary to execute these tasks.

■ Notes 4.0 Database Management and Security Features

Notes 4.0 has a host of new tools to assist the database manager in regular tasks associated with managing Notes databases. The following is a list of some general information about the tools covered in greater detail later in this chapter.

- *Local encryption of databases*—requires a user to have the correct ID file and password for that ID file to open a database. This feature is excellent as a tool for protecting information on unprotected servers as well as laptops. For example, if a database stored on a server is encrypted with the public key of the server anyone directly accessing the database would need the server's private key to decrypt and read the database. This means they would need the password(s) for the server's ID file. Workstation clients accessing this database through the server will be able to read the information because the server will decrypt it before passing the information to the client.

- *New access control list options*—allows the database manager to specify access to shared and private folders, views, agents, and LotusScript agents.

- *Database Access Control list changes logging*—enables a database manager to see a history of changes made to the access control list. This is an excellent security management tool for answering questions about how an ACL was changed as well as by whom.

- *Local access control list compliance*—limits a user's activities on a local replica of a database to those that he or she would have access to on the server replica. Note: This feature is used to eliminate confusion and not as a security feature, as users can work around local ACL compliance.

- *Automatic server updates of the access control list*—updates the ACL based on changes made to the corporate Name and Address Book. This feature helps manage the access control list by updating it with changes, such as user deletions, made to the Name and Address Book.

- *Database User Type identification*—permits the database administrator to include the type of user as well as the level of access in the Access Control list. This feature has many ramifications including preventing a server ID file from being used for activities that are only appropriate for users, preventing someone with access to the Name and Address Book from creating a Group Document with the name of a user or server with high access to the database and putting his or her name in it to gain access to a database.

- *Uniform Access Controls*—enables the database administrator to force all access control lists for all replicas to be replicated. This limits the possibility of unauthorized access to data across all replicas.

- *The V-4 Database analysis feature*—provides detailed information about many facets of the database collected from the database itself and from the server log file. The information reported by the database analyze feature includes user activity, replication additions, deletions and update, replication history, and mail messages delivered to the database. Information may include information on replicas of the database on other servers and is recorded in a Notes database that can be full text searched.

- *Field level replication*—reduces the amount of time necessary to replicate a document as only the fields that have changed are replicated. Application developers can use this feature in conjunction with a form setting to automatically resolve some replication conflicts.

- *New database capacity*—allows for databases to reach 4 gigabytes in size.

- *Database quotas*—allows the database manager, or server administrator, to set a maximum size for the database and prevent users from entering information if the database exceeds this size.

- *New full text index features*—allows the database manager to set up full text searching for attached documents and encrypted fields.

- *User restrictions*—enable the ability to prevent users from printing, copying, and forwarding a form. This is not a security measure as users could work around this setting, but it does help in limiting data movement.

■ Using Access Controls

The database manager is responsible for controlling access to a Notes database and the information contained within it. As in earlier versions of Notes, all settings for Access Controls are stored in the database itself. It is important to limit Manager access to those who are charged with adjusting these settings.

Notes 4.0 provides seven levels of access to every Notes database as did Notes 3.0. Enhancements have been made to the access control function to provide granular control over new functionality as well as old functionality. The seven basic levels a database manager may assign to a user, server, or group are: No Access, Depositor, Reader, Author, Editor, Designer, and Manager.

Additional controls for each of these access levels enhance the control a database manager has over a user's access to documents, agents, shared views and formulas and other features of the database.

As with earlier versions of Notes, it is important to include servers in Access Controls (and roles) if the database is to be replicated. Access Controls, including roles, limit and grant privileges to servers very much as they do users. If a server is not listed in an Access Control list of a database, it may not be able to replicate information properly with other Notes servers or Notes workstation clients. For example, if Server A is listed in the ACL of a database on Server B as Editor, only document changes will replicate from Server A to Server B. A design change made to Server A's replica of the database will not get replicated with Server B because A is only listed as an Editor not a Designer in the database stored on Server B.

Setting Access Controls

To set access controls in Notes 4.0:

1. Select the database whose access control list you wish to change.

2. Choose File Database Access Control or click the right mouse button and select Access Control on the context-sensitive menu.

3. Enter your user password if necessary. You will see a dialog box similar to Figure 28.1.

Figure 28.1

Access Control dialog box.

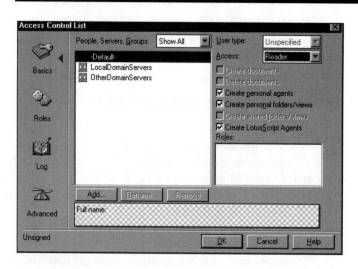

Understanding the Dialog Box

On the left side of the dialog box shown in Figure 28.1, you are given a graphical representation of the types of settings you can change. On the right are fields to change them. If you do not have Manager access to the database, the options for changing access controls will be grayed out and you will not be able to make changes. Another user who is designated as a Manager will need to give you Manager access or make the changes.

Adding a User

To add a user to the access control list:

1. Select the Basic Icon on the left side of the dialog box (default). Notice the list of the users, servers, and groups currently in the access control list for this database similar to the list shown in Figure 28.1.

2. Click the Add button in the lower left of the dialog box. A pop-up field will prompt you for the name to add.

3. Type the name of the person, group, or server you wish to add to the database. You should always use the fully distinguished name of the user, including their common name as well as the organizational unit and organization certifier names. This will minimize the possibility of the wrong person (with the same common name) gaining access. Use the pop-up list of users from the Public Name and Address book to ensure correct spelling.

4. Click OK.

   or

5. Click the icon to the right of the Add User field to get a list of names from the address book from which you may choose a user, group or server to add.

6. Select the user, group or server you wish to add.

7. Click the Add button to put that user in the list displayed on the right.

You may use the Open button to show you the full information about the user, group or server you have selected or choose New to type a new name.

Finding Users to Add   If you do not see the name you want to add:

1. Click the down arrow in the upper left corner of the dialog box.

2. Select another Name and Address Book from which Notes will display names if one is available.

NOTE. *Follow the procedures described above to select the users, servers, and groups you want to add to the access control list.*

3. Click OK to return to the access control list dialog box.

Assigning Types to Entities in the Access Control List

Using the User Type feature in access controls will enable you to limit functionality to what is appropriate for a given user type. For example, designating an entry in the access control list as a Server or Server Group prevents a user from accessing the database from a Notes workstation using the server ID and being granted the access assigned to the server. Note: This is a filtering mechanism rather than security measure as it is possible for a program created with the Notes API to use the server ID and circumvent the limitations imposed on ID files based on User Type.

To assign a type of user to the entries in the access control list:

1. Select an entity in the access control list.

2. Click the down arrow in the upper-right corner of the access control list dialog box that is labeled User Type.

3. Choose the designation for this entity.

Assigning Access Levels

Once you have added the user, group, or server to the access control list you must assign an access level to that entry:

1. Click on the down arrow in the field labeled Access.

2. Choose one of seven levels of access just as in Notes 3.x.

Additional Controls for Access Levels

In addition to setting the access level, you may set other options within that access level. For example, if you select Author, you may also want to select Delete Documents to enable that user to delete documents he or she creates. In addition to Create Documents and Delete Documents, Notes 4.0 provides controls that help manage access to new features that were not previously available. Most of these options provide controls to help the database manager make better use of server resources such as disk space and processor cycles. Different access levels have different additional controls that may be placed upon them.

New in Notes 4.0: Options for Access Levels

In addition to new features, Notes 4.0 adds controls for managing these new features as well as enhancements for using features available in older versions of Notes. The following are database access controls available in Notes 4.0 file format databases.

Create Personal Agents This option allows Designers, Editors, Authors, or Readers to create personal agents on the server copy of the database.

Managers always have this access. Personal agents require disk space and processor cycles that you may wish to conserve. Users not granted access to create Personal Agents on the server copy of a database may still run Personal Agents which will be stored on their workstation in the Desktop.dsk file.

Notes administrators may prevent people from running personal agents on a server via the Server Document in the Corporate Name and Address Book.

If the Notes server administrator denies users this access, that setting in the Server Document will take precedence over the database Access Control setting set here in the database.

Create Personal Folders and Views   This option allows Designers, Editors, Authors, or Readers to create personal folders and views in a database on a server. Managers always have this access. Personal folders and views stored on a server copy of a database are more secure. Users accessing multiple Notes servers from different workstations will have these Folders and Views available regardless of their location. Another advantage is that administrative agents can be used to operate on folders and views stored on a server copy of a database. Without this access granted, personal folders and views created by users will be stored on their local workstations in the Desktop.dsk file. Not granting this access for some or all users will save disk space on the server.

Create Shared Folders and Views   This option allows Designers and Editors to create shared folders and views. Managers always have this access. Server disk space is saved by not granting this access. Furthermore, limiting this access will prevent users from creating views that you do not want published. This is only a filtering mechanism—Document Reader Name fields should be used to prevent access to documents.

Create LotusScript Agents   This option allows Designers, Editors, Authors, and Readers to create LotusScript agents. Managers always have this access. LotusScript agents may take up significant server processing cycles so you may want to limit this access.

NOTE. *Notes administrators may prevent people from running LotusScript agents on a server via the Server Document in the Corporate Name and Address Book. If the Notes server administrator denies users this access, that setting in the server document will take precedence over the database Access Control setting in the database.*

Managing Access Controls   The Access Control dialog box offers new tools to simplify the management of Access Controls by sorting the entries in the access list by type of access granted:

1. Select the Basics icon in the upper-left corner of the Access Control dialog box.

2. Click the down arrow in the upper center of the dialog box in the field labeled "People, Servers, Groups."

3. Choose the type of access by which you would like to sort.

Roles

A role is a group within the access control list of a database that is created and used to simplify the management of a database. Database managers (the only users with the authority to change any Access Control of a database) can create roles that will be used by the database Designer. The Designer can use these role names when designing the database so that access to information can be granted to users in these roles automatically. For example, if a database manager creates a role called [ContactEditors] and enters some users (who are listed as Authors in the database access control list) for the database into this role, the database designer may then create an Author field in all "Contact" documents so that anyone in the ContactEditors role may edit any "Contact" document in the database. This may be useful for certain administrative positions that need to keep the information in the database current. These editors would not, by necessity, have access to other documents (such as "Revenue" or "Status") in the contact management database. Managing access to the database is simplified by using roles to grant privileges into specific components of the database such as forms and views. The Database manager simply adds and removes users, servers, and groups from the roles for these privileges.

Roles could also simplify managing document security by limiting access. For example, a database Designer might code the role [MarketingReaders] into Readers field in the properties of a form so that every document created with that form has a Reader Names field listing the role [MarketingReaders]. This will grant users, servers, and groups who are members of this role access to that set of documents. The database manager can then grant read access to those documents by adding additional user names to the role called [MarketingReaders]. To do this without roles, the database manager would have to edit each document and add the user's name to the Reader Names field. Simply put, roles make using granular controls to database components easier to manage.

Creating Roles

To create a role:

1. Select the database to which you want to add the role.

2. Choose File Database Access Control or click the right mouse button and choose Access Control.

3. Select the role icon on the left side of the dialog box to view role options.

4. Click the Add button and type the name of the role you wish to add. Role names cannot exceed 15 characters.

5. Click OK.

The role will be displayed in the window within brackets []. You can rename or remove roles by selecting the role in this same dialog box and clicking the appropriate button.

Adding a User to a Role

To add a user or server or group to a role that has been created:

1. Select the Basics icon in the left side of the dialog box.

2. Select the user, server, or group you wish to include in a role by clicking on the name in the center window of the dialog box. The user, group, or server must already be listed in the access control list of the database.

3. Select the role into which you want to put the entry

A check mark will appear next to the role name indicating that the selected user, server, or group is now been added to the selected Role as depicted in Figure 28.2.

Read Access Lists for Documents

Individual documents can have access lists determining which users, servers, and groups may and may not access that particular document. This information is stored in a Readers field created either by the designer of the database or by individual users.

Notes will store the field as $Readers in the document itself. Database designers use read access fields to automate security of particular documents. For example, a Designer may set up a form to put a role into the Reader Names field so that only users assigned to that role can access documents created with that form. The designer can create this field in two ways, one will automatically place a role or user name in the Reader field based on a formula, and the another will allow this field to be edited by the user. If this

Figure 28.2

Access control list dialog
box with a user included
in a role.

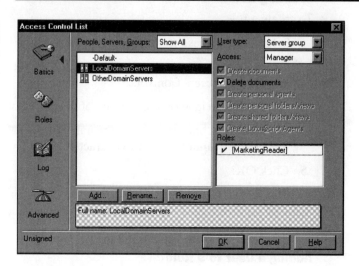

field is editable, when creating or editing a document, anyone may insert a list of readers to a document.

NOTE. *A user must have server and database access to read a document in addition to a presence in the Reader Names field of the document.*

Adding a User to the Read Access List of a Document

To add a user to the list of readers for a document:

1. Select a document.

2. Select Edit Properties.

3. Choose Document as the type of properties to edit.

4. Click the tab with a key icon.

5. Uncheck the box labeled "All Readers and Above."

6. Select from the list of users, servers,and groups in the access control list the entities to whom you wish to grant access.

If you do not see a name in the list that you would like to add, click the person icon to add names from the Name and Address Book. Figure 28.3 illustrates manually adding a user to the read access list of a document.

Using Access Controls to Limit Access to Data

Adding reader names to documents enables users, designers, and database managers to limit the access to particular data elements within the database. It is a good practice for the database manager to consider the forms that will

Figure 28.3

Adding a user to the read access list of a document.

be used to create documents in the database and consider which users, servers and groups should be able to access that information. Once the database manager has determined the appropriate access for given bits of data, he or she should have the developer implement roles within the read access list to automate the access to data.

■ Managing Database Size

Managing database size is, like many issues in Notes, a function of several specialties including system administration, database design, and database management.

From the database managers' perspective, managing database size has a few purposes:

- It makes data more useable by limiting the amount of information through which users will need to sift and search

- Improves performance so users spend time working with information rather than waiting for windows to open

- Saves disk space and transmission costs

- Complies with file system space allotments made by the server administrator

Notes 4.0 offers tools to help the database manager control database size. These tools fall into two categories: prevention and automation.

Limiting the Size of a Notes 4.0 Database

Database managers can use the new size limit setting for Notes 4.0 to limit users' ability to enter information if the database grows too large. Limiting the maximum size of a database may be done when a database is created as a new database, a copy of a database, or a replica of a database or using the server administration tools, if available to the database manager. To limit the size of a database already in use, follow one of the following procedures:

- *Create a replica copy of a database, one that will replicate with other replica copies of the database on other servers.*

    1. Select the database icon whose size you want to limit.

    2. Select File/Replication/New Replica from the menu.

    3. Enter the name of the server on which the database will be located, the title of the database and the file name of the database.

    4. Click on the size limit button.

    5. Click on the down arrow and select a size from 1 to 4 gigabytes as displayed in Figure 28.4.

Figure 28.4

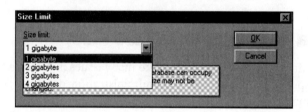

- *Use the Server Administration Tool to Set Database Size and Warning Thresholds.*

    1. Choose File/Tools/Server Administration.

    2. Click on the name of the server on which the database you wish to limit in size resides.

    3. Click on the tile labeled "Database" in the lower-right corner of the screen.

    4. Select Database/Quotas.

    5. Select the database whose size you wish to limit.

    6. Click on the button labeled quota and enter the maximum size to which you want to allow this database to grow. If the database reaches this size, a message will appear in the Notes Log in the Miscellaneous Events view to warn you of the problem, but it will not stop users from entering more data into the database.

    If you would like the Notes server to issue a warning that the database is approaching its maximum size, select the "Warn If" button and a size to trigger the warning. When the database gets to the size that will trigger the warning, users will get an error message ("Cannot allocate database; object-database would exceed its disk quota") when they attempt to add documents to the database and may not be allowed to add their information.

Compacting a Database to Reclaim Unused Space

Notes databases retain space used by documents that were deleted. You can reclaim this unused space by compacting the database.

NOTE. *Notes server administrators often compact databases on a regularly scheduled basis so manual compacting may not be necessary. In general, the server administrator will have the Compact program set up to run at times when the server's resources are not in great demand by users or other processors.*

Before compacting a database, check to see how much space you will reclaim by doing so:

1. Select the database icon on the workspace that you wish to compact.

2. Choose File/Database/Properties or click with the right mouse button and choose Database Properties.

3. Click on the Information icon.

4. Click on the % Used button to determine the amount of space used in the database as shown in Figure 28.5.

Figure 28.5

Using the Database Properties dialog box to check the amount of unused space in a database.

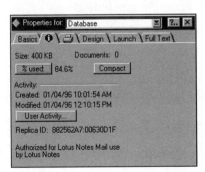

NOTE. *If the amount of space used exceeds 90% it may not be worthwhile to compact the database. You may also check the amount of space used in the server Log in the Database Sizes view.*

Note. Compacting the database is processor-intensive and should be done at a time when the server is not being tasked with a great deal of user access. If a user is currently using the database you want to compact you will get an error message telling you the database is currently in use; the server will queue your request until the database is not being accessed. The Notes server creates a copy of the database, temporarily, in the compacting process, so there must be sufficient disk space for this second copy.

If you decide to compact the database, click on the compact button to have Notes compact the database and reclaim unused space.

Remember, Notes database files contain all of the security, design elements and data but indexes are not created until the view which that index supports is accessed by a user. As a result, the temporary copy of the database will not be quite as large as the original, unless its views had not been accessed.

Automatic Removal of Documents

Some documents do not need to be kept for extended periods of time. For example, a discussion database may get heavy usage but the information stored in it may only have value for 90 days, after which time the discussions are no longer current or relevant.

To address database size you have several options including using database settings as well as building agents to archive documents. Notes will automatically remove (delete) documents from the database based on the amount of time that has elapsed since the last time a document was edited. Once documents are deleted, they cannot be retrieved unless there is a backup of the database or a replica copy of the database on another server which has not yet received the deletions via replication.

To set a database for automatic deletions of documents, select the icon for the database whose documents you would like to have automatically removed. Follow these steps:

Note. Notes will remove the documents without further prompting and, thereafter, will remove documents that have not been modified in the last 90 days. Changing the "Remove documents not modified in the last ** days" setting will also affect how long deletion stubs remain in the database.

1. Choose File/Database/Properties

2. Click on the Basics tab

3. Click the Replications Setting button

4. Select the Space Savers Icon in the upper-left corner of the dialog box.

5. Check the box labeled Remove documents not modified in the last ** days.

6. Enter the number of days after which you would like Notes to delete the documents in the field provided. The default is 90.

7. Click OK.

Using Selective Replication to Limit the Size of a Notes Database

Another technique for limiting the size of the database is to use selective replication. Notes 4.0 still lets you use selective replication formulas to limit the amount of information that will replicate from another replica copy of a database. In addition, Notes 4.0 has simplified this filtering process by allowing the database manager to replicate only specified views and folders and/or allowing the database manager to select a creation date for documents it will accept from other copies of the database. Using the latter feature limits the documents a database will receive to those that were created on or after a specified date. For example, if you are located in a remote sales office with limited server disk capacity, you could set up your replica of the corporate sales database to only receive customer documents that were created in the last year. By making this setting, you will receive only documents that are relevant to the current sales process while all of the historical information (contacts, meetings) will remain in the headquarters replica and may still be used by the marketing department there.

Specifying Views and Folders to Limit Database Size

A new and simpler Notes 4.0 way to limit the amount of information that is replicated to a database is to select the views and folders you want to replicate. For example, if there is a view "By State of California" in the database, you can have Notes 4.0 replicate only documents in that view to your replica of the database.

NOTE. *This is not a security feature, as replication formulas can be changed by local administrators.*

To set up replication that is limited to a view or folder:

1. Select the database icon whose replication you wish to filter.

2. Choose File/Replication/Settings or click the right mouse button and select Replication Settings from the context sensitive menu.

3. Click the icon called Space Savers in the upper-left hand column of the Replication Settings dialog box.

4. Click on the check box marked Replicate a Subset of Documents.

5. Click once on the folders and views you would like to be included in the replication as shown in Figure 28.6. Your selections will retain a highlight box around them.

Using Selective Replication Formulas to Limit Database Size

Database managers can specify replication formulas to choose which documents to replicate. This is not a security feature as replication formulas can be changed by local administrators. To specify a formula that will control what is replicated:

1. Select the database icon in which you want to place a selective replication formula.

Figure 28.6

Selecting documents to
replicate using folders
and views.

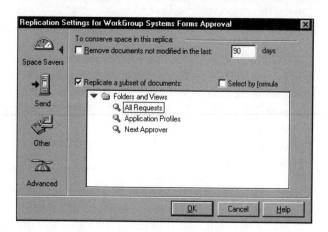

2. Choose File/Replication/Settings.

3. Click the check boxes marked: Replicate a Subset of Documents and
   Select by Formula.

4. Enter a selection formula to choose which documents will be replicated.
   For example: The San Francisco sales office server may want to replicate
   only contact documents for the State of California. If this is the case, the
   San Francisco server replica of the database would have a replication formula that specifies that only documents that were created with the Contact form and have California in the state field should be replicated. The
   formula would look something like: SELECT Form="Contact" &
   State="CA." Figure 28.7 shows the Selective Replication dialog box and
   a sample formula that might be used.

Receiving Truncated Documents

Another means of limiting the size of a database is to replicate only portions
of documents. This is not usually recommended for server copies of databases as it requires more time and effort on the part of the many users who
may be accessing server replicas. However, sometimes a location may not
need all of the information, and truncating documents will save considerable
disk space.

  To specify that a database only replicate a portion of each document:

1. Choose File/Replications/Replicate.

2. Replicate with options and OK.

3. Click the down arrow under Receive documents from server.

Figure 28.7

Using a selective
replication formula in the
Selective Replication
dialog box.

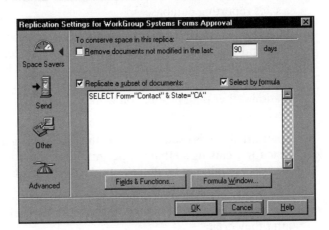

4. Choose either Receive summary and 40kb of rich text or Receive summary.

The other option was to have chosen Receive summary and 40kb of rich text only when you first created the replica.

Using Archiving Documents from an Active Database

An archive database is one which stores old documents from another database. The purpose is to keep the production database as small in size as possible so that user access is not hampered. It make particular sense to archive databases that have high usage levels. Archive databases in Notes are easy to create and can be useful going forward as knowledge repositories as well as for statistical analysis of information spanning a period of time. Archive databases can be easily created and maintained using Notes 4.0 Agents.

Considerations Regarding Archiving

- If you plan to archive (move from one database to another) documents, you should notify users that documents in the database will be moved to the archive database at given intervals so they know where to look for information. You may do this notification to users via electronic mail or in the About This Database Document.

- Consider how often the database needs to have documents moved out of production and into the archive. A database that stores information which stays relevant to users for a long period of time, such as a contacts database, should probably have its documents archived less frequently than a database that has documents whose information is timely, such as a sales reporting database.

- Plan in advance which users should be able to access the archive database and with what level of access. It usually makes sense to set default access to the archive database to Reader access. Usually once information is stored for historical lookup purposes it is used for reference information rather than production work so updates to documents will not be necessary.

- Since archiving is usually done by the server using an agent, establish a time for archiving so that the performance of the server, during peak user access, will not be deteriorated (on weekends, for example).

- Check the replication schedule and plan archiving so that it precedes replication so that other replicas of the database receive the deletions soon after they occur.

- Compact the database after archiving to reclaim unused space in the database.

- Design the archive database for performance. It will store large amounts of documents so limiting the number of views, fields and agents will make using it faster.

- Take advantage of the archive database by including design elements that will provide useful information. Make the views in the archive database relevant to how it (as opposed to the production database) will be used. For example, if the database is a Sales Tracking application, you may want to include a view that shows yearly revenue by customer. This view may not be helpful in the production database used by the sales people day to day but may be extremely useful for management and marketing people looking at the archive database for historical information.

Creating an Archive Database

The first step in using any archiving strategy is to create a database that will store the documents to be archived. Follow these steps to create an archive database:

1. Create a new copy of the database with a new replication ID number by selecting the working database with documents you wish to archive, choosing File/Database/New Copy. It is important that the archive database, the one to retain the old documents, has a different replica ID number so that it does not exchange document additions and deletions with the production, or current, copy of the database. Using the File/Database/New Copy command will create a database with the same design features: forms, views and agents with a *new replica ID number*.

2. Specify the server on which the archive database is to reside as shown in Figure 28.8. The default will be the server where the current database resides.

Figure 28.8

Creating a new database in which to store archived documents.

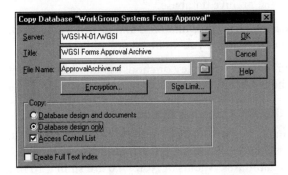

NOTE. *You must have Create Database privileges on the server to create a new copy and locate it on the server.*

3. Give the database a new name for the file system and title to appear on the database icon in the fields provided.

4. Select the radio button "Database Design Only." Notes will create a new database with the same forms and views, providing easy viewing of documents, without copying any of the actual documents (data).

5. Choose OK. Notes will create a new database on the server you specified and give it the file name and title you typed in step 3.

Manually Archiving

To manually archive a database you are simply taking a document from one database and putting it into another database as you would move a paper document from one file drawer to another. Manually archiving databases is effective for smaller databases with less activity as well as larger databases for which a criteria for removing documents is more difficult to determine. To manually archive a database, follow the steps below:

1. Open the database which contains documents you wish to move elsewhere for storage.

2. Select a view that shows all the documents you will want to move.

3. Select the documents to be archived by clicking in the left margin next to the document.

4. Select Edit/Copy to copy the documents into the clipboard.

5. Choose Window/Workspace and open the database you created in Step 5 of the section "Creating an Archive Database."

6. Select Edit/Paste to paste the documents into the archive database.

7. Check to make sure all the documents you want to archive now appear in the archive database.

8. Close the archive database and return to the working database where the documents you archived are still selected.

9. Press the Delete key or choose Edit/Clear to delete the documents from the working copy of the database.

Creating an Archiving Agent

If granted the privilege by the server administrator, the database manager may use an Agent running on the server to archive information stored in Notes databases. Agents in Notes 4.0 are similar to macros in earlier versions of Notes but provide much more functionality.

The following example shows the steps necessary to create a simple archiving agent. This agent is stored in the database which is to be archived and should be run only on one server. Other replicas of the database will receive the deletions via replication. The database to which the documents are archived may be replicated to other servers if users at those locations need access to the historical information.

NOTE. *Since your agent will delete documents, it is very important to test the agent before putting it into production.*

1. Select the working database (the one from which you want to create an archive) and select Create/Agent.

2. Name the Agent by typing in the field labeled "Name."

3. Click on the down arrow in the field labeled "When should this agent run?" and select "On schedule..." and choose the frequency (hourly, daily, weekly, monthly) with which you want this agent to run. You may click on the Schedule button to specify particular days and times for the Agent to run as well as the server on which you want the agent to run. Remember, you only want the Agent to run one server.

4. Click on the down arrow in the field labeled "Which documents should it act on?" It probably makes sense to choose the "New and modified documents since last run" option so the Agent has fewer documents to process, conserving server resources. Initially, you may want to have the agent act on "All documents."

   In this way you will archive, on the first run of the agent, all documents that are older than 90 days old. Documents that are not new and haven't been modified since the last run will be properly archived during the initial run of the agent.

5. Click Add Search and specify a criteria. For example, you may want to choose "By Date" in the "Condition" field and then "Date Modified" in the "Search for documents whose" field and "Is older than" as the conditional expression and enter 90 days in the field provided as shown in Figure 28.9.

Figure 28.9

Adding search criteria to the archiving agent.

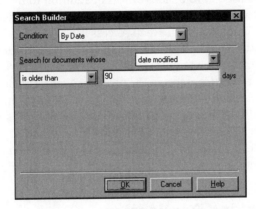

6. Click OK.

7. Click the button labeled "Simple action(s)" under "What should this agent do?"

8. Click the Add Actions button and then click the down arrow in the field labeled "Actions."

9. Select the action "Copy to database."

10. Click the Choose Database button and select the archive database you created in step 5 of the section "Creating an Archive Database."

11. Click on Select and then click on OK.

12. Click Add Actions again and select "Delete from database."

13. Close and Save the Agent.

14. Select the database and choose View/Agents, select the agent just created.

15. Click Actions/Test to preview how the agent will run.

16. Click OK.

NOTE. *Every time an Agent runs it writes information to a log to provide a history of what happened to the database the last time the Agent ran. You can check the log by clicking on the database, selecting View/Agents, selecting the Agent whose log you want to see and selecting Agent/Log.*

Using Access Controls to Limit Database Size

Access controls are usually used as a security measure rather than a means to limit database size. However, in some circumstances, it may make sense to solve two problems at one time. Let's assume that you have contacts database that is used in four sales offices in addition to the headquarters location. One good way to limit the exchange of documents via access controls is by using roles and document Read Access list.

By putting field office server names only into roles for certain documents (WestContacts, for example) the server will not receive any documents that do not have WestContacts in the "Region" field. The headquarters server can be in all roles and therefore receive all documents from all servers. In addition to *limiting* the amount of data on the local servers, this approach *secures* documents. Where selective replication is a method of *filtering* document exchange roles and document Read Access Lists *prevent* document exchange. See the section on Access Controls for more information.

■ Checking Replication

Notes servers exchange information in databases on a scheduled basis determined by the systems administration staff. Database managers should check the replication of databases they manage on a regular basis to make sure that documents are being passed from one server to another. If replication is not working properly, alert the server administrator responsible for maintaining connections to other servers. One simple way to check replication is to create a document in one replica of the database and check another replica after replication should have occurred to see if the document was copied to the other replica.

Using the Replication History

Each Notes database stores a replication history that details successful replications with replica copies of the database on other servers. This history can be useful when trying to establish if replication was successful.

Notes uses this same log to determine which documents to replicate when two servers connect for replication. When two servers connect to replicate, Notes checks the last time each database successfully replicated and exchanges only the changes that have occurred since that time. If the last successful replication between Server A and Server B was at 2:00 a.m. yesterday, only the changes that have occurred since that time will be exchanged. Figure 28.10 shows the Replication History of a database.

Figure 28.10

Viewing the successful replications of a Notes database.

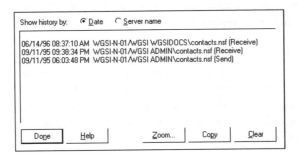

To check the replication history of a database, select the database icon of the database whose replication history you want to check. Then choose File/Replication/History or click the right mouse button and select Replication History. Notes displays the history of replication with each server and details whether documents were sent or received. You may choose to sort the list by date or by server name to assist in troubleshooting.

If a database has not successfully replicated, you may want to choose the Clear button to clear the history so that Notes will attempt to replicate the entire database the next time the two servers replicate. Clearing the history will tax the server so it should only be done when documents are not replicating.

Replication Problems and How to Solve Them

The following messages indicate that there has been a replication problem.

No Changes Have Been Made

Sometimes you won't see any changes in the database and the replication history will show a successful replication took place. In this case, check the copy of the replica on the other server to see if there are new documents, modified documents, or deleted documents that should have been replicated.

Replica IDs Are Not the Same

Notes determines what databases to replicate based on the replica ID number in databases. Two databases with the same replica ID number will exchange documents when the two servers on which they are located connect for a replication event. If a copy of a replica has been made with the File/Database/New Copy the database will look identical but will not replicate. If a new copy of a replica database is needed, use the File/Replication/New Replica command.

Replication Settings Are Set to Limit or Disable Replication

Check the Replication Settings dialog box to make sure that a replication setting such as a selection formula or "Temporarily Disable Replication" is not set to inhibit replication.

Problem with the Notes Network

Either a network operating system or Notes network error has occurred. Checking the replication history of the database will help you determine if this is the case. If the replication history does not show a successful replication, contact your systems administrator and ask him or her to check the network connections.

Other Server Is Not in the Database or Server or Directory Link Access List

Servers must be listed in the access list for databases, servers, and directory links just as are users. If a database does not appear to be replicating successfully, check the access list of the database and make sure the other server is listed either explicitly or in a group with a sufficient level so that it can exchange documents. You may also have to check with the server administrator and ask him or her to make sure that server and directory link access lists are set appropriately. Directory links allow server administrators to store Notes databases in directories other than those located under the Notes data directory in the file system hierarchy.

In addition to enabling Notes administrators to store database files on other file systems, Directory Links can include an access control list similar to the database access control list. Servers must be listed in this list just as would users for the server to gain access to the database to replicate with it.

NOTE. *All servers in the replication sequence must have appropriate access for documents to get passed to all replicas of the database.*

Replication and Save Conflicts

A replication or save conflict occurs when the same document is edited at the same time by different users. If the document is edited on different replicas of the same database, when the servers replicate that database the document that was saved the most recently is the main document and the other document a response document to it. If one document has been modified more times than another, it will become the main document. If the edits are done on the same replica of the database, the one that is saved first becomes the main document. The user saving the second version of the document will be notified that saving will cause a conflict and that his or her version will be saved as a conflict document.

Notes 4.0 enables a database designer to specify that Notes should merge conflicting edits into a single document. If the designer specifies that documents be merged, Notes will merge the two edited documents if the changes made by the users are to different fields in the same document. If the same field was edited in the same document, Notes saves one document as a main document and the other as a response document.

Resolving Replication and Save Conflicts

Resolving replication and save conflicts must be done manually using cut and paste or by an API program written to resolve conflicts. To resolve conflicts manually the database manager or someone else with editor access to the documents must copy from one document to the other so that all changes reside in one document, save that document and delete the conflicting document.

■ Using Replica Databases

Replica databases are identical copies of Notes databases that share a common replica ID number. When Notes servers connect to replicate information, they search databases for common replica ID numbers and exchange documents between those files. Replica databases, as in earlier versions of Notes, are useful for localizing information so that a live connection to a single file is not necessary. Notes 4.0 offers enhancements to the database file that improve security and usability of replicas. Database managers need to be fluent in the features and functions of setting up replicas as they may be the first line of support if users have difficulty.

NOTE. *We will assume that you have an icon on your workspace that represents a database on Server A. You want to put it on Server B so local users may start entering and using information. You have been granted the appropriate access to Server B by the server administrator.*

Before Creating a Replica

Consider who should be allowed to access this database and with what privileges. Check the access control list in the original database to make sure you are listed as a database manager. If you are, you can select the "Copy access control list" checkbox and make changes to the access controls later. If you are not listed as a database manager, either uncheck this box (and Notes will establish you and the server onto which you put this database as Managers of the database) or make sure that replication is properly configured so that the rightful manager of this database will be able to make changes either directly or through replication to this database.

If you are not sure that another manager will be able to make changes, temporarily make yourself the manager and ensure that this access level is not changed through replication with other servers by lowering the access privileges of other server to Designer until you have clarified how this replica will be managed. The key is to ensure that some person has manager access to the new replica, regardless of whether that person is local or at another location that replicates to the location where the new replica will reside. You can add additional entries to the access control list for users, servers and groups later.

NOTE. *You must be listed as the database manager in the access control list or you will not be able to make changes to it once the replica is on the server.*

Consider whether you want to create the replica "Immediately" or "Next scheduled replication." If you choose "Immediately," all the documents, design, and access controls will be copied while you wait. If you are creating a replica of a database that has significant amounts of data stored, your machine will be unavailable for some time. Choosing "Next scheduled replication" will create a placeholder for the new replica on Server B. The next time Servers A and B replicate, all the design elements and data will be copied to the new replica on Server B.

Notes 4.0 allows you to encrypt databases so that users who gain access to the database without going through the server will still need the correct ID file and password to see the information. If you want to enable this local encryption to prevent users from looking at the database when they get physical access to the server, click the Encryption button and choose Simple, Medium, or Strong encryption.

Consider placing a size limit on the database. If you want to force a maximum size for a database, click on the Size button and select a setting from one to four gigabytes.

Based on volume and content, determine whether the information in the database should be full text indexed. Full text indexes are the only component of a Notes database stored outside the .nsf file. They require extra disk space and processing power. Consider the kind of information stored, how the views and navigators in the database help users find the information they need and how much time can be saved by users if they have the ability to use full text search to find documents. If use of the database will be significantly enhanced by adding full text search capability to the database, click on the check box labeled "Create full text index for searching."

Determine what components of the database you want to replicate to the new replica. For example, if the new replica is for use by a field sales office, it may make sense to use replication settings to limit the documents received by this copy of the database to a specific state or series of zip codes.

Think about whether this database should be listed in the Notes database catalog and on the File/Database/Open menu. The Database Catalog database lists all the databases on the server or in the domain, helping users to find information. If the information is sensitive, you may want to keep the database unlisted. By default, all databases in a directory appear in a list when a user selects File/Database/Open. If you want to disable these listings, go to the Database Properties dialog box, select the Design tab and uncheck these options.

Make sure there is a Connection Document in the Public Name and Address Book specifying that the server on which you are placing the new replica will replicate with another server that has a replica of the database. You may do this by opening the Public Name and Address Book and choosing View/Server/Connections and looking to see if there is a Connection Document to or from your server to another server with a replica of the same database on it.

Finally, create a Policy Document for using the database that includes information about how to contact the database manager should problems arise.

To Put a Replica on a Server

Once you have addressed the items above, it is time to put the replica on the server. Follow the steps below to create a replica of a database on a server.

1. Add the database icon to your workspace.

2. Select the database icon and choose File/Replication/New Replica.

3. Click the down arrow in the "Server" field and specify the server on which you want to place the new replica.

4. Check the database title and file name entries and confirm that they are as you want them to be (they will default to the same as the original database).

5. Choose the settings you want for Encryption, Size, and Replication.

6. Select "Copy access control list" if it has you entered as a manager

NOTE. *If remote users will call this server to replicate local copies it is also important that the server be explicitly listed as a Manager so it can make changes to the users' local replica of the database. If the server is not listed, users may find that their local replica does not accept data and design changes to the database from the server in the future.*

7. Check "Create full text index for searching" if you want to enable this feature.

8. Select either "Now" or "Next scheduled replication" as the time to do the actual copying of database design and documents.

9. Choose OK.

Notes will create a replica copy of the database with the options you have set. The new database will appear on your workspace on top of the other replica icon.

■ Using Full Text Indexes

If you did not create a full text index at the time you initially created a replica of a Notes database, you can add one at any time. Remember, full text indexes may consume significant disk space. You can expect a database that has a large percentage of text to require an index that is about 30 percent of the size of the entire database. Databases with medium or less text as a percentage will require an index that is 25 percent to 12 percent of the size of the entire database. To calculate the approximate size of the index multiply the size of the database by one of these percentages. For example, if you have a database that is 100 megabytes and it has a large percentage of text, the index will be about 30 megabytes.

Index files are stored in a subdirectory under the one containing the databases. Servers are generally setup to update full text indexes each night when users will not perceive a performance degradation. Performance is difficult to gauge in advance as it is dependent upon the number of databases being indexed, what other processes are running on the server simultaneously as well as hardware and operating system configurations. Indexes stored on local file systems for use with locally stored databases must be updated manually for new documents to be indexed and thus, found during a search.

Indexing Options

When creating a full text index you will have many options that determine how the index will be created and how it may be used. To set up the index for maximum efficiency as well as usefulness, consider the options in advance and implement them after weighing the benefits of increased search capabilities versus conserved server resource.

Choosing the "Exclude words in Stop Word file" prevents Notes from indexing common words such as "and" and "or" to save space in the index—up to 20 percent. If you use a stop word file, users will not be able to search for words included in that file. If your stop word file included the word "of" users could not search for the phrase "nick of time." They could still, however, search on "nick" and "time." You can create your own Stop Word file to suit the vernacular of your organization or industry.

Choosing "Word Breaks only" will not allow users to limit their searches to one sentence or paragraph. Choosing "Word, Sentence and Paragraph" will allow users to search for words within these break points but takes more index space.

Bear in mind, you must have Manager or Designer access to a database to create or update full text indexes. This means that you should plan on using the index periodically to make sure it is working properly. Users will not have the authority to update it or make changes to it.

Creating the Full Text Index

Once you have determined how you will set up your index, you may follow the steps below. Remember, these steps must be carried out on each Notes computer on which you wish to enable full text searching as the full text search does not replicate as do the data, design, and security components of the database.

1. Select the database you want to full text index.

2. Select File/Database/Properties or click with the right mouse button and choose Database/Properties.

3. Select the tab labeled "Full Text."

4. Click the button labeled "Create Index."

5. Select what elements of the database you would like to index, if you want to use a stop file, and how Notes should tag index breaks. Notes 4.0 lets you index attachments and encrypted fields.

6. Choose OK.

Updating Full Text Indexes

Once you have created a full text index on the server you will need to update it periodically so that it adds new documents to the index so that they can be searched. The update process will need to run on every server where the full text index resides as this index is not part of the Notes database and therefore is not replicated. Database managers and designers can schedule Full text indexes that are located on servers to update automatically on a scheduled basis. To have the full text index for a server based database automatically updated:

1. Select the database whose full text index you want to automatically update.

2. Select File/Database/Properties and click on the Full Text tab of the properties box.

3. Click on the down arrow in the field labeled "Update Frequency" to determine how frequently the server should update the database.

You may chose several frequency options, including immediately, hourly, and daily. There is also complete flexibility in scheduling the index updates by using a Program documenting the Public Name and Address Book. Bear in mind that you will need to have appropriate access privileges (such as those usually granted to a server administrator) to create such a Program Document. Remember, if no Program Document in the Public Name and Address Book or setting in the NOTES.INI file runs the Updall program the database will not be updated.

■ Deleting Databases

Only the database manager or someone with direct access to the server file system can delete a database. Before deleting a database consider whether any information stored in that database will have value down the road. It may make sense to have your server administrator backup the database before you delete it. Bear in mind that the database will need to be deleted on every server as replication will not delete a file. In addition to deleting the database, you should ask a system administrator with appropriate access to remove any Documents referring to the database from the Public Name and Address Book. For example, if Program Documents have been created to run API programs on this database or if a Mail-In-Database Document has been created so that documents may be mailed to this database or if a Connection Document has been created to replicate this database exclusively, all of these documents should be deleted from the Public Name and Address Book. *If one of these documents is not deleted, the server will waste processing resource and an error will appear in the server log database.* To delete a database in Notes 4.0, select the database you wish to delete and choose File/Database/Delete from the menu.

■ Monitoring Usage

As with earlier versions of Notes, 4.0 allows the database manager to view user activity. This assists in determining if the database should be removed because it is not being used or if it should be enhanced. To check user activity:

1. Select the database whose usage you want to check.

2. Select File/Database/Properties or click with the right mouse button and select Database/Properties.

3. Click on the information tab

4. Click on the User Activity button.

By default Notes databases do not record user activity, but you may choose to turn this option on by checking the option in the User Activity properties window for the database. When activity has been recorded, the dialog box that appears will detail who used the database as well as whether they read or wrote to the database. This information can also be found in the server log database in the Database Usage or Usage by User view if the Log All Client Events setting was turned on during server setup. If this setting was not enabled, you may use a Server Configuration Document to turn it on.

■ Analyzing the Database

Notes 4.0 has a database analysis feature that allows the database manager to create a summary of information regarding user access, replications and other information that can assist in the routine tasks of managing the database. This tool is especially useful in resolving replication and access control issues especially since it can report on replicas on other servers.

To create a database analysis:

1. Select File/Tools/Server Administration.

2. Click on the icon labeled "Database."

3. Select "Database Analysis."

4. Click on the button labeled "Source Database" and choose the database you want to analyze.

5. Click on the button labeled "Results Database" and designate a name and title for the database into which Notes should put the results and choose OK.

6. Select the components of the database on which Notes should report and select "Start."

Notes will create a database in the location you specified with the results of the analysis.

■ Index